Christian Perspectives on
Legal Thought

# Christian Perspectives on Legal Thought

Edited by
Michael W. McConnell
Robert F. Cochran, Jr.
Angela C. Carmella

Yale University Press

New Haven & London

Set in Garamond and Stone Sans types by The Composing Room of Michigan, Inc. Printed in the United States of America by Edwards Brothers, Inc.

Library of Congress Cataloging-in-Publication Data

Christian perspectives on legal thought / edited by Michael W. McConnell, Robert F. Cochran, Jr., Angela C. Carmella.
      p.   cm.
Includes bibliographical references and index.
    ISBN 0-300-08749-7 (cloth : alk. paper) — ISBN 0-300-08750-0 (paper : alk. paper)
    1. Christianity and law.    I. McConnell, Michael W.    II.  Cochran, Robert F., 1951– .   III. Carmella, Angela C.
    BR115.L28 C475   2001
    261.5—dc21                                                    2001001783

A catalogue record for this book is available from the British Library.

The paper in this book meets the guidelines for permanence and durability of the Committee on Production Guidelines for Book Longevity of the Council on Library Resources.

10  9  8  7  6  5  4  3  2  1

To my colleagues and students.
—Michael W. McConnell


To those who have encouraged me to think Christianly about the world, especially my parents, Bob and Jo Cochran, and my teachers, Jim Houston and Tom Shaffer.
—Robert F. Cochran, Jr.


To my parents, Angelo and Lillian Carmella, my first and greatest teachers. To my husband, Paul Hauge, my true love and greatest friend.
—Angela C. Carmella

# Contents

# Foreword

*Harold J. Berman*

Both Christian and non-Christian students, teachers, and practitioners of the law should be delighted that a substantial number of highly
qualified American legal scholars have joined together to produce a
book that views legal thought from various Christian perspectives. It's
about time!

With rare exceptions, American legal scholars of Christian faith
have not, during the past century, attempted to explain law in terms of
that faith. Indeed, in the vast majority of scholarly writings on the vast
majority of legal subjects, and in almost all classroom teaching of
those subjects, Christianity is not mentioned. Is this because most
contemporary American legal scholars see no connection between law
and Christianity? Or is it because Christianity has been a taboo subject in twentieth-century American legal education?

As one who has sought answers to these questions ever since becoming a student at Yale Law School in 1940, I may perhaps be permitted to give some examples from personal experience.

The first example does not involve the use of the word *Christianity*
but rather the use of the closely related word *justice*. I recall vividly my

last law-school class—it was in June 1947 (I had returned to law school after military service overseas)—when Professor Eugene Rostow, in the course in corporate finance, somehow brought the discussion around to the day's news of the failure of a South Carolina grand jury to indict persons charged with carrying out the lynching of a black man, though the evidence against them was overwhelming. "Is that justice?" Professor Rostow asked. "What *is* justice?" I remember it particularly because it was the first time the word *justice* had been mentioned in any of the courses I had taken during three years of law study.

That was Yale in the heyday of so-called legal realism, when in many of the courses law was said to be essentially an argumentative technique and judicial decisions were said to be based principally on the prejudices of the judges.

At Harvard Law School the concept of justice was taken more seriously in those days, but there too Christianity was rarely, if ever, mentioned. In 1951, as an assistant professor, I asked the formidable Dean Erwin Griswold whether it would not be a good idea to introduce a course in law and Christianity, since Christianity had had such an important influence on the origin and development of our legal institutions. He replied, "Well, perhaps it could be an extracurricular seminar, not for credit."

And I recall in 1974 sending copies of my newly published book, *The Interaction of Law and Religion,* to the eight of my fifty or so Harvard Law School colleagues who I thought might have at least a faint interest in the subject. I received not one acknowledgment of the gift—not a single "Thank you, I look forward to reading it." It was simply an embarrassment to them for a colleague to link law with religion, and especially with Christianity.

One could tell other more recent stories to the same effect. On the other hand, in the 1980s and 1990s a number of Christian legal scholars have come out of the closet. The formation of the Christian Legal Society, though intended primarily for legal practitioners, has drawn some law teachers into its conferences and publications. Christian legal scholars played a major part in founding *The Journal of Law and Religion* in 1983 and subsequently in contributing articles to it and in establishing and contributing to programs in law and religion at some law schools, starting with Emory in the early 1980s. And now this book brings together for the first time a wide variety of Protestant and Roman Catholic perspectives presented by almost thirty avowedly Christian law teachers, some of whom have not previously acknowledged Christian influences on their scholarship.

What gives the book its unity is less its theology—indeed, there are only a few chapters in it that address major theological questions directly—than its philosophy, and more particularly, its moral philosophy. And of its moral philosophy there are two parts: one is the analysis of law in general, and of various branches of law, from the perspective of Christian concepts of justice and injustice; the other is the critique of major contemporary schools of legal thought which, in the guise of pragmatism, reflect (in the words of Albert W. Alschuler) "the vices of atomism, alienation, ambivalence, self-centeredness, and vacuity of commitment [that are] characteristic of our culture." One can hear in this an echo of Jesus' reprimand, "Woe unto you lawyers, for you tithe mint and dill and cumin but neglect the weightier matters of the law, which are justice and mercy and good faith" (Matthew 23:23).

But Jesus added: "These"—that is, the weightier matters—"you should have done, without neglecting the others," that is, without neglecting the "mint and dill and cumin," the technical subject matter of legal practice that helps to maintain order in society.

In a short but important essay in the middle of the book, Robert F. Cochran, Jr., draws on H. Richard Niebuhr's *Christ and Culture* to classify traditional Christian perspectives on law to be amplified in subsequent chapters. He identifies the role of Roman Catholic theology in adding concepts of justice—especially the Thomist theory of natural law—to legal philosophy; the role of Calvinist theology in challenging communities to reform law in the direction of Christian charity; the role of Anabaptist and contemporary evangelical theology in exposing the sinful nature of all law and exalting nonlegal virtues of forgiveness and self-sacrifice; and the role of Lutheran theology in separating law from faith in the human quest for wholeness and holiness. These four traditions of legal thought correspond to Niebuhr's categories of Christ *added* to culture, Christ *converting* culture, Christ *separated from* culture, and Christ *in tension with* culture.

Left hanging, however, in this section of the book, is Niebuhr's fifth category, Christ *of* culture. Can we not say that God has revealed Himself in existing legal institutions, and that he continues to reveal Himself in the development of those institutions, insofar as they reflect justice and mercy and good faith? Is there not a Christian dimension *of* existing laws, which, like the Ten Commandments, prohibit stealing, murder, adultery, defamation, lying? As I said in my 1993 book *Faith and Order,* from a Christian perspective, the purpose of our existing body of property law, criminal law, family law, tort law, and other branches of law is to create conditions in which sacrificial love of God and of neighbor, the kind of love personified by Jesus Christ, can take root in society and grow.

The final section of *Christian Perspectives on Legal Thought*, dealing with individual branches of the law, raises most sharply the question of the extent to which our existing system of positive law reflects Christian beliefs and Christian values. Here the historical dimension of law, its process of growth from century to century and from generation to generation, must be studied to determine whether we can indeed discern in it the working of divine providence.

This is a book that should be read in what were once called "perspective courses" in law schools—courses in jurisprudence, legal history, comparative law, legal method, and related subjects. Also, its chapters on specific branches of the law—family law, criminal law, environmental law, professional responsibility, contracts, and torts—should be assigned in courses on those subjects. Above all, it should be read by both law teachers and legal practitioners—especially by those who have seen no relationship between Christianity and law and those for whom Christianity has been a taboo subject in the classroom.

Finally, it is important that this book be read by scholars in disciplines taught outside of law schools—in political science, in history, in philosophy, in religion. It will enrich those courses, which sorely need to include in their content the study of legal institutions. Moreover, it will ultimately be in response to pressures from those other disciplines that legal scholars will be forced to "locate" themselves, as it is put in one of the chapters of this book, in the fundamental presuppositions, the implicit belief-systems, that underlie and determine their scholarship.

# Acknowledgments

It is impossible to thank all of the people who are responsible for this project, but we will name a few. Our thanks to Dean Scott Matheson of the University of Utah College of Law, Deans Ronald F. Phillips and Richardson Lynn of Pepperdine University School of Law, and Deans Ronald J. Riccio and Patrick E. Hobbs of Seton Hall University School of Law for their support and encouragement; to Lara Heimert, Dan Heaton, and John Covell of Yale University Press for their wise and patient editorial assistance; to Michelle Pirozzi, Stacey Rock, Beth Nunnick, Tammie Carpenter, and Tami Lumm of Pepperdine Law School, and Maja Basioli, Eileen Denner, and Kathleen McCarthy of the Seton Hall Law Library for their research support; and to Candace Warren and Sheila McDonald of Pepperdine Law School for their assistance in manuscript preparation.

More than half of the essays in this book were originally presented at conferences of the Law Professors' Christian Fellowship. Our thanks to the participants in those conferences for their thoughtful comments and suggestions. A special thanks to those people who helped to plan the conferences. They include (in addition to several of

In the legal academy today, there is no shortage of voices answering Jesus' questions. "What is written in the law? How do you read it?" We hear economic interpretations of law, feminist interpretations, anthropological interpretations, Kantianism, utilitarian theories, theories grounded in the experience of race, sex, and sexuality, and virtually everything else. The answers reveal something about those who offer them, and the conversations that ensue reveal something fundamentally important to all of us about the meaning of the law.

But in the midst of this multifarious conversation there is a strange silence on the part of Jesus' own followers. Where can one hear the expression of Christian perspectives on law and legal theory? There are books and articles galore on legal theory from every conceivable philosophy, ideology, and identity. But there are surprisingly few books or articles applying the gospel of Jesus Christ, other than in a few specialized areas like legal ethics and church-state law. Much the same is true in the classroom. Professors encourage law school students to analyze law from a variety of perspectives and points of view, but religious views are oddly absent. A student in criminal law, for instance, is unlikely to question modern criminological theory from the standpoint of sin and redemption. If a student did offer such a critique, many professors would not know how to react. There would likely be an awkward silence, followed by a polite change of subject.

This book is intended to break that silence. We have put together a collection of essays to introduce readers to Christian perspectives on legal thought. The editors come from different traditions within Christianity—from Roman Catholic, evangelical, and mainline Protestant churches. We are keenly aware that the religious orientation of our traditions is relevant not only to our personal lives but to our understanding of the world and ultimately to the ways we teach, write about, and practice law.

As Thomas H. Groome has suggested in *Educating for Life,* religious thinking is not confined to speculations about the transcendent but typically provides an anthropology; a cosmology; a sociology; an understanding of text, history, and tradition; an epistemology; a spirituality; an ecclesiology; and an understanding of justice. Throughout Christian history, men and women have reflected on such questions as the nature of the human person and of our role in the world, on the nature of good and evil and of grace and sin, on texts and various traditions of interpretation, on efforts of reform and renewal, on the role of reason and its relation to faith, on authority and institutions, and on what it means to be a just society. Much of this reflection has a bearing on law, because law is similarly concerned with these very questions.

We are persuaded that Christian understandings of law will serve both to illuminate the underpinnings of our legal order, which was heavily influenced by the Christian culture from which it emerged, and to provide a perspective from which to criticize that order. Democracy needs both. It is important for a free people to connect the positive law to their ideals of a higher good. Unless they perceive such a connection, the people will resist compliance with the law, and the state will be forced to turn to naked coercion. Because many people in this country derive their most fundamental sense of moral order from their religious faith, it is essential to democracy that the connections between that faith and the law be explored and understood. Yet it is equally important that a democratic people retain a critical stance from which to examine the practices of our culture and political life. Again, for the many people whose understanding of the moral order is shaped by religious faith, religion may be the most promising foothold for a critical stance.

Some might suggest that giving attention to Christian perspectives on law will exacerbate an already disturbing degree of disunity and divisiveness in legal thought, but it could also lead to areas of mutual understanding and common ground. In fact, it could lead to understanding in areas where secular perspectives have led only to division. Religious identity cuts across the racial and sexual divides of America. Christian discourse may serve as the basis for understanding between many who have little else in common with one another. A Christian conversation may enable many to find a common agenda for human well-being. As Anthony Cook has said of Martin Luther King, Jr., "He showed us that as we go deeper into our particularities, we discover commonalities."

We believe, therefore, that Christian understandings of the law might help in the wider project of restoring a sense of public right and justice—of "commonwealth"—to the American political culture. Whatever their differences, many thoughtful Americans of various religious and political stripes share a deep concern that modern life, including public life, has become dominated by selfish, shallow, materialistic, cruel, and nihilistic values. Christianity, along with other faiths, may be an antidote to this great moral failing of our time. Christ teaches us to love our neighbor, to have compassion for the poor and the alien, to love justice, and to walk humbly before God. If believers do not base their view of law on their deepest moral insights, they are likely to base it on their most selfish instincts. To ignore Christian (and other religious) perspectives on law is like ignoring a life raft on an endangered vessel.

This is not to suggest that there is a single "Christian" perspective. There has been no shortage of disagreement within the Christian fold. Agreement on a few first principles has led to a rich and diverse conversation on a host of other questions. In this book, by gathering authors who write from a wide variety of Christian traditions, we have tried to reflect the diversity of attitudes, doctrines, and approaches found within the broader Christian community. Indeed, the diversity is greater and more complex than even the number of different traditions might suggest. If we were to poll the authors of the essays in this book, the only common belief might be the original church's confession that "Jesus is Lord" (1 Corinthians 12:3). That, of course, was the confession that got the members of the early church into trouble. They were unwilling to say that "Caesar is Lord." The key question of this book may be, "What does it mean in America today to say that Jesus, rather than Caesar, is Lord?" Our hope is that our common bond in Christ will enable us to better understand one another and to move toward greater knowledge of what Christ would have us do.

We realize that some will view a book of this sort with skepticism or even with alarm. In this multicultural world, there is surprising resistance to the idea that Christianity is a legitimate perspective from which to address issues of the secular world. We believe this resistance to a Christian voice in legal theory has its roots in three different periods in American intellectual history. In part, the resistance is a reaction to the premodern era, in which Christianity was understood to be the privileged and sacrosanct basis for law. As late as 1844, Justice Joseph Story could write an opinion presupposing that Christianity is part of the common law (*Vidal v. Girard's Executors,* 43 U.S. [2 How.] 127 [1844]). Much of the progress of a liberal and democratic understanding of law required a break from this past—a recognition that no religion could enjoy a privileged and hegemonic status in a democratic society. We suspect that some resistance to self-consciously Christian voices in the legal conversation today is based on a fear that these would be the opening wedge in a program to reassert Christian hegemony. To that concern, we can only offer the assurance that none of us, and few in America today, entertain the notion that Christianity is entitled to a privileged status in American life. We enter into public discussion on equal terms and seek only the right that others have in equal measure: to explain our premises, to participate in the conversation, and to offer arguments on the merits.

A second source of the resistance, we think, is a throwback to the modern or "scientific" period of legal thought. During this period, leading legal scholars attempted to base the study of law on an analogy to the natural sciences. Dean Christopher Langdell of Harvard, who developed the case method in the 1870s, viewed law as a science consisting of "principles and doctrines": "Written opinions in cases were the legal scientist's specimens or 'data.'" Under this view, a "Christian perspective" on law is objectionable because religion is said to be based on faith rather than reason. Religion is subjective, and science is objective. This view suffers from two fundamental flaws. First, for many Christians, faith and reason are not in opposition but are compatible and complementary. Second, even if science is an "objective," "rational" endeavor, the notion that law is or can be a science was discredited long ago. Underlying the law of any culture will be the pretheoretical beliefs of that culture. Those beliefs are necessarily rooted in culture, tradition, identity, and other sources of conviction. Even science itself, according to one view, is based on pretheoretical assumptions that are logically equivalent to faith. This is a lesson that Augustine taught long ago: faith precedes and conditions understanding. Before we can process data, before we know what it means to be "thinking," we require a theoretical standpoint or framework for understanding the world. That is why legal thought is now so open to diverse voices and perspectives, not all of them "rational" in any narrow "Enlightenment" sense of that term. The dream of many is of a legal academy that reflects the multicultural world in which we live. If the world of the legal academy is to be truly inclusive, if we are to have a broad-based conversation about our lives together, religious people and religious ideas need to be part of that conversation.

A third source of resistance, we think, has its source in the politics of our own time. In recent years the most vocal proponents of Christian perspectives on law and politics have come from the religious right, and they have plenty of opposition within the modern academy. The fear of many in the American academy is that a Christian view of law will yield an authoritarian conservative regime, to the detriment of gay rights, abortion rights, women's rights, children's rights, and "progressive" causes of all sorts. To this we offer two responses. First, this is an inaccurate caricature. Christians can be found at most points in the ideological spectrum. Historically, evangelical Christians have been in the forefront of "progressive" causes like abolition, women's suffrage, and universal education—as well as "conservative" causes like Prohibition and the restoration of "family values." The Catholic Church in America has been a vigorous opponent of capital punishment and a warm supporter of labor, social welfare, and immigration, as well as a supporter of protections against abortion and euthanasia. But even if religious voices were reliably antithetical to a particular brand of progressive politics, democrats (with a small d) should recognize that it is unprincipled and undemocratic to exclude or marginalize fellow citizens on the mere expectation that they will vote the wrong way.

This book has two intended audiences. First, we hope that these essays will help Christian lawyers, legal scholars, students, citizens, and lawmakers to think more deeply about the connection between the truths of the gospel, the lived experience of Christian communities throughout history, and the legal questions that face this world. It is not good to live a compartmentalized existence: one life (and one set of values) in church on Sunday and another life (and another set of values) in the office during the week. By bringing these issues into the open, those who work in the law may be able to live lives of greater understanding and greater integrity. Second, we hope that non-Christian lawyers, legal scholars, citizens, and lawmakers will find these essays an illuminating introduction to ways of thinking about law that they may never have encountered before. Perhaps they will be inspired to reflect on their own deepest beliefs and the implications of those beliefs for our legal system. With respect to both audiences, we hope that this book will promote a conversation in which people of many different faiths (including modern secular faiths) can better understand one another, and better understand the law.

In Part I, authors reflect on prominent schools of thought within the legal academy: liberalism, legal realism, critical legal studies, feminism, critical race theory, and law and economics, from Christian perspectives. In Part II, we introduce readers to the ways that various Christian traditions have understood law. In Part III, legal scholars apply the insights and perspective of faith to concrete legal issues arising in various substantive areas of the law: family, criminal, environmental, professional responsibility, contract, and tort. They do so in ways that critique, find commonality with, and mark new directions for legal thought.

Our purpose, in short, is to introduce the secular world of legal thought to major themes and diverse paths within Christianity. We hope this will make it easier for people of all faiths and beliefs—but most particularly fellow believers in the gospel of Christ—to address those ancient questions: "What is written in the law? How do you read it?"

# Part I  Christian Perspectives on Schools of Legal Thought

In considering Christian faith as a basis for thinking about law, we begin with essays that reflect upon the currently dominant schools of thought in American jurisprudence. These essays provide critiques—some more positive, some more negative—of those schools from Christian perspectives, and thus suggest how Christian perspectives on law might differ from, or complement, current modes of thinking.

# Section 1 Enlightenment Liberalism

Liberalism, though born of Protestant Christianity, seems to have become hostile toward religion. Liberalism teaches that human beings are individuals, whose rights are supreme, and who have little claim on one another aside from the claim to be free from aggression. Christianity teaches that human beings are brothers and sisters under the Headship of Christ, bound together in community, with responsibilities to one another. How inevitable is this tension between liberalism and Christianity?

Because of the importance of liberal theory to the modern condition, we present four authors with different perspectives on the matter. Michael W. McConnell emphasizes the difference between early liberalism, which was rooted in Protestantism and congenial to religious conscience, and modern secular liberalism, which is not. He urges Christians and other people of faith not to abandon liberalism but to "take it back." Stephen L. Carter writes more pessimistically of the effects of modern secular liberalism on religious commitment in the public, and sometimes even the private, sphere. Elizabeth Mensch provides an intellectual history of the paradoxical relation between liberalism and Christianity. H. Jefferson Powell addresses three features of modern liberalism—individual rights, centralization, and governmental secularism—from an Augustinian perspective. He notes the problematic cultural effects of each but argues that a "chastened version" of each is defensible as a strategy for achieving social peace.

# Old Liberalism, New Liberalism, and People of Faith

*Michael W. McConnell*

In many circles, religion is seen as an illiberal phenomenon in our public life—a challenge to the rational and tolerant ethos of modern liberalism. Liberal democracy, it is said, is predicated on "reason," which is said to be antithetical to faith. Religion is alleged to be authoritarian, divisive, irrational, and exclusionary. The suggestion that religion—as opposed to secular philosophies or ideologies—might be entitled to special protection in our legal system is thus foreign to many modern secular liberals. One scholar has called the Free Exercise Clause "a limited aberration in a secular state."[1] Indeed, it is often said that providing special protection for religion violates the neutrality that lies at the heart of the liberal state. This point of view is linked to a tradition in intellectual history which traces liberal democratic theory to a struggle against the chains of feudalism and Christian ideological hegemony. In this view, liberal democracy represented the triumph of the secular Enlightenment over the powers of priest and king.

1. Suzanna Sherry, *Enlightening the Religion Clauses*, 7 J. of Contemp. Leg. Issues 473, 477 (1996).

Some Christians have accepted this claim and have concluded, as a result, that Christians cannot be liberals.[2] They perceive a hostility between liberalism and Christianity—indeed, any serious religion that claims to be based on truths that are beyond rational and empirical demonstration—and believe that secular liberalism is a prescription for a society based on materialism, atomistic individualism, and ultimately nihilism.[3] Thus some Christians have become critics of the liberal regime.

I think it is a mistake for Christians to give up on liberalism, and that it is an arrogant pretension on the part of secular liberals to attempt to relegate Christianity, or any other religion, to the sidelines of public life. Liberalism in its original form was more a product of the Reformation than of the Enlightenment, and it placed respect for the primacy of conscience at the center of the political project. Long before liberalism was conceived in theory or in practice, the division between temporal and spiritual authority in Christian thought gave rise to what would become the most fundamental features of liberal democratic order: the idea of limited government, the idea of individual conscience and hence of individual rights, and the idea of equality among all human beings. These ideas came about not in rebellion against religion, but in defense of religion against the encroachments of the state. If religion has become controversial again in our liberal society—and it has—this is not because religion has changed or the idea of liberty has changed, but because liberalism has changed. And not for the better.

I am not arguing that liberalism—in any of its forms—is an inescapable deduction from Christianity. Christianity is not, at bottom, a political doctrine, and sincere believers over the centuries have deemed it compatible with a wide variety of regimes. Some Christians are not liberals. Nor am I arguing that liberalism is exclusively a product of Christian thinking. Like John Rawls, I think that liberal democracy in the United States can be, and is, defended on the basis of a number of different comprehensive doctrines, of which Christianity is only one.[4] Many liberals are not Christians. I am arguing, however, that certain

2. *See, e.g.,* Stanley Hauerwas and Michael Baxter, *The Kingship of Christ: Why Freedom of "Belief" Is Not Enough,* 42 DePaul L. Rev. 107 (1992).

3. I use the terms *liberal* and *liberalism* in their broad sense, as denoting supporters of a regime in which the state is committed to preserving essential liberties among the people rather than to promoting a particular understanding of the good life. This sense of the term should not be confused with the more partisan sense, as an advocate of the policies of the left wing of the Democratic Party.

4. *See* John Rawls, *Political Liberalism* 134 (1993); *see also id.* at 147.

doctrines of mainstream Christianity point in the direction of liberalism, and that historically, liberalism was a product of those Christian impulses. It is, in short, no accident that liberalism arose when and where it did, in the lands of the Protestant Reformation. It is time to reclaim the noble ideal of liberalism from the secularists.

## THE FOUNDATIONS OF LIBERALISM

Let us consider some of the ways in which the foundational beliefs of liberalism find support in Christian doctrine and experience.

### Original Sin and the Rejection of Utopianism

Perhaps the most fundamental connection between liberalism and Christianity is their common belief in the pervasive and ineradicable nature of sin. That may sound surprising. Some believe that liberal democracy is a hopeful doctrine, predicated on the view that the people can and will rule wisely and justly. This is a misunderstanding. The central insight of liberal politics is that all human beings and human institutions are prone to abuse of power. That is why liberal constitutionalism insists on dividing power and on creating checks and balances. Liberals do not believe in philosopher kings. If they did, they would advocate not liberal democracy but enlightened despotism. Nor do liberals believe in philosopher peoples. If they did, they would create governments of direct democracy, along the lines recommended by Condorcet and other French revolutionaries. Nor do liberals think that governments can be trusted to dominate and control the most important things, such as religion and family life. If they did, they would create a civil religion, as Rousseau recommended and Robespierre tried to do. Better to allow many millions of people to make mistakes each in their own way than to license the civil magistrate to foist error on the entire nation.

The Christian idea that government must be created in recognition of the sinfulness of mankind pervades *The Federalist Papers* (to take one example of a liberal text). Madison's analysis of the problem of government is based on the existence of faction, and the "latent causes of faction," he says, are "sown in the nature of man." "As long as the reason of man continues to be fallible, . . . different opinions will be formed. As long as the connection subsists between his reason and his self-love, his opinions and his passions will have a reciprocal influence on each other." Note that this statement presupposes that human reason is inherently fallible, and that human reason is distorted and influenced by selfishness, which is at the heart of human sin. This is familiar Calvinist doctrine, and stands in sharp contrast to the naive faith in "reason" found among epigones of the secular Enlightenment. Moreover, Madison's prescription for government—to rely on the clash of "opposite and rival interests" to remedy "the defect of better motives"—is similarly based on this pessimistic view of human virtue. "It may be a reflection on human nature that such devices should be necessary," Madison wrote. "But what is government itself but the greatest of all reflections on human nature? If men were angels, no government would be necessary. If angels were to govern men, neither external nor internal controls on government would be necessary."[5]

The Christian understanding of human sin leads, therefore, to the idea that Christian politics should be antiutopian in character. We will not bring about the Kingdom of Heaven on this earth through our political efforts. If we allow our governments to try, the result will be tyranny. Liberals take human nature as given, and make modest efforts to improve community life at the margin. That disposition is closely aligned with the Christian view that we must not rely on earthly institutions for our salvation or for our regeneration. Utopian politics is dangerous and deceptive. More importantly, it is a kind of idolatry.

### Limited Government and the Separation of Church and State

A second aspect of the doctrine and experience of the Christian religion that is part of the foundation of liberalism is the separation between church and state, or what medievalists were more likely to call *libertas ecclesiae,* the "freedom of the church." This separation was a reality long before it was an idea. In Christian Europe after the fall of Rome, there were many warring nations but only one catholic Church. This stubborn geopolitical reality persisted despite, not because of, ideological commitments—whether they be the romantic ideal of Christendom, reflected in Charlemagne's Holy Roman Empire, or the imperial vision of Marsilius of Padua. No one seemed to favor the separation. But it would not go away. And it had consequences. No king, however powerful, could dominate a church that existed beyond his own borders. Like multinational corporations today, a multinational Church defied effective regulation

5. Madison et al., *The Federalist Papers,* No. 10 at 78–79 (Madison) (New American Library ed. 1961); *id.* No. 51 at 322 (Madison).

and control. This meant, moreover, that the Church could serve as a counter-vailing power within every state. The king may have commanded more troops, as well as the power of legal coercion, but bishops had normative authority. They translated the will of God to man, and enforced it, if necessary, through powers of absolution and excommunication. This was a more equal division of powers than one might at first expect. Think of Henry II and Becket.

Later, when the Protestant Reformation divided the church into many different bodies, the danger of a genuine union between church and state increased. The Church of England lost its independence in a way that the Church of Rome never could. But when the formula of "one prince, one church" broke down into "one prince, many churches," statesmen acquired an incentive to extend some measure of equal treatment to members of different denominations. If they did not, differences in religion (which could not be eradicated) might become occasions for treason. A policy of evenhandedness toward the different principal religions was the easiest way to create loyal citizens. This led to a different kind of "separation"—separation based on neutrality rather than on competition.

Although this division between spiritual and temporal authority began in practice rather than theory, it was soon articulated in theological, and later in constitutional, terms. It found expression in papal teachings as early as the fifth century and was elaborated in the two-kingdoms theology of the Lutheran and Calvinist traditions. Two-kingdoms theology conceived of humans as owing allegiance to two sets of authorities, the spiritual and the temporal. "God has appointed two kinds of government in the world," explained Isaac Backus, a Baptist leader and one of the most influential advocates of religious freedom at the Founding. These governments "are distinct in their nature, and ought never to be confounded together; one of which is called civil, the other ecclesiastical government." In this view, religious freedom comes into being not as a result of ontological individualism but as a result of the jurisdictional separation between these two sets of authorities. Elisha Williams, a New Light Congregationalist and Rector of Yale, drew an analogy to one king attempting to govern the people of another kingdom: "If Christ be the Lord of the conscience, the sole King in his own kingdom; then it will follow, that all such as in any manner or degree assume the power of directing and governing the consciences of men, are justly chargeable with invading his rightful dominion; He alone having the right they claim. Should the king of France take it into his head to prescribe laws to the subjects of the king of

Great Britain; who would not say, it was an invasion of and insult offer'd to the British legislature."[6]

The two-kingdoms view is at the heart of our First Amendment. The first paragraph of the most important document explaining the Founders' conception of religious freedom, James Madison's *Memorial and Remonstrance Against Religious Assessments,* reasons as follows: "It is the duty of every man to render to the Creator such homage, and such only, as he believes to be acceptable to him. This duty is precedent both in order of time and degree of obligation, to the claims of Civil Society. Before any man can be considered as a member of Civil Society, he must be considered as a subject of the Governor of the Universe: And if a member of Civil Society, who enters into any subordinate Association, must also do it with a reservation of his duty to the general authority; much more must every man who becomes a member of any particular Civil Society, do it with a saving of his allegiance to the Universal Sovereign." Madison's view of the grounding of religious freedom was thus surprisingly similar to Elisha Williams's. It was not a deduction from the personal autonomy of the individual but an inference from the sovereignty of God and the duty of human beings to obey God as they understand Him. Religious exercise, under this view, is an inalienable right because it follows from the duties owed to God by His creatures. "It would be sinful for a man to surrender that to man which is to be kept sacred for God," according to Madison's constituent, the Baptist leader John Leland.[7]

While theological in its origin, the two-kingdoms idea lent powerful support to a more general liberal theory of government. The separation of church from state is the most powerful possible refutation of the notion that the political sphere is omnicompetent—that it has rightful authority over all of life. If the state does not have power over the church, it follows that the power of the state is limited. The extent of state power need not be left to the discretion of the rulers. And once limits are conceived in this way, it becomes possible to craft further limitations on the scope of governmental authority, in service of broader liberal ends.

6. Isaac Backus, *An Appeal to the Public for Religious Liberty* (1773), reprinted in *Political Sermons of the American Founding Era* 334–35 (Ellis Sandoz ed., Liberty, 1991) [hereinafter *Political Sermons*]; Elisha Williams, *The Essential Rights and Liberties of Protestants* (1744), reprinted in *id.* at 51, 65–66.

7. James Madison, *Memorial and Remonstrance Against Religious Assessments* § 1 (1785), reprinted in *Everson v. Board of Educ.,* 330 U.S. 1, 64 (Rutledge, J., dissenting); John Leland, *The Rights of Conscience Inalienable* (1791), reprinted in *Political Sermons, supra* note 6, at 1079, 1085.

Nowhere is the connection between church-state separation and the more general idea of liberal government so clear as in the writings of John Locke. His *Essay on Toleration* and his *Second Treatise on Government* address different problems but propose precisely the same solution. For the protection of religious liberty, Locke "esteem[ed] it above all things necessary to distinguish exactly the business of civil government from that of religion and to settle the just bounds that lie between the one and the other." The "whole jurisdiction" of government, he wrote, is confined to "civil concernments," which consisted of protecting the "life, liberty, health, and indolency of body; and the possession of outward things, such as money, lands, houses, furniture, and the like." Compare this formulation to his delineation of the legitimate scope of government in the *Second Treatise*. There Locke insisted that the "great and chief end" of government is the protection of "property," which he defined as including "life, liberty, and estate." When government is confined to this end, freedom is secured. In Lockean theory, there was no tension between liberalism and religious freedom—they were essentially the same. They meant government limited in its powers.[8]

Of course, these ideas—the separation of church and state and limited government more generally—had their detractors. Hobbes, for instance, would have no part of it. Large sections of his *Leviathan* are devoted to the principle that the sovereign must be "Supreme Pastor" as well as civil ruler. He must have power to determine the doctrines, sacraments, and personnel of the church. Hobbes recognized that if citizens perceive a contradiction between the commands of God and the commands of the sovereign, they will be inclined to obey that of the higher authority. This is the main cause of "Sedition, and Civill Warre" in Christian nations. The solution to this problem, Hobbes argued, is to vest spiritual and temporal authority in the same sovereign. This would not conflict with any rightful claim of conscience, he said, because all that is necessary to salvation is faith in Christ and obedience to the laws.[9]

Rousseau was even more radical in his rejection of the separation between church and state. He wrote in *The Social Contract* that under Christianity "men have never known whether they ought to obey the civil ruler or the priest." Christianity gave men "two legislative orders, two rulers, two homelands," and

8. John Locke, *Essay on Toleration*, in 6 *The Works of John Locke* 1, 9, 10 (Locke 1823 and photo. reprint 1963); John Locke, *The Second Treatise of Government* ¶¶ 124, 87 [1690] (Thomas P. Peardon ed., Macmillan, 1952).

9. Thomas Hobbes, *Leviathan*, Part III, ch. 42–43, at 567–71, 609–10 [1651] (C. B. Macpherson ed., Penguin, 1968).

it put them under "two contradictory obligations." This division, of course, is precisely what commends separation to the liberal. But to Rousseau, "all that destroys social unity is worthless; all institutions that set man in contradiction to himself are worthless." He thus would establish a new civil religion, which would "bind the hearts of the citizens to the State," and he advocated banishment of all citizens who refuse to conform. To be sure, Rousseau insisted that citizens "owe the Sovereign an account of their opinions only to such an extent as they matter to the community," but that is scant comfort, for he also maintained that "the Sovereign is sole judge of what is important . . . for the community to control."[10]

Rousseau's position is more radical than Hobbes's because his project for society is more ambitious. For Hobbes, the great end of government is to prevent civil disorder. As it relates to religion, that objective requires no more than that the commands of religion be consistent with those of the sovereign. This can be accomplished without great change, as Henry VIII demonstrated, through adoption of an erastian form of Christian ecclesiology. Indeed, though Hobbes does not say so, a shrewd prince in the school of Machiavelli will make as little change in the religious customs of the nation as reasons of state will permit. Rousseau, by contrast, wishes to create a new society in which social solidarity, or fraternity, is profound—so profound that the citizens become "aware . . . of their own existence merely as a part of that of the State."[11] That requires a wholly new religion, and banishment or death for any who adhere to the traditional faith of France, Roman Catholicism.

Hobbes and Rousseau are not wrong. A liberal society does pay a price for its separation of the two kingdoms of church and state. Hobbes is right that religious difference is a potent cause of sedition and civil war. Rousseau is right that religious difference is an obstacle to social unity. But in response to Hobbes, we might say that this division between priest and king is also a potent protection against tyranny, and for the same reason. It is no accident that the most effective resistance to tyranny in this most tyrannical of centuries has come from men and women of the cloth and institutions of the church— whether in Poland or South Africa, Selma or Managua or Tibet. But what can we say to Rousseau? What do citizens of liberal regimes get in return for their

10. Jean-Jacques Rousseau, *The Social Contract* 179–81 (Maurice Cranston trans., Penguin 1968); *id.* at 121; *id.* at 27.

11. Jean-Jacques Rousseau, *A Discourse on Political Economy,* in *The Social Contract and Discourses* 249, 268 (Dutton 1913).

loss of fraternity? The answer to that question is based on the idea of conscience, the idea to which I will now turn.

## Conscience and Rights

A third theological notion at the foundation of liberalism is the idea of primacy of conscience. This is the belief that faith, to be valid and acceptable to God, must be uncoerced. Under this view, it is literally impossible as a theological matter for government power to improve a citizen's spiritual state. In the words of Elisha Williams: "That faith and practice which depends on the judgment and choice of any other person, and not on the person's own understanding judgment and choice, may pass for religion in the synagogue of Satan, whose tenet is that ignorance is the mother of devotion; but with no understanding Protestant will it pass for any religion at all. No action is a religious action without understanding and choice in the agent."[12] Under this view, it is worse than useless—it is blasphemous—for an outside party, the government for example, to presume to supplant the free act of God.

The origins of the idea of the primacy of conscience are clouded. Thomas Aquinas invoked Paul's Letter to the Romans ("Everything that is not from faith is sin") in support of the proposition that we are always obliged to do what our conscience discerns, even though the conscience might be mistaken.[13] The same doctrine was incorporated into medieval canon law. Later, in Protestant thought, the primacy of conscience was connected to the doctrine of salvation through grace: the only way that unregenerate man can come to faith and salvation is through the intervention of God. One of the rallying cries of the Reformation was "God Alone is Lord of the Conscience."

If the practice of church-state separation (of a sort) preceded the theories that supported it, it must be said that the practice of respect for conscience lagged far behind. Augustine, however reluctantly, mounted a defense of the punishment of heretics, and many of his successors showed no reluctance in carrying the idea to its logical conclusion. It was easy to understand the idea of conscience within Christian orthodoxy, but it was difficult to extend that idea to others. Luther cooperated with coercion of dissenters in states with Lutheran princes, and Calvin commanded the execution of the Anabaptist Michael Servetus. Yet it must be said that the *idea* of respect for conscience

12. Williams, *supra* note 6, at 62.

13. Thomas Aquinas, *Summa Theologiae,* pt. 1.2, quest. 19, art. 5 (Thomas Gilbs, trans., McGraw-Hill, 1964–73).

the church. In its secular garb, the notion of covenant lies behind the political idea of the consent of the governed. If all persons are equally capable of perceiving the good and acting on it, then no one has a natural right to rule over another, and just government can be based only upon consent. In this sense, democracy was a secularization of the movement away from a hierarchical church structure and toward congregational ecclesiology.

Consider the sermon preached by the Baptist leader John Leland, entitled "The Rights of Conscience Inalienable." Leland considered the proposition "that the ignorant part of the community are not capacitated to judge for themselves" and responded: "Has [God] not hidden the mystery of gospel truth from [the wise] and revealed it unto babes? Does the world by wisdom know God? Did many of the rulers believe in Christ when he was upon earth? Were not the learned clergy (the scribes) his most inveterate enemies? . . . Is not a simple man, who makes nature and reason his study, a competent judge of things? Is the bible written (like Caligula's laws) so intricate and high that none but the letter-learned (according to common phrase) can read it?" Even within Protestantism, spiritual egalitarianism was more pronounced in the revival tents of New Lights, Baptists, and evangelicals than in the more scholarly circles of traditional Congregationalism or Anglicanism. The Great Awakening—the religious revival that swept the colonies in the mid-1700s—represented an outpouring of the spirit on the common people of America and prepared the ideological soil for the Revolution. But even in more restrained circles, such as Presbyterianism, the idea of the presence of the Holy Spirit in each believer's life gave rise to a "common sense" philosophy with dramatically democratic implications. Unlike reason, which was unequally distributed, this common sense was potentially present in all. It was "purely the gift of heaven," according to James Wilson. Thus egalitarianism (of a sort) was concomitant to Protestantism. Even Gordon Wood, who is hardly a partisan of religion, has noted the connection: "By the early nineteenth century, America had already emerged as the most egalitarian, most materialistic, most individualistic—and most evangelical Christian—society in Western history." In effect, Wood explains, Americans "secularized the Christian belief in the equality of all souls before God."[16]

16. John Leland, *The Rights of Conscience Inalienable,* in *Political Sermons, supra* note 6, at 1083, 1090; James Wilson, *Lectures on Law,* in 1 *The Works of James Wilson* 213 (Robert Green McCloskey ed., 1967); Gordon Wood, *The Radicalism of the American Revolution* 230, 235 (1991).

### Religion and Liberalism

In sum, in the early years of the American republic few would have perceived any conflict between a religious citizenry and liberal republicanism. On the contrary, both the First and Second Great Awakenings were politico-religious movements that spurred the nation toward a more liberal, egalitarian, populist self-understanding. Liberal democracy, with its protection for religious freedom, was good for religion; and religion, in turn, provided the moral and cultural underpinnings for liberal society. Tocqueville, writing in the 1840s, observed that the Christianity of America was "what I can only describe as democratic and republican" and suggested that the religious character of America was one of the social "fact[s]" that "singularly favored the establishment of a temporal republic and democracy." Indeed, he reported that "for the Americans the ideas of Christianity and liberty are so completely mingled that it is almost impossible to get them to conceive of the one without the other." Tocqueville reported that French intellectuals viewed this connection between religion and liberty as "an obvious mistake" and thought that the only defect in the "freedom and human happiness" of the United States was its religious spirit. Perhaps in this they anticipated the perspective of the secular left of our day. To his countrymen, Tocqueville responded: "I have really no answer to give, except that those who talk like that have never been in America and have never seen either religious peoples or free ones."[17]

### THE MOVEMENT TOWARD SECULAR LIBERALISM

How, then, did American liberalism undergo the transformation from a set of ideas rooted in Christian theology and congenial to religious institutions to an ideology hostile to or suspicious of religion, at least in its more common traditional forms? How did we move from Madison to Rousseau? Let me suggest three political and intellectual developments that contributed to the shift.

### The Shift from Political to Comprehensive Liberalism

In its early phase, liberalism was not a comprehensive ideology, in the sense of offering answers to questions about the nature of the good life. To borrow a distinction from John Rawls without necessarily embracing his conception of it,

17. Alexis de Tocqueville, *Democracy in America* 288, 293–94 (J. P. Mayer ed., 1969).

early liberalism was a "political" liberalism. A "political" conception of justice, according to Rawls, is one that applies only to "the framework of basic institutions," whereas a "comprehensive" doctrine is one that addresses nonpolitical life as well, including "conceptions of what is of value in human life, and ideals of personal character, as well as ideals of friendship and of familial and associational relationships, and much else that is to inform our conduct."[18] The constitutional principles of the early American republic were a form of political liberalism because they did not purport to direct the people how they should live. The Constitution limited the government in the way it should conduct the public business. The First Amendment, for example, begins "*Congress* shall make no law . . ." The constitutional order created by the founders did not restrict—indeed it protected—the ability of citizens to take sides in religious disputes, favor their own interests or those of their group, and to be prejudiced or enlightened in accordance with their own lights. The Constitution was an attempt to create a government strong enough to keep the peace and promote economic prosperity but *without* the power to affect or coerce the ordinary lives or beliefs of a heterogenous people. The Religion Clauses of the First Amendment, in particular, were designed to enable people of many diverse views to live together in a political community in relative harmony, with the least possible imposition on their consciences, consistent with peace and good order.

Elements of this liberal polity were state neutrality, tolerance, and the guarantee of equality before the law. Neutrality meant, fundamentally, that the government would not take sides in the religious and philosophical disagreements among the people. "If there is any fixed star in our constitutional constellation," wrote Justice Robert Jackson, "it is that no official, high or petty, can prescribe what shall be orthodox in politics, nationalism, religion, or other matters of opinion."[19] Tolerance meant something like "live and let live." It did not mean that everyone in the nation was expected to approve of the conduct or beliefs of everyone else. It meant that everyone would refrain from using public power or private violence to force one another to conform. Equality under the law meant that our rights as citizens did not depend on belonging to the right religion—or later, to the right race, gender, or nation of origin. We could be equal fellow citizens with people with whom we shared no other value.

It seems obvious that something has changed. Today there is a widespread sense that not only should the government be neutral, tolerant, and egalitarian,

18. Rawls, *supra* note 4, at 13.
19. *West Virginia Bd. of Educ. v. Barnette,* 319 U.S. 625 (1943).

but so should all of us, and so should our private associations. Open-minded-ness, not conviction, is the mark of the good liberal citizen. Indeed, there is something suspect in those who are sure that they are right, for it might imply that someone else is wrong. From a religious point of view, however, open-mindedness in itself is a largely instrumental virtue—a way station in the search for Truth. Once a person has experienced the presence of God, faith—not open-mindedness—joins hope and love in the triad of theological virtues. For this and other reasons, the new ideal of the liberal citizen seems to conflict with the ideal believer in religion or any other comprehensive faith or ideology. To the extent that the state uses its power to inculcate and enforce this new vision of the liberal citizen, religious freedom is endangered. Indeed, liberalism in the old sense is itself endangered, for liberal government becomes not a set of political arrangements by which people of widely differing views can live together in relative harmony, but an essentially sectarian program enforcing its dogmas by force. It ceases to embody a genuine separation between church and state and comes to be the establishment of a particular view toward religious matters, the establishment of secularism.

We can see the origins of this new secular liberalism—this liberalism as a comprehensive ideology—in Rousseau. Rousseau insists that it is not possible to distinguish what he calls "civil" toleration from what he calls "theological" toleration. In the terms we have been using, he suggests that there can be no distinction between political and comprehensive liberalism. Listen to Rousseau: "Those who distinguish civil from theological intolerance are, to my mind, mistaken. The two forms are inseparable. It is impossible to live at peace with those whom we regard as damned; to love them would be to hate God who punishes them: we positively must either reclaim or torment them." We hear the same message today from scholars like Stanley Fish, who insist that a "committed Christian," to be consistent with his own principles, should want to "disband" the "marketplace of ideas" and replace it with "a regime of virtue." Because committed Christians are not "theologically tolerant"—they believe that their faith is true—it is not consistent for them to be civilly tolerant, or "liberal," according to Fish, echoing Rousseau. We likewise hear the same message more crudely put by those who demonize the so-called religious right—as if those whose understanding of justice and the common good are religiously informed are suspect. Rousseau was characteristically blunt about the consequences of his position. Traditional religions must be persecuted: "Whoever dares to say: Outside the Church is no salvation ought to be driven from the State." All religions must be required to embrace toleration—meaning theological toleration, the view that all religious positions are equal—under threat of banishment.[20]

In America we do not live up to Rousseau's exacting standard. But there is more than a hint of Rousseau in Amy Gutmann's argument that all schools, including private religious schools, should be forced to teach liberal dogma concerning "toleration" and "mutual respect," in Yale University's refusal to allow the Christian Legal Society to recruit on campus because it favors Christians, in the insistence by some universities that traditionalist students live in university dormitories despite their conscientious objection to the loose and immoral environment of the dorms, in the attack on the tax-exempt status of churches that have all-male clergies, and in the attempt by gay-rights groups, supported by many of the pillars of the American establishment, to force the Boy Scouts of America, a private voluntary association, to accept an avowed homosexual as an assistant scoutmaster.[21]

The logical misstep here is not in the identification of neutrality, tolerance, and equality as proper guiding principles for liberal government. It is the projection of political principles onto private persons and associations. This is not merely overextension. It is inversion. When government comes to insist that all citizens should be neutral, tolerant, and egalitarian, it ceases to be liberal government. As Rawls has commented, government should not "seek to cultivate the distinctive virtues and values of the liberalisms of autonomy and individuality, or indeed of any other comprehensive doctrine. For in that case it ceases to be a form of political liberalism."[22]

### The Decline of Limited Government

A second important development is that liberalism ceased to be understood as standing for limited government. Welfare-state liberalism has so eclipsed Lockean liberalism that the latter is no longer even denominated "liberalism" in common speech. With the rise of the welfare-regulatory state, the spheres of re-

20. Rousseau, *Social Contract, supra* note 10, at 121–22; Stanley Fish, *Why We Can't All Just Get Along,* First Things 18–26 (Feb. 1996).

21. Amy Gutmann, *Democratic Education* 118 (1987); Letter from Dean Anthony Kronman, First Things 2 (Aug.–Sept 1997); *Rader v. Johnston,* 924 F. Supp. 1540 (D. Neb. 1996) (evangelical Christian student at University of Nebraska); John Garvey, *The Yale Five,* 128 Commonweal, No. 13, at 7 (July 17, 1998) (Orthodox Jewish students at Yale); Mary Becker, *The Politics of Women's Wrongs and the Bill of "Rights": A Bicentennial Perspective,* in *The Bill of Rights and the Modern State* 453, 484–85 (Geoffrey Stone et al. eds., 1992); and *Boy Scouts of America v. Dale,* 120 S. Ct. 2446 (2000) (U.S. Supreme Court).

22. *See* Rawls, *supra* note 4, at 200.

ligion and government were no longer distant and distinct, with the government in charge of commerce and civil order and the churches in charge of charity and the inculcation of goodness and truth. The state extended its regulatory jurisdiction over broad aspects of life that formerly had been private and frequently religious, creating conflicts both with religious institutions and with the religiously motivated activity of individuals.

It should be remembered that when the First Amendment was proposed and ratified, the government had little or no involvement in education, social welfare, or the formation and transmission of culture. These functions were predominantly left to the private sphere, and within the private sphere religious institutions played a leading role. As the government has assumed wider and wider responsibility for the funding and regulation of these functions, the idea of a "secular state" has become more and more ominous. When the state is the dominant influence in the culture, a "secular state" becomes equivalent to a secular culture. Religious influences are confined to those segments of society in which the government is not involved, which is to say that religion is confined to the margins of national life—to those areas not important enough to have received the helping or controlling hand of government.

The growth in the governmental role makes achievement of religious freedom far more difficult. As long as the domain of collective decisionmaking is small and of little philosophical import, religious freedom is protected as it were naturally—as a byproduct of a limited state, as Locke supposed. As the domain of government increases in scope, government involvement in religious activity becomes necessary if religious exercise is to be possible at all. The Lockean prescription of privatizing religion and secularizing government ceases to work as a protection for religious liberty. More sophisticated and more contentious devices, based on self-conscious religious pluralism even within the public realm, become essential. That is why the old paradigm of "strict separation" under the Establishment Clause has had to give way to such ideas as "equal access," "neutral funding," and "accommodation." If it had not, the expansion of government power, combined with the old insistence on "strict separation," would have been a relentless engine of secularization.

### Neutrality and Secularism

A third development that has contributed to the transformation of early liberalism has been the conflation of "neutrality" and "secularism." Genuine neutrality is pluralistic in character, allowing many different and contending voices to be represented in public discourse. Religious ideas, however, are often

liberalism as a hostile ideology. I believe this is a mistake for both groups. Liberalism, in its original form, was consistent with (and in many respects drawn from) major strains of Christian doctrine. Perhaps the most important function of liberalism was to enable people of faith—of different faiths—to coexist in civil society with the greatest possible freedom to live according to the dictates of conscience. To a great extent, this spirit of pluralistic liberalism still survives, and should be cultivated. But the word *liberalism* has been increasingly captured, in recent times, by a less tolerant political movement that wishes to mold public opinion in accordance with that movement's own conception of the good. Christians and citizens of other faiths would be wrong to retreat into our own brand of illiberalism. Liberalism properly understood is the form of government most consistent with the gospel, and most conducive to living in harmony with God and our neighbors. We should take it back.

# Liberal Hegemony and Religious Resistance: An Essay on Legal Theory

*Stephen L. Carter*

In *God's Long Summer,* Charles Marsh's splendid book on religion in the civil rights movement, the theologian recounts a fascinating anecdote about Fannie Lou Hamer, a founder and the guiding spirit of the Mississippi Freedom Democratic Party.[1] In the summer of 1964 the MFDP waged a challenge to the credentials of the lily-white Mississippi slate of delegates to the Democratic National Convention, a slate chosen by the lily-white Mississippi Democratic Party. The MFDP offered an integrated slate of delegates, many of whom, like Mrs. Hamer herself, had tried to register to vote and had been punished for it. The controversy terrified President Lyndon Johnson, who wanted no blot

1. A longer version of this essay formed the basis of the Zabriskie Lectures, delivered at the Virginia Theological Seminary in October of 1998. A shorter version was delivered at the annual meeting of the *Journal of Law and Religion* in October of 1999. An earlier draft was also delivered at the faculty workshop of the University of Minnesota Law School in October of 1999. A part of the argument, as well as the story about Mrs. Hamer, also appears in Stephen L. Carter, *God's Name in Vain: The Wrongs and Rights of Religion in Politics* (New York: Basic, 2000).

All scriptural references are taken from the Holy Bible, New International Version.

on the celebration of his nomination. So he sent his vice president–in–waiting, Hubert Humphrey, to visit Mrs. Hamer, with orders to buy her off.

Humphrey, believing that he was undertaking a political negotiation, asked Fannie Lou Hamer what she wanted.

Mrs. Hamer, a devout evangelical Christian, responded: "The beginning of a New Kingdom right here on earth."

Humphrey, evidently stunned, explained that his political future was on the line if he could not close a deal with her to end the credentials challenge. He apparently wanted her to understand that his nomination would create a strong voice for racial equality at the highest levels of the White House, reason enough to compromise. Fannie Lou Hamer, who had survived beating and torture in a Mississippi jail for insisting on her constitutional rights, was unimpressed. This was her reply: "Senator Humphrey, I know lots of people in Mississippi who have lost their jobs for trying to register to vote. I had to leave the plantation where I worked in Sunflower County. Now if you lose this job of vice president because you do what is right, because you help MFDP, everything will be all right. God will take care of you." This alone must have been hard on Senator Humphrey, who had fought for civil rights long before it became fashionable in the Democratic Party, and whose speech on the subject at the 1948 convention is one of the most important moments of twentieth-century political history. Mrs. Hamer, however, was relentless: "But if you take [the vice presidential nomination] this way, why, you will never be able to do any good for civil rights, for poor people, for peace or any of those things you talk about. Senator Humphrey, I'm gonna pray to Jesus for you." And that, according to Marsh, was the end of the Johnson administration's negotiation with Hamer.[2]

I begin with the story of the attempt to make a deal with Mrs. Hamer because it has much to teach us about what can happen when strong religious commitment runs up against the world of secular politics—and secular politics is, of course, the world that produces law.[3] It is my assigned task to say

2. This account is drawn from Charles Marsh, *God's Long Summer: Stories of Faith and Civil Rights* (Princeton: Princeton University Press, 1997), pp. 39–40. For a shorter version of the same story, somewhat more sympathetic to Humphrey, see Taylor Branch, *Pillar of Fire: America in the King Years 1963–65* (New York: Simon and Schuster, 1998), pp. 465–66. Branch's account has both Humphrey and Hamer in tears as she promises to pray for him. Marsh sees the two of them as adversaries, with Humphrey's eye fixed rigidly on his political ambitions.

3. Actually, I am persuaded by the work of Stanley Hauerwas that the concept of *secular* is an illusion, that the "secular world" does not exist. See *Dispatches from the Front: Theological Engagements with the Secular* (Durham: Duke University Press, 1994). In this essay, however, I shall pass that point.

something about the relation of religion generally—and Christianity in particular—to the liberal theory of law. The rule of law is a fundamental principle of
liberal democracy. The exercise of political and personal freedoms and the
functioning of the market economy both rely on and are constrained by the necessity of obedience to law. Liberal theory in turn relies on rules of recognition
to tell us what counts as a law—we develop ways to distinguish between a bill
to raise taxes that is passed by the state legislature and signed by the governor on
the one hand and, on the other, an order from Joe down at Joe's Diner raising
taxes because he thinks it is a good idea.

In liberal theory, however, legal legitimacy cannot rest simply on the process
through which a law is enacted. Liberal democracy rests also on the idea that
there are fundamental principles of justice to which laws should cohere. At
minimum, these principles enable us to tell good laws from bad ones, so that
we know which laws to favor and which to oppose. In addition, some theorists
believe that the principles of justice enable us to impose a just order on the society, notwithstanding contrary acts that meet all the requirements to be recognized as laws. In other words, a law's inconsistency with the principles of justice
on which the society rests can be proof of its invalidity. This notion underlies,
to take the most obvious example, the contemporary model of constitutional
law. It is therefore unsurprising that in political philosophy, identifying the
principles of justice to which the apparatus of governance should (or must)
conform has become nearly the entire game. Contending theorists have created
an enormous literature, arguing for and against various ways of deriving the
principles. The literature shares two admirable commitments: first, to liberal
principles, and, second, to the rule of law.

From the Christian point of view, however, these commitments, while important, are insufficient. The first and highest duty of the individual Christian
believer is to Christ. What this means for the community in which the believer
lives has been a matter of sharp debate among theologians for centuries. Some
have opted for a society run according to Christian mores—for example, the
medieval Catholic Church, the early followers of the Reformed tradition, the
preachers of the "Christian America" movement in the nineteenth century,
some liberation theologians of the twentieth, and, of course, the conservative
Christian political organizations that have, over the past two decades, so shaken
the national political scene. Others have simply insisted that the society should
be well ordered, should not require of the believer what Christ forbids, and
should basically leave the believer alone to go his own way—for example, some
of the very early Christians, the Anabaptists (and their American descendants,

including the Mennonites and the Amish), the dissenting preachers of the First Great Awakening in the eighteenth century, and many evangelicals even in the twentieth. (Lately, a fair number of conservative Christian political activists in the United States have also gravitated from the first group into the second.[4])

Mrs. Hamer, like so many religious activists in the nation's history, fell into the first group: she wanted to reorganize American society along the lines that she believed the Lord required. In this she stood in the shoes of the abolitionists and the prohibitionists alike, who also wanted to repair human damage to God's creation. Johnson and Humphrey shared a more modest goal: they simply wanted to win the election. They wanted Mrs. Hamer on board, but only if they could first transform her activism into a more familiar category, so that her religious commitments might either be submerged or be turned to the political purposes of the Democratic Party.

More important to the present purpose, the story may also do service as a metaphor for a larger conversation. Mrs. Hamer may play the part of the unapologetically religious voice in our public councils; Johnson and Humphrey may stand in for liberal theory. In their roles, they could accept only part of what Mrs. Hamer desired—the part justifiable in liberal terms. Insofar as her argument was couched in illiberal terms, however, they could not accept it and, indeed, could not really acknowledge it. And according to contemporary liberal theory, what made Mrs. Hamer's argument illiberal was not its goal but its nature: she insisted on pressing a religious case in the public square.

The liberal state is uncomfortable with deep religious devotion—and, for the most part, so is its product, liberal law. Religious belief is reduced to precise parity with all other forms of belief, an act of leveling that is already threatening to religion itself. In practice, liberalism often reduced religion to an even smaller role than other belief systems, seeking to limit or shut off its access to the public square and often deriding the efforts of the religious to live the lives they think the Lord requires when those efforts seem to conflict with other liberal goals.

## BELIEF AND ILLIBERAL LIBERALISM

The discomfort of contemporary liberal theory with strong religious commitment poses a particular challenge for me, as a committed Christian, teaching at

4. See, for example, the discussion in "Is the Religious Right Finished? An Insiders' Conversation," *Christianity Today,* September 6, 1999, p. 43. I discuss the evolution of the idea of retreat in *God's Name in Vain,* especially chapters 3 and 8.

a university that, despite its religious roots, is committed to a vigorously secular ethos. Unfortunately, like so many secular institutions, Yale now and then loses track of what makes distinctive religion valuable to nonreligionists, and thus falls into the common liberal trap of leveling, trying to force everyone into accepting a given set of meanings that the institution prefers. So in the late 1990s Yale rejected the petition of a group of Orthodox Jewish students who wanted to live off campus (because they believe that the atmosphere in the dormitories encourages premarital sex, which they believe God wants them to avoid) and the request by the Christian Legal Society for the freedom to recruit at the law school while hiring only . . . well, Christians.[5]

It may be that the reader will disagree with my view that Yale was wrong in both cases. But I do not cite these examples to argue against what the university did. Rather, I suggest that Yale's reactions in both these cases mirror the tragedy of liberal theory when it meets religious commitment. The basic response of liberal theory to religiosity is to try to speak words that seem to celebrate it (as a part of the freedom of belief, or conscience, or the entitlement to select one's own version of the good) while in effect trying to domesticate it . . . or, if that fails, to try to destroy it.

This accusation might sound overstated, but it should be unsurprising. Liberalism is a theory of the state in its relationship with individuals, but not just a theory of the organization or output of the state; liberalism also seeks to explain how the state should both stimulate and regulate the search for meaning. Religions, too, seek to provide meanings to their adherents, meanings of a deep and transcendent sort. What is religion, after all, but a narrative a people tells itself about its relationship with God, usually over an extended period of time?[6] And if the narrative is truly about the meaning God assigns to the world, as Chris-

5. Each of these disputes has spilled into public view. The Orthodox Jewish students sued, claiming violations of, among other things, the Fair Housing Act and the antitrust laws, but the case was dismissed by a federal judge in August 1998. See *Hack v. President and Fellows of Yale College,* 16 F. Supp. 2d 183 (D. Conn., 1998). (At this writing, it is on appeal.) The Christian Legal Society controversy has been much discussed on the Internet and was also the subject of much argument and correspondence in the magazine *First Things.*

6. I defend the definition of religion as narrative in my Oliver Wendell Holmes Lecture. See Stephen L. Carter, "Parents, Religion, and Schools: Reflections on *Pierce,* 70 Years Later," *Seton Hall Law Review* 27 (1997): 1194. Obviously, the consequence of this view is that there is no such thing as a religion of one—or a religion founded just yesterday. Until the belief system develops both facets of the definition, a people and an extension over time, it may be an interesting set of ideas about God, those ideas may even involve a strong faith commitment, they may even be true—but it is not a religion.

tianity is, the follower of the religion, if truly faithful, can hardly select a different meaning simply because the state says so. If Religionist believes that God's love does not allow some human beings to enslave others, no amount of teaching by the merely mortal agency of the state should cause Religionist to change. Quite the contrary: Religionist, if she believes that the state is committing great evil, has little choice but to try to get the state to change.

I should make clear that I do not believe, as some do, that conflict between liberalism and religious commitment is inevitable. The liberalism of the Enlightenment, for example, is generally compatible with a Christian view of the world. Christianity is not, in its essence, opposed to representative democracy, to a regime of individual rights, or to the principle that we should, for the most part, be left alone by the state so that we can pursue individual visions of the good. Quite the contrary: Christianity probably could not survive in the absence of these fundamental assumptions of liberal democracy. Democracy has been good for Christianity. (The distorted Christianity of the Middle Ages, when the church tried to create, as the historian Paul Johnson says, a "total Christian society" in Europe, soon was barely recognizable as Christian.)

Similarly, the process-based liberalism that formed the heart of legal theory for a large chunk of the second half of the twentieth century is entirely consistent with a Christian view of the world. For the process theorist, law was recognized by its compliance with certain "rules of recognition." Morality and law were not entirely separate, but their spheres were not thought to be identical. One could recognize a valid law even though it required or allowed something that was wrong; one could recognize a valid realm of private conduct even though my actions within it contradicted the moral judgment of others. Christianity, precisely because the first allegiance of every Christian is to God, must have a reliable basis for comprehending the state's commands. It is God's instruction that Christians obey the constituted authorities, the leaders of the state, who hold their offices from God in trust, except when the commands of the state are inconsistent with the demands of the Lord. But one can neither give allegiance to the constituted authorities on earth nor defy them for Christ's sake until one knows just what the authorities have commanded.

Yet neither Enlightenment liberalism nor process-based liberalism represents the entire story of contemporary liberal philosophy. Liberalism as a theory cannot help but take on a triumphal character, for the ideals of liberalism have largely triumphed in the political world; the state is nowadays a liberal state. The trouble is that the state and the religions are in competition to explain the meaning of the world. When the meanings provided by the one differ from the meanings provided by the other, it is natural that the one on the losing end will do what it can to become a winner. Often, especially in today's mass-produced world, characterized by the intrusion into every household of the materialist interpretation of reality, religions are just overwhelmed, which leads most of them to change and many of them to die.[7] But more subtle tools are available in the assault on religious meaning. Indeed, all through history, the state has tried to domesticate religion, sometimes by force, simply eliminating dissenting faiths; sometimes through the device of creating an official, "established" church; sometimes—as in twentieth-century American experience—through reducing the power of religion by confining its freedom within a state-granted, state-defined, and state-controlled structure of constitutional rights.[8]

Religion, however, is no idle bystander. If the state tries to domesticate religion, its most powerful competitor in the creation of meaning, then religion tries simultaneously to subvert the state.[9] Liberalism sees this as one of religion's dangers, which it is: history has demonstrated time and again the mischief the institutional church can cause (especially for its doctrinal purity) when it grabs for the reins of secular authority. But the tendency of religion, at its best, to subvert the state is also one of religion's virtues. Every theory of the state—at least when put into practice—tends toward hegemony. When theory becomes law, it becomes power, and power works to sustain itself. Another lesson history teaches us is that every state seeks to restrict or eliminate competing

7. For two quite different accounts of the process of that change, see Harold Bloom, *The American Religion: The Emergence of the Post-Christian Nation* (New York: Simon and Schuster, 1992), and Nathan O. Hatch, *The Democratization of American Christianity* (New Haven: Yale University Press, 1989). Bloom believes that the strange workings of American individualist ideology have reduced almost all of religion to a form of Gnosticism. Hatch argues that the tug of democracy has altered the hierarchical structures that characterized most European religions, greatly enhancing the importance and the power of the lay member. Although Bloom's polemic is, as always, fascinating, and what he says is surely true of many mainline Protestant churches, my scholarly sympathies lie with Hatch.

8. For a useful discussion of the ways in which the offer of establishment was used very early to seduce Christian believers away from Christian truth, see Hugo Rahner, *Church and State in Early Christianity*, trans. Leo Donald Davis (San Francisco: Ignatius Press, 1992) (originally published in German, 1961). I discuss the problem of domestication through the granting of rights in greater detail in my Brennan Symposium Lecture. See Stephen Carter, "Religious Freedom as if Religion Matters: A Tribute to Justice Brennan," *California Law Review* 87 (1999): 1059.

9. I borrow the image of religion as subversive of the state it inhabits from the work of the liberation theologians, especially David Tracy. See David Tracy, *Plurality and Ambiguity: Hermeneutics, Religion, Hope* (San Francisco: Harper and Row, 1987).

centers of meaning. Thus every state, however noble the theory on which it is constructed, needs its subversives.

The liberal state is no exception to the general rule. Liberalism, too, tends toward hegemony. Not content to serve as a theory of organization of the state, it has grown into a theory of organization of private institutions in the state. If the state itself cannot discriminate among its citizens on the basis of race or sex or religion, then private institutions, it seems, should not do so either. One need not support any of these forms of discrimination to see the obvious conceptual difficulty: a theory that developed in order to explain the organization of the state (from which there is no simple exit for dissenters or subjects of discrimination) becomes a theory about organization of everything. And that, I think, is the true source of the supposed conflict between liberal theory on one side and religion on the other. Religion resists. Let us think about that.

## RELIGION'S SUBVERSIVE POWER

There are in the United States of America a number of private colleges that accept only women as students. As of this writing, there is but one that accepts only men. A few decades ago there were significant numbers of both. The change in numbers is an artifact of the liberal idea that private organizations should follow the lead of public ones. (The democracy that the theorists of pluralism celebrated in the fifties and sixties believed exactly the opposite, but that is a rather moot point.) If it is wrong for public organizations to discriminate on the basis of sex (specifically, against women), then it is wrong for private organizations to do so. This idea is often dressed up in plausible theoretical garb—private male-only organizations may be conceptualized, for example, as supporting bulwarks for women's oppression—but no matter how it is dressed, it remains the same animal. That animal is hegemony. Its enemy is diversity.

I have no particular brief for male-only colleges. I would never have dreamed of attending one and would not wish it for my son. But I am not prepared to say that no rational, public-spirited parents could ever decide that such a school would be better for their son than a sexually integrated campus would be. Certainly enough parents think that way for the choice to be one that the market would support. But it is the tendency of liberalism, as for all successful theories of the state, to find danger in competing systems of meaning, and so to strive to eliminate them. Consequently, male-only colleges, male-only private clubs, and (on many campuses, including my own) male-only bathrooms have all died, or are on the way to dying, sacrificed to the public virtue of sexual equality. One may celebrate the public virtue and, at the same time, mourn the death of private diversity.

Democracy needs diversity because democracy advances through dissent, difference, and dialogue. The idea that the state should not only create a set of meanings, but try to alter the structure of institutions that do not match it, is ultimately destructive of democracy because it destroys the differences that create the dialectic. Yet the idea is a popular one—and religions, precisely because the meanings they offer can be so radically different from those proposed by the state, often bear the brunt of hegemony. Thus, for example, America's anti-Catholicism during the nineteenth and early twentieth century was not simply a matter of private discrimination; the state, especially through the curriculum of the public schools, was heavily involved in what might fairly be described as an effort to wean Catholic children away from the "un-American" religion of their parents.[10] The reason? The meaning thought to be basic to the Catholic way of life was inconsistent with the meaning thought to be basic to the American (in this case, Protestant) way of life. (Some of the most prominent voices of the early Republic expressed doubts that Catholicism was even covered by religious freedom, for religious freedom was the freedom to practice a free religion, which Catholicism, according to its critics, was not.[11])

To take a more recent controversy, the Platform for Action and Beijing Declaration, adopted at the close of the Fourth World Conference on Women in September 1995, seems to commit the signatories to undoing centers of power, including private ones, in their own countries that are oppressive of women as the phrase is understood politically in the West—a proposition that traditional religionists, men and women, all over the world see as a threat to their freedom

10. See the somewhat depressing discussions in Warren A. Nord, *Religion and American Education: Rethinking a National Dilemma* (Chapel Hill: University of North Carolina Press, 1995); Robert Handy, *Undermined Establishment: Church-State Relations in America, 1880–1920* (Princeton: Princeton University Press, 1991); and Jay P. Dolan, *The American Catholic Experience: A History from Colonial Times to the Present* (Garden City, N.Y.: Doubleday, 1985).

11. Critics of Catholicism included such prominent dissenting colonial Baptists as Isaac Backus, as well as such influential members of the founding generation as John Jay. For the critics, "free" religion meant religion free of the corrupt and worldly churches of Europe: in a word, Catholicism. For a discussion of Backus, see, for example, William Lee Miller, *The First Liberty: Religion and the American Republic* (New York: Knopf, 1986), pp. 211–16. For a discussion of Jay, see Gerard V. Bradley, "The Religious Test Clause and the Constitution of Religious Liberty: A Machine that has Gone of Itself," *Case Western Reserve Law Review* 37 (1987): 674.

to build communities of meaning independent of the state. By liberal standards, Roman Catholicism, Orthodox Judaism, a variety of Bible-centered Protestant communities, and the Sunni and Shia branches of Islam are all oppressive of women. One reading of the Beijing Declaration is that the signing states must try to alter the substantive content of these religious traditions.

But why not set out to change the religion of the people? No state is truly interested in preserving independent communities of meaning. States, historically, have been interested in preserving themselves. The liberal state should be different, because of its supposed neutrality among competing conceptions of the good; but in practice, and more and more in theory, the liberal state is just as insistent as any other that everybody should believe the same basic things . . . as long as they are liberal things.

It is not surprising that the conference seemed to view religion as a special danger to its effort to impose a single set of meanings on the world, because religion has been one of the few institutions that has had modest success in resisting the hegemonic pull of liberalism. I do not mean to suggest, obviously, that no religion can have tenets that are politically "liberal," or that an institutional religion always errs when it reinterprets traditional doctrine in light of the lived experience of God's people. Quite the contrary. Religions always understand the Will of God imperfectly; consequently, they may come to a richer understanding of that Will with the passage of time; and thus does doctrine evolve. Moreover, for all that critics may deride traditional religion for purportedly antiquated understandings of sexuality and the role of women, the Western religious traditions have often been, and are today, well to the left of the American norm on such matters as sharing the wealth and caring for the oppressed.

On the other hand, some Western religions have caved in to the pressure to organize according to the meanings propounded by the state, more or less agreeing with the proposition that the same rules that guide the state should also guide private institutions within the state, and so they have decided to change their teachings to fit the changing beliefs of the people—they have tried to be, in a word, popular. As a Christian, I find mysterious the notion that God's will can be decided by majority vote, because it seems to confirm the ancient critique of religion, that man has created God in his own image. When religion surrenders to the political or cultural passion of the moment, whether a passion of the left or a passion of the right, it yields the transcendent character that marks the religious sense as potentially distinctive among ways of understanding the world. One sees this process at work, for example, among those politically active conservative evangelicals who seem confident that there is a correct biblical position on everything from building a strategic missile defense system to cutting the capital gains tax; and also among those progressive Protestants who seem to believe that only a shameless homophobe, rather than a careful student of God's word, could possibly oppose the blessing of same-sex unions.

The conflict with liberal theory, however, is posed not by those faith traditions that surrender to the pull of the world but by those that struggle against it, exercising their power of resistance. These resisting faiths, as we might call them, are those that insist on teaching different meanings from those imposed by the state, even in the face of public disapproval or, in many cases, actual state pressure. The resisting faiths have insisted on their right (and perhaps their responsibility) to be different, to teach different meanings, and, in some cases, have amassed sufficient political clout to remain so.

In America, Christianity has sometimes been a resisting faith, and has sometimes surrendered to the culture instead.[12] Yet Christians are, without question, called to resist: "Do not conform any longer to the pattern of the world, but be transformed by the renewing of your mind" (Romans 12:2). The resistance to which Christians are called is not necessarily active dissent, though it sometimes may be.[13] The more important form of resistance is active difference, living life in a way that sets the Christian apart from the culture. Active difference is necessarily resistance in an era when cultural, political, and legal pressures combine in an effort to influence fundamental values.

For a resisting faith to survive and thrive, political clout is often crucial. The courts are not usually helpful because, as Frederick Mark Gedicks has pointed out, no adherent to a non-Christian, nonmainstream faith has ever won a First

12. For a discussion of the link between surrender to the culture and the desire to fill the seats, see the sociologist Peter L. Berger's classic analysis, *Noise of Solemn Assemblies: Christian Commitment and the Religious Establishment in America* (New York: Doubleday, 1961).

13. Romans 13:1 reads: "Everyone must submit himself to the governing authorities, for there is no authority except that which God has established. The authorities that exist have been established by God." Some Christians read this language to say that Christians may never rise up in rebellion, even against an unjust government (Paul wrote these words at a time of persecution). Others argue that the word "authority" presupposes "legitimacy"— that is, a government that is too anti-Christian might not possess authority. Most Christians, in any case, would agree that submission to authority does not mean obedience to unjust laws. Christians must disobey laws requiring them to act in ways contrary to God's edicts, even if to do so means punishment, for the will of God is superior to the will of authority, even when authority has been established by God.

Amendment religious freedom case in the Supreme Court.[14] Dissenting Christians have not fared well either, notably in recent years, as the courts have more or less abandoned any serious protection of religious liberty as a distinct constitutional right. In particular, the federal judiciary has all but abandoned the once-lively theory of accommodation, under which, in certain circumstances, the dissenting religionist is excused from compliance with a law that applies to others. This theory was used in the nineteenth century, for example, to allow churches to hire pastors from abroad in defiance of restrictions on immigration; and it was used in the twentieth to permit Amish parents to keep their children home from school after the eighth grade.[15] But from the mid-1980s onward, the theory has largely disappeared, so the Supreme Court had no trouble, in 1986, allowing the Air Force to punish a Jewish officer for refusing to remove his yarmulke indoors.[16] Today's judges have forgotten what yesterday's recalled: that religious freedom is nothing if it is not the freedom to be different. The different meanings of life that religions at their best supply translate into different ways of living—in short, into diversity—if the state allows believers sufficient space.

With the courts largely out of the picture, the legislature has become the principal battleground of religious freedom, as different traditions jockey for advantage, or at least survival, resulting in all the favoritism and all the discrimination that one would expect.[17] The devolution upon the legislature of the duty to carve out exceptions from general laws for the benefit of religious liberty helps explain why, for example, the Roman Catholic Church maintains its freedom to ordain only men as priests, notwithstanding the nation's antidiscrimination laws, but adherents of Santería are often prosecuted when they sac-

14. Frederick Mark Gedicks, *The Rhetoric of Church and State: A Critical Analysis of Religion Clause Jurisprudence* (Durham: Duke University Press, 1995). One non-Christian tradition has won a Fourteenth Amendment case, claiming discrimination; *Church of the Lukumi Babalu Aye v. City of Hialeah*, 508 U.S. 520 (1993).

15. *Church of the Holy Trinity v. United States*, 143 U.S. 457 (1892); *Wisconsin v. Yoder*, 406 U.S. 205 (1972).

16. *Goldman v. Weinberger*, 475 U.S. 503 (1986).

17. I have argued elsewhere that religious believers, particularly dissenters, may be too court-dependent. If the courts continue to retreat from serious protection of religious freedom, the religious may have to rely on God for their survival. See Carter, "Religious Freedom as if Religion Matters." I am not advocating judicial abandonment of the job of protecting religious dissenters, I am simply pointing to the risks to traditions that come to see judges as their principal protectors.

rifice animals (as their faith requires) in violation of animal rights ordinances.[18] It is not that we value animals more than women but that we value Catholics more than Santeros.

Resisting faiths have been an important source of dissent in our democratic polity, and sometimes the dissenters have prevailed. The abolitionist and civil rights movements are the most prominent examples, but they are far from the only ones. Liberal theory tends to celebrate the results achieved by those movements—an end to slavery, the development of formal legal protection against racial discrimination—without ever having very much to say about the actual source of the power of resistance. But the source matters. Not only do religions often teach different meanings than the state does, but religion, because it is at its heart a communal rather than an individual exercise, provides moral and spiritual support to the dissenters, strengthening them to stand against a tide of public disapproval. Sometimes, the lonely religious dissenter helps spark a movement that changes America, as did Fannie Lou Hamer. At other times, the lonely dissenter, along with the resisting faith, drowns in the sea of hegemonic meaning, as many Native American and African religious traditions did in the nineteenth century, and as the Mormons nearly did at the same time.

But the resisting faiths, at their best, are able to survive, and sometimes even to thrive, in the face of state pressure. As the legal scholar Robert Cover once pointed out, it is at the moments when official disapproval is greatest that the resisting faith learns most firmly what constitutes its core.[19] The subversive power of religion is tested precisely at the moment when the meaning it teaches and the meaning the state teaches are most sharply opposed. If the state teaches the virtues of enslaving human beings and the resisting faith preaches the opposite, those who hear the Word will be forced to choose. Sometimes the nation will choose to continue to do whatever the religion, through its witness, seeks to end. But more often than many observers realize, the resisting faith will persuade citizens outside the faith that its set of meanings is (on one issue, at least) the correct one; and if the resisting faith persuades enough citizens, the state is forced to change.

This last point matters. Although some liberal philosophers have argued that

18. The Supreme Court, in *Lukumi Babalu Aye*, held only that Santeros had to have the same opportunity as others to gain exemption from animal rights laws, not that the laws could not be applied to the church at all.

19. See Robert M. Cover, "The Supreme Court, 1982 Term—Foreword: *Nomos* and Narrative," *Harvard Law Review* 97 (1983): 4.

religious language in public debate will lead only to cacophony, history suggests otherwise: at times, the religiously defended proposition prevails. The philosopher Charles Taylor argues that liberal uneasiness with strong religious commitment rests in large measure upon this historical truth, or its contemporary resonance.[20] According to Taylor, an important reason that so many theorists of the present age seek to design rules for public argument from which religious language is absent is that religious language often wins. Unfortunately, it does not always win on behalf of good (that is, liberal) causes. The obvious solution is to inhibit the ability of religious commitment to alter the nature of the state.

Yet is such a goal attainable—let alone desirable? Let us ponder for a moment what has become a commonplace of liberal theory: that actions must be justified according to principles that are accessible, through dialogue, to all citizens. Different writers have different visions of what this means, but all of them seem to agree on the need, whether as a thought experiment or an actual model of dialogue, for the development of a mediating language in order to facilitate a conversation open on the same terms to all citizens. To such theorists, religious arguments on behalf of $P$ or $Not P$ make dialogue more difficult. And when the institutions of the state (and sometimes citizens themselves) actually act publicly out of religious commitment, a deeply illiberal moment has arrived. In liberal theory, the argument that the society should do $P$ because God wills it is not merely wrong in the sense that it is insufficiently justified—it is, literally, incomprehensible.

Why incomprehensible? Consider the approach of Bruce Ackerman, who offers the following hypothetical.[21] Suppose that two citizens are having a conversation. The first of them, Diviner, has before him a black box. He says that the black box has authoritatively determined which policy the state should pursue—let us continue to call it $P$. The black box, he adds, is in direct communication with God, so, really, it is God who has determined that we should do $P$. How is his fellow-citizen to respond? According to Ackerman, it is sufficient for his skeptical fellow citizen (Ackerman calls him Democrat) to point out that he himself is unpersuaded that the black box is in communication with God. Therefore even if it happens that Diviner is right about the content of God's will, he must find a way to justify $P$ that will persuade the skeptical Democrat.

20. Charles Taylor, *Sources of the Self: The Making of Modern Identity* (Cambridge: Harvard University Press, 1989), pp. 96–98 and elsewhere.

21. This example is drawn, with certain modifications that I hope do not change the original intention, from Bruce Ackerman, *Social Justice and the Liberal State* (New Haven: Yale University Press, 1980).

And so, in the end, the supporters of $P$ must repair to the tools of secular political argument.

As an observation about practical politics, Ackerman's account is entirely persuasive; that is, members of a given resisting faith are unlikely to persuade skeptics of other faiths, or of no faith, simply by consulting their sacred black box and then repeating, "God commands it!" Perhaps that is why relatively few groups that have any actual access to the levers of decisionmaking power behave this way. Even the Christian Coalition, that great bogeyman of contemporary liberalism, no longer couches many of its public appeals in biblical terms. The Contract with the American Family, the public platform of the Christian Coalition in the mid-1990s, reads, almost in its entirety, as a secular political document that any conservative organization might have produced. (The Contract with the American Family should not be confused with the Contract with America, the Republican platform in the 1994 midterm elections.) Both the goals the Contract with the American Family proposes and the arguments offered to promote them read like secular policy analysis. This result should scarcely be surprising: if one wants to prevail in politics, one must do what politics requires.

Some liberal critics of the Christian Coalition have argued that, by creating public documents that do not discuss religion, the group is concealing its true motivation. I agree with this criticism and am profoundly troubled by it—but I do not think political liberals should be. In contemporary liberal theory, religionists who wish to enter the public square are *supposed* to restate their arguments in the language of secular politics. The Christian Coalition should be applauded by liberals for its willingness to do what liberal theory requires.

Why, then, am I troubled? For the same reason I am always concerned when the people of the garden decide that the wilderness is attractive.[22] As C. S. Lewis pointed out many years ago, the practical need to be other than itself is one of the reasons that a religious organization should be wary of engaging in partisan politics.[23] He was writing against the establishment of a "Christian

22. The metaphor of the garden and the wilderness to describe the church and the world originated with Roger Williams and is probably the antecedent of the "wall of separation" metaphor. For a discussion see Mark DeWolfe Howe, *The Garden and the Wilderness: Religion and Government in American Constitutional History* (Chicago: University of Chicago Press, 1965).

23. See C. S. Lewis, "Meditation on the Third Commandment," in C. S. Lewis, *God in the Dock: Essays on Theology and Ethics* (Grand Rapids, Mich.: William B. Eerdmans, 1970), p. 196.

Party" in England, and his argument was persuasive. In a multireligious democracy, the need for political compromise is so extreme that the putatively religious organization that decides to be actively political will, inevitably, be transformed into a political organization that was once religious—in the same way, for instance, that Yale is a secular university that was once religious. This, I believe, is what is happening, or perhaps has already happened, to the Christian Coalition. Democrat is prevailing over Diviner: the Christian Coalition is learning not to talk too much about the will of God. That is why liberal theorists who oppose religious language in politics should be pleased that Christian Coalition has gained such power in the Republican Party: the process of domestication of politically active white conservative evangelicals is well under way, and may be irreversible.[24]

But perhaps we have erred in considering the story only from Democrat's point of view. Diviner might not be quite so ready to accept dialogic defeat. For example, Diviner might persuade a majority of his fellow citizens that the voice emanating from the box is indeed the voice of God. Then the majority would have a perfectly adequate reason to follow the voice . . . or perhaps we should say the Voice. Moreover, our analysis assumes the stability of Democrat's preferences when, in practice, who knows? Democrat himself might be converted to Diviner's faith, and so accept the judgment of the box.[25] In other words, there is no reason, a priori, to suppose that Diviner cannot persuade the majority of his fellow citizens, or perhaps all of them, that the Voice is to be obeyed *simply because it is the Voice.* If the goal is to find a language that all citizens might in principle accept, the language of the Voice might turn out to be it.

But even if a society-wide religious conversion is theoretically possible, liberal theory need not concede that the possibility is relevant. The dialogue liberalism envisions is, for the most part, a hypothetical one—that is, a thought experiment. Ackerman, for example, need not be read as seeking to demonstrate how an actual conversation between Democrat and Diviner might flow. He is trying to show why the individual (or the state) already committed to liberal principles should not act on a proposition merely because the Voice has commanded it. The question, therefore, is not whether a majority of citizens agrees with what the Voice commands, but whether what the Voice commands is itself

24. I discuss this proposition further in *God's Name in Vain,* especially chapter 3.

25. The legal scholar Abner Greene has made this suggestion in an analogous context. Abner Greene, Review of John Rawls's *Political Liberalism, George Washington Law Review* 62 (1994): 646, 659–660.

justified according to the principles of the liberal state.[26] In short, it is not the actual dialogue of the liberal state but the work of the liberal state that must, in its formal justification, be liberal.

Consequently, it may matter less what language citizens use in arguing over policy than whether it is possible, through a dialogue according to liberal principles, to justify the policy itself. Liberalism, as a political theory, is nowadays about output, not input; ends, not means. This in turn suggests that the liberal concern about religion in public dialogue is at least partly misplaced. It turns out not to matter much what language citizens actually use in arguing over policy; what matters is liberal analysis of the policy itself. One can therefore, consistently with Ackerman's thesis, envision two separate dialogues—one among the citizens, who are trying to govern themselves, and the other by the actual instrument of organized state power, as it tries to justify what it has done. What matters is the work of the state, not the reasoning behind it. And although I suspect that my colleague and friend Bruce Ackerman and I would often test the output of the state against somewhat different principles, I think we agree on this point.

But it is not a point liberal theorists generally are prepared to accept. Ackerman's vision might ultimately be about ends, not means, but many theorists seem perfectly serious in trying to set forth limits for real debate. The philosopher John Rawls, whose fine book *A Theory of Justice* is taught to undergraduates everywhere as a thought experiment, strongly implies in his more recent book *Political Liberalism* that he is serious in trying to design an actual dialogue, not a hypothetical one.[27] Even writers otherwise sensitive to the need to preserve the distinctive religious sphere against liberalism's assault—I have in mind, for example, the legal scholar Kent Greenawalt—have been unambigu-

26. This argument is consistent with the views of some philosophers who have argued that even if God exists, we must evaluate his commands according to a coherent moral theory in order to decide whether they are worthy of obedience. See, for example, the discussion in Bernard Williams, *Ethics and the Limits of Philosophy* (Cambridge: Harvard University Press, 1985), pp. 32–33. The Christian tradition, of course, is otherwise, for God is, in the Christian view, the very definition of moral truth.

Williams, I should add, is not persuaded that God must be obeyed only if humans decide that His will fits human definitions of the good. Williams thinks we need not obey God because he thinks God does not exist.

27. See John Rawls, *Political Liberalism* (New York: Columbia University Press, 1993). For a similar argument, see Thomas Nagel, "Moral Conflict and Political Legitimacy," *Philosophy and Public Affairs* 16 (1987): 215.

ous in their preference for a public square in which debate is carried on in a secular political language.[28]

If the language of public debate must be secular, religious citizens are required, as Michael Perry has put it, to "bracket" their religious selves, leaving behind, before entering the public square, the very aspect of personality that lends meaning to their lives.[29] The idea that religious citizens must remake themselves before joining debate might have an abstract logical appeal, but in practice it simply represents another form of official pressure on the religious to be less than their full selves. Why should anybody be surprised? It is harder to build a liberal public order (or any official public order) in the face of powerful sources of resistance. Despite disclaimers, I have always believed that this is one of the reasons that liberal theory worries so about religion: it might indeed seek to destroy the state. Better to destroy religion first. The destruction may be subtle, as in the morally nonsensical idea that it is possible for schools to teach sex education without moral content, even though few if any religions teach that sexuality is amoral. (Certainly the Christian tradition does not.[30]) Or the destructive urge can be quite direct, as in the notion, presented by a growing number of political theorists but really going back to Dewey, that the state should wean children away from any illiberal religions their parents might try

28. See especially Kent Greenawalt, *Religious Convictions and Political Choice* (New York: Oxford University Press, 1988), and Suzanna Sherry, "Responsible Republicanism: Educating for Citizenship," *University of Chicago Law Review* 62 (1995): 131.

29. See Michael Perry, *Morality, Politics, and Law: A Bicentennial Essay* (New York: Oxford University Press, 1988), pp. 72–73.

30. Many school districts wisely allow parents to excuse their children from sex education classes, but those that refuse fight furiously for their authority to teach the children as facts whatever the latest political trend believes. The courts are firmly against the parents (and thus against the survival of the religious narrative) in these matters. See, for example, *Ware v. Valley Stream High School*, 75 N.Y.2d 114, 550 N.E.2d 420 (N.Y. 1989).

I have argued elsewhere, however, that the right to excuse one's children from objectionable courses of instruction is not necessarily a sufficient protection for the religious parents seeking to project their narratives into the future. See Stephen L. Carter, *Civility: Manners, Morals, and the Etiquette of Democracy* (New York: Basic, 1998), particularly chapter 13. Opponents of classroom prayer often point to the exclusionary effect on dissenting children who know that others are engaging in an activity—prayer—from which they themselves are abstaining. There is no reason to think that the effect on dissenting religious children, who do not want to study sex education, for example, is any less. One important argument in favor of vouchers to cover part of the cost of private education, including religious education, is to spare both families and educators the difficulty of resolving these dilemmas.

to teach them.[31] Liberal theorists seem to believe that deep faith commitments pose serious threats to the order they are trying to create. I hope they are wrong. If they are right, then the order is not worth preserving.

Which brings us back to the summer of 1964 and Lyndon Johnson's sabotage of the Freedom Democrats, led by Fannie Lou Hamer.

## ARTICULATING THE BASIC QUESTION

Fannie Lou Hamer's solidly Christian faith, as Charles Marsh meticulously details, was the wellspring of her public activism. She believed herself to be answering a divine call. Yet what happened after the abortive negotiation with Humphrey is quite instructive. Rebuffed by Hamer, who claimed to be guided entirely by her faith, the party turned to other leaders of the MFDP, people who were better educated than Hamer and who were, in Johnson's eyes, easier to handle. They knew how the game was played in a way that Hamer did not. A compromise was worked out behind her back, the lily-white delegation was seated, and the brief challenge to the segregationist Democrats was turned back by a president who despised them.

It is fascinating to think that most Americans who have heard of her consider Fannie Lou Hamer a hero. In contemporary liberal theory, Mrs. Hamer could perhaps be viewed as a villain in her effort to use openly religious language in a nefarious scheme to impose a frankly religious order on the nation, and Humphrey and Johnson as heroes for going behind her back, sabotaging her inspirational leadership in order to negotiate with more practical MFDP members to destroy their leader and their movement. If Hamer is viewed heroically rather than villainously, then perhaps Charles Taylor is correct, and the purported liberal distaste for religious voices in political dialogue is simply a distaste for a particular set of political results that those voices, as articulated today, might conjure.

Let us, in any event, make no mistake: the mass protest wing of the civil rights movement, the part that was moved by religious inspiration and in turn inspired a nation, did not truly achieve its goal. America was reformed but not remade. The state did not come to revolve, as Hamer hoped and Martin Luther King, Jr., preached, around a Gospel of Love; rather, it retained its capitalist

31. See Amy Gutmann, *Democratic Education* (Princeton: Princeton University Press, 1987).

core and widened somewhat the set of beneficiaries. The state came to see its job, not as permanently changing the nation in a fundamental way in the search for a greater vision of love (for Hamer, Christian love), but rather as the permanent establishment of vast civil rights bureaucracies to monitor those aspects of equality that are measurable. The existing order was not subverted; it was reformed in minor ways that siphoned off enough support from the more radical aspects of Hamer's vision (and King's) so as to avoid grappling with the more fundamental challenges that the civil rights movement posed. The state, in short, refused to allow itself to be subverted by the resisting faith. It was a lot cheaper to invent affirmative action and buy people off.

I hope that this does not seem unfair, but it is easy to forget that Hamer was hardly alone in understanding racial oppression in religious terms. The civil rights era, it is easy to forget amidst the strange quasi-constitutional rhetoric of the present day, was a time when the fabled separation of church and state utterly dissolved, as if by some divine magic. In those heady years, the nation's politics was moved by the openly religious appeals of the *Reverend* Martin Luther King, Jr., head of the Southern *Christian* Leadership Conference. True, we saw the wonderful courage of heroic lawyers and heroic political leaders and heroic judges—but it was the remarkable heroism of ordinary black folk, facing police dogs and assassins' bullets, that captured the popular imagination.[32] And many of those ordinary black folk believed profoundly that their cause was just because God was on their side. They saw no need, as philosophers today seem to think is the better course in a liberal democracy, to reconfigure their arguments in terms of secular morality.[33] On the contrary: to speak in some other, more acceptably secular language would have been to leave their own best selves behind. So they marched and suffered and praised God, and, in some ways, changed America forever. This, surely, was a resisting faith in action.

Why was it necessary to go behind Fannie Lou Hamer's back? America, it seems, was not prepared to receive the message she insisted on bringing. Nei-

32. Those who continue to think that King's rhetoric was more secular than Christian should peruse, for example, Richard Lischer, *The Preacher King: Martin Luther King, Jr., and the Word that Moved America* (New York: Oxford University Press, 1995). For a thoughtful and scholarly analysis of the role of religion in inspiring black activists throughout the nation's history, see Albert J. Raboteau, "Martin Luther King, Jr., and the Tradition of Black Religious Protest," in Rowland A. Sherrill, ed., *Religion and the Life of the Nation* (Urbana: University of Illinois Press, 1990), p. 46.

33. See generally the discussion in Marsh, *God's Long Summer*.

ther was the Democratic Party. In particular, neither Johnson nor Humphrey was prepared to receive a message that did not result in the two of them getting precisely what they wanted. And this is at the heart of liberalism's notion that committed religionists are dangerous in the public square because it is hard to do business with them: what is meant is, they may be hard to persuade and, therefore, we might not get what we want.

The *what we want* of contemporary liberal theory is the exercise of our freedom of choice; or, more properly, our *freedoms* of choice. Modern liberalism shares its ideological foundations with free-market capitalism, because both envision human beings as bundles of preferences. The role of the liberal state (like the role of the market) is to create spaces in which the maximum number of preferences can be pursued, with the minimum amount of interference with the pursuit by others of their own preferences. In contemporary partisan politics (not to be confused with liberal theory), all sides have surrendered to this ideology. The fact that Republicans seem to think the preferences that matter most are economic and the Democrats seem to think the preferences that matter most are sexual and reproductive should not blind us to the simple truth that both parties are up to the same mischief: in real America today, as in the hypothetical America of liberal theory, it is the individual, unconnected to any sense of self-restraint, who matters most.

The point bears emphasis. The seeming incompatibility between liberal democracy and strong religious commitment is said, by the theorists of liberalism, to be about means. But it is really about ends. Much of liberal theory before the middle of the twentieth century focused on the question that has driven the Western religions from their founding— *What is best for man?*—and thus was about ends. This should scarcely be surprising, because the supposed humanism of such thinkers as Kant, and certainly the dogmatic liberalism of Locke, was shaped by the experience of religious ferment in a Europe in which the answer to this question (what I will call the basic question) carried abiding political and social significance. The project of the Enlightenment, like the project of the Protestant Reformation that preceded it and in most ways inspired it, did not hold that the basic question had no proper answer, or that all answers were equally good; the Enlightenment project held, rather, that human reason was sufficient to discover what the answer was.

Contemporary liberal theory has built from the Enlightenment project an ideal of process, pushing the state into the background, not because the state is unimportant but because the individual is more important—a valuable and still mostly unlearned lesson. But liberalism has gone past this sensible point, pressing for a reinterpretation of the basic question itself. If each of us, in the exercise of individual reason, has the ability to answer the basic question, the state, say today's theorists, should not interfere (beyond a carefully prescribed minimum, designed to maximize the freedom of others) with our freedom to live whatever answer we happen to have found. But note what has changed in liberalism. No longer is the basic question that each of us must ask the communal and perhaps even transcendent *What is best for man?* Now the basic question is *What is best for me?* (What we might call basic question primed.) The role of the liberal state is not to provide us with a space in which to reason together about the answer to the question—an answer that might then suffice for an entire community—but to provide us with the space to invent our own glorious diversity of answers, among which the state, with rare exception, will assiduously refuse to choose.

Many contemporary theorists—I have in mind, for example, Stephen Macedo and William Galston—seem willing to discard the solid post-Rawlsian liberal tenet that the state must be neutral among competing conceptions of the good. In order to create a world in which citizens are able to pursue their own answers to basic question two— *What is best for me?*—it is important, evidently, to develop citizens who themselves see the pursuit of basic question two as important. Education for democracy, or for liberal citizenship, is the way the proposition is sometimes put: children must be trained, from the time they are young, to accept liberal precepts, including the central importance of basic question two. That is why so many liberal theorists are so scathing in their attacks on *Wisconsin v. Yoder,* a 1972 decision in which the Supreme Court allowed the Old Order Amish to remove their children from school after the eighth grade.[34] The Amish, and the Supreme Court, saw further formal education as a threat to the Amish tradition, which is based in the terrible suffering of the Anabaptist experience and thus quite understandably preaches separation from the world. The critics, led by Justice William Douglas, argued that the refusal of Amish parents to send their children to school for ninth grade and beyond harmed the children—by denying them the tools they would need to lead lives in pursuit of the answer to basic question two.

Contemporary liberalism has constructed a worldview that exalts the individual self as a bundle of desires, the fulfillment of those desires in turn protected by rights. This criticism of liberalism is hardly new, and many theorists

34. 406 U.S. 205 (1972).

would not consider it a criticism at all. But Christianity, almost by its nature, must reject the liberal edifice, for Christianity constructs a worldview exalting not the individual but the connection—connection to other humans and, ultimately, to a transcendent God.[35] The Christian tradition teaches that the believer must die to self in order to live in Christ, and must reject the world for Christ's sake. Christianity, in short, is more about duty than choice. Parents who raise their children to understand their lives this way are training them to be other than what liberal theory says they should be; but a liberal state that tries to interfere is one that many committed Christians are likely to see as the enemy.

**THE MECHANISM OF CHOICE**

There is something chilling, as the theologian Stanley Hauerwas has pointed out, in the inability of liberal theory to give an account of why bearing and raising children is a positive good—children are mere choices, the outcomes of the exercise of rights—or, for that matter, to find a stronger explanation on what is wrong with murder than the argument that the victim of the murder is deprived of his or her rights.[36] Most people would see the value of children or the horror of murder without the need for explanation. It is not merely an instinct but a part of their vision of the good.

The orthodox Christian vision of the good is that goodness is exactly coextensive with the will of God. Humans do not create good and, except through God's grace, do not do good either. In the words of the 1801 articles of faith of the Episcopal Church, "Works done before the grace of Christ, and the inspi-

35. But what about religions that do not contemplate a connection to a transcendent God—the more refined forms of Buddhism, for example? I do not consider them here, because I do not think they offer much challenge to liberal hegemony. Pope John Paul II raised hackles several years ago when he speculated that belief systems that lack a sense of the transcendent should perhaps not be considered religions at all. See Pope John Paul II, *Crossing the Threshold of Hope,* ed. Vittorio Messori, trans. Jenny McPhee and Martha McPhee (New York: Knopf, 1994). For a response, see Ram Swarup, *Pope John Paul II on Eastern Religions and Yoga: A Hindu-Buddhist Rejoinder* (New Delhi: Voice of India, 1995). I have argued elsewhere that the pope was overstating a mainly theoretical point, not demeaning a religious claim. I do believe that religion needs a definition and, although I do not offer one here—I have done it elsewhere—honesty compels any would-be definer to concede that somebody's "religion" will be left out.

36. See Hauerwas, *Dispatches from the Front.*

ration of the Spirit, are not pleasant to God; . . . we doubt not but they have the nature of sin."[37] For Christians the vision of the good is the faith-guided and Spirit-inspired vision of God's will. But Christianity, unlike liberalism, does not treat this vision as a choice.[38] One does not *decide* to be a Christian. One is *called* to be a Christian. Christians differ sharply on whether mortals have the power to resist God's call, but Christianity has never taught that it is possible to become a follower of Christ if the call itself is absent.

The dedication to this worldview is created in Christian community. Parents who are serious about their Christianity consider it a responsibility to teach it to their children, not as one of several possible options but as truth. Nor are Christians alone in resisting the liberal idea that children should be raised to be neutral (as Rawlsian liberalism properly believes the state should be) among competing conceptions of the good. Few people want selves quite as unencumbered as many liberal theorists seem to propose. Such theorists as Michael Sandel and Alasdair MacIntyre have been forceful advocates for the proposition that there may after all be little value to the life lived in radical separation from others, in which all obligations are voluntary and all choices are available to be made.

Choice is not wicked. Choice is the essence of freedom, and liberalism has done more than any political idea in history to promote and protect it. Liberalism, however, is like neoclassical economics: a theory about the availability of choice without a theory about the virtue of good choices. It should not be surprising, then, that the liberal state has generated a market that produces all the gore and horror people demand. When the heavy metal group Cannibal Corpse sings about masturbating with the severed head of a murdered child, liberal theory possesses no tools with which to explain why such music is bad and is unable to accept the notion that people who derive utility from listening to such music should be discouraged from doing so. What religion provides, and liberalism by its nature cannot, is a mechanism for selecting among the available choices. The mechanism of choice is morality. If our day-to-day ac-

37. "Articles of Religion as Established by the Bishops, the Clergy, and the Laity of the Protestant Episcopal Church in the United States of America, in Convention" (Sep. 12, 1801), Art. XIII, reprinted in *The Book of Common Prayer* (New York: Seabury, 1979), p. 867.

38. For a discussion of this distinction in traditional religion, see Michael Sandel, "Freedom of Conscience or Freedom of Choice?" in James Davison Hunter and Os Guinness, eds., *Articles of Faith, Articles of Peace: The Religious Liberty Clauses and the American Public Philosophy* (Washington, D.C.: Brookings, 1990).

tivities are unmediated by morality, the same market that produces the cars and shampoos and breakfast cereals that people want will also produce the child pornography, the blackmailers, and the Klan hoods that a morally unencumbered public might demand.

Most Americans, of course, do not want these things, and the reason is the operation of the moral sense, honed since childhood, that helps us to understand the difference between good and evil, even among choices we might legally make. And although it is possible to raise moral children without the aid of religion, few Americans are interested in making the attempt. Most Americans are people of religious faith, and most people of religious faith learn right and wrong with the aid of their faiths. Liberal theory can explain neither why there are bad reasons to want a billion dollars nor why there are bad reasons to want an abortion, but the great majority of Americans would have no trouble identifying bad reasons to do either. For the Christian, the point is particularly sharp. There are no actions that I take beyond the sight of God and, therefore, no actions I take beyond the scope of moral judgment. "Everything that you do, do for the sake of God," wrote the Jewish philosopher Moses Maimonides.[39] The orthodox Christian teaching is identical: "Whatever you do, do it all for the glory of God" (1 Cor. 10:31). Even though this famous epigram may seem impossible to live thoroughly, it nevertheless presents an approach to living, to understanding the good, that is sharply distinct from the self-seeking self of liberalism.

Systems of secular morality (if one rejects the contention of Hauerwas and others that the secular is a myth) can also provide reasons to choose among alternatives. But precisely because secular morality is not linked to any sense of the transcendent, its hold on human personality is often weaker than the hold of religion. I do not contend that the hold is always weaker, any more than I contend that religious moral systems always generate better choices than secular ones; history refutes that idea. I contend only that virtuous adult citizens could believe quite rationally (*pace* Hume) that their religious faith is the appropriate source of values to guide both private and public actions, and that a theory of the state that implies that it isn't will neither win, nor deserve, their adherence.

39. Quoted in Abraham Joshua Heschel, *Maimonides,* trans. Joachim Neugroschel (New York: Doubleday, rpt. 1991), p. 203. (Translation first pub. 1982; original German version pub. 1935.)

## THE TRAINING OF CHILDREN

Liberal theory, of course, is a theory; it need not be psychologically accurate; it need not deal with people as they are; it can consider people as they should be. So when Stephen Macedo, for example, suggests that liberalism should set out to combat illiberal religions, we can take him quite seriously.[40] He is uninterested in constructing the state for the benefit of the people. He would rather construct the people for the benefit of the state. That is the reason that liberal theory focuses so heavily on public education. The theory pretends that education will give children the tools they need as citizens, tools of critical analysis, for example.[41] In practical operation, however, the liberal theory of education means competing actively with families for the privilege of creating meaning in the lives of children—more fundamentally, trying to wrest the children from the grasp of the religion of the parents, thus denying the putatively illiberal religion the opportunity to extend itself into the future.[42]

In the Christian vision, children are to be raised not for the purposes of the state but for the purposes of God. "Train a child in the way he should go," admonishes the Proverb, "and when he is old he will not turn from it" (Pr. 22:6). And how are young Christians to be trained? For one thing, Christians are to focus their minds only on what is good and noble (Phil. 4:8). They are to be "living sacrifices," to resist conformity to the world (Rom. 12:1–2). And they are, in the traditional Christian teaching, to die to self, to seek Christ rather than the fulfillment of their own desires. But in the liberal vision, the horizons of the traditionally trained Christian child must seem narrow indeed. And the agents of that illiberal constraint are the parents.

Small wonder that the schools are the great contemporary battlegrounds for the struggle over the role of religion, not only in our public life but in our private lives. This essay is not the place to recapitulate the sad history of the use of compulsory education laws as weapons for the destruction of religions opposed

40. This is the implication, for example, of Stephen Macedo, "Liberal Civic Education and Religious Fundamentalism: The Case of God vs. John Rawls," *Ethics* 105 (1995): 468.

41. See, for example, the discussions of education in Ackerman, *Social Justice and the Liberal State,* pp. 150–58, and Gutmann, *Democratic Education,* pp. 1–70. See also Macedo, "Liberal Civic Education."

42. Two thoughtful discussions of this difficulty are Nomi Maya Stolzenberg, "'He Drew a Circle that Shut Me Out': Assimilation, Indoctrination, and the Paradox of Liberal Education," *Harvard Law Review* 106 (1993): 581, and Stephen G. Gilles, "On Educating Children: A Parentalist Manifesto," *University of Chicago Law Review* 93 (1996): 937. Both writers owe an obvious debt to Robert Cover.

by the state, especially Roman Catholicism.[43] Rather, I simply wish to note that the educational approach preferred by liberal theory, with its emphasis on critical skills that enable the child to choose what to believe, flies in the face of the traditional Christian understanding of family responsibility: the Christian child is trained to follow God's commands, not to question them.

What can one make of this? Simply that liberal political theory, for all its virtues, is woefully incomplete because of its persistent refusal to accept the force of religion as a genuine and vital expression of human personality. Few Americans see religious faith as an aberration, in the way that many leading theorists of liberalism do. Few religious Americans (and most Americans are religious) will likely value a theory of the state that not only dismisses their most cherished beliefs from the public sphere but even tries, through the device of public education, to make it harder for those beliefs to function in the private sphere.

Yet there are obviously limits on how accommodating public education can be. In a multireligious democracy, it would be difficult, and sometimes wrong, for the schools to embrace traditional religious notions of right and wrong—at least if the embrace is explicit. Character education, for example, although generally popular among parents, leaves some evangelicals uneasy. How is it possible to teach moral rules, they wonder, if one fails to mention the source of all morality? This difficulty helps explain why so many parents support vouchers and other forms of tax support for private education. (Nearly four out of ten parents of public school children say they would put their children in private schools if they could afford to do so.[44]) I do not think that vouchers, even for

43. The most striking example of this tendency is the largely successful effort by nativist Protestants during the nineteenth century to craft public education into a device to wean Catholic children from their parents' religion, an effort that led to the rapid rise of the Catholic schools—and to the invention of the constitutional principle denying them the public assistance that had theretofore been available to other religious schools. I discuss some of this history in Stephen L. Carter, *The Dissent of the Governed: A Meditation on Law, Religion, and Loyalty* (Cambridge: Harvard University Press, 1998), pp. 36–45. For more detail see, for example, Warren A. Nord, *Religion and American Education: Rethinking a National Dilemma* (Chapel Hill: University of North Carolina Press, 1995), pp. 71–74, and the history discussed in Charles Leslie Glenn, Jr., *The Myth of the Common School* (Amherst: University of Massachusetts Press, 1988). For general background on anti-Catholicism (including the school controversy), see Jay P. Dolan, *The American Catholic Experience: A History From Colonial Times to the Present* (Garden City, N.Y.: Doubleday, 1985).

44. Data are taken from Lowell C. Rose and Alec M. Gallup, "31st Annual Phi Delta Kappa/Gallup Poll of the Public's Attitude Toward the Public Schools," (1999), available at:

religious schools, pose any interesting constitutional problems.[45] There is reason to believe, moreover, that the traditional resistance to vouchers among liberal policymakers is softening a bit.[46] Even should we ultimately reject a system of school vouchers, the strong support for it suggests that the state has an obligation to ponder why its public schools, once the glory of our nation, are making so many parents so unhappy.

African Americans are particularly unhappy. Black Americans are among the nation's strongest supporters not only of vouchers to assist poor parents in purchasing private education for their children but also of classroom prayer, even more powerfully anathema to liberal theory.[47] It is mere stereotyping to suppose that the reason for these data is simply that the public schools black children overwhelmingly attend do not do a good job at basic education, although that, sadly, is true. A better explanation, consistent with the rest of what we know, is that the data reflect the abiding evangelical Christianity that is the dominant faith within African America. Black Americans understand, often better than white Americans, the deadly danger in raising children without the aid of the tight moral cocoon that religions of genuine power can still offer. But this bit of unfinished business from the civil rights movement—assisting African Americans in the moral education of their children—is one that the liberal state cheerfully ignores.

Undeniably, religion can be dangerous to the basic human liberties of believers and unbelievers alike. But religion is not uniquely dangerous. The state itself poses a threat to basic human liberties, and the secular ideological wars of the twentieth century killed far more people than all the religious wars of history combined. Yet secular ideologies are not banned from the liberal public square because of their dangers.

Naturally, a liberal public order must set limits on what religion is able to ac-

---

<http://www.pdkintl.org/kappan/kpol9909.htm#2a>. Other surveys have indicated that many of those parents who would prefer to leave the public schools (about one out of six in the Phi Delta Kappa poll) would base their choice on the moral values being taught in each school. The Phi Delta Kappa survey, however, did not include morality as one of the choices for parents who were asked why they would choose a private school.

45. For some of the reasons I find the constitutional questions uninteresting, see Carter, "Parents, Religion, and Schools."

46. See, for example, the discussion in Peter Schrag, "The Voucher Seduction: The Issue Liberals Can't Ignore," *American Prospect,* Nov. 23, 1999, p. 46.

47. See, for example, the data discussed in "Black Magic," *The Economist,* July 15, 2000.

complish through the legislative process—but it is not obvious why those limits must be different from the limits on what any other powerful force is able to accomplish. It is foolish, and fruitless, to try to assess the validity of a public policy according to the motivation underlying it, as the Supreme Court has too often tried to do. It is unwise, and perhaps unfair, to single out religious motivations as belonging to the set of evil state motives, like racial bigotry, which some liberal theorists have tried to do. Far better to assess the work of the state by what it actually does, so that the Civil Rights Act of 1964 is perfectly acceptable in the liberal state even if, as the evidence suggests, many supporters considered it a religiously necessary piece of legislation; and organized classroom prayer is impermissible even if, as is certainly plausible, a school adopts it for a secular reason, such as the studies suggesting that people who pray regularly live longer, healthier lives.

What the liberal state should never do, however, is design a way of testing either the input or the output of the state that freezes out Americans like myself, people who believe that their understanding of God's word is the appropriate guide for both their public and their private actions. Certainly a state that freezes us out, or that demands that we pay for the privilege of having our children attend public schools that will seek to wean them from our faith, has no serious claim on our allegiance.

Little of this analysis is new. Critics of liberalism have made many of these points for years. Liberal theory, however, continues to be unwilling to accommodate itself to the systems of meaning preferred by the most religiously committed citizens of the nation. Instead, liberalism has grown ever more muscular, pressing theories about education and the public square that few religious citizens will ever support. That is a flaw in liberal theory, not a flaw in religion. For serious religion understands that the life lived without attention to the basic question is life not worth living. In traditional Christianity, discerning God's will and doing it is prior to everything else. If God's will is that we suffer, the Christian must suffer. If God's will is that we change, the Christian must change. If God's will is that we fight, the Christian must fight. Even when, in secular terms, the battle the Christian is fighting seems to be an appealing one, the Christian's motive for the struggle must always be to glorify God—and the Christian must never be afraid to say so.

That was the import of Fannie Lou Hamer's answer to Hubert Humphrey's awkward attempt to buy her off in 1964. Liberal theory can only find her response incomprehensible. Most Americans, however, would probably find it heroic. Luckily for America.

# Christianity and the Roots of Liberalism

*Elizabeth Mensch*

Liberalism stands in paradoxical relation to Christian theology. In Christianity liberalism finds much of its origin and sustenance, yet also pockets of stubborn resistance to its most basic presuppositions. Conversely, Christianity finds in liberalism both its own reflection and, simultaneously, a starkly conceived and alien antagonist. The complexity of this relation derives from centuries of Western thought during which theorists tried to explain and justify political power by reference to a largely Christian vocabulary. Liberalism is inexplicable except as an outgrowth of that history.

The prevailing model of liberalism is the model of the autonomous private individual confronting a democratic state whose power is limited by the neutrality and rationality of law. This model presupposes a clear legal boundary between a limited sphere of public governance and a sphere of private ordering within which autonomous individuals make freely willed choices based on their own subjective value preferences: moral values may be freely chosen precisely because they lack objective content. In the United States, liberalism has placed religion, like the market, within the sphere of private ordering. Arguably, that placement has trivialized religion by treating it as merely a subjective belief preference without public or political dimension; but, as with the market, it has also invigorated religion by freeing it from the debilitating effects of direct government supervision.[1]

*Public* and *private,* however, are notoriously elusive and collapsible categories. What some consider a subject of obvious public concern will seem to others purely a matter of private choice. (Abortion is an oft-debated example.) Moreover, activities labeled private can in fact form a powerful part of our collective life—as with the market, perhaps our most visibly public, as well as most global, reality. In the particular case of religion, the label *private* obscures the extent to which, as traced in this essay, Christianity has shaped Western discourse about the meaning of politics itself. Paradoxically, the liberal model of public political ordering is, in no small measure, an outgrowth of the very Christianity which the same model now so insistently labels private.

To point to influence and interpenetration, however, is not to suggest congruence. Christians, over time, challenged prevailing models of political life and helped to mold new ones. In so doing they introduced elements we would now label liberal, but sometimes in the service of decidedly "illiberal" goals. The process was dialectical, not linear. When traced over centuries, even briefly and superficially, as here, the result is a series of shifting and unstable configurations that, even in their untidy malleability, contain extraordinary evocative power—power to both inspire and delude.

## EARLY CHRISTIANITY

Nothing is more basic to the liberal model than the boundary of protection separating the individual from the state. That radical separation of self from polity is now so familiar that its largely Christian roots in the Roman Empire are easily forgotten. The Romans borrowed from the Greeks the micro/macrocosm imagery of individual/household/polity—the same manly virtue that gave the well-bred Roman citizen a rational, measured control over the otherwise undifferentiated urges of the body also brought governance and definition to an otherwise formless household of wife, children, and slaves, and further provided structured authority for the shifting, stirring populace of the city.[2]

1. Peter Berger, *The Sacred Canopy* 137–48 (1967).
2. *E.g.,* Plato, *Republic,* Book II. *See also* David George Hale, *The Body Politic: A Political Metaphor in Renaissance English Literature* 19 (1971); Patricia L. Mackinnon, The Analogy of the Body Politic in St. Augustine, Dante, Petrarch, and Ariosto (Ph.D. diss.) 13–18 (1988).

Self and polity were so inextricably linked that each, reciprocally, gave definition to the other. Thus an infant had value only when accepted (given political
definition) by the father of the household, which is why infanticide was allowed before the influence of Christianity.

An extraordinary effect of early Christianity was to separate the meaning of
personhood from the Roman political order. Christianity meant that one's primary identity came, not from the Roman polity, but from participation in a
death-defeating narrative about self-sacrifice and resurrection. Martyrdom was
a powerful symbol of that separation; so too was celibacy, which represented a
refusal to enter into Rome's defiance of mortality through the empire's own
heroic continuity in historical time. The continuity of Rome required citizen
participation in the mini-polity of the household, where childbearing imposed
an especially heavy and dangerous burden on women. While not usually taken
to be a model of the liberal self, the celibate body, especially when female, became a powerful image of a self barricaded off from the assigned roles of the
political order.[3]

This apolitical self was not apolitical in a liberal, individualist sense, however. Early Christians were called away from the pagan body politic by an alternative membership in the body of Christ, which Paul described by drawing
directly, albeit paradoxically, on pagan body politic imagery. Thus Paul reinforced conventional political wisdom, but he also upended it: he reversed traditional status gradations (greater honor went to "inferior" members) and
obliterated conventional dualities (slave/free, Jew/Gentile, even male/fe-
male).[4] Though capable of purely mystical interpretation, uniting believers of
all times and places in a kingdom not of this earth, the body of Christ was also
capable of concrete (if always imperfect) political embodiment, as in the religious orders that recognized the God-given worth of each individual in almost
liberal fashion. Those orders insisted, however, that the individual's unique
gifts could be realized only in (illiberal) obedience and communal self-giving.[5]

3. For an extraordinarily vivid description, here relied upon, *see generally* Peter Brown, *The
Body and Society: Men, Women, and Sexual Renunciation in Early Christianity* (1988), especially 10–12, 62, 83–84.

4. 1 Corinthians 12:12–27, Galatians 3:28. *See* Wayne A. Meeks, *The Origins of Christian
Morality: The First Two Centuries* 134 (1993).

5. For attempts to translate the Benediction spirit into modern vocabulary revealing the
complexity of similarity and difference, *see, e.g.,* Kathleen Norris, *The Cloister Walk* 14–22
(1996); Joan Chittister, *The Rule of Benedict: Insights for the Ages* (1997).

The celibate orders, theoretically barricaded from the world's demands and from the pagan virtues of heroic militarism, were at the same time utterly open to the world in charity. To give of oneself, however, is to reach out to the world, including the polity. During the early fourth century CE, church and polity would, in the fateful pact with Constantine, envelop each other in warm but not always chaste embrace. The result was a decidedly illiberal unity of church and polity, but from that unity emerged a (liberal) confidence in reason and law, as well as the first glimmerings of a liberal constitutional order.

No theorist, however, complicated the Western political thought more than St. Augustine, who remains today a persistent influence. As a post-Constantinian bishop during the waning days of the Roman Empire, Augustine exercised both political and ecclesiastical power, and he wielded church authority to influence public officials. He also used political coercion (albeit reluctantly) to try to quash potentially powerful intellectual tendencies in Christian thought, thereby forever implicating Christian theology with state power.[6]

Paradoxically, however, Augustine so brilliantly undercut the self-glorifying claims of the polity that the exercise of state force thenceforward always posed a problem of legitimacy. What are kingdoms, Augustine asked, but "great robberies," whose size and coercive power convey impunity to rulers but keep them forever estranged from their subjects—a theme of alienated sovereignty Hobbes later elaborated. (According to Augustine, when a pirate captured by Alexander the Great was asked what he meant by keeping "hostile" possession of the sea, he retorted, "What thou meanest by seizing the whole earth; but because I do it with a petty ship, I am called a robber, whilst those who dost it with a great fleet art styled emperor."[7]) Over time the haunting problem of ethical legitimacy for the polity's alienating exercise of violent, coercive force came to be called, simply, the Augustinian dilemma—a dilemma that liberalism veils but does not solve by invoking the principle of legality.

Augustine acknowledged no such legally based solution. Instead, he argued that the political order is inevitably caught up in contradiction. In an irremediably sinful world, violent force is absolutely necessary to ward off chaos. The reality of sin makes the wistful longing for the utopian state (or the Marxist state that withers away) mere fantasy. Yet the political order can deal with sin only by invoking the very sins that make earthly authority necessary—the lust for

6. *See, e.g.,* William Connolly, *The Augustinian Imperative: A Reflection on the Politics of Morality* 83–85 (1993); Peter Brown, *Augustine of Hippo* 212–43, 345–52 (1969).

7. Saint Augustine, *City of God* 112–13 (Modern Library ed. 1993) (Bk. 4 § 4).

power, for violence, for property, and for domination. Although the exercise of political and economic power is necessary, it is never untainted. Moreover, Augustine deepened and intensified the old pagan micro/macrocosm relation of individual and polity by describing inevitable divisions in household and kingdom as, in effect, the self-divided Adamic soul writ large. These were the same divisions, the same Augustinian realities, which Americans recognized after the Revolution, when the New Eden so quickly lapsed into self-interested factions, requiring a national government to bring order out of chaos.[8]

Augustine juxtaposed this earthly city to the City of God, setting in motion the grand antitheses that dominated political thought for centuries. The foundation for the City of God was laid by Christ's universalistically conceived loving and innocent self-sacrifice, in contrast to the fratricide and civil warfare that mark political foundation myths, as with Romulus and Remus. At the microcosmic core of the City of God is a self healed by grace rather than a self divided against itself and against God. Augustine described the "healed" microcosmic self as radically separated from the external, habit-bound world, a separation achieved by the inner search for God. The search inward was one of Augustine's powerful contributions to Western thought, arguably laying a foundation for modern conceptions of self. Augustine's self, however, realized its freedom only through *caritas,* the result of reconciliation with God and the human community. The earthly macrocosmic realization of that self would be a world at perpetual peace rather than at war.

Augustine never believed that the City of God was realizable on earth, even within the church. Rather, both church and polity contained a radical intermixture of sin and grace ("In truth, these two cities are entangled together in this world and interunited until the last judgment effect their separation."[9]) Therefore in this "present age" no precise moral judgments or fixed legal standards could sort out the justified from the unjustified exercise of coercion.

Liberalism learned from Augustine not to try to turn the polity into the City of God. As an important example, the more muted Madisonian goal was to contain sin, not achieve perfection.[10] Liberalism did, however, yearn to solve the problem of legitimacy, which it tried to do by relying on reason and the law, a reliance it learned from the (illiberal) medieval church.

8. See Gordon Wood, *The Creation of the American Republic 1776–1787* 504–5 (1969).

9. Augustine, *supra* note 7, at 38 (Bk 1 § 35).

10. *See supra* Michael W. McConnell, Old Liberalism, New Liberalism, and People of Faith.

## MEDIEVALISM

The early Middle Ages were marked by intense struggles between rulers and ecclesiastical officials. Christianity was a more unifying force than political allegiance, and Charlemagne set an important precedent by receiving his crown from the pope in 800 CE. Nevertheless, kings routinely turned clergymen into mere crown functionaries, and the reality of temporal power over religion was symbolized by the emperor's investment of bishops. Pope Gregory VII condemned the practice in 1075, and Henry V finally renounced it in 1122, after a century of conflict. Henry's renunciation laid an important foundation for the liberal notion of limited government and separation of spheres.[11]

On the other hand, arguments for ecclesiastical autonomy quickly led to the church's claim to its own supremacy, based on the successful assertion of centralized ecclesiastical authority as against both local churches and Europe's wide variety of competing political forms. (There was no "state" in anything like the modern sense—except, perhaps, the church.[12]) The result was the all-encompassing medieval conception of organic unity within a simultaneously spiritual and political body modeled symbolically on the body of Christ. This imagery suggested that all of humanity was a single divinely constituted universal body—an extraordinary moral vision of human worth and interconnection, which also led naturally to the view that the head of such a body must be Christ, whose vicar on earth was the pope. A wholly independent emperor would mean the monstrosity of a body with two heads. Arrangements were bound to be hierarchical (a head sat higher than the feet on a human body and was meant to rule), but organic interconnection offered notions of apportionment and interrelation that cut against absolutism. Members of the organic/ political body, including pope and political ruler, should serve the welfare of the whole; and because the whole lives only in and through the members, loss of even one member is a loss to all.

Central to this conception was the idea of "mediate articulation." Individuals were not separated, atomized individuals confronting each other and the state, as in later liberal formulations, but were socially grouped by function; groups (for example, gentry or artisans) had their own unities as wholes, even

11. Steven Ozment, *The Age of Reform 1250–1550: An Intellectual and Religious History of Late Medieval and Reformation Europe* 86, 138 (1980).

12. See Harold J. Berman, *Law and Revolution: The Formation of the Western Legal Tradition* 114–15 (1983).

while being, collectively, members of the larger body.[13] The decline of this notion of mediating structures was a hallmark of an emerging liberalism.

The great unifying theorist of the High Middle Ages was Thomas Aquinas, who almost suggested that the Augustinian gulf between the City on Earth and the City of God might be closed through the church. He replaced Augustine's dialectical method of posing antitheses with a methodology that closed gaps, eased contradiction, and unified dualities, suggesting a polity in which Christian grace would perfect but not overturn the natural virtues of the pagan polity.

The perfected and the natural came together through an Aristotelian epistemology in which knowing was a process achieved by internal natural reason operating in relation to external sense data that were themselves part of a natural, moral ordering ordained by God's own reason. The Thomistic celebration of natural reason, which laid the groundwork for a "reasoned" Enlightenment liberalism, thus presupposed an (illiberal) ontological relation between divine reason, the human mind, and a morally ordered world. The individual was not an autonomous actor selecting his/her own moral viewpoint, as in later liberalism. Rather, God, humans, and the natural were ethically interconnected by the very structure of reality itself—an ontological relationship which meant that the organically conceived universal polity on earth could actually approach the City of God.[14]

Reality thus understood provided the basis for considering relationships in legal and eventually constitutional terms. The central, essentially teleological (illiberal), concept was of a natural law grounded in the being of God and directing all things to their appointed ends. Human beings, through natural reason, were capable of apprehending this substantively moral natural law, which was supplemented by revelation (divine positive law) and also by human positive law, which bore the nature of "law" only if it did not violate natural law.[15]

13. See Otto Gierke, *Political Theories of the Middle Age* 4–22 (F. W. Maitland trans., 1900). Gierke's is the classic text on medieval political conceptualism, relied upon here.

14. For a relatively modern account of the underlying presuppositions of the Thomistic approach, *see* A. P. d'Entreves, *The Case for Natural Law Re-Examined,* 1 Nat. L.F. 5 (1956); on the political implications of grace perfecting nature, *see* Ozment, *supra* note 11, at 147–48. On Thomistic ontology, *see id.* at 54–55; on medieval law as reconciliation of opposites and contradictions and ultimately of God and human, *see* Berman, *supra* note 12, at 132–43, 163–64. For the link between the church as mystical body and the "natural" body, *see* Ernst Kantorowicz, *The King's Two Bodies: A Study in Medieval Political Theology* 194–218 (1957). Kantorowicz traces much of what follows herein.

15. *See, e.g.,* Francis Oakley, *Natural Law, Conciliarism and Consent in the Late Middle Ages: Studies in Ecclesiastical and Intellectual History* 65–83 (1984).

The medieval church employed the methodology of law to construct itself as a vast, legally constituted political entity. Moreover, by epistemologically combining the mystical and the legal, it invented a number of concepts still central to liberal legalism. For example, with the church as the first case in point, medieval canonists described a corporate body sufficiently of the present age to own property and enter contracts, yet sufficiently like the body of Christ to survive the death of any particular church official. From thence emerged the modern corporation, which has an existence apart from the mortality of any individual CEO or group of shareholders.[16] Similarly, canonists produced something like a theory of representation: the pope was head of the church, with authority over members because he "embodied" the whole church, which was in him. The obvious model was Christ, who was head of the Church, which was his body, and at the same time was the whole body, head and members together. The concept of embodiment was a first step toward a theory of representation: because the many were mysteriously present in the one, the one could legitimately make decisions on behalf of many.

In turn, representation moved the church toward a conception of constitutionalism. Inevitably, difficult situations arose that tested the meaning of representation. When the papacy was vacant, for example, the church did not cease to exist; the corporate body of the faithful remained, with Christ as the true head. In such cases the power of the papacy seemed to revert, or escheat, to the community, and thus to the cardinals, who chose a new pope.[17]

The more telling case was the problem of the heretical pope. Canonists actually affirmed the power of the whole body of the church to depose a head who deviated from the faith and therefore was spiritually dead. Once this exception was allowed others suggested themselves, so that it came to be said that ultimate church authority existed in the whole mystically conceived *congregatio fidelium,* the corporate association of members under Christ.[18]

Such notions came to the fore during the great schism, when three compet-

16. 1 Sir Frederick Pollock and Frederic W. Maitland, *The History of English Law Before the Time of Edward I* 501 (1968); *see also* Frederick Maitland, *Selected Essays* 73–103 (Hazeltine et al. eds., 1936).

17. Gierke, *supra* note 13, at 41, 49–50, 154 n. 174.

18. Ozment, *supra* note 11, at 161. The major study of the power of the notion of *congregatio fidelium,* especially in the conciliarist period, is Brian Tierney, *Foundations of the Conciliar Theory: The Contribution of the Medieval Canonists from Gratian to the Great Schism* (1955).

ing popes were each backed by political allies. Obviously no body could have three heads. In the resulting conciliar struggles, language that once exalted the papacy served to limit individual popes. Although language of limitation was employed with equivocation, and amid much practical failure, conciliarist language was later echoed during political struggles with secular rulers, as, for example, during the English Civil War.[19]

Medieval law thus emerged from within a Christian worldview that linked the juridical to the spiritual, the natural to the mystical, the external world to the mind of God, and the "self" to an organic polity of almost infinite mediating wholes within wholes where the spiritual so interpenetrated the actual that the two became virtually indistinguishable. It is a world the modern liberal can barely comprehend, yet from which liberalism has derived some of its most indispensable constructs.

For a time, however, the ecclesiastical vocabulary of simultaneous exaltation and limitation was borrowed by secular rulers to inflate their own authority. Bracton described a king who, in the famous protoliberal formulation, was both above and below the law; as Bracton explained, with obvious (illiberal) comparison to the pope, the king was *Vicarious Dei* only if and so far as he submitted to the law "like the Son Himself."[20] By the thirteenth century the legal profession was called a "priesthood," a parallelism, repeated often in early American legal culture, which helped to constitute the "virtual holiness" of the legally constituted secular state.[21]

Eventually many theological constructs were grafted onto the kingship, giving it a mystical existence, like the church's, separate and apart from any existing king or set of institutions and thereby dividing, in modern terms, the office from the person. Thus the king in his "body politic" or in the "dignity" of the crown, did not die with the natural death of the king, and the king who was obligated to no man was nevertheless obligated to the dignity of the crown, which was, like the mystical body of Christ or the congregation of the faithful, perpetual. So, too, the king incorporated in his person the whole body politic, of which he was at the same time only its head, as his subjects were the members. Just as Christ was both head and head-and-members, as well as both God and man, so too the king was both body natural and body politic, both king and

19. Oakley, *supra* note 15, at 804–5.

20. Kantorowicz, *supra* note 14, at 157.

21. *Id.* at 124, 128–29. On this phrase in early American legal culture, *see* Mensch, History of Mainstream Legal Thought, *in The Politics of Law* 14 (D. Kairys ed., 1990).

king-and-parliament, and also the embodiment of the whole polity as a *corpus republicae mysticum.*[22]

A more democratic version of the transfer of religious vocabulary to the secular realm occurred as theorists began to upend all hierarchy by arguing that if the true mystical body of Christ was the *congregatio fidelium,* then true authority belonged with the lay members. The laity, in turn, could be found most directly and concretely in the polity. Thus emerged, from constitutional language within the church, an (illiberal) argument for complete political control over ecclesiastical institutions, including confiscation of land. ("For with food and raiment the priests should be content," Marsilius announced, a position which led Pope John XXII to denounce him for heresy in 1327.) Such arguments would be repeated in the court of Henry VIII.[23] In effect, the ultimate language of exaltation—the pope's role as Vicar of Christ and head of a universal, organic, church-state unity—by its own inner logic became an argument for total political takeover of the church.

## REFORMATION

Neither political control over church nor papal authority over polity allowed for the liberal separation of church and state. The move toward separation is commonly attributed to the Reformation, but the real separation that occurred during the Reformation occurred at a deeper level and did not lead directly to church-state separation at all. Rather, it entailed a separation of individual faith from the sacralized, integrative ordering of the High Middle Ages and a return to the Augustinian insistence on a radical disjuncture between God and human beings. Reformation theorists, drawing on nominalist strands in Catholic thought, blasted through the whole elegantly conceived organic/epistemological/juristic medieval unity by emphasizing the free will of God, not his reason, an emphasis that underscored the corresponding subjectivity of the individual believer. This emphasis on God's unfettered will meant that God related to humans not because of any ontological unity linking his reason to ours but rather by the words he has chosen to utter *(sola scriptura)* and the undeserved grace *(sola gracia)* he has freely willed to confer on the faithful *(sola fides).*

22. Kantorowitz, *supra* note 14, at 385–87, 399. On the probable influence of canon law even on the Magna Carta, that classic document of English common law, *see* R. H. Helmholz, *Magna Carta and the Ius Commune,* 66 U. Chi. L. Rev. 297 (1999).

23. Ozment, *supra* note 11, at 151–55.

The Reformation rejection of the sacral Aristotelianism of the medieval period was crucial for Enlightenment individualism. The emphasis on God's words rather than reason, for example, meant that God related to the world through a series of disparate linguistic events, requiring no institutional mediation. Replacing organically conceived unities within unities was the starkness of the individual confronting a normatively neutral material world.

Although this starkness almost defines liberalism, its most obvious implication was in fact absolutism, as Hobbes ruthlessly argued. Scripture, Hobbes explained, described the history of Israel and of Christ's appearance in actual historical time to proclaim the Second Coming. During this interim period, between the First and Second Coming, we have been left by God with only the biblical text. Furthermore, to avoid the atomization of a multitude of prideful individual textual interpretations, the church must humbly submit to whatever interpretation the sovereign provides.

Other than a text, we have only the (desacralized) materiality of our own existence in an atomized world of objective forces of attraction and repulsion—which is all we can mean by "good" or "bad." As a result, all existing political authority is rendered contingent, provisional, and without spiritual significance. Its very contingency, however, renders it absolute—because its legitimacy depends solely on the force it can exert, it is required to respect no ecclesiastically based ethical limits. Hobbes the Protestant had no patience for the mystical legal language that simultaneously exalted authority and limited it. The materialized and atomized self, in a one-time alienation of sovereignty, consented to authority for the sake of self-preservation, the state's sole (but totally sufficient) source of legitimacy that carried with it no normative limitation.[24]

At the opposite Protestant extreme were the Puritan radicals of the Civil War period, feared by Hobbes. They were eager to experience in participatory democracy itself a kind of apocalyptic infusion of grace, making them a people being and acting "as itself before God," without need for the mediation of legal

24. See J. G. A. Pocock, *Politics, Language and Time: Essays in Political Thought and History* 148–201 (1971), and for a somewhat different interpretation, Joshua Mitchell, Thomas Hobbes: On Religious Liberty and Sovereignty, *in Religious Liberty in Western Thought* (Noel B. Reynolds and W. Cole Durham, Jr. eds., 1996). For a somewhat different account of the importance of the "religion books" (III and IV) of *Leviathan see* S. State, *Hobbes and Hooker; Politics and Religion: A Note on the Structuring of Leviathan,* 20 Canadian J. Pol. Sci. 79–96 (1987). For the reduction of morality to forces of appetite and aversion, *see* Thomas Hobbes, *Leviathan* part 1, chapter VI at 41 (A. Lindsay ed., 1950). Although Hobbes posited a right of self-preservation against Leviathan, its only normative basis lay in the aversion to being destroyed.

limits or political authority.[25] Similarly, James Harrington, the English republican theorist who powerfully influenced the American colonies, described the
participatory republic, modeled after ancient Israel, as itself, Christlike, a perfect dual-natured mediation between heaven and earth.[26] Much of this (illiberal) ecstatic Protestant spirit swept through the colonies during the Great
Awakening, igniting a powerful (liberal) democratic spirit.[27] Not illogically,
some have found in politicized Protestantism a source of totalitarian impulses.
Rousseau provides the secular version: the new Adam as citizen, obeying only
himself, unites himself with the collectivity and thereby achieves a moral/po-
litical transformation, finding his "true self" in the state.[28]

Within such political/religious apocalypse, any liberal "legal" limit to
democracy constituted an artificial, illegitimate restraint to religiopolitical purity. The church, in particular, required no legal protection because the true
polity and the true church were one. Harrington and Hobbes, the republican
and the absolutist royalist, agreed in their antilegalism and anticlericalism.
Both were, in that sense, decidedly "illiberal." Nevertheless, liberalism combined, however illogically, the Hobbesian atomized individual in a material
world with a contradictory Harringtonian faith in democratic process as a self-
justifying moral good. Both are elements of modern liberalism.

No single model of church-state relations emerged from Reformation theology, which was more concerned with how the church should relate to the world
than with how the polity should relate to the church. Models ranged from complete separation (Anabaptist) to unity under the crown (Anglican).[29] In between were complex notions of duality, with the dual nature of the self (redeemed but still sinner) replicated in the church (pure mystical church and
inevitably sinful institutional church), which served in turn as a model of
church and state (voluntary community under Christ and coercive polity).[30]

25. J. G. A. Pocock, Introduction, *The Political Works of James Harrington* 373 (1977); J. G.
A. Pocock, *The Machiavellian Moment: Florentine Political Thought of the Atlantic Republic
Tradition* 372–73 (1975).

26. See W. C. Diamond, *Natural Philosophy in Harrington's Political Thought,* 16 J. Hist.
Phil. 396–97 (1978).

27. See Elizabeth Mensch, *Religion, Revival and the Ruling Class, A Critical History of Trinity Church,* 36 Buff. L. Rev. 427, 456–62.

28. See d'Entreves, *supra* note 14, at 25.

29. See John Tonkin, *The Church and the Secular Order in Reformation Thought* (1971).

30. See W. D. J. Chargill Thompson, The "Two Kingdoms" and the "Two Regiments":
Some Problems of Luther's Zwei-Reiche-Lehre, *in Studies in the Reformation: Luther to Hooker*
(1980); W. J. Torrance Kirby, *Richard Hooker's Doctrine of the Royal Supremacy* 41 (1990).

Largely following Augustine, Luther described the polity as only a necessary (but therefore divinely ordained) dike against chaos; and, especially in his early writings, he recognized no conceptual basis for legal limits to a ruler's power. He conceded all coercive jurisdictional power to the prince, including power even over ecclesiastical appointments and property. The prince's acts should be treated as a gift of God, he stated, an argument that served chiefly to legitimate political absolutism in early modern Europe. Luther did lay down principles of duty which a godly prince should follow, and advocated passive resistance if a ruler commanded unchristian acts, yet he denied a right to active resistance. Tyranny is "not to be resisted but endured." Calvin, by contrast, found some moral worth in both law and polity, and at least some warrant for a "right" to resist despotism, as would later Calvinists and Lutherans as well. [31]

Notably, however, the first articulation of a natural right in the "subjective" sense most familiar to liberalism—as a sphere of individual choice—emerged not with the atomizing effect of the Reformation, nor with Locke and the Enlightenment, but rather with twelfth-century canonists who had noted that *jus* could mean not just "rightness" in the Thomistic sense of objective justice but also the "power" that one person could licitly exercise, as with property or self-protection. This subjective notion had been developed in the fourteenth century during a protracted dispute concerning the intelligibility of the Franciscan claim to imitate Christ by relinquishing all property rights. The pope declared the claim incoherent: because neither Christ nor the Franciscans starved themselves, he argued, they necessarily exercised at least a simple use right over what was eaten.

Both sides to the quarrel debated the meaning of subjective rights without suspecting that the concept itself might be, as we now assume, incompatible with either "objective" Thomistic natural law or an organic/mystical community modeled after the body of Christ. The idea of subjective rights was further developed by subsequent Catholic theorists and was familiar to Thomistic counterreformation scholars of the Spanish "second scholasticism." Grotius provided the bridge to Protestants and to the Enlightenment. [32]

Thus by the time of Locke, the "rights" conceptualism so often associated with him had, in fact, a long Catholic history. Locke did, however, base his

31. See Quentin Skinner, *The Foundations of Modern Political Thought*, vol. 2, *The Age of Reformation* 15 (1978).

32. For the complete history, from which this account is drawn, *see* Brian Tierney, *The Idea of Natural Rights: Studies on Natural Rights, Natural Law and Church Law 1150–1625* (1997).

analysis of rights on a conception of natural reason sharply different from that of the Thomists. Locke did not describe a reason that discovered in nature a substantive moral order reflecting God's wisdom or divinely ordained teleological ends. Rather, as with Descartes, Locke's reason was the disengaged, instrumental reason that came to characterize the Enlightenment generally, a reason that confronted and dominated an objectified material world—corresponding to the individual right to property as derived from human industry and the capacity to control.[33]

Paradoxically, although Locke is usually taken to have established the individual's natural rights as *against* the state, this Lockean conception of disengaged, instrumental reason is closely associated with the emerging capacity of the Enlightenment absolutist state to regulate and discipline vast fields of human endeavor, from trade, to health, to mores, and even to modes of piety.[34] The individual exercising reason instrumentally is mirrored by a Benthamite bureaucracy capable of extraordinary instrumental power—the conceptual relationship is one of reciprocity and symbiosis, rather than true limitation. In effect, the transcendent Protestant God of unfettered freedom created its own image, as it were, in both a state and an individual that were free to exercise reason instrumentally in relation to a desacralized world.

Notably, moreover, although Locke (illiberally) recognized important religiously based exceptions to the individual rights he described, with respect to religion itself he was tolerant only in a very modern sense. He recognized freedom of conscience as an inalienable right (like life itself, which was a gift from God), but this right extended only to belief, not to practices that violated reasonable state regulations. Locke assumed a neat congruence between reasonable religious practice and those reasonable laws that a polity of sensible and industrious property owners would enact. In case of noncongruence, Locke made no exception for protecting what we now label free exercise.[35] Thus on the American constitutional law question of religious exemption as opposed to strict neutrality, Locke advocated a standard of neutrality—consistent with Jefferson and current doctrine, but arguably contrary to the Madisonian conception of religious liberty as a recognition of prior membership in the king-

33. See John Locke, *An Essay Concerning Human Understanding* chapter 3 at 6–9, chapter 4 at 7, chapter 28 at 7–13 (P. Nidditch ed., 1975); John Locke, *Essays on the Law of Nature* 161, 153, 135 (W. von Leyden ed., 1954).

34. Charles Taylor, *Sources of the Self: The Making of the Modern Identity* 159–76 (1989).

35. John Locke, A Letter Concerning Toleration (1689), *in* 6 *The Works of John Locke* I at 44–45 (photo reprint 1963) (1823).

dom of God.[36] Indeed, when religion posed a political threat, Locke's famous toleration ended. Atheists were not tolerated because they could not be trusted to honor oaths, nor were those who might be drawn to foreign political loyalties (Muslims, or by implication, Catholics). Locke thus enunciated liberalism's version of religious toleration, which quickly becomes pacification of true difference and resistance.[37]

Perhaps the most influential articulation of the liberal argument for the legal protection of individual autonomy derived, however, not from Locke, but rather from Kant, who did not actually urge that his model of individual ethical reasoning be a basis for law or politics at all.[38] More radically than Locke, Kant sought a definition of moral reasoning freed from the claims of religious authority and also from instrumentalist, consequentialist reasoning. The two points were related. Kant, unlike Locke, argued that the exercise of instrumental reason is not necessarily an exercise of freedom. Whereas Locke assumed a God who had freed humans to exercise their instrumental reason in a world designed precisely to reward consequentialist calculation, Kant saw in such calculation only enslavement to desire—enslavement to the longing for the desired consequence.[39]

In contrast, Kant postulated freedom as the freely willed choice to act disinterestedly, in accord with the duty-defining dictates of human reason itself—dictates of internal consistency, principled universality, and utter impartiality. In effect, full autonomy again becomes (illiberally) a matter of obedience—obedience, however, not to God (traditional Christianity) nor to the democrat-

36. See Michael W. McConnell, *The Origins and Historical Understanding of the Free Exercise of Religion,* 103 Harv. L. Rev. 1409 (1990). On Locke specifically, *see id.* at 1434 n. 134. McConnell's reference to Locke's belief in freedom of conscience in this volume should be read in light of McConnell's prior insights as well. For current doctrine, *see City of Boerne v. Flores,* 521 U.S. 507 (1997).

37. Locke, *supra* note 35, at 52. On the power and significance of this resistance, *see* Stephen Carter, Liberal Hegemony and Religious Resistance, *supra.*

38. See Hannah Arendt, *Lectures on Kant's Political Philosophy* (R. Beiner ed., 1982) (discussing especially the "Third Critique"). For perhaps the most systematic effort to construct liberal theory at least partly on Kantian assumptions, *see* John Rawls, *A Theory of Justice* (1978). For Rawls on the role of religion in the modern liberal state, *see* John Rawls, *Political Liberalism* (1993). For analysis of Rawls on religion and of recent critical commentary, *see* Leslie Griffin, *Good Catholics Should Be Rawlsian Liberals,* 5 L. & S. Cal. Interdisc. L.J. 297 (1997).

39. See Walter Lowe, *Theology and Difference: The Wound of Reason* 104 (1993).

ic polity (Rousseau) nor even to one's own desires but only to the internal requirements of one's own reason. Kant thus solved a difficult problem of Christian ethics—Catholic thought bound God, as well as humans, to natural law, arguably in denial of divine freedom, whereas Protestant thought bound humans to divine commands with no guarantee that those commands were just or reasonable. In contrast to both, Kant described a conception of duty that seemed capable of summoning our accord without violating either God's freedom or ours.[40]

Kant himself, however, never assumed that people were perfectly self-sufficient moral reasoners. Humans were drawn by desire for the sake of their very survival, which depended on their (imperfect) capacity for consequential reasoning. Therefore the human condition was one of ambiguity, and what judgment required in the complex particularity of history might differ from the pure consistency required by individual ethical reasoning.[41] In fact, Kant's description of the divided human self is (illiberally) Augustinian, and by holding out the elusive possibility of the unity between duty and desire he might almost be describing a state of grace.[42] Notably, however, the conflict Kant identified between consequentialism and the protection of autonomy pervades modern legal thought, with no promise of graceful resolution in sight.

The early English theorists most identified with (liberally) defending either democracy or the rights of the individual were those least open to the claims of legal traditionalism. The Enlightenment's impatience with the quirky forms of the ancient common law is evident, for example, in both Locke and Harrington. Indeed, one of Blackstone's great goals was to reconcile common-law practice with the Lockean "logic" of natural rights.[43]

For purposes of American law, a primary influence in effecting that reconciliation was the earlier Richard Hooker, an Anglican theologian and legalist whose influence on early, largely Episcopalian, American legal culture tends to be overlooked. Hooker's (illiberal) purpose was to defend the Anglican church against the challenge of the English Puritans, who argued for greater separation. Even while defending the Anglican establishment, however, Hooker

40. See J. B. Schneewind, *The Invention of Autonomy: A History of Modern Moral Philosophy* 508–13 (1998), for the theological dilemma Kant thus solved.

41. See Lowe, *supra* note 39 and Arendt, *supra* note 38.

42. See Taylor, *supra* note 34, at 58.

43. Duncan Kennedy, *The Structure of Blackstone's Commentaries,* 28 Buffalo L. Rev. 209 (1979).

achieved a complex reconfiguration of traditional and modern ideas that has provided American constitutional liberalism with much of its force.[44] Hooker paid deference to the natural ethical and communal virtues of medieval Aristotelianism, but he then located the true basis of government in the liberal notion of consent—specifically, the consent given to government for the (Augustinian) purpose of containing sin. The emphasis he gave to consent predated Locke, who took the idea, in fact, directly from Hooker, turning it into an original contract.

By consent, however, Hooker did not mean direct, participatory democracy of the ecstatic Puritan variety that alarmed Hobbes; yet he also did not mean the one-time, fearful alienation of sovereignty Hobbes described. Instead, Hooker meant the more complex but still familiar notion of consent to authority as it is distributed among the institutions of the polity conceived as a corporate body, making possible the medieval but also modern constitutional idea of consent by "the people" as a whole, which is different from majoritarian rule at any particular time. Here Hooker not only echoes the medieval church but also foreshadows John Marshall on the legal meaning of the sovereign people who consent to limits even to their own consensual power.

The (medieval) foreshadowing of Marshall, and of modern liberalism, is even more apparent when Hooker links the consent of the people to law, which he describes (illiberally) as echoing the voice of the angels and representing the perfected and immortal side of the body politic.[45] Drawing on Protestant imagery of the two realms within the self (the redeemed and the still sinful) as they were replicated in the church, Hooker (liberally) separates, within the polity itself, the realm of law and the realm of politics more dramatically than ever had been done in the past.

In spite of Hooker's seeming emphasis on the perfection of law, he was no pure medievalist. He acknowledged the substantive morality of natural law, as reflecting on earth the reason that God ordains, but most actual laws he described as being of mere "probability," not necessity, and therefore not rooted in the substantive law of natural reason at all. Instead, reflecting the growing influence of common-law theorists in England, Hooker describes the real foundation of law as resting on the English people's consent, in history, to being governed as a corporation bound together by the long tradition of constitu-

44. See Elizabeth Mensch, *Images of Self and Images of Polity in the Aftermath of the Reformation,* 3 Graven Images 249 (1996), from which the following argument is taken.

45. Richard Hooker, Laws of Ecclesiastical Polity, *The Works of Mr. Richard Hooker* 285 (J. Keble ed., 7th ed. 1988; reprint 1970).

tionalism and customary common law. Hooker would carefully describe spheres of governance with boundaries as laid down not by natural reason but by the particularity of English custom and constitutional law—areas where the king's power was absolute, areas where Parliament must give consent, and also an area that, however so much it might be under the crown, was nevertheless reserved for the church and into which the king could not legally intrude.[46]

The language of a political consent to a corporate body that transcends historical time and popular will is markedly similar to language describing the church as a mystical body whose existence is outside time and place, or the crown as containing both a body natural and a perpetual, Christlike body politic. Such (illiberal) language was oddly necessary for (liberal) constitutionalism, which to the Framers seemed to represent a kind of political transubstantiation: a text written and politically ratified by one group of men in the particularity of historical time becomes the corporate act of a Sovereign People creating a body politic whose continuity—and legal authority—transcends the mortality of individual human beings.

Even after overtly religious vocabulary ("priests at the temple of justice," for example) dropped out of American legal rhetoric, belief in the liberal constitutional tradition provided jurists with a kind of secular liberal faith, a source of meaning and hope in an otherwise disenchanted age. Even now, when faith in the ideals of the Constitution seems muted, there is an odd similarity between the postmodern notion of law as a cultural practice with no "real" foundational referent except the practice itself, and the assumption that the church "makes real" the body of Christ in historical time solely through its own faithful practice.[47]

When the polity thus appropriates the forms of religion it learns some of its highest ideals. That has been the case with liberalism, and has been part of the long creative tension in centuries of church-state relations. Nevertheless, as Augustine insisted, Christian identity is not based in the polity, and Christian virtues are not identical to the habitual virtues of the Roman (or the liberal) state. However much liberalism appropriated the forms and values of Christianity, for example, law inevitably entails the exercise of coercive force; in spite

46. See Harold Berman, *The Origins of Historical Jurisprudence: Coke, Selden, Hale,* 103 Yale L.J. 1651 (1994); W. Chargill Thomson, "The Philosopher of the Politic Society": Richard Hooker as a Political Thinker, *in Studies in Richard Hooker* 47 (W. Speed Hill ed. 1972); W. J. Torrance Kirby, *Richard Hooker's Doctrine of the Royal Supremacy* (1990).

47. See Pierre Schlag, *Hiding the Ball,* 71 N.Y.U. L. Rev. 1681, 1703–4 (1996).

of liberalism's claims to neutrality and process rationality, its foundational premise remains the premise of inevitable conflict that can be contained only by law's implicit threat of violence. In Robert Cover's stark phrase, "Legal interpretation takes place in a field of pain and death."[48]

By contrast, Christianity holds out the hope of a different community, one formed on a promise—the promise that the learned practice of forgiveness can replace coercion and that a life lived for God and the neighbor can replace a life lived in the egoistic, competitive pursuit of gain and privatized comfort. The realization of that promise entails a radical reorientation of the self, of a kind that simply lies outside the bounds of the liberal framework of rights. Necessarily, therefore, that promise exists in some disruptive tension with the liberal political order, which virtually by definition cannot be an exemplar of agape.[49]

In that sense, attempts to show that liberalism is fully consistent with Christianity are misguided, but so too are attempts to "Christianize" the liberal state. After the long history of religious warfare in Europe, Christianity cannot claim that it has solved the problem of politics. Rather, history seems to suggest that Christianity and the polity will inevitably exist in some tension with each other, not in a state of complete congruence. That tension can be creative, but only if churches have the courage to retain faith in their own distinct inflexible promise, in their own disruptive hope.

Even now, the liberal Enlightenment model of the autonomous self has lost much of its hold on current thinking, displaced by an antifoundational and largely Nietzschean postmodernism, and also by a global market that may be rapidly changing our conception of the liberal nation-state itself. In the face of those changes, Christianity still, as it has for centuries, stubbornly holds out a different story and a different hope—about the renunciation of power rather than its exercise, and about *caritas* rather than *cupiditas*. The challenge now faced by Christians, it would seem, is not how to influence the liberal state but how, simply, to stay stubborn.

48. Robert Cover, *Violence and the Word,* 95 Yale L.J. 1601, 1601 (1986).

49. See Thomas L. Shaffer, *Faith Tends to Subvert Legal Order,* 66 Fordham L. Rev. 1089 (1998). For others who emphasize continuing "difference" *see, e.g.,* Stanley Hauerwas, *After Christendom? How the Church is to Behave if Freedom, Justice, and a Christian Nation Are Bad Ideas* (1991); John Howard Yoder, *Politics of Jesus: Vicit Agnus Noster* (1972); John Milbank, *Theology and Social Theory: Beyond Secular Reason* (1990); Douglas John Hall, *The End of Christendom and the Future of Christianity* (1997) (the latter with an emphasis on being "in but not of the world" rather than on complete discontinuity, but sharing their emphasis on the break with the Constantinian order and set of assumptions).

# The Earthly Peace of the
# Liberal Republic

*H. Jefferson Powell*

"Give me a place to stand and I will move the world," boasted the ancient mathematician, at once giving voice to a proposition of elementary physics and to a presupposition of critical thought. The presupposition, if not the proposition, appears to hold even in our allegedly postmodern world, and critics of contemporary society often look far indeed in search of adequate footing for their analyses. For would-be Christian critics of contemporary American society, this search for an adequate foundation for analysis is particularly important and, I think, particularly difficult. Christian social criticism must serve the universal Christian commitment to truthful vision, and certain features of the situation in which Christians in the United States find themselves complicate that task. As American Christians are increasingly aware, our comfortable accommodation with American society long ago became a virtual Babylonian captivity to which American Christians have willingly submitted our thought and practice. In this dangerously seductive environment, merely to recover a sense of Christian distinctiveness requires an effort. At the same time, in our quest for the necessary critical distance from secular culture there is a risk that we will ignore the truth of our necessary involvement in that culture. Christian social criticism of secular society must rest on a distinctively theological basis in order to be Christian, but by that very token (I shall claim) it cannot be the product of an alienated and radical detachment from that society.

In this essay I propose the social theology of St. Augustine as an appropriate theological basis on which to build a Christian social critique of contemporary American society.[1] Augustine's mature thought, I shall argue, provides the necessary critical distance to ground a distinctively Christian vision of this society. I shall also attempt to show the way in which Augustine demonstrates the need for the Christian social critic to be, in a genuine if peculiar sense, a connected critic, one whose criticism is shaped in part by his or her connections to secular society.[2] My own essay in Augustinian social criticism will focus on an aspect of our society with which I have great professional concern: the liberal political and legal structure through which, in part, the society organizes itself. More particularly, I will analyze three features of that structure: its focus on individual rights, its centralizing tendencies, and its partial exclusion of religion from the processes of government. In each case, I contend, an Augustinian perspective demands significant concern over the cultural effects of these aspects of American liberalism while inviting Christian support for a chastened version of them as strategies for social peace.

## AUGUSTINE'S MAGNUM OPUS

Augustine's great treatment of society, his *City of God,* was, as he wrote in the preface *magnum opus et arduum,* "a long and difficult task."[3] He published the

1. I am far from the first person to make this proposal. See, for example, the very interesting book by Graham Walker, *Moral Foundations of Constitutional Thought: Current Problems, Augustinian Prospects* (1990). Looming behind projects such as Walker's and mine is, of course, the immense figure of Reinhold Niebuhr and his classic *The Nature and Destiny of Man* (2 vols. 1941, 1943). The ultimate failure of Niebuhr's later work to bring theological commitments to bear on American reality with real critical force is a warning that Augustinian thought can be (unintentionally) domesticated. See Stanley Hauerwas's powerful critique of Niebuhr in *Against the Nations* 29–33 (1985).

2. In contrasting the radically detached from the connected critic, I am drawing of course on the work of Michael Walzer. See especially his *Interpretation and Social Criticism* (1987) and *The Company of Critics* (1988).

3. *De civitate Dei* I, praef. (8). In this essay I shall ordinarily quote the *City of God* from the readily available Penguin Classics translation by Henry Bettenson (1972, reprinted with new

first five books in 413, followed with installments in 415, 417, 418, and 420, and he finally completed the work in 425.[4] Over the course of that extended period, Augustine continued the process of working through his theological analysis of society that he had begun long before, with some of his earliest writings as a Christian, and thus neither Augustine's corpus as a whole, nor the *City of God* in particular, is entirely consistent. In this essay I shall be drawing primarily on the later books of the *City of God,* not only because they reflect Augustine's mature thought on the subject but also because they seem to me the most powerful theologically.

### The Limits of the Classical Tradition

In the *City of God* Augustine developed his theological analysis of society in reaction to the many centuries of classical reflection on the nature and goals of social and political life. Particularly in the Roman version of classical political thought with which Augustine was most immediately concerned, this tradition laid great stress on the role of common justice and common good in the constitution of political society. "Scipio in Cicero's *On the Republic* . . . gives a brief description of the commonwealth as 'the interest of the people.' . . . He defined a 'people' as a multitude 'united in association by a common sense of right and a community of interest.' He explains in the discussion what he means by 'a

---

introduction 1984) and cite to book and chapter with the page number in Bettenson in parentheses: e.g., I, praef. (5). In quoting from Bettenson I have silently changed *man* and *men* to gender-neutral terms except where Augustine's point seems gender-specific: doing so is more faithful, I think, both to Augustine's Latin and to his meaning. *See* Jean Bethke Elshtain, *Public Man, Private Woman* 73 (1981) ("Augustine, taken all in all, is one of the great undoers of Greek misogyny"). On a very few occasions I provide my own translation with a standard citation.

4. The course of the *City of God*'s writing and publication can be followed through the latter chapters of Peter Brown's classic biography *Augustine of Hippo* (1967). Of the discussions of the overall theological objectives of the *City of God* that I have read, the writings of R. A. Markus, John M. Rist, and Rowan Williams have been the most helpful. *See* Markus, *Saeculum: History and Society in the Theology of St. Augustine* (1970); Rist, *Augustine: Ancient Thought Baptized* (1994); Williams, *Politics and the Soul: A Reading of the "City of God," 19/* 20 Milltown Studies 55 (1987). I should note that these scholars are in significant disagreement over the correct interpretation of Augustine's social theology. Another work should be mentioned: Jean Bethke Elshtain's *Augustine and the Limits of Politics* (1995) is a wonderful restatement of Augustine's social vision in relation to certain contemporary questions in political thought.

common sense of right,' showing that a state cannot be maintained without justice." Augustine commends Cicero's "most vigorous and powerful argument on behalf of justice against injustice."[5]

As Augustine readily acknowledged, the classical tradition had served as the basis for quite searching criticisms of society and politics. The historian Sallust, for example, had chronicled the rapid decline of the Roman Republic into moral corruption and civil war following the Third Punic War: "Sallust proceeds to dwell on the vices of Sulla, and comments on other depravities in the community. Other writers agree with him on this subject." "Now those historians judged it a part of honourable freedom not to keep silence about the evils of their country." Philosophers too had employed their normative account of what a commonwealth or *res publica* is in order to support harsh judgments about the condition of the empirical state. The classical, pagan tradition of social critique had needed no novel Christian analysis to reach the famous equation of the unjust state and the criminal mob, and its judgment on that issue was one Augustine fully endorsed. "Remove justice, and what are kingdoms but gangs of criminals on a large scale? What are criminal gangs but petty kingdoms?"[6]

Critical as it could be, however, the classical tradition was inadequate in Augustine's view, unable truly to perceive the state of society, the problems of politics, or their sources. The launching point for Augustine's accusation is his claim that the pagan critics systematically understate how radical the results ought to be of applying their own analyses. In criticizing the moral and political degeneration of his own era, for example, Sallust had contrasted it with the preceding period, "a time, according to Sallust of sound morality and of a great measure of concord in Rome." But that very period, Augustine points out, was the setting for evils of a similar severity to those Sallust denounced among his contemporaries: political ingratitude and injustice, the introduction of novel forms of "license and debauchery," and blatantly inequitable legal discrimination against women. Similarly, Cicero had put his denunciation of his contemporaries in terms of their decline from the "ancient morality and the men of old," but Augustine charged him with suppressing his own realization that in the earliest period the Roman commonwealth "was not even then a living reality in human behaviour, but merely a fancy picture." While Augustine granted the critical side of Cicero's claim that the Roman state had degenerated, he went to great lengths to relate the cruelties, bloodshed, and injustice

5. XIX, 21 (881) (translation altered; the original text reads *Breviter enim rem publicam definit esse rem populi*); XIX, 21 (882).

6. II, 18 (69); III, 17 (112); IV, 4 (137).

that had characterized the very period that Cicero eulogized as the golden age.[7]

The admirable candor of the pagan historians and philosophers, it seems, had its limits—why? By the time he came to write the later books of the *City of God*, Augustine had concluded that the problem was in part moral, in part epistemological, and in both parts theological. Inscribed into the foundation of the pagan social critique was a fundamental affirmation of pagan society, an affirmation demanded by their moral inability or unwillingness (hardly opposite terms for Augustine) to achieve true critical distance from their society. This moral defect in their social critique was at the same time an intellectual or epistemological error: one that rendered them fundamentally unable to see either social good or social evil clearly. And the moral and intellectual failure of the pagan social critique stemmed from its unavoidable theological shortcomings.

Augustine analyzed the moral mistake at the heart of the pagan tradition through a close reading of Cicero's normative definition of the state as constituted by the "common sense of justice and [the] community of interest" that can be maintained only by justice. Although Cicero wielded the definition to good effect in attacking the generalissimos whose ambition had wrecked the Republic, the definition depended for its effectiveness on a fundamentally positive evaluation of society and the state: it was the just *res publica* of theory and the (falsely) imagined just Republic of history that gave Cicero's criticisms their bite. But a critical stance ultimately determined by its allegiance to the critic's object must eventuate either in social nihilism, perhaps tinged by nostalgia, or in the celebration of a renovated status quo. Both outcomes are false, and thus the moral failing is an intellectual one as well. This is manifest in Cicero's denial of the brutal reality of the idealized past, but it is equally clear on an Augustinian perspective when the brutal reality of the present is misdescribed either in nihilistic or celebratory tones. "Let us strip off the deceptive veils, remove the whitewash of illusion and subject the facts to a strict inspection," Augustine urges his reader: the society and empire of his day can neither be imagined away nor uncritically commended. Even the greatest of the pagan critics ultimately succumbed to the temptation to do one or the other because they lacked an ultimately critical—because ultimately truthful—theological perspective.[8]

7. III, 21 (121–22); II, 21 (74–75); *see* III, 14–21 (103–22).

8. III, 14 (105). *Cf.* III, 17 (112): "Now those historians judged it a part of honourable freedom not to keep silence about the evils of their country, which in many places they have been constrained to praise in terms of the highest eulogy, since they have not another City which is a truer one than theirs, one whose citizens are chosen for eternity?"

## The Implications of Creation and Fall

The most fundamental principle of Augustine's theological understanding of human beings is that we are creatures, radically contingent, entirely dependent for our existence on the Creator and part of a created, temporal order that is ontologically and temporally finite. Against the Manichaeans and certain strains in Platonic thought, Augustine maintained the common Christian belief in the goodness of creaturehood, despite its mutability and lack of self-subsistence. But doing so, as Augustine realized, committed him to locating neediness and lack in our very nature, as created by God. "You have made us and drawn us to yourself, and our heart is restless until it rests in you," as he prayed famously at the beginning of the *Confessions:* the need and desire that are for Augustine intrinsic to love are anterior to, not the product of, human sin. Human action, including human social action, was created by God to be oriented toward that which human beings love. Human sinfulness—that primal and pervasive disorientation of human existence that is the second–most important principle of Augustine's anthropology—complicates and darkens this picture without changing its basic outlines, so that for Augustine "the problem of the life of the two cities is, like every other question presented to the theologian, inextricably linked with the fundamental issue of what it is to be a creature animated by desire, whose characteristic marks are lack and hunger, who is made to be *this* kind of creature by a central and unforgettable absence, by lack and hunger."[9]

An adequate, truthful theological basis for social critique must, in Augustine's view, start from the theological truths of human sinful creatureliness. "To help us form our judgment let us refuse to be fooled by empty bombast, to let the edge of our critical faculties be blunted by high-sounding words like 'peoples,' 'realms,' 'provinces'"; human society and human politics are constituted around the reality of what actual human beings love, of how they respond to their creaturely and fallen lack and hunger. Therefore Augustine proposes an expressly theological alternative to Cicero's definition of a people. "A people is the association of a multitude of rational beings united by a common agreement on the objects of their love. . . . It follows that to observe the character of a particular people we must examine the objects of its love. And yet, whatever those objects, if it is the association of a multitude not of animals but of rational beings, and is united by a common agreement about the objects of its love, then there is no absurdity in applying to it the title of a people." Augustine immediately draws out the critical advantages of this proposal. Most importantly,

9. Williams, *supra* note 4, at 69.

of course, it brings God and the human need for God into the analysis. By definition secular society is not organized around the final human good, obedience to God, and so even the most just secular society is, ultimately, unjust.[10]

Furthermore, Augustine's proposal surmounts the moral and epistemological problem that impaired the pagan critical tradition. Unlike the pagan critics, he has no need to deny either evils of the past or the realities of the present. He does not have to pretend there was a golden age in order to criticize the present, nor denigrate the present in order to vindicate his critical stance. "Obviously, the better the objects of this agreement, the better the people; the worse the objects of this love, the worse the people. By this definition of ours, the Roman people is a people and its estate indubitably a commonwealth." Injustice and the absence of a true community of interest, for the pagan philosopher proof that the object of political thought and action had simply disappeared, were for Augustine data about the ends toward which a community's love is directed, not "a reason for asserting that a people is not a people or that a state is not a commonwealth."[11]

Analyzed under the more searching scrutiny of Augustine's theological critique, the immediate source of Roman society's ills turned out to be identical with its central principle (rather than, as the pagan critics believed, a deterioration from that principle): the *libido dominandi,* the love or lust for domination and power. "The lust for power . . . of all human vices was found in its most concentrated form in the Roman people as a whole." The Roman commonwealth rested on a mutual agreement to pursue the self-aggrandizement of the will, an agreement manifest in Roman imperialistic aggression, civil disorder, acquisitive materialism, and a debauched "public" life. The disorganizing thrust of the *libido dominandi* was checked in turn by the early Romans' efforts to obtain glory and freedom and their successors' efforts to maintain social peace—efforts to which Augustine gave due credit—but the central truth about Roman society remained the ultimately individualistic nature of "the objects of its love." The Roman state was a commonwealth, all right, but a commonwealth dedicated to what are, in the end (or rather, End), hellish purposes.[12]

10. IV, 3 (138); XIX, 26 (890). A secular society is unjust both in that it denies to God the sacrifice that is His due, XIX, 24 (891), and because in doing so it leaves its members "alienated from . . . God" and by that fact "wretched" XIX, 26 (892).

11. Williams, *supra* note 4, at 59.

12. I, 30 (42). The theme is pervasive in the earlier books of the *City of God* that expressly examine Roman society. *See, e.g.,* III, 14 (104–5); IV, 15 (154–55); V, 19 (212–13). Augustine

## The Search for Peace

At this point, a reader new to Augustine might well suspect that his social critique can only eventuate in an unremittingly negative conclusion: secular society is a "covenant with death" from which the Christian can only flee.[13] But Augustine did not draw that conclusion, and his refusal to do so was not the result of a failure on his part to carry through on the logic of his position. To understand why, and to grasp the extent, limited but real, of Augustine's approbation of society and state, we must look for a moment at some of the specific details of his moral judgments.

A consistent theme in the *City of God* is Augustine's abhorrence of violence. Again and again, Augustine expresses horror at physical brutality and bloodshed and compassion for their victims. The *Pax Romana,* Augustine reminds his reader, was purchased at a hideous price: "Think of the cost of this achievement! Consider the scale of those wars, with all that slaughter of human beings, all the human blood that was shed!" Even those wars that justice requires the wise man to wage are occasions for great sorrow. "Surely, if he remembers that he is a human being, he will rather lament the fact that he is faced with the necessity of waging just wars," involving as they do "horror and cruelty."[14]

Augustine's revulsion at violence is paralleled by his almost visceral dislike of human injustice, and particularly the injustice perpetrated by the strong against the weak. "I am sick of recalling the many acts of injustice which have disturbed the city's history; the powerful classes did their best to subjugate the lower orders." At the same time, Augustine's social pessimism does not prevent him from valuing human justice, flawed as it may be, as a means toward the "temporal peace . . . that consists in . . . fellowship with one's kind." Augustine's theologically critical vision does not blur the real distinctions between the

---

generally puts it more briefly but no less emphatically in the later books. *See, e.g.,* XIV, 16 (577); XIX, 24 (891).

13. Isaiah 28:15.

14. XIX, 7 (861–63). The *City of God* is replete with expressions of Augustine's revulsion at violence. *See, e.g.,* II, 25 (81) ("the crime of civil war" involved the fighting of "loathsome battles . . . with frightful bloodshed"); III, 7 (94) ("What crime had poor Ilium committed that, when the civil wars were raging, she should be destroyed by Fimbria [a general of Marius during the civil war between Marius and Sulla] with greater savagery and ruthlessness than she had suffered from the Greeks?"); III, 20 (119) ("In the midst of all the horrors of the Second Punic War nothing was more lamentable, nothing more deserving an outcry of compassion than the destruction of Saguntum. . . . Even to read of its end fills one with horror").

more and the less just: Vespasian and Titus, "the most attractive emperors," are distinguishable from Domitian, "the most ruthless tyrant."[15]

The connecting thread among the moral judgments Augustine expresses about society and the state is that they are judgments concerning created and fallen beings. As creatures, human beings are naturally incomplete, drawn out of themselves by their needs, and above all on earth by their need for one another. Fallen as they are, they also need protection against the lusts of others and, indeed, from their own wayward wills. The great emptiness at the heart of the earthly city is its refusal to acknowledge the human need for God, but the inheritors of the city of God can display no corresponding disdain: their very allegiance to that city demands of them concern for their own and their neighbor's earthly needs as well. "God, our master, teaches two chief precepts, love of God and love of neighbor."[16] Human suffering, human injustice—and the always flawed efforts of humanity to reduce suffering and correct injustice—are of the greatest concern to the Christian because the neighbor is and ought to be an object of love. The earthly city is radically flawed not because it cares too greatly for human, temporal good but because it cares too little for what is truly good in the here and now as well as eternally.

Augustine's comprehensive term in the *City of God* for that which answers human need, the true human good, is *peace,* and he uses it both for "the peace of the Heavenly City" and for the earthly peace that consists of the absence of suffering and the existence of this-worldly concord and "fellowship with one's kind": "Peace is so great a good that even in relation to the affairs of earth and of our mortal state no word ever falls more gratefully upon the ear, nothing is desired with greater longing." Human sin warps but cannot erase the universal thirst for peace; even the acts of the *libido dominandi* are a perverted attempt to satisfy human neediness by creating a "peace" in which all other creatures serve the self's appetites. Human society thus is not, as for the pagan critics, a source alternately of (self-) glorification or despair. Freed of any need to posit the fundamental goodness of any society other than the City of God, Augustine is also free of the temptation either to idolize or demonize society and the state. He can see them for what they are in truth, the site of the ongoing, universal hu-

---

15. II, 18 (67); XIX, 13 (872); V, 21 (216).

16. XIX, 14 (873). The Christian community, in terms of Augustine's definition of a "people," is constituted by its "common agreement about the objects of its love," God and the neighbor, and thus Augustine's ecclesiology necessarily includes a positive as well as critical engagement with society.

man search for the "temporal peace" that is God's greatest gift "suitable to this life."[17]

The pagan critics lamented human folly and human suffering; the Christian critic, animated as he or she must be by the law of love, knows that lamentation is not enough. "For this reason [the Christian] will be at peace, so far as lies in him or her, with all people, in that peace among human beings, that ordered harmony." As Augustine immediately points out, to seek that peace requires positive action on the Christian's part, who thus is, for theological reasons, an active participant in the life of secular society and of the state. "Thus even the Heavenly City in her pilgrimage here on earth makes use of the earthly peace and defends and seeks the compromise between human wills in respect of the provisions relevant to the mortal nature of humanity, so far as may be permitted without detriment to true religion and piety." As Augustine's careful wording shows, the Christian's loyalty to society and state is strictly limited and critical: all claims that cultural achievements or earthly politics are the modality of ultimate human fulfillment are excluded, and secular institutions must limit themselves to the penultimate resolution of issues involving "the things relevant to mortal life." But within those limits, and with respect to those goals, Christians share their pagan fellow citizens' obligation to seek the common good, even at the cost of involvement in the "darkness that attends the life of human society." Even "a people alienated from . . . God . . . loves a peace of its own, which is not to be rejected," and even in the midst of a society alienated from God "prayers should be offered for Babylon, 'because in her peace is your peace'—meaning, of course, the temporal peace of the meantime, which is shared by good and bad alike."[18]

The essential elements of Augustine's theologically grounded social critique are now in place. The primary question to be asked by an Augustinian social critic concerns the character of the society he or she is seeking to understand. The society's underlying nature will be shaped and revealed by the human needs that it identifies and the manner in which it seeks to fulfill them, by (in Augustine's terms) the implicit or explicit "common agreement about the objects of its loves" that unites it. In our fallen world, the overlap between true human needs and those canonized by a given society will inevitably be less than perfect, but there are greater and lesser degrees of imperfection. The objects around which a society is organized will be largely determinative of the answer

17. XIX, 13 (870, 872); XIX, 11 (866); XIX, 13 (872).

18. XIX, 14 (873); XIX, 17 (878); XIX, 17 (877); XIX, 6 (860); XIX, 26 (892), quoting *Jeremiah* 29:7.

to a second question that must be asked: how far do the society's forms and institutions actually achieve temporal peace, avoid violence, relieve suffering, and achieve justice? In asking this second question, the Augustinian critic will take care to avoid either uncritical acceptance of the society's pretensions or pseudocritical assumptions about its moral bankruptcy. Only a truthful account of the society's failures and successes can serve the Christian and critical task of furthering that earthly peace that Christians must seek for all humanity: "There is earthly work to be done in the name of peace."[19]

## AN AUGUSTINIAN CRITIQUE
## OF AMERICAN POLITICS

Both the cultural forms and the institutional structures of modern American liberalism have undergone sustained attack for the past three decades. The attacks have come from many directions, including some Christian ones, and have run the length and breadth of American liberalism's history, present performance, and theoretical attractiveness. As I noted in the introduction to this essay, I am going to narrow my focus to three features of the formal political/legal structure of the United States: its focus on individual rights, the centralizing tendencies of its national institutions, and its partial exclusion of religion from government. Each has been heavily criticized; with respect to each, I believe that an Augustinian perspective will illuminate what is convincing about the criticisms while indicating the positive value of these aspects of the American political order when understood as strategies for the achievement of the Augustinian earthly peace.

### 'It's My Right'

One of the most prominent features of the political and legal order of the United States is the importance that it accords to individual rights. While most polities in the post–Cold War era are at least formally committed to the protection of some set of personal liberties, the American fascination both cultural and legal with the rights of the individual is, I think, essentially without parallel. Americans deal with an astounding array of social and economic issues by asking who has an individual right to do or not do something. It is perfectly intelligible, in American living rooms, legislatures and courts, to ask that question in controversies over the location of cable TV attachments and public ac-

19. Elshtain, *supra* note 4, at 105.

cess to public beaches, over the identity of a child's father and the identity of one's associates, over the administration of life support technologies and the administration of life-ending drugs, over the length of a student's hair and the absence of a teacher's tie, over high-tech methods of selling sexual activity and low-tech methods of distributing newspapers.[20] The point is not that Americans or their courts uniformly agree over the right answers (they don't), but that they assume, often without debate, that it makes sense to think about the issues as questions of individual rights.

The broad cultural acceptance of "rights talk" as a primary vehicle for discussing an ever-widening range of issues about which people disagree has been the object of harsh criticism in recent years.[21] The American fascination with individual rights often diverts public attention from addressing real social problems to the expensive resolution of rarified legal disputes. It transfers the locus of public decision from democratically responsible legislatures to countermajoritarian courts. The constant refrain "it's my right" undermines efforts to promote a sense of loyalty to society. Most fundamentally, the American fetish of individual rights reenforces and furthers the tendencies to selfish and antisocial behavior that underlie and warp American society. The solution, the critics usually suggest, is to reduce the social and legal role of individual rights. The community, not the individual, must resume its proper place at the center of social thought and action. Judicial activism in the service of expanding the individual's freedom from social norms should give way to judicial deference to society's articulation of what is expected of the individual. The American political and legal system should be reoriented away from the encouragement of American selfishness and toward the fostering of American values.

From an Augustinian perspective, the critique of the American focus on individual rights, while it contains a great deal of truth, is insufficiently radical and, paradoxically, overly negative. It is insufficiently radical because it rests on a basically positive evaluation of American society that is in fact false. The crit-

20. Respectively, *Loretto v. Teleprompter Manhattan CATV Corp.*, 458 U.S. 419 (1982); *Nollan v. California Coastal Comm'n*, 483 U.S. 825 (1987); *Michael H. v. Gerald D.*, 491 U.S. 110 (1989); *Dawson v. Delaware*, 503 U.S. 159 (1992); *Cruzan v. Director, Missouri Dep't of Health*, 497 U.S. 261 (1990); *Washington v. Glucksberg*, 521 U.S. 702 (1997) and *Vacco v. Quill*, 521 U.S. 793 (1997); *Holsapple v. Woods*, 500 F.2d 49 (7th Cir.), *cert. denied*, 419 U.S. 901 (1974); *East Hartford Educ. Ass'n v. Board of Educ.*, 562 F.2d 838 (2d Cir. 1977); *Reno v. ACLU*, 521 U.S. 844 (1997); and *City of Lakewood v. Plain Dealer Publ'g Co.*, 486 U.S. 750 (1988).

21. See, for example, Mary Ann Glendon's seminal *Rights Talk: The Impoverishment of Political Discourse* (1991).

ics assume that there was a healthy American society in the past (and that we lost it), or that there is one in the present (if only we could remove the individualistic veils that hide it), or that there could be one in the future (if we would but build it). Rights talk thus is a perversion of what America was or could be.

But this evaluation of American society's "essence" is, I think, erroneous. Let us ask Augustine's primary question: what is the "common agreement about the objects of its loves" that unites American society? The answer, I suggest, is that American society is united by its shared commitment to individual acquisition and "self-actualization." The accumulation of private possessions, the rejection of intrusive social impositions, and the assertion of individual autonomy are constitutive elements of American society, and have been so for most if not all of the nation's history. American society implicitly identifies the human good with the comfortable, materialistic life of late-twentieth-century individualists, and is organized around the endless reproduction of that lifestyle for those with the means, and with the provision of simulacra for those without.

If my claim is correct, the usual criticism of the American fascination with individual rights does not go far enough.[22] American rights talk is not a perversion or denigration of American values: it is, rather, the natural expression of those values. The United States is dedicated—as indeed was said at the nation's birth—to the "inalienable rights" of the individual and above all to the individual's right to pursue happiness as he or she sees fit. The legalistic mode in which Americans so often discuss social matters in and out of court is the logically appropriate discourse of a society that identifies the good with the "liberty . . . to define one's own concept of existence, of meaning, of the universe, and of the mystery of human life." Talk about "the right of every individual to the possession and control of his own person" merely restates the point that society can enable the individual to define his or her own concept of existence only through conferring "the right to be let alone, the most comprehensive of rights and the right most valued by civilized men."[23] Those who seek a refuge from excessive individualism in the shared values of the American community will find only that from which they are fleeing.

In addition to being insufficiently radical, from an Augustinian perspective the usual critique of American rights talk is inappropriately negative. The critic

22. I fully recognize that I am asserting rather than establishing my claims about the objects of love in American society, and for the purposes of this essay can only ask the reader to consider whether the claims resonate with his or her own perceptions.

23. *Planned Parenthood v. Casey*, 505 U.S. 833, 851 (1992); *Cruzan*, 497 U.S. at 269: *Olmstead v. United States*, 277 U.S. 438, 478 (Brandeis, J., dissenting).

mistakes the focus on individual rights as a warping of American community and thus prescribes a reduction of the sphere of individual rights as a means of rendering the community healthier. But the prescription not only would not work, because the community itself is constituted by the very individualism expressed in rights talk, but would be likely to render the American political order more unjust. The American obsession with rights has many unfortunate consequences, but the language of individual rights is at the same time the most effective means—often the only effective means—of raising questions about social justice and social peace. A truly Augustinian attitude toward the American focus on individual rights will therefore be one of guarded support, based on a truthful appreciation of the actual role the judicial protection of individual rights plays in reducing violence and injustice. I do not think that such an appreciation leads one to an uncritical endorsement of broad judicial interference with majoritarian politics or an equally uncritical attack on the legal enforcement of individual rights.[24]

For all the questionable decisions American courts have made in elaborating the current constitutional law of individual rights, the overall effect of much of that law has been "to promote the well-being of the common people" by imposing procedural and substantive restraints on the government's use of violence, by imposing significant limitations on government's ability to exclude identifiable groups from equal treatment, and by prohibiting most governmental interference with criticism of government.[25] These are very real and meaningful accomplishments, particularly insofar as they provide some protection for the substantial body of Americans whose economic status is marginal and, indeed, increasingly precarious. To the extent that the critics of rights talk would roll back or undercut these accomplishments, their critique would have most unfortunate consequences.

The Augustinian, then, has good theological reasons to support the legal enforcement of certain individual rights as a strategy for protecting and promoting the temporal peace of American society. At the same time, it would be a mistake to ignore the negative impact cultural rights talk has on the members of American society, including that society's Christian members. The baleful effects of conceptualizing social issues as in their essence questions of individual rights can be traced throughout much of American Christianity. A large segment of the Christian community, or at least of its vocal leaders, appears to

24. I make a first attempt to draw the appropriate distinctions in Powell, *The Moral Tradition of American Constitutionalism: A Theological Interpretation* 260–92 (1993).

25. Quotation: XIX, 19 (880).

endorse uncritically notions about the sanctity of private property and the illegitimacy of governmental interference with it that cannot easily be reconciled with traditional Christian teachings about the role of wealth and the obligations of the well-off to the poor. In other corners of American Christianity, an uncritical appropriation of the idea that "the mystery of human life" is a matter of individual choice threatens the coherence of traditional Christian doctrine. One great task for Christian social criticism in the twenty-first century must be to find effective ways to weaken the link between the socially valuable role of legal rights and the socially destructive effects of the cultural obsession with individual liberty.

### Concentration of Power

The strong centralizing tendencies of the political and legal order of the United States perhaps are not quite as prominent as its focus on individual rights, but they are long-standing and perhaps equally important features of that order. The early constitutional history of the republic was dominated largely by the struggle between the localist tradition that was initially dominant and its nationalist opponents. From the late nineteenth century on, the nationalist deployment of central governmental power (and its analogues in the private sphere) became increasingly active and, after the New Deal crisis, essentially unquestioned. The Supreme Court, to be sure, has of late displayed considerable interest in putting some limits on the formal scope of central legislative power, although it remains to be seen whether these limits will have much practical significance.[26] It should be noted that the Court has shown no sustained interest (the occasional eccentric justice to the contrary) in putting major limits on the scope of central judicial power.[27] Major reductions in the overall

26. See *New York v. United States,* 505 U.S. 144 (1992); *United States v. Lopez,* 514 U.S. 549 (1995); *City of Boerne v. Flores,* 521 U.S. 507 (1997).

27. The Court's disinclination to limit the reach of its own authority is clearest in its unwillingness to put clear limits on the range of individual rights it protects against state and local government. In the recent assisted-suicide cases, for example, the Court rejected the particular claims before it but made a point of noting that its holdings did not foreclose the possibility that the Court would uphold "a more particularized challenge." *Glucksberg,* 521 U.S. 702 at 735 n.24. I do not think that the Court's recent Eleventh Amendment cases, which on their face do constrain the power of the federal courts, require a significantly different conclusion. The primary effect of the Court's most far-reaching decision, *Seminole Tribe v. Florida,* 517 U.S. 44 (1996), was to reduce somewhat the power of Congress vis-à-vis the courts, because the decision did not question the constitutionality of the *Ex parte Young* alternative means of applying national judicial power to state officials. The most recent

power of the national government are unlikely, furthermore, not only because of institutional concerns but because the power of the central government and the culture of individual rights are mutually dependent; the primary means by which that culture is given legal reality is through the exertion of central power against local officials.

The American system's centralizing features are often censured by the same critics who attack its concern over individual rights, and once again the critics make a powerful case. The central government's swollen ambitions and bureaucracy place a heavy regulatory and financial burden on local governments and on private individuals and groups, reducing the latter's ability to address local issues and maintain local community. The flow of power from municipal and state governments to Washington has impaired the sense of mutual responsibility between the governed and the governors that is essential to a healthy democratic system. And in much that they do, national institutions are overtly hostile to the preservation of the more localized structures that can mediate between the lonely individual and the national leviathan. The solution, the critics usually suggest, is to reduce the size and capacity of central power, to devolve responsibility and authority to local institutions.

Once again, I think that an Augustinian perspective highlights weaknesses in the usual critique. The criticisms of national power are a mirror image of those addressed to individual rights, and properly enough, given the interdependency noted above between these two elements in the American political and legal order. But by the same token, for an Augustinian this means that the usual critique of centralization is partly erroneous. The existence of powerful central institutions is unlikely to be the primary cause of the weakness of social structures in a culture as individualistic as this one.[28] On an Augustinian account, what is specifically negative about central power is its heightened capacity for violence and oppression, and its ability to mobilize public support for violent or unjust actions. At the same time, the exercise of central authority through

---

Eleventh Amendment case modestly extended the amendment's protection of state autonomy from federal court process while producing surprisingly strong reaffirmations of *Young* by seven justices. See *Idaho v. Coeur d'Alene,* 521 U.S. 261, 291–93 (1997) (O'Connor, J., concurring in part and in the judgment); *id.* at 297–99 (Souter, J., dissenting). I discuss the other exception, the Court's drastic limitation of the availability of federal habeas corpus for state prisoners, below.

28. *See* Hauerwas, *supra* note 1, at 124, where Hauerwas criticizes as fundamentally liberal the concept of mediating institutions and argues that it is liberal individualism that "warps the moral reality of such institutions as the family."

the creation and enforcement of individual rights has been with some frequency the means by which entrenched local injustice has been undermined.

The Augustinian therefore will attempt to discern the actual consequences of reducing national power and will find, I believe, cause for concern about a general and indiscriminate enthusiasm for decentralization. Translated into political reality, the "return" of power to state and municipal government does not automatically create enhanced local democracy. Most state government is as faceless and distant from the persons it governs as is the national government, and very few contemporary American county and city governments are run along the lines of the New England town meeting, that beguiling image that often shapes the rhetoric of the advocates of decentralization. Similarly, there is little reason to believe that narrowing the reach of central power will in itself reinvigorate the mediating institutions that the critics favor. The dissipation rather than the relocation of communal action seems at least as likely a result.

More disturbingly, the attack on national power sometimes stems from hostility to the very features of that power's exercise that Christians have reason to endorse. Two controversial examples will make the point. Over the past decade the Supreme Court has sharply restricted the availability of federal court review of the legality of state criminal convictions (federal habeas corpus), a process recently furthered by Congress as well.[29] To the extent that the restriction of federal habeas corpus leads to increased official misbehavior in the administration of the criminal law, the Augustinian will find cause to regret the Court's and Congress's actions. More recently, Congress has engaged in major revisions of the nation's programs for addressing the problems of poverty, revisions that consist in large part in turning the problems over to the state governments. Given the existence of significant hostility not just to the former federal programs (which certainly were flawed) but to governmental aid to the poor in general, there is an obvious danger that the result of decentralization will be negative.

Because of its constant concern for the actual consequences for human good and ill of social arrangements, an Augustinian social critique of the centralizing forces in American society can not adopt a basically negative stance, not even in the name of a supposedly theological principle of subsidiarity. The different "levels" of American government, and indeed the national hierarchies of other American institutions as well, are all products of a liberal society and as such

---

29. *See, e.g., Teague v. Lane,* 489 U.S. 288 (1989); *Graham v. Collins,* 506 U.S. 461 (1993); Anti-Terrorism and Effective Death Penalty Act of 1996, Pub. L. No. 104–132, 110 Stat. 1214.

none of them has any *a priori* claim to Christian support. The question of where social authority is best exercised in this society is always a strategic or prudential question about where the most appropriate outcomes are most likely to be reached. And in light of American history the answer will often be that central power bears the most promise—or creates the smallest risks.[30]

### 'Because God Does Not Rule There'

I turn now briefly to the American political and legal order's relation to public religious exercise. Many forms of religious expression and practice are entirely absent from the activities of government, in part because of judicial interpretation of the First Amendment's ban on "establishments" of religion. At the same time, American political life is saturated with expressions of religious belief. Many American Christians are hostile to the partial exclusion of religion from government and welcome political invocations of deity on the assumption that they address the God Christians worship. I believe that Augustine's social theology leads us, properly, to reverse those judgments.

The Augustinian case against the introduction of religion into government must begin with his assertion that "God is not the ruler of the city of the impious, because it disobeys his commandment that sacrifice should be offered to himself alone. And because God does not rule there the general characteristic of that city is that it is devoid of true justice."[31] By deliberately forbidding public sacrifice to God, American liberalism ensures that its polity is devoid of true justice. But the logic of Augustine's thinking, if not entirely of his practice, cuts against drawing a distinction between a formally irreligious polity and one that fosters religion.[32] Traditional pagan society was full of religious expression, much of it governmentally sanctioned or commanded; Augustine viewed the Christian Empire's suppression of this public religion with unalloyed approval.

30. Perhaps the most obvious example is the role of centralized power in undermining the formal structures of racial caste through the Civil Rights Act of 1964, the Voting Rights Act of 1965 and the judicial decisions invalidating *de jure* racial segregation.

31. XIX, 24 (891).

32. I do not think that even the most generous allowance for Augustine's context renders his support of governmental coercion of heretics compatible with Christian ethical commitments or, indeed, with Augustine's own fundamental account of those commitments. Augustine, as he himself well knew, could err. "Let those, therefore, who are going to read this book not imitate me when I err, but rather when I progress toward the better." Augustine, *Retractiones* praef., 3, *in The Retractions* 5 (Mary Inez Bogan trans., 1968).

Augustine would have viewed with horror a polity in which governmental processes are indifferently employed in the worship of whomever or whatever individual officials choose.

Whatever Augustine may have thought about the possibility of a genuinely Christian political order, he thought that non-Christian polities should be limited in principle to this-worldly concerns.[33] Such a society ought to limit "the harmonious agreement of citizens concerning the giving and obeying of orders," in other words the domain of governmental action, "to the establishment of a kind of compromise between human wills about the things relevant to mortal life." The laws of the best-constituted secular society regulate "those things which are designed for the support of this mortal life" rather than the worship of God that is the object of "the Heavenly City." A society resting on liberal premises is literally incapable of engaging in true worship: any religious exercises under the auspices of a liberal government would necessarily be idolatrous and grounds for Christian dissent, not Christian approval. "The Heavenly City could not have laws of religion in common with the earthly city, and in defence of her religious laws she was bound to dissent from those who thought differently and to prove a burdensome nuisance to them."[34] It is only insofar as the government avoids involvement in religious practices that Christians can "defend and seek the compromise among human wills" that is the proper object of secular politics.

By the same token, the professions of carefully "nonsectarian" religious belief that permeate American government—the national motto "In God We Trust," the prayer at the opening of the legislature, the "God bless you" at the end of the official speech—ought to provoke Christian outrage. Rather than greeting these expressions of American "civic religion" with a kind of relief, as though they were a welcome reminder of some underlying equation of the United States and the biblical city on the hill, Christians should view them as objectionable, an attempt to manipulate public sentiment that is as cynical as it is essentially blasphemous. We need to educate politicians who are practicing Christians about their Christian duty not to engage in this type of profanity.

33. Markus's conclusion, convincing to me, is that by the time Augustine began the *City of God,* he "had already perceived that the idea of a Christian society was a mirage." Markus, *supra* note 4, at 100. As Williams argues, Augustine's praise of certain Christian emperors, *see* V, 24–V, 26 (219–24), points to "those features of [their reigns] least congenial to an ideology of the emperor's sole authority and unlimited rule." Williams, *supra* note 4, at 64.

34. XIX, 17 (877); XIX, 17 (878); *id.*

The pattern of Christian practice is shaped by our calling to love God and to love our neighbors. Our calling demands of us distance from practices that are not shaped according to that pattern, including the social and political institutions of the secular society of which we are part. At the same time, our calling demands of us engagement with that society, for it is, after all, made up of our neighbors. In our search for a Christian social presence in the American liberal republic that is critical and (by that very fact) appropriately involved, we have much to learn from Augustine's theological critique of his own, very different, earthly city.

## Section 2 Legal Realism

Legal realists hold that law is not a reflection of any preexisting normative reality. They generally reflect deep skepticism about the possibility of moral reasoning—reasoning about the nature of justice and injustice, good and evil. Albert W. Alschuler's essay suggests that the skepticism of the realists now infects all the most common schools of jurisprudence, from critical legal studies on the left to law and economics on the right (if that is indeed where they are situated). He argues for a return to moral reasoning, which, he says, will enable us to think more clearly about law and at the same time reconcile faith and reason.

# A Century of Skepticism

*Albert W. Alschuler*

The left and the right in American legal thought are more alike than different. They are united in their skepticism, especially their skepticism concerning values. Justice Holmes sounded the principal theme of twentieth century jurisprudence when he wrote that moral preferences are "more or less arbitrary. . . . Do you like sugar in your coffee or don't you? . . . So as to truth." Judge Learned Hand added that values "admit of no reduction below themselves: you may prefer Dante to Shakespeare, or claret to champagne, but that ends it." Hand insisted that "our choices are underived" and that "man, and man alone creates the universe of good and evil."[1]

Taxonomies of legal scholarship place both law and economics and public choice theory on the political right and feminist jurisprudence, critical legal studies, and critical race theory on the left. Nearly all of the scholars associated with all of these movements, however—like

1. Holmes to Lady Pollock, Sept. 6, 1902, *in Holmes-Pollock Letters*, at 105 (Mark DeWolfe Howe ed., 2d ed. 1961); Learned Hand, *The Spirit of Liberty: Papers and Addresses of Learned Hand* 261, 118, 121 (Irving Dilliard ed., 3d ed. 1977).

most of the pragmatists and functionalists in the center—echo Holmes and Hand.

Justice Holmes's letters and speeches revealed the depth of his skepticism:

- I don't see why we mightn't as well invert the Christian saying and hate the sinner but not the sin. Hate . . . imports no judgment. Disgust is ultimate and therefore as irrational as reason itself—a dogmatic datum. The world has produced the rattlesnake as well as me; but I kill it if I get a chance, as also mosquitos, cockroaches, murderers, and flies. My only judgment is that they are incongruous with the world I want; the kind of world we all try to make according to our power.
- I think "Whatsoever thy hand findeth to do, do it with thy might," infinitely more important than the vain attempt to love thy neighbor as thyself.
- I see no reason for attributing to a man a significance different in kind from that which belongs to a baboon or to a grain of sand.
- I take no stock in abstract rights . . . [and] equally fail to respect the passion for equality.
- I think that the sacredness of human life is a purely municipal ideal of no validity outside the jurisdiction. I believe that force, mitigated so far as may be by good manners, is the *ultima ratio.* . . . Every society rests on the death of men.
- Doesn't this squashy sentimentality of a big minority of our people about human life make you puke? [That minority includes people] who believe there is an onward and upward—who talk of uplift—who think that something in particular has happened and that the universe is no longer predatory. Oh bring me a basin.
- You respect the rights of man—I don't, except those things a given crowd will fight for.
- All my life I have sneered at the natural rights of man.[2]

2. Holmes to Lewis Einstein, May 21, 1914, *in The Essential Holmes: Selections from the Letters, Speeches, Judicial Opinions and Other Writings of Oliver Wendell Holmes, Jr.,* at 114, 114 (Richard A. Posner ed., 1992); Holmes, Speech at a Dinner Given to Justice Holmes by the Bar Association of Boston, Mar. 7, 1900, *id.* at 77, 79; Holmes to Frederick Pollock, Aug. 30, 1929, *id.* at 108, 108; Holmes to Harold Laski, Aug. 1, 1925, *id.* at 142, 142; Holmes to Frederick Pollock, Feb. 1, 1920, *id.* at 102, 102–03; Holmes to J. H. Wigmore, Nov. 1915, *quoted in* Sheldon M. Novick, *Honorable Justice: The Life of Oliver Wendell Holmes* 469 n.11 (1989); Holmes to Harold Laski, June 1, 1927, *in* 2 *Holmes-Laski Letters* 948, 948 (Mark DeWolfe Howe ed., 1953); Holmes to Harold Laski, Sept. 15, 1916, 1 *id.* at 21, 21.

Although Holmes said that he had values and called these values his "can't helps," his values were difficult to identify. They included only one political cause, his "starting point for an ideal for law": "I believe that the wholesale social regeneration which so many now seem to expect, if it can be helped by conscious, coordinated human effort, cannot be affected appreciably by tinkering with the institution of property, but only by taking in hand life and trying to build a race. That would be my starting point for an ideal for the law."[3]

Holmes wrote of "substitut[ing] artificial selection for natural by putting to death the inadequate" and of his contempt for "socialisms not prepared . . . to kill everyone below standard." He declared, "I can imagine a future in which science . . . shall have gained such catholic acceptance that it shall take control of life, and condemn at once with instant execution what now is left for nature to destroy." He spoke of the possibility of a future civilization "with smaller numbers, but perhaps also bred to greatness and splendor by science," and he wrote, "I can understand saying, whatever the cost, so far as may be, we will keep certain strains out of our blood."[4]

Recent writings about Holmes describe him as "the great oracle of American legal thought," "the only great American legal thinker," and "the most illustrious figure in the history of American law."[5] Holmes's view that rights are the bones over which people fight has found many champions in the academy.[6]

On the left, members of the critical legal studies (CLS) movement are the heirs of Holmes. They take as their motto, "Law is politics," an aphorism that does not seem to refer to the politics of civic virtue. For CLS scholars, politics is who you cheer for. The white male elite who wrote the laws cheered for themselves; CLS cheers for their victims. That is all there is to it.

3. Oliver Wendell Holmes, *Ideals and Doubts,* 10 Ill. L. Rev. 1, 3 (1915).

4. Holmes to Clare Castletown, Aug. 19, 1897, *quoted in* Sheldon M. Novick, *Justice Holmes's Philosophy,* 70 Wash. U.L.Q. 703, 729 (1992); Holmes to Lewis Einstein, Aug. 6, 1917, *quoted id.* at 729; Holmes, The Soldier's Faith, *in The Essential Holmes, supra* note 2, at 87, 88; Holmes, Speech to the Harvard Alumni Association of New York, Feb. 15, 1913, *quoted in* Liva Baker, *The Justice From Beacon Hill: The Life and Times of Oliver Wendell Holmes* 485 (1991); Holmes, Law and Social Reform, *in The Mind and Faith of Justice Holmes: His Speeches, Essays, Letters, and Judicial Opinions* 401 (Max Lerner ed., 1945).

5. Thomas C. Grey, *Holmes and Legal Pragmatism,* 41 Stan. L. Rev. 787, 787 (1989); Morton J. Horwitz, The Place of Justice Holmes in American Legal Thought, *in The Legacy of Oliver Wendell Holmes, Jr.* 31, 31 (Robert W. Gordon, ed., 1992); Richard A. Posner, Introduction, *The Essential Holmes, supra* note 2, at ix.

6. See Oliver Wendell Holmes, *Natural Law,* 32 Harv. L. Rev. 40, 42 (1918) (declaring that, just as people will fight for their rights, "[a] dog will fight for his bone").

Many radical feminists and critical race theorists are also the heirs of Holmes. They deny the possibility of a principled response to the unprincipled subordination of minorities and women. "Feminism does not claim to be objective, because objectivity is the basis of inequality," writes Ann Scales. "Feminism is result-oriented. . . . When dealing with social inequality there are no neutral principles." Catharine MacKinnon adds, "When [sex inequality] is exposed as a naked power question, there is no separable question of what ought to be. . . . In this shift of paradigms, equality propositions become no longer propositions of good and evil, but of power and powerlessness, no more disinterested in their origins or neutral in their arrival at conclusions than are the problems they address." Kimberle Crenshaw, a founder of critical race theory, describes this movement as "grounded in a bottom-up commitment to improve the substantive conditions" of minorities rather than in opposition to "the use of race . . . to interfere with decisions that would otherwise be fair or neutral."[7]

On the right, "public choice" theorists are the heirs of Holmes. They see most legislation as the product of the capture of the legislature by whatever group bid highest.[8] Among the themes of public-choice studies have been that laws ostensibly designed to prevent securities fraud were the product of bankers' fears of losing savings deposits, that the votes of federal trial judges on the constitutionality of sentencing guidelines were affected by the prospects of the judges' appointment to appellate courts, that nineteenth-century politicians allowed fires to rage out of control to encourage the establishment of patronage-generating fire departments, and that members of Congress have supported the creation of federal bureaucracies in order to gain political support by aiding constituents who would be treated unfairly by these bureaucracies.[9]

7. Ann Scales, *The Emergence of Feminist Jurisprudence: An Essay,* 95 Yale L.J. 1373, 1385, 1390 (1986); Catharine A. MacKinnon, *Feminism Unmodified: Discourses on Life and Law* 43–44 (1987); Kimberle Crenshaw, A Black Feminist Critique of Antidiscrimination Law and Politics, *in The Politics of Law: A Progressive Critique* 195, 201 (David Kairys ed., rev. ed. 1990).

8. Compare Holmes, The Gas-Stoker's Strike, *in The Essential Holmes, supra* note 2, at 583–84 ("[Legislation] is necessarily made a means by which a body, having the power, put burdens which are disagreeable to them on the shoulders of somebody else").

9. Jonathan R. Macey and Geoffrey P. Miller, *Origin of the Blue Sky Laws,* 70 Tex. L. Rev. 347 (1991); Mark A. Cohen, *Explaining Judicial Behavior, or What's "Unconstitutional" About the Sentencing Commission?* 7 J. of Law, Econ., and Organization 183 (1991); Fred C. McChesney, *Government Prohibitions on Volunteer Fire Fighting in Nineteenth-Century America: A Property Rights Perspective,* 15 J. Legal Stud. 69 (1989); Morris P. Fiorina, *Congress: Keystone of the Washington Establishment* 46–47 (1977).

In their normative writings and in their descriptions of common-law doctrine, law and economics scholars generally moderate the view of law as an unprincipled dogfight that characterizes their analysis of the work of legislatures and administrative agencies. The economists substitute a milder version of the skeptical creed, a perspective commonly described as "applied utilitarianism." But the most prominent of the law and economics scholars, Richard Posner, resists this characterization. Posner maintains that welfare economists seek the maximum satisfaction not of all human desires but only of desires backed by wealth. He claims that by adding a wealth constraint to classical utilitarianism, he has made his moral relativism less troublesome than Jeremy Bentham's. In Bentham's utilitarian world, a sadist who derived enough pleasure from torture to outweigh his victim's suffering would be justified in tormenting her. Jeremy's joy could excuse Alice's anguish. As Posner describes his own vision of justice, however, a sadist "would have to *buy* [his or her] victims' consent, and these purchases would soon deplete the wealth of all but the wealthiest sadists."[10]

As Arthur Leff summarized both Posner's bottom line and Bentham's, "Each of the Seven Deadly Sins is as licit as any of the others, and as any of the Cardinal virtues."[11] In the absence of an external source of value, all human desires have become, for economists and many others, equivalent to one another. The pleasure of pulling the wings off flies ranks as highly as that of feeding the hungry. For economically minded scholars, the function of law, the market, and other social institutions is to achieve the maximum satisfaction of human wants regardless of their content (or, if you prefer Posner's variation, to achieve the maximum satisfaction of desires backed by wealth).

Without the possibility of God, writers like Posner see no escape from their moral skepticism, yet their viewpoint falsifies everyday human experience as much as it does religious tradition. As the theologian James Gustafson ob-

10. Richard A. Posner, *The Economics of Justice* 82 (1983) (emphasis in the original). *But see* Richard A. Posner, *1997 Oliver Wendell Holmes Lectures: The Problematics of Moral and Legal Theory*, 111 Harv. L. Rev. 1637, 1670 n. 62 (1998) (denouncing all moral theories articulated by academics and conceding that his own theory was "doomed").

11. Arthur Allen Leff, *Unspeakable Ethics, Unnatural Law*, 1979 Duke L.J. 1229, 1244. *See* Robert H. Bork, *Neutral Principles and Some First Amendment Problems*, 47 Ind. L.J. 1, 10 (1971) ("[T]here is no principled way to decide that one man's gratifications are more deserving of respect than another's or that one form of gratification is more worthy than another. Why is sexual gratification more worthy than moral gratification? Why is sexual gratification nobler than economic gratification? There is no way of deciding these matters other than by reference to some system of moral or ethical values that has no objective or intrinsic validity of its own and about which men can and do differ").

serves, people are "valuing animals." They use their mental capacities to reflect about principles, duties, obligations, and ends. They examine critically the objects of their valuation. They rank desires on more than a scale of intensity. They sense that some desires are not simply stronger but more worthy than others, and they struggle toward a proper ordering of the objects of desire.[12]

The skepticism of welfare economists and utilitarians, however, is only partial. They attempt to put on the brakes before skidding into skeptical free fall. Although utilitarianism views all desires as commensurable with all other desires (and although law and economics treats all desires as commensurable with money), utilitarianism remains an *ethical* system. It is egalitarian, ranking everyone's happiness as highly as the king's. (Richard Posner's wealth-driven version of the creed, however, abandons this virtue.) Moreover, utilitarianism sometimes demands altruism—for example, by requiring a not-very-happy middle-aged person to sacrifice her life to save the lives of two blissful children on the opposite side of the globe, and thereby maximize the aggregate amount of happiness.

But what makes this system just? Despite Jeremy Bentham's insistence that "natural rights are simply nonsense . . . nonsense on stilts," does even this subjectivist ethical system require external justification?[13] Can utilitarianism, wealth maximization, or any other ethical system make sense in the absence of "a brooding omnipresence in the sky"?[14] Can one truly brake ethical skepticism halfway down? What's so great about egalitarianism, altruism, and human (or hippopotamus) happiness anyway?

In the absence of external justification, the desire that everyone's desires be satisfied is just another desire, and utilitarianism can be no more than a taste. Jeremy Bentham and his followers hoped to maximize happiness; Richard Posner and his followers seek to maximize wealth; and Oliver Wendell Holmes preferred taking in hand life and trying to build a race. Different strokes for different folks. People give up a lot when they give up on God.

Legal scholars of both the left and the right have tilted from Socrates on the issue that marks the largest and most persistent divide in all of jurisprudence. In Athens, four hundred years before Christ, Socrates contended that justice was not a human creation but had its origin in external reality. Thrasymachus disagreed; he insisted, "Justice is nothing else than the interest of the stronger."

12. See James M. Gustafson, 1 *Ethics from a Theocentric Perspective* 284–87 (1981).

13. Jeremy Bentham, Anarchical Fallacies, *in* 2 *Works of Jeremy Bentham* 105 (J. Browning ed., 1962).

14. See *Southern Pac. Co. v. Jensen*, 244 U. S. 205, 222 (1917) (Holmes, J., dissenting).

Ethical skepticism had a number of champions in the centuries that followed—for example, Thomas Hobbes, who wrote in 1651: "Whatsoever is the object of any man's appetite or desire, that is it which he for his part calleth *good:* and the object of his hate and aversion, *evil.* . . . For these words of good [and] evil . . . are ever used with relation to the person that useth them: there being nothing simply and absolutely so."[15]

Throughout Western history until the final third of the nineteenth century, however, the views of moral realists like Cicero, Gratian, Accursius, Bonaventure, Duns Scotus, Thomas Aquinas, Hugo Grotius, Samuel Puffendorf, Edward Coke, John Locke, William Blackstone, Thomas Jefferson, and Abraham Lincoln dominated European and, in later centuries, American law. The twentieth century may have given moral relativism its longest sustained run in Western history. (As I use the term, *moral realism* refers to a belief in mind-independent moral principles. I use this term and the term *natural law* interchangeably. Similarly, I do not distinguish between *moral skepticism* and *moral relativism.* I use both terms to denote the view that moral principles are the product of individual or group preferences without any grounding in external reality.)

I am not knowledgeable enough to confirm or refute the claim that the decline of societies always has coincided with a weakening or abandonment of the idea of natural law. Similarly, I do not know the extent to which intellectual movements shape society or whether they do at all. Nevertheless, "the nation's mood is sullen."[16] The vices of atomism, alienation, ambivalence, self-centeredness, and vacuity of commitment appear characteristic of our culture.[17] And when Perry Farrell, the lead singer of Porno for Pyros, shouts the central lyric of twentieth-century American jurisprudence, "Ain't no wrong, ain't no right, only pleasure and pain," another storm cloud may appear on the horizon.[18] Perhaps, amid signs of cultural discouragement and decay, one should expect to hear this lyric from orange-haired, leather-clad rock stars as well as from Richard Posner.

The current ethical skepticism of American law schools (in both its utilitarian and law-as-power varieties) mirrors the skepticism of the academy as a whole. Many pragmatists, abandoning the idea that human beings can perceive

15. Plato's *The Republic* 19 (B. Jowett trans., Vintage undated); Thomas Hobbes, *Leviathan* 32 (Michael Oakeshott ed., Basil Blackwell 1957).

16. Albert Borgmann, *Crossing the Postmodern Divide* 6 (1992).

17. See Jeremy Waldron, *Minority Cultures and the Cosmopolitan Alternatives,* 25 Mich. J. L. Ref. 751, 764–65 (1992).

18. Greg Kot, *Porno for Pyros' Act a Fizzled Freak Show,* Chi. Trib., June 14, 1993.

external reality (right, wrong, God, gravity, suffering, or even chairs), maintain that the only test of truth is what works or what promotes human flourishing. At the end of a century of pragmatic experimentation, that standard has given us a clear answer: pragmatism and moral skepticism don't. They are much more conducive to despair than to flourishing. They fail their own test of truth.

As pragmatism foundered, twentieth-century philosophy supplied a new and better test of truth. This epistemology goes by many names—coherency, reflective equilibrium, holism, and inference to the best explanation. (I do not suggest that these terms are synonyms—only that they have much in common and that they capture aspects of the same reasoning process.) As Michael Moore describes the core idea, "Any belief, moral or factual, is justified only by showing that it coheres well with everything else one believes. . . . One matches one's own particular judgments with one's more general principles without presupposing that one group must necessarily have to yield where judgments and principles contradict each other."[19] In effect, current epistemology portrays analogy, induction, and deduction as a single continuous process. It emphasizes the complex, holistic, provisional, and nonfoundational nature of human reasoning.

How people regard the process of knowing (epistemology) bears on what kinds of things they think exist (ontology), and today's epistemology has the potential to reshape moral reasoning and law. Older images of human reasoning set up morals for a kill. They suggested that "logic" always could be pushed to a "premise" and that reaching this premise ended the game. At this end point, it was everyone for herself.

As Justice Holmes expressed this viewpoint: "Deep-seated preferences cannot be argued about—you can not argue a man into liking a glass of beer—and therefore, when differences are sufficiently far reaching, we try to kill the other man rather than let him have his way. But that is perfectly consistent with admitting that, so far as it appears, his grounds are just as good as ours."[20]

Whether one claimed that her premises came from God or admitted that she made them up, her values were the product of "can't helps"—of leaps of faith unaided by reason. In the end, one could merely assert her own personal, exis-

19. Michael Moore, *Moral Reality,* 1982 Wis. L. Rev. 1061, 1112–13. *See* Nelson Goodman, *Fact, Fiction, and Forecast* 64 (4th ed., 1983) ("[R]ules and particular inferences alike are justified by being brought into agreement with each other. A rule is amended if it yields an inference we are unwilling to accept; an inference is rejected if it violates a rule we are unwilling to amend"); John Rawls, *A Theory of Justice* 20–21 (1971).

20. Holmes, *Natural Law, supra* note 6, at 40–41.

tential faith—a faith that might not move any other rational person and that she was likely to assert apologetically and without conviction or with indefensible conviction. Unreasoning faith appeared unavoidable for everyone engaged in normative discourse, religious believer or not.

Religious believers today (the coherentists among us anyway) rely less on blind faith. We despair far less of human reason. People who consider us more dependent on faith and less committed to reason than our disbelieving colleagues often have things backward. More than four hundred years ago, John Calvin recognized the holistic and experiential basis of theological reflection: "Nearly all the wisdom we possess, that is to say, true and sound wisdom, consists of two parts: the knowledge of God and of ourselves. But, while joined by many bonds, which one precedes and brings forth the other is not easy to discern."[21]

Today's coherentist epistemology emphasizes that premises do not come from nowhere. They are usually the products of efforts to generalize our experience of the world. We may do this job of inference well or poorly—perceiving patterns sharply or dimly, misperceiving them, or missing them altogether. We move from induction to deduction to induction to deduction in continuous and, we hope, progressive spirals. We generalize, test our generalizations against new experience, then generalize again. Human reasoning does not resemble the operations of a hand-held calculator as much as it does the workings of a computer ranging over a large set of ever-changing data to determine a "best fit" line.

Gilbert Harman puts it this way: "If we suppose that beliefs are to be justified by deducing them from more basic beliefs, we will suppose that there are beliefs so basic that they cannot be justified at all." Traditional images of human reasoning portray the most important of our beliefs as the least justified. Harman underlines the new epistemology's response: "These skeptical views are undermined . . . once it is seen that the relevant kind of justification is not a matter of derivation from basic principles but is rather a matter of showing that a view fits in well with other things we believe."[22]

One implication of this holistic vision of human understanding is that we need no longer mark a sharp divide between faith and reason. Older views declared that unless some "proof" of the existence of God was conclusive, belief in God could rest only on faith or revelation. At the beginning of the twenty-

21. John Calvin, 1 *Institutes of the Christian Religion* 35 (Ford Lewis Battles trans., Westminster 1960) (1559 ed.).

22. Gilbert Harman, *Thought* 164 (1973).

first century, however, the name of the game is not hogchoker "proof"; it is in-ference to the best explanation.

This vision offers a clearer perspective on many theological issues—among them, the argument from design. It does so at the same time that twentieth-century science has multiplied the evidence in support of this classic argu-ment.[23] As scientists reveal phenomena as wondrous as anything in the Book of Genesis, we begin to perceive a more awesome God than God the Watchmaker, the already inspiring God of Newtonian physics. God, more fully revealed but ever more mysterious, is the God of the big bang and the expanding universe and of order in chaos and chaos in order. Moreover, the new epistemology, by emphasizing the unity of emotional and cognitive ways of knowing, has ended the banishment of our sense of wonder, reverence, dependence, and gratitude from our "reasoning" process.

Twentieth-century philosophy suggests the partial collapse of induction and deduction, of cognition and emotion, and of faith and reason. It also suggests the collapse of fact and value. Once we understand that we come to moral con-clusions in the same way that we come to empirical conclusions, ascribing a higher ontological status to judgments of fact than to judgments of value can-not be justified.

An illustration may make this proposition less abstract:

I once saw a man beat a horse. Among my thoughts on that occasion were:
  1. That is a horse.
  2. The horse is in pain.
  3. The man's act is cruel.
  4. The man's act is wrong.
Which, if any, of these things did I know?

Rays of light stimulated my optic nerves, and my brain interpreted the re-sulting electronic impulses, saying, "That is a horse." Yet my interpretation of the world could have been erroneous. I might have seen a mule, or it might have been a hologram. It might even have been a sensory impression fed to me, a brain in a vat, by a mad scientist.

Although people in my culture could have constructed other taxonomies, they had taught me a useful category, *horse*. In an instant and without bringing most of the process to consciousness, I considered the available data—color, size, configuration, movement, and more. I determined that the "horse hy-

23. See, e.g., Paul Davies, *The Mind of God* (1992); John Polkinghorne, *The Faith of a Physicist* (1994); John Polkinghorne, *Belief in God in an Age of Science* (1998).

pothesis" fit. As Nelson Goodman observes, "Facts are small theories, and true theories are big facts."[24] Facts and theories are both interpretations of experience, but it does not follow that one interpretation is as good as another. Someone who saw what I saw and said, "Why, that man is beating a frog," would not have gotten it right.

I often revise my interpretations of the empirical world. At one time, I might have thought that the stick protruding from the beaker of water was bent. I now infer that the same stick is straight. Whole cultures do what I do. Everyone once believed that the world was flat and the sun went around it; those hypotheses offered the simplest explanations of what they saw. But careful people then made closer observations. The old hypotheses did not fit, and the culture accepted new ones.

I knew that the horse was in pain in the same way that I knew it was a horse. The word *pain* gives a single name to many experiences. It speaks of a pattern in the world just as the word *horse* does. I envisioned what I would have experienced had the man whipped me, and some of the horse's visible responses to the whip were like those I might have exhibited. I inferred that the horse and I were members of the same interpretive community; we both knew the meaning of the whip. My judgment that the horse was in pain was, like most other judgments about the world, a potentially fallible inference, but I have enough confidence in this inference to call it *knowledge*. I *knew* that the horse was in pain.

When I concluded that the man's act was cruel, I again inferred a creature's state of mind from external circumstances. This time it was the man's state of mind rather than the horse's. Like many other words, the word *cruel* combines an empirical and a normative judgment within a single concept. Words with this characteristic are sometimes called *thick ethical concepts*. They illustrate that people rarely pause to distinguish fact from value in trying to make sense of their experience.

People who have followed me this far may get off before the last stop. They may agree that horses are real, that pain is real, and that cruelty is real. But right and wrong? Those things are not "real." They're subjective, they're relative, contingent, and socially constructed. If someone does not believe that horses are real, that horses can experience pain, or that people can be cruel, that person is crazy. But if this person does not believe that beating horses is wrong, why, that is her choice. Right and wrong are matters of personal or, at most, community taste.

24. Nelson Goodman, *Ways of Worldmaking* 97 (1978).

It's a strange place to get off. The thought that the man's act was wrong rushed into my mind as quickly and forcefully as the thoughts, "That is a horse," "The horse is in pain," and "The man's act is cruel." Moreover, the word *wrong* categorizes and simplifies experience in the same way that the words *horse, pain,* and *cruelty* do. In what sense could the latter terms, but not the former, be regarded as capturing external reality? Why should I give greater credence (or different credence) to the first three judgments than to the last? What error lies in regarding all of the words that leapt to my mind as capturing genuine characteristics of what I saw?[25] People consider the unseen forces of Einstein's physics real because hypothesizing these forces unifies and explains a variety of human experiences. I believe in God, right, and wrong for precisely the same reason.

On March 18, 1989, when I was forty-eight, I knelt beside two other men of equally advanced age and became a Christian. My baptism would have astonished most of the people who had known me in my adult life. It was prompted partly by circumstances of the sort that commonly lead adults to reconsider their direction (in my case, concern and guilt about a child in trouble and distress about a recently failed romance). It was prompted too by a teacher, J.B., who succeeded in making sense of things that never had made sense to me before. Finally, odd though it may seem, my conversion from agnosticism to Christianity was prompted by long-standing dissatisfaction with legal and other academic thought as I had experienced it throughout my career. My professional experience had taught me that law not grounded on a strong sense of right and wrong was lousy law.[26] Thinking about law, like thinking about most things, can lead one to God.

In recent years, a resurgence of legal and philosophical writing about moral realism has made natural law respectable again.[27] As I have suggested elsewhere, the image of returning may be appropriate.[28] A child's trust in her parents is likely to give way to adolescent rejection; and when the child becomes an

25. For a much fuller development of the argument sketched here and for a careful consideration of some objections to it, see two articles by Michael Moore. Moore, *Moral Reality, supra* note 19, and Michael Moore, *Moral Reality Revisited,* 90 Mich. L. Rev. 2424 (1992).

26. See, e.g., Albert W. Alschuler, *Failed Pragmatism: Reflections on the Burger Court,* 100 Harv. L. Rev. 1436 (1987); Albert W. Alschuler, *Preventive Pretrial Detention and the Failure of Interest-Balancing Approaches to Due Process,* 85 Mich. L. Rev. 510 (1986).

27. See, e.g., Symposium, *Natural Law,* 4 S. Cal. Interdisc. L.J. 455 (1995); Symposium, *Natural Law,* 90 Mich. L. Rev. 2203 (1992); Symposium, *Perspectives on Natural Law,* 61 U. Cin. L. Rev. 1 (1992); *Natural Law Symposium,* 38 Clev. St. L. Rev. 1 (1990).

28. Albert W. Alschuler, *Rediscovering Blackstone,* 145 U. Pa. L. Rev. 1, 55 (1996).

adult, her adolescent rejection is likely to give way to a new and wiser appreciation of her parents' virtues. In the same way, lawyers of our new century may develop a new, more mature appreciation of their natural-law heritage—a heritage that lawyers of the past century mostly dismissed as "transcendental nonsense."[29] The iconoclasm and skepticism of the twentieth century then may yield to a new idealism and a new spirituality.

In the interim:

> There is only the fight to recover what has been lost
> And found and lost again and again; and now, under conditions
> That seem unpropitious. But perhaps neither gain nor loss.
> For us, there is only the trying. The rest is not our business.[30]

29. See Felix Cohen, *Transcendental Nonsense and the Functional Approach,* 35 Colum. L. Rev. 809 (1935).

30. T. S. Eliot, East Coker, *in The Complete Poems and Plays, 1909–1950* 128 (1952).

# Section 3 Critical Legal Studies

The critical legal studies movement burst onto the legal academic scene in the mid-1970s. Like the legal realists, critical legal studies theorists argued that there is no internal logic within the law that compels particular decisions in cases; the law is indeterminate. They accused judges and legal academics generally of determining those rules in ways that serve the wealthy classes. Like the Hebrew prophets, critical legal studies leaders condemned the legal establishment for its treatment of the poor. The legal analysis in the academy was, as Roberto Unger put it in his 1986 book *The Critical Legal Studies Movement,* merely "one more variant of the perennial effort to restate power and preconception as right." Critical legal studies theorists brought the tools of postmodern literary criticism and neo-Marxist social thought to the legal academy. They saw law merely as politics and sought to tear down the existing structure. What is not so clear is what they would put in its place.

In the following essay, David S. Caudill identifies a close parallel between the critical legal studies recognition that ideology underlies law and the insights of the early-twentieth-century Dutch Calvinist thinker Herman Dooyeweerd. Both saw that beneath any legal system there is a system of beliefs that guides and directs it. There is no neutral ground. Other authors in this book who have been associated with or influenced by critical legal studies include Elizabeth Mensch and Thomas L. Shaffer.

# Law and Belief: Critical Legal Studies and Philosophy of the Law-Idea

*David S. Caudill*

The critical legal studies (CLS) movement, much discussed in 1980s legal academe, seemed by the year 2000 to have dissipated into various other schools of critical jurisprudence. These include law and literature studies, feminist legal theory, and critical race theory, so references to CLS are often about the past—the recent past, an influential past, but nevertheless the past. In this essay I shall highlight one major theme in the literature that was associated with CLS and in more recent critical jurisprudence, namely the ideology critique and specifically the idea of disclosure of "belief-systems" (clusters of assumptions to which faithlike commitments are made) in legal theory and practice. This aspect of CLS drew on other intellectual movements, including Frankfurt School Neo-Marxism, the "new" history and philosophy of natural science, and recent developments in literary theory and criticism. Of particular interest, however, is the similarity of CLS methodology to the *Wijsbegeerte der Wetsidee* (roughly, "philosophy of the law-idea"), a critical Christian and Calvinist perspective arising in Holland in the early 1900s and relatively unknown in American legal scholarship. The goal of belief-disclosure, which CLS shares with the philosophy of the law-idea, represents one of the primary virtues of CLS and provides a key response to certain criticisms of the movement.

One such criticism is that CLS (or, for example, the philosophy of the law-idea) is just another belief system, with no more or less justification or foundation than the targets of its critique. I will suggest the nature and elements of one debate that follows from the acknowledgment that all philosophers of law are believers. The label *believers* does not imply that legal philosophers worry that others will not share their vision of law, or that they do not try to test their beliefs against reality. Rather, the point is that fundamental commitments play a vital role in the construction of legal theories, even in the theorist's conception of reality and standards concerning what "makes sense."

To appreciate the affinity between CLS and the philosophy of the law-idea, one must understand the concept of ideology broadly, in the sense of worldview, rather than in the narrower sense of specific political systems or in the pejorative sense associated with orthodox Marxism.[1] The characteristics of ideology have been described by CLS scholars in four related forms. First, the term *ideology* is used variously to describe a worldview or coherent set of communal beliefs and interpretations, including a tacit value system, our habits of thought, and society's shared assumptions (for example, about the nature and role of law and legal institutions). Second, such belief structures appear natural and necessary to their holders, thereby hiding contradictions and limiting cultural options. Third, an ideology (and a legal ideology) is constitutive rather than reflective of social realities—it stabilizes, confirms, maintains, and justifies society. In its normative conception, ideology legitimates the status quo, including existing power structures. Last, ideology can operate to replace, or play the role of, religion; for example, the liberal belief in the autonomy of consciousness is revealed as an undisclosed commitment in mainstream jurisprudence. These aspects of ideology are coexistent, not exclusive, and together parallel the identification and critique of belief structures by certain Christian philosophers.

## CRITICAL LEGAL STUDIES AS IDEOLOGY CRITIQUE

To some, identifying CLS might seem no more difficult than naming scholars who use the abstract words associated with the movement: indeterminacy, le-

1. *Cf.* David Ray Papke, *Neo-Marxists, Nietzscheans, and New Critics: The Voices of the Contemporary Law and Literature Discourse* (book review) 1985 Am. B. Found. Res. J. 883, 889 (discussing concept of ideology among CLS and Neo-Marxists).

gitimation, trashing, and demystification. While precise meanings of these words are not consistently established in CLS literature, conceiving the movement as a critique of ideology gives some meaning to the unique terminology, as well as to the concept of ideology in general.

## The Disclosure of Belief Structures

A firmly entrenched system of shared beliefs in any culture makes it difficult for its members to imagine that life could be different. The law and its institutions may comprise one such cluster of beliefs, shared interpretations, or "cultural codes" that tend to be accepted as givens. One of the fundamental themes in early CLS literature was that social reality, in fact constructed by its members, too often is externalized and placed above human choice, thus producing an imagined necessity. CLS sought to expose such ideological presuppositions: legal rules can be shown to be historically contingent; legal categories can be shown to be arbitrary; legal necessity can be empirically disproven. The latter is an immanent critique of mainstream legal theory and practice—by its own terms and methodology, doctrine is shown to be incoherent or contradictory. For example, rules "can be applied quite differently in quite different circumstances, sometimes 'paternalistically,' sometimes strictly, sometimes forcing parties to share gains and losses with each other, and sometimes not at all."[2]

The perceived necessity, or false consciousness, identified by CLS is not overt but operates at a level where options are dismissed as unthinkable, or never even conceived. The resulting tacit value system must be re-created first for the sake of awareness, then to permit a deeper criticism of the system itself—not just particular theorists, legislators, or judges. Borrowing from new historians and philosophers of science, the CLS critique discloses an ideological system that is not seen as closed or deterministic because there is room for breakthroughs, paradigm shifts, and revolutions.[3]

CLS scholars accuse traditional legal scholars of contrasting the objective and rational adjudicative process to the arbitrary decisions in the political sphere. Under CLS scrutiny, no form of legal reasoning distinguishes itself from political dialogue. "Law is simply politics dressed in different garb; it neither operates in a historical vacuum nor does it exist independently of ideological strug-

2. Robert W. Gordon, New Developments in Legal Theory, in *The Politics of Law: A Progressive Critique* 287–89 (David Kairys ed., 1982).

3. *See* G. Edward White, *The Inevitability of Critical Legal Studies*, 36 Stan. L. Rev. 649, 652–54, 670 (1984).

gles in society."[4] In contemporary legal discourse, an appeal is often made to conventional morality for a source of norms, to fundamental rights that "are purported to exist independently of conventional morality and to inhere within a liberal society," or to "an economic thread that neatly ties together and justifies the seemingly illogical jumble of legal doctrine." For the CLS scholar, however, there are no such foundational givens: one must inescapably choose between values.[5] At this point, given that few scholars endorse rigid objectivism or formalism, asserting the role of values in law is like kicking in an open door. Nevertheless, CLS methodology can be further explored, and its claims made more compelling, by conceiving the movement as a critique of ideology.

### The Concept of Ideology

Ideology, in one contemporary construction, provides its holders with both an intelligible description of the world and guidelines for action in that world. For CLS, the real power of legal ideologies is "their tendency to establish a dynamic of their own and to confer on legal doctrine a false air of naturalness."[6] Recall that neo-Marxian critical theory, a parent of CLS, "declared that the chains that most strongly bind an oppressed class are ideological in nature, *i.e.,* the habits of thought that tend to make both the master and the slave accept the existing situation as justified or inevitable."[7]

Raymond Geuss, in his helpful assessment of the Frankfurt School, distinguishes between the descriptive and pejorative senses of the term *ideology.* In the purely descriptive sense, ideology can mean "the beliefs the members of a group hold, the concepts they use, the attitudes and psychological dispositions they exhibit, their motives, desires, values, predilections, works of art, religious rituals, gestures, etc."[8] In its pejorative sense, ideology can refer to delusion or false consciousness, hence the phrase *end of ideology* for projects that attempt to demonstrate the delusion. Such false consciousness is sometimes considered an

4. Allan C. Hutchinson and Patrick J. Monahan, *Law, Politics, and the Critical Legal Scholars: The Unfolding Drama of American Legal Thought,* 36 Stan. L. Rev. 199, 202, 206 (1984).

5. *See id.* at 208.

6. *See id.* at 215, 217; *see also* Duncan Kennedy, *The Structure of Blackstone's Commentaries,* 28 Buffalo L. Rev. 205, 272 (1979) (Blackstone made liberalism "look like the product of a linear process of accretion of truths or, at worst, like a timeless way of understanding the world").

7. *See* Phillip E. Johnson, *Do You Sincerely Want to Be Radical?* 36 Stan. L. Rev. 247, 251 (1984).

8. *See* Raymond Geuss, *The Idea of A Critical Theory: Habermas and the Frankfurt School* 5 (1984).

ideology by "virtue of the function or role it plays in supporting, stabilizing, or legitimizing certain kinds of social institutions or practices. Habermas regularly speaks of ideology as a 'world-picture' which stabilizes or legitimizes domination or hegemony *(Herrschaft)*."[9] Additionally, a form of consciousness that "mask[s] social contradictions" or hinders "maximal development of the forces of material production" can be called an ideology in this second sense.[10]

In what sense is the term ideology used by CLS? Some suggest that critical legal theorists "condemn legal ideology not because it is morally wrong or instrumentally inappropriate . . . but because it is false."[11] This pejorative sense of ideology is integral to the concept of legitimation, because if a person believes that a social structure is natural or given and it is not, that person's belief is false *and* it serves to legitimate that social structure. The term *hegemony* in Antonio Gramsci's and CLS writings refers to this control and extraction of consent by ideological means.[12]

However, with respect to law, the term *ideology* often refers descriptively "to beliefs that individuals hold about law or to a set of beliefs, ideas, and values embodied in the legal institutions and legal materials (cases, regulations, and statutes) of a particular society." The ideology embodied in the law might mean (1) a particular set of beliefs expressed in laws that do not necessarily influence behavior or beliefs, (2) the arguments and reasons that legal institutions use to justify actions, or (3) a set of beliefs that change the desires of individuals or limit their available choices in certain ways. CLS seems to use the term in this third sense, but the idea of limiting choices has a pejorative and not just a descriptive edge. The law, again, functions to legitimate certain social arrangements and to affect nonlegal actors directly:[13] "People respond optimally to their environment in light of their known self-interests. Ideology distorts their knowledge of their own self-interests and consequently leads people to act contrary to their 'true' interests. . . . The primary task of Critical legal theory is to reveal to people their true interests."[14] Not only are choices limited, but knowledge is distorted and true interests lie hidden. CLS finds it difficult to retain a purely descriptive sense of ideology because of the conviction that a monolithic belief system effaces something—choices, freedom, and alterna-

---

9. *See id.* at 11–12, 15 (footnote omitted).

10. *See id.* at 18.

11. Lewis A. Kornhauser, *The Great Image of Authority,* 36 Stan. L. Rev. 349, 372–73 (1984).

12. *See id.* at 376.

13. *See id.* at 376–77.

14. *Id.* at 378–79.

tive visions.[15] Ideology must be linked to domination—to asymmetrical distribution of power and resources—in order to develop its critical potential.[16]

The negative, critical approach to ideology seems to have two constructions: (1) a strong, almost dogmatic, allegiance to the allied Marxian concepts of domination, class struggle, and legitimation of oppression, and (2) a weaker, modest approach that emphasizes option-limiting belief structures and their disclosure. The latter seems to be a descriptive approach because it lacks confidence that one set of social structures is more correct than another. The effort nevertheless can be labeled critical because it seeks to disclose hidden belief systems, to open up for free discussion that which is unquestioned. Ideology is, for this modest school, not something false that hides the oppressor's chains; instead, ideology is an inevitable perspective or tilt typical of all nonreflective or uncritical—perhaps everyday—thought. The social critic here does not judge between true and false political or legal orders except in the sense that people who freely discuss and decide matters make true choices and those who believe the social world cannot change have a false impression.

Several scholars associated with CLS employ the modest strand of ideology critique. Boyle, for example, clearly links current legal knowledge with power, critique with liberation. His references to a "pre-existing delusion," "structural prejudice," and "collective fantasies" are pejorative, not descriptive. However, Boyle also endorses "a partial, nonprivileged account of particular areas of life" and a method of disclosing invisible ideological constraints. He is intensely aware that CLS'ers who demonstrate the failure of others to ground or justify their legal theory are themselves implicated in the process: "how do we know our structure is *the right structure?*" According to Boyle, we don't; we make up "partial, local maps that sometimes seem to work and sometimes do not."[17]

Joseph Singer, even more than Boyle, represents the modest strand of CLS ideology critique. Because legal doctrine is a matter of beliefs and commitment, not logic and rationality, the critical project can succeed by disclosing in law the contingencies, contradictions, and indeterminacy that appear other-

---

15. *But see* John B. Thompson, *Studies in the Theory of Ideology* 5 (1984) ("[I]t seems more likely that our societies, in so far as they are 'stable' social orders, are stabilized by virtue of the diversity of values and beliefs and the proliferation of divisions between individuals and groups"). See also David McLellan, *Ideology* 73 (1986) (a dominant ideology is likely to be accepted by the ruling class alone).

16. *See* Thompson, *supra* note 15, at 4, 76.

17. *See* James Boyle, *The Politics of Reason: Critical Legal Theory and Local Social Thought,* 133 U. Pa. L. Rev. 685, 740, 749, 769–80 (1985).

wise. Responding to the charge of nihilism, Singer explains that the postaware-ness void can be filled with imaginative discussion and joint reconstruction of social life. The CLS critique rejects nothing that was not already gone. The foun-dations of legal doctrines and institutions are beliefs, and CLS disturbs any pre-tensions to the contrary. Singer has standards—he advocates the use of the law to prevent cruelty, alleviate misery, democratize illegitimate hierarchies, and end loneliness—but the critical bite in his work comes from reducing all of us to believers.[18]

Finally, Gary Peller's work attempts to demonstrate the social and contin-gent character of language and knowledge in general. Specifically, legal lan-guage and knowledge are ideological, characterized by "shared conventions and codes of meaning" and not by the representation of some objective reality. Nevertheless, "we come to associate social conventions with 'true knowledge' and accordingly lose sight of the contingency of status quo social patterns." Be-cause we have "lost sight," some knowledge becomes institutionalized, some social relations reified, some descriptions "taken as fact rather than 'mere' opin-ion or ideology." By implication, critique can make visible the "traces of con-tingency in existing social relations" and "demonstrate the marginalized sense that things could be otherwise." Facing the inevitability of politics in the fullest sense, we recognize that we either reproduce or resist the social order without confidence that any course is the right one.[19]

Some leftists perceived of ideology as false or as bourgeois consciousness (for example, Marx) or as the opposite of science (for example, Engels). Such con-ceptions, outdated in contemporary society and academia, at least preserved the link with domination and might be preferred over a mere mapping of social reality as so many systems of belief, none open to criticism.[20] A middle ground, however, appears between the pejorative and descriptive conceptions of ideol-ogy. Instead of beginning by identifying and criticizing oppressive social struc-tures or illegitimate hierarchies, which exercise might appear dogmatic, one may instead disclose the marginalization of alternative viewpoints, the social character of knowledge, or the hidden assumptions of legal theory and prac-tice.

18. *See* Joseph William Singer, *The Player and the Cards: Nihilism and Legal Theory*, 94 Yale L.J. 1, 35, 59–70 (1984) (criticized in John Stick, *Can Nihilism Be Pragmatic?* 100 Harv. L. Rev. 332 (1986)).

19. *See, e.g.,* Gary Peller, *The Metaphysics of American Law*, 73 Cal. L. Rev. 1151, 1164, 1177–81, 1275, 1290 (1985).

20. McLellan, *supra* note 15, at 83.

## Law and Doctrine as Legitimating Ideology

For CLS, the ruling class or dominant legal culture does not simply impose itself on society. An important distinction can be made between the argument that the United States Supreme Court is "carrying out a right-wing political program" that is shrouded in "a complex structure of ideological justifications that mask the political nature of the activity," and, on the other hand, the view that "the Supreme Court is fundamentally a figment of the cultural imagination and that its true role is to be found not in the direct practical consequences of the outcomes of its decisions—with the politics of these outcomes being mystified by ideology—but rather in the ideology itself as a set of cultural images that are intended to give a false political legitimacy to the social order."[21] This is a fine distinction between ideology as hiding an agenda and ideology as legitimating a false consciousness. In the latter view, the Supreme Court's role is "to pacify conflict through the mediation of a false social-meaning system, a set of ideas and images about the world which serve today as the secular equivalent of religious ideology." The highest legal institution here operates to maintain that worldview not simply by making decisions consistent with it but by constructing and confirming an otherwise indeterminate system as necessary. Legitimation is most successful when "we are led to believe that it is 'our' political institutions that actually create the social and economic hierarchies in the first place," and that the law merely conforms with our choice.[22] Legal thought, however, actually constructs social realities rather than merely reflecting them.[23]

## Methodology: Delegitimation and Trashing

Liberation and enlightenment, or at least open discussion and criticism, are aided by unfreezing the world as it now appears. Delegitimation (or "trashing") therefore has validity as a form of legal scholarship. Its purpose "is to destabilize a variety of theoretical world views (and thus, one would hope, related common sense world views) that imply the beneficence or inexorability of social life

21. *See* Peter Gabel, *The Mass Psychology of the New Federalism: How the Burger Court's Political Imagery Legitimizes the Privatization of Everyday Life,* 52 Geo. Wash. L. Rev. 263, 264 (1984).

22. *See id.* at 265.

23. *See* Robert M. Hayden, *Rules, Processes, and Interpretations: Geertz, Comaroff, and Roberts* (Book Review), 1984 Am. B. Found. Res. J. 469, 476 (citing Clifford Geertz, *Local Knowledge* 232 (1983)).

as we see it."[24] The conception of delegitimation or trashing constitutes the belief-disclosure methodology of CLS. That which appears as given, natural, and real in the legal system is shown to be ideological—the result of belief structures that are socially and historically contingent.[25]

## CONTRASTING GOALS OF THE CRITIQUE

Two vaguely distinct versions of the critique of ideology of law emerge from the CLS canon, which might be termed *normative* and *methodological.* The normative critique attempts to disclose the ideological assumptions in the legal system that are wrong. Legal ideology is conceived as a "cloak" hiding and maintaining tensions, contradictions, and, most important, oppression of a powerless class or classes by a powerful ruling class. Some scholars say that CLS is linked to a radical political agenda because of the normative critique, in which the disclosure of tilt is a call to revolution. The legal system, parading as neutral, is shown to have hidden interests in a particular class, even though the members of the ruling class may be ideologically unaware of the boundaries upon thought that protect them. The false consciousness that "all is well" may be shared by all. Once the normative critique demonstrates the inconsistency and incoherency of the ruling ideology (which all aware people should agree is wrong), and then discloses the tilt in favor of a ruling class (which the lower class should agree is wrong), the stage is set for emancipation from the ideology. The normative critique typically does not focus on the ideology of the critics, or the new ideology that will replace the old ideology. Rather, it tends toward a pejorative use of that term. Significantly, the normative critique seems to endorse revolution and violent change, depending upon how large the oppressed class is in comparison with the ruling class.

---

24. *See* Mark G. Kelman, *Trashing,* 36 Stan. L. Rev. 293, 327–28 (1984). Trashing "is designed to counter beliefs (which appear quite clearly in daily life) that the world is running smoothly." *See id.* at 329.

25. One introductory account of the methodology of trashing sets forth the steps as follows: (1) separate logic from perception, then focus on the logic and show political choices that have been repressed by quasi-formalist beliefs; (2) sketch out paradigms of legal consciousness that are legitimating visions which the legal elite uses; (3) do a concrete analysis of a frozen slice of a particular worldview; and (4) show the political slant of all postrealist attempts to deny subjectivity. *See* Jamie Boyle, *Critical Legal Studies: A Young Person's Guide, in* Information Packet and Readings, Nat'l CLS conf. (March 15–16, 1984), at 15–16.

The methodological critique, on the other hand, emphasizes disclosure of ideological tilt for purposes of awareness, discussion, and criticism. Where a legal system parades as neutral or given, the methodological critique shows that political and moral neutrality is a myth and that nothing is given or natural—everything is made by people. Legal theory is shown to reflect a particular set of tacit values and a particular vision of society that together form an ideology which constitutes our world by legitimating and justifying its institutions. Nevertheless, our habits of thought can be broken by the methodological critique's demonstration that legal rules are historical, legal categories are arbitrary, and legal necessity a lie. The ultimate goal seems to be open communication; the emancipation seems to take place on the level of thought. That is, people should be free to choose or re-create their legal system. The revolution is one of paradigms, and thus the violent overtones are absent. The battle here seems tame and academic because it is among scholars and not on the streets.

The distinction between the normative and the methodological critique of ideology highlights my thesis that the most valuable contribution of CLS is in its methodological critique. This is not to deny the value of the normative critique, for example, in its initial disclosure of inconsistent assumptions. The exercise, however, is often not constructive. The conclusion that all of legal doctrine is manipulable and incoherent leaves no legal doctrine, no basis to build a new doctrine, and a suspicion that the critic's proposals are just as manipulable and incoherent. Likewise, in the normative critique's emphases on disclosing class interests and oppression, one senses an undisclosed ideology on the part of the critics (the political agenda identified by some) in the words *oppressed, ruling class*, and *false ideology.*

Of course, the methodological critique is not without problems. The normative critics may consider awareness of and communication regarding beliefs directionless and relativistic. The linking of ideology with domination provides a standard, a goal, for the critical project. The methodological critics seemingly have no basis to criticize anything. The methodological critics might answer that they attack the oppression of silence and the marginalization of alternatives, not the oppression of a ruling class.

In the next several sections of this essay, I shall show that CLS's methodological critique has a certain affinity with the philosophy of the law-idea, a movement critical of Marxism and all other theorizing that fails to confess its own fundamental belief structures. Significantly, neither CLS's methodological critique nor the philosophy of the law-idea is an attempt to escape or rise above ideology or belief. Rather, each attempts to critically and self-critically disclose the inevitable tilt in all theory, including legal doctrine.

## THE PHILOSOPHY OF THE LAW-IDEA AS IDEOLOGY CRITIQUE

Like any intellectual movement, CLS builds on other movements, thus the similarity of CLS to other contemporary approaches is to be expected, as is the criticism that CLS is not "new." However, the similarity of CLS to a philosophy that is neither young, nor leftist, nor American is somewhat surprising, and, more important, indicates a potential common ground for discourse between CLS and its critics.

A more typical or predictable response to CLS by Christian philosophers might be to see little common ground. After all, Christians are variously committed to revealed truth, natural-law principles, and other stabilizing ideas that seem to run counter to notions of social construction, historical contingency, the manipulability of doctrine, and law as power and politics. Indeed, for those Christians who claim a foundation outside faith—in revelation, natural law, or "reality"—the CLS methodological critique seems relativistic. For those Christians who see finality and legal truths as functions of faith *and* are concerned that secular theorists contrast faith with rational thinking, attention to reality, and common sense, however, the methodological attempt to level the playing field is empowering.

### Dooyeweerd and the Transcendental Critique

Herman Dooyeweerd (1894–1977), a well-known legal philosopher in his native Holland, remains relatively unknown in the United States. Many of his books and essays have been translated into English, and his name, if not the details of his philosophical perspective, is quite familiar to scholars—especially theologians and philosophers—in the Christian Reformational or Calvinistic tradition. Dooyeweerd was raised in a Calvinist home, studied law in Amsterdam, and served in various political positions before returning to the Free University of Amsterdam as a professor of legal philosophy.[26] He is considered one of the most important Dutch philosophers, alongside Erasmus of Rotterdam (1469–1536), Grotius (1583–1645), and Spinoza (1632–77). Dooyeweerd's ma-

---

26. *See* Bernard Zylstra, Introduction, in L. Kalsbeek, *Contours of a Christian Philosophy* 14 (Bernard Zylstra and Josina Zylstra eds., 1975).

jor significance lies in his contribution to the development of Christian philosophy in general, and not merely Christian jurisprudence.[27] Of his publications, which number more than two hundred, the most significant is *De Wijsbegeerte der Wetsidee,* the book whose title soon became the generally accepted name of a new philosophical movement: the philosophy of the law-idea.[28] Dooyeweerd and his colleague Dirk H. T. Vollenhoven are considered the founders of that philosophical movement, which grew in numbers and significance in Holland between the two world wars.

As with CLS, the attempt to summarize briefly the major themes of a philosophical movement appears feeble. One published bibliography of the philosophy of the law-idea is thirty-six pages long and contains only twenty-four of Dooyeweerd's publications.[29] Nevertheless, before narrowing my focus to the "disclosure of belief structures" central to the philosophy of the law-idea, it is important to acknowledge at least some of the breadth and complexity of the movement.

The critical aspect of the philosophy of the law-idea follows from its search for the philosophical foundations of science, including both the social and natural sciences. "Philosophy is not an independent, metaphysical speculation about ultimate reality which is then brought to bear on the sciences as an 'outside' determiner. Rather, each science, by the very nature of its attempt to abstract and isolate a special field, should be driven back to reflect on its own foundations."[30] Such critical reflection will reveal the basic philosophical suppositions that "underlie, precede, and make possible the special scientific investigations that are already under way." Immediately apparent is the similarity between Dooyeweerd's critique and, for example, Neo-Marxism's identification of ideologies and CLS disclosure of belief systems.

27. Two primary influences on Dooyeweerd's scholarly development can be identified in the work of Guillaume Groen Van Prinsterer (1801–76), a historian, statesman, journalist, and essayist, and Abraham Kuyper (1837–1920), a theologian and follower of Groen Van Prinsterer and his successor in the Dutch parliament. *See infra* this volume David S. Caudill, A Calvinist Perspective on the Place of Faith in Legal Scholarship.

28. Published in English as the four-volume Herman Dooyeweerd, *A New Critique Of Theoretical Thought* (David H. Freeman and William S. Young trans., 1953).

29. *See* Bernard Zylstra, Bibliography, in Kalsbeek, *supra* note 26, at 307–45 (listing English, French, and German titles). Zylstra, writing more than twenty years ago, claimed that a complete bibliography of the philosophy of the law-idea would cover more than three thousand titles.

30. James W. Skillen, *Herman Dooyeweerd's Contribution to the Philosophy of the Social Sciences,* J. Am. Sci. Affiliation, Mar. 1979, at 21.

Dooyeweerd's preoccupation with theoretical presuppositions led James Skillen, a political scientist inspired by Dooyeweerd's philosophy, to draw a rough analogy between Dooyeweerd's critique and Thomas Kuhn's approach to natural science. Dooyeweerd's work does indeed question the assumption in modern philosophy that theoretical thought, or scientific reason, provides an autonomous, self-sufficient starting point. Skillen explains that Dooyeweerd studied the historical development of philosophy and some of the sciences "with a view to identifying the *pre-theoretical* 'perspectives,' 'motives,' and 'world views' which drive and mold them."[31] Such *Religieuse Grondmotieven* (religious ground-motives) are frames of reference that encompass "a community of human beings in all their activity, including their scientific study." Significantly, the term *motive* does not refer to the personal biases or psychological motivations among those engaged in an otherwise objectively neutral science.[32] Rather, the reference is to foundational pretheoretical commitments, shared by a social group and guiding experience and interpretation of experience.[33]

Of primary importance to the present study is the philosophy of the law-idea's attempted transcendental critique, which is, in simplest terms, the discovery of an "intrinsic and necessary connection between religion and science."[34] As with Kant, the discovery is by means of an inquiry into the structure of scientific thought itself. Dooyeweerd distinguishes between the presupposita, or the conditions of all theoretical thought, and the pretheoretical suppositions or prejudices that will "have very different contents in the case of different philosophical tendencies." If one does not identify and account for the pretheoretical suppositions in one's analysis, the result is a dogmatic, uncritical assumption that such suppositions are universal conditions of thought. For example, Kantian premises "about the spontaneity of understanding (the logical function of thought) as a formal legislator in respect to 'nature,' [and] about understanding and sense as the two sole sources of knowledge" are not theoretical axioms, but rather fundamental, dogmatic prejudices. Dooye-

31. *See id.* at 21–22.

32. *See* Skillen, *supra* note 30, at 22.

33. Coincidentally, Duncan Kennedy uses the term *motives* in his analysis of tort and contract law to describe a legal decisionmaker's appeal to distributive, paternalistic, and efficiency ideals. *See* Duncan Kennedy, *Distributive and Paternalistic Motives in Contract and Tort Law, with Special Reference to Compulsory Terms and Unequal Bargaining Power,* 41 Md. L. Rev. 563, 571–74 (1982).

34. *See* Herman Dooyeweerd, *Transcendental Problems of Philosophic Thought,* v (1948).

weerd's transcendental critique does not require abandonment of such prejudices as postulates; instead it directs that such postulates should be identified as pretheoretical suppositions and not as criteria of a scientific character. Thus, the philosophy of the law-idea "submits every possible starting point of philosophical thought to a fundamental criticism."[35]

### Disclosure of Ground-Motives

It is clear that, for Dooyeweerd, philosophical analysis or activity is driven by "religious" ground-motives, a reference not to organized religions but to the pretheoretical commitment involved, which is most like the faith of believers. In an effort to investigate his thesis, Dooyeweerd identifies four basic religious motives in the history of western civilization: the Greek matter-form dialectic, the Christian worldview of creation-fall-redemption, the Roman Catholic nature-grace dualism, and the freedom-nature dialectic of modern humanism.[36] Such a scheme of categories inevitably appears simplistic, and the validity of such a criticism could be tested only by carefully analyzing the hundreds of pages in which Dooyeweerd develops his thesis. The late Hendrik van Eikema Hommes, a student of Dooyeweerd and his successor to the Chair of Jurisprudence at the Free University, attempted to identify and criticize the religious ground-motives of western schools of jurisprudence using Dooyeweerd's scheme.[37]

Although Dooyeweerd's systematic philosophy concerns itself with accounting for scientific theorizing, his popular work reveals the beginnings of an ideological account of social beliefs. Dooyeweerd writes that a religious ground-motive can be discerned because it "places an indelible stamp on the culture, science, and social structure of a given period" and "determines profoundly" the worldview of the members of a culture. A religious ground-motive is communal and "governs its individuals even when they are not fully conscious of [it] or when they do not give an account of it."[38]

The critique of the pretended autonomy of rational thought is ever present

35. *See id.* at 22–23, 36.

36. *See* Herman Dooyeweerd, *Roots of Western Culture: Pagan, Secular and Christian Options* 15–22 (J. Kraay trans., 1979) [hereinafter *Roots of Western Culture*].

37. Hendrik Jan Van Eikema Hommes, *Major Trends in the History of Legal Philosophy* (J. Kraay and P. Brouwer trans., 1979), reviewed in *Booknote,* 18 Hous. L. Rev. 391 (1981) (written by David S. Caudill).

38. *See Roots of Western Culture, supra* note 36, at 9; see also 1 Dooyeweerd, *supra* note 28, at 61.

in Dooyeweerd's conception of religion: "Religion grants stability and anchorage even to theoretical thought. Those who think they find an absolute starting point in theoretical thought itself come to this belief through an essentially religious drive, but because of a lack of true self-knowledge they remain oblivious to their own religious motivation."[39] The appeal to an "impersonal" science as an arbiter in the resolution of social and individual crises is therefore inappropriate, because the very answers that science gives to philosophical questions are religiously biased.[40] Additionally, the religious aspect of culture cannot be reduced to a sociological, economic, psychological, moral, legal, or historical explanation. Dooyeweerd acknowledges that a religious ground-motive receives particular forms in history but insists that its meaning transcends history. A reductionistic, historical explanation is therefore circular because it presupposes a supratheoretical starting point that is determined by a religious ground-motive distinct from empirical history.[41]

The significance of Dooyeweerd's thesis for the present essay is in his unique view that belief or faith is an essential dimension of human thought and personality and therefore is not operative only in religious people or members of organized religions. Albert Wolters, a student and follower of Dooyeweerd, writes that "man is by nature a creature of commitment—he seeks and finds a certainty and bedrock foundation to his life, whether that be formulated in myths, philosophy or theology. . . . To be human is to believe."[42] Curiously, however, historians of Western philosophy often exclude the religious order as an operative factor, favoring instead sociological, cultural, or psychological explanations. Even in their review of patristic and medieval philosophy, in which religious factors are clearly present, historians misinterpret these factors as questions only of faith and theology and give them little weight.[43] Dooyeweerd's treatment of the history of philosophy clearly attempted to restore religion as a foundational element, and not just a factor, in all scientific thought. The use of the term *religion* here has a special meaning that warrants further discussion.

An important distinction is made in the philosophy of the law-idea between such activities as philosophy, theory, and science, on the one hand, and the re-

39. *Roots of Western Culture, supra* note 36, at 8.

40. *Id.* at 15.

41. *See* 1 Dooyeweerd, *supra* note 28, at 61.

42. Albert M. Wolters, *Facing the Perplexing History of Philosophy* 6 (1978) (A.A.C.S. booklet, Toronto).

43. *See* Wolters, *supra* note 42, at 14.

ligious or foundational aspect of philosophy, theory, or science. The latter is not to be confused with the common meaning of religion, usually referring to particular ideas of God. Indeed, it is much closer to the concepts of ideology or worldview.

### Life- and Worldview

Dooyeweerd specifically addresses, without endorsing, the German concept of *Lebens- und Weltanschauung* (life- and worldview) in his analysis of religious ground-motives, in an effort to illustrate the basis upon which antithetical philosophical positions can communicate and cooperate on the same philosophical task. The classification of worldviews is popular in philosophical discourse even today to indicate the limited perspectives of various cultures or thinkers. Dooyeweerd accepts as inevitable the limitations of a worldview but speaks of the importance of "competition between all philosophical trends without discrimination" and without claiming "a privileged position" for his own views.[44]

Dooyeweerd's analysis is directed against the conception that neutral, theoretical thought can rise above and replace individual and communal worldviews originating in myth or religion. He does not simply argue that it cannot. He also argues that the entire conception is confused. Theoretical thought is never neutral regarding religion. It necessarily proceeds from a commitment to pretheoretical suppositions. Moreover, theoretical thought does not rise above or replace worldview but coexists with worldview by shifting its vision from immediate, everyday experience to systematic abstraction.

In summary, Dooyeweerd and his followers urge the disclosure of foundational beliefs present in communal and scholarly understanding. Some beliefs, when disclosed, may appear unjustified, illogical, inconsistent, or nonsensical to their holders, and thereafter may be discarded. The most fundamental belief structures, however, those necessary for initiating a particular discourse or analysis, are matters of commitment. The nobility of the debate following disclosure of such beliefs is in the fairness of it all—no one has an edge in appealing to logic, common sense, or "nature" at the level of faith. Critics may not agree on what is logical, commonsensical, or natural. Therefore the historical and social limits of such standards will be exposed.

44. *See* 1 Dooyeweerd, *supra* note 28, at 115, 117. "For even the Christian ground-motive and the content of our transcendental ground-Idea determined by it, do not give security against fundamental mistakes." *Id.*

## Disciples and Revisionists

The philosophy of the law-idea can be conceived of as an ideology or world-view critique, similar to that of CLS'ers Boyle and Singer. Dooyeweerd's disclosure of ground-motives that drive theoretical inquiry has been replaced by a broader conception of religious motives as driving nontheoretical thought and practice as well as theoretical thought. Among disciples of Dooyeweerd, the beliefs that compose an ideology or worldview are no longer only philosophical presuppositions but involve beliefs about society, politics, and law.[45]

In *Creation Regained,* Albert Wolters explores the Christian worldview in a way that implies the inevitability of worldviews for all individuals and society.[46] Wolters believes that Dooyeweerd pioneered an understanding of the centrality of religious commitment for all human thought and conduct. Wolters, however, recognizing that education, social conditioning, the structures of society, and other factors influence knowledge and action, cautions that such a system of principles, ideals, or values is not the only factor in determining the world. Nevertheless, Wolters, like Dooyeweerd, perceives a decisiveness in the basic beliefs of individuals and the shared beliefs of a society.[47]

James Olthuis also generally follows Dooyeweerd in emphasizing the centrality of religious motivations in all of life. Significantly, Olthuis argues that

45. Bob Goudzwaard, whose writings in the field of economics show the profound influence of the philosophy of the law-idea, illustrates this broader conception of ground-motives. The belief in progress, integral to the success of capitalism, finds its expression in the everyday beliefs of the members of contemporary capitalist societies (not just in the beliefs of philosophers and economic theorists). *See* Bob Goudzwaard, *Capitalism and Progress: A Diagnosis of Western Society* (Josina Van Nuis Zylstra trans. and ed., 1979). In the history and philosophy of art, the late Hans Rookmaaker drew inspiration from Dooyeweerd, *see* Hans Rookmaaker, *Modern Art and the Death of a Culture* (1970), and Calvin Seerveld continues to explore the legacy of Dooyeweerd for aesthetic theory. *See* Calvin Seerveld, Dooyeweerd's Legacy for Aesthetics: Modal Law Theory, *in The Legacy of Herman Dooyeweerd: Reflections on Critical Philosophy in The Christian Tradition* 41–79 (C. McIntire ed., 1985) (hereinafter *Legacy*). The late Bernard Zylstra developed his political theories using the general outlines of Dooyeweerd's systematic philosophy. *See* Bernard Zylstra, *Modernity and the American Empire,* Int'l Reformed Bull. 3 (1st and 2d qtrs. 1977). *See also* C. T. McIntire, Dooyeweerd's Philosophy of History, *in Legacy, supra,* 81–117.

46. Albert M. Wolters, *Creation Regained: Biblical Basics for a Reformational Worldview* (1985).

47. Albert M. Wolters, The Intellectual Milieu of Herman Dooyeweerd, *in Legacy, supra* note 45, at 5, 17.

not only do individuals find the certainty (necessary to live) in this commitment or orientation to a motivating vision but that communities also are maintained by a common spirit or vision. Olthuis refers to such communal, motivating visions as worldviews and also uses the phrase "religious paradigms" to express the same concept in his translation of Dooyeweerd's work.[48]

Jacob Klapwijk, a student of Dooyeweerd and philosopher at the Free University of Amsterdam, recently posited the idea of a transcendental-hermeneutic critique that improves on Dooyeweerd's philosophy. In this new conception, Klapwijk emphasizes both the role of worldviews and the need for communication and contact between various worldviews. Although the tradition of reformational philosophy emphasizes the antithetical difference between Christian and secular motivating visions, overemphasis of that difference renders communication and cooperation nearly impossible, a position that seems incompatible with "transformative" efforts. The hermeneutical revision of Dooyeweerd's transcendental critique can help resolve this tension. Klapwijk also attempts to avoid Dooyeweerd's orientation to Western philosophy, and to take instead a "concrete historical cultural situation, including its intellectual heritage as [a] hermeneutical starting point"; in this sense, the hermeneutical critique attempts to be a "local" theory of any culture. Klapwijk thereby acknowledges the significance of worldviews for everyday thought as well as for theoretical reflection.[49]

## THE SUBSTANCE OF THINGS HOPED FOR

### Faith

If historians of Western philosophy have ignored the religious aspect in their assessments of the various thinkers, critical legal theorists generally have not.[50] Legal reasoning does not exhaust the source of legal results, because these "results come from those same political, social, moral, and religious value judg-

48. James Olthuis, Dooyeweerd on Religion and Faith, *in Legacy, supra* note 45, at 25, 36 (quoting translation of Herman Dooyeweerd, *Kuyper's Wetenschapsleer,* 4 Phil. Ref. 217 (1939)).

49. *See generally* Jacob Klapwijk, *Reformational Philosophy on the Boundary Between Past and Future* 9, 44–62 (D. Morton trans., 1986).

50. For subheading, *cf.* Hebrews 11:1 (faith is "the substance of things hoped for, the evidence of things not seen").

ments from which the law purports to be independent."[51] Although much of the CLS canon appears to reduce everything to politics, the analysis is richer in scope. A historical analysis of American law discloses that the particular ideals or ways of thinking about the world in any period are not inevitable or natural. They are "created and constructed by people"—that is, by commitment and (perhaps unenlightened) choice.[52] According to Phillip E. Johnson, "One might even say that the notion that religion and law are radically distinct categories is itself a pillar of liberal ideology, a pillar that Critical reflection upon the arbitrariness of the legal definition of 'religion' tends to undermine. Religious questions have to do with our perceptions of ultimate reality, our sense of what life is really about. Such beliefs form our values, and law reflects those values."[53]

The methodology that seeks to disclose tilt is primarily an attack on the pretense of neutrality, which "obscures the real choices made."[54] When the collective faith of a society legitimizes a legal institution, two problems may arise. First, the institution may thereby be clothed with necessity, naturalness, and objectivity, such that few or no alternatives can be seen. Second, and related but distinct, the faith itself may be hidden, such that its adherents are unaware of their commitment. These two conceptions are intertwined in CLS scholarship. The weaker, methodological strand of critical scholarship is designed to avoid both problems by disclosing (hidden) tilt and presenting the alternatives. A theory that does only the first is not intellectually (or socially) liberating; a theory that does only the second is not critical—that is, it does not account for the way institutions are legitimized.

### Self-consciousness

Although CLS should not be characterized as merely skeptical or nihilistic, the very accusation points up one significant program that follows from CLS literature. One might conclude

---

51. *See* David Kairys, *Law and Politics,* 52 Geo. Wash. L. Rev. 243, 247 (1984). "Thus, it is the context, it is a function of values and judgments based on social, political, ideological, moral, religious, and a variety of other factors, that determines the outcome of cases." *Id.* at 248.

52. *See id.* at 259.

53. Johnson, *supra* note 7, at 288–329.

54. *See* Steven H. Shiffrin, *Liberalism, Radicalism, and Legal Scholarship,* 30 UCLA L. Rev. 1103, 1165 (1983).

that the critical project, the constant demonstration of indeterminacy, incoherence, and contradiction, is, at present, the most politically effective form of radical legal scholarship. Though perhaps initially dismissed as so much tilting at windmills, criticism would eventually challenge complacency by increasing self-consciousness in the discipline and making each scholar aware of the problematic character of his political assumptions. Demystification, "exposure of the contingency of events as cultural constructions rather than natural conditions," might engender social and political change simply by removing the sense of necessity inherent in perceptions of the present social order.[55]

The end result of a critical project that attempts to disclose belief structures parading as neutral principles does not, at first glance, solve any problems. One might say that such a program is destructive, because things are torn down and nothing is put in their place. Such criticism of CLS, common in law reviews, misses an important point. If every social community is a community of believers whose ideas and practices are based upon and driven by ideology, then genuine communication and debate can begin only with awareness and acknowledgment of that situation. The self-critical program of CLS consists of disclosing tilt without denying the foundational presuppositions giving rise to both the critique and whatever solutions are offered.

The philosophy of the law-idea originated in an effort to identify religious ground-motives or belief structures in history and in contemporary culture. Although CLS may mean many things to many of its adherents, its program of ideology critique shares Dooyeweerd's concern with disclosing the most fundamental faiths that direct culture. And although scholars associated with CLS and the philosophy of the law-idea bring rigorous critiques of the status quo, when they acknowledge that their views are based on different belief structures, there is at once a less threatening goal of open communication and a comforting humility on the part of the critic concerning absolute truth that accompany the ideology critique.

A significant contribution of CLS, as with the philosophy of the law-idea, is its restatement of a theoretical controversy in terms of commitment and ideology.

55. Note, *Round and Round the Bramble Bush: From Legal Realism to Critical Legal Scholarship*, 95 Harv. L. Rev. 1669, 1684–85 (1982) (quoting Thomas Heller, *A Brief Rejoinder to the Discussion of CCLS*, 1 Zeitschrift Für Rechtssoziologie 126, 130 (1980) (footnotes omitted). Yet there is risk: "Relentlessly pursued, contradiction can be self-perpetuating—the end product of a scholarship that disables the critic from utopian speculation, prey to his own devices." *Id.* at 1685.

The appeal to universal principles grounded in human rationality simply provides no foundation to legal scholarship. For CLS, rationality itself is historically and culturally situated.[56] For the philosophy of the law-idea, theoretical thought always begins with pretheoretical suppositions accepted, of necessity, by faith. The differences between the philosophy of the law-idea and CLS methodology are many, and much could be written (and perhaps should be) by turning their critical methods toward each other. Much of the ideological foundation of traditional legal theory, which CLS tries to uproot, has a religious origin; conversely, the faithlike commitments that a philosopher of the law-idea wants to disclose are rampant in CLS. Yet a persistent commonality arises in their belief-disclosing methods and their goals of open communication regarding worldviews.[57] Moreover, the goal of communication is, or should be, shared with legal scholars of any persuasion. Such communication is problematic and troublesome, but necessary if some degree of self-awareness is to be attained in contemporary legal discourse.

56. *See* Singer, *supra* note 18, at 63; *see also* Boyle, *supra* note 17, at 690 ("our ideas of rationality are themselves incoherent, authoritarian, or politically tilted"), 705 ("the very concept of reason assumes a political tilt"), 715–16 ("it seems as though we must challenge not only liberal legalism but our very notion of rationality").

57. "What now is the fruit of this transcendental critique? . . . It can pave the way for a real contact of thought among the various philosophical trends." 1 Dooyeweerd, *supra* note 28, at 70; *see also* Boyle, *supra* note 17, at 737 ("The more one 'does' social theory and reads hard books, the more one comes to believe that it is actually useful and liberating to find out about the philosophical structures behind the richly textured justifications for 'the way things are' in every area of social life").

# Section 4 Critical Race Theory

In response to the failures of the civil rights movement of the 1960s, critical race theory came on the scene in the mid-1970s with the writing of law professors Derrick Bell (an African American) and Alan Freeman (who is white). As Richard Delgado explains in the introduction of his 1995 book *Critical Race Theory: The Cutting Edge,* the major themes of this school of thought include "the call for context, [a] critique of liberalism, [the] insistence that racism is ordinary not exceptional, and the notion that traditional civil rights law has been more valuable to whites than to blacks."

Attention to these issues has not been confined to the legal academy. W. Burlette Carter's essay traces the parallels between African-American legal and theological critical race theory scholarship. Combining the insights of race theory in both law and theology, her inquiry centers on Christ's second great commandment: what does it mean to love our neighbors across the lines of racial difference and prejudice? Davison M. Douglas finds similarities between the work of Reinhold Niebuhr, a white theologian writing in the middle of the twentieth century, and that of the critical race theorists. Douglas shows in his essay how Niebuhr's analysis of the abuses of power by dominant groups, emerging from his Augustinian emphasis on the sin of pride, helps to explain the persistence of racial subordination. José Roberto Juárez, Jr. discusses the Latino-Critical Studies movement in his essay. He decries the insistence by many within the movement that religious voices be excluded from critical race discourse. Juárez argues that Catholicism, as a fundamental part of Hispanic culture, is a source of Hispanic empowerment and a vehicle for justice.

# What's *Love* Got to Do with It?
# Race Relations and the Second
# Great Commandment

*W. Burlette Carter*

African Americans have to be very careful when making public state-ments about race.[1] When our description of race relations diverges from the norm prevailing among whites in our society—that America no longer has a race problem—we are sometimes met with a glower. We are troublemakers; we are overly sensitive; we are combative; we don't ever acknowledge progress; we are harsh and simplistic; we are negative; we are paranoid; we are mired in victimhood; maybe even, we are racist ourselves.

Well-meaning whites may invite us to be open and honest, but as our descriptions of our experiences and perspectives unfold, our lis-teners too often turn silent. The promised dialogue becomes mono-logue. Some are simply tired out by the weight of the discussion, the burden made heavier by the fact that it is not their life. Our most con-

1. I extend my deepest appreciation to Drs. Charles Long and Charles Shelby Rooks, Dr. Jeffrey Haggray and the Rev. Shelby Haggray, Professor Bradford Clark, and Hazel Bland Thomas. Discussions with them contributed greatly to shaping my thoughts in this article. The opinions expressed are, of course, solely my own.

133

cerned listeners are often stunned by a guilt that they are not sure is their own, but that they feel as deeply as if it were. And we are left angry—at ourselves for expecting mutual vulnerability—and at them for, once again, we believe, shifting the focus of our comments from our pain to their guilt. And so the next time, to avoid the unease of those we might otherwise hold dear as friends or to avoid rejection by or even retribution from those interested in our stories only if it confirms their truths, we simply say nothing at all. In this fashion, the facade that everything is fine where race is concerned is continued in the public sphere, and the seeds of deep and enduring relationships between African Americans and whites shrivel up and die. Upon leaving the venues where African Americans are forced to accept a world that acknowledges, primarily, the experiences of whites—their jobs, schools, the public places—they often return to their respective private places—their homes and neighborhoods, their churches—to speak about their own lives in America with a freedom and a comfort they rarely encounter in the public sphere. The more hostile the public places are to recognizing their own racial experience, the more precious the private places become.

From where I sit, the preceding paragraph accurately describes most discussions about race in America when they occur—or fail to occur—between white people and African-American people. The concession that the racial experience of African Americans is significantly different from that of whites in America seems too painful or too risky for many whites—the proposition that public policy, if it is to be fair, should reflect this fact in an affirmative way, even more foreign.

True, occasionally, race grabs a corner of the discussion that occurs in the public places. But too often the impetus is an indefensibly horrible act of violence against a minority group member, an affront that shocks the conscience and presents circumstances that make it difficult for American whites to conceive of explanations other than racism. Absent such extreme cases that compel whites to distance themselves publicly from the offender, the negative day-to-day reality of race in America is not a subject that whites spend much time thinking about. And many whites erroneously take the fact that race is not discussed as a sign that there is no problem.

By now many white readers are pausing, I suppose. One white friend reading a draft of this essay stated the frustration: "You begin this piece with your views, and readers cannot respond to you." This is true enough. But in my experience, when whites write and speak rarely do they pepper their statements with the perspectives of other racial groups. Just for now, I exercise the same privilege, for this piece is an attempt to identify a perspective. To measure it by whether or not it responds to the dominant perspective is to defeat its very purpose.

This essay is an attempt, in the brief pages allotted, to address the impasse that African Americans know exists between them and whites in public conversation, an impasse indicative of a larger life separation. First, it takes on the question of how race matters. Here I want to offer the results of a very simple empirical study. I want to examine how much attention white American scholars in both law and religion have historically given to race issues and compare that to the attention given to the same subject by African Americans. The point is not that all whites or all African Americans think alike but rather that racial experience does correlate with outcomes. For whites and for blacks, race significantly impacts one's interpretation of a present situation, as well as one's priorities for future action.

Second, having considered how race matters, I will seek to connect these thoughts to the concept of Christian love, and specifically, what Jesus called one of the two greatest commandments: that one should love one's neighbor as thyself.[2] Here I want to explore the difficulties whites and African Americans experience in extending neighborly love to one another. I shall also attempt to surmise how these difficulties translate more generally into other interracial relations, but my focus is America's obsession with the black-white dichotomy.

A few comments are necessary to frame my perspective. First, I approach this piece as one whose ancestors were American slaves. Thus when I speak of African Americans or blacks, I mean my fellow descendants of slaves, not other persons of color or black immigrants. Although important similarities exist, these groups' stories are significantly different from mine. Second, regarding one concern whites may have, I do recognize that some whites might object to being called "white." They might say, "I am Italian-American, or Irish-American, or Jewish, or just American." There is some merit to this complaint, I acknowledge. But when the world considers my rights and interests relative to their rights and interests, the world considers them white and me black. The differences among them when compared with me are treated as inconsequential. To deny the dichotomy, then, is to deny my own experience.

2. *E.g.,* Mark 12:31. All biblical citations are to the New International Version (Zondervan, 1995).

## WRITING IN BLACK AND WHITE

Is there such a thing as a "black voice" or a "white voice"? Certainly, it is true that not all blacks have the same point of view, nor all whites. But generally speaking, black Americans do share a common racial experience, and their white counterparts share the same among themselves vis-à-vis blacks. For blacks it is the experience of being negatively affected and excluded because of their perceived race; for whites it is the experience of being benefited and included for the same reason.

A few years ago, in preparation for an article, I began a survey of legal scholarship. I reviewed the indexes of some of the oldest university-based law journals—Harvard, Yale, Michigan, Columbia—from their origin in the late 1800s and early 1900s into the mid-1980s. When I set out on that journey, I hypothesized that during the period in which there were no African-American law professors on the faculties of majority law schools, and before the litigation in *Brown v. Board of Education,* generally speaking, racism against persons of color would either be ignored in legal scholarship or treated as a marginal issue. The *Brown* litigation is a key point of reference.[3] In the final *Brown* decision, the U.S. Supreme Court mandated that states could not set up separate public schools for black and white schoolchildren. Thus that litigation brought race relations directly into the zone of interest of whites and heralded the civil rights era of the 1960s. One would expect, therefore, that after *Brown* and throughout the sixties, more whites would attend to race as a subject matter because more whites would perceive that race issues affected them. I further hypothesized that African-American law professors hired as a result of the gains in the civil rights movement would give more serious treatment to racism in their scholarship, particularly racism as it affected their racial group.

My hypothesis was confirmed. When one examines these early law journals, one sees quite starkly that, with rare but notable exceptions, the discussion of race or racism against people of color was absent before the *Brown* litigation. Only a small number of the articles that appeared in law reviews even acknowledged that race discrimination of any kind existed, and some of these sought to downplay its impact or to justify its existence and perpetuation. With rare exceptions, white full-time law professors—whose job it was to think and write

3. *Brown v. Board of Educ.,* 347 U.S. 483 (1954) (hereinafter *Brown I*); *Brown v. Board of Educ.,* 349 U.S. 294 (1955) (hereinafter *Brown II*) (remanding to district courts and ordering school desegregation "with all deliberate speed").

about important legal issues and who dominated legal scholarship—did not write about race.[4]

The American civil rights movement, both its litigation component led by lawyers and its social consciousness component led by religious leaders, changed the face of legal scholarship by creating opportunities for African-American scholars. The first professor of color to be hired at a majority law school to a tenured or tenure track position was the civil rights attorney William R. Ming, who joined the faculty of the University of Chicago Law School in 1947 and received tenure in 1951.[5] In 1949 Ming published "Racial Restrictions and the Fourteenth Amendment: The Restrictive Covenant Cases."[6] Was it mere coincidence that Ming published an article about racism early in his professorial career or even that he had dedicated his life to civil rights? C. Clyde Ferguson, an African American, was hired to the Rutgers Law School faculty in 1955.[7] Ferguson established himself as a specialist in matters of international law, evidencing a strong commitment to issues of human rights and racial discrimination both at home and abroad. In 1957 he cowrote a book, *Desegregation and the Law,* with fellow Rutgers professor A. P. Blaustein.[8] Was Ferguson's emphasis on issues of human rights and race discrimination mere coincidence?

After the hiring of Ferguson and Ming, other majority law schools hired professors of color. African Americans Charles Quick (Wayne State, 1958), Ronald Davenport (Duquesne, 1963), John Wilkins (University of California, Berkeley, 1964), and Derrick Bell (Harvard, 1969) entered the academy. The first

4. For example, student articles aside, in the sixty-plus years from the late 1800s up to 1953, I found fewer than fifteen articles expressly addressing America's problems with racism against persons of color (that is, racism with respect to any American group of color) in either the *Harvard Law Review* or the *Yale Law Journal.* Other journals follow this pattern. A brief review of the early treatment of racism by the *Harvard Law Review* is found in A. Leon Higgenbotham, *The Life of the Law: Values, Commitment, and Craftsmanship,* 100 Harv. L. Rev. 795, 808–11 (1987). But *see, e.g.,* Eugene Rostow, *The Japanese American Cases: A Disaster,* 54 Yale L.J. 49 (1944–45) (Rostow was then a professor at Yale).

5. For more on Ming *see Rites Tuesday for Civil Rights Lawyer Ming,* Chi. Sun Times, July 2, 1973.

6. William Robert Ming, Jr., *Racial Restrictions and the Fourteenth Amendment: The Restrictive Covenant Cases,* 16 U. Chi. L. Rev. 203 (1949).

7. *See, e.g., In Memoriam: C. Clyde Ferguson, Jr.: A Brilliant Career,* 97 Harv. L. Rev. 1253 (1984).

8. A. P. Blaustein and Clarence Clyde Ferguson, *Desegregation and the Law* (1957).

tenure-track African-American female at a major law school was Joyce Hughes, who joined the University of Minnesota's faculty in 1971.

For sustained race theory scholarship, the most notable hire among these was probably Bell, who was Harvard's first tenure-track African-American law professor. Bell, a former civil rights attorney, began writing expressly about race and racism and even developed a course on the subject.[9] As the numbers of nonwhite professors in the legal academy grew, a distinct pattern became apparent in the scholarship that they produced: race and racism appeared as significant themes in their work. This certainly is not true of all of their writing, but the correlation between articles addressing race and racism and the presence of American persons of color on law faculties was as obvious as the long-standing correlation between the dominance of scholarship by whites and the absence of race or racism as important issues in scholarship. These new professors of color were writing from their own racial experience. But they were not doing anything new. The white professors who preceded them in the legal academy had been doing the very same thing.

Apart from subject matter, the writings by the newly hired minority faculty also were distinct in their approach to the subject of racism. Race was not limited to the constitutional questions traditionally considered as civil rights issues; rather, the work of these scholars suggested that race was a factor that operated across the legal landscape. Some of these new writers often controversially jettisoned the preestablished restrictions on the proper subjects of legal scholarship, the appropriate modes of discourse, the sources worthy of citation, and the assumption that a long-standing principle was presumptively credible. Indeed, some of them claimed that such structures were merely props holding up a status quo that perpetuated race discrimination. In the 1980s some advocates of this latter view chose to formally label themselves "critical race theorists," and they were joined by writers from other racial and ethnic groups and even some white writers.[10]

Today a major controversy is swirling among scholars at America's law schools. At its center are the writings of American scholars of color.[11] Critics claim that these writings collectively and individually lack merit according to

9. See Derrick Bell, *Confronting Authority* 33–34 (1994) (discussing his hiring at Harvard).

10. For attempts to classify critical race theory *see Critical Race Theory: The Cutting Edge* (Richard Delgado ed., 1995) (hereinafter *The Cutting Edge*); *Critical Race Theory: The Key Writings That Formed the Movement* (Kimberle Crenshaw et al., eds., 1995).

11. *See, e.g.,* Daniel Farber and Susanna Sherry, *Beyond All Reason: The Radical Assault on Truth in American Law* (1997).

purely objective scholarly standards. But others argue that such objections, though couched in terms of "scholarly merit," are in reality rejections of the idea that race is an important subject for scholarly discussion. Moreover, they argue that the critique is based upon an assumption that the only valid approaches are those grounded in the experience of being white in America or those that have otherwise been previously validated by whites. A wide spectrum of black writing that references race is caught up in this firestorm. The debate is important not only because it affects black academic freedom but also because it affects whether black scholars are hired, promoted, or receive tenure. More important, it affects whether the black community's voice will be authentically represented—in all its variations—in public debates about law or whether it will be represented only by voices that conform to white scholars' views about the appropriate stress on race and appropriate approaches to writing about it.

For my purposes here, there is no need to defend critical race theory in particular, or any specific approach to black writing about race. What is at issue for black scholars—indeed, for all scholars of color—is the right to deem the subject matter of race important enough to write about, not just as whites would write about it but from one's own experience, just as whites do. The proposition is that whenever blacks write, and however they write, considering their works collectively, and comparing it collectively to that of whites, race is acknowledged as more significant in black writing than in writing by whites. Its impact is perceived as broader, the need for remedy more crucial. If I am correct, we are compelled to inquire to what extent white judgments about the quality of black writings about race are affected by the dominant community's life experience with race: the expectation that race will be relegated to small corners of discussion or that the writings of persons of color will be governed by standards that have been adopted in a context where race operates predominantly as an accepted silent privilege. Could it be that, precisely because whites have shaped the dominant discourse using their own racial perspective, the emerging approaches informed by African-American experiences now appear as loose threads in the otherwise tightly woven fabric of scholarly discourse?

The correlation between race and attention to race with respect to legal writings is also confirmed when one considers the evolution of theological writing by Americans. Of course, religious scholarship does not shape religious policy to the same extent that legal scholarship shapes law. There is, for example, no religious Supreme Court to cite the opinions of religious scholars and translate them into policy to apply to all Americans. We can concede the different roles religion and law play in society and still draw parallels; indeed, the higher tolerance for diversity among religions may offer an alternative approach to any insistence that law must spring from a single cultural root.

Considering American theological journals and periodicals from their beginnings, the dominant approach of white American writers was that racism was either not mentioned at all or, when it was mentioned, its effects were downplayed. Before the sixties, those in the "social gospel" movement concerned themselves primarily with class difference and poverty; race discrimination was rarely addressed directly. There were no articles specifically addressing race in the *Harvard Theological Review* between its inception in the nineteenth century through 1971, when the university's divinity school hired Preston Williams, its first black permanent faculty member. More popular periodicals also reflected the absence of race-specific discussion, but occasionally one can find articles by whites that seek to justify black oppression or minimize its impact. The *Hartford Seminary Record,* which in its early days was more like a biweekly newspaper, had a few more race-related articles, but the number was still small and the approach clearly responsive to white concerns. The Index to Religious Periodical Literature published by the American Theological Library Association confirms the dearth of articles written from nonwhite racial perspectives.[12] As with the articles of white scholars in the field of law, the articles that white religious leaders wrote reflected their own life experience.

Lawyers and religious leaders in the civil rights movement also had an important impact upon religious scholarship. That movement propelled African-American students into predominantly white higher educational institutions and eventually produced the African-American graduates who joined the faculties of majority religious seminaries and divinity schools. Before the 1950s there were no African Americans on the faculties of majority theological schools. By 1960 only five white seminaries had any African-American faculty: Drew University in Madison, New Jersey (Professor George D. Kelsey); Garrett Theological Seminary of Northwestern University (Professor Grant Shockley); the University of Chicago Divinity School (Professors Nathan Scott and

12. *See, e.g.,* J. C. Mitchell, *Five Factors in the Negro Problem,* 15 Hartford Seminary Rec. 35 (1904). *See also* Edward A. Steiner, *The Race Problem in A Changing World,* The Christian, June 13, 1931 (slavery has benefited Negroes, but under it whites have become arrogant taskmasters, not teachers); Alva W. Taylor, *Inter-Racial Conciliation in the South,* Christian Century, Apr. 27, 1922, at 531–32 (if whites participated in interracial committees they would find that Negroes were "reasonable" and were not demanding social equality as so many whites feared).

Charles Long); Wesley Theological Seminary (Professor John Satterwhite); and the University of Pittsburgh (Professor Gayraud Wilmore).[13] But the tide changed, due not only to the civil rights movement but also to a determined effort by the Fund for Theological Education, led by Dr. Charles Shelby Rooks, to recruit African Americans to graduate programs in theology and to find funding for their studies.[14] Union Theological Seminary (Columbia University) hired its first African-American faculty member in 1965, Lawrence Jones, dean of students with the rank of associate professor. William R. Jones joined the Yale Divinity School faculty in 1970. Harvard Divinity School hired Preston Williams as a tenured professor in 1971. By 1988 there were 186 African Americans teaching either part- or full-time on the faculties of the predominantly white theological schools.[15]

Among many black writers, preachers, and teachers, an alternative vision of God's work began to take shape, one in which that work was interpreted through blacks' own racial perspective. Certainly, well before the doors of majority religious institutions opened to black faculty, giants like Benjamin Mays and Howard Thurman, as well as institutions like Howard Divinity School, led the way in developing a body of religious writing that took account of the black experience.[16] And of course, long before Martin Luther King, Jr., became a name well known to whites, black preachers were interpreting God's work through that experience. But when the doors of majority institutions began to open, what was done in the private places became public.

With the arrival of black faculty at theological schools, we see an evolution in theological scholarship that parallels the evolution in legal writing. In 1969, a year after Derrick Bell joined the full-time faculty at Harvard Law School, James Cone, then a professor at the Union Theological Seminary at Columbia University, published *Black Theology and Black Power;* a year later he published *A Black Theology of Liberation.* In these works, Cone argued that Christian whites had created a "white theology," one that assessed God's priorities in light

13. Charles Shelby Rooks, *Revolution in Zion* 91 (1990).

14. See generally *id.*

15. Rooks, *supra* note 13, at 175. The numbers of full-time faculty are not listed separately.

16. Mays was the dean of the Howard University School of Religion and later the sixth president of Morehouse College. In 1953 Howard Thurman became dean of Marsh Chapel at Boston University, the first black dean at a majority religious school. Both wrote and spoke extensively on matters of racial justice.

of the white man's needs and experiences. The resulting "God," according to Cone, was one indifferent to the racial oppression of African Americans.[17]

Just as black legal scholars later urged a racial critique of law, newly minted scholars of religion urged what one could call a racial critique of theology. Some who joined in the attempt to bring a black perspective to scholarly religious discourse adopted the label "black theologians" or "black liberation theologians," reflecting their parallels with liberation theology.[18] Like those who sought to conceive of law through the black racial experience, these black writers sometimes disagreed with each other.[19] But the significance of this influx of African Americans speaking about religion in the public sphere was noted by theologian C. Eric Lincoln in 1990: "The significance of the present new movement of black liberation theology is that for the first time in American religion, a group of Christian theologians in major divinity schools and theological seminaries have attempted to construct systematic theologies from a black perspective."[20]

## THE SIGNIFICANCE OF THE CORRELATION

The question must be asked: why didn't white legal scholars or white theologians address race in their scholarly works before the civil rights movement? The reason, it seems, is that white writers wrote from their own racial perspective, and in their experience, racism directed against people of color, though perhaps intellectually disturbing, had no perceived direct negative effects on their lives. Perhaps the benefits of racism for the white majority made the pain it brought to victims' lives difficult to see or easy to rationalize; perhaps the widespread acceptance of dominant modes of scholarly discourse among whites rendered challenging those modes too lonely a course. Thus the fact of these white writers' whiteness determined what subjects did and did not receive the

17. James Cone, *Black Theology and Black Power* (1969); James Cone, *A Black Theology of Liberation,* twentieth anniversary edition (1970) (hereinafter *Liberation*).

18. *See, e.g., Black Theology: A Documentary History* (James Cone and Gayraud Wilmore eds., 1993, 2 vols.).

19. *Cf., e.g.,* Preston N. Williams, *James Cone and the Problem of a Black Ethic,* 65 Harv. Theological Rev. 483 (1972), *and* Randall Kennedy, *Racial Critiques of Legal Academia,* 102 Harv. L. Rev. 1745 (1989).

20. C. Eric Lincoln and Lawrence H. Mamaye, *The Black Church and the African-American Experience* 178 (1993). C. Eric Lincoln was another pioneering black member of the faculty at Union Theological Seminary.

benefits of their efforts and, moreover, what approaches they would take in their work. This principle seems to hold true whether or not these writers actually ever consciously thought a single racist thought—in other words, the principle is true irrespective of whether they individually harbored any specific racist intent.

The correlation observed here between race and the approach to race in scholarship is reflected in other fields as well.[21] Such evidence confirms that there is such a thing as a racial experience, at least in America, where race has unique historical import. There is a life experience—a culture, if you wish— that correlates closely with race in America, and that experience shapes our lives. Just as important, it shapes our points of view.

Perhaps it will be posited that in modern times barriers have been broken down and that what was once true of white and black approaches to race is no longer true. Although progress certainly has been made, all evidence points away from such a conclusion. One can leave the pristine world of ivory-tower scholarship and look to opinion polls, which regularly show that on many issues race still correlates strongly with point of view. One can step inside the private places and hear the discussion that blacks have among themselves—on black radio, or black talk shows, in black magazines, and in black churches— and compare the content to so-called mainstream discussion in the public places, where white perspectives dominate the discussion.

In 1979, in his classic work *Brown versus Board and the Interest Convergence Dilemma,* Derrick Bell made an observation that was criticized by several white scholars. The backdrop for his statement was an article published twenty years earlier by the prominent white scholar Herbert Wechsler, who, while he sympathized with the plight of African-American schoolchildren in segregated schools, argued that in ordering desegregation the Court in *Brown v. Board* abandoned "neutral" principles of law.[22] At the time the article was published

21. *See, e.g.,* Donald Gibson, *The Politics of Literary Expression: A Study of Major Black Writers* (1981) (rejecting the application of "formalistic" modes of literary criticism to the writings of black writers arguing that they often proceed from different assumptions than do white writers); Albert Boime, *The Art of Exclusion: Representing Blacks in the Nineteenth Century* (1990) (discussing how the work of privileged white artists in the nineteenth century reflected their racial perspectives); Guy C. McElroy, *Facing History: The Black Image in American Art, 1710–1940* (1990) (discussing *inter alia* how the racial experiences of artists affected their presentation of the images of blacks).

22. Herbert Wechsler, *Toward Neutral Principles of Constitutional Law,* 73 Harv. L. Rev. 1 (1959).

several prominent white scholars agreed with Wechsler, while others challenged the argument, essentially defending the "neutrality" of the decision.[23] Twenty years later Bell rejected the very idea that such neutrality existed with respect to race. Instead, he argued that whites see the world *as whites* and that whites would address African Americans' needs only when those needs intersected with those of whites. He called this the *interest-convergence dilemma*. Appellations are important to many in legal academia. Wechsler's piece was originally delivered as a lecture at the Harvard Law School, with no intent toward publication, but some viewed the comments important enough (or their author significant enough) to publish as an "article." By contrast, years later, the same law review classified Bell's responsive work as an "essay."[24]

Viewed broadly, Bell's interest-convergence thesis is an observation about the willingness of people to use their power to overcome their own self-interest. The view is quite pessimistic. According to Bell, the majority will consider the needs of those from another racial experience only when the majority's needs are also advanced in so doing. Consider, then, instances of repeated police misconduct against blacks. Under the theory, it seems, the majority will take action to curb police misconduct only when (1) it also affects significant numbers of white people; (2) riots or other civil unrest in response to such misconduct threaten whites' own public safety; or (3) the misconduct is so brutal that it shocks the conscience of whites, eliminating potential excuses as to possible justification and creating a personal or political need for whites to publicly distance themselves from the offender. What is lacking from Bell's observation is any faith that the simple goodness of people might be sufficient to cause them to investigate their neighbor's well-being and to trigger a remedial response to the pain of persons in a group to which they do not perceive themselves as belonging. Was he—is he—correct?

### WHAT'S *LOVE* GOT TO DO WITH IT?

When asked to name the greatest commandment, Jesus responds by giving the two. "'Love the Lord your God with all your heart and with all your soul and with all your mind.' This is the first and greatest commandment. And the second is like it: 'Love your neighbor as yourself.' All the Law and the Prophets

23. *See, e.g.,* Charles L. Black, Jr., *The Lawfulness of the Segregation Decisions,* 69 Yale L.J. 421 (1959–60) (rejecting Wechsler's view).

24. Derrick Bell, *Brown versus Board and the Interest Convergence Dilemma,* 93 Harv. L. Rev. 518 (1979).

hang on these two commandments."[25] In another account, when asked by an expert in the law what one can do to inherit eternal life, Jesus gives the same response.[26]

Not fully satisfied, the same expert in the law asks another question: "And who is my neighbor?" Jesus responds with the parable of the Good Samaritan. A Jew traveling from Jerusalem to Jericho is attacked, robbed, and left for dead along the side of the road. A priest and a Levite, both Jews, cross over to the other side of the road to avoid the man. A passing Samaritan, however, gathers up the man, bandages his wounds, and takes him to a local inn. He cares for the Jew for a day and then, upon leaving, pays the innkeeper to look after him, promising more money later if needed. After finishing the parable, Jesus asks: "Which one of these three was a neighbor to the man who fell into the hands of robbers?"[27] The obvious answer is the Samaritan, who, despite a history of hatred between Samaritans and Jews, stopped to help.

That we should all behave like the Good Samaritan is a nice ideal, of course, but its simplicity ignores the true difficulty. One of my students in a Sunday School class of teenagers summed up the problem for me when I asked him to compare his less-than-desirable behavior to that of Jesus. Appropriately named Levi, my student emphatically responded, "But Jesus was *divine*." I could not argue with him about that. Though fully man, fully divine, Jesus knew all his neighbors' business before they told him, and he nevertheless loved them.[28] We are more like the Apostle Paul, who said, "For I have the desire to do good, but I cannot carry it out."[29]

And Levi would surely have asked, "What if there were no inn and this had

25. Matthew 22:37–40. See also Mark 12:29–31.

26. Luke 10:25–29. Actually, the original Ten Commandments received by Moses had two commandments dealing with one's neighbor. The ninth provided "You shall not give false witness against your neighbor," and the tenth provided "You shall not covet your neighbor's house . . . your neighbor's wife . . . or anything that belongs to your neighbor." Exodus 20:16–17. Jesus' identification of the second great commandment appears to be an extension of these two principles. Also related may be Jesus' "new command" given to the disciples at the Last Supper: "As I have loved you, so you must love one another. By this all men will know that you are my disciples." John 13:34.

27. Luke 10:29–37.

28. *See, e.g.*, John 4:18 (Jesus telling the Samaritan woman at the well, "The fact is, you have had five husbands; and the man you now have is not your husband"); Mark 14:27–31 (Jesus predicting Peter's denial of him); Mark 14:17 (Jesus predicting his betrayal by a disciple).

29. Romans 7:18.

happened in Samaria? Would the Samaritan have taken the man to his own home and insisted that his family and neighbors take the Jew in? Or what if the Samaritan were on his way to a job interview and stopping would surely make him late? Would the Samaritan *then* have helped?"

Such questions remind us that there are practical difficulties in crossing over group lines. As Gordon Allport noted in his classic work *The Nature of Prejudice,* humans instinctively love that which is most like themselves and instinctively dislike that which is different from themselves. "Birds of a feather flock together" not only because of imagined differences but also because of real differences among us, as each group adopts certain ways of doing things that best suit its needs.[30] Some of the differences yield wonderful results; they are the source of tacos, fettuccine, jazz, and Irish music. But groups are also centers of power; sometimes membership requirements satisfy perceived political needs; the need to reinforce the dominance of one group over others, the need to protect a minority group against being overcome by a more dominant one. Publicly bringing a Jew into one's Samaritan community has consequences that privately helping the Jew does not.

Our group associations themselves—whether the result of our choice or society's designation—can change to match our convenience. The point was brought home to me on a trip to Los Angeles, during a convention of a major African-American religious organization. I was standing in a line to purchase a sandwich inside the conference center during a break in activities. Practically all of the persons attending the conference were African-American. As we were standing there, a white male in a three-piece suit passed by the line. I assumed that he was conference center staff; he had no conference attendee badge, and his walk was determined and directional. As he passed us, an African-American woman turned to me and said with a sigh, "Finally—an American." I asked of whom was she speaking. She nodded her head toward our servers, who, I suddenly noticed, appeared to be Latino. I had noticed that all of the maids I had encountered at the hotel—where she was, no doubt, also staying—were also Latinas. Nodding my head in our servers' direction, I asked her, "What makes you think that these people are not American?" She responded, "Oh, you know what I mean, a *real* American." I then said—calmly, I promise—"What makes *you* a real American? If I recall correctly, your people came over on the slave ship with my people."

Ever since I was a little girl I have had a big mouth. That statement ended our

30. *See* Gordon Allport, *The Nature of Prejudice* 4, 19 (1954). Allport was Jewish.

conversation. To her credit, she looked sufficiently embarrassed and even waved to me from her table half an hour later as she left the eating area. I have since reflected many times upon the irony of the conversation. Certainly, if she and I had been discussing racism directed against us, she might have called herself black or African-American. But vis-à-vis these new faces, strange to her, she was *an American,* aligned with the white man we had just seen. She was in the dominant group.

To get on with the business of being Good Samaritans or, in legal terms, to arrive at a true vision of equality under the law, we need a broader understanding of how group prejudice operates in our lives. We must accept that we all think in terms of groups, that often we do it unconsciously, and moreover that regardless of our own individual intent, there are those bent on determining rights and privileges on the basis of group memberships. Those who want a better world must accept that it takes a special consciousness to be fair to groups to which we do not belong, particularly when the other group is in some way subordinated. To arrive at that consciousness, we need the help of those who are different from us. We need it not only to help them, but to help ourselves; we need it to ensure a fair and just society. There seems no better argument supporting measures to ensure racial diversity in matters affecting the distribution of rights and privileges.

We must accept that assumptions and norms based upon our group experience may suit us, but they will not accommodate others outside our group and may even disadvantage them. If we are dominant, we have the power to impose our assumptions and norms on others and to call those assumptions and norms neutral. But that power alone does not make them so.

Moreover, when dominant groups assert their power to determine the rules no matter what, they essentially transform the public sphere into their own private place. They diminish the less powerful group's ability to participate in the processes that affect it, and in so doing, they make the less powerful group more vulnerable to extremists. Members of excluded communities who are able may adapt by attempting to pass as a member of the dominant group and at least publicly adopting its norms. Those for whom "passing" is impossible may withdraw to private places to seek affirmation among their own kind and form independent power centers for protection.

Consciousness also requires a reexamination of the notion that intent to discriminate should be the litmus test for whether a remedy for discrimination is desirable. Focusing only upon intentional prejudice does not identify unconscious prejudice that lies deep within our brains awaiting its stimulus. It ignores the instances in which the majority race unsuitably imposes its own subjective manners and customs on others. It places on a minority group not only the burden of the prejudice, if it exists, but also the burden of demonstrating its effect and of proving its conscious existence in the mind of the actor. It compels remedial action only when the discrimination is obvious to the dominant group, regardless of how long it damages the victimized one. In the meantime, day-to-day injustices—arguably as damaging to the minority community as a whole as the specific horrific acts that attract media attention—go unrecognized and unremedied. Finally, focusing upon intent destroys avenues for reconciliation. Those who suffer from discrimination are required to make a highly personal charge against those who benefit from it in order to establish the need for a remedy. Some accusers may resent the burden and fear backlash from the exposure. Some may use the accusatory obligation to level the playing field. Meanwhile, the accused resent the accusation, however it is delivered.

We should embrace the positive aspects of groups more openly. This approach requires distinguishing affirmative groups from negative ones. The mantra of a negative group is that other groups do not matter, or even that they must be destroyed. By contrast, affirmative groups are self-affirming for members, without negating the worth of nonmembers. Affirmative groups are needed by those who feel that their needs are not wholly met in the outside world. Both within and without groups, we can celebrate affirmative groups without embracing negative ones.

I began this piece by talking about how African Americans and whites talk about race, suggesting an impasse. I have argued that the majority status of whites often shields them from the realities of racial privilege in America. That shielding, in turn, leads to an arrogance of perspective, a belief by whites that their approaches to race are neutral and the expectation that others, if neutral, will speak about race in the same way that whites do. There are, of course, whites who do not fit this generalization, and African Americans who understand that if broad brushstrokes completely mask the individual exceptions, we have become what we claim to detest. Without denying the reality of race in America, then, we must learn to celebrate the heroes who every day violate group injunctions by shuttling acts of kindness across racial lines. We must encourage the increase in such heroes within our groups and seek to imitate them. When we take these risks, we diminish the negative potential of groups, we find love in places that we did not know love existed, and we come closer to understanding what both the second great commandment and the notion of equality under the law really mean.

# Reinhold Niebuhr and Critical

# Race Theory

*Davison M. Douglas*

In spite of a long history of racial oppression, African Americans have enjoyed significant legal gains during the past four decades: the eradication of *de jure* school segregation; the statutory prohibition on racial discrimination in the workplace, housing, and public accommodations; and the protection of the right to vote. Many Americans view these gains as evidence that the United States has finally confronted its history of racial discrimination and has embraced the American creed of equal treatment for all. Although many observers would acknowledge that some racial discrimination still exists in America, they are likely to describe it as "rare and aberrational rather than . . . systemic and ingrained." As one legal scholar has noted: "Most Americans, black and white, view the civil rights crusade as a long, slow, but always upward pull that must, given the basic precepts of the country and the commitment of its people to equality and liberty, eventually end in the full enjoyment by blacks of all rights and privileges of citizenship enjoyed by whites."[1]

---

1. *Critical Race Theory: The Key Writings that Formed the Movement* xiv (Kimberle Crenshaw et al. eds., 1995) (hereinafter *Key Writings*); Derrick Bell, *Race, Racism, and American Law* 13 (3d ed. 1992).

Not everyone agrees with this optimistic view of racial progress in America. Indeed, during the past two decades, a group of scholars known as critical race theorists has sharply questioned prevailing orthodoxies about race relations in the United States. To these critics, racism is not aberrational. Rather, it remains deeply embedded in our social and institutional structures. Moreover, many critical race theorists are profoundly pessimistic about the ability of America to make significant changes to patterns of racial oppression, referring instead to what critical race theorist Derrick Bell calls the "permanence of racism." As Bell has written: "Black people will never gain full equality in this country. Even our most successful efforts will produce no more than temporary 'peaks of progress.' Given this unassailable truth, blacks need to acknowledge the permanence of their subordinate status."[2]

Although critical race theorists concede that the civil rights legislation of the 1960s made some headway against discrimination, they argue that it has not overcome the long-established oppression of African Americans and other people of color. Because racism is an ingrained aspect of our culture, critical race theorists contend that traditional antidiscrimination legal measures, which aspire to achieve "colorblindness," are insufficient and simply reinforce existing patterns of racial power. As Richard Delgado has noted: "Formal equal opportunity—rules and laws that insist on treating blacks and whites (for example) alike—can thus remedy only the more extreme and shocking sorts of injustice, the ones that do stand out. Formal equality can do little about the business-as-usual forms of racism that people of color confront every day and that account for much misery, alienation, and despair." To critical race theorists, "colorblind" legal rules that appear neutral in fact favor "insider" groups who enjoy social, economic, and political power. As Bell has written, antidiscrimination laws "could do little more than bring about the cessation of one form of discriminatory conduct that soon appeared in a more subtle though no less discriminatory form."[3]

While critical race theorists have focused on demonstrating the enduring presence of racial discrimination, they have paid less attention to the question why this discrimination persists despite our claims as a society that racial discrimination is immoral. Some critical race theorists, such as Bell, identify white

2. Derrick Bell, *Faces at the Bottom of the Well: The Permanence of Racism* (1992); Bell, *supra* note 1, at 62 (italics deleted).

3. Richard Delgado, Introduction, in *Critical Race Theory: The Cutting Edge* xiv (Richard Delgado ed., 1995); Bell, *supra* note 1, at 62.

self-interest as a barrier to racial reform but do not fully explain why white self-interest continues to subvert racial reform in light of America's rhetorical and legal commitment to equal treatment.[4]

One answer to the question of why racial discrimination might persist despite America's commitment to racial equality can be found in the writings of Reinhold Niebuhr, arguably the most influential American theologian of the twentieth century. Writing during the 1930s in response to secular and religious liberals who believed that education, science, and moral instruction would lead to a new era of social justice, Niebuhr articulated a powerful theory of group self-interest to explain the ongoing oppression of racial and other disfavored minority groups. Niebuhr's critique of liberal optimism evokes much of critical race theory's contemporary critique of liberal faith in antidiscrimination law as the cure for racial discrimination. Racism persists, Niebuhr's social ethics suggests, because the self-interest of majority groups prevents a full embrace of the racial outsider.

## THE NIEBUHRIAN CRITIQUE OF LIBERAL OPTIMISM

Religious liberals during the early twentieth century championed the ability of humanity to be "redeemed" and sought to establish a "kingdom of God" on earth, marked by social justice for all groups. These liberals, writing from various Protestant traditions, "were confident that a new age of social Christianity was about to begin, transforming the raw realities of life in industrial cities and ushering in an era of international peace by the application of Christian love." Walter Rauschenbusch, the leading proponent of the Christian social gospel movement, claimed that "for the first time in religious history, we have the possibility of so directing religious energy by scientific knowledge that a comprehensive and continuous reconstruction of social life in the name of God is within the bounds of human possibility." Other liberal apologists extended this optimism to class and race relations. The Presbyterian theologian William Adams Brown wrote in 1930 that "in relations between races, in strife between

---

4. One such effort is Charles Lawrence's use of cognitive psychological theory to explain the "deeply ingrained" nature of racism in our culture. Charles Lawrence, The Id, The Ego, and Equal Protection: Reckoning with Unconscious Racism, *in Key Writings, supra* note 1, at 238.

capital and labor, in our attitudes toward the weaker and more dependent members of society we are developing a social conscience, and situations which would have been accepted a generation ago as a matter of course are felt as an intolerable scandal."[5]

Secular liberals shared the optimism of their religious counterparts in the ability of science and education to lead to greater progress and the mitigation of human suffering. These liberals, such as the philosopher John Dewey, believed that social injustice had "its main roots in ignorance—which must itself gradually yield before the extension of enlightenment through education and before the power of moral suasion."[6] They developed a theory of history that emphasized an upward trajectory of human moral development.

Niebuhr, however, held that liberal optimism in moral progress was profoundly misplaced. Influenced by the devastations of the First World War and the travails of his working-class parish in Detroit during the 1920s, Niebuhr expressed pessimism about the "moralistic utopianism of the liberal Church" that in his view failed to grasp the dark realities of human nature. Niebuhr elaborated: "The sum total of the liberal Church's effort to apply the law of love to politics without qualification is really a curious medley of hopes and regrets. The Church declares that men ought to live by the law of love and that nations as well as individuals ought to obey it. . . . These appeals to the moral will and this effort to support the moral will by desperate hopes are politically as unrealistic as they are religiously superficial." Niebuhr cited the liberal embrace of the new League of Nations as an example of this unfounded optimism: "glorification of the League of Nations as a symbol of a new epoch in international relations has been very general, and frequently very unqualified, in the Christian churches, where liberal Christianity has given itself to the illusion that all social relations are being brought progressively under 'the law of Christ.'" As Nathan A. Scott, Jr., has observed, Niebuhr also criticized "the secular tradition of Locke and Jefferson and Stuart Mill and John Dewey [that] appeared to [Niebuhr] to be very largely the ideological expression of the characteristic utopianism of bourgeois mentality" with its belief that rationality would triumph over self-interested behavior. Indeed, Niebuhr targeted Dewey for spe-

5. Robin W. Lovin, *Reinhold Niebuhr and Christian Realism* 5 (1995); Walter Rauschenbusch, *Christianity and the Social Crisis* 209 (1924); William Adams Brown, *Pathways to Certainty* 246 (1930).

6. Nathan A. Scott, Jr., *Reinhold Niebuhr* 14 (1963).

cial criticism, ridiculing Dewey's notion that ignorance was the main cause of injustice as opposed to "our predatory self-interest."[7]

Niebuhr offered his most significant attack on the misdirection of liberal optimism in his 1932 book *Moral Man and Immoral Society,* which "sent a series of shockwaves through America's liberal Protestant community." Niebuhr targeted his book at "the moralists, both religious and secular, who imagine that the egoism of individuals is being progressively checked by the development of rationality or the growth of a religiously inspired goodwill and that nothing but the continuance of this process is necessary to establish social harmony between all the human societies and collectives." Liberal reviewers in turn suggested that Niebuhr's "emphasis on sin made him a traitor to progress."[8]

Niebuhr conceded that individuals, despite their sinful nature, may on occasion be capable of moral behavior in the sense that they are "capable, on occasion, of preferring the advantages of others to their own." But this capacity for moral behavior among individuals was far less prevalent among social groups. Niebuhr believed that "human groups, classes, nations, and races are selfish, whatever may be the moral idealism of individual members within the groups." Niebuhr argued that selfishness of human groups is natural; though an individual may occasionally modify his or her self-interested behavior, "every human group which benefits from a present order of society will use every ingenuity and artifice to maintain its privileges and to sanctify them in the name of public order; that political life is, in short, a thinly veiled barbarism." To the argument that human reason will check the unjust actions of the group, Niebuhr replied that "in collective behaviour reason serves largely to rationalize group egoism."[9]

Noting that secular and religious liberals believed that deep-seated self-interest could be controlled either through "the development of rationality" or "the

7. Reinhold Niebuhr, *An Interpretation of Christian Ethics* 155, 160–61 (1958); Reinhold Niebuhr, *Moral Man and Immoral Society: A Study in Ethics and Politics* xxi, xiii (1941 ed.) (hereinafter *Moral Man*); Scott, *supra* note 6, at 14.

8. Daniel F. Rice, *Reinhold Niebuhr and John Dewey: An American Odyssey* 17 (1993); *Moral Man, supra* note 7, at xii; Taylor Branch, *Parting The Waters: America in the King Years, 1954–63,* 84 (1989).

9. *Moral Man, supra* note 7, at xi; Reinhold Niebuhr, *Moralists and Politics,* The Christian Century (July 6, 1932), *reprinted in Essays in Applied Christianity* 79 (D. B. Robertson ed. 1959); Langdon Gilkey, Reinhold Niebuhr as Political Theologian, *in Reinhold Niebuhr and the Issues of Our Time,* 168 (Richard Harries ed., 1986) (hereinafter *Issues*).

growth of religiously inspired goodwill," Niebuhr was emphatic that the tendency of groups to self-interest was too great to overcome through education or moral instruction:

> Social intelligence and moral goodwill . . . may serve to mitigate the brutalities of social conflict, but they cannot abolish the conflict itself. That could be accomplished only if human groups, whether racial, national or economic, could achieve a degree of reason and sympathy which would permit them to see and to understand the interests of others as vividly as they understand their own and a moral goodwill which would prompt them to affirm the rights of others as vigorously as they affirm their own. Given the inevitable limitations of human imagination and intelligence, this is an ideal which individuals may approximate but which is beyond the capacities of human societies.

Thus scientists "who dream of 'socializing' man and religious idealists who strive to increase the sense of moral responsibility . . . are not conscious of the limitations in human nature which finally frustrate their efforts." Years later, Niebuhr would explain white resistance to the civil rights initiatives of the 1950s and 1960s as due to the overwhelming power of group identification that allowed southern whites to reject the moral and legal claims of African Americans.[10]

Recognizing that Christianity articulates self-sacrifice as a central ethic, Niebuhr argued that this ideal "is achieved only rarely in individual life and is not achieved in group life at all. No nation, race, or class sacrifices itself. Human groups make a virtue of the assertion of self-interest and will probably do so until the end of history."[11] Moreover, individual loyalty to the group, honored as altruistic and hence characterized as moral behavior, unwittingly disguises the self-interested activities and attitudes of the group. Although Niebuhr articulated this theory of group identity more than sixty years ago, recent experiences of ethnic identification in Africa and the Balkans demonstrate the ongoing vitality of the power of group identity.

Accusing liberalism of embracing a "romantic overestimate of human virtue and moral capacity," Niebuhr complained that "what is lacking among all these moralists, whether religious or rational, is an understanding of the brutal char-

---

10. *Moral Man, supra* note 7, at xi–xiii, xxiii–xxiv. *See* Reinhold Niebuhr, *The States' Rights Crisis,* 41 The New Leader 6, 7 (Sept. 29, 1958); Reinhold Niebuhr, *Man, the Unregenerate Tribalist,* 24 Christianity and Crisis 133, 133 (July 6, 1964) (hereinafter *Unregenerate Tribalist*).

11. Niebuhr, *supra* note 9, at 83.

acter of the behavior of all human collectives, and the power of self-interest and collective egoism in all intergroup relations."[12]

Niebuhr's critique of liberal optimism in *Moral Man and Immoral Society* was primarily a social and political critique, with limited concern for the theological underpinnings of his claims. During the late 1930s and early 1940s, however, Niebuhr developed a theological basis for his earlier social critique, primarily in his monumental two-volume work *The Nature and Destiny of Man.* Surveying classical, biblical, and modern views of human nature, Niebuhr concluded that modern thinkers were too optimistic about the essence of human nature: "Modern man has an essentially easy conscience; and nothing gives the diverse and discordant notes of modern culture so much harmony as the unanimous opposition of modern man to Christian conceptions of the sinfulness of man. The idea that man is sinful at the very centre of his personality . . . is universally rejected. . . . If modern culture conceives man primarily in terms of the uniqueness of his rational faculties, it finds the root of his evil in his involvement in natural impulses and natural necessities from which it hopes to free him by the increase of his rational faculties." This optimistic view of human nature, according to Niebuhr, led to the "notion that human society can move toward perfection through some force in nature, increasing rationality, or elimination of specific evils in religious, political, economic, or cultural life." As the critical race theorists speak of the "permanence of racism," Niebuhr spoke of "evil as a permanent aspect of the human character." Niebuhr would continue to accuse liberals of being "in perfect flight from the Christian doctrine of sin."[13]

By contrast, Niebuhr articulated an Augustinian notion of human sin that manifests itself as pride. Niebuhr identified three types of pride that humans exhibit as a means of dealing with the anxieties and insecurities of life: pride of power, pride of knowledge, and pride of virtue. Expanding on certain ideas about group behavior that he had previously introduced in *Moral Man,* Niebuhr argued that this tendency toward pride was particularly nefarious when exhibited in groups: "Collective pride is thus man's last, and in some respects most pathetic, effort to deny the determinate and contingent character of his existence. The very essence of human sin is in it. . . . Collective egoism and group pride are a more pregnant source of injustice and conflict than

12. *Moral Man, supra* note 7, at xx.

13. Reinhold Niebuhr, *The Nature and Destiny of Man: A Christian Interpretation,* 23 (1941); Charles C. Brown, *Niebuhr and His Age: Reinhold Niebuhr's Prophetic Role in the Twentieth Century* 76 (1992); Branch, *supra* note 8, at 82.

purely individual pride." Niebuhr cautioned that individuals, but especially groups, have a "disposition to hide self-interest behind a stated devotion to values transcending self-interest," a tendency that leads to all sorts of social mischief.[14]

Thus for Niebuhr the "source of evil is not inadequate education or social or economic arrangements," but rather is located in human nature itself, in our "tendency to seek [our] own interests before the interests of others."[15] The ramifications of this understanding of human nature suggest that self-interest, coercion, and the struggle for power are inevitable in human relations. Although Niebuhr's views evolved over time on a number of issues, he retained a belief throughout his life in the corrupting influence of human nature, particularly when exacerbated by group identification.

## NIEBUHR AND THE PERSISTENCE OF RACISM

Although racism was by no means the primary focus of Niebuhr's social ethical writings, he wrote extensively about the treatment of African Americans in this country, influenced in part by his work with southern black migrants in Detroit during the 1920s. Indeed, in 1927 Niebuhr called racial discrimination "one of the greatest challenges to the spirit of real Christianity. The whole validity of the Christian faith is in the balance as men try to solve the race problem."[16]

Niebuhr conceived of racial discrimination as due to the exercise of group power by whites. During the late 1950s, for example, Niebuhr wrote that southern white resistance to school desegregation "was caused by the ineradicable tendency of men to build integral communities upon the sense of ethnic kinship and to exclude from that kinship any race which diverges too obviously from type. In the white South, the Negro's primary offense is that he is black." In commenting on the difficulties of securing antidiscrimination legislation during the early 1960s, Niebuhr noted: "The effort . . . to give Negroes the full and equal status of citizenship and of a common humanity was bound to prove more difficult than even the most realistic idealists imagined . . . [because]

14. Niebuhr, *supra* note 13, at 188, 213; Timothy W. Floyd, *Realism, Responsibility, and the Good Lawyer: Niebuhrian Perspectives on Legal Ethics,* 67 Notre Dame L. Rev. 587, 603 (1992).

15. Floyd, *supra* note 14, at 602, 603.

16. Reinhold Niebuhr, *Race Prejudice in the North,* 44 The Christian Century 583, 584 (May 12, 1927).

Western man—in common with all men—remains an unregenerate tribal-ist."[17]

Niebuhr also believed that efforts to combat racial discrimination by relying solely on moral appeals would be of limited utility. Commenting on ongoing "efforts at interracial cooperation," Niebuhr concluded that these efforts "accomplish little more than spin a thin veil of moral idealism under which the white man does not really hide his determination to maintain the Negro in a subordinate position in our civilization." Moral idealism alone, Niebuhr wrote in 1932, would never be sufficient to overcome the deeply entrenched self-interest of majority groups: "It is hopeless for the Negro to expect complete emancipation from the menial social and economic position into which the white man has forced him, merely by trusting in the moral sense of the white race. . . . However large the number of individual white men who do and who will identify themselves completely with the Negro cause, the white race in America will not admit the Negro to equal rights if it is not forced to do so. Upon that point, one may speak with a dogmatism which all history justifies." In words evoking the later pessimism of the critical race theorists, Niebuhr concluded that "there are, in other words, no solutions for the race problem on any level if it is not realized that there is no absolute solution for this problem." Niebuhr's reason: "It is not possible to purge man completely of the sinful concomitant of group pride in his collective life."[18]

For the remainder of his life, Niebuhr retained his pessimism about the possibilities of meaningful racial reform. Writing in 1963 at the height of the civil rights movement, Niebuhr responded critically to Robert Kennedy's suggestion that African Americans, like the Irish, would eventually overcome discrimination and enter the political and economic mainstream: "The analogy is not exact. The Irish merely affronted us by having a different religion and a different place of origin than the 'true' Americans. The Negroes affront us by diverging from the dominant type all too obviously. Their skin is black. And our celebrated reason is too errant to digest the difference." While much of liberal America hailed the passage of the Civil Rights Act of 1964 as a triumph of the American creed, Niebuhr remained decidedly pessimistic. Writing on the eve

17. Niebuhr, *The States' Rights Crisis, supra* note 10, at 7; *Unregenerate Tribalist, supra* note 10, at 133.

18. Niebuhr, *supra* note 9, at 80; *Moral Man, supra* note 7, at 252, 253; Reinhold Niebuhr, The Race Problem, *in Love and Justice: Selections from the Shorter Writings of Reinhold Niebuhr* 130–31 (D. B. Robertson ed., 1957).

of the enactment of the landmark 1964 civil rights legislation, Niebuhr noted: "It will be a crisis-filled decade and century before the nation has solved—or even taken the most rigorous steps toward the solution of—this 'American dilemma.' The dilemma is actually wider than our national life; it is the dilemma of validating the humanity of man despite the strong tribal impulses in his nature." Niebuhr's profound pessimism about human nature and the ability of white America to fully embrace African Americans earned him rebukes from many racial liberals who criticized Niebuhr for being "too pessimistic about [the possibility of] radical social change."[19] Niebuhr, who since the 1920s had steadfastly urged racial reform, certainly welcomed the civil rights legislation of the 1960s. But his view of the profound human tendency toward self-interest prevented him from sharing the enthusiasm of many racial liberals about the ultimate significance of those legislative gains.

What, then, in Niebuhr's view, should African Americans do in the face of persistent discrimination? Niebuhr contended that "the relations between groups must therefore always be predominantly political rather than ethical, that is, they will be determined by the proportion of power which each group possesses at least as much as by any rational and moral appraisal of the comparative needs and claims of each group." For Niebuhr, the "outsider," such as the African American, must "develop both economic and political power to meet the combination of political and economic power which confronts him." Niebuhr specifically recommended that African Americans engage in various cooperative arrangements such as economic boycotts to confront majority power: "Boycotts against banks which discriminate against Negroes in granting credit, against stores which refuse to employ Negroes while serving Negro trade, and against public service corporations which practice racial discrimination." Niebuhr's understanding of the importance of power to social and political relations bears similarities to those critical race theorists who question the ability of racial minorities to make significant gains absent activity grounded in the realities of the distribution of power in America.[20]

Niebuhr, however, also recognized that moral suasion plays a role in the quest for social justice. To Niebuhr politics is "an area where conscience and

19. Reinhold Niebuhr, *Revolution in an Open Society,* 46 New Leader 7, 8 (May 27, 1963); Reinhold Niebuhr, *The Struggle for Justice,* 47 New Leader 10, 11 (July 6, 1964); Ronald Preston, Reinhold Niebuhr and the New Right *in Issues, supra* note 9, at 90.

20. *Moral Man, supra* note 7, at xxiii; Niebuhr, *supra* note 9, at 81; *Moral Man, supra* note 7, at 254.

power meet, where the ethical and coercive factors of human life will interpenetrate and work out their tentative and uneasy compromises." Although Niebuhr did not believe that moral appeals alone could compel the white majority to share power with "outsider" groups, he recognized that moral argumentation should nevertheless be used to undermine racial discrimination. Writing in the 1940s, Niebuhr argued that those interested in furthering justice claims "must use every stratagem of education and every resource of religion to prompt humility and charity in the life of the majority."[21]

Like many contemporary critical race theorists, Niebuhr expressed skepticism about the ability of legal rules barring racial discrimination to alter patterns of long-standing behavior. Writing in 1950, Niebuhr questioned the efficacy of proposed fair-employment legislation, concluding that even if Congress passed such legislation, "it probably could not be enforced. . . . In stating such a conclusion we are flying in the face of an almost unanimous 'liberal' opinion, inside and outside the churches. But liberal opinion has again and again failed to observe that the potency of law has its limits." In 1963, at the height of the civil rights movement, Niebuhr counseled against undue optimism about the power of legislative enactments to alter racial attitudes: "Laws cannot finally change the recalcitrant. Their prejudices dictate customs that are at war with the explicit law of the land and the law that is written into the heart."[22]

Niebuhr had a profound impact on Martin Luther King, Jr., and King's view of the nature of white resistance to demands for racial equality. Drawing on Niebuhr, King wrote in 1952 that liberalism "vainly seeks to overcome injustice through purely moral and rational suasions. . . . Perfect justice will not come by a simple statement of the moral superiority of brotherhood in the world, for men are controlled by power, not mind alone." King wrote that Niebuhr had helped him to "recognize the illusions of a superficial optimism concerning human nature and the dangers of a false idealism." King wrote in 1958, "Niebuhr's great contribution to contemporary theology is that he has refuted the false optimism characteristic of a great segment of Protestant liberalism." Indeed, one King scholar has concluded that "the Christian realism of Reinhold Niebuhr

21. *Id.* at 4; Reinhold Niebuhr, *The Children of Light and the Children of Darkness* 143 (1944).

22. Reinhold Niebuhr, *Fair Employment Practices Act,* 15 Christianity and Society 3, 3 (Summer 1950); Reinhold Niebuhr, *The Mounting Racial Crisis,* 23 Christianity and Crisis 121, 122 (July 8, 1963).

. . . was probably . . . the greatest sobering influence upon King's optimistic anthropological assumptions."[23]

## NIEBUHR AND CRITICAL RACE THEORY

Niebuhr's pessimistic analysis of the problems confronting African Americans is strikingly similar to the analysis of contemporary critical race theorists. Derrick Bell, for example, one of the most prolific and influential critical race theorists, has consistently argued that the oppression of African Americans in this country's history has continued in significant measure because it has served majoritarian group interests and that white elites have and will continue to recognize certain rights of African Americans "only when such recognition serves some economic or political interests of greater importance to whites." Bell argues that the desegregation and antidiscrimination initiatives of the past half-century have succeeded to the extent those initiatives have served white interests, creating what Bell labels an "interest convergence" that makes racial reform possible.[24] Several civil rights gains of the twentieth century illustrate Bell's theory.

President Franklin Roosevelt's establishment of the Fair Employment Practice Committee (FEPC) in 1941, for example, has been duly noted as one of the first important steps by the federal government in the campaign against racial discrimination. Although the FEPC did help reduce racial discrimination in wartime industry, President Roosevelt undeniably created the FEPC in order to thwart a potentially embarrassing "march on Washington" that threatened to reveal the extent of racial discrimination in the American workplace at a time when such revelations would have harmed U.S. foreign policy interests. Similarly, during the late 1940s, a number of northern states and cities enacted legislation and ordinances barring racial discrimination in public accommodations, employment, education, and housing. These measures were motivated in significant part by the desire of white elites to capture political support from

23. Martin Luther King, Jr., Reinhold Niebuhr's Ethical Dualism, *in* 2 *The Papers of Martin Luther King, Jr.* 146 (Clayborne Carson ed., 1992); Martin Luther King, Jr., *Stride Toward Freedom: A Leader of His People Tells the Montgomery Story* 99, 96 (1958); Lewis V. Baldwin, *There Is a Balm in Gilead: The Cultural Roots of Martin Luther King, Jr.* 78 (1991).

24. Derrick A. Bell, Jr., *California's Proposition 209: A Temporary Diversion on the Road to Racial Disaster*, 30 Loy. L.A. L.Rev. 1447, 1452 (1997); Derrick A. Bell, Jr., *Brown v. Board of Education and the Interest-Convergence Dilemma*, 93 Harv. L. Rev. 518, 523 (1980).

the growing number of black voters and to stem burgeoning racial tensions triggered by wartime urban riots. During the early 1960s some southern cities enacted antidiscrimination ordinances or initiated token school desegregation plans to defuse economically embarrassing demonstrations and to avoid experiencing economic losses from racial unrest such as those suffered in Little Rock and Birmingham.[25]

One cannot understand the civil rights movement of the twentieth century without appreciating the ability of blacks (and many whites) to frame their arguments for racial justice in ways that appealed to those in power. Some whites supported civil rights initiatives because of sincere moral commitments, but many civil rights gains would not have been possible absent the ability of African Americans to use civil disobedience to appeal to majoritarian interests in avoiding civil unrest and embarrassment. Niebuhr's forecast of the need for African Americans to eschew exclusive reliance on "the moral sense of the white race" and to exercise "power" to alter majoritarian behavior has proven remarkably prescient.

Furthermore, critical race theorists generally share Niebuhr's concern with the distribution of power in society and the most effective means of challenging that power. Civil rights activists have relied in significant measure on litigation to win racial reform. Many contemporary critical theorists, however, influenced by the legal realists of the 1920s and 1930s who argued that "purportedly neutral and objective legal interpretation . . . [is] really based on politics," contend that the efficacy of litigation campaigns has been overstated. As Richard Delgado has written, "Virtually all of Critical Race thought is marked by deep discontent with liberalism, a system of civil rights litigation and activism characterized by incrementalism, faith in the legal system, and hope for progress." Instead, in a manner that recalls Niebuhr's earlier observation that "relations between groups must . . . always be *predominantly* political rather than ethical," many critical race theorists urge minorities to pursue community-based private and political initiatives that seek to maximize economic and political power. Although critical race theorists generally remain skeptical of the possibility of ethical argument influencing majority power, Niebuhr, though he did urge mi-

25. See Paul Burstein, *Discrimination, Jobs, and Politics: The Struggle for Equal Employment Opportunity in the United States Since the New Deal* 69 (1985); Davison M. Douglas, *The Limits of Law in Accomplishing Racial Change: School Segregation in the Pre-Brown North*, 44 UCLA L. Rev. 677, 719–20 (1997); Davison M. Douglas, *Reading, Writing, and Race: The Desegregation of the Charlotte Schools* 96–103 (1995).

nority groups to emphasize the "political rather than the ethical," recognized the vitality of a convergence of "ethical and coercive factors."[26]

This nation's treatment of persons of color, particularly African Americans, has been a source of discomfort for those who celebrate the moral idealism of the American creed and its vision of equal justice. Most Americans, however, believe that the legal reforms of the civil rights era have largely dealt with our nation's long failure to live up to our ideals and that any ongoing racism is aberrational. Contemporary opponents of affirmative action, for example, reject the notion that systemic racism continues.

More than fifty years ago, Reinhold Niebuhr sharply challenged liberal faith in moral progress and confronted us with the insidious influence of human sin that manifests itself in expressions of individual and group self-interest. Although Niebuhr welcomed the legal advances of the 1960s, he retained his pessimism in the possibilities of racial justice given the sinful nature of the human character. When contemporary critical race theorists write of the profound difficulties of eliminating racial discrimination in America, they build on the ethical and theological understandings of Niebuhr.

26. *Key Writings, supra* note 1, at xviii; Delgado, *supra* note 3, at 1; *Moral Man, supra* note 7, at xxiii (emphasis added); *see, e.g.,* Gerald D. Lopez, *Rebellious Lawyering: One Chicano's Vision of Progressive Law Practice* (1992); Giradeau Spann, *Race Against the Court* (1993); Charles F. Abernathy, *When Civil Rights Go Wrong: Agenda and Process in Civil Rights Reform,* 2 Temp. Pol. and Civ. Rts. L. Rev. 177, 201–2 (1993); *Moral Man, supra* note 7, at 4.

# Hispanics, Catholicism, and the Legal Academy

*José Roberto Juárez, Jr.*

"You're too defensive."

I had been accused of this before, usually during a discussion of a difficult issue involving race, and almost always by a white person. The proponent was usually someone who, not having been subjected to discrimination on the basis of race, was claiming an "objectivity" that I, as a victim of racial discrimination, was not entitled to claim.[1]

"You're too defensive."

The accusers this time were different, mostly Hispanics who were keenly sensitive to subordination on many different grounds: race, gender, sexual orientation, and class. The accusation was from Hispanic law professors gathered at the second annual LatCrit conference

1. I am indebted to current and former colleagues who discussed the issues I raise here and offered helpful suggestions: Barbara Bader Aldave, Yvonne Cherena Pacheco, Cecelia Espenoza, Elise García, Emily Fowler Hartigan, Marsha Cope Huie, Ana Novoa, and Reynaldo Anaya Valencia. I also thank Angela Carmella, Robert Cochran, and Michael McConnell for their invaluable assistance throughout the editing process.

163

in May 1997.[2] The accusation was also from Asian and African-American law professors attending LatCrit II. I couldn't dismiss the accusation as one being made by persons unfamiliar with subordination.

"You're too defensive."

The accusation was made in a room at the Center for Legal and Social Justice of St. Mary's University School of Law. St. Mary's is a Catholic law school, and the center houses the law school's clinical programs as well as nonprofit organizations working to empower the poor and the oppressed in our society, all in a building formerly operated as a spiritual retreat center by Marianist nuns.[3] This session of LatCrit II was held in a room at the center in which several religious tapestries hang on the walls, one of which depicts the Last Supper.

During one of the conference presentations, anger and frustration that had been pent up among some of the conference participants was finally expressed. Lesbian and gay participants voiced their unhappiness with the setting of the discussion in a room containing symbols of the Catholic Church, an institution that has a long history of oppression of lesbians and gays. Other conference events, such as invocations at the conference dinners and a talk by a Chicana nun on Hispanas and the church, had precipitated their unhappiness.[4] They viewed the images on the wall as still one more slap in the face.

It is difficult to convey the power of the statements made by the lesbian and gay participants as they described the oppression and pain inflicted upon their community by institutional Christianity. Theirs was a power I had seen and admired in others who have refused to accept oppression in their lives. But in the

2. Professor Richard Delgado has described Latino-critical scholars, or "LatCrits," as "applying the powerful insights of Critical Race Theory to the situation and problems of Latinos." Richard Delgado, *Rodrigo's Fourteenth Chronicle: American Apocalypse,* 32 Harv. C.R.-C.L. Rev. 275, 275 (1997). The Lat Crit conference gathers Hispanic and non-Hispanic legal academics to explore issues affecting the Hispanic community using Latino-critical theory. LatCrit I was at the University of San Diego School of Law in 1996. LatCrit II was at St. Mary's University School of Law in 1997.

3. St. Mary's University is owned and operated by the priests and brothers of the Society of Mary (Marianists). The nuns of the Daughters of Mary Immaculate (also Marianists) have worked closely with the University. Organizations housed at the Center for Legal and Social Justice have included the Texas headquarters of the Appleseed Foundation, Partners for the Common Good, Hispanas Unidas, and offices for Béxar County Legal Aid staff.

4. Sister Grace Walle, F.M.I., the St. Mary's Law School's campus minister, gave a nondenominational invocation at the opening dinner. A Native American gave an invocation in his native language at the second dinner. The LatCrit II participants expressed objection only to Sister Grace's invocation.

course of their expressing this pain, some of these participants asserted that their pain and the history of oppression demanded the exclusion from the Lat-Crit conferences of religion in general, and Catholicism in particular.

Exclusion of Catholicism from any conversation regarding the empowerment of Hispanics in the United States is unacceptable to me, and I (and others) said so during the course of the discussion that morning at LatCrit II. I described the importance of Catholicism to a majority of Chicanos in the United States. I described the role Catholicism had played in empowering Chicanos, and the crucial importance of Catholicism to the social justice work undertaken by St. Mary's Law School under the leadership of then-Dean Barbara Bader Aldave. And I described how St. Mary's had been attacked by critics inside and outside the law school for our efforts to empower the oppressed—including gays and lesbians. The response was:

"You're too defensive."

The friends and colleagues who made this accusation were right. I was too defensive because religion, like racial discrimination, is an issue of great importance for me. The relation between religion and Hispanics, and the role that relation can or should play in the empowerment of the Hispanic community, should be of importance to the legal academy.[5] It certainly was of great importance to the participants in the discussion at LatCrit II. I wish to set forth my views on these questions—with what I hope is less defensiveness than I apparently expressed at LatCrit II—in the hope of continuing the important discussion begun at that conference.

My views derive from my life experiences before joining the legal academy and have been reinforced by my experiences as a professor at St. Mary's University School of Law. A brief description of those experiences is therefore in order.

## MY CATHOLICISM

I am a Roman Catholic. Like most Chicanos, I am a descendant of the Spaniards who brought Catholicism to the Americas, and of the native peoples and Africans who were forcibly converted to Catholicism. Some of my "Spanish" ancestors were probably Sephardic Jews who were also forcibly converted and

5. The disparity between the religiosity of the nation and the secularism of the legal academy is well known. Emily Fowler Hartigan, *Practicing and Professing Spirit in Law,* 27 Tex. Tech. L. Rev. 1165, 1172 (1996) (describing dismissals of religious talk at the national convention of law professors as ranging from "the supercilious to the irrationally hostile").

fled from Spain to Mexico.[6] I thus know all too well from my own family history that the Catholic Church has often been a force of oppression that cooperated with the Spanish military and political authorities to enslave and oppress millions of indigenous and African slaves.[7]

Moreover, as an imperfect institution directed by humans, the church hierarchy continues sometimes to exclude the marginalized. Women continue to be excluded from the priesthood.[8] Although the church no longer prohibits the ordination of Indians, Africans, mestizos, and mulattos, as it did in 1536, Hispanics continue to be underrepresented among the clergy.[9] Notwithstanding the church's teachings prohibiting discrimination against homosexuals, many within the church continue such discrimination.[10] For many gays and lesbians, the church's continuing prohibition against physical expression of their sexuality is deeply painful.[11] The response of many intellectuals is to reject the Catholic Church entirely. In many ways, my life would be much easier if I could only do so. But like most Hispanics, I continue to claim Catholicism as my faith.

In part, my faith is a gift from my ancestors. My parents, who attended Catholic schools through college, shared this gift with me. In part, my faith is a gift of the nuns who taught me in Catholic elementary school and showed how powerful a force the message of Jesus Christ can be when taken seriously. In part my faith is a gift of the many people of faith who have demonstrated

6. The web site of the Leona G. and David A. Bloom Southwest Jewish Archives of the University of Arizona Library discusses the Jewish heritage of Chicanos in the Southwest. <http://dizzy.library.arizona.edu/images/swja/crypto.htm>

7. Virgil Elizondo, *Guadalupe: Mother of the New Creation* 54 (1997) (noting the Church's role in justifying the newly established Spanish order in the Americas).

8. Catechism of the Catholic Church ¶1577 (1994) (stating that "the ordination of women is not possible").

9. Elizondo, *supra* note 7, at 57.

10. Catechism, *supra* note 8, at ¶2358 (stating that homosexuals "must be accepted with respect, compassion, and sensitivity. Every sign of unjust discrimination in their regard should be avoided"). *See also* Bishops Urge Parents of Homosexuals to Accept their Children, Themselves, Church Teaching on Human Dignity (visited Mar. 1, 1998) <http://www.nccbuscc.org/comm/archives/97-208.htm> (noting that U.S. Catholic Bishops' pastoral letter urges all to "strive to eliminate any form of injustice, oppression, or violence against" homosexuals).

11. *See, e.g.,* Paul Halsell, Silence=Death (visited Mar. 1, 1998) <http://www.bway.net/halsall/lgbh/lgbh-silence.txt>.

throughout my life the power of that faith. And in large part, my faith is a gift of the Spirit, who for whatever reason, has chosen to bless me—an imperfect human who sins frequently and regularly—with this faith.

My faith is a gift shared by most Hispanics. Religion is a fundamental part of Hispanic culture. Within Hispanic culture, faith is not something that is thought about only on Sundays. It permeates everyday life. Pictures of religious figures, such as Jesus Christ and the Virgin Mary, hang in the living room. Chicanos still utter freely, in Spanish, phrases such as "God willing" that sound strange in the secular English of today's United States: *Si Dios quiere* and *Dios mediante.* Moreover, despite inroads by other religious groups, Catholicism continues to be claimed by most Hispanics as their religion.[12] Given the dramatic increase in the Hispanic population in the United States, the Catholic Church finds itself struggling to meet the needs of a group that will soon dominate the U.S. Church.[13]

For me as a Chicano growing up in Texas at a time of blatant racial discrimination against Chicanos in both the public and private sectors, the church was a source of empowerment. As in the rest of the nation, the struggle to end racial segregation in Texas was often led by African-American clergy, joined by clergy of many races and faiths. After the abolition of the poll tax, voter registration drives were organized in the Chicano parishes. We marched behind an image of La Virgen de Guadalupe in the mid 1960s, when we joined farmworkers from the Río Grande Valley who had marched to Austin to ask Governor Connally to assist them in their efforts to secure a living wage. No Chicano movement protest or march during the 1960s and 1970s would have been complete without a banner displaying the image of Guadalupe that Catholics believe miracu-

12. A 1990 survey by the City University of New York found that one-third of Hispanics are now Protestants. Daniel J. Lehmann, *Surprises Surface in Religion Study,* Chi. Sun-Times, Apr. 7, 1999. The 1990 census, however, estimated that 80 percent of U.S. Hispanics were baptized Catholic. *The Catholic Almanac* 457 (Matthew Bunson, ed., 2000).

13. Hispanics will constitute a majority of U.S. Catholics within the next twenty-five years. Office of Communications, Nat'l Conf. of Catholic Bishops/U.S. Catholic Conference, Hispanics' Fourth Encuentro in Year 2000 Approved by Bishops (visited Feb. 16, 1998) <http://www.nccbuscc.org/comm/archives/97-251.htm>. The National Conference of Catholic Bishops and the United States Catholic Conference have established a Secretariat for Hispanic Affairs that seeks to "integrate the Hispanic presence into the life of the Catholic Church and society." Secretariat for Hispanic Affairs, Nat'l Conf. of Catholic Bishops/U.S. Catholic. Conf., Mission (visited Jan. 24, 1998) <http://www.nccbuscc.org/hispanicaffairs/mission.htm>.

lously appeared on the *tilma* (cloak) of the Mexican Indian Juan Diego in 1531.[14]

Nor is this a new phenomenon. The church has long been a powerful force in the lives of Chicanos. The dominant icon among Chicanos, even among those who rarely attend church services, continues to be La Virgen de Guadalupe, the Indian mother whose apparition before Juan Diego was a seminal event in the conversion of the natives of Mexico by the Spaniards.[15] The Chicano scholar (and priest) Virgil Elizondo points out that La Virgen "has been a source of energy and inspiration for many who have struggled for liberty and justice in the Americas: for Father Miguel Hidalgo, César Chávez, Dolores Huerta, Adelita Navarro, Samuel Ruiz, and for many others who have found their heroic strength for survival within her."[16] Millions continue to ask the brown-skinned Virgen to intercede with God, often invoking one of her traditional titles: *abogada nuestra*—our lawyer.[17] Some Christians who are not Catholic, and some U.S. Catholics who are not Hispanic, have questioned this devotion to La Virgen, wondering whether this devotion diverts Hispanics from worship of Jesus Christ. Pope John Paul II has no such qualms: "This is not so. Through Mary, we come to her Son more easily. Mary is held up as a

14. A description of Juan Diego's *tilma,* together with a summary of the scientific studies conducted on it, can be found in Spanish at <http://webdemexico.com.mx/religion/ guadalupe/ tilma.html>. An English-language translation of portions of the original Nahuatl (Aztec) relation of the apparition of Guadalupe, the *Nican Mopohua,* can be found at <http://ng.netgate.net/norberto/materdei.html>. For a detailed analysis of this account of the Virgin of Guadalupe, see Elizondo, *supra* note 7.

15. *See, e.g.,* César Martínez, *Hombre que le Gustan las Mujeres* [Man who likes women], *reproduced in* John Beardsley et al., *Hispanic Art in the United States: Thirty Contemporary Painters and Sculptors* 98 (1987). The painting depicts a Chicano with a small tattoo of a nude woman on his right arm, a small tattoo of his sweetheart on his left arm, and a large tattoo of the Virgin of Guadalupe on his chest. See generally Elizondo, *supra* note 7.

16. Elizondo, *supra* note 7, at 135.

17. *See, e.g.,* the prayers found at Novena en Honor de Nuestra Señora de Guadalupe (visited June 19, 2000) <http://ng.negate.net/norberto/novena-spanish.html> ("Oh Santísima Virgen de Guadalupe! Que bien se conoce que eres Abogada nuestra en el tribunal de Dios. . . . Haces también oficio de abogada, rogando y procurando a favor nuestro" [Oh most holy Virgin of Guadalupe! How well is it known that you are our lawyer in God's court. . . . You also take on the role of lawyer, pleading and obtaining in our favor]); and at Entronización de la Imagen de la Virgen de Guadalupe (visited June 19, 2000) <http://207.248.192.11/pithprensa.com/spanish/addmat/enthron.htm> ("Señora, abogada nuestra!" [Lady, our lawyer!]).

model for the believer and for the whole Church called to respond to the Lord with her own 'yes.' She is the Mother who intercedes for all: for souls thirsting for God and for those who are groping in the darkness of doubt and disbelief, for those who are suffering in body or tired in spirit, for those who yield to the attraction of sin and for those who are struggling to escape its clutches. Her motherly concern overlooks no one."[18]

## CATHOLICISM AND THE CATHOLIC LAW SCHOOL: AN OFTEN UNCOMFORTABLE FIT

I went to law school because I saw the law as a means of continuing the struggle I had long engaged in: to empower my community. My work as a civil rights lawyer with the Mexican American Legal Defense and Educational Fund (MALDEF) was a dream come true for me; I went to work every day happy to be able to participate in my community's struggles for justice.

After working as a civil rights lawyer for nine years, I received a phone call from my former constitutional law professor and soon-to-be dean, Barbara Bader Aldave, inviting me to apply to join the faculty at St. Mary's University School of Law. I accepted the invitation largely because St. Mary's was a Catholic law school whose mission statement explicitly set forth its goal to carry out the social justice work of the Catholic Church and Dean Aldave was committed to that work.

I quickly discovered that St. Mary's, although Catholic, was a law school with few Catholics on the faculty and with no historic emphasis on the Catholic Church's social-justice teachings. At one of my first faculty meetings, a fundamentalist Protestant colleague argued that as a Catholic law school, St. Mary's had to object to the American Bar Association's accreditation standard prohibiting law schools from discriminating on the basis of sexual orientation.[19] I rose in opposition to any objection to the standard, noting that it was fully consistent with Catholic teaching, which prohibits discrimination against

18. John Paul II, Mary is the Mother Who Intercedes for Everyone (visited June 19, 2000) <http://www.cin.org/jp960505.html>.

19. American Bar Ass'n Section of Legal Education and Admissions to the Bar, Standards for Approval of Law Schools and Interpretations, Standard 210 (1996) ("A law school shall foster and maintain equality of opportunity in legal education, including employment of faculty and staff, without discrimination or segregation on grounds of race, color, religion, national origin, sex, or sexual orientation").

homosexuals.[20] Colleagues approached me afterward—both supporters and opponents of the ABA's ban on discrimination—and asked with amazement whether my statements on Catholic teaching in fact were true.

I soon learned that the church's teachings on discrimination were not the only ones unknown to many of the law school's faculty, students, and alumni. Consistent with the church's opposition to the death penalty, St. Mary's established a capital punishment clinic, which provided students the opportunity to assist in the representation of inmates on death row.[21] The clinic was soon attacked as inappropriate for a Catholic law school! Similar attacks were made on the law school's civil justice, immigration, human rights, and community development clinics.

These attacks were made by politically conservative individuals who accused the school of seeking to foist a "liberal" agenda on the law school. What these critics failed to understand is that Catholicism does not fit within the secular categories of liberal and conservative. The perception of opposition to the death penalty in the current secular political climate of the United States as "liberal" is of no moment to the church. Nor does the church care that the exercise of its preferential option for the poor is perceived in the United States as "liberal"—just as it does not matter that the church's opposition to abortion is perceived as "conservative." Former Dean Aldave has explained:

> We at St. Mary's University School of Law are virtually obliged to sponsor the particular clinical programs that we have initiated, I aver. After all, for whom is our school named? Once we strip away the heavily romanticized tradition that surrounds her, what does Mary mean to us as Catholics? In the early part of the New Testament, Mary is introduced to us as an unmarried pregnant teenager. When last we hear of her, she is an old woman, at least by the standards of her time—a widow who looks

20. *See* National Conference of Catholic Bishops Committee on Marriage and Family, Always Our Children: A Pastoral Message to Parents of Homosexual Children and Suggestions for Pastoral Ministers (visited June 20, 2000) <http://www.mu.edu/um/Bishops.htm> (noting that "[n]othing in the Bible or in Catholic teaching can be used to justify prejudicial or discriminatory attitudes and behaviors").

21. Office of Social Development and World Peace, Nat'l Conf. of Catholic Bishops/ U.S. Catholic Conf., The Death Penalty and the Catechism (visited June 18, 2000) <http://www.nccbuscc.org/sdwp/national/criminal/cappunishment.htm> (announcing modifications to the *Catechism* that clarify that the cases in which the execution of an offender "is an absolute necessity 'are rare, if not practically non-existent'") (quoting John Paul II, *Evangelium Vitae* 56 (1995)).

to friends for sustenance and support. Between her major appearances, she has searched for shelter, fled from persecution, and watched the execution of her son. Somehow I have to believe that such a woman, whom I view as a strong and courageous figure, would heartily approve of programs—instituted at the only law school bearing her name—that are designed to aid the poor and the homeless, immigrants and refugees, the young and the elderly, and inhabitants of death row.[22]

Similarly, the tremendous strides St. Mary's has made since 1989 in increasing the diversity of its student body, faculty, and staff have nothing to do with politics. The Marianists who founded St. Mary's were French priests and brothers who came in the mid-nineteenth century to serve the people of south Texas. This goal of service continues to be reflected in the university's mission statement and to be supported by the leadership of the institution. Given its location in a region in which a majority of the population is Chicano, it is entirely appropriate that the university reflect the region it serves. A majority of the undergraduate population is now Hispanic. As of 1998 St. Mary's Law School had more Chicano students and faculty than any other law school in the country. In the post–Proposition 209 and *Hopwood* climate, these achievements have been attacked within and without the law school.[23] Yet St. Mary's University has remained committed to continuing to increase the diversity of the student body, the staff, and the faculty.

This is the context in which the discussion at LatCrit II took place. For the St. Mary's participants, the last few years have often been painful as the law school's critics have sought to undo the progress of recent years and to return it to its former status as a nominally Catholic but effectively secular institution. Having been subjected to repeated criticism from secular "conservatives" because we take the church's teachings seriously, I looked forward to LatCrit II as an opportunity to gather strength from colleagues from around the country who, whether they shared our faith or not, shared our goal of empowerment of Hispanics and others who have been oppressed.

22. Barbara Bader Aldave, *The Reality of a Catholic Law School,* 78 Marq. L. Rev. 291, 294–95 (1995).

23. Proposition 209, adopted by the voters of California in 1996, prohibits the consideration of race, and therefore the use of affirmative action, in "public employment, public education, or public contracting." Cal. Const. art. 1, § 31. In *Hopwood v. Texas,* the United States Court of Appeals for the Fifth Circuit held that the affirmative action program at the University of Texas School of Law violated the Equal Protection Clause of the Fourteenth Amendment. 78 F.3d 932 (5th Cir. 1996).

## CATHOLICISM AS A FORCE FOR CHANGE

The discussions at LatCrit II strengthened me—even the discussions with those who objected to the inclusion of religion in LatCrit II. I continue to be troubled, however, by the attempted exclusion of religion at a gathering purporting to seek the empowerment of Hispanics. It is illegitimate for those who expressly seek to empower Hispanics to ignore a fundamental part of Hispanic culture, religion. Moreover, as a strategic matter, I find it incomprehensible that anyone seeking to empower Hispanics would not actively seek to understand the transformative potential of the Catholic Church within the Hispanic community. However extensive the church's history of oppression, it has also been a force for positive change in the Americas. It is not only unfair, but strategically shortsighted, for the legal academy to ignore this aspect of the church's relationship with Hispanics in the United States.

The history of Chicanos in the Southwest reveals the dual nature of the church's legacy. The Spanish missions of Arizona, California, New Mexico, and Texas share a legacy of often brutal conversion of the native peoples to Catholicism. Yet it was Father Miguel Hidalgo, a Catholic priest, who led the fight for Mexico's independence from Spain. After the conquest of northwestern Mexico by the United States, Father José Antonio Martínez led the Taos revolt of 1847 in New Mexico, which sought to challenge the dispossession of neo-Mexicanos from their lands by Anglo immigrants.[24] Although the Catholic Church had to be prodded at first, it became one of the most important sources of support for the United Farm Workers in the 1960s and 1970s. The rallying cry of the farmworkers was "Justicia para los campesinos y viva la Virgen de Guadalupe!" (Justice for farmworkers and long live the Virgin of Guadalupe!).[25] Reies López Tijerina, the leader of the Alianza Federal de las Mercedes in New Mexico, which sought to enforce the guarantees of the Treaty of Guadalupe Hidalgo in the 1960s, was able to elude authorities in New Mexico because local *penitentes* (religious lay brotherhoods) protected him.[26]

Catholicism remains a potent force today, as I was reminded several years ago when researching the church's position on immigration in preparation for giving a lecture on Catholic social justice and immigration. As a MALDEF lawyer, I quickly became accustomed to being perceived by xenophobic advo-

24. F. Arturo Rosales, *Chicano! The History of the Mexican American Civil Rights Movement* 155 (1996).

25. *Id.* at 139.

26. *Id.* at 158.

cacy groups and politicians as a "radical" simply because MALDEF fights to protect the rights of documented and undocumented immigrants. The church's
teachings on immigration challenged me to do much more to support my im-
migrant brothers and sisters. The church rejects principles that are accepted
without question in the political arena of the United States, such as a nation's
sovereign right to control its borders.[27] As Pope John Paul II emphasized in his
last visit to the United States, "La Iglesia es el lugar donde a los inmigrantes ile-
gales se les recibe como hermanos" (The Church is where illegal immigrants are
received as brothers and sisters).[28]

Some of the LatCrit II participants seemed to view the church as a continuing obstacle to ending the marginalization of gays and lesbians in our society. I
view the church as potentially one of the most powerful means of helping Hispanics to transform our culture—a culture that is generally warm, welcoming,
and loving—into one that warmly welcomes and loves our homosexual brothers and sisters. The church's teaching prohibiting discrimination against our
homosexual brothers and sisters challenges the body politic. The challenge is
posed even more forcefully to Hispanic Catholics, for traditionally our culture
is vehemently homophobic. I believe that the very institution that has hurt so
many Hispanic gays and lesbians—the church—can in fact help to begin eradicating the traditional homophobia of the Hispanic community. This task will
not be an easy one, for the challenge posed to many Hispanics by the church's
teachings prohibiting discrimination against homosexuals is as daunting as the
challenge posed to many non-Hispanics by the church's teaching on welcoming immigrants.

## THE NEED FOR DIALOGUE AND
## UNDERSTANDING

The tapestry of the Last Supper on the wall of the Center for Legal and Social
Justice illustrates what is, to me, the central message of Christianity: that Jesus

27. U.S. Catholic Bishops' Conf., Policy Statement on Employer Sanctions (1988) (asserting that "[t]he right to migrate for work cannot be simply ignored on the exercise of a nation's sovereign right to control its own borders. In this regard, Catholic social teaching sets
a higher ethical standard for guarding the rights of the undocumented within our borders
than do current U.S. law and policy").

28. Juan Vicente Boo, Católicos norteamericanos, una Iglesia marcada por el éxito y la fi-
delidad, ABC (Madrid), Oct. 14, 1995, available at Noticias de la Santa Sede, 1–15 Octubre
de 1995 (visited June 19, 2000) <http://www.christusrex.org/www1/news/octubre1-95.
html>.

Christ adopted human form in a distant land more than two thousand years ago to save all humanity and to call on all of humanity to love each other. He came for Jew and Greek, for slave and free, for man and woman, for Anglo and Chicano, for rich and poor, and for straight and gay. The power of the message of Jesus Christ for all who are marginalized today is great—if those of us who claim to follow Him take that message seriously.

My LatCrit II colleagues who were disturbed by that same tapestry, however, did something very important by expressing their discomfort. For it is easy to overlook the diversity of experiences, even within the Hispanic community. We must not forget why others may see these same images as symbols of oppression. And their cry reminds us that our work in holding the church—and ourselves—accountable is not over.

I seek to hold them accountable as well. Legal academics seeking to empower Hispanics must see that it is essential for us to work to see the same power in those religious symbols that a majority of Hispanics do. To fail to do so is to engage in the kind of elitism that critical race theorists purport to reject. Religion, and particularly Catholicism, is an integral part of the Hispanic community and of the Hispanic story. To exclude religion is to fail to give voice to the very community that LatCrit participants seek to empower.[29] To exclude religion is to ignore the source of much of Western thinking about justice. To exclude religion is to ignore what the church can teach us today about what justice is. At best, to exclude religion is a strategic error because it fails to utilize a potentially powerful source of support. At worst, to exclude religion risks making the legal academy irrelevant to the population we purportedly want to empower.

We have been blessed at St. Mary's with an environment in which those of us who are Catholic are able to come together to pray in our faith tradition. One colleague has been inspired to join the Catholic Church. Several others who were "lapsed" Catholics have begun to attend services on an occasional basis. But what is especially satisfying to me is the willingness of non-Catholics to respect the peculiarities of Catholic traditions and to join us enthusiastically in carrying out the Catholic and Marianist missions of the Law School. Protestants, Jews, Muslims, Hindus, agnostics, and even a few atheists have played critical roles. Diversity poses challenges, and paradise on earth does not exist,

29. Cf. Anthony V. Alfieri, *Reconstructive Poverty Law Practice: Learning Lessons of Client Narrative*, 100 Yale L.J. 2107, 2111 (1991) (noting that "[l]awyer storytelling falsifies client story when lawyer narratives silence and displace client narratives").

even at St. Mary's University School of Law. Yet through daily interaction and collective work, this group of very diverse individuals has found a way to respect each other's traditions without denigrating the Catholic nature of St. Mary's. We have begun to understand each other.

"You're too defensive."

Defensiveness doesn't help in achieving understanding. Dialogue does. However difficult that dialogue may sometimes be, it is imperative that the dialogue on religion continue among those within the legal academy who seek to empower Hispanics. Working together on the common goal of empowerment, I believe we can begin to understand each other.

## Section 5 Feminism

Feminist legal theory, like critical legal studies and critical race theory, developed vigorously over the last quarter of the twentieth century. Feminist legal thought received considerable intellectual impetus from feminist thinking in fields outside law, such as literature and history. Because feminists have emphasized the importance of women's experience, no single position represents "the" feminist perspective. The essays in the following section illustrate this point. Although both authors are Catholic women, they disagree about feminist insights on faith and law.

Teresa Stanton Collett and Leslie Griffin struggle with the fundamental issue of sameness versus difference, of laws that treat men and women the same versus those that reflect difference. Relational feminism (drawing on an image of male-female complementarity and on the particularity of women's experience) and liberal feminism (drawing on the individualism and universalism of liberalism) provide the framework for both discussions. Collett asserts a compatibility between Christianity and relational feminism, while Griffin argues that feminist theology suggests that feminist legal theory should not abandon liberalism's gains.

# Independence or Interdependence? A Christian Response to Liberal Feminists

*Teresa Stanton Collett*

In considering the relation between orthodox Christianity and feminism, one is struck by the diversity of thought and emphasis within each of these "communities of faith." Christians divide over such questions as whether salvation is primarily communal or individual; the role of grace and works in salvation; even what texts should be included as Holy Scripture. Yet despite this diversity, there is unity arising from Christians' common beliefs. Christians believe that God created the universe in accordance with a divine plan, that people are estranged from God, and that God's plan included the life, death, and resurrection of Jesus Christ as the means of reconciling Creator and created.

Like Christianity, feminism contains diverse views. Liberal feminists believe that each individual has the moral "right" to create a "life story" pleasing to that individual.[1] They attack social structures as un-

---

1. "At the heart of liberty is the right to define one's own concept of existence, of meaning, of the universe, and of the mystery of human life. Beliefs about these matters could not define the attributes of personhood were they formed under compulsion of the State." *Planned Parenthood of Southeastern Pennsylvania v. Casey,* 505 U.S. 833, 851 (1992).

just, permitting men the freedom to fashion their individual stories, while compelling women to act out preordained scripts that largely cast them as bit players in men's dramas.[2] This restricted role for women forms the primary complaint of liberal feminists. They argue that a just society allows each individual to determine the activities she or he wishes to pursue, free from any prescribed role. They demand the elimination of social and legal barriers to women's full participation in the economic, intellectual, and political life of society.[3]

In contrast, relational feminists assert that although men and women are persons of equal moral worth, fundamental differences exist between the sexes, and a just society must reflect those differences.[4] These feminists claim that past social structures are unjust because they ignored or undervalued women's views and virtues in structuring our common life. Unlike liberal feminists, who argue that no relevant differences exist, relational feminists argue that present social structures reflect a harmful misunderstanding of the relevancy of genuine sexual differences.[5] They measure their success by the public sphere's inclusion and valuing of women, and of the special characteristics and contributions of our sex.

Although other schools of thought exist within the feminist movement, theories developed by liberal and relational feminists dominate the legal and political debate in this country.[6] Feminists, antifeminists, and policymakers have struggled with the question: are men and women essentially the same or essentially different, and where differences exist (whether essential or individual), how should those differences be accounted for in law and society?

What unifies the feminist movement is not a particular answer to this question but rather a belief that the present social order has not justly accounted for whatever differences exist. Feminists are united in their beliefs that contemporary society is hierarchical, that women are subordinated to men in the hierarchy, and that this subordination is "not good, not ordained by nature, and not inevitable."[7] Any attempt to move beyond this negative definition of femi-

2. John Stuart Mill, *Subjection of Women* 232–33 (1869).

3. *Id.* at 243.

4. *E.g.,* Robin West, *Jurisprudence and Gender,* 55 U. Chi. L. Rev. 1 (1988).

5. *See* Sylvia A. Law, *Rethinking Sex and the Constitution,* 132 U. Pa. L. Rev. 955, 969–83 (1984).

6. Martha Minnow, *Introduction: Finding Our Paradoxes, Affirming Our Beyond,* 24 Harv. C.R.-C.L. L. Rev. 1, 2–3 (1989).

7. *Feminist Jurisprudence* 3 (Patricia Smith ed., 1993).

nism, and define the movement by what it proposes rather than opposes, risks gross inaccuracy.[8]

Yet absent an affirmative intellectual agenda, feminism risks becoming captive to hedonism, radical individualism, shallow egoism, or political opportunism. None of these approaches has contributed to the creation of a just society when pursued by men, and there is no evidence that a different outcome will be achieved if they are pursued by women. Christianity offers the affirmative vision of women's participation in the world needed by contemporary liberal feminism.

## A BRIEF INTELLECTUAL HISTORY OF THE
## NATURE OF WOMAN

At the core of liberal feminism is the demand for recognition of the equal dignity of men and women. In contemporary America, such a claim seems beyond argument. Yet this has not been the case throughout history.

In early Greek philosophy, the moral equality of men and women was disputed. Plato argued in favor of equality on the basis that sexuality was not an essential aspect of the person. He reasoned that the human person was composed of body and soul. The body was merely the material manifestation of the person, and sexual identity was simply one aspect of that manifestation. The soul was the true nature of the person, and was neither male nor female, as evidenced by the ability of both men and women to acquire wisdom and virtue.[9]

Aristotle rejected Plato's dualistic understanding of the human person, arguing that the soul did not exist free from the body. The body, as an integral part of the person, necessarily was either male or female. Because men and women were members of the same species, he accounted for their differences by categorizing them as contraries or opposites. In Aristotle's metaphysics, opposites were defined by the absence of a characteristic found in the other. Thus he came to define woman as a person deprived of the essential characteristic of maleness, "the female is as it were a deformed male."[10] This deprivation manifested itself in women's failure to conform their behavior to the judgments reached through their deliberative faculty. Women were capable of reasoning,

8. *Id.* at 8.

9. *Id.* at 80. Plato's views of the sexless soul were subsequently espoused in Mary Astell, *Essay in Defense of the Female Sex* (1697).

10. Aristotle, *Generation of Animals* 725 at 25–28, *discussed in* Sr. Prudence Allen, R.S.M., *The Concept of Woman: The Aristotelian Revolution, 750 BC–AD 1250* 97–98 (1985).

but their nature precluded reason directing their activities in an ordered way. Thus virtuous women were to submit to their fathers or husbands because men were capable of directing their actions through deliberation.[11]

Augustine was critical of both Plato's conclusion that equality exists due to the absence of sexual identity and Aristotle's conclusion that women are inferior. Although traces of both approaches can be found in his writings, in the *City of God* Augustine argued that people will be resurrected in their male and female forms.[12] This led to his belief that men and women could be both equal and different. Unfortunately, Augustine did not fully develop this theory, instead limiting the sexes' equality to heaven, and continuing Aristotle's claim that, in this world, women reflected perfection only when joined with their husbands.[13]

Thomas Aquinas also discounted women's earthly existence in his discussion of "whether woman should have been made in the first production of things?"

As regards individual nature, woman is defective and misbegotten, for the active power in the male seed tends to the production of a perfect likeness according to the masculine sex; while the production of woman comes from defect in the active power, or from some material indisposition, or even from some external influence, such as that of a south wind, which is moist, as the Philosopher observes. On the other hand, as regards universal human nature, woman is not misbegotten, but is included in nature's intention as directed to the work of generation. Now the universal intention of nature depends on God, Who is the universal Author of nature. Therefore, in producing nature, God formed not only the male but also the female.[14]

In discussing whether women would be resurrected in their feminine form St. Thomas echoed Augustine's idea, and advanced it by arguing that woman achieves perfection through grace acting upon her feminine nature rather than upon that part of woman's nature that had no sexual identity.[15] This recognition of women's capacity to be perfected through grace while maintaining their sexual identity was a significant improvement over Aristotle's theory of women's general inferiority.[16]

11. *Id.* at 113.

12. Augustine, *City of God*, bk. XII, § 17. The significance of this is discussed in Allen, *supra* note 10, at 219–21.

13. Allen, *supra* note 10, at 222, quoting Augustine, *De Genesis ad Litteram*.

14. Thomas Aquinas, *The Summa Theologica*, ques. 92, art. 1. *See also id.* at ques. 93, art. 4.

15. Allen, *supra* note 10, at 385.

16. See Michael Nolan, *What Aquinas Never Said About Women*, First Things, Nov. 1998, at II–12.

Although other concepts of the nature of sexual identity existed in Aquinas's time, his views came to dominate western European discourse about the nature and role of women.[17] How these ideas affected the day-to-day lives of men and women is more complicated.

> Particularism [the belief that each being had a discrete telos and should aspire to the specific forms of excellence appropriate to its own kind] presupposed a commitment to hierarchy in society as well as in nature: some men naturally ruled over others, and all men ruled over the women of their own family. That hierarchical vision, while consigning women to the rule of men, offered them discrete opportunities to excel as women and, because it envisioned the rights of collectivities as prior to the rights of individuals, even opportunities to serve as delegates or representatives of their communities. Thus a woman might, in the absence of her husband or father, (temporarily) occupy the role of "lord of the manor."
>
> . . .
>
> Thus noble women, although outranked by noble men, themselves outranked peasant men as well as bourgeois and peasant women. The difference between women and men was taken as a constitutive aspect of all social groups and even of comprehensive ideologies or religious beliefs, but was not taken as an overriding or universal principle of social organization.[18]

Nowhere is this distinction between treatment based upon class rather than sex more apparent than in the successful reign of Elizabeth I in England from 1558 to 1603.[19]

In the seventeenth century liberal thinkers began to contest the notion that social status should determine the right to command, arguing that the individual was the source of all natural rights and authority.[20] In early liberal discourse, it was assumed that the individual was male and little attention was directed to the status of women.[21] At the close of the eighteenth century, this began to change as arguments emerged in favor of women's equality.

17. The work of Hildegard of Bingen provided a rival conception of sexuality premised upon the complementarity of the sexes. Allen, *supra* note 10, at 292–315, 410–12.

18. Elizabeth Fox-Genovese, *Feminism Without Illusions: A Critique of Individualism* 116 (1991). This is confirmed in Mill, *supra* note 2, at 230.

19. The idea that a woman might rule as queen was not without detractors. *See* John Knox, *First Blast of the Trumpet Against the Monstrous Regiment of Women* (1558) *quoted in* George Catlin, Introduction, *in* Mary Wollstonecraft, *Vindication of the Rights of Woman* (1792) and Mill, *supra* note 2.

20. *E.g.,* Thomas Hobbes, *Leviathan* (1651), John Locke, *Two Treatises of Government* (1690), and one of their intellectual successors, Charles Montesquieu, *The Spirit of the Laws* (1748).

21. Fox-Genovese, *supra* note 18, at 123.

In 1792 Mary Wollstonecraft published *A Vindication of the Rights of Woman.* She argued that God created people as rational creatures so that they might, through the exercise of reason, move from self-love to the discovery of God's wisdom and goodness, and thus enjoy "a more godlike portion of happiness."[22] To encourage this movement toward God, society should seek to educate its young to "enable the individual to attain such habits of virtue as will render it independent."[23] Women, as well as men, were in need of this education, both for their individual improvement and for the economic protection of their families and themselves.[24]

## THE CHRISTIAN ACCOUNT OF THE MORAL
## EQUALITY OF THE SEXES

As originally formulated, many of Mary Wollstonecraft's ideas are confirmed in the Christian understanding of the nature and needs of women. Christ, too, lived in a time and place that refused to recognize the equal dignity of women. He also was offended by the creation and exercise of male prerogatives that left women without support and status.

This offense is evidenced by Jesus' exchange with the Pharisees concerning divorce.[25] Although wives were not permitted to divorce their husbands, Jewish law permitted husbands to divorce their wives if the circumstances met the requirements of Mosaic law.[26] The content of these requirements was disputed at the time. Followers of the Hillel school believed that divorce was permitted if "a man's wife should burn his food or even be less pleasing to him than another woman."[27] Members of the Shammai school required that the wife commit adultery or some sexual offense before divorce was permitted.[28]

A group of Pharisees approached Jesus, asking Him, "Is it lawful for a man to divorce his wife for any cause whatever?" Jesus responded, "Have you not read that from the beginning the Creator 'made them male and female' and said,

22. Wollstonecraft, *supra* note 19, at 17–18.

23. *Id.* at 25.

24. *Id.* at 56, 70, and 72.

25. Matthew 19:1–9 and Mark 10:2–12. See also John Paul II, *On the Dignity and Vocation of Women* ¶ 12 (1988).

26. *A New Catholic Commentary on Holy Scripture* 782 (Reginald C. Fuller et al. eds., 1969) ("Divorce was a privilege of the husband alone").

27. *Id.* at 937 citing Rabbi Aqiba c. CE 120.

28. *A New Catholic Commentary on Holy Scripture, supra* note 26, at 782, 927.

'For this reason a man shall leave his father and mother and be joined to his wife, and the two shall become one flesh'? So they are no longer two, but one flesh. Therefore, what God has joined together, no human being must separate."

This response seemed contrary to Jewish law, which clearly recognized the husband's right to divorce his wife, so the Pharisees asked, "Then why did Moses command that the man give the woman a bill of divorce and dismiss [her]?"

Jesus' response reveals His understanding that divorce was desired by men, harmed women, and was contrary to God's original plan for humanity. "Because of the hardness of your hearts Moses allowed you to divorce your wives, but from the beginning it was not so. I say to you, whoever divorces his wife (unless the marriage is unlawful) and marries another commits adultery."[29]

By his answer, Christ restores the original relationship of permanent union by marriage. Neither spouse is permitted to destroy that union. In this way, He reestablishes the equal duty of husband and wife to live out the commitment made in marriage.

By His reference to "the beginning," He directs the Pharisees to the Genesis accounts of the creation of man and woman. He reminds them of Genesis 1:27, "God created man in his image; in the divine image he created him; male and female he created them." From this passage, it is clear that God willed the creation of both man and woman—and both are created in His image. Neither is a defective or "misbegotten" version of the other.

Christ also directs the Pharisees to the second, yet older, creation account, Genesis 2:18–25. In this account man is created first, but after his creation God concludes "It is not good for the man to be alone. I will make a suitable partner for him."[30] This verse can be interpreted in many ways. It may be read as reflecting the social nature of the person and the universal need for human companionship.[31] It also can be understood more specifically to reflect the need of man for woman.[32]

---

29. Matthew 19:3–9.

30. Genesis 2:18.

31. "Being a person in the image and likeness of God thus also involves existing in a relationship, in relation to the other 'I.'" John Paul II, *supra* note 25, at § 7 (1988).

32. Both interpretations are suggested by Calvin in his commentary on Genesis. 1 John Calvin, *Commentaries on Genesis*, pt. 6 available at <www.iclnet.org/pub/resources/text/ipb-e/epl-01/cvgn1–06.txt>. Additional reflections on this verse can be found in John Paul II, *Original Unity of Man and Woman* 43–54 (1981).

"So the Lord God cast a deep sleep on the man, and while he was asleep, he took out one of his ribs and closed up its place with flesh. The Lord God then built up into a woman the rib that he had taken from the man."[33] The reference to Adam entering a deep sleep before the creation of woman has led to speculation that God re-created the human person into the complements of man and woman. "Perhaps, therefore, the analogy of sleep indicates here not so much a passing from consciousness to subconsciousness, as a specific return to non-being (sleep contains an element of annihilation of man's conscious existence), that is, to the moment preceding the creation, in order that, through God's creative initiative, solitary 'man' emerge from it again in his double unity as male and female."[34] This interpretation avoids any moral primacy of the male due to his creation earlier in time.

The significance of God's using a rib of Adam to create Eve has also been read to support the equal dignity of women. Thomas Aquinas propounded a specific question on this passage: "Whether the woman was fittingly made from the rib of man?"[35] "It was right for woman to be made from a rib of man. First, to signify the social union of man and woman, for the woman should neither use authority over man, and so she was not made from his head; nor was it right for her to be subject to man's contempt as his slave, and so she was not made from his feet. Secondly, for the sacramental signification; for from the side of Christ sleeping on the Cross the Sacraments flowed—namely, blood and water—on which the Church was established."[36] By this answer Aquinas responds to those who might argue that equality requires that woman be made from dust as was man, or that the creation of woman from man renders man incomplete, and thus imperfect.

This creation story next reveals Adam's recognition of woman as one like himself. "When he [the Lord God] brought her to the man, the man said: 'This one, at last, is bone of my bones and flesh of my flesh; This one shall be called 'woman,' for out of 'her man' this one has been taken."[37] Scripture thus provides an eloquent answer to those who seek to deny woman's worth because of her differences from man. The true measure of woman's dignity and moral value lies in her direct creation by God in the divine image, and her shared humanity with man.

33. Genesis 2:21–22.
34. John Paul II, *supra* note 32, at 64.
35. Aquinas, *supra* note 14, at ques. 92, art. 3.
36. *Id.*
37. Genesis 2:22.

This passage concludes "That is why a man leaves his father and mother and clings to his wife, and the two of them become one body."[38] This verse explains the divine plan that men and women attain their mutual fulfillment in communion with one another. It provides the basis for the Christian claim that authentic equality of the sexes must be founded upon personalism and complementarity, rather than the exaggerated individualism that appears to lie at the heart of contemporary liberal feminism.

## INDIVIDUALISM AND LIBERAL FEMINISM

Liberal feminists ground their claims for women's equality in the ideal of individualism. Individualism developed as a response to the then-existing political and social order in which the rights of the individual derived from his or her relationship to others. In the early feudal system, the standing of the family and local community determined the status of the individual. This hierarchical order, in turn, arose from "the belief that each being had a discrete telos and should aspire to the specific forms of excellence appropriate to its own kind."[39]

The proponents of liberal philosophy disputed the existence of a discrete telos to be found in the person's "station in life." Instead, they argued that the political and social rights of man arose by virtue of the social contract wherein people exchanged their natural state of freedom for the protection of the collectivity. Society was born not as a divinely created hierarchy but as a human arrangement in furtherance of individual peace and security.[40]

Underlying this theory of political society was an understanding of human nature that elevated reason above all other characteristics. Reason was that which distinguished the person from all other creatures, and thus it was reason that defined the nature of the human person. This understanding of rationality as the essence of the human person was not new to philosophy. Plato, Aristotle, Augustine, and Aquinas each recognized rationality as the hallmark of humanity. The innovation found in liberal philosophy was the assertion that because there is a universal capacity to reason, there should be an equality of natural rights. Although this affirmation of each person's intrinsic value and the right of the individual to participate in communal decisionmaking is desirable, the

38. Genesis 2:22–23.

39. Fox-Genovese, *supra* note 18, at 116.

40. Hobbes, *supra* note 20, at 100 and Jean-Jacques Rousseau, *The Social Contract or Principles of Political Right* (1762) *reprinted in* Monroe C. Beardsley, *The European Philosophers from Descartes to Nietzsche* 330 (1960).

unintended consequence of liberal political philosophy was a flattening and loosening of the social ties binding families and communities together.[41]

Social ties loosened because communal structures of support and obligation like the family, the church, and the community, previously understood as pre-existing the individual and having independent moral significance, were reinterpreted as voluntary associations for personal fulfillment.[42] The good of these social structures increasingly came to be understood as the aggregate of the good of the individuals participating within them.[43]

The good of the individual came largely to be defined as the goals the person sought after reasonable deliberation. As each person was equally capable of reason, each could best discern the ends he or she should seek.[44] Though not logically required, this conclusion led to the further conclusion that if each should be free to pursue his own ends, there is no basis to dispute the individual's choice of one end over others.[45] The best form of government, then, avoided interference with any act of the individual unless interference was necessary for the protection of others.[46] Thus "the individual is not accountable to society for his actions, in so far as these concern the interest of no person but himself."[47]

Contemporary liberal feminists built upon this limited account of the human person and community, arguing that women were capable of reason and thus entitled to equal inclusion in political society. They defined their political agenda as one of "liberating women" from what they characterized as unjust so-

41. "Individualism flattened particularistic distinctions by positing a single, uniform, and universal model of excellence—the individual—and overthrew particularistic premises by assuming that the individual preceded all groups, which could only derive their meaning and legitimacy from their conformity to and respect for individual rights." Fox-Genovese, *supra* note 18, at 116.

42. Contemporary political liberalism sees people as "free and independent selves unclaimed by ties antecedent to choice." Michael Sandel, Freedom of Conscience or Freedom of Choice? *in Articles of Faith, Articles of Peace* 76 (James Davison Hunter and Os Guinness eds., 1990).

43. See Gregg Temple, *Freedom of Contract and Intimate Relationships,* 8 Harv. J.L. and Pub. Pol'y 121, 150 (1985) ("Where marriage once served a variety of institutional functions, the current marriage is a vehicle for personal happiness and fulfillment").

44. John Stuart Mill, *On Liberty* 95 (1859).

45. *Id.* at 76.

46. *Id.* at 9.

47. *Id.* This vision of the human person underlies what Justice Brandeis described as the "right to be left alone." *Olmstead v. United States,* 277 U.S. 438, 478 (1928).

cial structures that forced women out of the "meaningful" sphere of public life, and into what they perceived as passive and infantilizing domesticity.[48]

This agenda simultaneously emphasized the universality of reason as the measure of human value, and the individuality of woman as the source of her rights, in opposition to the historical treatment of women as universally "other" from man. Liberal feminists embraced "noninterference" as the ultimate political goal to be attained. The "right to be left alone" or the "right of privacy" became the passwords adopted by these feminists seeking access to the political and economic structures of the United States. The goal of noninterference explains the embrace of no-fault divorce and unlimited access to abortion by liberal feminists.[49]

## EQUALITY GROUNDED IN PERSONALISM AND COMPLEMENTARITY

This ideal of noninterference as a primary norm of political community is contrary to the Christian understanding of human nature and human community. "You shall love your neighbor as yourself" requires something different from the liberal command "You shall not interfere with the liberty of another."[50] In large part the difference between these two visions arises from differing understandings of human nature and human community.

Unlike liberalism, which asserts rationality as the essence of the person and therefore grounds the rights and equality of the person in the ability to reason, Christianity understands the essence of the person to be found in his or her relationship to God. People are distinct from animals by virtue of God's continuing involvement in our creation, our bearing of his divine image, and our eternal destiny to live with him after this life. Through our relationship with God, we come to recognize all people as our neighbors, having a moral

48. Simone de Beauvoir, *The Second Sex, excerpted in The Feminist Papers: From Adams to de Beauvoir* 674–704 (Alice S. Rossi ed., 1988) (analogizing women's situation in the 1940s to that of black slaves in pre–Civil War United States); Betty Friedan, *The Feminine Mystique* (1963).

49. It also explains the failure of liberal feminism to anticipate the harms visited upon women once these policy choices were implemented. *E.g.,* Lenore J. Weitzman, *The Divorce Revolution: The Unexpected Social and Economic Consequences for Women and Children in America* (1985), and Thomas R. Eller, *Informed Consent Civil Actions for Post-Abortion Psychological Trauma,* 71 Notre Dame L. Rev. 639 (1996).

50. *See* Matthew 22:39.

claim upon us, independent of the positive law or the requirements of citizenship.[51]

This ordering of relationships, and the nature of the claims arising from them, are described in Scripture: "[A scholar of the law tested Jesus] by asking, 'Teacher, which commandment in the law is the greatest?' [Jesus] said to him, 'You shall love the Lord, your God, with all your heart, with all your soul, and with all your mind. This is the first and greatest commandment. The second is like it: You shall love your neighbor as yourself. The whole law and the prophets depend on these two commandments.'"[52] The first and primary relationship for every person is his or her relationship with God. Through this relationship we learn who we are, that we are valued, and that the proper form of relationships is mutual love. This understanding of the human person is referred to as "personalism" in theological and philosophical literature.[53]

The human person is innately social. Relationships with others are a constitutive aspect of each person. God's relationship with the human person forms the Christian's understanding of self, and acts as the model for relationships with others. As God's response to us is love, our proper response to one another is love.

Christians understand the absence of relationships as isolation and a product of human failure. This is best seen in the second account of creation and the story of the fall of Adam and Eve. In the second chapter of Genesis, God creates man and sets him in the Garden of Eden to care for it with this charge: "You are free to eat from any of the trees of the garden except the tree of knowledge of good and bad. From that tree you shall not eat; the moment you eat from it you are surely doomed to die." Soon after this, God creates woman because "it is not good for the man to be alone." The chapter concludes with Adam's immediate recognition of Eve as "bone of my bones and flesh of my flesh."[54]

In both creation accounts, God and humanity exist in loving communion with each other. It is not until the third chapter of Genesis that Creator and created, as well as man and woman, become estranged. Eve and Adam transgress

51. Dietrich Bonhoeffer, *The Cost of Discipleship* (1959). "We are separated from one another by an unbridgeable gulf of otherness and strangeness which resists all our attempts to overcome it. . . . Christ stands between us, and we only get into touch with our neighbours through him." *Id.* at 98.

52. Matthew 22:34–40. *See also* Mark 12:28–34.

53. E.g., Jacques Maritain, *The Person and the Common Good* (1946).

54. Genesis 2:2–20.

the one law that God pronounces before giving them dominion over all the earth. They eat the fruit of the tree of the knowledge of good and evil.[55]

By violating the law of God, both man and woman act contrary to full communion with God. Instead of eagerly joining Him when He walks in the garden, they seek to hide themselves from God.[56] Thus even before divine judgment, Adam and Eve evidence their separation from God. "The Lord God then called to the man and asked him, 'Where are you?' He answered, 'I heard you in the garden; but I was afraid, because I was naked, so I hid myself.' Then he asked, 'Who told you that you were naked? You have eaten, then, from the tree of which I had forbidden you to eat!' The man replied, 'The woman whom you put here with me—she gave me fruit from the tree, so I ate it.' The Lord God then asked the woman, 'Why did you do such a thing?' The woman answered, 'The serpent tricked me into it, so I ate it.'"[57]

This exchange illustrates the harm done by the original sin, and foretells the future conflict between men and women. By his answer to God, Adam attempts to isolate himself from Eve, blaming her for his disobedience. He suggests that God, himself, is also blameworthy for placing this "temptress" in his life. For her part, Eve denies responsibility by blaming the serpent, suggesting that she did not understand the import of her actions—"the serpent tricked me into it." Neither Adam nor Eve are willing to acknowledge their responsibility for the sin and seek God's forgiveness for their transgression. This failure of the first parents of humanity results in the same harm every evil inflicts; a disruption of unity with God and between persons.

God then pronounces judgment for their sin. The serpent is condemned to slither on his belly and be the enemy of woman.[58] Woman is destined to experience pain in childbirth, "yet your urge shall be for your husband, and he shall be your master."[59] Man will now be required to toil against natural adversity his entire life in order to survive, and in the end he will die, returning to the dust from which he was made.[60] Thus hardship and human mastery are introduced into the world, not as part of God's original plan but as the result of the original sin of Adam and Eve.

Before original sin, Scripture reveals an essential equality and delight be-

55. Genesis 3:1–7.
56. Genesis 3:8.
57. Genesis 3:9–13.
58. Genesis 3:14–15.
59. Genesis 3:16.
60. Genesis 3:1–19.

tween woman and man. This joy is repudiated when Adam and Eve each seek to evade the consequences of their sin by blaming the other. Mutual concern and responsibility are replaced with claims of individual justification. Thus a new order between men and women is introduced. This new order is based not upon interdependence and delight but upon claims of independence and mutual suspicion.

God recognizes the personal culpability of each yet continues to deal with them as husband and wife. In the creation of Eve, both God and Adam recognized man's need for woman.[61] Woman's need for man is implicit in the fact that she was created as his companion and helpmate, but it remains unspoken until God's judgment: "Your urge shall be for your husband, and he shall be your master."[62] In this judgment, the interdependence that is present in the original creation becomes a hierarchy based upon the mutual need of man and woman.

This mutual need has often been distorted into mutual use of each other, as the means to sexual, material, or emotional self-gratification. What is common to wrongful relationships is not the nature of the needs met through the interaction of man and woman but the form the interaction takes. "The values of being are replaced by those of having. The only goal which counts is the pursuit of one's own material well-being. The so-called 'quality of life' is interpreted primarily or exclusively as economic efficiency, inordinate consumerism, physical beauty and pleasure, to the neglect of more profound dimensions—interpersonal, spiritual and religious—of existence."[63]

The hierarchy of husband and wife described in God's judgment resembles that of men and women described by Aristotle, when Aristotle concluded that virtue for women consisted of submission to men, because men were more fully able to direct their actions by reason. Eve defended her actions as motivated by a lack of understanding; thus she was subjected to the tutelage of her husband.[64] Universalization of this norm within marriage as a norm requiring submission

61. "It is not good for the man to be alone. I will make a suitable partner for him." Genesis 2:18.

62. Genesis 3:16.

63. Pope John Paul II, *The Gospel of Life* ¶ 23 (1995).

64. The form of this tutelage is best described by St. Paul's oft-misunderstood passage on marriage, in which he instructs wives to submit to their husbands, and husbands to love their wives "as Christ loved the church." Ephesians 5:22–33. Rarely do non-Christian commentators focus on the standard imposed upon husbands, a standard of loving self-sacrifice, even unto death.

of all women to all men and abuse of the marriage relationship are the source of many of the practices and attitudes that feminists legitimately decry.

Liberal feminists are correct in asserting that women and men are of equal dignity. They also are correct in their claims that women often are unjustly excluded from aspects of the political, economic, and social life of the community by barriers constructed for no greater purpose than the personal comfort and advantage of particular men or a class of men. The error of contemporary liberal feminism lies not in these claims but in the attempt to achieve equality through a false relativism, and freedom through denial of human relationships and the mutual dependence of men and women.

By embracing individualism as the means to equality, liberal feminists deny those aspects of the human person that lie beyond reason, and seemingly demand no greater opportunity than the opportunity to make the same egoistic mistakes that men have made in the abuse of their freedom. In demanding the "right to be left alone" liberal feminists deny the relational aspect of the human person, thrusting women into isolation from their fathers, brothers, husbands, and children. Neither women nor men can prosper under such a regime.

What the Christian account of human nature and community offers liberal feminists is an affirmation of the equal dignity of all human persons, and a truer foundation for crafting authentic equality between the sexes. By focusing upon the natural complementarity of women and men, and by seeking to restore the original friendship of both with God, feminists will have a firmer foundation for their efforts to help build a society characterized by mutual respect and solidarity between the sexes, and love and concern between individuals. It may be that relational feminism, with its recognition of the importance of relationships and its recognition of the differences between men and women, is more compatible than liberal feminism with the Christian vision of community and the complementarity of the sexes.

The intrinsic worth of a woman does not lie in her ability to reason. Nor does it arise from any "work of her hands" or "work of her womb." It is not dependent upon any recognition by authorities or individuals. Each woman's worth derives from God's creation of and continuing love for her person.

Concern for that person is not merely the mandate of political solidarity with those who are our mothers, sisters, wives, or daughters. Nor is it only the product of enlightened self-interest, by which we recognize the risk to ourselves when we validate oppression of others. It is a part of our obligation to God, each other, and ourselves. Contemporary feminism has much to gain by embracing this understanding of the human person and replacing the present demand for "the right to be left alone" with "the right to be respected as one of God's children."

As Pope John Paul II has said, "In transforming culture so that it supports life, women occupy a place, in thought and action, which is unique and decisive. It depends upon them to promote a 'new feminism' which rejects the temptation of imitating models of 'male domination,' in order to acknowledge and affirm the true genius of women in every aspect of the life of society, and overcome all discrimination, violence and exploitation."[65]

God created man and woman in His image. The talents and gifts of each are necessary to the success of society. Just as a child best prospers when cared for and loved by both mother and father, human society flourishes when the social, political and economic structures reflect the thoughts and efforts of both men and women. This is the insight Christianity offers feminism, and this is the insight that will lead to authentic equality.

65. John Paul II, *supra* note 63, at ¶ 99.

# Citizen-Soldiers Are Like Priests:
# Feminism in Law and Theology

*Leslie Griffin*

Does feminist theology contribute to American legal theory?[1] The academic disciplines of political science, psychology, and philosophy have been more influential in feminist legal theory. For example, Carol Gilligan's *In a Different Voice,* with its identification of women's and men's differences in moral reasoning, has influenced reflections on the meaning of legal equality. Her models of justice and care raise significant questions, for example, about whether equality requires the same or different treatment for men and women. Feminist theology's relation to law is less developed and less apparent. Nonetheless, its history offers some reminders to feminists that liberalism remains an important component of any feminist legal theory. Feminist theology reminds us that "a broader-based ideal for both women and men that combines virtues and desirable traits traditionally associated with women with virtues and desirable traits traditionally associated with men" is unlikely to occur absent women's access to traditionally male institutions.[2]

1. This essay is dedicated to Margaret Farley, who teaches feminist theology with justice and with care.
2. James P. Sterba, *Justice for Here and Now* 80 (1998).

Christian feminist theology shares with other feminisms a three-stage process of the critique, retrieval, and reformulation of tradition. In theological writings the critique stage has been the most vigorous. The retrieval of feminist aspects of the Christian tradition and the reformulation of the Christian tradition in light of feminist principles have proven to be more difficult.

I begin with the critique. Feminist theologians have criticized those aspects of the Christian tradition that do not promote the well-being of women (and thus of all human persons). A classic article in feminist theology—a theological precursor, if you will, to Gilligan's psychological analysis—is Valerie Saiving's 1960 essay "The Human Situation: A Feminine View." Saiving began her essay: "I am a student of theology; I am also a woman." Thirteen years earlier, at the beginning of her studies, she had seen no need to assert her "sexual identity." By the time of publication, however, she had decided that identity mattered, and that it was significant that "theology has been written almost exclusively by men."[3]

Thus Saiving's criticism: women's voices have been excluded from Christian theology. Her solution: women's experience must now be included in theological reflection.

Saiving argued that the incorporation of women's experience would upset traditional formulations of Christian theology. Her own contribution was to the doctrine of sin. She argued that Christian theologians' identification of sin with pride was rooted in men's experience and inadequate to women's experience. Like Gilligan, Saiving noted many caveats against employing the different definitions of men's and women's experience too restrictively. Nonetheless she identified a woman's sin, distinct from man's:

> For the temptations of woman *as woman* are not the same as the temptations of man *as man,* and the specifically feminine forms of sin—"feminine" not because they are confined to women or because women are incapable of sinning in other ways but because they are outgrowths of the basic feminine character structure—have a quality which can never be encompassed by such terms as "pride" and "will-to-power." They are better suggested by such items as triviality, distractibility, and diffuseness; lack of an organizing center or focus; dependence on others for one's own self-definition; tolerance at the expense of standards of excellence; inability to respect the boundaries of privacy; sentimentality, gossipy sociability, and mistrust of reason—in short, underdevelopment or negation of the self.[4]

3. Valerie Saiving, The Human Situation: A Feminine View, *in Womanspirit Rising: A Feminist Reader in Religion* 25, 25 (Carol P. Christ and Judith Plaskow, eds., 1979).
    4. *Id.* at 37.

Underdevelopment or negation of the self—the sin that Christian theologians ignore by neglecting the experience of women. Women are tempted to devalue themselves; Christianity reinforces this deficiency by urging them not to be proud. Note that this problem is not merely one of neglect but of potential harm to women. If a woman with an underdeveloped self listens to Christian theology, "she will try to strangle those impulses" that encourage appropriate independence or autonomy.[5] Saiving's thesis exemplifies the criticism phase: a tradition that ignores women's experience does harm to women and conflicts with feminism's fundamental commitment to the well-being of women.

Since 1960 feminist theologians have focused on chronicling and interpreting women's experience; experience has been the watchword of feminist theology. That emphasis on experience helps to explain why stages two and three—the retrieval of texts about women and the reformulation of contemporary Christian life—have posed difficult questions of interpretation and implementation. Women criticize a tradition for its exclusion of women's experience but then must determine how to recover the missing voices. First, they search to discover whether that experience can be gleaned from the historical record. Then they ask, for example, whether the experience of women in Scripture or in the early church is normative for Christians in the twentieth century. They question whether current experience is a theological source, canonical in its own way. If it is, then women's experience provides the standard by which to reject scriptural texts and the teachings of church authorities, and the foundation upon which to construct a reformulated Christian tradition that promotes the well-being of women as well as men.

This emphasis on experience, however, has provoked a new critique: that white middle- and upper-class women theologians (like men before them) privilege their own experience at the expense of other women's. New feminist theologies have emerged—womanist and mujerista as well as feminist, Asian and African as well as European and American.[6] Now all these experiences are brought to bear on such traditional theological doctrines as sin and grace, Christology and ecclesiology. The preeminent task for feminist theology has been the inclusion of a broad range of women's experiences in theological reflection.

This recognition of the diversity of women's experience has posed an addi-

5. *Id.* at 39.

6. Serene Jones, Women's Experience Between a Rock and a Hard Place: Feminist, Womanist and Mujerista Theologies in North America, *in Horizons in Feminist Theology* 33, 33–53 (Rebecca S. Chopp and Sheila G. Davaney, eds., 1997).

tional problem for the third stage of the reformulation of the Christian tradition for the present life of the church. Feminist theology is practical. As Lisa
Sowle Cahill writes: "Virtually by definition, feminist theology is 'moral' theology or ethics. It emerges from a practical situation of injustice and aims at social and political change."[7] Feminism's emphasis on diverse experience, however, poses many problems for practical moral questions. Feminist ethics begins
with a normative opposition to the exclusion and oppression of women. Yet
once one emphasizes the diversity of women's experience, how can one generalize about women's experience and draw normative ethical conclusions from
it? Because such generalization may exclude women's voices anew, some feminists resist universal claims. As Cahill phrases it, "A nagging relativism plagues
feminism insofar as it appeals to 'experience' precisely on the grounds that no
'universalist' definition of women has been genuinely adequate to women's reality."[8]

The relativism–universalism debate is ongoing. Many feminist theologians
focus on the description of a broad range of women's experiences. Others argue
that feminist theology must retain normative commitments to the well-being
of women. Theologians, with other feminists, ponder and debate essentialist
and nonessentialist accounts of human and woman's nature. They ask whether
feminism, with its fundamental commitment to the equal dignity of all human
persons, can abandon universalism.

In response to such questions, Susan Frank Parsons, for example, recommends that Christian feminism develop an "appropriate universalism that will
sustain and nourish a feminist ethic."[9] Some universalism is needed to protect
the rights of women because "a reluctance to speak normatively about human
life, and about gender, can have unfortunate consequences for feminism in actually obscuring the hierarchies which their emphasis on heterogeneity is meant
to overcome."[10] Margaret Farley writes that feminists have reasons "both to reject and to promote belief in a common or universal morality."[11] On the one
hand, theories of common morality have been antifeminist in the past when
they have applied male standards to women in the name of universality. As
Saiving explained, a universal male norm may do harm to women. Yet feminists

7. Lisa Sowle Cahill, *Feminist Ethics,* 51 Theological Studies 49, 50 (1990).

8. *Id.* at 63.

9. Susan Frank Parsons, *Feminism and Christian Ethics* 181 (1996).

10. *Id.* at 195.

11. Margaret A. Farley, Feminism and Universal Morality, *in Prospects for a Common
Morality* 170, 170 (Gene Outka and John P. Reeder, eds., 1993).

also have good reasons to support a common morality; "if theories of universal morality have been distortive and harmful, theories of unmitigated relativism are no less so."[12] Unmitigated relativism cannot foster the well-being of women.

Thus Farley recommends that some norms about the treatment of women "can and ought to cross (though not ignore) the boundaries of culture and history"; some voices should be rejected as untrue.[13] Because she recognizes the strengths and limitations of theories of common morality for women, Farley challenges Gilligan's "Care-Versus-Justice" approach.[14] Farley advocates a feminism that does not "insist on the *inevitability* of a dichotomy" between justice and care.[15] "The problem, one might say, is whether and how caring may be just."[16]

Thus my summary of feminist theology. It begins with criticism of traditions that exclude women, with some initial retrieval of the missing voices. The retrieval is incomplete, both in the quest for historical sources about women and in the characterization of women's present experience. Finally the reformulation has stalled with difficult questions of how one respects women's diverse experience while maintaining ethical standards that protect all women.

In this account of feminist theology, it is difficult to discern what is distinctive about theological feminism. Feminist theologians have borrowed from philosophy and other disciplines in order to critique Christian theology and to construct a modern theology that recognizes the rights of women. This appropriation of other subjects often obscures theology's contribution.

What makes any theology distinctive, of course, is its commitment to a particular tradition. Christian feminists have developed their theologies within the context of the history of Christianity and the ongoing life of the churches. In this history are lessons about the particularity and universality of theological commitments. For example, in the twentieth century many Christians of different denominations struggled to respect the diverse interpretations of the gospel while seeking unity in their faith in Jesus Christ. One noteworthy account of such ecumenism is the book that provides the framework for this anthology, *Christ and Culture*. H. Richard Niebuhr therein provided one influential interpretation of how Christians can acknowledge the diversity of

12. *Id.* at 178.
13. *Id.*
14. *Id.* at 183.
15. *Id.* at 184.
16. *Id.*

Christian experience while remaining unified by the Absolute. After presenting his five models, Niebuhr concluded that "it must be evident that neither extension nor refinement of study could bring us to the conclusive result that would enable us to say 'This is the Christian answer.'"[17] Indeed, seeking *the* Christian answer "would be an act of usurpation of the Lordship of Christ."[18]

Christian feminists have had a similar response to the diversity of women's experience. They understand that women's experience is womanist and mujerista as well as feminist, Asian and African as well as European and American. They recognize in those very different experiences the same attempt to respond to the gospel.

Niebuhr also faced the "nagging relativism" question. He argued that faith in the Absolute provides a unifying point for Christians in the midst of their relativities: "In the presence of other relativities men seem to have three possibilities: they can become nihilists and consistent skeptics who affirm that nothing can be relied upon; or they can flee to the authority of some relative position, affirming that a church, or a philosophy, or a value, like that of life for the self, is absolute; or they can accept their relativities with faith in the infinite Absolute to whom all their relative views, values and duties are subject."[19] So too might Christian feminists who overemphasize experience become skeptical of any ethical norms. Or they might absolutize one description of women's experience into an essentialism that is too limiting. The "appropriate universalism" or "universal morality" sought by Christian feminists reflects this struggle for unity in Jesus Christ amid diversity of experience. Christian feminists strive for an acceptance of relativity that retains faith in the infinite Absolute. Their experience may be a model for other feminists who seek some unity amid diversity in legal and political systems.

Another important feature of feminist theology is that it develops within actual communities and institutions. Theology has been practical and institutional, not only conceptual or theoretical. Christian feminists have faced divergent responses to their proposals across Christian churches. This institutional experience offers rich insights that feminist philosophy and psychology may be unable to provide.

In 1960, when Saiving wrote, "I am a student of theology; I am also a woman," she addressed more than the content of Christian theology. At that time, women's access to theological study was circumscribed, and they were

17. H. Richard Niebuhr, *Christ and Culture* 231 (1951).

18. *Id.* at 232.

19. *Id.* at 238.

barred from the ministry or priesthood in many Christian churches. Readers of Saiving might now focus on her interesting intellectual account of sin. Yet her article was also an argument for the participation of women in traditionally male institutions and jobs. Feminist theology has never aimed only at a theory of women's experience. It has advocated a greater role for women in the life of the church.

The implementation of feminist theology requires a greater role for women in the churches. Women's role in some denominations has changed; however, this development has not occurred in all Christian churches. For example, in Roman Catholicism, although the literature of feminist theology has expanded, the magisterium's opposition to the ordination of women has strengthened.

The church prohibits the ordination of women for a variety of reasons. First, it argues that the church's "constant tradition," "so firm in the course of the centuries" has forbidden women's ordination.[20] Although Jesus challenged the customary treatment of women in his day, he did not choose to ordain them. Thus the church may not ordain women in the twentieth century.

The church also employs theological arguments against women's ordination. For example, the priest represents Christ, "taking the role of Christ, to the point of being his very image."[21] Because the priesthood is of a "sacramental nature," the priest must be a perceptible and recognizable sign to the faithful. As the image of Christ, the sign to the faithful, the priest must be a man: "There would not be this 'natural resemblance' which must exist between Christ and his minister if the role of Christ were not taken by a man: in such a case it would be difficult to see in the minister the image of Christ. For Christ himself was and remains a man."[22] This different role for men and women does not connote the inequality of men and women. "Diversity of mission in no way compromises equality of personal dignity."[23]

Roman Catholic feminists have expressed vigorous (stage one) criticism of this interpretation of Catholic tradition. "Credit for first raising the issue of the ordination of women in the public forum of the Church goes to the original

20. Congregation for the Doctrine of the Faith, Inter Insigniores, *in From "Inter Insigniores" to "Ordinatio Sacerdotalis"* 21, 25–27 (United States Catholic Conference, 1998).

21. *Id.* at 41.

22. *Id.* at 43.

23. Concerning the Reply of the Congregation for the Doctrine of the Faith on the Doctrine Contained in the Apostolic Letter "Ordinatio Sacerdotalis," *in From "Inter Insigniores" To "Ordinatio Sacerdotalis"* 199, 201 (United States Catholic Conference, 1998). Hereinafter Reply of the Congregation.

Catholic feminist organization, the St. Joan's International Alliance founded in 1910 in Britain by Catholic women working for women's suffrage."[24] By 1959 the alliance requested greater participation of women in the church in anticipation of Vatican II. "A request that the diaconate be opened to women was adopted in 1961."[25] Petitions for ordination were submitted in 1963 after Pope John XXIII's encyclical letter *Pacem in terris* appeared.

In ensuing years, Catholic feminists have challenged the accuracy of the magisterium's account of the historical tradition, noting that even the Pontifical Biblical Commission concluded that nothing in Scripture precludes the ordination of women. In addition to historical arguments, they have relied on arguments about women's equality to insist that women and men should be treated equally—in the same way—concerning ordination. The church has consistently rejected any argument that women's ordination is an issue of equality.

The church also rejects feminist arguments about the experience of women. Perhaps those arguments have a nagging subjectivity: "It is sometimes said and written in books and periodicals that some women feel that they have a vocation to the priesthood. Such an attraction however noble and understandable, still does not suffice for a genuine vocation. In fact a vocation cannot be reduced to a mere personal attraction, which can remain purely subjective."[26]

Finally, the church warns women that they should not claim ordination as a right because priestly ordination is a matter of service. For example, a commentary to Pope John Paul's apostolic letter *Ordinatio Sacerdotalis* explains: "Whoever, man or woman, conceives of the priesthood in terms of personal affirmation, as a goal or point of departure in a career of human success, is profoundly mistaken, for the true meaning of Christian priesthood, whether it be the common priesthood of the faithful or, in a most special way, the ministerial priesthood, can only be found in the sacrifice of one's own being in union with Christ, in service of the brethren."[27]

This teaching, that ordination is not a matter of personal right or of social equality, is a fundamental theological tenet of the magisterium. Consider this argument in juxtaposition with Saiving's article on women's and men's sin. Is it

24. Rosemary Ruether, The Roman Catholic Story, *in Women of Spirit: Female Leadership in the Jewish and Christian Traditions* 373, 373 (Rosemary Ruether and Eleanor McLaughlin, eds., 1979).

25. *Id.* at 374.

26. Inter Insigniores, *supra* note 20, at 51.

27. Reply of the Congregation, *supra* note 23, at 201.

the sin of pride for women, but not for men, to claim ordination? Such papal texts remind us that feminist theologians like Saiving not only argued for a catalogue of women's experience but also demanded a public voice in the fora traditionally reserved to men.

The church now teaches that the prohibition of women's ordination is not open to debate, critique, retrieval, or reformulation. It must be "definitively held" by all Catholics.[28] "It is a matter of full definitive assent, that is to say irrevocable, to a doctrine taught infallibly by the Church."[29] The tradition is constant, it has been retrieved consistently throughout the centuries and it is not reformulable. In Niebuhr's terms, the authority of one position has become absolute. As we have seen, faced with such an absolute, many Catholic feminists have insisted that women's experience is authoritative, even in its diversity.

In contrast to the Roman Catholic experience, American feminist legal theory has undergone all three stages of critique, retrieval, and reformulation of tradition. A nineteenth-century Supreme Court opinion about women lawyers, for example, echoes the magisterium's arguments about ordination. The State of Illinois refused to grant Myra Bradwell admission to the state bar because she was a woman.[30]

The Supreme Court rejected Bradwell's argument that the state's action violated Article IV and Fourteenth Amendment privileges and immunities. More interesting is Justice Bradley's concurrence, which rejected the "supposed right of every person, man or woman, to engage in any lawful employment for a livelihood." There is no such "right of every person" because men and women have very different natures which equip them for different tasks. "The natural and proper timidity and delicacy which belongs to the female sex evidently unfits it for many of the occupations of civil life. . . . The constitution of the family organization, which is founded in the divine ordinance, as well as in the nature of things, indicates the domestic sphere as that which properly belongs to the domain and functions of womanhood. . . . In the nature of things it is not every citizen of every age, sex, and condition that is qualified for every calling and position."[31] In court and church we hear a similar argument: no personal right of every person to advocacy or ordination.

28. John Paul II, *Ordinatio Sacerdotalis, in From "Inter Insigniores" to "Ordinatio Sacerdotalis"* 185, 191 (United States Catholic Conference, 1998).

29. Reply of the Congregation, *supra* note 23, at 202.

30. *Bradwell v. Illinois*, 83 U.S. 130 (1872).

31. *Id.* at 141–42.

In the twentieth century, the Court has employed the Fourteenth Amendment's Equal Protection Clause to reformulate the law's treatment of women and men. The Supreme Court retrieved the Fourteenth Amendment and applied it to treat men and women equally—in the same way. Indeed, equal protection cases brought on behalf of male plaintiffs helped to establish the principle of equality. For example, Mississippi violated the Equal Protection Clause when it denied admission to nursing school to male applicants in part because such a policy "tends to perpetuate the stereotyped view of nursing as an exclusively woman's job."[32] Equal protection tests must be applied "free of fixed notions concerning the roles and abilities of males and females."[33]

Equality as sameness offers some benefits to women. In a legal system that excludes women from the legal profession or regulates women's working conditions under different rules from men's, sameness can be an improvement. Catholic feminists have argued for this type of equality in the church but have never attained it. The church continues to teach that men and women are equal but different in their capacity to serve the church in the priesthood. In contrast, American law has offered women some equal opportunity of access to jobs traditionally held by men.

Some American feminists have challenged the adequacy of this legal interpretation of equality because it does not take account of the biological and cultural circumstances of women. It might achieve for men access to a women's school and yet fail to improve women's lives. Questions of reproduction, including the treatment of pregnancy in the law, have focused feminists' attention on the alternative concept of equality in difference, leading them to ask what legal reforms can protect the different needs of women. These theorists echo feminist theology's constant cry for attention to the particular voices of women. In contrast to Catholic feminist theologians, feminist legal theorists have occasion to ask whether the law's inclusion of women in traditionally male roles betrayed feminism by abandoning the distinctive needs of women.

Some of the ongoing tensions in feminist legal theory are evident in the Virginia Military Institute case in which the Supreme Court ruled that the "Constitution's equal protection guarantee precludes Virginia from reserving exclusively to men the unique educational opportunities VMI affords."[34]

How should the state educate citizen-soldiers? Virginia had several options:

32. *Mississippi University for Women v. Hogan,* 458 U.S. 718, 729 (1982).
33. *Id.* at 724–25.
34. *United States v. Virginia,* 518 U.S. 515, 519 (1996).

"Admit women to VMI; establish parallel institutions or programs; or abandon state support, leaving VMI free to pursue its policies as a private institution."[35] Virginia developed the Virginia Women's Institute for Leadership at Mary Baldwin College. The men's program was "adversative," the women's school was "cooperative." The schools were also different in academic offerings, methods of education, financial resources, SAT scores, and faculty training.

Equality as sameness or equality as difference?

The District Court and the Fourth Circuit upheld the parallel programs, but the Supreme Court reversed. Justice Ginsburg concluded that equal protection required the admission of women to the all-male school because VMI and Mary Baldwin were not comparable. VWIL was a "'pale shadow' of VMI in terms of the range of curricular choices and faculty stature, funding, prestige, alumni support and influence."[36] In dissent Justice Scalia argued for the diversity of an educational system that includes single-sex colleges: "Virginia's election to fund one public all-male institution and one on the adversative model—and to concentrate its resources in a single entity that serves both these interests in diversity—is substantially related to the State's important educational interests."[37]

*VMI* suggests that feminist theology's contribution to American law and legal theory is quite limited. Psychology, educational theory or military history are more likely sources of insight for this case, even though feminist principles are at stake. Theology has limited resources for considering the adversative education of citizen-soldiers.

Catholic feminist theologians who read the VMI opinion, however, may conclude that citizen-soldiers are like priests: their role is distinctive and influential. Catholic feminists have argued that there is no equality for women in the church as long as they are excluded from the church's central institution of priesthood. They have reason to favor Justice Ginsburg's vision of equality over Justice Scalia's defense of all-male institutions.

Some feminist legal theorists may complain that the admission of women to male institutions cannot meet the specific needs of women. The experience of Catholic feminist theologians suggests that feminism advances little absent such entry. As Susan Moller Okin has noted: "Though by no means all contemporary feminists are liberals, virtually all acknowledge the vast debts of feminism to liberalism. They know that without the liberal tradition, feminism

35. *Id.* at 525–26.
36. *Id.* at 553.
37. *Id.* at 579.

would have had a much more difficult time emerging."[38] Contemporary feminism has criticized liberalism's emphasis on individualism and autonomy, its view of social and political relations, and its view of a neutral state, thus "outgrow[ing] its parent tradition in significant respects."[39]

Catholicism, too, is a critic of liberalism's emphasis on individualism and autonomy, its view of social and political relations, and its view of a neutral state. Mary Segers explains: "Catholicism would have to be seen as lagging behind liberalism because it has not yet granted women the signs and symbols of basic respect, individual dignity, and equal opportunity necessary to the full inclusion of women in social life. . . . Catholic thought has yet to appropriate fully those positive elements of the liberal tradition that would help to promote women's greater recognition and self-value as individuals."[40]

Segers concludes that both Catholicism and liberalism have lessons to learn from the insights of "liberal feminism." My own conclusion is a little different: that feminist legal theorists have a lesson to learn from the experience of feminist theologians. As feminist lawyers outgrow liberalism, they should with Justice Ginsburg remain wary of any stereotypes of women's nature and experience. Feminist justice "requires that the traits that are truly desirable in society be equally open to both women and men or, in the case of virtues, equally expected of both women and men."[41] Feminist justice requires that women and men have an equal opportunity to be citizen-soldiers as well as priests.

38. Susan Moller Okin, *Justice, Gender, and the Family* 61 (1989).

39. Mary C. Segers, Feminism, Liberalism, and Catholicism, *in Feminist Ethics and the Catholic Moral Tradition* 588, 590 (Charles E. Curran et al., eds., 1996).

40. *Id.* at 606–7.

41. Sterba, *supra* note 2, at 80.

# Section 6  Law and Economics

The law and economics school of thought dates from the early 1960s but came into its own in the 1970s. It brought the tools of economic analysis to law school. For some, law and economics scholarship is descriptive, merely identifying the economic effects of various rules of law, and perhaps providing the unexplained justification for many of the rules that courts adopted in centuries past. For other law and economics scholars, the discipline is normative—they argue that the law should be efficient, that it should be utilitarian, providing greater goods for all to enjoy. Some have applied efficiency theories to matters not normally associated with economics—to the allocation of adopted children and human organs and to the efficiency of criminal punishment and suicide. Critics argue that it is generally those who already have who get to do the enjoying under many of the rules that law and economics scholars favor, and that the principle of exchange should not dominate all spheres of human relations.

In this section, Stephen M. Bainbridge presents a defense of the Christian's use of economic analysis in legal reasoning. George E. Garvey argues that law and economics' focus on efficiency can leave behind the poor, who are God's special concern. Neither is simply an apologist nor a critic.

# Law and Economics:

# An Apologia

*Stephen M. Bainbridge*

Law and economics is the school of jurisprudence in which the tools of microeconomic analysis are used to study law. Those of us who practice it have a deceptively simple task. We translate some legal doctrine into economic terms. We then apply a few basic principles to the problem—cost-benefit analysis, collective action theory, decision-making under uncertainty, risk aversion, and the like. Finally, we translate the result back into legal terms. These tasks have both a positive and a normative component. Positive economic analysis simply asks whether the law is efficient, while normative law and economics commands that the law ought to be efficient.

In trying to make behavioral predictions, positive law and economics does nothing more than to apply modern microeconomic tools to legal rules. If we think of legal sanctions as the cost of engaging in certain activities, changing a legal rule is no different from any other change in price. A legal rule is just as subject to analysis under price theory as is the price of a commodity. Imposing a more onerous legal sanction on the use of illegal drugs is functionally no different from charging more for tobacco. Just as people respond to higher prices by consuming less of the good (here tobacco), they should respond to greater legal sanctions by engaging in less of the regulated activity (here consuming illegal drugs). Nothing about this sort of analysis strikes me as theologically problematic. Instead, the more troubling questions have to do with the rational-choice model of human behavior that undergirds this analysis: Is rational choice a valid account of human behavior? Is rational choice a morally palatable account of human behavior?

The bedrock principle of normative economic analysis is wealth maximization; that is, law should seek to increase social wealth, as measured by the dollar equivalents of everything in society. Although both the objections to and defenses of wealth maximization are getting a little shopworn, it remains the essential starting point for any evaluation of law and economics, especially in light of our faith's teachings on wealth. I follow the Chicago School convention of focusing on wealth rather than utility maximization, which follows from the premise that one cannot make interpersonal comparisons of subjective utility. Wealth maximization avoids that problem by focusing solely on preferences capable of being monetized. As a result, however, we are faced with two moral decisions: (1) are we content with a norm that ignores preferences that cannot be reduced to a monetary value; and (2) are we content with the initial distribution of wealth?

In this essay I take up the following questions. First, whether wealth maximization is an appropriate moral norm on which a Christian legal scholar may draw. Second, whether the rational-choice model of human behavior is consistent with the Christian understanding of man as a fallen creature of God.

## WEALTH MAXIMIZATION

At first blush, the wealth maximization norm ought to strike Christians as unpalatable, at best. Is not "the love of money a root of all evil"? (1 Timothy 6:10) Did not Christ himself tell us that we "cannot serve both God and money"? (Luke 16:13) Does not the Bible repeatedly teach us that there are many things more important than wealth, not least of which is the fear of the Lord? How then can Christians associate themselves with a normative principle explicitly intended to maximize wealth and whose measurement of wealth includes only those preferences having monetary values? Good questions all. Three responses suggest themselves: evade the objection's moral force by redefining the norm; rise in defense of wealth maximization; or concede part of the objection, while seeking to preserve a role for economic analysis.

### Evasive Maneuvers

There are a couple of moves by which one can pull the teeth from objections to the wealth maximization norm, of which changing the terminology is easiest. *Wealth maximization* is a poor choice of words. It implies a normative principle calling for society to squeeze the maximum possible wealth out of every opportunity for profit. A better term might be *wealth optimization,* which takes a longer-term view. As a societal norm, wealth optimization would consider many factors besides immediate wealth maximization. Indeed, wealth optimization might even take into account preferences having no knowable monetary value.

Alternatively, we could shift the focus from wealth maximization to efficiency, which we might define as acting "without wasting money."[1] The wealth maximization norm thus transforms into the more palatable proposition that, as we move toward whatever goals society chooses, we should do so without wasting money. This move shifts the burden of proof to opponents of the norm and, moreover, leaves them the unpalatable task of advocating rules that waste money. It is also attractive because it acknowledges that law and economics is an instrumental mode of reasoning that must be constrained and guided by exogenous norms.

### In Defense of Wealth Maximization

A defense of wealth maximization as a moral norm might begin with pragmatic arguments about the size of the economic pie. Those who favor distributional concerns over wealth maximization often give short shrift to the positive effects of social wealth maximization. In contrast, I prefer the old adage "a rising tide lifts all boats." Whatever distribution scheme society adopts, everyone is likely to be better off if the pie to be distributed is larger. From this perspective, wealth creation and distribution are two independent questions. Society's first task is to set up wealth maximizing rules so as to encourage wealth creation. Only then should society consider distributional questions.

One thus need not deny the relevance of distributional concerns in order to believe that care should be taken to address them in a manner that does no harm (or minimal harm) to wealth creation. Critics of neoclassical economics often fail to take into account the secondary unintended effects of regulating economic activity. Because the secondary effects are often counter to and larger

---

1. *See* Robert D. Cooter, *The Best Right Laws: Value Foundations of the Economic Analysis of Law,* 64 Notre Dame L. Rev. 817, 817 (1989).

than the primary intended effects, much social legislation makes matters worse, not better. This is so even if the public-choice arguments made below are discounted, because the law of unintended consequences inevitably follows from the bounded rationality of human minds.

Wealth maximization can be defended, however, on grounds that go beyond mere expansion of the economic pie. Experience with the failures of mercantilism and, more recently, command economies teaches that society succeeds only when individuals are free to pursue the accumulation of wealth. Economic liberty, in turn, is a concomitant of personal liberty—the two have almost always marched hand in hand. The pursuit of wealth has been a major factor in destroying class distinctions, moreover, by enhancing personal and social mobility. At the same time, "the manifest failure of socialist systems to deliver reasonable standards of material well-being has undermined collectivism as an alternative" to capitalist societies in which wealth maximization is a paramount societal goal.[2] Accordingly, "wealth maximization may be the most direct route to a variety of moral ends."[3]

To be sure, many Christians disagree with this view of the wealth maximization norm. As Michael Novak observes, however, theological discourse on the relation between social justice and economic concerns tends to use distributional arguments for left-liberal ideological purposes.[4] All too often, arguments against wealth maximization serve only to give aid and comfort to the Leviathan state.

I intend to be rather provocative here: religiously premised objections to the wealth maximization norm are a specific incarnation of the broader attack launched throughout this century against capitalism by a number of prominent Christian scholars and intellectuals—a worldview captured by Paul Tillich's claim that "any serious Christian must be a socialist."[5] As Novak argues, however, Christian scholars tend to be poorly trained in economics and inexperienced with the business world. They "are likely to inherit either a pre-capitalist or a frankly socialist set of ideals about political economy."[6] As a result, Christian intellectuals "are more likely to err in this territory [economic justice] than in most others."

2. Paul Johnson, *Blessing Capitalism,* Commentary, May 1993, at 33, 34.

3. Richard A. Posner, *The Problems of Jurisprudence* 382 (1990) (hereinafter Posner, *Jurisprudence*).

4. Michael Novak, *Toward a Theology of the Corporation* 12–14 (rev. ed. 1990).

5. Quoted in Richard John Neuhaus, *Doing Well and Doing Good* 47 (1992).

6. Novak, *supra* note 4, at 59.

To be clear, I am not arguing that a godly society promotes wealth maximization at all costs. Here I take the liberty of paraphrasing Paul Johnson's defense of capitalism: "The divine plan was indeed that we should enjoy the fruits of the earth and of our own industry, and [wealth maximization] is the best way we have yet devised to organize the latter. But it was equally the divine plan that God should be worshiped and obeyed and, not least, feared. The fear of the Lord, in short, is the beginning of [economic] wisdom, as of any other kind."[7] In sum, there must be a balance, which leads to the need for a partial concession to the objections to wealth maximization as a moral norm.

## A Partial Concession

When law and economics was a young academic discipline, some of its prominent practitioners rejected the notion that wealth maximization could be trumped by distributional considerations or other values. Contrary to what many believed, these scholars did not ignore the humanitarian considerations that underlie distributional claims. They asserted, however, that strict adherence to the wealth maximization norm was a more effective means of accomplishing altruistic goals. This view was famously articulated by Judge Richard Posner: "A society which aims at maximizing wealth . . . will produce an ethically attractive combination of happiness, of rights (to liberty and property), and of sharing with the less fortunate members of society."[8]

Almost from the beginning, however, important law and economics scholars asserted that the wealth maximization norm could be trumped by what Guido Calabresi called "Other Justice" norms.[9] That position now prevails in the law and economics community. Even Judge Posner concedes (albeit with qualifications) that economic analysis sometimes can be trumped by noneconomic norms.[10]

Again, it may be useful to draw an analogy between the problems presented by law and economics and the broader debate within the Christian community

7. Johnson, *supra* note 2, at 36.

8. Richard A. Posner, *The Ethical and Political Basis of the Efficiency Norm in Common Law Adjudication*, 8 Hofstra L. Rev. 487, 487 (1980).

9. Guido Calabresi, *About Law and Economics: A Letter to Ronald Dworkin*, 8 Hofstra L. Rev. 553, 559 (1980).

10. *See, e.g.,* Posner, *Jurisprudence, supra* note 3, at 376–80; Thomas S. Ulen, *The Prudence of Law and Economics: Why More Economics Is Better*, 26 Cumb. L. Rev. 773, 797 (1995–96) (efficiency "is certainly not the only legal norm and probably not even the most important legal norm").

relating to the ethical organization of a capitalist society. Consider the long line of Catholic social justice thought arguing that the enormous societal forces unleashed by capitalism must be circumscribed by laws that place the capitalist economy at the service of human freedom.[11] The core of human freedom in this perspective is ethical and religious, not economic. Instead, the freedom to pursue wealth is simply one aspect of the totality of human freedom. A Christian legal scholar could approach law and economics in precisely the same manner, viewing the normative claims of economic analysis as merely a subset of the full panoply of ethical and moral principles by which we are called to live as Christians.

At first blush, such an approach might prove quite attractive to Christian legal scholars. It appears to offer a mechanism for striking precisely the sort of balance that needs to be struck between wealth maximization and Christian virtues. On closer examination, however, we run into the thorny problem of implementation. As such, although in theory I acknowledge the need to permit other normative values to trump wealth maximization, in practice I am deeply suspicious of claims that Other Justice norms should prevail. (Note that my analysis focuses on regulation of markets and other economic activity, which has been the dominant subject of economic analysis. As discussed below, considerations other than efficiency may dominate in nonmarket contexts.)

Note carefully: this part of my argument does not depend on a claim that wealth maximization is an ethically superior norm by which to guide societal decisionmaking. Instead, my argument here is premised on prudential considerations. While the partial concession gambit is philosophically attractive, it proves operationally problematic. Specifically, legal institutions are more effective when they promote wealth maximization than when promoting wealth redistribution.

At the outset, it is important to carefully specify the role one wishes distributional considerations to play in analysis. The two principal competing alternatives are (1) the proposition that social policy ought explicitly to be based on notions of distributional justice—put another way, that Other Justice norms are appropriate independent evaluative norms by which social policy ought to be judged—and (2) the proposition that economic analysis should be based on a more expansive notion of welfare economics that includes a taste for fairness and related Other Justice concerns within the relevant utility function. The lat-

11. *See* Stephen M. Bainbridge, *Corporate Decisionmaking and the Moral Rights of Employees: Participatory Management and Natural Law,* 43 Villanova L. Rev. 741 (1998).

ter approach has the virtue of being based on a complete account of human behavior, which reflects the full range of tastes and preferences. As such, this broader conception of welfare responds to the emerging evidence that human behavior not infrequently diverges from that predicted by rational-choice theory, as by preferring perceived fairness to efficiency. While defensible, however, such a move is problematic due to interpersonal noncomparability and because expansive definitions of welfare tend to render cost-benefit analysis wholly indeterminate.

Whatever problems inhere in expanding our notion of utility to include concerns beyond wealth maximization, however, pale in comparison to those using distributional concerns as independent evaluative norms. In our society, questions of distributive justice have been taken out of the hands of individuals (be they believers or not) and reserved for the government. In particular, distributive justice is usually a matter for the legislative branch. Common-law judges normally take the initial distribution of wealth as a given. This is just as well, because judicial powers are better suited to enforcing wealth-maximizing rules than to redistribution. Indeed, the common law has what Judge Posner calls an "implicit economic logic."[12] At least *arguendo*, I therefore assume herein that judicial decisions are likely to be concerned with wealth maximization, while legislative decisions are more likely to be concerned with distributive justice.

To complete the circle, however, economic analysis of the legislative process has given us a robust and disheartening perspective on legislative solutions to distributive problems. Public choice is the branch of law and economics relevant here. Public choice's basic tenet is that politically influential interest groups use their influence with lawmakers to obtain legal rules that benefit themselves at the expense of larger, more diffuse groups.[13] In other words, legislative decisions are driven not by distributive justice but by interest group pressures.

If my defense of wealth maximization has evolved into a defense of the limited state, that move should be neither surprising nor troubling. Here I draw on the tradition that finds its purest expression in the Calvinist principle of sphere sovereignty.[14] Social institutions—including the state—are organized horizontally, none subordinated to the others, each having a sphere of authority

12. Richard A. Posner, *Economic Analysis of Law* 251 (1992).

13. Daniel A. Farber and Philip P. Frickey, *Law and Public Choice* 23–24 (1991).

14. J. Budziszewski, *The Problem with Conservatism*, First Things, Apr. 1996, at 38, 42; see *infra* this volume, Robert F. Cochran, Jr., Tort Law and Intermediate Communities: Calvinist and Catholic Insights.

governed by its own ordering principles. Expansion of any social institution beyond its proper sphere necessarily results in social disorder and opens the door to tyranny. In our era, the state's expansion beyond those functions prescribed by custom and convention into the pervasive nanny state has become the principal threat to personal liberty.

Although sphere sovereignty is a creature of Reformation theologians, there are scriptural passages that presaged it. The strongest scriptural example of this principle doubtless is Samuel's speech to the people of Israel when they desired a king. Indeed, I suspect that many modern people would be grateful if the government would content itself with "a tenth of [our] seed and of [our] vineyards."[15]

To be clear, I do not claim that all legislative choices are driven solely by naked self-interest. Public-choice theory has enormous explanatory power, but it has difficulty accounting "for ideological politicians like Reagan and Thatcher."[16] This is all the more true when public-choice theory confronts religiously motivated actors. Any sensible account of modern politics must take into account not only naked self-interest but also the possibility that ideology and morality matter, even in the halls of Congress. As James Q. Wilson observes, "Something in us makes it all but impossible to justify our acts as mere self-interest whenever those acts are seen by others as violating a moral principle." Rather, "We want our actions to be seen by others—and by ourselves—as arising out of appropriate motives."[17] Hence legislators may choose to act consistently with their ideological principles, even when doing so puts them at odds with important interest groups.

I am merely claiming that we need to be suspicious of legislators who claim to be acting in the name of distributive justice. Ideology and morality often serve as cover for self-interest. Worse yet, "human nature may incline even one acting in subjective good faith to rationalize as right that which is merely personally beneficial."[18] When we conclude that a wealth maximizing judicial outcome is socially undesirable, let us therefore be very careful to ensure that asking the legislature to reverse that outcome does not lead to an even more undesirable result.

15. 1 Samuel 8:15.

16. Farber and Frickey, *supra* note 13, at 24.

17. James Q. Wilson, *What Is Moral and How Do We Know It?* Commentary, June 1993, at 37, 39.

18. *City Capital Assocs. v. Interco Inc.,* 551 A.2d 787, 796 (Del. Ch. 1988) (emphasis deleted), *appeal dismissed,* 556 A.2d 1070 (Del. 1988).

In sum, it is not the wealth maximization norm that leads to socially undesirable outcomes. An ungodly society will have socially undesirable outcomes irrespective of its guiding norm. The challenge for Christians therefore is to build a godly society in which the wealth maximization norm is tempered by the fear of the Lord.

## RATIONAL CHOICE

Law and economics is the most successful form of intellectual arbitrage in the history of jurisprudence. The movement's greatest successes have come in business law fields, such as corporate law, securities regulation, and antitrust. In my field, corporate law, it is now impossible to find scholarship that is not informed by economic analysis. Even the small handful of corporate-law scholars who reject economic analysis spend most of their time responding to those of us who practice it. Perhaps the most telling evidence of the success of law and economics in my field, however, is that many of our leading corporate-law judges and lawyers are now adept at using economic analysis. Both judicial opinions and practitioner publications are filled with the jargon of law and economics. This is a claim no other modern school of jurisprudence can make.

Why has law and economics been so successful? Traditional forms of legal scholarship were mostly backward looking. One reasoned from old precedents to decide a present case, seemingly without much concern (at least explicitly) for the effect today's decision would have on future behavior. Yet law is necessarily forward looking. To be sure, a major function of our legal system is to resolve present disputes, but law's principal function is to regulate future behavior. The law and economics movement succeeded because it recognized that judges cannot administer justice solely retrospectively. They must also consider what rules their decisions will create to guide the behavior of other actors in the future. Even more important, however, law and economics gives judges a systematic mechanism for predicting how rules will affect behavior. Indeed, as I will argue herein, no other interdisciplinary methodology offers judges or lawyers a more robust model for making these predictions.

It is precisely this aspect of law and economics, however, that might give Christian scholars pause. As with any model claiming predictive power, law and economics rests on a theory of human behavior. "Economic Man" is an autonomous individual who makes rational choices that maximize his satisfactions. The question before us is whether the economic view of human nature is consistent with that of Christianity.

One can anticipate at least three faith-based objections to the rational-choice model. First, some deny that rational choice provides a plausible account of human behavior, especially insofar as nonmarket behavior is concerned. Second, as members of a faith community, many Christians have a strong communitarian streak. Religious communities, local communities, and other mediating institutions serve as a buffer against the pervasive power of the central state and, perhaps even more important, against the power of the debased cultural elites who set the moral tone of secular society. Finally, our faith calls us to aspire to the Christian virtues. At bottom, virtue is a willingness to act against interest, something Economic Man never does. Because Economic Man is both an autonomous individual and pure rational calculator, the model of human behavior provided by Economic Man fails to account either for the importance of mediating institutions or of virtue. This is not an appropriate forum for an extended discourse on the merits of communitarianism or the role of virtue in human behavior.[19] Instead, I simply want to suggest that neither objection is fatal to the law-and-economics project. Among other things, both critiques arguably rest on a caricature of rational-choice theory. Economic Man is not driven by purely pecuniary incentives but rather by all incentives to which humans respond, including such things as risk aversion and even a generalized sense of fairness.

## (Mis)Understanding the Claims of Rational Choice

If rational-choice theory were offered up as a moral norm, I would readily concede its inconsistency with the Christian understanding of human nature. Judge Posner claims that Economic Man "is a person whose behavior is completely determined by incentives; his rationality is no different from that of a pigeon or a rat."[20] This is a perspective on human nature essentially identical with that of the evolutionists: man is just an animal, morally indistinguishable from any other animal. Indeed, Posner's Economic Man is a feral monster wholly lacking in the Christian virtues. As a tool of moral debate, moreover, rational-choice theory inevitably turns conversations about rights or human dignity into mere dickering over prices, which Christians ought to find abhorrent.

Rational-choice theory, however, emphatically is not a moral norm. Instead, it is just a policymaking tool useful for predicting how people respond to regu-

19. *See* Stephen M. Bainbridge, *Community and Statism: A Conservative Contractarian Critique of Progressive Corporate Law Scholarship*, 82 Cornell L. Rev. 856 (1997).

20. Posner, *Jurisprudence, supra* note 3, at 382.

lation. Although the term *rational* as used in everyday speech has both normative and expressive implications, in economics rationality has mostly descriptive connotations: "The hallmark of rationality, as taught to economics graduate
students, is that consumers have transitive preferences. This means that if, at
any given moment of time, some good or bundle of goods denoted A is preferred to another good or bundle of goods denoted B and B is preferred to a
third good or bundle of goods denoted C, then it must be the case that A is preferred to C. By contrast, if it were the case that A is preferred to B, B is preferred
to C, and C is preferred to A, we would find that distinctly odd—indeed, irrational."[21] So defined, rational choice scarcely resembles the bogey man its
critics sometimes make it out to be. Indeed, this definition of rationality is so
benign that economists are understandably puzzled by those who find it objectionable.

To be sure, people do not always behave rationally. People make irrational
choices, even if all we mean by that statement is that their choices sometimes
reflect intransitive preferences. But that is far from fatal for the law-and-economics project. Although those of us who practice law and economics claim
that Economic Man is a useful construct, we recognize that Economic Man is
not intended to describe real people embedded in a real social order. Instead, it
is simply a theory we claim has general predictive power. Such a theory is properly judged by its predictive power with respect to the phenomena it purports
to explain, not by whether it is a valid description of an objective reality. As
such, "the relevant question to ask about the 'assumptions' of a theory is not
whether they are descriptively 'realistic,' for they never are, but whether they
are sufficiently good approximations for the purpose in hand."[22] The proper
question thus is not whether rational-choice theory is a defensible moral norm
but rather whether rational-choice theory makes sufficiently accurate predictions about human behavior to justify its use as a guide to public policy.

In recent years, the predictive claims of rational-choice theory have been
challenged by a burgeoning literature known as behavioral economics.[23] Draw-

21. Thomas S. Ulen, *Rational Choice and the Economic Analysis of Law*, 19 Law and Soc. Inquiry 487, 488 n.2 (1994).

22. Milton Friedman, The Methodology of Positive Economics, in *Essays in Positive Economics* 23, 30 (1985).

23. *See generally* Christine Jolls et al., *A Behavioral Approach to Law and Economics*, 50 Stan.
L. Rev. 1471 (1998); Donald C. Langevoort, *Behavioral Theories of Judgment and Decision
Making in Legal Scholarship: A Literature Review*, 51 Vand. L. Rev. 1499 (1998); Cass R. Sun-
stein, *Behavioral Law and Economics: A Progress Report*, 1 Am. L. and Econ. Rev. 115 (1999);

ing on empirical work by cognitive psychologists and experimental economists, this literature has identified a variety of cognitive errors and systematic decisionmaking biases that result in systematic departures from the behavior predicted by rational choice. It is the systematic nature of these departures that is significant. Rational-choice theory has always assumed that individual actors depart from rationality, but also that such departures are random and, so to speak, come out in the wash. In contrast, behavioral economics claims that some departures from rationality are not random but rather predictable.

To take but a single example, studies of the so-called endowment effect show that experimental subjects sometimes place a higher monetary value on items they own than on those that they do not own, even if the two items have the same market value. Accordingly, subjects must be paid more to give up something than they would be willing to pay to acquire the same object. The endowment effect appears to be a specific example of a more general phenomenon known as the status quo bias.[24] All else being equal, decisionmakers favor maintaining the status quo rather than switching to some alternative state. The status quo bias can lead to market failure where decisionmakers' preference for the status quo perpetuates suboptimal practices.

The extent to which behavioral economics calls into question more traditional modes of economic analysis remains sharply contested within the law and economics community. On the one hand, it seems clear that attention must be paid to the possibility that a behavioral economics analysis will shed light on legal problems. On the other hand, it also seems clear that behavioral economics mostly modifies rational-choice theory rather than displacing it.[25]

One of the distinguishing characteristics of behavioral economics is the emphasis on empiricism. Although this might strike one as a virtue, on closer examination it may prove a significant vice. In many cases, identified cognitive errors may simply be an artifact of experimental design. "Most individuals, including virtually all university students—the principal experimental subjects of behavioral economics, which relies much more heavily than standard economics does on experiments—are buyers but not sellers. When we do have

Robert B. Thompson, *Securities Regulation in an Electronic Age: The Impact of Cognitive Psychology,* 75 Wash. U. L.Q. 779 (1997).

24. *See generally* Russell Korobkin, *The Status Quo Bias and Contract Default Rules,* 85 Cornell L. Rev. 608 (1998); Russell Korobkin, *Inertia and Preference in Contract Negotiation: The Psychological Power of Default Rules and Form Terms,* 51 Vand. L. Rev. 1583 (1998).

25. *See generally* Stephen M. Bainbridge, *Mandatory Disclosure: A Behavioral Analysis,* 68 U. Cin. L. Rev. 1023 (2000).

something to sell, we usually sell through middlemen, such as real estate brokers, rather than directly to the ultimate consumer. Experimental situations in which the subjects are asked to trade with each other are artificial, and so we cannot have much confidence that the results generalize to real markets."[26] A related problem is that the results of many studies are not robust. Small tweaks in experimental design can make the endowment effect disappear, for example.

A second major limitation of behavioral economics literature is that we need far better evidence as to the persistence of these biases over time. As a general matter, the corrective powers of market forces and learning by decisionmakers remain contested. It seems reasonably well-settled, however, that the corrective effect of such forces is contextual, varying from one setting to another. A critical question thus is whether purported systematic biases will persist over an extended period of time, such that a persistent market failure plausibly can be posited.

Finally, even where one can tell a plausible behavioral economics story identifying a systematic departure from the predictions of rational choice, the rational-choice model may still be a superior alternative on which to base public policy. There seems to be a strong temptation to use behavioral economics too glibly. Advocates of government intervention are tempted to jump from positing the status quo bias, citing endowment effect studies, to an assertion that the government needs to shake up the status quo, without demonstrating that the bias is truly valid in the specific setting at hand. Although behavioral economics is not intrinsically ideological, it is regularly invoked by scholars telling market failure stories that purport to justify legal intervention. In light of this phenomenon, and my earlier argument that the Christian tradition is consistent with a preference for a limited state, one appropriately ought to be skeptical of behavioral economic arguments.

Indeed, one of the oddities of behavioral economics loops back on itself. In claiming that law can correct market failures caused by decisionmaking biases or cognitive errors, much behavioral economics scholarship treats regulators as exogenous to the system. Private actors are asserted to be subject to decision-making biases, which results in market failure requiring state intervention. The problem is that the state is endogenous rather than exogenous. Judges, bureaucrats, and other state actors are themselves subject to systematic cognitive errors and decisionmaking biases. When coupled with the insight of public-choice

26. Richard A. Posner, *Rational Choice, Behavioral Economics, and the Law,* 50 Stan. L. Rev. 1551, 1566 (1998).

theory that the decisions of government actors often are influenced by interest group politics, the policy-prescriptive powers of behavioral economics seem likely to prove less robust than those of rational choice.

In sum, we might usefully compare rational choice to Newtonian physics. Both capture an important part of the phenomena they seek to explain, but neither is fully explanatory. Just as Newtonian physics adequately models the behavior of a falling rock, the economic model of behavior adequately explains the behavior of large masses of people engaged in exchange.[27] Just as Newton's theories lose their explanatory power at some point and thus give way to relativity and the other accoutrements of modern physics, economics doubtless cannot explain all human interaction. In my field of corporate law, which by its nature is concerned with the behavior of actors in the markets, rational-choice theory not only seems plausible, but has considerable empirical support. As applied to those areas of the law regulating nonmarket interactions, however, rational-choice theory on its face seems less plausible and, moreover, lacks empirical support. We know, for instance, that habitual criminals behave in ways inconsistent with rational-choice theory. As such, I doubt very much whether economic analysis is a particularly useful tool in nonmarket areas of the law, especially those involving serious moral questions, but at least for now I shall leave that difficult issue to those with greater expertise (and interest) in such areas.

### Is a Theological Understanding of Human Nature Inconsistent with Rational Choice?

"So what" is thus my initial response to the claim that Economic Man is an imperfect model of human behavior. If it takes a theory to beat a theory, critics of the rational-choice model fairly may be asked to put forward an alternative methodology that can better assist us to understand the real-world effects of legal rules than economics. As fleshed out by the insights of behavioral economics, the economic model offers a robust set of tools for predicting behavior. Do sociology, psychology, or literature offer a more robust theory of behavior than economics? More to the point, at least for present purposes, does theology offer any more robust insights than economics?

That question presupposes that theological insights on human nature lead to different behavioral predictions than those premised on Economic Man. But is that necessarily true? Consider a restaurant located on one side of a busy street.

27. Posner, *Jurisprudence, supra* note 3, at 366.

Although crossing the street is dangerous, some people will nonetheless do so in order to eat at the restaurant. Basic economic theory tells us some things about the likelihood that people will do so. The more dangerous the crossing becomes, the less likely people are to venture across. Conversely, the more attractive the restaurant becomes, the more risk people are willing to bear. And so forth. All of which seems quite obvious, but these predictions about human behavior, when extrapolated and generalized, become the foundation for price theory. Here's the kicker: price theory tells us how people will choose, but as R. H. Coase notes, "it does not tell us why people choose as they do. Why a man will take a risk of being killed in order to obtain a sandwich is hidden from [economists] even though we know that, if the risk is increased sufficiently, he will forgo seeking that pleasure."[28] In other words, economics has no good account of the character or origins of human preferences.

For me, however, as a Christian practicing law and economics, faith brings something to the table in grappling with the question of preference formation. Christianity is not a utopian faith but rather is quite realistic about human beings. In particular, our central doctrine of the Fall of Man tells a coherent story about the nature and origins of human preferences in an unredeemed world. In my view, the assumptions about human behavior made by economists are largely congruent with the fallen state of man. If Economic Man is a fair description of Adam after the Fall, the rational-choice model used in economics is not a bad model for predicting the behavior of fallen men. At the same time, however, because Christianity's account of how man fell and the consequences of that Fall provide an answer to Coase's question about human preferences, our faith gives Christian practitioners of economic analysis a more fully realized account of human behavior.

To be sure, Christians are called to a higher standard of behavior than that of fallen man. If the purpose of economic analysis is to predict how people will respond to changes in legal rules, however, can we assume Christian behavior by the masses of a secular and Godless society? No realistic social order can assume "heroic or even consistently virtuous behavior" by its citizens.[29] A realistic social order therefore must be designed around principles that fall short of Christian ideals. In particular, the rules must not be defined in ways that effectively require every citizen to be a practicing Christian. Christian visions of justice therefore cannot determine the rules of economic order. Instead, legal rules and

28. R. H. Coase, *The Firm, the Market, and the Law* 5 (1988).
29. Novak, *supra* note 4, at 28.

predictions about human behavior must assume the fallen state of Man, which is precisely what I have tried to suggest Economic Man permits us to do.

I do not want to overstate the case for law and economics. Although rational choice remains a robust predictive tool, we may nonetheless hope that no one uses it as a philosophy of life. Only someone bemused by reductions and abstractions would deny that there are all sorts of noneconomic communities, principles, and activities that exercise a powerful influence on life choices. In all aspects of life, there are always relations of trust, unspoken understandings, settled expectations, and commitments whose reality and importance lie largely outside the reach of economic analysis. As I have tried to demonstrate herein, however, a Christian legal scholar may rely on both positive and normative economic analysis with confidence that it is both a powerful analytic tool and one that is consistent with his or her walk with God.

# A Catholic Social Teaching

# Critique of Law and Economics

*George E. Garvey*

Among the jurisprudential schools emerging over the past several decades, "law and economics" has surely been the most influential. We better understand law, and are better able to predict the consequences of new and changing rules, because the law-and-economics movement brought powerful analytical methods to the study of law. It would indeed be hard to exaggerate the impact that law and economics has had on modern legal thinking and practice. In this essay I shall measure some of the more significant underlying principles of this influential movement against the benchmark of Roman Catholic social teaching.[1]

1. Significant contemporary law-and-economics publications include *Chicago Lectures in Law and Economics* (Eric A. Posner ed., 2000); Avery Wiener Katz, *Foundations of the Economic Approach to Law* (1998); Nicholas Mercuro and Steven G. Medema, *Economics and the Law* (1997); Ugo Mattei, *Comparative Law and Economics* (1997); Thomas J. Miceli, *Economics of the Law* (1997); Cass R. Sunstein, *Free Markets and Social Justice* (1997); Richard A. Posner, *Economic Analysis of Law* (4th ed. 1992); David W. Barnes and Lynn A. Stout, *Cases and Materials on Law and Economics* (1992); Charles J. Goetz, *Law and Economics: Cases and Materials* (1984); A. Mitchell Polinsky, *An Introduction to Law and Economics* (1983); and *The Economics of Legal Relationships* (Henry G. Manne ed., 1975).

To critique law and economics from the perspective of Catholic social teaching presents quite a challenge. It is not possible to bring a monolithic Catholic view to bear on a unified economic theory of law. The relevant, modern social teachings of the Catholic Church lack doctrinal precision, and they have evolved, together with the world's societies, over the past hundred or so years. Economists, for their part, are not a homogeneous group, and they bring diverse methods and philosophies to the study of law. Catholic social teaching and the mainstream law-and-economics movement, however, share several goals. Though rooted in radically different value systems—Catholic social teaching seeking to mediate the message of the gospel to the modern world and law and economics promoting efficiency as a compelling value in its own right—both are ultimately concerned about the allocation of material resources in ways that maximize social utility and create wealth. Both are also concerned with the respective roles of individuals and governments in that allocative process.

It is easy—too easy—to identify controversial positions presented by economic analysts, such as the creation of a marketplace for the adoption of babies, and dismiss the entire movement as antithetical to the basic values of a Catholic philosophy rooted in the inherent and inalienable dignity of each human being. At the other extreme, one may present the champions of law and economics merely as technicians, the practitioners of morally neutral tools applied within value structures created by others whose judgments must bear the brunt of moral scrutiny. Neither extreme is tenable. Economic analysts of the law have not led U.S. policy to illogical and immoral extremes: babies do not yet go to the highest bidder. These analysts, however, are not mere technocrats. Normative economic prescriptions for society have had significant impact on the development of modern U.S. law and policy. A reasonable critique, therefore, must identify the core attributes of the movement, those that have in fact had impact on law and policy, and weigh them against the core of the Catholic social vision.

## LAW AND ECONOMICS: AN OVERVIEW

As already noted, economists are members of diverse and conflicting camps. Simply attempting to identify a universally accepted definition of "economics" demonstrates the difficulty of the present task. Ronald Coase, for example, has written that he considered "the definition of economics which Boulding attributed to Viner, and has often been repeated, 'economics is what economists do,' as essentially sound if it were accompanied, which it never is, by a description of the activities in which economists actually engage."[2] One text defines economics simply as "the study of how human beings satisfy their material needs and wants."[3] Paul Samuelson concludes that "economics is the study of how we choose to use scarce productive resources with alternative uses, to better meet prescribed ends."[4] These various definitions demonstrate that the magnitude of the economic enterprise is striking.

One additional definition is particularly significant for any discussion of law and economics. Judge Richard Posner, surely the most influential scholar associated with law and economics, defines economics as "the science of rational choice in a world—our world—in which resources are limited in relation to human wants."[5] Addressed to an audience of noneconomists—lawyers—this definition conveys a certainty that may in part explain the success of the movement over the past several decades. Defining economics as a science suggests an objectivity and precision that the more comprehensive definitions do not. As practitioners of the "science of rational choice," economic analysts of the law would seem to merit special deference and respect. Economists, however, are quick to acknowledge the limitations of their discipline. Samuelson captures the limitations well: "Because it cannot employ the controlled experiments of the physicist, economics raises basic problems of methodology: subjective elements of introspection and value judgment; semantic issues of ambiguous and emotional meanings; . . . fallacies of reasoning and fallacies of inference."[6] Other prominent economists share Samuelson's concern about attributing to economics the characteristics of the hard or natural sciences.[7] The point is simply that economics has the characteristics of a behavioral science, such as psychology or sociology, rather than a natural science. It is art as well as science.

There are, moreover, major philosophical divisions within economics. The range of historically significant camps include, among others, classical, neoclassical, Marxist, Keynesian, and various intellectual schools of economic thought identified with Chicago, New Haven, and Austria. The presumptions

2. R. H. Coase, *Economics and Contiguous Disciplines,* 7 J. Leg. Stud. 201, 202 (1978).

3. Roger Chrisholm and Marilu McCarty, *Principles of Economics* 2 (2d ed. 1981).

4. Paul A. Samuelson, *Economics* 12 (11th ed. 1980).

5. R. Posner, *supra* note 1, at 3.

6. Samuelson, *supra* note 4, at 12.

7. *See* James M. Buchanan, *Liberty, Market, and State* 14–17 (1986); Coase, *supra* note 2, at 207–08; Goetz, *supra* note 1, at 2; Robin Paul Malloy, *Law and Economics: A Comparative Approach to Theory and Practice* 60 (1990).

and methodologies of the various schools sometimes overlap, but often they conflict. Not surprisingly, therefore, law-and-economics scholars have brought diverse analytical methods to the law. Major contributors to our understanding of law have used the tools of neoclassical analysis, industrial organization economics, game theory, public choice, transaction cost analysis, and, increasingly, econometrics. Given the philosophical and methodological diversity, any attempt to critique law and economics must abstract common principles from this complexity and, in the process, lose some of the rich texture that economics has brought to legal analysis.

This critique focuses primarily on the "Chicago School" of law and economics because it has been the most influential champion of the movement. The Chicagoans brought the tools of neoclassical or welfare economics to bear on legal matters. Scholars associated with the University of Chicago, most notably Ronald Coase and Gary Becker, demonstrated how methods used by economists to analyze markets and market transactions could be applied productively outside of the realm of traditional economic markets.[8] Posner's scholarship in particular made the approach of the Chicago School widely accessible to legal academics, jurists, and law students.

When the methodology of the Chicago School is applied to legal matters, individuals and institutions are presumed to be wealth maximizers who act rationally in their own self-interest. The ultimate goal of society is to maximize social welfare by ensuring the best possible allocation of scarce resources. Because wealth is a function of individual utility (a subjective measure) rather than simply money (an objective measure), the allocative function is best achieved through individual transactions.

Neoclassical economists are particularly concerned with the role that the pricing mechanism plays in the allocation of resources through free-market transactions.[9] In perfectly competitive markets, with all-knowing consumers and producers, resources can be expected to flow to their highest valued uses through individual exchanges. Much of economic analysis is focused on the operation of markets where competition is faulty, knowledge is imperfect, or other barriers to transactions exist. The basic model, however, which assumes away such factual complexities, is analytically powerful.

The law-and-economics movement brought its presumptions about human

8. *See* R. H. Coase, *The Problem of Social Cost,* 3 J. L. and Econ. 1 (1960); Gary S. Becker, *The Economic Approach to Human Behavior* (1976) and *The Economics of Discrimination* (1957).

9. *See* George J. Stigler, *The Theory of Price* (3d ed. 1966).

behavior to the study of law. To the economic analyst, the purpose of law is to regulate relationships—*transactions* to use economic terminology—between individuals, facilitating and encouraging some forms of conduct while deterring others. Whether we are dealing with property law, contracts, criminal law, torts, or other major divisions within our legal system, rules can be reduced to applications that are capable of analysis as if they were private transactions between two or more rational, utility-maximizing individuals. Sound legal rules should naturally reduce the costs of engaging in socially desirable transactions while imposing costs on socially undesirable conduct. Beneficial transactions, for example, are generally promoted by leaving the conduct to the realm of private decision making—that is, to the market—or by adopting rules that minimize the costs of negotiating or enforcing complex transactions. When markets for various reasons are not expected to work smoothly, the state may intervene in various ways to improve the situation. Government, for example, may create enforceable rights for intellectual property in order to facilitate market transactions, encourage desired activities by providing subsidies, or provide at public expense goods needed for society's well-being such as national defense and public transportation. Undesirable transactions on the other hand—for example, torts or crimes—are deterred by increasing the costs of engaging in unacceptable behavior through the imposition of punitive civil awards and criminal sanctions.

Economic analysis may be either positive or normative. Positive analysis is descriptive. It seeks to better understand and explain how the law does in fact operate. The Chicagoans have applied the neoclassical economic model to the common law and concluded that the rules of the common law foster allocative efficiency. Posner, for example, states that "the common law is best understood not merely as a pricing mechanism, but as a pricing mechanism designed to bring about an efficient allocation of resources."[10] It is not clear whether this is a product of judges consciously or intuitively seeking the efficient outcome or of processes that, over time, induce litigants to invest more resources to challenge inefficient rules, but the Chicago School analysts believe that the commitment of the common law to efficiency is demonstrable.

In addition to positive or descriptive analysis, there is a normative component to the economic study of law. The normative analyst not only seeks to understand the law but to modify legal rules in order to better satisfy the efficiency norm. The law *should* foster allocative efficiency. To neoclassical economists, fa-

10. Richard A. Posner, *The Law and Economics Movement*, 77 Am. Econ. Rev. 1, 5 (1987).

cilitating the use of free-market forces to bring all resources to their highest valued use maximizes social welfare, and therefore allocative efficiency should stand as a first principle of law.

At the risk of oversimplification, the basic elements of the Chicago School's law and economics may be summarized as follows: The law may be studied as a pricing mechanism whose ultimate goal is and should be to maximize aggregate social wealth or welfare. Scarce societal resources—including labor, capital, and material goods—are allocated most efficiently by free markets responding to pricing stimuli. The market accepts as a given the current distribution of wealth, and society should ordinarily allow redistribution to occur through operation of the market. Finally, government should generally intervene in private exchange relationships only to facilitate efficient transactions—that is, to reduce transaction costs.

Some scholars associated with law and economics equate efficiency with justice, but to many a market-based social order is considered morally preferable to alternative economic regimes not simply because it is efficient. Market transactions foster the public good because they are neutral, they foster individual liberty and responsibility, and they reward such social virtues as creativity, prudence, and thrift. Government-dictated transactions, by contrast, are viewed as inefficient and biased. They tend to reward political influence and to promote the interests of entrenched groups rather than enhance the public weal.

Although the focus of this discussion has been on legal analysis associated with the University of Chicago, another school merits mention. The "New Haven School" provides an interesting contrast to some aspects of neoclassical analysis. Scholars of this school, which is rooted in seminal works by Yale's Guido Calabresi, generally agree that markets allocate resources efficiently, but they see market failure as a pervasive phenomenon. The modern administrative state is accordingly accepted as a necessary reality, and the focus of analysis is on the regulatory structure. Unlike the Chicagoans, analysts associated with New Haven view prudent regulation as more likely to achieve efficient outcomes than does the common law and, most notably, they consider justice and fairness to be higher values than efficiency. Given this framework, the inequitable distribution of wealth is a matter of concern that law and policymakers cannot simply leave for correction through market transactions. The administrative state has a role to play in establishing a just and equitable society, not merely one that is efficient.[11]

11. Mercuro and Medema, *supra* note 1, at 89–90.

As the law-and-economics movement has grown in sophistication and influence, other economic approaches like those associated with Yale have challenged the dominance of the Chicago School. Coase had in fact predicted that the primacy of economists would diminish with time. He stated that once experts from other disciplines "have acquired the simple but valuable truths which economics has to offer, economists . . . will have lost their main advantage and will face competitors who know more about the subject matter."[12]

Whether or not economists in general, and the Chicago School in particular, will have less influence in the future over the development of law remains to be seen. For purposes of this essay, it is important only to recognize the extraordinary influence that economists and economic analysis have had over the past several decades. The efficiency norm seems to have attained a status in legal analysis that was once occupied by notions of "justice" and "equity." Much future scholarship, as perhaps already evidenced by the work at Yale, will struggle with reconciling these norms. In this essay I attempt to bring the teachings of the Roman Catholic Church to that task.

## CATHOLIC SOCIAL TEACHING

Is there *a* Catholic or Christian economic model? Certainly not in the sense that all Catholics or Christians of good faith would agree on a single ideal economic order. The Gospels contain a radical message about earthly goods: "Jesus said to him, 'If you wish to be perfect, go, sell what you have and give to the poor, and you will have treasure in heaven. Then come, follow me.'"[13] As described in the Acts of the Apostles, the socioeconomic order of the earliest Christians was characterized by communal living: "The community of believers was of one heart, and mind, and no one claimed that any of his possessions was his own, but they had everything in common. . . . There was no needy person among them, for those who owned property or houses would sell them, bring the proceeds of the sale, and put them at the feet of the apostles, and they were distributed to each according to need."[14] The ideal of the gospel, therefore, as well as the practices of Christians of the apostolic era, hardly fits a model characterized by rationally self-interested wealth maximizers.

The first Christians, however, believed that the Kingdom of God was at hand, and they had no reason to be concerned about either their own or their

12. Coase, *supra* note 2.
13. Matthew 19:21.
14. Acts 4:32–35.

progeny's material well-being. As generations passed, Christians accepted the fact that they required material goods sufficient to care for self and family. Various Christian denominations have developed different views about the relation between the material and spiritual worlds, between wealth and salvation. The Protestant tradition, particularly that associated with Calvin, is seen as more sanguine than Catholicism with the underlying premises of a market economy. Max Weber, for example, identified Calvinism as the moving force in the development of the spirit of capitalism.[15]

The starting point for this analysis is the latter half of the nineteenth century, a time of turmoil in continental Europe. Central Europe was racked by revolution, the restoration of monarchies, and the rise of Marxism. The working class was restless, and the struggle between capital and labor was raging. The evils of unrestrained capitalism were apparent to many, but at the same time, fear of socialism was great. In this context, the Roman Catholic Church adopted fundamental policies to address the socioeconomic problems of the day. The Catholic response was embodied in Pope Leo XIII's 1891 encyclical *Rerum Novarum*.[16]

The church, *Rerum Novarum* taught, would not be content in that age of social upheaval merely to address the spiritual needs of the faithful. It would speak to the most pressing economic and social needs of the day, the struggle between capital and labor, or, in Leo's words, "the worker question." The encyclical addressed the fundamental struggle between capitalism, perhaps more accurately "liberalism," and socialism, the two great competing economic ideologies of the times. The church could find complete justice in neither economic order.

Pope Leo struck a balance. He recognized that the central problem of the day was the extraordinary gap between the opulent lifestyles of the wealthy and the crushing poverty of the working class. There would be no peace in society until this extreme gap was narrowed. To Leo, peace could be built only on a foundation of justice, including economic justice. He could not, however, countenance socialism as it was emerging, with its tendency toward atheism and its propensity for violence. The pope also challenged the prevailing doctrines of western liberalism or capitalism. To many western European economists, the rules of the marketplace were part of the natural order; they were the normal

15. Max Weber, *The Protestant Ethic and the Spirit of Capitalism* 44 (1958).

16. Pope Leo XIII, *Rerum Novarum,* Encyclical Letter on the Conditions of the Working Classes, May 15, 1891, *reprinted in Catholic Social Thought* 11 (David J. O'Brien and Thomas A. Shannon eds., 1992).

route to freedom and prosperity. The laws of supply and demand were, to liberals, as natural as the laws of gravity. Surely, the Catholic Church, with its traditional commitment to natural law, would appreciate that unrestrained capitalism reflected the natural and progressive economic order. Pope Leo would have none of this.

*Rerum Novarum* developed several themes that have influenced all subsequent Catholic social thought. To the surprise of many at the time, the pope declared that it was the responsibility of the church to weigh in on significant social, economic, and political issues. It would apply the principles of the gospel and of its conception of natural law to the pressing issues of the world and suggest practical solutions to foster peace and justice. The church's goal was to reconcile the classes by calling all people to a higher level of moral sensitivity. The message was not intended solely for a faithful Catholic audience, but rather the encyclical and all subsequent Catholic social teachings have attempted to capture universal principles that are instructive to men and women of all faiths.

Work, according to Pope Leo, is not simply a burden, it is a right and source of dignity. One's labor is one's own property; it may be employed to achieve individual advantage and to foster the well-being of family and society. In the context of the working class, the right to work is no less than the right to survive. Every individual, Leo stated, "has a right to procure what is required in order to live; and the poor can procure it in no other way than by work and wages."[17] As a corollary of this fundamental right to work, workers have a right to a living wage, one that will support themselves and their families. They are also entitled in justice to safe and humane working conditions, appropriate to the circumstances. Workers must be given adequate time for rest and leisure to recuperate from their labors. Children must not be forced prematurely into the workforce. Women have a special calling to care for the well-being of the home and children. Employers are morally bound to provide for these essentials—a living wage and humane working conditions—regardless of the market for labor. Neither market conditions (the availability of excess, relatively fungible, workers) nor contractual rights could justify the abuse of workers.

*Rerum Novarum* suggests several concrete remedies for the "worker problem." Pope Leo believed in the right of individuals to own and accumulate private property. Wage earners who choose to be prudent and frugal should be free to acquire property, "for every man has by nature the right to possess property

17. *Id.* at 34.

as his own."[18] The gulf between the wealthy and poor would over time diminish if individual workers were free to turn their industry into property. The socialist solution—elimination of private property—would merely dull incentive and diminish personal responsibility. Workers in the emerging industrial order, however, if left to their own devices and individual bargaining strength, would be at the mercy of unscrupulous employers. *Rerum Novarum,* therefore, insisted on the right of workers to form associations.

The encyclical obliged the state, as well as employers, to address the problems of the working class. Government may not favor one class over another, but must protect the rights of all citizens. "Among the many and grave duties of rulers who would do their best for their people, the first and chief is to act with strict justice—with that justice which is called in the schools *distributive*—toward each and every class. . . . Justice, therefore, demands that the interests of the poorer population be carefully watched over by the administration, so that they who contribute so largely to the advantage of the community may themselves share in the benefits they create—that being housed, clothed, and enabled to support life, they may find their existence less hard and more endurable."[19] While espousing neutrality in principle, *Rerum Novarum* was advocating that the state intervene on behalf of any class being denied justice. It was the working class that needed the support of the state; the rich could take care of themselves.

To summarize, this seminal instrument of Catholic Social Teaching established various principles: Men and women have a *right* to work; they have a *right* to a living wage for that work; they have a *right* to humane working conditions; they have a *right* to convert their labor into private property; and they have a *right* to freely associate to promote their interests as workers. In return, they have an obligation to give a fair day's work for a fair day's pay and to respect the rights and property of their employers. Employers may use their property as they see fit, subject to the obligation that they not subordinate through economic coercion the rights of the workers to a fair wage and safe conditions. Finally, the state has an obligation to intervene, particularly on behalf of society's poor, to promote distributive justice.

There was plenty in *Rerum Novarum* to make both the capitalist and the socialist wince. Leo shared the socialists' view that there was a great and inequitable chasm between the "haves" and "have nots" of that time. He shared

18. *Id.* at 5.
19. *Id.* at 27.

their view that those with capital were often callously oppressing the working-class poor. The pope rejected, however, the socialists' call for the violent overthrow of one class by another and the elimination of private property rights. The classes could live in harmony so long as justice was maintained, a state in which every individual could, through personal labor, achieve an adequate standard of living. This would be accomplished by calling the wealthy to sound Christian moral values (conversion); through peaceful but collaborative efforts by the working class; and by state intervention when necessary to protect the rights of all citizens, particularly those social and economic rights defined in *Rerum Novarum.*

Catholic social thought has naturally developed since *Rerum Novarum.* Through a series of papal encyclicals, documents of the Second Vatican Council, and the statements of Bishops' Conferences, the church has continued to apply the underlying principles of *Rerum Novarum* to evolving social and economic conditions.[20] Though never providing a universal "blueprint" for reform, which must reflect the needs and circumstances of individual societies, the church's social teachings continue to make specific, practical recommendations to help resolve the problems that foster social and economic injustice in the world. Several major themes have developed over the years.

The primary significance of Catholic social teaching is that it applies religiously based values, those of Catholic tradition, to the pressing social and economic conflicts of the day. *Rerum Novarum* and all subsequent Catholic social teaching is built largely on one overarching principle: that every human being, every man, woman, and child, is possessed of inherent dignity, a principle well-grounded in Catholic philosophy and theology. Pope John Paul II states that "beyond the rights which man acquires by his own work, there exist rights which do not correspond to any work he performs, but which flow from his essential dignity as a person."[21] The Catholic belief in the universal dignity of the human person is a function neither of individual merit nor of basic human nature. Observed individual and collective behavior may explain many phenom-

20. Significant contributions to Catholic social thought include Pope Pius XI, *Quadragesimo Anno* (1931); Pope John XXIII, *Mater et Magistra* (1961); Pope John XXIII, *Pacem in Terris* (1963); Second Vatican Council, *Gaudium et Spes* (1965); Pope Paul VI, *Populorum Progressio* (1967); Pope Paul VI, *Octagesima Adveniens* (1971); Pope John Paul II, *Laborem Exercens* (1981); Pope John Paul II, *Sollicitudo Rei Socialis* (1987); and U.S. Catholic Bishops, *Economic Justice for All* (1986).

21. Pope John Paul II, *Centesimus Annus,* Encyclical Letter on the Hundredth Anniversary of Rerum Novarum, May 1, 1991, 11 (hereinafter *Centesimus Annus*).

ena—it surely helps to explain the operation of the marketplace—but it hardly leads inevitably to a notion of inherent dignity. That belief is grounded in the transcendental, the parenthood of God, and, to Christians, the brotherhood of Christ. It is neither earned nor deserved, but simply given.

One contemporary text identifies twelve "major lessons" of modern Catholic social teaching.[22] Several of these lessons have particular significance for the topic of this essay. First, all human beings possess certain inalienable rights, both political and economic. Second, the church has identified a "preferential option for the poor." Society, under the principle of solidarity—the obligation to promote the common good—has a special duty to protect those who cannot protect themselves, the poor.[23] Moreover, the principle of solidarity applies across national boundaries. The world's wealthiest nations are bound to promote the well-being of impoverished nations. Third, all individual rights must be subordinated to the common good. Fourth, the Church has promoted the concept of "subsidiarity." Under this principle, "responsibilities and decisions should be attended to as close as possible to the level of individual initiative in local communities and institutions. Mediating structures of families, neighborhoods, community groups, small businesses, and local governments should be fostered and participated in."[24] Fifth, economic justice requires that human labor not be considered just one more factor of production. It must take precedence over technology and capital. Just wages, humane working conditions, and the right of workers to organize are essential aspects of economic justice. Finally, the right to private property is essential, but all property is held in stewardship. The world's resources must be shared and respected.

To abstract even further from this list, the core of Catholic teaching seems to embody a dual commitment to freedom and responsibility. Society must recognize and protect certain individual rights, both political and economic, but individuals must exercise their freedoms with due regard to the rights of others. The church and the state must act when individual liberties, particularly economic rights, are used by one class to impose an unjust economic status on others. The church must teach and cajole; the state must coerce through law if necessary.

The most significant recent chapter in the church's social teaching came on the hundredth anniversary of *Rerum Novarum.* In *Centesimus Annus,* Pope John Paul II demonstrates the continued vitality of the church's approach to

22. Peter J. Henriot et al., *Catholic Social Teaching: Our Best Kept Secret* (1989).

23. *Centesimus Annus, supra* note 21, at 15.

24. Henriot, *supra* note 22, at 21.

pressing economic and social problems. John Paul begins with the opening theme of *Rerum Novarum,* the "new things" of the title. Leo, according to John Paul, was responding to the new things of his day, namely the struggle between capital and labor. *Rerum Novarum* responded to the evils generated by the emerging industrial economic order. John Paul continues the tradition. He applies the same natural-law principles to the new things born of the current era. The sweat shops of nineteenth-century Europe and urban America have largely disappeared, though there is compelling evidence that the emerging international economic order may have simply moved them to new venues in the developing world. The minimum requirements demanded by Leo—a living wage and humane working conditions—have long been met in the industrialized world. But the current socioeconomic order generates other new things that assault the dignity of the individual.

It is fortuitous that a Polish pope could write the encyclical demonstrating that Leo's concerns about socialism had proven to be true. The socialist system, at least as it had developed in Eastern Europe and the Soviet Union, was authoritarian, stifled individual initiative, and deprived workers of their dignity. It could not even meet the prime secular economic test: socialism was inefficient. In any case, whether for spiritual, political, or economic reasons, the socioeconomic system rejected by Pope Leo in 1891 collapsed of its own weight in 1989.

Again, following the lead of Leo, John Paul turned to the economies that emerged from the liberal, capitalistic tradition. At an earlier time, there was only land and labor. In Leo's time, a new property emerged: capital. John Paul suggests that there are new forms of property today: know-how, technology, and skill. If not completely new, they certainly have achieved an extraordinary prominence in the contemporary economic order. As a result, the fundamental right to work—to obtain the resources needed for a free and productive life— is dependent on access to knowledge and training. Pope Leo's command that society provide the framework for safe working conditions and adequate wages gives way to Pope John Paul's call for society to ensure the availability of training and education, including retraining for those who are displaced by new technology or patterns of production or consumption.

Leo equated peace with justice. John Paul adds a variant more suited to the realities of the modern industrial world: "Another name for peace" the Pope states "is *development.*"[25] What must be developed if peace is to prevail? *Cen-*

---

25. *Centesimus Annus, supra* note 21, at 52.

*tesimus Annus* suggests the former communist nations, the Third World, and the so-called Fourth World—the underclass of the industrialized societies—all need to be developed. The principle of solidarity continues to call each nation to provide its own citizens with the tools needed to thrive in productive society— access to education and training. The principle of global solidarity requires wealthy nations to transfer the means of modern productivity to poor nations.

The growth of Catholic social thought as it relates to work can be seen in the following statement from *Centesimus Annus:* "It is a strict duty of justice and truth not to allow fundamental human needs to remain unsatisfied, and not to allow those burdened by such needs to perish." This is a basic restatement of the Leonine teaching. But John Paul continues, "It is also necessary to help these needy people to acquire expertise, to enter the circle of exchange, and to develop their skills in order to make the best use of their capacities and re- sources."[26]

John Paul also identified the "phenomenon of consumerism" as a product of the modern economy. "It is not wrong," the pope teaches, "to want to live bet- ter; what is wrong is a style of life which is presumed to be better when it is di- rected towards 'having' rather than 'being,' and which wants to have more, not in order to be more but in order to spend life in enjoyment as an end in it- self."[27] The encyclical suggests that decisions to invest, produce, and consume are all moral decisions and should be made with the common good in mind. Ultimately, John Paul states that education is the answer to the problem of con- sumerism. Consumers should be educated so that they better appreciate the so- cial responsibility that attaches to their "power of choice." Producers and the mass media in particular should develop a strong sense of responsibility for the consequences of their decisions.

John Paul also attributes modern environmental problems largely to con- sumerism. The principle of stewardship requires that mankind use the earth's resources wisely, for the common good, including the welfare of future genera- tions. Producers seeking to satisfy consumer desires, however, are exploiting the earth for short-term gains.

At the time of *Rerum Novarum* the primary issue, the "worker question" as Pope Leo stated it, was one of human survival. Workers could neither be ex- posed to unreasonable danger nor denied a subsistence wage. Pope John Paul II is less concerned with survival and more with alienation, at least in the context

26. *Id.* at 34.
27. *Id.* at 36.

of economically developed nations. Clearly the Leonine model still fits in many parts of the world, and John Paul continues to apply it in the context of global solidarity, but capitalism has taken care of survival where it has thrived. For that matter, even socialism achieved that level of success. The dilemma of the industrialized world is alienation, which, in the pope's words, "happens in consumerism, when people are ensnared in a web of false and superficial gratifications rather than being helped to experience their personhood in an authentic and concrete way."[28] Alienation occurs in the workplace when "through increased isolation [a worker is caught] in a maze of relationships marked by destructive competitiveness and estrangement, in which he is considered only a means and not an end."[29]

Catholic social teaching is in many ways quite compatible with the major tenets of the mainstream law and economics movement, that associated primarily with the Chicago School. It favors private-property rights and is not antagonistic to the accumulation of individual wealth. The fairly conservative political bent of the Chicago School shares with Catholic teaching a belief that individuals should assume responsibility for their economic destinies and should be free to make choices about the employment of their labor, capital, and other property. Catholicism of course adds the admonition that all such choices must reflect the actors' moral obligations. The church and Chicago School economists are also suspicious of excessive governmental intervention in areas where individuals, families, or local community groups should be free to act. And the Catholic Church naturally has no quarrel with efficiency as such. At first glance, therefore, Catholic teaching poses no great challenge to the law-and-economics scholars.

Upon closer examination, however, economic analysis and Catholic teachings are quite divergent. The *summum bonum* of neoclassical economic analysis is efficiency, certainly as practiced by members of the Chicago School. The church first faced, and rejected, this philosophy in *Rerum Novarum*. John Paul has characterized the issue presented to his predecessor, Leo, as follows: "A *new form of property* had appeared—capital; and a *new form of labour*—labour for wages, characterized by high rates of production which lacked due regard for sex, age or family situation, and were determined solely by efficiency, with a view to increasing profits. . . . In this way labour became a commodity to be

28. *Id.*
29. *Id.*

freely bought and sold on the market, its price determined by the law of supply and demand, without taking into account the bare minimum required for the support of the individual and his family."[30] In *Rerum Novarum* the church called capitalists, employers, the state, and itself to higher principles. It continues to do so today.

In Catholic doctrine, there is room for all of the elements of a market-based economic order: private property, profits, the accumulation of wealth, and individual initiative, freedom, and enterprise. The market, however, must "be appropriately controlled by the forces of society and by the State, so as to guarantee that the basic needs of the whole of society are satisfied."[31] The market cannot treat human beings as just one more factor of production, like technology and know-how. People must have the opportunity to work—it is a source of dignity—and to attain the skills needed to be meaningfully employed in modern productive society. Those with resources, both individuals and nations, have a moral obligation rooted in justice to provide for the truly destitute and a duty founded on Christian charity to share from their abundance with those who have much less. In short, maximizing the aggregate wealth of society is not a morally acceptable goal if it results in a grossly inequitable distribution of that wealth.

Just as people cannot be treated as commodities in the market for productivity, they cannot be converted solely into consumers. Economic models tend to place people on either the demand or supply side of a calculus, as producers or consumers. When individuals start to value themselves based on what they possess or do, however, as opposed to who they are, they lose track of the Christian message about the fundamental object of their being.

Ultimately, Catholic social teaching seems to take up where economic analysis ends. A capitalistic, market-based economic order does foster many of the goals identified by Catholic social teaching as desirable. Individuals are allowed to employ their own resources, capital, knowledge, or labor in productive ways. A sense of personal dignity is enhanced by engaging in work that contributes meaningfully to society's well-being while providing the resources needed to care for one's self and family. One may also accumulate wealth—that is, convert one's labor into real property and capital, which may be enjoyed and put to further productive uses. Economic analysts have shown how the law may best accommodate these goals.

30. *Id.* at 4.
31. *Id.* at 35.

Unlike many economists, however, the Catholic Church does not accept the expansion of society's wealth as an end in itself. Economic growth is, to be sure, a good if it is achieved in ways that respect human dignity and when the benefits are distributed in ways that are just. A society that expands its aggregate wealth, however, by reducing human beings to productive or consuming things is morally impoverished, at least from the Catholic perspective.

While expressing deep concern over the dehumanizing aspects of a strident and unqualified commitment to private property and free markets, the church also cautions against undue intervention by government. Efforts by states to achieve a forced economic equality by denying individuals control over their own lives and property have proven to be as dehumanizing as capitalism at its worst.

The Catholic focus is on wealth as a means to promote human development. The principle of solidarity does not permit indifference to the impact of growth-promoting policies on any individual or class of individuals. An economic "underclass" cannot be tolerated as a price for the growth of aggregate wealth. The solution is not merely to provide the necessities of life to those who are impoverished, though that is surely a moral imperative. Experience seems to show that endless government payments breed dependency and a sense of alienation as debilitating as the most demeaning jobs. The solution promoted by modern Catholic teaching is to provide individuals with the tools they need to obtain meaningful jobs. Those who have been excluded from the economic mainstream must be helped to experience the sense of self-worth that comes with productive employment. The engines of economic growth and efficiency must work to ensure at least minimal participation by all in society in the benefits of the economic order rather than simply and indiscriminately promoting the growth of wealth.

# Part II **Christian Traditions and the Law**

Historically, as H. Richard Niebuhr suggested in his 1951 book *Christ and Culture,* Christians have understood law from five basic perspectives. Synthesists reconcile the natural law with Christian teaching; conversionists seek to transform the law through Christian insight; separatists separate themselves from the world and its law; dualists support law as a necessary evil in a fallen world; and culturalists find the law of their culture consistent with Christian teaching. Whereas Niebuhr evaluated the approach of each of these groups to culture generally, in this part we present essays written from the first four of these perspectives as they apply to law. (Because the culturalist does not see a conflict between Christian teaching and law, this perspective does not bring a specifically Christian critique to the law.) First, however, Robert F. Cochran, Jr., provides a more developed introduction to the five Christian perspectives on law.

# Christian Traditions, Culture, and Law

*Robert F. Cochran, Jr.*

Christians disagree about many things. One thing that we share is the earliest Christian confession that "Jesus is Lord."[1] This confession has meaning at several different levels. At a personal level, it is a commitment that the Christian will seek to obey Jesus—that Jesus will be the Lord of his or her life. At a metaphysical level, it is an acknowledgment that Jesus is sovereign over history. But there is great disagreement among Christians about its implications for the relationship between the Christian and law.

As Christians today seek to bring a Christian perspective to the law, we do not write on a blank slate. For almost two millennia, Christians of all sorts have sought to understand how God would have them approach the law. In this essay, I will consider the variety of views that Christians have taken toward law.

In his classic study *Christ and Culture,* H. Richard Niebuhr presents a helpful way of classifying the relationship of various Christian

1. *See* 1 Corinthians 12:3. Portions of this essay were adapted from my *Christian Perspectives on Law and Legal Scholarship,* 47 J. Legal Ed. (1997) and are used with permission.

traditions to law, as well as to other aspects of culture. Law, along with the arts, philosophy, values, language, customs, education, and social organization, is an aspect of culture. According to Niebuhr, Christians have established five different relationships between Christ and culture: (1) Christ plus culture, (2) Christ transforming culture, (3) Christ against culture, (4) Christ and culture in paradox, and (5) the Christ of culture.[2] In this essay, I will introduce each of Niebuhr's categories and discuss how each might relate to law. Finally, I will explore possible means of reconciling these viewpoints.

## SYNTHESISTS: CHRIST PLUS CULTURE

Under the Christ-plus-culture perspective, culture is good, but Christ has things of value to add to it. One who takes a Christ-plus-culture view synthesizes Christ and culture. Niebuhr's label for this category was "Christ above culture," but such a label is too easily misunderstood as one of Christ controlling culture. The view of those in this category is one of Christ adding things to culture rather than controlling it.

Thomas Aquinas gave the classic example of a Christ-plus-culture view. "In his system of thought he combined without confusing philosophy and theology, state and church, civic and Christian virtues, natural and divine laws, Christ and culture."[3] He took the wisdom of Athens and added to it the wisdom of Jerusalem. He took Aristotle's natural law and added to it divine law. He took the Aristotelian virtues (courage, justice, temperance, friendship, and truthfulness) and added to them the Christian virtues (faith, hope, and charity). He took reason and added to it faith. According to Aquinas, the ideal comes when we draw on the insights of both Christ and culture. Thomist thought has been passed on within the Catholic Church, but we find it among many Protestants as well.[4] In recent years there has been a resurgence of interest in Aquinas's theory of natural law.

If Aquinas were with us today, he would be likely to still argue for Christ plus

2. Niebuhr's label for the first category was "Christ above culture." H. Richard Niebuhr, *Christ and Culture* 116–48 (1951). I have amended his label for reasons that are explained immediately below.

3. *Id.* at 130.

4. *See, e.g.,* Charles E. Rice, *Fifty Questions on the Natural Law* (1993); John Finnis, *Natural Law and Natural Rights* (1980); *Natural Law Theory: Contemporary Essays* (Robert P. George ed., 1992) (Catholic); and J. Budziszewski, *Written on the Heart: The Case for Natural Law* (1997) (Protestant).

many aspects of culture. He believed in natural law, that human goods (things of value) are the same across cultures and that reason leads to common methods of achieving those goods. Natural law, discernible by human reason, can create a common legal agenda for Christians and non-Christians. But given today's culture—or its multiplicity of cultures—Aquinas, in some respects, might not be a synthesist. Aquinas synthesized Christ with the Greek culture that was influential in his day, but he might have difficulty synthesizing Christ with our culture (or cultures). It is likely that today he would find greater tension between Christ and many aspects of culture. As to Enlightenment liberalism, Aquinas would share its attention to reason, but not its exclusion of faith. (In some respects, Enlightenment liberalism undid what Aquinas did.) Aquinas also would not share Enlightenment liberalism's focus on individualism and its moral neutrality. Aquinas would be likely to share postmodernism's focus on community but not its rejection of reason. Today, to the extent that our culture is individualistic and nonrational, Aquinas might pursue an "Aristotle transforming culture" agenda while also seeking to add Christ to culture.

## CONVERSIONISTS: CHRIST TRANSFORMING CULTURE

The next three motifs, in contrast to that of the synthesist, see culture as radically sinful. They suggest that the mere addition of Christian insight to culture is insufficient to redeem culture. Even reason is fallen; "reason in human affairs is never separable from its egoistic, godless, perversion."[5] This recognition of the fallenness of culture has been present, to some extent, throughout the history of Christianity—it was a central theme of Augustine—but it received renewed emphasis at the time of the Protestant Reformation in the sixteenth century. From their agreement that culture is fallen, the reformers went in very different paths: John Calvin called for the transformation of culture; the Anabaptists rejected culture; and Martin Luther held Christ and culture in tension.

Calvin recognized that the fall (the entry of sin into the world) infected every aspect of life, but he looked before the fall, to creation, and found a basis for transforming culture. God originally created a good world. We are called to imitate God not only in His holiness but in His creativity as well. That creativity can renew God's creation. Calvin saw the state as "God's minister not only in a negative fashion as restrainer of evil but positively in the promotion of welfare."[6]

5. Niebuhr, *supra* note 2, at 156.
6. *Id.* at 217.

Whereas the natural law tradition recognized a substantial area of cultural agreement that we have as humans, Calvin saw much less common ground. His concept of common grace (a measure of grace given to all by God) recognized some potential agreement between Christian and non-Christian, but there was much less potential for agreement than under natural law theory.

In the nineteenth century, the Dutch Calvinists, anticipating aspects of postmodern thought, argued that all traditions start from their own presuppositions or foundational beliefs.[7] As Christians we seek to construct a view of the law and culture that is consistent with our presuppositions (as others do with theirs). At the end of the day, we hope, there will be enough agreement as to ends that different traditions can work together. To some extent, Dutch Calvinists would avoid conflict with other traditions under a doctrine of "sphere sovereignty" leaving many aspects of life under the authority of institutions other than the state (for example, family and religious community).[8]

Note the similarities between the Dutch Calvinist and the postmodern view of the world. Both reject the possibility of reaching agreement as to foundational beliefs between different traditions. The similarities between Dutch Calvinist and postmodern antifoundationalism illustrates the difficulty of placing a group clearly within only one of Niebuhr's categories today. To the extent that Dutch Calvinists share the postmodern view of the world, they may be synthesists. In the postmodern world, they may be the synthesists and the Thomists may be the conversionists.

## SEPARATISTS: CHRIST AGAINST CULTURE

In response to the evil of the world, separatists come apart from the culture. They emphasize the newness of the Christian life and reject the old life. "The political task of Christians is to be the church rather than to transform the world."[9] It is widely believed that the earliest Christians were separatists. Throughout the history of Christianity, many Christians have joined separatist monastic orders. The Anabaptist churches are the separatist branch of the

7. *See infra,* this volume, David S. Caudill, A Calvinist Perspective on the Place of Faith in Legal Scholarship; *supra,* this volume, David S. Caudill, Law and Belief: Critical Legal Studies and Philosophy of the Law-Idea.

8. *See, e.g.,* my essay in this volume *infra,* Torts and Intermediate Communities: Calvinist and Catholic Insights.

9. Stanley Hauerwas and William H. Willimon, *Resident Aliens: Life in the Christian Colony* 38 (1989).

Protestant Reformation. The Mennonites are an example of an Anabaptist community in modern America. In recent years several scholars outside of Anabaptist circles have shown interest in Anabaptist theology and its critique of the world. Prominent examples are Duke's (Methodist) theologian and law professor Stanley Hauerwas and Notre Dame's (Catholic) law professor Thomas Shaffer.[10]

Anabaptists are nonresistant—that is, they believe that Christians may not use force. Their separation from political and legal culture flows from their belief in nonresistance. A necessary element of government is the use of coercion and Christians are prohibited from using the sword. God may use people in governmental positions to restrain and punish evil, but these are not positions that Christians can occupy. Thus Anabaptists will not serve as soldiers or police.

For Anabaptists, some cultural problems are not the Christian's concern. For example, the Anabaptist does not have an answer to the question of how evil is to be restrained if the state cannot use force against criminals or invading countries. The Mennonite biblical scholar John Howard Yoder said that it is not the business of Christians to work out the ethical problems of Satan.

Some scholars take issue with Niebuhr's placing Anabaptists within the "Christ against culture" category. Hauerwas and William Willimon criticize Niebuhr's categories on the ground that under them "Christians are in an all-or-nothing relationship to the culture; that we must responsibly choose to be 'all,' or irresponsibly choose to be sectarian nothing."[11] Yoder argues that Anabaptists are "Christ transforming culture" Christians, but that they seek to transform it in ways other than the use of political and military power. They seek to transform culture by speaking truthfully to it, like the Hebrew prophets.[12] They also seek to transform it by building alternative communities that they hope will draw others to Christ. An example of such transformation within legal scholarship and the legal profession may be the recent influence of Anabaptist communities on the alternative dispute resolution (ADR) movement. Anabaptists have long made use of nonadversarial methods of dispute resolution, and they have been at the forefront of the ADR movement.[13] Al-

10. *See id.* and Thomas L. Shaffer, *American Lawyers and Their Communities* (1991).

11. Hauerwas and Willimon, *supra* note 9, at 41.

12. John Howard Yoder, A People in the World: Theological Interpretation, in *The Concept of the Believers' Church* 250, 252–83 (James Leo Garrett, Jr., ed., 1969).

13. *See* Andrew W. McThenia and Thomas L. Shaffer, *For Reconciliation,* 94 Yale L.J. 1660 (1985).

though it might be incorrect to place Anabaptists within the "Christ against culture" category, it probably is correct to give them a "Christ against law" label. They reject the use of the coercion that is an inherent part of law, but, as the ADR example illustrates, they work to find alternatives to the use of law.

## DUALISTS: CHRIST AND CULTURE IN PARADOX

Niebuhr's dualist category consists of those who see an incompatibility between Christ and culture, but who see a role for the Christian in each.[14] Martin Luther held Christ and culture uncomfortably in tension. He shared the Anabaptist view that culture is necessarily fallen and unredeemable. "The lust for power and the will of the strong . . . rationalizes itself in [law and social institutions]." Nevertheless, he believed that Christians appropriately play a role within the state. Political activity and service in the military are "necessary to the common life, and [are] therefore spheres in which the neighbor could be served and God be obeyed." The Christian should attempt to bring the law of Christ to culture, yet "no human self-culture, in obedience to [Christ's law] or any other, can avail to extricate man out of his sinful dilemma."[15] That must await Christ's return. Christians live in a tension, working to uphold a state that is necessarily evil. According to Luther, Christians live in both the kingdom of God and the kingdom of man. People are tainted by sin in both the church and the world (though they can be redeemed ultimately by God's grace).

Other dualists are less thoughtful than Luther. Some comfortably separate their Christian lives from their secular lives and see little connection between the two; they live one life at church and another life at the office, one life on Sunday and another life during the rest of the week. Some make inward change of the individual the focus of the Christian life and offer no Christian social ethic.

Dualist scholars might see no relationship between Christian teaching and their scholarship. Each operates under a different set of ground rules. Dualist legal scholarship might not look very much different from any other scholarship. At its worst, such scholarship might be slow to identify evil. Niebuhr is highly critical of some dualist views: "Dualism may be the refuge of worldly-minded persons who wish to make a slight obeisance in the direction of Christ, or of pious spiritualists who feel that they owe some reverence to culture. Politicians who wish to keep the influence of the gospel out of the realm of 'Real-

14. Niebuhr makes it clear that his dualist category is not to be confused with Manichaean dualism. *See* Niebuhr, *supra* note 2, at 149.

15. *Id.* at 156–57, 175.

Politik,' and economic men who desire profit above all things without being reminded that the poor shall inherit the kingdom, may profess dualism as a convenient rationalization."[16] Niebuhr notes that such views are abuses of Luther's doctrine, but they are dangers that accompany a compartmentalization of the Christian life.

## CULTURALISTS: THE CHRIST OF CULTURE

Whereas the dualist may have given up on redeeming culture, the culturalist draws no distinction between Christ and culture. Culturalists baptize culture in the name of Christ and see no need to transform it. "They feel no great tension between church and world, the social laws and the Gospel."[17] The danger is that one who takes this perspective will fail to see the ways that Christ should transform culture.

As Harold J. Berman has argued, there can be value to this perspective of culture and law.[18] It is fruitful to recognize areas of overlap between law and Christian teaching. Some of these areas of overlap may be a result of Christian influences on law in the past. Others may be a reflection of the law that is written on the hearts of all.[19]

From the perspective of history, examples of those who created a Christ of culture are clear. Niebuhr points to John Locke's *The Reasonableness of Christianity,* Kant's *Religion Within the Limits of Reason,* and Thomas Jefferson's edited version of the New Testament as examples of the Christ of Enlightenment culture.[20] Locke, Kant, and Jefferson gave us a Christian faith that looked very much like Enlightenment liberalism. Slaveholders and segregationists who justified their actions with the Bible, Marxist Christians who followed "Comrade Jesus," and American consumerist Christians who follow a Jesus who makes them rich all seem to follow culture more than Christ.

The temptations of cultural Christianity can also be great for those in Niebuhr's second category, those who intend to convert culture. The attractiveness of political power creates a strong incentive to compromise. Those within the National Council of Churches and those within the Christian Coalition would both identify themselves as Christ-transforming-culture Chris-

16. *Id.* at 184.
17. *Id.* at 83.
18. *See supra* Berman's foreword to this volume.
19. *See* Romans 2:15.
20. Niebuhr, *supra* note 2, at 91–92.

tians. But when the press releases of the National Council of Churches are indistinguishable from those of the Democratic Party and the press releases of the Christian Coalition are indistinguishable from those of the Republican Party, one wonders who is transforming whom.

There is an especially strong temptation for those who benefit from the laws of a culture to give it the blessings of religious faith. They thereby seek to use "civil religion" to reinforce the power structure that benefits them. There is great irony and sadness that the name of One who came to serve the poor and powerless can be used to serve the rich and powerful.

The danger that Christians will be cultural Christians, that we will merely call some aspect of culture "Christian" without viewing it critically, is a temptation for all Christians who interact with culture. I have cited several examples from history of groups who created a Christ of their culture. The tendency of these groups to exalt the Christ of their culture is obvious to those on the outside but may not be obvious to those on the inside. All Christians are probably guilty, to some extent, of letting "the world around [us] squeeze [us] into its own mold."[21] Short of heaven and perfect vision, our ability to see where we err is limited. Christians need humility, clarity of vision, courage, and each other if we are to remain true to Christ.

## SUMMARY

We might summarize the views of the first four traditions presented above by noting the different combinations of answers that each has to the following questions: (1) How much value is there in secular views of law? and (2) Do Christians have special insight into what the law should be? The answers that each of these groups gives are illustrated on the following chart:

|  | High view of the potential of secular legal analysis | Low view of the potential of secular legal analysis |
|---|---|---|
| Christians have special insight into what law should be | synthesists | conversionists |
| Christians do not have special insight into what law should be | dualists | separatists |

21. Romans 12:2 (Phillips New Testament).

Synthesists have a high view of the value of both secular and Christian perspectives on law—they believe that Christian teaching can be reconciled with the natural law. Conversionists have a low view of secular perspectives and a high view of Christian perspectives on law—they seek to transform law through Christian principles. Separatists have a low view of law, in whoever's hands it might be—they focus their attention on being the church rather than on law. And Dualists see value in secular law as a restrainer of evil in this fallen world, but view law as ultimately unredeemable. Culturalists do not appear on the chart because they do not have a special perspective on law; they adopt their culture's perspective on the place of religion in law.

## POSSIBLE LINES OF RECONCILIATION

In this essay I have focused on the differences between the legal perspectives of Christian traditions. There are some irreconcilable differences between these groups—the most obvious being that some separatists do not approve the use of force by the state. But the possibility may exist of reconciliation of some of the differences between the traditions' views on law. There are at least three possibilities: balance, "reading the times," and calling.

There are insights that all Christians can gain from each of the traditions. Synthesists remind Christians that we can learn from culture; conversionists remind us that we can have an impact on this fallen world; separatists remind us of the temptations (especially the temptation to pursue power) that accompany involvement with culture; dualists remind us that our views are also corrupted; and culturalists remind us of the ways in which culture may already coincide with Christian teaching. It may be that we should seek balance by drawing from the insights of each.

In the Bible we find believers making very different responses to very different legal systems: (1) Saul, David, Solomon, and other Hebrew kings governed the nation of Israel under the Mosaic legal code; (2) Hebrew prophets condemned the injustice of their own society, laws, and rulers, as well as the injustice of foreign rulers; (3) Joseph, Daniel, and other Hebrews served in administrative positions in the governments of foreign rulers; and (4) the Hebrews and the early Christians suffered under the persecution of foreign rulers.[22]

22. *See* Exodus 19–31 (Mosaic law); 1 Kings 21:15–29 (Elijah confronts King Ahab); Jeremiah 46–51 and Ezekiel 25–32 (prophets confront other nations); Genesis 41:37–57 (Joseph serving in Egypt); Exodus 1:8–2:25 (Hebrews enslaved by Egypt); Acts 12:1–19 (Christians persecuted by Rome).

Among these are examples of all of Niebuhr's approaches to culture. When Moses and Solomon drew from the wisdom of other cultures, they were synthesists.[23] When Hebrew kings used military power and Hebrew prophets used persuasion attempting to transform culture, they were conversionists. When the Jews and early Christians emphasized the importance of being distinct from the corrupting influences of the surrounding culture, they were separatists. When Daniel and Joseph served in the courts of foreign rulers while maintaining their religious commitments, they acted as dualists.

It may be that some cultures call for a particular response on the part of the faithful. The proper Christian response to a culture may be a matter of discerning the times. In some cases, it may be irresponsible for Christians *not* to use legal and political power. We might certainly criticize those within (my own) southern states who failed to take action against segregationist laws. The South's fault was in not putting into practice the teachings of its faith. One wishes that southerners had been more Christian in their courts, voting booths, and state legislatures.

At other times, it may be that the only place that a Christian can be faithful is outside of the culture. There may be no place for a Christian in a Nazi regime. A regime may be so evil that there is no hope of changing it from within. The difficulty is discerning the times—do they call for engagement or withdrawal?

What of the Christian in America today? I am confident that we do not live in Christian America and that the proper response is not to comfortably label what we have Christian. But who should be the model for Christians in modern America? David, leading Israel to reform? Amos, calling Israel to reform? Joseph, serving in the courts of Pharaoh's Egypt? The early Christians building their own communities in the catacombs of Nero's Rome? It may depend on whether we live in Israel, Egypt, or Rome. I must confess that I move in my thinking between the options suggested above. It may be that we live in a time of transition, when no one knows in what direction our culture will go or what response a Christian should make.

Finally, it may be that the proper Christian response to law and culture is a matter of calling. Within the same culture, God might call some to play one role and others to play another. God called David to be king and he called his prophet Nathan to challenge David's abuse of power. Within the same culture,

23. *See, e.g.*, John Bright, *A History of Israel* 172–73, 220 (3d ed. 1981) and sources cited therein.

possibly today's America, God calls synthesists to look for common ground with the surrounding culture, conversionists to seek to improve the culture through Christian transformation, separatists to build communities outside of the culture that might draw others to Christ, and dualists to work within the existing culture. It may be that, as Niebuhr suggests, Christ's answer to the question of culture "transcends the wisdom of all his interpreters yet employs their partial insights and their necessary conflicts."[24]

24. *See* II Samuel 12; Niebuhr, *supra* note 2, at 2.

## Section 1 Synthesists:

## Reconciling Christ and Law

To refer to Christians as synthesists is to focus on the compatibility rather than opposition of temporal and spiritual concerns. The synthesist approach, while evident in other theological traditions, is perhaps most clearly exemplified in Catholic social thought. The Catholic Church offers an organic worldview, with a harmony of elements: nature and grace, reason and faith, individual and community, world and church, natural law and gospel, temporal authority and spiritual authority. Although Catholics acknowledge tensions between these elements, they bring these realms together as a reflection of the complementarity between the human and divine in Christ.

Angela C. Carmella presents a general overview of Catholic social thought, which focuses on the philosophical and theological understanding of the human person. The "social teachings" of the Catholic Church, she writes, are grounded on a positive conception of the person, the society, the state, and its laws. The vision of the common good and justice, as informed by both natural law and biblical principles, attempts to safeguard and nurture the sacredness, dignity, rationality, freedom, responsibility, and sociality of all persons.

The Catholic tradition has a special connection to the philosophical tradition of natural law. Natural law is knowable by reason alone, accessible to all, binding upon all. Gerard V. Bradley's essay defends the possibility of natural law and presents its implications for society's laws. It illustrates the appeal of natural-law discourse, which enables conversation concerning the commonality of human experience among persons of different faiths and no faith. Other authors in this book whose essays are informed by Catholic social thought or by natural-law jurisprudence include José Roberto Juárez, Teresa Collett, Leslie Griffin, George Garvey, Thomas Shaffer, Joseph Allegretti, Catherine Mc Cauliff, and Robert Cochran.

# A Catholic View of Law
# and Justice

*Angela C. Carmella*

What do Jesus and his mission mean for our common life together in a pluralistic society, and ultimately for our vision of justice in that society?[1] The Catholic Church has reflected on questions of this sort throughout its two millennia and, with extraordinary directness, in its social teachings of the past century. In an attempt to summarize this reflection, I offer an overview of Catholic social thought as it proposes a view of the person, society, and the state, and ultimately of law and justice. I also offer a brief description of several theological positions concerning the nature of Christ, the nature of the world, and the nature of the Christian community, which serve as the foundation for Catholic social thought. Ultimately, the answers to these questions

1. I would like to thank Michael Ambrosio, John Coverdale, the Rev. Nicholas Gengaro, Paul Hauge, Catherine Mc Cauliff, Maureen O'Brien, and William Toth for their comments on earlier drafts of this essay, and William Baton for his research assistance. My deep gratitude also goes to the Rev. J. Bryan Hehir, whose lectures in the course Catholic Social Tradition and Catholic Social Teaching, given at Harvard Divinity School in 1995, have greatly influenced the structure and substance of this essay and serve as a source of information throughout, particularly in the areas of theology, natural law, and the nature of the state.

must be found in the church's understanding of the relationship between Jesus and the human person, for "Christ, the final Adam, by the revelation of the mystery of the Father and His love, fully reveals man to man himself and makes his supreme calling clear."[2]

## THEOLOGICAL BASES FOR CATHOLIC
## SOCIAL THOUGHT

During the Catholic Church's long history of involvement in temporal affairs, large-scale social, political, and legal issues have often been within the sphere of its competence and control. In particular, during the Middle Ages, the church in Europe enjoyed an ascendancy as "the guardian of culture, the fosterer of learning, the judge of the nations, the protector of the family, the governor of social religion."[3] Although it has not had such widespread sociopolitical dominance for centuries, and no longer seeks it, the church continues to be concerned institutionally and intellectually with the welfare of the whole of humanity and the world, as though both were within its care.

This posture of engagement with the world, developed through encounters between faith and culture over the millennia, is exemplified by the social teachings of the past one hundred years. These teachings are addressed *to* the world and locate the church in the thick of social issues, offering a critique of political and economic systems, a catalogue of human rights and duties, and a vision of a just global order. Furthermore, the church places itself squarely *within* the world, as seen in its announcement at the Second Vatican Council that it "is at the same time the sign and safeguard of the transcendence of the human person," witnessing to the sacredness of all persons and the stewardship of creation.[4] Additionally, it speaks of itself as a "servant church," with a gospel "duty

2. Second Vatican Council, *Gaudium et Spes (Joy and Hope: Pastoral Constitution on the Church in the Modern World)* (1965) 22, *reprinted in* The Pope Speaks, Summer 1966, at 259, 272–73. Many documents I cite in this essay (for example, individual papal encyclicals, the ecumenical council of Vatican II, and statements of bishops' conferences) constitute authoritative church teaching and are the primary sources, along with the Bible, for Catholic social teachings.

3. H. Richard Niebuhr, *Christ and Culture* 129 (1951).

4. *Gaudium et Spes* 76, *supra* note 2, at 312–13. The Second Vatican Council, 1962–65, represented the church's renewal in light of changes in the world. Its goals were twofold: the retrieval of and return to historical sources both biblical and traditional and the modernization or updating of the church in light of the modern world.

to put herself at the service of all."[5] Such a servant church must be open to the world, in conversation with the world, learning from it, teaching it—for the purpose of promoting the dignity of the human person. And if one's purpose is the promotion of human dignity, "it is impossible to accept that . . . one could or should ignore the importance of . . . justice, liberation, development and peace."[6]

Why this posture of engagement with the world, this concern for every person? It is not simply a vestige of a prior historical period when the church's influence on and responsibility for temporal affairs were considerably more direct. Theologically, the church is world-focused in its understanding of the nature of Christ, the nature of the world, and the nature of the Christian community. Catholics understand Jesus as first and foremost the Redeemer of all of creation, of all of humanity. Because redemption is universal, nothing and no one is beyond the reach of being transformed by grace. Everything is consecrated in Christ, including the market, the state, and the law. Thus, because of the mystery of redemption, "every man . . . is entrusted to the solicitude of the Church. Her solicitude is about the whole man and is focused on him in an altogether special manner. The object of her care is man in his unique unrepeatable human reality, which keeps intact the image and likeness of God Himself."[7] This emphasis on redemption is the source of a well-developed theological and philosophical anthropology at the center of the Church's social doctrine.

Although some other Christians tend to emphasize the pervasiveness of sin and the fallen nature of the world, Catholics argue that creation, though fallen, is redeemed, and essentially good; so good, in fact, that creation is "not simply a reminder of God, but the medium through which God's grace is present to humankind."[8] Because the Word has become flesh, things of the earth can carry the mystery and power of God—as the seven sacraments of the church show by using such simple elements of creation as water, oil, bread, and wine to

5. Pope Paul VI, *Octagesima Adveniens* (*A Call to Action on the Eightieth Anniversary of Rerum Novarum*, 1971) 5, *reprinted in The Gospel of Peace and Justice* 265, 267 ( J. Gremillion ed., 1975) (hereinafter *Peace and Justice*).

6. Pope Paul VI, *Evangelii Nuntiandi (An Apostolic Exhortation on Evangelization in the Modern World, 1975)* 31 *quoted in* Philip S. Land, *The Social Theology of Pope Paul VI,* America, May 12, 1979, at 392, 394.

7. Pope John Paul II, *Redemptor Hominis* (*The Redeemer of Man*, 1979) 13, *reprinted in The Encyclicals of John Paul II* 46, 65 ( J. Michael Miller, C.S.B. ed., 1996) (hereinafter *Encyclicals*). *See also* Teilhard de Chardin, *The Divine Milieu* (1960).

8. Thomas H. Groome, *Educating for Life: A Spiritual Vision for Every Teacher and Parent* 129 (1998).

mediate God's presence. But even beyond the specific sacraments, Catholics hold a "sacramental consciousness" about the whole world. "God mediates Godself to humankind, and we encounter and respond to God's grace and desire for us through the ordinary of life—through nature and the created order; through human culture and society; through our minds and bodies, hearts and souls; through our labors and efforts, our creativity and generativity; in the depths of our own being and through our relationships with others; through the events and experiences that come our way; through what we are doing and what is 'going on' around us; through everything and anything of our world."[9]

In keeping with this theological openness to a redeemed creation, the church considers reason to be capable of yielding new theological and moral wisdom, as well as aiding in the explication of doctrine. (This contrasts with other Christian traditions' regard for Scripture as the sole source of theological and moral wisdom.) Within the church's ecclesial life, "Tradition," mediated through human reason, stands alongside the Bible as a source of theological understanding forming a single deposit of faith.[10] And in the church's conversations with the world, primarily through its social teachings, "natural law" philosophy stands alongside the Bible as a source of moral understanding. The natural-law emphasis in Catholic social thought, denoted the "purely human" perspective by John Paul II, employs nontheological language and a philosophical anthropology to enable the church to address all people of goodwill on temporal matters affecting human dignity. Beginning with the Second Vatican Council, this philosophical language has increasingly given way to a language that also includes theological ideas. The church's social teachings have become more expressly biblical and christological, incorporating a theological anthropology of the person and retrieving an older, richer vision of justice. This development is intended to complement and enhance philosophically based natural-law teaching.

The clear theological sense of immersion in the world and of movement toward its transformation through the promotion of human dignity should provide some context to the church's seemingly triumphalist claim that it is "the sign and safeguard of the transcendence of the human person."[11] It must be stressed that this claim does not imply a political ministry for the church. The

9. *Id.* at 125 (italics omitted).

10. Yves Congar, *Tradition and the Traditions* (1963).

11. *Gaudium et Spes* 76, *supra* note 2, at 312–13. For a discussion of the "extensive implications" of this phrase, see John Courtney Murray, S.J., *The Issue of Church and State at Vatican Council II,* Theological Studies, Dec. 1966, at 580, 602–3.

church's own ecclesiology, its self-understanding, makes "action on behalf of justice and participation in the transformation of the world . . . a constitutive dimension of the preaching of the Gospel."[12] At the core of the church's identity—recognized as essential, not optional, aspects of that identity—are found the social teachings: the protection of human dignity and human rights, the provision of a deep sense of meaning for every human activity, and the promotion of the human family. Thus as part of its religious ministry, the church must be in the thick of social issues because its "evangelizing mission has as an essential part action for justice and the tasks of the advancement of man."[13] This ministry may (and should, according to the church) have consequences for the secular world, because the church exists in history, lives in the world and tries to influence it through dialogue and service. But any influence it has in temporal matters is a by-product of its religious ministry. "If the Church makes herself present in the defense of or in the advancement of man, she does so in line with her mission, which although it is religious and not social or political, cannot fail to consider man in the entirety of his being."[14]

The church offers an organic worldview, with a harmony and complementarity of elements—nature and grace, reason and faith, world and church, natural law and gospel, temporal and spiritual spheres—which are often considered adversarial in other religious or political systems of thought. Although tensions between them are acknowledged, these realms are brought together as a reflection of the complementarity between the human and divine in Christ. The categories are neither collapsed nor held in radical opposition. God's grace does not destroy human nature but instead perfects it; faith does not destroy human reason but complements it; the church exists in, and manifests itself through, a world created and consecrated by God. Keeping in mind the pervasively sacramental sense of the world, the church's role as servant and partner with the world in promoting human dignity, the universality of God's love, God's saving will, and God's self-disclosure, it should not be surprising that the

12. Third International Synod of Bishops, *Justitia in Mundo* (*Justice in the World*, 1971) 6, *reprinted in Catholic Social Thought: The Documentary Heritage* 513, 514 (D. A. O'Brien and T. A. Shannon eds., 1992) (hereinafter *Heritage*).

13. Pope John Paul II, *Address at Puebla*, Origins, Feb. 8, 1979, at 530, 536.

14. *Id.; see also Gaudium et Spes* 40–42, *supra* note 2, at 283–85. On the autonomy and independence of church and secular sphere, see id. at 76; John A. Coleman, S.J., Neither Liberal nor Socialist: The Originality of Catholic Social Teaching, in *One Hundred Years of Catholic Social Thought: Celebration and Challenge* 25, 36–37 (John A. Coleman ed., 1991).

social teachings built upon these theological foundations contain positive, harmonious, and organically interconnected conceptions of the person, society, the state, and law.[15] We now turn to those themes.

## THE PERSON, SOCIETY, AND STATE IN
## CATHOLIC TEACHING

Building on the fundamental conviction that all creation is essentially good, Catholic teaching recognizes four universal characteristics of the human person: dignity, rationality, free responsibility, and sociality. Though classical and biblical in its origins, this anthropology has been developed most explicitly in the past hundred years in response to the conditions and challenges of modern and postmodern society. The ongoing explication of this Catholic anthropology, particularly in the writings of the Second Vatican Council and subsequent theological reflection, and with extraordinary intensity and vigor in the writings of John Paul II, reveals the church's understanding of society (its sociology), the state (its political theory), and civil law within society (its jurisprudence).

### A Catholic Anthropology

The person is sacred and good. Taking seriously the claim that each person "is truly a visible image of the invisible God," the source of this conviction is the threefold action of God-in-history: the Creation, the Incarnation, and the Resurrection.[16] These events affirm human personhood in that they reveal God's profound love for each of us and great desire for relationship with us now and for eternity. In particular, they point to a central attribute of the human person: dignity. "The root reason for human dignity lies in man's call to communion with God. From the very circumstances of his origin man is already invited to converse with God."[17] The Incarnation shows God's regard for us, in that "human nature, by the very fact that it was assumed, not absorbed, in [Christ], has been raised in us also to a dignity beyond compare."[18] Redemption, through the Incarnation and Resurrection, "has definitively restored his dignity to man and given back meaning to his life in the world, a meaning that was lost to a

15. Groome, *supra* note 8, at 136–39. See also James Hitchcock, *Recovery of the Sacred* (1974).

16. The quotation is a reference to Christ, made in Colossians 1:15, that is applied to all persons in *Justitia in Mundo* 34, *supra* note 12, at 520.

17. *Gaudium et Spes* 19, *supra* note 2, at 269–70.

18. *Redemptor Hominis* 8, *supra* note 7, at 57.

considerable extent because of sin."[19] Although we are fallen and need to be cleansed of "original sin," we also have "original grace"—the capacity to know and respond to God's revelation in history. Thus although our proclivity to sin is recognized, the church considers us "more capable of good than evil precisely because the *imago Dei* is never lost to us."[20]

This fundamentally positive conception of the human person—sacred, good, and dignified—is ultimately bound up with the church's notions of law and society. In fact, the first step on the road to a Catholic jurisprudence is the vital centrality of human dignity to the social teachings. The dignity that comes from God's action in salvation history, the action that consecrates and transforms the human person, is obviously not bestowed by government or status, nor derived from certain conduct. As the theologian David Hollenbach has written, this dignity is a transcendental characteristic possessed by each one of us that must be recognized and respected in all concrete historical situations; we demand and enjoy recognition and respect of our worth by making moral claims upon one another, which are set forth as "universal, inviolable and inalienable" human rights.[21] Human dignity, the source of all human rights, thus becomes the standard by which the political, legal and economic structures are measured. Societal structures are "properly ordered" only when they serve all persons. The church's social teachings attempt to specify such a proper ordering "'to make human life ever more human' and [to] make every element of this life correspond to man's true dignity."[22] The church has taken the effort so seriously, in fact, that it radically amended its own centuries-old doctrines of Catholic privilege when it came to see that human dignity demanded religious freedom.[23]

The second universal human attribute is "the transcendent capacity of human reason." Based on its acceptance of the goodness of creation, the church has long held a positive conception of reason that undergirds the complementarity of reason and faith. No contradiction between them is possible because

19. *Id.* at 10, at 59.

20. Groome, *supra* note 8, at 78. For a discussion of original grace *see id.* at 228.

21. David Hollenbach, *Claims in Conflict* 90 (1979). Quoted language is from Pope John XXIII, *Pacem in Terris* (*Peace on Earth*, 1963) 9, *reprinted in Peace and Justice, supra* note 5, at 201, 203.

22. *Redemptor Hominis* 14, *supra* note 7, at 67, quoting in part from Pope Paul VI, *Populorum Progressio* (*On the Development of Peoples*, 1967), *reprinted in Peace and Justice, supra* note 5, at 240; Hollenbach, *supra* note 21, at 42–47, 90.

23. Second Vatican Council, *Dignitatis Humanae* (*Declaration on Religious Freedom*, 1965), *reprinted in The Documents of Vatican II* 672 (W. M. Abbott ed., 1966).

"the God of creation is also the God of salvation history . . . who establishes and guarantees the intelligibility and reasonableness of the natural order of things . . . and who reveals himself as the Father of our Lord Jesus Christ."[24] This contrasts on the one hand with the Protestant tendency to highlight the limits of reason and its incompatibility with faith, and on the other hand with the secular tendency to aggrandize reason and marginalize faith.

God created the human mind with the capacity for self-knowledge, which includes assessing our experiences, learning from our environment, and exercising judgment. Most significantly, the church teaches that our ability to reflect on our nature and experience can yield knowledge of universal and binding moral principles, without special revelation. The conviction that we can know "natural law" is based upon the premises that the person "is intelligent, that nature is intelligible, and that nature's intelligibilities are laws for the mind that grasps them."[25]

An intelligible moral order means that the positive law of a society can be measured against those moral principles, and that the dignity of all persons can be recognized and respected through the legal specification of universal moral claims (for example, human rights). Reason surely is affected by sin, which means that any attempt to discern natural law is fraught with the peril that we are simply accepting (even sanctifying) the status quo.[26] Yet despite these dangers, the search for objective moral principles remains important and necessary in the church's social thought. For if no intelligible moral order exists, then the transcendent worth of all persons cannot be acknowledged and promoted. In that case, the positive law would simply reflect power inequities and justify political, social, and economic exploitation and oppression.[27]

Inextricably connected to our transcendent dignity and our capacity to reason is our free will. A third attribute of the person is thus freedom coupled with responsibility, or human agency. The person is "an active participant in the fashioning of his [or her] own social and political destiny."[28] The person is not

24. Pope John Paul II, *Fides et Ratio* (*On the Relationship Between Faith and Reason*, 1998) 34 reprinted in The Pope Speaks, January–February 1999, at 1, 20.

25. John Courtney Murray, S.J., *We Hold These Truths: Catholic Reflections on the American Proposition* 298 (1960). *See generally*, Pope John Paul II, *Veritatis Splendor* (*The Splendor of Truth*, 1993) *reprinted in Encyclicals, supra* note 7, at 674.

26. *See* Charles E. Curran, *New Perspectives in Moral Theology* 78 (1976).

27. *Veritatis Splendor* 99, *supra* note 25, at 754.

28. John Courtney Murray, S.J., *The Problem of Religious Freedom*, Theological Studies (1964) 503, 545; *see also* Groome, *supra* note 8, at 85.

"a merely passive element in the social order," but is "its subject, its foundation and its end."[29] The image is not of the lone individual divorced from actual social context, nor of an individual who is the mere product of his or her surroundings, but rather of the person actively engaged in shaping and creating that context in dialogue and collaboration with others.[30]

A final fundamental characteristic of the person is sociality. The person is by nature a social being and becomes fully a person only within and through community. Catholic teaching sees the person embedded within concentric social circles: the family, the civil society of the nation, and the global human family. These relations are not contractual but organic. Because we are "meant to live with others and to work for one another's welfare," a positive conception of society emerges, one that safeguards human dignity through the specification of correlative rights and duties universal to all.[31] This emphasis on sociality differs radically from political theories that presuppose an autonomous individual who freely contracts to enter into social obligations or that subordinate the individual to the community.

The Catholic emphasis on the person-in-society is neither individualist nor collectivist but "personalist." Personal dignity is "mediated socially . . . [and imposes] duties which bind other persons, society and the state."[32] Thus to protect human dignity we must "respect the multiple social, economic, intellectual, interpersonal and religious conditions of personal development . . . [which] can be achieved only in society and through social collaboration . . . through its institutions."[33] The theologian Thomas Groome sums it up best when he writes, "We have our identity, but we have it in community; our autonomy, but in interdependence; our freedom, but with responsibility."[34] The church's social teachings on the economy exemplify this personalism, in which work is understood not only in terms of the larger economy but also of its effects on the person. An economic system must allow the person to preserve the awareness that one's work is profoundly "for oneself," because "man is the source, the center, and the purpose of all economic and social life."[35] If the economic system does not recognize this fundamental truth, "incalculable damage

29. *Pacem in Terris* 26, *supra* note 21, at 206. *See also id.* at 9, at 203.

30. Groome, *supra* note 8, at 79–81.

31. Quotation from *Pacem in Terris* 31, *supra* note 21, at 207.

32. Hollenbach, *supra* note 21, at 96–97. *See also* Coleman, *supra* note 14, at 37.

33. Hollenbach, *supra* note 21, at 78–79.

34. Groome, *supra* note 8, at 81.

35. *Gaudium et Spes* 63, *supra* note 2, at 302.

is inevitably done throughout the economic process, not only economic damage but first and foremost damage to [the person]."[36]

Given our essential dignity, intelligence, free will, and social character, Catholic social doctrine offers a catalogue of rights and duties that "flow[] directly and simultaneously from [our] very nature."[37] These rights are claims to distinct goods that are essential to human dignity. The duties are correlative, binding upon each person, group, and institution to create the conditions that will enable the realization of corresponding rights. The church recognizes the right to life and to the basic necessities (including medical care and social services) "for the proper development of life"; the right to respect and to reputation, to search for truth, to express opinions and to pursue art; the right to be informed and educated; the right to worship God and profess faith publicly; the right to choose a state in life and set up a family; the right to employment, to decent labor conditions, and to a just wage; the right to own and use property (subject to social duties); the right to organize, associate and collaborate with others; the right to move freely within and outside one's nation; the right to participate in public affairs and contribute to the common good; and the right to juridical protection of these rights.

These personal and political liberties concerning "forms of injustice in the field of the spirit" seem familiar to American lawyers because they have their analogs in what we call civil liberties coming out of a natural rights tradition.[38] But rights in Catholic social thought differ in important ways from those derived from the natural-rights tradition. First, because Catholics see a social person embedded in relationships, rights flow from prior duties owed to others. Natural-rights theories have an individualistic conception of the person who possesses rights but who owes only duties voluntarily undertaken. Second, Catholics view the state primarily as necessary and helpful in the promotion and articulation of rights and duties; natural-rights theories view it primarily as the person's adversary.

The Catholic emphasis on socioeconomic entitlements, the "material rights," is harder for American lawyers to grasp because these entitlements emphasize the responsibilities of institutions and social structures to create the conditions

36. Pope John Paul II, *Laborem Exercens* (*On Human Work*, 1981) 15, *reprinted in Heritage*, *supra* note 12, at 352, 374. *See also* David L. Gregory, *Catholic Labor Theory and the Transformation of Work*, 45 Wash. and Lee L. Rev. 119 (1988).

37. *Pacem in Terris* 9, *supra* note 21, at 203. The list that follows is found at *Pacem in Terris* 11–27, at 203–6.

38. Quotation from Pope John Paul II, *On Pilgrimage*, Origins, Oct. 11, 1979, at 258, 264.

for full development of the person. The church has been concerned for most of its history with the distribution of material goods and with what has been referred to in the social teachings as "the universal destination of all the goods of the earth." The goods of creation are intended for the entire human family, and the catalogue of rights and duties dealing with socioeconomic matters shows how these goods are to be distributed throughout human society. The teachings on private property exemplify this concern for the whole human family. The right to property is always a qualified right—property must be used in ways that recognize the moral claims of others in society.[39]

The four essential characteristics of the person—dignity, rationality, agency, and sociality—together with the universal human rights and duties that this anthropology demands, have inevitable implications for an understanding of society, politics, and law. To that we now turn.

## A CATHOLIC SOCIOLOGY AND POLITICAL THEORY

The Catholic theory of society holds first that human society is a natural outgrowth of our social character and that society is good. "Civil society" refers to the multidimensional reality of the social, economic, cultural, political, religious, and legal life of the nation. It includes all intermediate groups within society: the family, local community, professions, occupational groups, cultural groups, and various other group affiliations.[40] In accordance with the anthropology described above, the purpose of civil society is to promote the common good, "a set of social conditions which facilitate the realization of personal good by individuals."[41] Significantly, and consistent with the personalist emphasis of Catholic teaching, these social conditions are intended to guarantee (not frustrate) these individual rights. In fact, to determine the common good, one first looks at the specific goods claimed as rights. For instance, because food, housing, health care, and education are considered basic rights, it follows

39. *Pacem in Terris* 21–22, *supra* note 21, at 205. For a discussion of the universal destination of material goods, *see* Pope John Paul II, *Centesimus Annus* (*On the Hundredth Anniversary of Rerum Novarum*, 1991) 30–32, *reprinted in Heritage, supra* note 12, at 439, 461–63. For commentary on the many encyclicals discussing the right to property, see Charles E. Curran, *The Changing Anthropological Bases of Catholic Social Ethics,* in *Readings in Moral Theology 5* 188, 204–9 (Charles E. Curran and Richard A. McCormick eds., 1986).

40. Murray, *supra* note 25, at 334.

41. Hollenbach, *supra* note 21, at 64.

that a decent and growing economy must be part of the common good. Thus the common good is the totality of goods that create the conditions in which persons flourish. In its fullest sense, the common good describes social conditions designed to enable the "total human development" of the person, such as human rights for individuals, social health and development of the community, and a just, stable, and secure order.[42]

Second, Catholic social thought distinguishes sharply between civil society and the state. The state is composed of a particular set of institutions within civil society, possessing political authority through law. The church offers a positive conception of the state as it does of the person and society. Unlike much Protestant thought, which attributes the necessity of government to our sinfulness and views its main role to be the coercive restraint of evil, Catholic doctrine attributes its necessity to our sociality and views its role to be the affirmative promotion and coordination of the common good.[43] The state, through its exercise of "political power . . . is the natural and necessary link for ensuring the cohesion of the social body."[44] Despite such major social responsibility, all government authority is inherently limited because all authority is derived by delegation from God; governmental actions are limited to the furtherance of the common good and must be consistent with natural law.[45] Further, given the freedom and responsibility that inhere in the human person, the state must exercise its power "with the moral participation of the society or people" because they "are master and sovereign of their own destiny."[46]

Although both civil society and the state share the normative purpose of promoting the common good, the state does so primarily by coordinating the larger social effort. In fact, the state is considered necessary to the very existence of society precisely because the collaboration that constitutes "civil society" relies upon a center of authority. Because human dignity "makes a genuine moral demand" upon public life, the protection of human rights—those material and spiritual rights that are inherent in the person and antecedent to the state—is possible only with government involvement.[47]

The state protects and coordinates, but does not wholly define or control,

42. United States Catholic Conference, *Catechism of the Catholic Church nos. 1906–1909* (1994).

43. Hollenbach, *supra* note 21, at 57.

44. *Octagesima Adveniens* 46, *supra* note 7, at 282.

45. Coleman, *supra* note 14, at 36–37.

46. *Redemptor Hominis* 17, *supra* note 7, at 76.

47. Hollenbach, *supra* note 21, at 55.

the common good. Rather, the state takes responsibility for a subset of the common good: those "elements of the common good that are committed to the power of the state."[48] The state properly "intervenes to protect the common good, which consists in the mutual respect of rights and the fulfillment of duties by all citizens, . . . [and] defends the rights of the poor and the powerless."[49] This vital protective and coordinative role means that the state is both activist and limited. Moreover, because the state's function is related to the common good, its limited, activist role is a moral one as well: it must act in accordance with natural-law principles. In fact, although Catholic teaching favors a constitutional democratic form of government, majority decision cannot change universal rights and duties.[50]

Determining what aspects of the common good are properly within the state's function and what should be left to civil society may vary from culture to culture, but that function always includes the maintenance of public peace, public morality, and minimum standards of justice. "It is the function of government to intervene to assure that all the rights and duties of citizens are brought into the harmony of a moral order, thus assuring public peace. The state must protect freedom, and to this end freedom may be regulated. . . . It may regulate, which is to say it may order, human interaction. . . . Order is an ordering of freedom."[51] But this function of promoting and protecting the inviolable rights of the person is not limited, as Americans might think, to their judicial enforcement. The determination of what should be within the state's purview involves an analysis based on two concepts: subsidiarity and socialization.

Subsidiarity is a normative principle that refers to the attempt to address social issues first by using private, intermediate groups within civil society (unions, neighborhoods, families, churches, professional associations, and so on) at an appropriately decentralized level to encourage and support a local response. It reflects the presumption that, with respect to social issues (such as the economy and health care) that are outside the narrow scope of the state's public order function, groups within civil society and not the state should be the primary actors. Subsidiarity also reflects the coordinative role of state, in that state intervention is intended primarily to assist rather than displace those

48. Murray, *supra* note 28, at 544–45.

49. Hollenbach, *supra* note 21, at 48–49. *See also* Murray, *supra* note 25, at 325–26.

50. Pope John Paul II, *Evangelium Vitae* (*The Gospel of Life*, 1995) 70, reprinted in *Encyclicals, supra* note 7, at 792, 860–61.

51. Hollenbach, *supra* note 21, at 77.

groups within civil society in the roles they play, coordinating those groups in civil society toward the larger common good. "Wherever the welfare of a community requires concerted common action, the unity of that common action must be assured by the state. . . . [But] even when the state legitimately and necessarily intervenes . . . to 'encourage, stimulate, regulate, supplement and complement' the action of intermediate groups, Catholic social thought assumes that, as much as possible, the state should act in ways that utilize and favor rather than simply supplant voluntary associations."[52] Thus, in contrast to a common usage of the term that equates it with autonomy for nongovernmental groups vis-à-vis the state, subsidiarity in Catholic thought contains an important element of relation, even partnership, with the state. The state places political and economic resources and the force of law behind efforts toward the common good, which give rise to public-private partnerships that exemplify the state's coordinative role. The state is not conceived of as the exclusive protector of civil rights and enforcer of civil duties. Every person, every voluntary association, every professional group, and every institution bears responsibility for the common good.

Despite the weighted presumption against large-scale government intervention expressed in the concept of subsidiarity, Catholic social thought also recognizes the phenomenon of socialization, which is marked by the increasing interdependence among persons, social systems, and nations, and by the growing complexity of social issues. In the face of such changes, government must respond to address such issues adequately and comprehensively.[53] Although it is inevitable that with socialization "an increasing number of problems fall within the scope of governmental interest," subsidiarity remains a bulwark against wholesale takeover of social issues by the state.[54] State power continues to be conceived of as intervention that "does not deprive individuals and intermediary bodies of the field of activity and responsibility which are proper to them."[55]

52. Coleman, *supra* note 14, at 38. *See also Octagesima Adveniens* 46, *supra* note 5, at 282. Murray, *supra* note 25, at 334.

53. *See generally* John XXIII, *Mater et Magistra (Mother and Teacher: Christianity and Social Progress,* 1961) 51–58, *reprinted in Peace and Justice, supra* note 5, at 143; *Gaudium et Spes* 25, *supra* note 2, at 274–75. *See also* Hollenbach, *supra* note 21, at 73–74.

54. Quotation from Jean-Yves Calvez, S.J., *The Social Thought of John XXIII: Mater et Magistra* 45 (1964).

55. *Octagesima Adveniens* 46, *supra* note 5, at 282.

Some theorists could use the principle of subsidiarity to argue against "big government," but the Catholic analysis has nothing to do with a critique of size. Because the state's purpose is tied to the promotion, protection, and coordination of the common good, its role is essentially a moral one, with the principles of subsidiarity and socialization helping to determine the scope and extent of its action and the character of its relations with nonstate actors. Even with the state's limited, coordinative role, Catholic thought supports active government involvement in the economy, education, health care, housing, opposition to discrimination, and the environment—virtually every field modern political systems address.

This limited, activist, moral state described in Catholic social teachings rejects both the liberal conception of a limited, "umpire" or proceduralist state and a totalitarian state that makes a total claim to the person. It is ultimately bound by natural law: the state must recognize and respect the rights and duties of the person, as those define the meaning of the common good, enforcing them through law whenever their realization within civil society is inadequate. Furthermore, the state must recognize human dignity outside of its borders. An outgrowth of the church's emphasis on sociality has been the concept of our "solidarity" with the global human family.[56] All our social, cultural, economic, political, and legal decisions must be viewed in light of their impact on the rights and duties not only of members of the civil society of one nation but of the entire human community. Our international interdependence means that the common good is not only for the civil society of the nation but for the entire human family.

## CIVIL LAW AND JUSTICE

### A Catholic Jurisprudence

The transcendent dignity, intellect, freedom, and sociality of the person remain at the center of Catholic jurisprudence, just as they remain at the center of its sociology and political theory. A Catholic analysis and critique of the civil or positive law of a society (that is, all law promulgated by judicial, executive and legislative branches of government at all levels) starts from the premise that there is a natural law written on the human heart that is intelligible through

56. Pope John Paul II, *Sollicitudo Rei Socialis (On Social Concern, 1987)* 38–48, *reprinted in Encyclicals, supra* note 7, at 426, 461–76.

reason, and knowable without revelation, against which all civil law is measured.[57] This natural (or "moral") law thus serves as "the obligatory point of reference for civil law itself."[58]

The positive conception of the person, society, and state continues in the Catholic understanding of law. Law is "necessary for social existence, not only to restrain wrongdoers, but to channel human energies toward cooperative relationships, and to teach the basic values of the society."[59] Thus a society's law not only plays a coercive role but also has community-building and didactic functions as well—not surprising when we recall that the state's primary role is to coordinate efforts promoting the common good and that law is the typical mechanism for such coordination. Ultimately, law "guarantee[s] an ordered social coexistence in true justice . . . [and] ensure[s] that all members of society enjoy respect for certain fundamental rights which innately belong to the person."[60] And what of the situations in which the positive law does not reflect the moral law? "If civil authorities legislate for, or allow, anything that is contrary to [the moral order] and therefore contrary to the will of God," that law cannot bind "the consciences of the citizens."[61] Thus, as is the case with any natural law theory, positive law is never the final word and so conscientious objection remains an available, though rarely invoked, option.

Although the civil law must correspond to the moral law, civil law is more limited in scope because civil law reflects the limited function of the state. In fact, the political-legal community of a nation must determine whether, when, and how the rights and duties that must be promoted within the larger common good should be incorporated into the positive law of a society. Said another way, the larger community must decide when state action is appropriate

---

57. There exists an enormous literature on natural-law philosophy, both secular and religious. *See generally* 1 and 2 *Natural Law* (John Finnis ed., International Library of Essays in Law and Legal Theory, 1991).

58. *Evangelium Vitae* 70, *supra* note 50, at 861.

59. M. Cathleen Kaveny, *Listening for the Future in the Voices of the Past: John T. Noonan on Love and Power in Human History,* J.L. and Relig. 203, 210 (1994–95).

60. *Evangelium Vitae* 71, *supra* note 50, at 862. *See* Spring 1999 Symposium issue of the *South Texas Law Review* for a thought-provoking look at "the lawyer's duty to promote the common good."

61. *Pacem in Terris* 51, *supra* note 21, at 212. Note, however, that a legislator "could licitly support proposals aimed at limiting the harm done by such a law and at lessening its negative consequences at the level of general opinion and public morality. This does not in fact represent an illicit cooperation with an unjust law, but rather a legitimate and proper attempt to limit its evil aspects." *Evangelium Vitae* 73, *supra* note 50, at 864.

and necessary, noting in particular whether law will "support and strengthen forms of social interrelation . . . based on a mutual recognition and respect for the dignity of the human person."[62] If government involvement is necessary, we must decide whether it should take the form of law or whether it should take the form of political aspirational speech or formation of public opinion or education of society. Not everything within the state's jurisdiction needs a legal response, for "public authority can sometimes choose not to put a stop to something which—were it prohibited—would cause more serious harm."[63] But if a legal response is necessary, we must still determine the form of that response. Should it originate in executive, legislative, or judicial power and processes? Should it be made at the local, state, federal, and/or international level? Should it occur indirectly through incentives or directly by coercion? What sorts of remedies should be fashioned? Should the response emphasize individuals, or should it focus on structures, systems, and institutions? Should its vehicle be the development of common law, statutes, regulations, or constitutional interpretation?

Though the church's social teachings quite boldly proclaim many rights and duties and offer sophisticated social critique and reconstruction, they give no blueprint to answer these questions relating to the precise specification of the state's political-legal function. The silence is intentional, to respect national differences and give flexibility for problem solving, with the hope that the particular legal implementation is significantly informed by the principles of subsidiarity and socialization. But the church does caution us against viewing law as the final answer to every social ill, because the promotion of human dignity is the task of all of civil society, not just of the state through its laws. "If, beyond

---

62. Hollenbach, *supra* note 21, at 57. *See also* Murray, *supra* note 25, at 328–29. Many laws are considered necessary to human dignity. In economic matters, law forbids or regulates what is contrary to human dignity: "theft, deliberate retention of goods lent or objects lost, business fraud, unjust wages, forcing up prices by trading on the ignorance or hardship of another, the misappropriation and private use of the corporate property of an enterprise, work badly done, tax fraud, forgery of checks and invoices, excessive expenses, waste, etc." *Veritatis Splendor* 100, *supra* note 25, at 755. And in the political sphere: "truthfulness in the relations between those governing and those governed, openness in public administration, impartiality in the service of the body politic, respect for the rights of political adversaries, safeguarding the rights of the accused against summary trials and convictions, the just and honest use of public funds, the rejection of equivocal or illicit means in order to gain, preserve, or increase power at any cost. . . . These are principles which are primarily rooted in . . . the transcendent value of the person." *Id.* at 101, at 755.

63. *Evangelium Vitae* 71, *supra* note 50, at 862.

legal rules, there is really no deeper feeling of respect for and service to others, then even equality before the law can serve as an alibi for flagrant discrimination, continued exploitation, and actual contempt. Without a renewed education in solidarity, an overemphasis on equality can give rise to an individualism in which each claims his own rights without wishing to be answerable for the common good."[64]

### The Meaning of Justice

What is "justice" in Catholic social thought? The two sources of moral wisdom in the social teachings, revelation and reason, each yield a vision of justice. The natural law and biblical visions of justice are complementary, with the biblical vision "build[ing] upon and perfect[ing]" the vision produced by reason.[65] Catholic natural-law philosophy contains all the traditional categories of justice: commutative, distributive, and social. More broadly speaking, justice in this philosophical framework is the promotion and realization of the common good. That, of course, is no small task. That vision of justice is one in which the dignity of all persons is recognized and respected, and one in which all social, political, legal, economic, and cultural preconditions for the full flourishing of every person in every society of the world are present.

But justice for Christians is more than commutative, distributive, and social justice, more than the promotion of the common good. This is so because "Christianity combines justice with the great commandment of love, convinced that God's relationship with humankind should be the model of our relationships with each other."[66] As the American bishops have written of the Hebrew Scriptures, "People are summoned to be 'just,' that is, to be in proper relation to God, by observing God's laws which form them into a faithful community. Biblical justice is more comprehensive than subsequent philosophical definitions. It is not concerned with a strict definition of rights and duties, but with the rightness of the human condition before God and within society. Nor is justice opposed to love; rather, it is both a manifestation of love and a condition for love to grow."[67] God "is a God of justice" (Isaiah 30:18) and requires

64. *Octagesima Adveniens* 23, *supra* note 5, at 273–74.

65. This is a variant on Thomas Aquinas's statement that "faith builds upon and perfects reason." *Fides et Ratio* 43, *supra* note 24, at 25–26.

66. Groome, *supra* note 8, at 363.

67. National Conference of Catholic Bishops, *Economic Justice for All: Pastoral Letter on Catholic Social Teaching and the U.S. Economy* 39, at 22 (United States Catholic Conference, 1986). The quotations that follow are from 37–38, at 20–21.

justice from those in covenant with him. Justice is faithfulness to the covenant; and this "fidelity . . . joins obedience to God with reverence and concern for the neighbor." And this reverence and concern for neighbor demands protection of the most vulnerable. God hears their cries and treats them with special favor, and so must his people. "The justice of a community is measured by its treatment of the powerless in society, most often described as the widow, the orphan, the poor, and the stranger (non-Israelite) in the land." The result of living in right relation with God and others is a rich vision of social harmony, or "shalom" (peace).[68] Obviously, a close connection between justice and shalom exists, as is expressed in the command of Micah 6:8 to "do justice, love kindness, and walk humbly with your God."

The Christian Scriptures sound similar themes. The cornerstone of Jesus' preaching was the Kingdom of God, an image rooted in the shalom vision of justice and peace. This reign of God demands justice and "symbolize[s] God's shalom intentions for humankind and all creation."[69] After the Resurrection, "the Risen Christ symbolizes God's ultimate guarantee that God's loving will of shalom for all will be finally realized."[70] Jesus calls for a right relationship with God and neighbor, and he does so always with special concern for the poor, the oppressed, the marginalized. In fact, those who care for the vulnerable are "just"—because reverence and concern for one's unfortunate neighbor is the reverence and concern for Jesus himself.

Before the Second Vatican Council, the church's social thought articulated the goal of justice in natural-law terms. This was so because social teachings began in the late nineteenth century, at a time when a major revival of Thomist thought was under way. Thus the Catholic "language" of addressing contemporary justice concerns became that of natural law—of dignity, of rights and duties, and of the common good. The biblical language of justice—the language of covenant, of right relation, of shalom, of the Kingdom of God—was absent. Based upon Aquinas's conviction that the church should not speak a language that the polity would not understand, the church articulated its social doctrine, addressed to the world, in a language accessible to all—a language of philosophy rather than of theology. Natural law enabled the church to converse with people of all faiths and of no faith, because the reasoned discourse offered by natural law was considered universal to all persons. Yet this lack of explicit reliance on theological discourse did not mean that Scripture and theology

68. *See generally* Groome, *supra* note 8, at 365–68.
69. *Id.* at 368.
70. *Id.*

played no role. On the contrary, the social doctrine has always been deeply rooted in theological reflection on our Creation in God's image, and Christ's redemptive action in the Incarnation and Resurrection. But the social teachings were thought to be separable from these roots and capable of expression through natural law.

By the mid-twentieth century, and at the time of the Second Vatican Council in the 1960s, many theological currents of change were under discussion, including the retrieval of the Bible as a central resource for the renewal of the church's life. The implication of this wider movement for Catholic social thought was that biblical sources (and the vast reserves of Scripture scholarship and commentary) could be drawn upon more explicitly, to broaden the language and the vision of the social teachings. Given the fact of the council's determination that the social teachings were now deemed central to the identity and mission of the church, advocacy on behalf of the dignity of the person had to be articulated theologically. And so, with a more explicit acceptance of the inextricable link between holiness and justice found in the Bible, church documents on its social teachings have become in the past forty years more theological in tone and content.

The explicit biblical and theological reflection on the social concerns of our time has enriched the social teachings in several ways. First, the biblical justice described above has provided a "deeper vision of God, of the purpose of creation, and of the dignity of human life in society."[71] The importation of the scriptural image of the Kingdom of God into the social teachings, with its demand for "right relation" with God and neighbor and service to the poor, and its symbiotic connection between justice and peace, has had an important impact on the Catholic understanding of justice. The Kingdom of God "proclaimed and embodied by Jesus" offers a view of Christian discipleship as intimately connected to God's desire for justice.[72] It brings about a richer sense of the "common good" because of the vision of a society in which not only are all rights and duties fulfilled but God's generous compassion, mercy, and steadfast love are reflected in our treatment of each other. In fact, John Paul II has been instrumental in building upon the work of the Second Vatican Council to develop a theological language beyond natural law for the social teachings. The Catholic voice in the conversation with the world is now more explicitly tied to the Jesus narrative and the central demand of justice found in both Hebrew

71. *Economic Justice for All* 29, *supra* note 67, at 16.
72. Quotation *id.* at 53, at 29.

and Christian Scripture, more explicitly a reflection on the ways in which "Christ reveals man to man himself."

The biblical emphasis on the vulnerable in the social order adds synergy to a concern for the poor already present by way of the church's sacramental consciousness. Both the Bible and the church's sacramental sense call on Christians to see Jesus in the despised, the poor, the weak, and the "useless." Together the biblical and sacramental foundations make it possible for the church to place justice passionately at the center of its life for those who find themselves at the social, political, cultural, and economic margins. Because every person "is truly a visible image of the invisible God and a brother of Christ, the Christian finds in every [one] God himself and God's absolute demand for justice and love."[73] Thus it is not surprising that the social teachings have focused increasingly on the unjust distribution of material goods within and among nations. All groups in society, the state and its laws, and all nations "in coordinated cooperation" are called upon to protect the poor in special ways, to overcome social, political and economic injustices—essentially to ensure the universal destiny of the goods of creation to serve the needs of all.[74] This "preferential option for the poor" is a demand of justice and not an act of charity. In the biblical context, alleviating poverty was seen as a way to "be faithful to the Lord who has given the goods of the earth as common possession of all and be faithful to others in the human community who have equal claim to these goods."[75] It is also not surprising, given the emphasis on the marginalized, that the church calls for the protection of life through its positions against abortion, euthanasia, and the death penalty.

The biblical vision of justice has also enabled the church to articulate a more sophisticated acknowledgment of sin. Natural law lacked a developed notion of sin, due in large part to what had become an exaggerated optimism about human reason and the essential goodness of the person. It became apparent that one could not understand the immense suffering experienced in social, political, and economic contexts—the very stuff of the social teachings—without focusing on sin. In this way, exclusive reliance on natural-law language had actually constrained the social doctrine's analytical possibilities. With a new emphasis on theological reflection, the church has even gone beyond individual sinfulness to explore the concepts of "social sin" or "structures of sin,"

73. *Justitia in Mundo* 34, *supra* note 12, at 520.

74. Quotation from *Pilgrimage,* supra note 38, at 264.

75. John R. Donahue, S.J., Biblical Perspectives on Justice, in *The Faith that Does Justice* 68, 84–85 (J. C. Haughey ed., 1977).

which refer to the interrelated political, economic, social, and/or cultural structures responsible for human degradation.[76] This also corrects a tendency in natural-law thinking to be overly solicitous of the state, by allowing a firmer critique of abuses of power by political authority.

This renewed emphasis on biblical justice by no means entails a rejection of natural law. Catholic teaching has become more deeply cognizant of its long-standing conviction that we rely on both reason and revelation. As the theologian Thomas Groome puts it, natural law gives analytic precision to the biblical passion for justice.[77] And the rights and duties specified through natural-law analysis continue to be central to an understanding of justice. "Christian love of neighbor and justice cannot be separated. For love implies an absolute demand for justice, namely a recognition of the dignity and rights of one's neighbor."[78] We have returned to the anthropology of the person—dignified, intelligent, free, and social—which is ultimately rooted in Christ who consecrates all that is human, and who reveals us to ourselves and makes clear our calling to love and serve one another.

76. *Sollicitudo Rei Socialis* 35–38, *supra* note 56, at 459–63.

77. Groome, *supra* note 8, at 369–70.

78. *Justitia in Mundo* 34, *supra* note 12, at 520.

# Natural Law

*Gerard V. Bradley*

Natural *law* refers to principles and norms that have prescriptive force for human choosing, norms and principles that do not depend for their existence or validity upon human choice or decision.[1] *Natural* law refers to what reason can discover about rectitude in human choosing; these discoveries are not the product of revelation or the decrees of authority. Natural moral law might simply be called reason; observing it is a matter of doing what is "reasonable." Natural law is antecedent to all human choosing. But God is also antecedent to all human choosing. In what sense, then, does the natural moral law depend for its validity or existence upon God? The revealed word of God tells us that there is a natural moral law. Ask a Christian about the scriptural basis for believing that there is a natural moral law, and he will very likely quote this passage from St. Paul's letter to the Christians at Rome: "When Gentiles who have not the law do by nature what the law requires, . . . they show that what the law requires is writ-

1. I gratefully acknowledge the generous support of the Earhart Foundation during preparation of this essay.

ten on their hearts."[2] Ask a Christian about the content of the natural law, and he will very likely cite the Ten Commandments, and some of the specific moral duties of which Jesus spoke in the Sermon on the Mount.[3]

The natural moral law can be, and is, known apart from revelation or religious authority, save in the extended sense of revelation indicated by the notion of its being "written on their hearts." This sense is that God is the author (creator) of all there is, including what humans discover "on their hearts" by using their (created) capacity to reason.

There is a crucial distinction between natural law and all natural-law theories. Given what the natural law is, it obviously can have no history, just as the laws of physics have no history. But there is a history of scientific discovery and of human uses of scientific knowledge. Human recognition and (much more) human observance of the truths of natural law likewise have a history, including an especially eventful history among the ancient Israelites.

The natural moral law is objective; it is categorical, universal. Because its prescriptions are knowable by unaided reason, they are accessible to all persons as rational creatures, and bind persons as rational creatures.

Natural-law theories are efforts to give specific content to the natural law, and to show how that content (and, by implication, the possibility of there being a natural law at all) is true. Natural-law theories can thus be seen as attempts to verify the proposition asserted by Saint Paul: how is it the case that apart from the "law" people can know what is right? Of natural-law theories there is a history, a story of innovation, advance, declension, desuetude, and revival. One can write of medieval natural lawyers and their theories, "neoscholastic" or otherwise, and of the new classical theory of Germain Grisez, John Finnis, and Joseph Boyle.[4]

### THE 'NATURALISTIC FALLACY'

The central argument against the possibility of a natural moral law and, as far as intellectual history is concerned, the chief explanation for the emergence of contemporary skepticism, is Hume's "naturalistic fallacy." Hume famously observed:

> In every system of morality, which I have hitherto met with, I have always remarked, that the author proceeds for some time in the ordinary way of reasoning, and estab-

2. Romans 2:14–15.
3. *See* Matthew 5–7.
4. *See infra* text accompanying notes 12–16.

lishes the being of a God, or makes observations concerning human affairs; when of a sudden I am surprised to find, that instead of the usual copulations of propositions, *is,* and *is not,* I meet with no proposition that is not connected with an *ought,* or an *ought not.* This change is imperceptible; but is, however, of the last consequence. For as this *ought,* or *ought not,* expresses some new relation or affirmation, it is necessary that it should be observed and explained; and at the same time that a reason should be given, for what seems altogether inconceivable, how this new relation can be a deduction from others, which are entirely different from it . . . this small attention would . . . let us see, that the distinction of vice and virtue is not founded merely on the relations of objects, nor is perceived by reason.[5]

How much difference to the acceptance of the possibility of a natural moral law has Hume's claim made? A great deal. Most of those who believe that Hume is right reject, for that reason, the possibility of a natural moral law. Many others hold the view that because there is a natural moral law (perhaps because Scripture says that there is), Hume must (therefore) be wrong, and that one must be able to deduce or derive moral norms from nature. In both cases, the assumption is that a teleological view of nature, perhaps an Aristotelian metaphysics, is indispensable and prior to the natural moral law. Here are the apparent alternatives: Hume is wrong, and natural-law theories founded upon some basis that violates the "naturalistic fallacy" may be sound. Or Hume is right, and a sound natural-law theory, if there is one, will have to avoid the naturalistic fallacy.

The first possibility: Is there a cogent natural-law theory that depends upon what Hume criticized? The most formidable defense of this possibility of natural law has been presented by Alasdair MacIntyre.[6] MacIntyre denies the irreducible distinctiveness of theoretical and practical reason upon which Hume's claim rests. Hume sharply distinguished, as we see in the excerpt above, what is from what ought to be. MacIntyre instead defends the interdependence of these two orders of reality. Note well: neither MacIntyre nor Hume is here making a moral claim. Whether there are distinct orders of theoretical and practical reason, as Hume holds and as MacIntyre denies, is a question about the deep structure of reality, a question investigated by metaphysics.

MacIntyre's response to Hume relies crucially upon the idea of "functional concepts," terms whose meaning includes a purpose or function that the thing defined is characteristically expected to serve. MacIntyre thus essentially links

5. D. Hume, *A Treatise of Human Nature,* book III, part i, sec. 1, quoted in J. Finnis, *Natural Law and Natural Rights,* 36–37 (1980).

6. *See* Alasdair MacIntyre, *After Virtue* 57–59 (2d ed. 1984)

intelligibility and ends. He supplies the example of a watch, a thing that is understandable only as an instrument for telling time accurately: the concept of *watch* is inseparable from its goodness—a watch and a good watch are not conceptually independent of each other. MacIntyre borrows another illustration from A. N. Prior: A sea captain ought to do what a sea captain should—a sea captain should navigate safely toward his destination, keep order among the crew, and perhaps do the occasional wedding. If so, have we not derived some "oughts" from the single fact that one is a sea captain?

Yes. But the sea captain example shows only that one can get nonmoral evaluative conclusions from theoretical premises. That is not to say, however, that factual premises by themselves can entail moral evaluative conclusions. A baseball pitcher is one whose goal is to retire opposing batters without allowing runs to be scored. We judge pitchers as good or bad according to their success in doing so. A pitcher's earned run average (ERA) is an evaluative criterion: good pitchers have low ERAS. But having a low ERA does not make anyone morally good. Many pitchers with low ERAS have, in fact, been miserable fathers, inveterate drunks, and promiscuous lovers. And nothing in the concept of *pitcher,* with its built-in functional evaluative criteria of ERA, can tell anyone whether it is good for one to be a pitcher. If being a pitcher does not seem potentially morally controversial, consider the functional concept *sea captain*—of a ballistic missile submarine.

MacIntyre concedes that Prior's example lacks a conclusion with substantive moral content. He presses his challenge by expanding his use of "functional concepts." According to MacIntyre, the classical, Aristotelian tradition—Greek and medieval—involved a functional concept of man "as having essential nature and an essential purpose or function." "'Man' stands to 'good man' as 'watch' stands to 'good watch.'" MacIntyre observes that in the classical tradition, "to be a man is to fill a set of roles each of which has its own point and purpose: member of a family, citizen, soldier, philosopher, servant of God."

> The presupposition of this use of "good" is that every type of item which it is appropriate to call good or bad—including persons and actions—has, as a matter of fact, some given specific purpose or function. To call a something good therefore is also to make a factual statement. To call a particular action just or right is to say that it is what a good man would do in such a situation; hence this type of statement too is factual. Within this tradition moral and evaluative statements can be called true or false in precisely the way in which all other factual statements can be so called. But once the notion of essential human purposes or functions disappears from

morality, it begins to appear implausible to treat moral judgments as factual statements.[7]

MacIntyre might well have hold of a sound historical story; at least, it might be true that one or more traditions of moral reasoning relied upon a functional concept of humankind. But that settles nothing about the truth of Hume's criticism. Rather, it helps to identify (I presume) a historical situation in which moral reasoning proceeded handily because the premises were both loaded and, as a matter of historical fact, uncontroversial. For it is obviously sound logic to draw the conclusion that Bill ought to worship God from these two premises: (1) Man is a being who ought to worship God, and (2) Bill is a man. But are the premises true? How can they rationally be defended? MacIntyre does not satisfactorily say.

### RORTY AND CORRESPONDENCE THEORY

Many people who accept, as Hume did, the irreducible distinctiveness of theoretical and practical reason conclude that the natural moral law exists if and only if there is some reality "out there" that verifies the moral propositions that constitute it. This way of thinking is obviously attractive; it would seem, after all, that only on grounds independent of the finitude, fallibility, and uncertainty of human reasoning could perennial, universal norms be affirmed. But contemporary critics of natural law say that if there is such a reality (and there probably is not), there is no Olympian perspective from which humans could ever acquire confident knowledge of it. The critic will grant and perhaps concede that God (if there is a God) has such a view. But then persons could acquire their knowledge (and confidence in their knowledge) of natural law only via some divine communication—through revelation. But then it would not be *natural* law at all.

The criticism implicitly assumes that, apart from logical fallacies, natural law presupposes a "correspondence" theory of knowledge. Richard Rorty took aim at this target in his *Philosophy and the Mirror of Nature*. According to Rorty, to know, the classical tradition in philosophy held, is to represent accurately what is outside the mind. Truth consists of correspondence of the picture within the knowing subject's mind to a mind-independent reality outside it. Rorty criti-

7. *Id.* at 59.

cized all claims that rest upon the notion of knowledge as an accurate mental imprint (in here) of reality (out there), knowledge as "mirror of nature."

Rorty's criticism depended upon a simplistic account of his target. He conflated the separate inquiries of alethiology (theory of the nature of truth) and ontology (theory of what there is), and treated them (undifferentiated) as epistemology (roughly, the study of human knowing). The correspondence theory is strictly an alethiological theory, an account of what it would take to verify a proposition as true (sound, valid). Propositions about what there is, independent of human thought (Pluto, oxygen), *are* true by virtue of adequation to what there is out there. How could it be otherwise? So correspondence is the correct alethiological theory for propositions in the domain of theoretical knowledge.

But it is not the case that the moral norm that prohibits murder is true because it is an accurate picture of something outside our minds. That and other moral norms are not a picture of anything. If not correspondence to some mind-independent reality in nature, what makes a moral norm true, sound, valid?

## GRISEZ'S INNOVATION

A broad range of contemporary moral theories, claiming to be or being called by others "natural law" theories, have sought to ground their truth claims within (one might say) practical reason itself. Some of these theorists conceive of natural principles of justice in terms of minimal conditions of agency, quite apart from religious or philosophical conceptions of a unified end for human action, and apart from membership in particular traditions of discourse. Other theorists, often termed Kantian, attempt to derive indubitable moral knowledge from the principles of rationality itself, like the logical truth that $A$ and *not A* cannot simultaneously obtain.

The most important development in recent natural-law theory is the new classical theory first articulated by Germain Grisez in 1965 and elaborated since then by Grisez in close collaboration with John Finnis and Joseph Boyle.[8] Their theory escapes the force of Hume's criticism by recognizing (as, Grisez says, both Aristotle and Aquinas did) that one cannot derive a moral "ought"—a conclusion about what one should do—from premises about what is, including premises drawn from such theoretical disciplines as metaphysics and philosophical anthropology.

8. *See* Germain Grisez, *The First Principle of Practical Reason: A Commentary on the Summa Theologiae, 1–2, Question 94, Article 2,* 10 Natural Law Forum 168 (1965); Germain Grisez et al., *Practical Principles, Moral Truth, and Ultimate Ends,* 32 Am. J. Juris. (1987).

Grisez and his collaborators hold that moral norms are not deduced from theoretical knowledge (metaphysics, anthropology), and that it cannot logically be otherwise. Theoretical knowledge is, indeed, to be tested by its adequation (or correspondence) to what is. But practical knowledge, including our knowledge of true moral propositions, is to be tested by different criteria. The orders of theoretical and practical rationality generate distinctive nontransferable criteria of truth. The truth of practical knowledge is, according to these contemporary theorists, its adequation to possible human fulfillment considered precisely insofar as that fulfillment can be realized through human action.[9]

Is there good reason to call this a natural-law theory? Is it the case that moral norms have no connection to, or grounding in, human nature? Has the logical truth to which Hume gave expression driven all objective moralities onto Kant's ground, the ground of idealism? The real issue, as Robert George has stated it, is whether agreement with Hume entails the proposition that morality is not grounded in human nature.[10] But that proposition is not so entailed. A methodology that avoids the naturalistic fallacy—essentially an epistemological move—does not imply that there is no ontological ground for human goods.

The new theory is grounded in what can well be called human nature. For were our nature different, what counts as a human flourishing would be different. John Finnis has argued that we can know man's nature by his capacities, and his capacities by his acts, and his acts by their objects.[11] So one can arrive at an understanding of human nature precisely by identifying the basic points or objects of human acts, ultimate reasons for acting. One grasps what one is doing in any human act by asking after its point. Eventually, the questioner will be satisfied that an answer calls for no further questions. No ulterior reason is necessary to explain the action. Such a resting point is a basic good, its intelligible point—a basic human good. These ultimate reasons for acting include such "basic goods" (the new theorists' term) as life, knowledge, play, and religion. And it is this plurality of basic reasons or goods that gives the Grisez, Finnis, Boyle theory its "thickness," the capacity to generate basic principles, intermediate modes of responsibility, and some concrete moral norms—a full-orbed morality. The content of the norms they derive and defend coincides with the biblical morality of Moses, Jesus, and the common Western tradition. Concep-

9. *Id.* at 115–17.

10. Robert George, Natural Law and Human Nature, *in Contemporary Essays* 34 (Robert George ed., 1992).

11. John Finnis, *Fundamentals of Ethics* 21 (1983).

tually they are breathtaking innovators, but when it comes to conclusions, the new theorists are traditionalists.

The most commonly misunderstood feature of the new classical theory is its strategically important appeal to self-evidence. The basic goods are ultimate reasons for action, but they, exactly speaking, are not self-evident. The practical principles that pick them out are self-evident. So the first practical principles are self-evident, and they are of the type, "knowledge is to be sought and pursued."

Here is the foundationalism of the new theory: all morally significant decisions about what to do, regardless of time and place, are built upon the ground formed by the first practical principles. But the new theory is not intuitionist. Intuitions are insight without data. But the basic goods—what they are and their status as basic—are derived from the data supplied by our awareness of human choices. That is to say: anyone with the relevant experience of choosing can see that the basic goods are ultimate reasons for acting.

## POSITIVISM'S PLACE

"Is there a necessary connection between law and morality?" The anthem of natural lawyers has been, it is said, that "an unjust law is no law at all." Denial of that proposition distinguished positivists. A set-piece battle was joined.

The battle was largely the product of misunderstanding; the parties could have agreed, for the most part, upon an answer. That is largely because the focal points of the theories—natural law and positivism—are different. Natural-law theory does not purport to be about the law of a particular community. Natural-law theory purports to provide the resources necessary to morally evaluate the laws of all communities. Natural-law theorists have never claimed that law should reproduce morality. Aquinas, for example, held for good reasons that only the more grievous immoralities, chiefly those harmful to others, should be legally interdicted. No natural lawyer has ever opined that all laws promulgated by public authorities actually were just.

Positivism originated in the work of Jeremy Bentham and John Austin. They hoped to develop an understanding—indeed, a science—that would enable one to identify the "law" of a given society without reference to disputed evaluative questions about the justice or wisdom of particular laws. The positivism of Austin, H. L. A. Hart, and Joseph Raz is a refined theoretical project devoted to developing the conceptual tools required to do legal anthropology. It does not purport to do the work—which it admits is valid and necessary—of natural-law theory, which is moral evaluation of legal systems. Positivism aims to provide the resources necessary to study a distinct cultural phenomenon: the law posited by human persons for the regulation of society. Positivism is a jurisprudential theory. Natural-law theory is not. Natural-law theorists investigate how it could be the case that there are moral norms knowable by reason, antecedent to and regulative of, all morally significant human choice, including the choice to lay down—posit—this law rather than that.

There can be, and are, some natural-law theories of law, or (the same thing) natural-law jurisprudential theories. As jurisprudence, natural-law theories of law treat precisely the same subject matter that positivist theories of law do: the human (declared, posited) law, and the conceptual tools (definitions, concepts) required to identify and describe law as a distinct cultural artifact. What, then, distinguishes natural-law jurisprudence? Here the reader must be referred to the pathbreaking first chapter of John Finnis's *Natural Law and Natural Rights*.[12] In those pages Finnis cogently argues that the selection of what he calls viewpoint decisively influences the content of a jurisprudential theory and that viewpoint is dependent upon the theorist's account of genuine human flourishing. Just as a cultural anthropologist must have in mind some notion of the permanent features of human existence, including recurring opportunities for human well-being, so, too, the legal anthropologist. The challenge to any social scientist, including the jurisprude, is to come up with justified criteria for the formation of general concepts.[13] As Finnis (citing Max Weber) states it, "Descriptive social theory . . . cannot in its descriptions do without the concepts found appropriate by men of practical reasonableness to describe to themselves what they think worth doing and achieving."[14] Finnis concludes that "if there is a viewpoint within which a specifically *legal* type of social order is presumptively required by practical reason," such a viewpoint should be used as the standard of reference by the theorist describing the features of legal order.[15]

In large part due to the important work of Finnis, Neil MacCormick (who is a positivist) wrote in 1992 that the battle between positivists and natural lawyers should be declared over.[16] In my view, the only remaining important question in the "debate" is, does the existence of a positive law, at least in a basically just

12. John Finnis, *Natural Law and Natural Rights* 3–22 (1980).

13. *Id.* at 18.

14. *Id.* at 16.

15. *Id.* at 15.

16. Neil MacCormick, Natural Law and the Separation of Law and Morals, in *Contemporary Essays, supra* note 10, at 106.

society, impose a prima facie morality to obey it? Natural lawyers characteristically hold that there is a *prima facie,* defeasible duty. Positivists deny that such a duty exists.

What distinguishes moral reasoning from legal reasoning? The answer to that question, in the very general terms with which I must treat it here, is that legal reasoning is practical reasoning, restricted by stipulated definitions, reasoning by analogy and from authority, and the need to make rules easily understood, common-sense terms so that the great mass of people—who are, after all, to be guided by the law—can figure out how to coordinate their activities. Another important distinguishing feature of legal reasoning is jurisdiction: the recognized competence to decide matters finally, in a way that binds all who are affected by the decision whether they agree with the decision or not.

## THE WOLFENDEN REPORT

A second great debate that was carried on for much of the same time as the first is related in some ways, but conceptually is quite distinct from it. The second debate centers on the propriety of adverse, especially criminal, prohibitions— of so-called "victimless immoralities." This debate started in its current form in 1957, when a blue-ribbon commission headed by Sir John Wolfenden recommended to the British Parliament that it decriminalize private homosexual behavior between consenting adults. The Wolfenden Report ignited the most celebrated jurisprudential debate of the twentieth century, which involved a series of scholarly exchanges between the Oxford legal philosopher H. L. A. Hart and High Court Judge Patrick Devlin.[17] The report's specific proposal about sodomy rested upon a controversial and sweeping claim: "It is not the duty of the law to concern itself with immorality as such."[18]

Devlin's basic criticism was that there could be no "theoretical" limit to the reach of the law; no act could be said to be, *a priori* and as a matter of principle, none of the law's business.[19] Hart, while saying little directly in favor of the Wolfenden Report's reasoning, attacked Devlin's position. Hart said that if the "no-theoretical limit" claim is taken as either an empirical assertion or as a necessary truth, it is false. Societies routinely survive changes in the basic moral

17. *See* the cogent analysis of the debate in chapter 2 of Robert George, *Making Men Moral* (1993).

18. Report of the Committee on Homosexual Offenses and Prostitution (1957), as quoted in Robert George, *supra* note 17, at 49.

19. Patrick Devlin, *The Enforcement of Morals* 14 (1965).

views of their members. It is absurd to suppose, Hart concluded, that when such a change occurs, we must say one society has disintegrated, and another has succeeded it.[20]

Devlin's apparently conservative criticism of the Wolfenden Report was hardly traditional. Devlin comes off, to put it just one way, as the one in moral hyperdrive. But he is no natural lawyer at all. He rejected the possibility of an objective morality; he was conservative in his social theory, but not in morals. Devlin criticized the traditional claim that law ought to inculcate virtue as "not acceptable to Anglo-American thought. It . . . destroys freedom of conscience and is the paved road to tyranny."[21] In fact, Devlin embraced a (limited) noncognitivism about ethics: basic moral truths are inaccessible to reason. There was, for Devlin, no objective truth of the matter about morals.

Without "theoretical limits," we can now appreciate, meant to Devlin that no particular type or category of act could ever be said to be "in principle" (*a priori* or categorically) incapable of posing a threat to social cohesion. Any action (eating meat, eating fish, polygamy, monogamy) might subvert a moral commitment around which people have integrated themselves, thus constituting a society. Morals laws are justified, Devlin argued, to protect society against the disintegrating effects of actions that undermine a society's constitutive morality—whatever it might be.

## ORIGINALISM AND POSITIVISM

Consider another set-piece battle, the one between Justices Scalia and Brennan over the autonomy of constitutional adjudication from moral and (more broadly) philosophical reasoning.[22] Justice Scalia would limit a judge's investigation of the meaning of the Constitution almost entirely to traditional legal sources: constitutional text and precedent, relevant common-law practice. Justice Brennan, on the other hand, would assimilate interpretation of some broadly phrased constitutional terms to unrestricted moral analysis. This situation has often caused Justice Scalia, who considers himself an originalist, to be viewed as a legal positivist. Thus positivism and originalism tend to be linked. Many have taken originalism to be positivist precisely because of its alleged autonomy from unrestricted reasoning about justice. John Hart Ely wrote in his classic *Democracy and Distrust:* "Interpretivism [read *originalism*] is about the

20. H. L. A. Hart, *Law, Liberty, and Morality* 50–52 (1963).

21. Devlin, *supra* note 19, at 89.

22. *See, e.g.,* their exchange in *Michael H. v. Gerald D.,* 491 U.S. 110 (1989).

same thing as positivism, and natural law [is] surely one form of noninterpretivism."[23] Scalia's position notwithstanding, is it the case that a natural lawyer may not consistently adhere to a positivist account of constitutional law?

Originalists are not the positivists, at least not necessarily, their critics say they are. They do not claim that law, including constitutional law, is beyond normative evaluation. Nothing in a sound originalism denies that there are natural or inalienable rights, some of them secured in the Bill of Rights. Originalism neither implies nor entails a moral obligation on the part of contemporary judges, legislators, or citizens to obey the will of the founders, no matter what.

Originalists do insist upon the proper autonomy of law, including constitutional law, from unrestricted practical reasoning. Put a bit more decisively, positivism (like natural-law theory) is not an interpretive theory. Originalism is. There are differences between the focal point of natural-law theory and the focal point of positivism, but neither is or purports to be a technique for resolving disputed questions of the law of a particular political community (say, the United States) at a particular time (say, now).

The important question—the one that does distinguish originalists (who may—like me—be natural lawyers) from most of their critics—is to what extent judges ought to invalidate legislation on the basis of principles of natural justice not fairly discoverable in (or inferrable from) the text. Originalists insist that this is a prudential question not significantly dependent on natural justice. Reasonable persons—anticipating the kinds of individuals who would sit on the bench, the intrinsic limits of the adjudicatory setting, the need for impartially administered justice and the inevitable diversity of views over the demands of practical reason, among other factors—might well constitute a government without judicial review at all. Such an arrangement would offend no tenet of natural justice. One cannot simply *deduce* either a requirement that judicial review be established or, if it happens to be established, its contours, from natural law or natural rights. For judicial review—its scope and its nature—is itself a political institution whose practice must find its legitimacy in positive sources, normally in the Constitution of the society in which the practice occurs.

## THE DEMANDS OF NATURAL LAW

I have said that originalism does not imply or entail an obligation on the part of those exercising public authority to adhere to the text—the Constitution—no

23. John Hart Ely, *Democracy and Distrust,* 1 (1980).

matter what. Can a judge who believes in natural law render judgment in accord with positive law even when the positive law in question is unjust? Yes. The natural lawyer distinguishes the law of a particular community from the requirements of natural justice. This limited positivism is a matter of separating what counts as law here or there from what is simply right, true, just. And such a distinction distinguishes what the law is from what anyone, all things considered, may—or must—do.

Does not natural-law theory say that a judge's duty is to give judgment according to the natural law in cases of conflict between natural and positive law? No, the question of how much legislative authority a judge has to translate the natural law into positive law by nullifying positive law that he believes to be unjust is a question of positive law, not natural law. Different political systems reasonably differ (both in theory and practice) as to how much legislative authority they confer upon judges. If, for example, a particular judge's views about duty make him a positivist, his positivism does not place him in conflict with the natural law.

According to natural-law theorists, judges are under the same obligations of truth telling that the rest of us are under. If the positive law is in conflict with the natural law, the judge may not lie about it. If his duty is to give judgment according to the positive law, then he must either (1) do so or (2) recuse himself. If he can give judgment according to immoral positive law without rendering himself formally or unfairly materially complicit in its immorality, and without giving scandal, then he may licitly do so, though he may also licitly recuse himself. If not, then he must recuse himself.

Let us take the case of abortion and the example of Justice Scalia, whom we will suppose believes that abortion is immoral, and that abortion-permissive laws are unjust. He holds that the Constitution has nothing to say about abortion; if Indiana restricted or prohibited abortion, it would be free to do so, as California would be to introduce abortion-on-demand. I do not think this correctly states the Constitution's view of the matter. I think the unborn have an equal right to the protection of the homicide laws. But if Justice Scalia honestly believes that the Constitution fails to protect unborn persons, and if his choice is to render a faithful construction of positive law and not in any way to further the pro-choice cause, he could give judgment in accord with (his understanding of) the Constitution. That some states would use their authority under the Constitution to enact unjust abortion laws does not necessarily indicate that Justice Scalia intends that they do so.

The moral norm that prohibits lying must condition the moral calculus here. Otherwise, the effect would be about the same as if unjust laws were not laws at all: if lying is permissible for, say, good or proportionate reasons, a judge holding the view that abortion is tantamount to murder could justify (to himself) some false assertion about the meaning of the Constitution, to avoid the unjust consequences of an honest statement of his views about the positive law. But unjust laws are laws nonetheless (though they do not bind in conscience the way just laws do), and if the judge's honest opinion about the relevant legal materials is that permissive abortion laws are constitutionally permissible, then that is it.

The real alternatives to giving judgment according to the (unjust) positivist law are to recuse oneself from the case or to resign the office. Either move should be accompanied by a clear public statement of the reasons for doing so; the people who trusted one with judicial responsibility are entitled to be told why this exercise of the judicial office cannot, in good conscience, be performed.

Given the intended audience of this volume, the aim of this essay has been to (re)introduce natural law to legal academics by addressing, however briefly, the leading objections to the possibility of natural law, and sketching some of the relations between natural law and the positive law. To some Christians the matter is of considerably greater import. The churches since the Reformation have carried on a lively debate about natural law—about the possibility of knowing what is right without revelation, and of the salvific consequences of different answers to the question.

I write as a convinced Roman Catholic. Here is what my church holds about the relation between natural law and faith, as stated by Pope John Paul II in his encyclical *The Splendor of Truth*:

> The Church knows . . . that it is precisely *on the path of the moral life that the way of salvation is open to all.* The Second Vatican Council clearly recalled this when it stated that "those who without any fault do not know anything about Christ or his Church, yet who search for God with a sincere heart and under the influence of grace, try to put into effect the will of God as known to them through the dictate of conscience . . . can obtain eternal salvation." The Council added: "Nor does divine Providence deny the helps that are necessary for salvation to those who, through no fault of their own have not yet attained to the express recognition of God, yet who strive, not without divine grace, to lead an upright life. For whatever goodness and truth is found in them is considered by the Church as a preparation for the Gospel and bestowed by him who enlightens everyone that they may in the end have life."[24]

24. Pope John Paul II, *The Splendor of Truth* 3 (1993).

## Section 2 Conversionists:

## Christ Transforming Law

John Calvin saw the world as radically fallen. In Calvin's view, the fall infected every aspect of human life, including our reason and our law. Nevertheless, he believed that the grace of God can redeem that fallenness. Calvin's pessimism about human nature was matched by an even more powerful confidence in the sovereignty of God, who works in human affairs. At the forefront of most reform movements in the United States have been Christians motivated by the faith that Christian insight can redeem culture.

Calvinist thought was especially influential in the founding of the United States. The Pilgrims sought to establish a Christian "city on a hill," an image that has inspired many Americans (for good and ill) throughout American history. Calvinist understanding of the fallenness of man inspired a fear of what rulers might do with power. Many of the American attempts to place limits on power, such as constitutional democracy, federalism, and the separation of powers, have their roots in a Calvinist distrust of power. Marci A. Hamilton's essay explores how the Calvinist, paradoxical belief in original sin and grace shaped the Constitutional Convention's debates. David S. Caudill's essay considers the influence that a Christian's faith should have on legal scholarship. He argues that one's scholarship cannot help but be based on a worldview, and that the Christian's scholarship will either be based on a Christian worldview or borrow from some non-Christian worldview. His Calvinism bears a surprising resemblance to the views of some postmodernists. Other authors in this volume who are influenced by a Calvinist perspective include Elizabeth Mensch, Michael McConnell, John Witte, Phillip Johnson, John Nagle, and Robert Cochran.

# The Calvinist Paradox of Distrust and Hope at the Constitutional Convention

*Marci A. Hamilton*

There was a paradoxical attitude at the Constitutional Convention that has received little attention but that illuminates the Constitution's foundation.[1] It is a distinctive combination of distrust and hope: the Framers repeatedly expressed distrust of any entity exercising power, while they labored with some optimism that they could fashion a scheme of government that would deter tyranny.

This marriage of distrust in individuals but hope in properly structured institutions is no mere historical accident but has its roots in the Reformation theology of John Calvin, the greatest systematic theologian of the Reformation. Others have made the more general case that Calvinist precepts permeated the culture at the time of the framing. Many of the Framers brought to the convention a background in Calvinist theology, with Presbyterians predominating among the Calvinists.

1. I would like to thank Princeton Theological Seminary, the Center of Theological Inquiry, and the Benjamin N. Cardozo School of Law for their generous support as I researched and drafted this essay, and Arti Tandon for her excellent research assistance.

Six of the Framers were Presbyterian, including a Presbyterian minister. The two most influential Framers on the question of the structure of the Constitution, James Wilson and James Madison, were steeped in the Presbyterian tradition, Wilson having been raised and educated as a Presbyterian in Scotland and Madison educated and mentored by the foremost Presbyterian theologian of the time at the College of New Jersey (now Princeton University), the Rev. John Witherspoon. More Framers attended the Presbyterian College of New Jersey than any other single educational institution, including Yale and Harvard. The ten who studied at the College of New Jersey—Bedford, Brearly, Davie, Dayton, Ellsworth, Houston, Madison, Alexander Martin, Luther Martin, and Paterson—were thoroughly educated on Calvinist principles through the curriculum and the compulsory twice-daily chapel.

### CALVINIST HOPE AND DISTRUST

At its core, Calvinism, more than any other Protestant theology, brings together the paradox that man's will is corrupt by nature but also capable of doing good. In this paradox are mingled dread, hope, and triumph. Calvin rejected the Platonic notion that knowing good produces good: "Much as man desires to follow what is good, still he does not follow it."[2] Rather, sin is necessary and inevitable—necessary, but also voluntary. "For man, when he gave himself over to this necessity, was not deprived of will, but of soundness of will." Anyone who is measured against the law falls far short. Indeed, "the wickedness and condemnation of us all are sealed by the testimony of the law."[3] Calvin explained, though, that the condemnation by the law does not counsel despair. Rather, one's inability to live up to the law forces one to look beyond the law for salvation, happiness, and reward. Reward in this life and after is not earned but rather offered by God "to attract us by sweetness of rewards to love and seek after him."[4] Thus success is possible even in the face of humans' natural corruption.

Only the presence of God's grace ensures that the human will can be exercised for good. Without grace, human will is corrupt and tends to evil.[5] Thus good and evil are both truly possible. In colloquial terms, we can hope for the

2. Jean Calvin, *Institutes of the Christian Religion*, bk. II, ch. II, § 26, at 286 (John T. McNeill ed. and Ford Lewis Battles trans., 1975) (hereinafter Calvin, *Institutes*).

3. *Id.* at bk. II, ch. III, § 5, at 295; *id.* at bk. II, ch. VII, § 8, at 356.

4. *Id.* at bk. II, ch. VII, § 7, at 356; *id.* at bk. II, ch. VIII, § 4, at 370.

5. *See id.* ("simply to will is of man; to will ill, of a corrupt nature; to will well, of grace").

best but expect the worst from each other and from the social institutions humans devise.

One of the dominating themes of Calvin's theology is this fundamental distrust of human motives, beliefs, and actions. On Calvin's terms, there is never a moment in human history when that which is human can be trusted blindly as a force for good. Humans may try to achieve good, but there are no tricks, no imaginative role-playing, and no social organization that can guarantee the generation of good: "Let us hold this as an undoubted truth which no siege engines can shake: the mind of man has been so completely estranged from God's righteousness that it conceives, desires, and undertakes, only that which is impious, perverted, foul, impure, and infamous. The heart is so steeped in the poison of sin, that it can breathe out nothing but a loathsome stench. But if some men occasionally make a show of good, their minds nevertheless ever remain enveloped in hypocrisy and deceitful craft, and their hearts bound by inner perversity." Thus Calvinism counsels in favor of diligent surveillance of one's own and other's actions, and it also presupposes the value of the law (both biblical and secular) to guide human behavior away from its propensity to do wrong.[6] Although Calvin's views later proliferated into a number of discrete sects with distinctive theologies and organizations, distrust of human nature runs through each.

As Calvinism counsels distrust, it teaches that there is no hierarchy of humans in the eyes of God. Every human, by nature, is sinful. Not even the head of the church is free from the distrust properly trained on all men. This was the hard lesson taught by the pre-Reformation excesses of the Roman Catholic Church: that even the church, and especially its leaders, could be corrupt.[7]

6. See generally id. at bk. II, ch. II, §§ 26–27, at 286–89, and bk. II, ch. III, §§ 1–14, at 289–309. This distrust should even extend to our views of ourselves. See id. at bk. II, ch. I, § 2, at 242 ("Man by nature inclines to deluded self-admiration"); id. at bk. II, ch. V, § 19, at 340; id. at bk. II, ch. VII, § 13, at 362. Although the law is a guide, it does not single-handedly open a pathway to redemption and away from sinfulness. Calvin speaks of the "feebleness of the law" in the face of human sinfulness. Human nature makes it impossible to fulfill the law's mandates, and, therefore, "if we look only upon the law, we can only be despondent, confused, and despairing in mind, since from it all of us are condemned and accused." Id. bk. II, ch. VII, § 4, at 352. The law is quite useful, however, because once one understands how deficient one is in the face of the law, one is led to seek God's forgiveness and salvation. See id. at bk. II, ch. VII, § 13, at 361–62, and bk. II, ch. VII, § 8, at 356–57.

7. See id. at bk. II, ch. V, § 17, at 338. As an interpretive matter, Calvin argued against the notion of a supreme papacy because such an institution was "utterly unknown to the ancient fathers." See generally id. at bk. IV, ch. II, at 1040–53 ("A Comparison of the False and the True Church").

Calvin's message was not complete with his undeniable emphasis on distrust. He simultaneously pointed to the fount of human hope—the Holy Spirit—to declare that great good could be done if the Holy Spirit is permitted to work through individuals. While the human baseline is sin, "with God all things are possible."[8] God's forgiveness and redemption make salvation and goodness real. So there is reason to have hope despite human nature.

Ultimately, then, Calvin's message was optimistic, though it proceeded from a less-than-happy philosophy. In particular, he placed great hope in the possibility that the magistrates, or representatives, could achieve "just rule." In fact, "civil authority is a calling, not only holy and lawful before God, but also the most sacred and by far the most honorable of all callings in the whole life of mortal men."[9] Calvin directed his efforts toward finding structural, institutional means to avoid mistakes of the past and believed that the principles he prescribed were equally applicable to church and secular government. He prescribed prophylactic measures intended to stem sinfulness and error (knowing full well that neither can be eradicated) by altering church organization and its relation to the people in the optimistic hope that the abuses of the pre-Reformation Catholic Church could be avoided. Specifically, he advocated a system of representation in the church for the purpose of making the church accountable to the faithful.[10] In the end Calvin taught deep humility in the face of human depravity and gratitude in the face of great, and undeserved, blessings. Calvin's socio-political-theological portrait of the human situation demanded despair and hope, distrust and celebration. This deeply pragmatic acceptance of man's shortcomings in the context of great hope was evident at the Constitutional Convention, where Calvinists and Presbyterian training predominated.

## DISTRUST AND HOPE AT THE CONSTITUTIONAL CONVENTION

It is all too easy to trace the genesis of the United States Constitution to the convention in Philadelphia. The country's governing structure, though, did not appear out of whole cloth in 1787; rather, the Constitution was a reformation of the states' original constitution, the Articles of Confederation, which in

8. *See id.* at bk. IV, ch. I–II, at 1011–53; *id.* at bk. II, ch. VII, § 5, at 354 (quoting Matthew 19:26).

9. *Id.* at bk. IV, ch. XX, § 4, at 1490.

10. *See id.* at bk. IV, ch. VII, § 19, at 1138–39.

turn was the governing structure crafted in the wake of the Declaration of Independence and the Revolutionary War. The Framers did not arrive at the
Constitutional Convention to inscribe a Constitution on a *tabula rasa,* nor did
they come flush with confidence after having just defeated a more powerful foe.
The Convention's atmosphere was more sober. They came self-consciously
armed with the states' ungratifying experiences under the Articles of Confederation, with the prospect of failure on all fronts quite imminent. In the spirit of
the Protestant Reformation, they sought to reform the existing constitution,
and they chose structural principles to effect that reform.

The success of the Revolutionary War had proven the righteousness of dis-
trusting a king and a supreme Parliament. Following the war, there was a Jeffer-
sonian impulse to trust the people. In those heady post-Revolutionary days, a
number of the states severely circumscribed executive power and chained the
state legislatures to the will of the people, thinking this was the road to liberty.
They trusted the people, through the legislatures, to bring greater wisdom to
government than either the king or Parliament had. Their experiment with
democracy, however, led to near anarchy, ineffectual trade policies, and serious
vulnerability to foreign attack. By the time of the Constitutional Convention,
the Framers distrusted the people's rule as much as they had distrusted the king
and the Parliament. Yet their distrust did not deliver them to Thomas Hobbes's
conclusion that benevolent tyrants rule best. Rather, they embraced distrust as
a tool to be employed in shaping the next governing structure. Madison's *Notes
of the Debates* are permeated with statements making clear that the Framers believed *all* humans with power must be distrusted and that distrust must be
built into the system, but that a system could be crafted that would deter the
vices of power.

A Calvinist lens was held to each social entity examined. Wherever the
Framers looked, they accepted as a fact that men could and would use their
power to accomplish evil ends, rather than good. In James Madison's words,
"The truth was that all men having power ought to be distrusted to a certain
degree." All those holding power, they believed, would be tempted to expand
it: "From the nature of man we may be sure, that those who have power in their
hands will not give it up while they can retain it. On the contrary we know they
will always when they can rather increase it."[11] Yet although they accepted the
fallibility of man and his institutions, they did so in the context of a steadfast,

11. James Madison, *Notes of Debates in the Federal Convention of 1787,* 272, 288 (Adrienne
Koch ed., Ohio Univ. Press 1966) (hereinafter Madison, *Notes of Debates*); *id.* at 266 (statement of Colonel George Mason).

if wary, optimism that they might craft a governmental structure that would preserve liberty.

The convention was, at its base, a contest in distrust. The Framers repeatedly couched their explanations for rejecting or accepting proposals in terms of which proposal would be least likely to permit a governmental entity to overstep its bounds. Because there was broad consensus on the end to be avoided—tyranny—the constitutional debates typically focused on the choice of the best means to avoid tyranny. Following the teachings of the Rev. John Witherspoon, they believed that properly structured governing institutions could deter overreaching if not wholly prevent it.

For the Framers, like Calvin, the appropriate exercise of power fell between two extremes. The one holding power could exercise it ineffectually or tyrannically. Either extreme was unacceptable. Thus James Wilson catalogued the types of tyrannical government as follows: "Bad governments are of two sorts. First, that which does too little. Second, that which does too much; that which fails thro' weakness; and that which destroys through oppression." The Articles of Confederation had produced a government that suffered from the former; the Framers were deeply concerned that they not repeat the errors of the Articles, but also that the more powerful federal government they were constructing not suffer from the latter.[12]

That they were consumed with identifying and preventing abuses of power (whether through inaction or overly aggressive action), did not mean that everyone at the convention agreed when a particular governmental structure would tend to tyranny and when it would not. In the context of discussing whether there ought to be popular elections, George Mason stated the matter bluntly: "At one moment we are told that the Legislature is entitled to thorough confidence, and to indefinite power. At another, that it will be governed by intrigue & corruption, and cannot be trusted at all." James Wilson responded that "the legislature might deserve confidence in some respects, and distrust in others."[13] In short, the disagreements at the convention did not arise from different assessments of human nature or different judgments regarding ancient and modern governments but rather revolved around the different empirical assessments made by each of the Framers with respect to each social entity examined.

12. *Id.* at 222. *See id.* at 222, 296 (statements of James Wilson). *See id.* at 201 (statement of Luther Martin) (stressing that the federal government's "powers ought to be kept within narrow limits").

13. *Id.* at 308; *id.* at 309.

The following is a taxonomy of the social structures examined at the Convention and the Calvinist attitudes employed.

### Distrust of Power

Edmund Randolph of Virginia was permitted to set the agenda for the Convention with what later would be called the Randolph Plan. In its most salient points it outlined the Constitution's future structure: a bicameral legislature, a national executive, a judiciary, dual sovereignty between federal and state governments, and republicanism (or a system of representation that limited the people's power) at both the federal and state levels.[14] Each aspect featured a division of power. This distrust of centralized power was shared by other Framers as well and, in fact, dominated the convention.[15]

### Distrust of the Legislature

There was general consensus at the convention that the most tyrannical branch of the federal government would be the legislature. Pierce Butler of South Carolina responded to Randolph that he had been opposed to granting power to Congress, but Randolph's plan, which divided power between two bodies, persuaded him they were on the right path. Butler distrusted a Congress with significant power, but he was willing to provide it some power if it was not concentrated in any single social entity. Legislatures were characterized repeatedly in negative terms. For example, "the legislature will continually seek to aggrandize & perpetuate themselves; and will seize those critical moments produced by war, invasion or convulsion for that purpose." Madison observed a "tendency in our governments to throw all power into the legislative vortex. The Executives of the States are in general little more than Cyphers; the legislatures omnipotent. If no effectual check be devised for restraining the instability & encroachments of the latter, a revolution of some kind or other would be inevitable."[16] In perhaps the most Calvinist moment at the Convention, Gouverneur Morris rejected the notion that the legislature should choose the na-

---

14. *Id.* at 28–30.

15. *See* Marci A. Hamilton, *Discussion and Decisions: A Proposal to Replace the Myth of Self-Rule with an Attorneyship Model of Representation,* 69 N.Y.U. L. Rev. 477, 540 (1994) (hereinafter Hamilton, *Discussion and Decisions*); *see also* Bernard Bailyn, *The Ideological Origins of the American Revolution* 162–63 (1967); Gordon S. Wood, *The Creation of the American Republic, 1776–1787,* 559 (1969) (hereinafter Wood, *The Creation*).

16. See Madison, *Notes of Debates, supra* note 11, at 34–35; *id.* at 322 (statement of Gouverneur Morris); *id.* at 312 (statement of James Madison).

tional executive on the ground that "it will be like the election of a pope by a conclave of cardinals."[17]

### Distrust of the People

The people were trusted no more than any governmental entity. On this score, the Framers followed the Presbyterian path out of early Calvinism, which endorsed a republican polity and rejected the town meeting–style democracy of the Congregational Calvinists and the hierarchical governmental form of the Episcopalian bishopric.[18] Though thought to be the source of all legitimate power, they were not trusted to be the sole or even primary exercisers of political power. Thus the Framers distrusted not only centralized power but also power wielded by the people qua the people. Popular decisionmaking, or democracy, was routinely denigrated in the debates. Roger Sherman stated the prejudice against popular decisionmaking succinctly: "The people . . . immediately should have as little to do as may be about the Government. They want information and are constantly liable to be misled." Elbridge Gerry chimed in, stating that "the evils we experience flow from the excess of democracy." Madison did not have faith in the competency of individuals to know the public interest and said that "they themselves . . . were liable to err also, from fickleness and passion. A necessary fence against this danger would be to select a portion of enlightened citizens, whose limited number, and firmness might seasonably interpose against impetuous councils." Colonel Mason compared the people to a "blind man" in rejecting the concept of popular elections.[19] The Constitu-

17. *Id.* at 306.

18. See James L. McAllister, Jr., *Francis Allison and John Witherspoon: Political Philosophers and Revolutionaries*, 54 J. Presby. Hist. 33, 52 (1976); *The Complete Works of Rev. Thomas Smyth: The True Origin and Source of the Mecklenburg and National Declaration of Independence* 43–44 (J. Wm. Flinn ed., R. L. Bryan 1908) (1847).

19. *See* Madison, *Notes of Debates, supra* note 11, at 75–77 (James Madison); Alexander Hamilton et al., *The Federalist Papers*, No. 46 (Mentor 1961) (1788) (James Madison) ("the majority, having such co-existent passion or interest must be rendered . . . unable to concert and carry into effect schemes of oppression"). *See* Madison, *Notes of Debates, supra* note 11, at 39 (statements of Roger Sherman and Elbridge Gerry); *id.* at 42 (statement of Edmund Randolph); *id.* at 64 (statement of Colonel George Mason); *id.* at 194–95 (statement of James Madison to guard against the danger of majorities over the minority based on republican principles); *id.* at 137 (statement of Alexander Hamilton) ("He sees evils operating in the States which must soon cure the people of their fondness for democracies"); *id.* at 39; *id.* at 194; *id.* at 308.

tion's explicit choice of representation (for the federal government and the states) over direct democracy confirms the presence of such distrust at the convention.[20]

## Distrust of Religion

No social entity was immune from the Calvinist distrust that permeated the convention. Religions were treated to the same attitude. Although the Framers acknowledged religion's power and potential goodness, they were more than a little concerned that religion could exceed its appropriate bounds in the political sphere.[21] This attitude toward religion was hardly surprising; many in the United States had fled Europe to escape religious oppression at the hands of established churches.[22] For the Framers religion manifested itself in the political culture as religious sects or factions capable of wielding significant power. The Framers valued religious liberty and therefore believed in protecting religion from a potentially tyrannical state, but they equally regarded it as potentially tyrannical. In their view religion is capable of applying political pressure in ways that are unacceptable in a republican democracy. Although this view is somewhat unorthodox in contemporary discourse, it follows naturally from the genesis of Protestantism, which was born out of an awareness that the church could do wrong.[23] This view of religion as simultaneously good for society and capable of overstepping its proper bounds echoes Calvinist precepts, which marry a faith in the good that human institutions can accomplish to an acceptance of the fact that all human institutions are inevitably fallible.

20. *See* U.S. Const. art. I and art. IV, § 4 (Guarantee Clause).

21. *See* Madison, *Notes of Debates, supra* note 11, at 210 (statement of Benjamin Franklin) (suggesting that the convention hire a chaplain to guide them in their deliberations). *See id.* at 76 ("Religion itself may become a motive to persecution & oppression") (statement of James Madison).

22. *See* Rodney J. Blackman, *Showing the Fly the Way Out of the Fly-Bottle: Making Sense of the First Amendment Religion Clauses,* 42 U. Kan. L. Rev. 285, 306–7 (1994).

23. *See* Calvin, *Institutes, supra* note 2, at bk. IV, ch. II, at 1041–53. For contemporary discourse, *see* Madison, *Notes of Debates, supra* note 11, at 76 (statement of James Madison); *id.* at 306 (statement of Gouverneur Morris) (identifying "faction" with "conclave of cardinals"). *See id.* at 76. *See id.* at 77 (statement of James Madison) (stating that "a republican system on such a scale & in such a form as will controul all the evils which have been experienced will be necessary to prevent a war on factions, including religious sects"); *id.* at 428 (statement of James Madison) (discussing influence of religious parties on British Parliament).

### Distrust of the Executive

The experience with a monarchy in Britain led many of the Framers particularly to distrust the executive and to worry over its power. Some feared that a single executive would be transformed into a "hereditary monarchy." In Randolph's memorable words, a one-man executive was "the foetus of a monarchy." James Wilson argued against Randolph in favor of a unitary executive. Butler, in turn, feared the executive's veto power, observing that "in all countries the executive power is in a constant course of increase. . . . Why might not a Cataline or a Cromwell arise in this Country as well as in others."[24] Randolph, Wilson, and Butler proceeded from the same principle: every human institution is capable of tyranny. They sought, through their crafting of executive authority, to find the best means of preventing tyranny.[25] Thus, although they disagreed on the empirical question of which organization would most likely lead to tyranny, they agreed that the avoidance of tyranny by the inappropriate exercise of power was the goal of the choice.

### Distrust of the Self-Interest of Representatives

The same logic of distrust was applied to the debates over compensation for federal legislators and the federal executive. The debaters sought to avoid tyranny because they distrusted those in power, but they differed on how best to avoid tyranny. Benjamin Franklin was permitted a lengthy speech in which he suggested that federal officials receive no compensation because otherwise the country would be governed by uncontrollable and avaricious men. Compensation would induce "the bold and the violent, the men of strong passions and indefatigable activity in their selfish pursuits [to serve]. These will thrust themselves into your Government and be your rulers." Franklin lost, but only because the other Framers believed that it was necessary to offer some remuneration to induce good and not just rich men to lead the country.[26]

### Distrust of the States

The experience under the Articles of Confederation led many of the Framers also to distrust the states. James Madison, in the course of arguing in favor of

24. Madison, *Notes of Debates, supra* note 11, at 312 (statement of Colonel George Mason); *id.* at 46; *id.* at 47; *id.* at 63.

25. *See id.* at 47 (statement of James Wilson) ("unity in the Executive instead of being the foetus of monarchy would be the best safeguard against tyranny").

26. *Id.* at 52–55; *id.* at 52. *See id.* at 198.

Congress's ability to preempt state law, provided a laundry list of reasons to distrust the states: "Experience had evinced a constant tendency in the States to
encroach on the federal authority; to violate national Treaties; to infringe the
rights & interests of each other; to oppress the weaker party within their respective jurisdictions." Madison's comments elicited an outraged response
from Gerry, who trusted the federal government less than he trusted the states,
and who predicted that a federal government with preemption authority would
"enslave the States" because the Congress would abuse its power to preempt.
Wilson responded that they could not successfully correct the Articles' errors
without a federal power that could preempt state laws, and Dickinson added
that they were forced to choose between "two things": "We must either subject
the States to the danger of being injured by the power of the Natl Govt or the
latter to the danger of being injured by that of the States."[27] While Dickinson
concluded that the "danger [was] greater from the States," everyone participating in this discussion assumed that one or both governments, federal or state,
deserved to be distrusted.

A great deal of the discussion at the convention centered on the means of selecting members of the two houses of the bicameral Congress. Some distrusted
the small states, some the large, and some neither. Wilson urged strongly the
election of both houses directly by the people, as "The General Government is
not an assemblage of States, but of individuals for certain political purposes—
it is not meant for the States, but for the individuals composing them; the *individuals* therefore not the *States,* ought to be represented in it."[28]

Paradoxically, in the midst of all this distrust, the Framers expressed sincere
hope and optimism regarding the success of their endeavors. They placed their
faith, as Calvin had, in the ability of well-structured systems to deter, even if
they could not halt, the human impulse to tyranny, and they believed themselves to be "providing for [their] posterity, for [their] children and [their]
grandchildren." Wilson stated, "We should consider that we are providing a
Constitution for future generations, and not merely for the peculiar circumstances of the moment."[29]

Gouverneur Morris sketched the hope-filled mission of the typical delegate
in the following terms:

27. *Id.* at 88; *id.* at 89–90; *id.* at 91; *see also* Hamilton, *supra* note 19, at No. 46, at 295–300.
28. *Id.* at 133; *id.* at 189; *see also* Hamilton, *Discussion and Decisions, supra* note 15, at 526–27.
29. *See, e.g.,* Madison, *Notes of Debates, supra* note 11, at 279 (statement of Gouverneur
Morris) ("He came there to form a compact for the good of America"); *id.* at 288 (statement
of Roger Sherman); *id.* at 376.

He came here as a Representative of America; he flattered himself he came here in some degree as a Representative of the whole human race; for the whole human race will be affected by the proceedings of this Convention. He wished gentlemen to extend their views beyond the present moment of time; beyond the narrow limits of place from which they derive their political origin. If he were to believe some things which he had heard, he should suppose that we were assembled to truck and bargain for our particular States. He can-not descend to think that any gentlemen are really actuated by these views. We must look forward to the effects of what we do. These alone ought to guide us.[30]

Given their inclination to distrust all holders of power, one can only marvel that the Framers did not walk away from their project. It was a faith in structural solutions to the problem of fallible man that helped them persist through the major and petty disputes over the many diverse provisions of the Constitution.

Their hope was not the helium-filled hope of the Enlightenment that would lead men to believe that they could, by reason alone, solve all problems. The Framers' hope was a Calvinist hope, always tethered to the anchor of human fallibility and sinfulness. Their view, expressed in the letter to Congress that accompanied the Constitution, was that they had done the best they could. They did not display false humility about their intellectual gifts and education but rather assumed that even when armed with such blessings they would produce an imperfect document. Knowing they could not render perfection, they included Article V, which mandates the procedures for amendment and makes clear that they anticipated the necessity of altering the document over the course of time. Like the Presbyterian Church's constitution, which was being written at the same time in Philadelphia and was built on the same architecture of distrust, they assumed that the Constitution was to be "reformed, always reforming."

It should come as no surprise that the Framers borrowed from their heritage a deep-seated theological construct to address the problems they faced. Theological precepts are as available to one as any other precept when one faces a challenge. There are sufficient parallels between the scenarios facing Calvin and the Framers to justify resort to similar principles.

The Framers were charged with a mission not unlike John Calvin's in the sixteenth century: to save a failing social organization from complete dissolu-

---

30. *Id.* at 240.

tion.[31] For Calvin it was the Christian Church that needed to be saved; for the Framers, the union of the states. Each faced a social institution that was expected at its formation to be capable of fulfilling its appointed role but that had failed. By Calvin's time the Roman Catholic Church had become a corrupt but influential behemoth, which had lost sight of its fundamental mission.[32] The confederation of states had degenerated into anarchy and an "excess of democracy," meaning that mob rule, unaccountable to higher ideals, had appeared.[33] The errant church had lost sight of the Holy Spirit, which was evidenced in the fact that church leaders had established personal fiefdoms and left behind their *raison d'être*, the saving of souls.[34] The states had lost sight of the goals set in the Declaration of Independence and had made a mockery of the many lives that had been lost for the purpose of securing independence.

Calvin and the Framers also viewed their missions as emergencies.[35] Although both missions were daunting in scope, each was approached with a confidence that defies common wisdom. In spite of the power amassed by the church and its pervasive influence, Calvin set his entire existence toward repairing the institution. In spite of the failure of the states' first constitution, the Articles of Confederation, the Framers accepted the charge to fix the confederation.[36] Each set out to bring back a state of affairs that had been intended but unrealized, to institute an order that could realize liberty. Thus each shared this

31. *See generally* Calvin, *Institutes, supra* note 2; *The Confederation and the Constitution* (Gordon S. Wood ed., 1978); Wood, *The Creation, supra* note 15, at 373–74; *see also* Madison, *Notes of Debates, supra* note 11, at 30 (resolutions proposed by Edmund Randolph); *id.* at 91 (statement of James Wilson) ("To correct [the articles'] vices is the business of this convention."); *id.* at 13–17 (Madison's preface).

32. Calvin found most "unbearable" the lack of accountability of the Roman Catholic see. *See, e.g.,* Calvin, *Institutes, supra* note 2, at bk. IV, ch. VII, § 19, at 1138 ("What is most unbearable of all [is that] they leave no jurisdiction on earth to control or restrain their lust if they abuse such boundless power. Because of the primacy of the Roman Church, they say, no one has the right to review the judgments of his see. Likewise: as judge it will be judged neither by emperor, nor by kings, nor by all the clergy, nor by the people").

33. Madison, *Notes of Debates, supra* note 11, at 39 (statement of Elbridge Gerry); *see also id.* at 42 (statement of Edmund Randolph).

34. *See* Calvin, *Institutes, supra* note 2, at bk. IV, ch. V, § 5, at 1089.

35. *See, e.g., id.* at bk. IV, ch. XX, § 29, at 1516–17 (counseling courage in the face of "great and present peril"); Madison, *Notes of Debates, supra* note 11, at 241 (statement of Gouverneur Morris) ("This county must be united. If Persuasion does not unite it, the sword will").

36. *See* Madison, *Notes of Debates, supra* note 11, at 222 (statement of James Wilson); *id.* at 240 (statement of Gouverneur Morris).

paradox: the phenomenon of hope in well-created institutions coexisting with a disillusionment leading to complete distrust. Of the theological traditions available to the Framers, the Calvinist tradition offered the most pragmatic solution to the problem of human shortfall: structural tools that could redress the failure of a faulty governing scheme.

For Calvin the only liberty was salvation. Humans could not effect this liberty. Indeed, human nature stood in the way. Salvation is a gift of God. The pre-Reformation church's efforts to sell salvation were treated to Calvin's most vehement rebukes. The tyrannical rule of church leaders had impeded its true mission. Thus Calvin set himself to restructuring the church to prevent this form of human tyranny from reappearing.[37] Although the experience with the pre-Reformation church taught him not to trust any humanly conceived and run institution, he had great hope that the church could find its way back to its original mission.[38]

For the Framers liberty also was freedom from human tyranny.[39] They believed that the convention might produce a form of government that tended less toward tyranny. Charles Pinckney captured the convention's mood as follows: "Our true situation appears to me to be this. A new extensive Country containing within itself the materials for forming a Government capable of extending to its citizens all the blessings of civil & religious liberty capable of making them happy at home. This is the great end of Republican Establishments."[40] The goal was conceived; the "materials" were available. The convention sought the right pragmatic structure to solve the problems posed by the Articles of Confederation and to prevent their recurrence.

In the back-and-forth of philosophical and political debates, we are often asked to choose between two conflicting options. Enlightenment-trained reason is supposed to be able to lead us to one or another.[41] Calvinist theology taught the Framers, in contrast, that the paradoxical elements of distrust and hope could be brought together to good effect.

---

37. *See* Calvin, *Institutes, supra* note 2, bk. IV, at 1011–1521.

38. *See id.* bk. IV, ch. XX, § 32, at 1520–21.

39. The words *tyranny* and *tyrannical* appear repeatedly in Madison's *Notes on the Debates. See, e.g.,* Madison, *Notes of Debates, supra* note 11, at 47, 48, 22, 308, 323, 615.

40. *Id.* at 185 (statement of Charles Pinckney).

41. *See generally* Steven Smith, *The Pride of Reason* (1997).

# A Calvinist Perspective on the Place of Faith in Legal Scholarship

*David S. Caudill*

As the title of my essay implies, I shall not attempt to represent *the* Calvinist vision of how scholarship reflects, or might or should reflect, a scholar's faith.[1] Given that the Reformation and the Reformed tradition are complex phenomena, respectively, in the history and in the current state of the Christian religion, numerous views on the relation between faith and theoretical knowledge could properly be character-ized as Calvinist. The position I will describe as neo-Calvinist is a par-ticular movement arising out of the Calvinist tradition in Holland (represented internationally now by Christian Reformed or Dutch Reformed churches). Neo-Calvinism in my terminology refers to those who trace their theology, and especially their views on the rela-tion between faith and scholarship, from Calvin to Groen van Prin-sterer to Kuyper to the philosophers Dooyeweerd and Vollenhoven, and finally to certain reformational philosophers of this generation.[2]

1. An earlier version of this essay appeared as *A Calvinist Perspective on Faith in Legal Scholarship,* 47 J. Legal Ed. 19 (1997), and is used with permission.

2. For a brief introduction to this particular neo-Calvinist movement, see Bernard Zylstra, Introduction, in L. Kalsbeek, *Contours of a Christian Philosophy* (Bernard Zylstra and Josina Zylstra eds., 1975).

Those names are associated with a school of thought that provides not only a normative method for integrating faith and intellectual pursuits but also a descriptive account of the necessary and inevitable relation between religion and all theoretical thought, including legal scholarship.

On the normative side, the Free University of Amsterdam, where I studied philosophy, was founded in 1880 by Abraham Kuyper (1837–1920) for the purpose of linking all disciplinary research to Christian belief.[3] That is where Herman Dooyeweerd and Dirk H. T. Vollenhoven taught philosophy—Dooyeweerd was a legal theorist.[4] The tradition of seeking a Christian perspective within each discipline remains important today at the Free University, even though it is now a state school with a diverse faculty, some of whom are quite hostile toward Kuyperian philosophy; the tradition continues as well in North America among many faculty members at the Institute for Christian Studies and at Redeemer College (both in Ontario), and to a lesser extent at Calvin College (Michigan) and Dordt College (Iowa), to name a few. Also in that tradition are the Center for Public Justice in Annapolis, a policy research and educational effort focusing on Christian political theory, its director James Skillen, and many of its members.[5]

On the descriptive side, I should at the outset highlight the unique and perhaps unfamiliar meanings attached, in what follows, to the terms *religion* and *faith*. In everyday discourse, the terms *religion* and *secularism,* taken to mean faith and unbelief, are antithetical, so that phrases like "the religion of unbelief" or "secular religion" are seemingly contradictory. In the neo-Calvinist tra-

---

3. Kuyper asserted that Calvinism is a worldview, with implications for all of life, and not merely a theological doctrine. See Abraham Kuyper, *Lectures on Calvinism* (1898).

4. Dooyeweerd's major work in Christian philosophy is the four-volume *A New Critique of Theoretical Thought* (David Freeman and William Young trans., 1953). For a summary of Dooyeweerd's views in this work and others, see David Caudill, *Disclosing Tilt: A Partial Defense of Critical Legal Studies and a Comparative Introduction to the Philosophy of the Law-Idea,* 72 Iowa L. Rev. 287 (1987). The "philosophy of the law-idea" (Wijsbegeerte der Wetsidee) is Dooyeweerd's term for his theoretical framework.

5. Skillen's book, *Recharging the American Experience: Principled Pluralism for Genuine Civic Community* (1994), reflects the influence of Kuyper in its argument for structural, as well as confessional, pluralism. *Structural* refers to various arenas of communal life (like family or schools) of which the state is only one limited example, a notion referred to as "sphere sovereignty" in Kuyperian literature. Skillen is also a student of Dooyeweerd; *see* James Skillen, *Herman Dooyeweerd's Contribution to the Philosophy of the Social Sciences,* J. Am. Sci. Affiliation, Mar. 1979, at 21.

dition, however, neither *religion* nor *faith* is limited by reference to theism, churches, the "great" world religions, or even conscious commitments to a set of theological doctrines or to a moral code. Rather, those terms are associated with the inevitable philosophical assumptions (or foundational presuppositions) that ground any human reflection, however those assumptions are systematized, and whether or not one is even aware of their functions in everyday or in theoretical thought. Thus faith and religion might be helpfully analogized to the popular terms *paradigm, steering field, discursive matrix, worldview,* and *ideology.* That is why neo-Calvinist philosophy in its descriptive aspect is properly identified with contemporary criticism of Enlightenment ideals of rationality, scientific objectivity, and the autonomous subject-in-control. (Of course, even in "descriptive" accounts of our dependence on ideological, pretheoretical commitments, there is an implied prescription that everyone should acknowledge that dependence in interideological discourse.)

Some readers may find it strange to classify neo-Calvinism, a historical religious perspective, along the lines of contemporary social constructivism, with its emphases on interpretive communities and on the narrativity of scientific knowledge. The analogy is justifiable but should be qualified. First, although Calvin is properly associated with this-worldly religion in his political activism and in his critique of Anabaptist otherworldliness, it would be wrong to associate Calvinism with rationalism or natural law in the Thomist tradition of Christian thought.[6] A recent book entitled *Rational Faith: Catholic Responses to Reformed Epistemology,* specifically critiques the views I offer below.[7] In reading that book, I realized how comfortable I am with the antifoundationalist, postmodern critique of rationalism, and how little I believe in the possibility of

6. See Michael Walzer, *The Revolution of the Saints* 28 (1965) (Calvin "firmly believed that the terrors of political life could be politically controlled [thus] he became an activist and ecclesiastical politician. . . . He promptly engaged in sharp polemic against the Anabaptists, whose goal was not so much reconstruction as the dissolution of the political world. . . . Calvinism was thus anchored in this worldly endeavor").

7. *Rational Faith: Catholic Responses to Reformed Epistemology* (L. Zagzebski ed., 1993). The chapter by Hugo Meynell, entitled Faith, Foundationalism, and Nicholas Wolterstorff, is a critique of Wolterstorff's *Reason Within the Bounds of Religion* (1976) discussed below. The Catholic critique of neo-Calvinism is in fact a response to Herman Dooyeweerd's criticism of Roman Catholic philosophy for its exaltation of human reason, which Dooyeweerd viewed as a compromise of synthesis between Greek and biblical worldviews. *See* Herman Dooyeweerd, *Roots of Western Culture: Pagan, Secular, and Christian Options* 115–32 (John Kraay trans., 1979).

determinative reason, even though I do not believe that "anything goes."[8] Second, the use of the term *religion* to describe every person's theistic or philosophical, confessional or hidden, pretheoretical commitments should not be read as a reduction of religion per se to an intellectual and individual affair—it only sounds that way in a discussion of the relationship of faith to theoretical thought. Calvinistic Christianity is devotional (if not mystical) in its orientation to prayer and worship and communal in its orientation to relationships, family, sectarian schools, and the church; indeed, even with respect to scholarship, the heritage of Protestant individualism is mediated by an orientation to intellectual traditions and communities in which scholars work.

At some risk of oversimplification, I should summarize several "theses" in the neo-Calvinist version of the Reformational perspective on the relation between faith and theoretical inquiry. First, the relation between faith and scholarship is unavoidable. Scholarship will always reflect faith, either a scholar's own consciously adopted ("confessional") faith or somebody else's faith, because all theoretical thought is based upon pretheoretical assumptions that are not ultimately verifiable except by faith. Second, and this is the flip side of my first thesis, there is no neutral or secular ground of principles to which scholars may appeal, no public reason in Rawlsian terms, and no common sense by which scholars can avoid faith.[9] There are, of course, shared experiences and common perceptual equipment and a shared language and form of logical argument, but the point is that these alone will not get you very far.[10] Setting aside the question of whether we can agree on how to build houses or cars without reference to faith, our views of justice and morality in law necessarily in-

8. See Meynell, *supra* note 7, at 80–81. ("I am troubled by the fact that, as it seems to me, no belief is so cognitively bizarre or morally frightful that it could not be defended on the basis of the kind of account that Wolterstorff advances. He strenuously denies—though he admits that the claim is often made—that 'anything goes' can validly be inferred from his anti-foundationalist position. But I am not convinced. . . . [On] Wolterstorff's view, no set of 'control beliefs' has foundations any more reliable than any other.") I think there is an assumption in the above criticism that the categories of *bizarre* and *frightful* are matters of reason; Wolterstorff, on the other hand, recognizes the social, historical, and discursive "foundations" upon which such judgments rest.

9. *See* David Caudill, *Pluralism and the Quality of Religious Discourse In Law and Politics,* 6 Fla. J.L. and Pub. Policy 135, 145–55 (1994), for a critique of Lawrence Solum's notions, following Rawls, of public reason and common sense.

10. *See id.* at 142 (citing J. M. Balkin, *Ideological Drift and the Struggle over Meaning,* 25 Conn. L. Rev. 869, 879 (1993)).

volve faithlike presuppositions.[11] Third, and finally, there is a religious aspect
to all legal thought and legal scholarship, such that scholars who belong, for example, to a theistic religious tradition need not feel that they are adding something foreign or interdisciplinary to law when they do legal analyses or criticism
on the basis of their "confessed" religious assumptions about humanity and
culture. That is not to say that Christian scholars, for example, should argue for
the legislation of biblical norms but rather that their fundamental commitments might (and perhaps should) affect their notions of justice and human
rights and liberty and even democratic pluralism. Of course, they might not—
a Christian scholar might be privately Christian but "secular" in his or her
scholarship, which in the neo-Calvinist perspective means that the Christian
holds two "religions"—a private confessional religion and a secular religion or
system of assumptions for scholarship.

These three theses, which are actually three ways of saying the same thing,
represent a vision of the relation of faith to scholarship with roots in an identifiable historical tradition. Although I think that this vision finds support in the
Bible, and in the writings of St. Augustine and Calvin, I begin with Guillaume
Groen van Prinsterer (1801–76), a Dutch politician who wrote about the
French Revolution in his major work *Unbelief and Revolution*.[12] Unbelief, it
turns out, is for Groen the religion that sustained the French Revolution, and
that religion turns out to be the antithesis of Reformational Christianity (the
"belief" in the word *unbelief* ).

Groen was not saying that civilization was Christian before the French Revolution; indeed, he traces the revolutionary ideals of liberty and equality from
Rome forward. His focus in nineteenth-century Europe was on the need to reassert a Calvinist vision of the state in opposition to the mainstream political
ideology of the day (which reflected atheism or non-Calvinist theism, both
"unbelief"). Groen, of course, did not oppose liberty and equality in the abstract, but he was critical of the particular interpretations given to those terms
in revolutionary politics. I emphasize here his belief that all theory is religious,
which led him to see on the one hand the need for a Christian political party
(later called the Antirevolutionary Party) as well as the need for Christian
schools that would be different from government schools, and on the other

11. *See* Caudill, *supra* note 9, at 162–66.
12. *See* Caudill, *The French Revolution as Phantom of the Opera*, 9 J. L. and Rel. 243 (1991)
for a review of Harry van Dyke's translation of and commentary on *Unbelief and Revolution*.

hand the necessity of doing scholarship (he was a historian) from a particular perspective; he believed that his religion gave him insights as to how ideas, not just events, drive history. Groen's transparency, his admission of a point of view, was, of course, viewed as a cardinal sin by fellow historians—he had lost his objectivity.

Groen's successor in Parliament in the late nineteenth century was Abraham Kuyper. In his 1898 Stone Lectures at Princeton, entitled "Lectures on Calvinism," Kuyper expanded Groen's arguments but stayed within the ideological dualism between Enlightenment Modernism and Calvinism. That is, Kuyper tended toward a vision of two worldviews in conflict—the reformed view, and everything else. Like Groen, Kuyper thought there should be a Christian political party and Christian schools, but he added everything else in culture to his list of ideology-based thinking. Not only history but art, all the humanities and sciences, all reflection on the family and morality, indeed, all thought proceeds on the basis of either a modernist worldview or a Calvinist worldview. (There is a clear bias here against all non-Calvinist Christian thought, which falls into the category of modernistic unbelief; for me that is a weak point in Kuyper's analysis.) The idea behind Kuyper's founding of the Free University of Amsterdam—free of government control—was that all disciplines could be taught on the basis of a Reformational Christian worldview. Kuyper was famous for saying that "there is not one square inch of life that should not be claimed for the Kingdom of Christ," by which he did not mean religious imperialism.[13] He meant that all of life is already religion, and Christians should not defer to another religion in their understanding of any aspect of life. Although critics wondered how Christian math or chemistry would proceed on the basis of grounds distinct from Enlightenment ideals of rationality, the university flourished and grew.

Herman Dooyeweerd redeveloped Kuyper's notion of unavoidable religious ideology. Many of Dooyeweerd's prize students became disciples and revisionists of his systematic Christian philosophy, which might be characterized as neo-Kantian and neo-Kuyperian. On the Kantian side—and I refer here to Kant's categorical tendencies: pure and practical reason, phenomenal and noumenal experience, and so on—Dooyeweerd developed a grand theory of all of the aspects of the "creation." He ended up with fourteen modalities of existence, beginning with the lowest, the numerical, then the spatial, then the physical,

13. *See* Kuyper, *supra* note 3, at 20, 72, 117.

which three roughly correspond to the objects of mathematics, of physics, and of inorganic chemistry. The fourth modality on the way up the ladder is the biotic, then the psychical, the logical, the historical, the linguistic—you can see that the modalities are getting more complex—then the social, the economic, the aesthetic, the juridical, the moral, and finally the highest modality of existence, the pistical or faith-oriented aspect of our lives.[14]

Of course, each such feature of the creation is represented by an academic discipline that focuses on that modality, and it is no coincidence that the Free University building in Amsterdam has fourteen floors, and that the fourteenth floor houses the theology department. Just under it is philosophy; the law faculty is a few floors below, above the art department, and so forth. This is perhaps the clearest concretization of an abstract philosophy in the world today. Roughly, the idea is that each discipline is seeking to discover God's laws for a particular aspect of reality; no discipline can explain everything or take priority, or you will by reductionism end up, for example, with historicism, or psychologism, or biologism.[15] The hierarchy is to suggest not that theology explains everything but only that it contains the highest of human ideals. Each thing in the world (for example, a rose, a painting, the U.C.C., the ideal of human freedom) functions primarily in one of those categories and requires everything below it to understand it (for example, a rose is biotic, a fourth-level phenomena, but it also has physical, spatial, and numerical aspects). That sort of systematizing is out of fashion nowadays, and most people think it ended with Hegel, but I mention it to show how seriously Dooyeweerd took Kuyper's neo-Calvinism. Dooyeweerd also took seriously the notion of worldviews in conflict, but he proposed four worldviews—the Greek, the Thomistic, the Reformational, and the Humanistic—and he proceeded to categorize the major figures of Western philosophy according to each one's fundamental ground-motive.[16] The weakness in that scheme is that it is overly philosophical—oriented to major philosophical figures and movements—and overly Western, for a large part of the world is left out.

That brings me to the neo-Calvinist perspective today, which inherited from Dooyeweerd a strong critique of Enlightenment rationalism, a suspicion concerning the natural sciences as the model for human knowledge, and a desire to

14. *See* Dooyeweerd, *A New Critique, supra* note 4, vol. 2 at 55–163; see also Skillen, *Herman Dooyeweerd's Contribution, supra* note 5, at 22.

15. *See e.g.,* 2 Dooyeweerd, *supra* note 3, at 200 (regarding historicism).

16. *See* Dooyeweerd, *supra* note 7, at 15.

identify fundamental belief-structures that guide theoretical thought, including legal theory and scholarship.[17] Nicholas Wolterstorff, a neo-Calvinist philosopher of religion at Yale, wrote a small book entitled *Reason Within the Bounds of Religion*—a play on Kant's *Religion Within the Bounds of Reason*—which is a primer on the notion of how belief functions in theoretical thought.[18] Wolterstorff argues that theoretical inquiry begins with a set of control beliefs, roughly analogous to a Kuhnian paradigm, and that the theories one is willing to accept are controlled or governed by these belief-structures.[19] Control beliefs might include fundamental assumptions about human nature, morality, human freedom, historical progress, and so forth. These control beliefs, significantly, produce neither the theory nor the data for the theory.[20] So taking the Christian religion as an example, Christian scholars might find their orientation in the Bible, but the Bible does not give them theories or data. They approach the data like everyone else, by observing and reflecting upon the world, and then come up with imaginative theories like everyone else, by weighing them against the data, but they are not likely to theorize that life has no meaning or that morality is only an aspect of social power, because of their control beliefs.

I was reading a marriage therapy book the other day in which the author included in the introduction a section entitled "Locating Myself."[21] There she confessed, for the benefit of the reader, who and what she was—a Jungian analyst, a married person committed to the family, a marriage therapist, and so forth; she then acknowledged the risk that someone might immediately reject the book: "Oh, she's one of *those*, so this book is about *that*."[22] In spite of that risk, it is apparent that all of us are "located"; legal scholars will not be influenced solely by their control beliefs, because we are also lawyers, and we view things from a certain society and class and race and sex, and we each have a personality to contend with.[23] Those aspects of our lives influence the way we interpret the world. Scholarship is personal, and one of the foundational presuppositions of neo-Calvinist philosophy is that every scholar places his experiences

17. *See* Caudill, *supra* note 4, at 345–48.

18. Nicholas Wolterstorff, *Reason Within the Bounds of Religion* (1976).

19. *Id.* at 74–75.

20. *Id.* at 74.

21. *See* Polly Young-Eisendrath, *You're Not What I Expected: Learning to Love the Opposite Sex* (1993).

22. *Id.* at 13–15.

23. Wolterstorff, *supra* note 18, at 79.

within belief-structures that make scholarship possible. Significantly, more than one theory may satisfy a set of control beliefs, so Christian scholars may disagree as to *the* Christian view of politics or law, and they will not always be able to refer to the Bible for answers, because the Bible does not function as a set of theories.[24] Thus theories represent a scholar's best efforts to work out the implications of his or her faith.

I find this scheme compelling but also complicated, and it is a complication often overlooked in the current law-and-religion debates, where the question is often asked whether a judge or legislator may impose her religious beliefs in legal decisionmaking. That question, for many liberal theorists, is whether the decisionmaker may use the Bible for a guide or should be limited to common sense and secular reason; from the Calvinist perspective the basis for a religious lawmaker's decision is neither of those two alternatives but rather is one of two other alternatives. That is, the Bible rarely gives a solution to a concrete legal controversy, and common sense rarely can offer such a solution. The question highlighted in neo-Calvinist criticism is whether the decisionmaker, if a Christian, was relying on a Christian perspective on the world or was relying on a perspective on the world that was controlled by another set of beliefs, perhaps the dominant beliefs of the American intelligentsia, which beliefs are just as "religious," in Groen's, Kuyper's, and Dooyeweerd's philosophy, as Christianity.[25]

The above example highlights as well the neo-Calvinist distinction between a confessional or consciously adopted "religion" and an influential yet hidden set of control beliefs, both of which may coexist in the hypothetical judge or legislator if he does not rely on his confessional religion in the activity of theoretical thought. A more authentic believer would theorize self-reflectively, on the basis of conscious commitments. The demand of neo-Calvinism is then upon Christians to align their confessional faith with their control beliefs in theoretical legal inquiry, and upon others to acknowledge their own control beliefs in debates over law and politics.

An example, perhaps oversimplified, might help at this point. If we consider homosexuality—and I could just as easily choose abortion or animal rights as

24. *Id.* at 74–75.

25. See Neil Duxbury, *Faith in Reason: The Process Tradition in American Jurisprudence,* 15 Cardozo L. Rev. 601, 703 (1993) ("The [process] tradition must be understood primarily as to embodiment of an attitude concerning the importance of rationality within a democracy. Process jurisprudence is . . . in essence, an attempt by lawyers to turn into theory the faith which they hold in common with other American intellectuals").

an example of how neither the Bible nor common sense (or public reason) give us answers to the legal questions involved—some Christians may theorize that it should be discouraged or prohibited by the government because of their belief that it is condemned in the Bible. But I might say that that is a bad political theory, and I might propose a political theory, for our pluralistic society, recommending not just that the government should be tolerant—for tolerance implies passive condemnation—but that the government should not be meddling in family and sexual life. (This example highlights another neo-Calvinist conception developed by Kuyper and Dooyeweerd, termed sphere sovereignty, which implies that families and schools and churches occupy spheres of authority that are distinct from the government and from each other.[26]) That theory is based on a Christian view (which I think is the best view for everybody) that people generally should not be forced to follow *any* interpretation of the Bible, so I am in fact arguing for a theory that is based on my beliefs. (I can't impose my views, but I can theorize about the best society.) When other scholars disagree with me or join me, on the basis of their own political theories, they are doing so on the basis of fundamental beliefs about tolerance or pluralism or liberty that function just as my beliefs did. If we disagree, we have demonstrated a conflict of worldviews. If we agree, we have not demonstrated that there is a realm of secular or rational principles to which all arguments may appeal; we have merely demonstrated an overlap of theory that is wonderful but that is also historically contingent, because we might end up disagreeing when we seek to apply our theories of liberty and pluralism to the abortion or animal-rights debates.

By way of self-criticism, I think a major shortfall of neo-Calvinist philosophy is its inattention, historically, to language systems (for example, legal discourse generally, or "rights" talk) as the carriers of hidden, pretheoretical assumptions or ideologies. Dooyeweerd has already been criticized for his orientation to major Western philosophical movements, and the hermeneutic turn in almost every discipline nowadays—in postmodern literary theory, in historiographical notions of emplotment (that is, history writing as fiction), in the critique of natural science as a narrative enterprise, and so forth—provides a framework in which to reconsider the unconscious operation of "control beliefs," which may have less to do with "religion" than with rhetoric and dominant systems of linguistic meaning.

26. *See* Kalsbeek, *supra* note 2, at 91–94, for a discussion of the doctrine of sphere sovereignty; *see also* Dooyeweerd, *supra* note 4, at 102–5, and Robert F. Cochran, Jr., Tort Law and Intermediate Communities: Calvinist and Catholic Insights, *infra* this volume.

In conclusion, I think that scholarship does reflect faith, though in the refor-mational perspective I have represented, there is a risk that everything becomes religion, and in fact Kuyper said that all of life is religion.[27] The danger is that we lose a lot of useful categories that help us analyze questions concerning the establishment of religion or government aid to religion or restrictions on wor-ship, so I want to confirm that I think we can distinguish between overtly reli-gious discourse and a more open-ended discussion between people from vari-ous perspectives. We can certainly distinguish between overt religious practices and everyday life, and we do share common modes of thought and communi-cation that are different from our diverse views on something like prayer. But when we're talking about scholarship, about our theories about how legal ques-tions and controversies should be handled, something like a religion, insofar as religion is associated with fundamental perspectives on who we are and what we should be doing, necessarily is involved in our written and spoken words.

27. *See* Kuyper, *supra* note 3, at 13–16.

## Section 3  Separatists: Christ Against Law

Throughout Christian history, there have been Christians who have wanted to have little to do with law. For some, the rejection of law has been a matter of Christian faithfulness. Anabaptists reject the use of law and the coercive power of the state as incompatible with Christ's teaching. For a look at the historical background of the Anabaptists, see David Smolin's essay at the beginning of section 4, in which he compares Anabaptist and Lutheran views of the state. Not surprisingly, there are few if any legal scholars who are members of the Anabaptist tradition. With the tension between their beliefs and law, Anabaptists may have a natural disinclination to go to law school. Nevertheless, the Anabaptist tradition has had a significant influence on some legal scholars from other traditions, and in some areas Anabaptists have had a significant influence on the law. Our first essay in this section is from Thomas L. Shaffer, who, though Catholic, has been greatly influenced by Anabaptist thought and has introduced it to legal scholarship. In the first essay below, Shaffer discusses the Christian view of forgiveness and its implications for law.

As Timothy L. Hall notes in his essay, Baptists in the United States are distant cousins to the Anabaptists. They share a distrust of the law, but for Baptists this distrust comes more from their history of being victimized by the law than from a theological aversion to using the law's coercive force. In response to religious persecution, Baptists sought protection from the state behind a high wall of separation and for most of their history have avoided political involvement. Hall's essay discusses Baptists' historical experience with law, as well as some of the recent tensions among Baptists over political activism.

In recent years, in response to the secularizing influence of the modern state, some Christians have sought to severely limit the power of the state. Libertarian Christians may not share the Anabaptist aversion to the use of force, but they do share their aversion to the state. Richard F. Duncan's Christian "libertarian" essay is representative of a new wave of Christians who just want the government to leave them alone.

# The Radical Reformation and

# the Jurisprudence of

# Forgiveness

*Thomas L. Shaffer*

> If it is as the apostles said, that Jesus Christ and not some other
> lord rules at the right hand of God over the powers of this world,
> then the purpose, goals, and standards of that rule can be no
> other than this same Jesus revealed to us, when in the flesh; he
> came not to destroy but to save.
> —*John Howard Yoder*

It seems to me possible to develop a Christian jurisprudence in, under, and around what I will call a politics of forgiveness.[1] Such a jurisprudence would for me be influenced by the Radical Reformation, the Anabaptist reform movement that began in the 1520s in Zurich. If, with that influence, such a jurisprudence is possible, it will be important to see that:

- The church is a community constituted by forgiveness.
- The church, from such a community, practices a politics of forgive-

---

1. This essay appeared in a slightly different form in Thomas L. Shaffer, *Forgiveness Disrupts Legal Order*, 4 Graven Image 127 (1998), and is used here with permission.

ness—not only for itself and its members but for everybody. "'Forgive us as we forgive' is the only petition in the Lord's Prayer to be conditional. It is the task for which Jesus empowers his disciples with the gift of the Holy Spirit (John 20:21 ff), the activity for which he himself has been most criticized by the authorities (Matthew 9:2 ff)."[2]

- Jesus is proclaimed by the church not only as prophet and priest but also as Ruler: "Of course, non-Christians will insist that we should keep our *religion* out of the way of their *politics*. But the reason for that is not that Jesus has nothing to do with the public realm; it is that they want nothing to do with Jesus as Lord."
- When what the church proclaims does not become law, it is because what the New Testament calls "the world" is in rebellion. "Infringements on the holy will of God in society can claim a certain formal legitimacy. The gospel does not immediately eliminate such from secular society, since, being noncoercive, the gospel cannot 'rule the world' in that way. . . . Something of the cross-bearing, forgiving love, and dignity which Jesus's life, death, and resurrection revealed to be the normative way to be human, must be the norm for all humans, whether they know it or not."
- The politics and the jurisprudence thus indicated for the church is a political and legal demand, but it is, if loud and clear, also nonviolent; it will, given the way things are, "necessarily work as salt and light."

Jesus told the story of two brothers who worked in their father's business. The younger brother said he wanted out of the business; he wanted his share of what he expected to get after his father died (Deuteronomy 21:17). Their father agreed; the younger son took his share in cash and squandered the money. He was then destitute, far from home, feeding a herd of pigs, wishing he could return to the family business—not as an heir, but as a hired hand. He set out for home, toward his father's house, to try to work that out.

His father greeted him with extravagant generosity, as if he were a guest deserving of unusual honor. "Quick, fetch a robe . . . and put it on him; put a ring on his finger and shoes on his feet. . . . Let us have a feast to celebrate the day." The elder son, not consulted until the party was under way, found out about the reception given his brother and was resentful. "I slaved for you all these years," he said to his father. "You never gave me . . . a feast for my friends." His

2. This and the following quotations are from John Howard Yoder, Against the Death Penalty, *in* H. Wayne House and John Howard Yoder, *The Death Penalty Debate* 179, 144, 141, 141 (1991). Yoder's essay is also the source of the epigraph.

father was not sympathetic: "Your brother here was dead and has come back to life, was lost and is found."[3]

In its traditional place as a New Testament forgiveness story, the parable of the prodigal son parallels Reynolds Price's version of Jesus' healing of the crippled man who was let down through the roof.[4] I remember the crippled-man story from images in Sunday School in the First Baptist Church, Fruita, Colorado, when I was a boy: Jesus is interested mostly in being a rabbi and is burdened by the fact that broken people come to him not to learn but to get over being sick. He takes refuge from a crowd of sick people in a house. Lawyers who hope to catch him breaking the law are also in the house. The crippled man has been kept out of the house. His brothers get him in by making a hole in the roof and lowering his pallet to "the spot where Jesus sat."

Jesus looks at him and says, "Son, your wrongs are forgiven." The crippled man is not impressed at being shriven. He nods. Jesus seems to have misunderstood: the crippled man is not worried about sin; he needs help for his ailment.

The lawyers are neither impressed nor amused. They say, "No one forgives real error but God." Jesus says, "So you know the Son of Man has power to forgive all wrongs—" He raises his hand; the crippled man is now somewhat more impressed, perhaps hoping the hand in the air is a healing gesture. Then Jesus says, "Stand, take your cot, and go." And the crippled man does. He is cured; he can walk.

"But the lawyers were scandalized," Price writes. "By their lights [Jesus] was not only breaking the laws of God but was dangerously attracting mobs that might yet boil into one more round of the common bloody quarrels with Rome. From that day they and Herod's henchmen"—that is, lawyers, judges, and officers of the law—"all plotted to silence Jesus or end him."[5] Told this way, and focused on forgiveness, both of these stories barely imply response from those who might have been serious about the Rule of Law. The lawyers in the crippled-man story are more concerned with power politics than with Torah politics, and the elder son in the parable gives no rationale for his resentment.

There is indication elsewhere in the New Testament of what legal concern based on power politics might have looked like in these stories. For example, in the realistic argument made by high priest Caiaphas in St. John's Gospel: The Council (the government) have a meeting, to decide what to do about the wan-

3. Luke 15:22–32. All bible quotations are from the New English Bible.
4. See An Honest Account of a Memorable Life, in Reynolds Price, Three Gospels (1996).
5. Id. at 251.

dering rabbi Jesus. "If we leave him alone like this the whole populace will believe in him. Then the Romans will come and sweep away our temple and our nation."[6] Which, of course, the Romans did, and not much later. The Council's small mistake as to timing was less a failure at realistic perception and future causation than the common ineptitude government shows in its practice of the ethics of consequences. John Howard Yoder argued that such a political ethic (1) makes the mistake of focusing all of its attention on power and then (2) supposing it can predict what will happen.[7]

There was nothing suppositious about the Council's concern for the common good. They were conscientious public officials. They needed a legal argument, though, and Caiaphas gave them one. He said, "It is [more] . . . to your interest"—that is, in the interest of legal order in service to power politics—"that one man should die for the people, than that the whole nation should be destroyed."[8] In other words, legal order here makes it necessary to kill somebody—a familiar situation in the history of Western law and, as to the high priest's point, a reasonable, sensible legal argument from a responsible public official. If Caiaphas's argument is heard in reference to the parable and the story of the crippled man, the point is that the politics of forgiveness would disrupt the legal order that serves the politics of coercive power.

I want to see here whether I can explore the jurisprudence that is in these three accounts. To introduce that, a modern story about forgiveness—and then back to the prodigal son (or, as modern preachers often have it, focusing on the father's forgiveness rather than the younger son's sinfulness, the prodigal father).

Joe Ross is a young priest in the Congregation of Holy Cross. He was until recently a rector in one of the men's residence halls at the University of Notre Dame and, by his own appointment, friend and counselor to forty-three death-row prisoners at the Indiana State Prison. His purpose was to practice a politics of forgiveness, to witness to and persuade those who are to be punished there for horrible crimes, who are waiting to be killed by the government. His agenda, he says, is that these forty-three men understand that they are forgiven by God, "completely and absolutely."

An interviewer from the campus radio station asked Father Ross, as students in such settings always ask, what a student could do in aid of his death-house ministry. His answer struck me as in part pastoral (become a pen pal with one

6. John 11:48–49.
7. John Howard Yoder, *Ethics and Eschatology*, 6 Ex Auditu 119, 119 (1990).
8. John 11:50.

of them, get connected to them) and in part activist (learn to confront lethal legal power; read about death row, and dispel the "monster image" of the people who are imprisoned there).

I suspect that Father Ross's relatively gentle practice of forgiveness would disrupt conventional legal order if it could—both in resistance to the death penalty (in general and in principle) and in asserting that the men in death row are forgiven, "completely and absolutely," by the Ruler of the Universe. There is no rational argument any longer to kill them—much less the common-good argument Caiaphas had for killing Jesus. Legal power, it seems, has to kill them anyway, if only because it would not be legal power if it didn't.[9] Law here cannot take the risk of forgiveness. Forgiveness would remove the fear, the accountability, and the responsibility that law provides—and thus, as law sees it, would invite chaos.[10]

The interviewer for the campus radio station asked Father Ross what he had learned from the condemned prisoners. "The deep and transforming power of forgiveness," he said; and the prisoners teach him about connectedness, as well as about forgiveness. They try to connect their isolated repentance to those they have harmed; they keep pictures of their victims in their cells, and they pray for their victims and the families of their victims. The prisoners are not allowed out of their cells for religious services, and Father Ross is not allowed to go into their cells, but he prays with them through the bars. One prisoner is—through the bars—studying religion with Father Ross in a formal course in Christian initiation for adults.

When Father Ross speaks about the "monster image" of the men he meets through the bars, he perhaps means that conventional legal power has a larger political agenda than its interest in killing these men. It also has an interest in keeping them alien, and representing them to the community as alien, as people so destitute of humanity, so completely removed from the community, that they cannot be allowed to go to church.

The parable of the prodigal son ends without a response from the elder son. The prodigal father gets the last word. The elder son must have had a response, though; I doubt that he slunk away in silence. But to get a response from him

9. See William J. Stuntz, *Pride and Pessimism in the Courts,* First Things, Feb. 1997, at 22, 27; *see also* Paul D. Carrington, *Law as "The Common Thoughts of Men": Thomas McIntyre Cooley,* 49 Stan. L. Rev. 495, 524 (1997).

10. Jose Porfirio Miranda, *Marx and the Bible: A Critique of the Philosophy of Oppression* 182, 229–53 (1974).

one has to fashion a midrash, a device that has become almost common among feminist theologians, that is what I will do.[11] A midrash written by a lawyer might correct and amplify the jurisprudential perspective from which the scriptural account is conventionally read, in this case the perspective St. Luke's Gospel generally takes, which, as Brueggemann argues, was not to rile the Roman authorities.[12] The lawyer's amplifying midrash might show—as it would if it were written by Caiaphas—how forgiveness disrupts legal order.

This is the midrashic response of the elder son:

The arrangement my brother and my father made here disrupted the legal order of property ownership and succession in our community and our culture. The law provided for division of the business at my father's death (Deuteronomy 21:17), but my father was not dead. My brother's demand for settlement was permitted, but it was unusual; it was the settlement a Jew made when he was leaving the Holy Land and going to some other place. The legal maneuver removed my brother, as a matter of law, from the family and the community. He was not supposed to be allowed back in.

My brother then made things worse; he engaged in behavior that would put him out of the family and community, even if he had not taken his inheritance and left us. He lived with and fed pigs. Pigs are unclean (Leviticus 11:7). The Rabbis teach that the person who keeps pigs is cursed.[13] My father accepted my brother's claimed repentance, both for the squandering and for the pigs, and he kissed him, so that he would know he was forgiven (2 Samuel 3:21, 14:33). But then my father upset sound social and familial order by treating my brother as he did:

- He put the ceremonial robe on him as if my wretched brother were an angel.
- The ring and the shoes are symbols not so much of sonship as of personal freedom (shoes) and authority, as if my brother was not only restored to the bonds of family life but also was going to take over (Maccabees 6:15).
- Dinner with meat is a rare thing in our house, or any other house in our community. That, and the singing, the dancing, and the cordial speech—are all

11. *See* Judith Plaskow, *Standing Again at Sinai: Jewish Memory from a Feminist Perspective, in* 1 Tikkun 28 (1986); Rosemary Radford Ruether, *For Whom, with Whom, Do We Speak Our New Stories?* Christianity and Crisis, May 12, 1985, at 183.

12. *See* Walter Brueggemann, A Social Reading of the Old Testament 108 (Patrick D. Miller ed., 1994).

13. Joachim Jeremias, *The Parables of Jesus* 129 n.74 (2d rev. ed 1963).

rare. They are extraordinary gestures. They do not fit the facts. My father asked me how I could help celebrating with this crowd. I *can* help celebrating; it is unnatural to celebrate; it is wrong.[14]

Finally, to all appearances, my father intends to restore ownership to my brother. He said that all he had (all that is left) is mine, but his extravagant treatment of my brother makes me wonder whether he will be able to deny my brother what I deserve, what the law provides for me, what I have labored faithfully to protect while my brother has been spending my father's wealth on whores.[15] I have learned to live with my brother's betrayal, and to shoulder the extra burden it put on me—only one son left to take care of business for an old man—but now my father will take what I have earned and give it to my wretched brother. I don't see why I should learn to live with that.

What my father really wants is for me to forgive my brother, as he did. I could do that, perhaps, if it meant learning to live with the proposal my brother made to my father—that he come back and become a hired hand. I am not vindictive. That arrangement would give me some relief, and would be consistent with the deal they made before he left. It might even be a just (if also merciful) resolution of the family situation—and, after all, it is what my brother says he wants. But my father has given every indication that he will not stop at accepting that arrangement. If it turns out that my brother is to regain his (my) wealth, I suppose my father will, as he does now, appeal to my conscience, to accept the arrangement. All I can say is that such a conscience would be as unfitting as this party is.[16]

14. Judaism, then and now, announces forgiveness—with, perhaps, more attention to repentance than Christianity. Shabbath, 1 *The Babylonian Talmud* 264–65, 781, 146–47 (London: Soncino, 1938). The elder brother's argument here, once it settles down a bit, becomes an argument about repentance.

15. *See* Jeremias, *supra* note 13, at 131–32. Jeremias likens this point to Matthew 21:28, where Jesus seems to have directed material gain to the brother who at first refuses to work for his father.

16. As it would be, as Judaism might teach can be and should be expected. But Judaism also contrasts legal order with precisely what the elder brother cannot bear: "When halakhic man approaches reality, he comes with his Torah, given to him from Sinai, in hand. He orients himself to the world by means of fixed statutes and firm principles. . . . The law with its sureness, with its very decisiveness, with its ability to encompass the holy, seduces even as it gives form, depth, and concreteness. The temptation is to submit totally to the authority of the law; to become God's judges and policemen, not His prophets and saints." David R. Blumenthal, *God at the Center* 227 (1998).

If that is what is to happen, I could even say I will try to forgive my brother, and even try to mean it, but this will not work unless the forgiveness changes both my resentful heart and the relationships in our family and community. That is, forgiveness, given the way things seem to be, means that I would not only accept my brother back, as my brother, but accept his being given what belongs to me. Otherwise my forgiveness would be a vapid gesture, like what Voltaire and the McGuire Sisters claim God does when He forgives: "God forgives because that is God's business," Voltaire said. Voltaire and I are not so sure it is our business. "Though it makes Him sad to see the way we live, / He'll always say, 'I forgive,'" the McGuire Sisters sang. Easy for God to forgive; it doesn't cost Him anything.

Cost is the point. Dietrich Bonhoeffer, waiting in prison for the hangman, said that forgiveness was for him costly, painful, and burdensome.[17] He did not say that it also disrupted Hitler's legal order—but it did, and it did in his case: Hitler's regime was a legal order. The very theory of forgiveness, let alone the practice, was disruptive of that legal order. The Nazis killed Bonhoeffer, which is what they had to do.

In addition to a sensible concern for what my forgiveness would do to our community, there is what it does to me. The conventional reading of the story of my father and my brother seems to endorse a kind of forgiveness that does not solve either the theological or the psychological mess my father put me in. The more natural course, and the healthier course, would be to hold on to my anger and my principles—not because it is a good thing to be angry but because otherwise my anger will be suppressed and I will turn it on myself. The natural and healthy course would be to *be* angry, because my anger is justified. The sentimental Christian reading of the story either ignores my rights or writes me off as a wimp.[18] I know what Bonhoeffer meant by costly forgiveness. His was a case like mine, and, like me, he found that he could not comfortably follow the natural course. To forgive, I would not only have to say and believe that the value of this person, my brother, transcends custom and law but I would have to give more than my extravagant and unreasonable father did. But I cannot not forgive, either, because I love my father.

17. *See* James William McClendon, Jr., *Systematic Theology: Ethics* 186–208 (1986).

18. Jones discusses Nietzsche's *On the Genealogy of Morals. See* L. Gregory Jones, *Embodying Forgiveness: A Theological Analysis* 244–46 (1995). There is a kind of refusal to forgive, which Nietzsche may have sometimes had in mind, that is an expression of love. Bronte's Heathcliff, for example, says to Catharine Linton, "I forgive what you have done to me. I love *my* murderer—but *yours!* How can I?"

My brother told our father that he repents of what he has done. I must say that was convenient repentance. I doubt that he would tell *me* he repents—not and mean it. Suppose, as seems likely, he does not repent of what he has done to me. That, too, would be like Bonhoeffer's case. And it would be, perhaps, a case where even those who endorse sentimental Christian notions of forgiveness would permit me retribution. I guess I should hope that he does not repent. That might let me off the hook.

Amplified to take account of what the elder brother has to say after his father tells him to rejoice at his brother's return, the story suggests that Christian religion is fundamentally at odds with the law on this matter of forgiveness.[19] That raises three problems:

## THE MANDATE TO FORGIVE

First problem: It puts a tension between forgiving in the community and order in the community. Its resolution of the tension depends on claiming membership in a community that is constituted by forgiveness rather than by force. The "addressing word," the mandate to forgive, as Gregory Jones puts it, "does not come to isolated individuals; it comes, rather, to the community."[20] The elder brother knows this; it is why he talks about order. "No longer is it necessary to live as if there is no alternative to the powers that feed on our fears, our lusts, our hopelessness," Stanley Hauerwas said in his Easter sermon in 1997. "There is an alternative kingdom to that rule of darkness—it is called forgiveness," rather than the community of law and order contemplated in the elder brother's midrash. "To be forgiven is not to be told that no matter what we may have done and did not do, it is all right with God. No, to be forgiven is to be made part of a community, a history." All of which is to say that the church is expected to be or to become a community of forgiveness. And that is jurisprudence, as well as politics.

## A COMMUNITY OF FORGIVENESS

That curious answer to the problem of disorder raises the second problem: To make any sense, such a notion about community has to demonstrate an an-

19. *See id.* at 241–78.
20. *Id.* at 11.

thropology that is consistent with its politics; it has to show that such a thing as a community constituted by forgiveness is conceivable, given what we know and what the elder brother in the parable knew, about the way people are, and thus to overcome what Avivah Zornberg writes about as the experience of *alilah*—being caught up in a "plot" without knowing what the plot is.[21]

Gregory Jones's answer to the second problem, and thus to the first, is to appeal to the last days of Dietrich Bonhoeffer. Bonhoeffer, like the elder brother in the parable, was all alone. The believing community he had served, and which had served him, was gone. (Or maybe it was, in a sad sense, also at a party that didn't fit.) From Bonhoeffer's perspective, the church had disappeared; he seemed to have no community other than the one the Nazis had made in Germany. The elder brother, in his appeal to his community's mores, thought he would have communal support—but he may have underestimated his father's influence on their neighbors, as resisting pastors in Hitler's Germany underestimated their influence on their congregations. Helmut Thielicke's autobiography provides many examples, though it is the story of a Protestant pastor in Nazi Germany who did more than most of the others to confront the evils of that government. He wrote: "Whatever the truth of Goethe's saying that those who act are always right, there can be no doubt that those who *observe*, that is, who cross the boundary and take a bird's-eye view, are always wrong."[22]

Bonhoeffer's story nonetheless suggests the persistence of a community of memory—a believing community that was not like the community the Nazis made—and of a discipline from that believing community. This was (from Bonhoeffer's perspective, waiting in prison to be killed) a community that *had been* and therefore *was*. Forgiveness, in the religious traditions Bonhoeffer inherited, including Judaism, contemplated a community in which, as Jones and Hauerwas say, forgiveness is a way of life. Jones shows how the community contemplated by the Hebrew prophets is a community that "knows about, experiences, and practices forgiveness."[23] Bonhoeffer came to understand that he did not need to see the darkness all around him as determinative, did not need to see that violence had priority over peace. A community constituted by forgiveness was available to him.

Bonhoeffer was thus able to fit his extreme situation into his religious heritage, and into his theology, which was a theology of costly discipleship. He

---

21. *See* Avivah Gottlieb Zornberg, *Genesis: The Beginning of Desire* (1995).

22. Helmut Thielicke, *Out of the Depths* 278 (1962).

23. Jones, *supra* note 18, at 49 *citing* Jeremiah 31:31–34.

wrote that his imprisonment and death were the cost of forgiveness, which seems to mean (1) a sharing of Jesus' passion, and (2) an acceptance of responsibility for what his Germany was doing—responsibility, in fact, for what he called "the apostasy of the western world."[24] He also saw this acceptance of cost as the traditional discipline of the believing community—penance—performed alone in prison because there was no believing community physically with him to do penance with. Finally, (3) he saw his forgiveness, in that extreme situation, as a political act—as disruptive of Hitler's legal order, even violently so. He referred, mysteriously, to "righteous action" and "the central events of life, which are not amenable to missionary demonstration."[25]

That anthropology and that theology have parallels in the history of the church. The practice of the skills of forgiveness among the Anabaptists of sixteenth-century Switzerland are an example. They took a stand, against the lethal, governmental force invoked both by the Roman Catholic Church of Christendom and against what they called the "magisterial reformers" (Lutherans, Calvinists, and Zwinglians). They invited and suffered the sort of response Bonhoeffer invited and suffered, and they did it communally; they had in suffering fellowship what Bonhoeffer found in memory. They formed and practiced their discipline in a community constituted by forgiveness.

For example, they dealt in a communal way with the Reformation doctrine that justification comes through grace and not through works. The Protestant problem was this: if God forgives sin and enters into fellowship with people purely because He wills to do so, and without regard to what people do—then what reason is there for this redeemed people to behave themselves? The Anabaptist answer was that reconciliation with God (salvation, justification) is more a process than an event, and that the process is communal—that is, it is a dynamic process, in a believers' church that is forgiven and that forgives. They "contended not for 'sinlessness' but for the possibility of living in victory over the inclination to evil." In their formulations of soteriology, they "preferred regeneration language to describe conversion."[26] They did not exclude the possibility that members might, as the Mormons of my boyhood used to put it,

24. *Quoted id.* at 25 from Bonhoeffer, *Ethics* 30 (E. Bethge ed. and N. H. Smith trans., New York: Macmillan, 1965).

25. *Id.* at 30, 30 n.72; *see also* McClendon, *supra* note 17, at 186–208. I sense a problem both Jones and McClendon have in coming to terms with Bonhoeffer's involvement in the plot to kill Hitler.

26. Luke L. Keefer, Jr., Armenian Motifs in Anabaptist Heritage, *in Within the Perfection of Christ* 150 (Terry L. Brensinger and E. Morris Sider, eds., 1990); *see also id.* at 146–55.

"backslide" from time to time. The important thing for and toward such people was to keep them in the community—membership, not perfection.

These practices disrupted legal order because the believers' church, a community constituted by forgiveness, sought to refrain from violence and to practice nonresistance. More important for jurisprudence, the Anabaptists saw themselves as, so constituted, ready for costly discipleship—ready for martyrdom as a probability, because discipleship was a noticeable and deviant way to live. To live as disciples was to invite lethal suppression from both Catholic Christendom and the magisterial reformers.

This, of course, meant that they answered this second problem, the problem of community, by realizing—slowly—that their believers' church would become separate from the society around them. They were killed for baptizing adults when the society around them baptized babies; they were killed for teaching that capital punishment was wrong; they were killed for refusing to accept military service. But through it all, and ever since among their spiritual descendants, they are an example of a community constituted by forgiveness—a separate community, finally, but separate more because the larger communities around them cast them out than because they seek to separate themselves.

This theological and anthropological response to the first two problems I posed for a community constituted by forgiveness has a negative historical argument to make, as well as these positive responses. The radical reformers did not concede that a civil community is necessarily constituted by force. A modern theologian in their tradition, the late John Howard Yoder, argued that (1) few political experiments in Western history show that the nonviolent alternative was attempted, and there is therefore little history of experimental failure of communities constituted by forgiveness; and (2) that the rare attempt to form a political community without violence had more success and more promise than conventional historians of church and state are willing to allow: "If it is the case that God is providentially in charge of history, even though that has not hitherto been visible, would not divine sovereignty be able to bless the believing obedience of a Caesar who, taking the risk of faith like any other believer, from his position of relative power, would love his enemies and do justice? Does the argument need to grant that if a Caesar had done that, in the context of authentic faith . . . the results would have been bad? What would have counted as bad results in that case?"[27]

27. John Howard Yoder, *The Priestly Kingdom* 145–46 (1984).

The notion that a civil community (everybody) might be constituted by forgiveness suggests, of course, a revolutionary anthropology—as revolutionary as Marx's and Engels's theory of primordial (in)justice. In that, though, it is closer to the anthropology of the Hebrew prophets than standard theology would allow, and, if revolutionary, nonetheless within what Catholics used to call "the deposit of the faith." (That is to say, of course, that Bonhoeffer and the Anabaptists found more in traditional Christianity than many Christians know to be there.) The anthropology of the prophets was revolutionary in this way in biblical Israel: the implicit "subversion (which means undermining and exposure to dismantling) is directed against a theology that knows too much, a God who is too strong, a church that is too allied with triumphalist culture, and a ministry that moves too much from strength," Walter Brueggemann says, as he surveys the modern situation in the United States from a biblical, prophetic perspective. Attention to the notion that God makes a covenant with a believing community constituted by forgiveness "exposes the failure of a remote God who has not triumphed, a church that has known too much, and a culture that has not kept its promises."[28]

In the midrash, the elder son understood that the critical boundary issue for such a community might be the biblical injunction to forgive enemies, an injunction in rabbinic Judaism as well as in the New Testament. "Even if the enemy come to your house to slay you, and he is hungry or thirsty," Rabbi Hanina bar Hama said, "give him food and drink; for thereby God will reconcile him to you."[29] These enemies are, by definition, not repentant. The elder son in the midrash argued, at the end, that if his brother did not repent of what he had done to the elder brother, the elder brother need not forgive. Much of modern Christian theology (particularly among "evangelicals") would support him in regarding his brother, his enemy, with "moral hatred," Dietrich Bonhoeffer to the contrary notwithstanding.[30] He would, as he (anachronistically) said, find some support among modern theological writers. Gregory Jones, on this point, admits that the psychology of righteous indignation may be too strong—and justifiably so, as Nietzsche argued—to lead to reestablished relationship with reprehensible people who refuse to repent. But even there, Jones says, the community constituted by forgiveness practices the disciplines of forgiveness—such skills as refusing vengeance, wishing the wrongdoer well, and

28. Walter Brueggemann, *A Social Reading of the Old Testament* 43 (Patrick D. Miller ed., 1994).

29. Thomas L. Shaffer, *Faith and the Professions* 64–65 (1987).

30. *See* Jones, *supra* note 18, at 241–78.

refusing to join in the world's deviance systems (for example, those practiced toward death row in the Indiana State Prison). In all of these ways, Jones says, the believing community is able to recognize reality, to avoid the separation that divides "issues of forgiveness and justice into the spheres of the personal and private and of the political and public," (which is what the elder brother in the midrash is trying to do).[31] The Rabbis point to II Kings 6:21–23: "'Shall I kill them?' 'No. . . . Give them something to eat and drink and let them return to their king.' So the king of Israel . . . sent them back to the king of Syria. From then on the Syrians stopped raiding the land of Israel."

There is also psychological wisdom, I think, in resisting the theology of "moral hatred." There is a sense—even a psychological sense—in which forgiveness precedes repentance: the elder brother in the midrash might consider that if he forgives his unrepentant brother, his brother will then repent. If this is so there is less moral comfort in deciding not to forgive him when he has failed to repent. The theological dimension here is another way forgiveness disrupts legal order: the believing community makes a mistake when it fastens too heavily on notions of pardon, which, as James McClendon—faithful to his own Anabaptist tradition—points out, is based not in forgiveness but in punishment, not in the anthropology of forgiving community but in an ecclesial analogue to the processes of the law.[32] Presidents and governors pardon offenders; the church forgives them.

As much as one might hope for and describe a civil community (everybody) constituted by forgiveness, history describes confrontations (as in sixteenth-century Zurich) between the communities constituted by forgiveness and everybody else. There are historical examples of this confrontation, more mainline examples perhaps, some of them more quaint than the sixteenth-century radical reformers. One is the biblical and medieval practice of asylum, in which the community provided a place of refuge for people who were fleeing from the consequences of having committed crimes.[33] Rabbinic Judaism extends the required arrangements to include putting up signs to show offenders the way to the cities of refuge, and the maintenance of roads that were straight and in good repair. Robert E. Rodes, Jr., describes a medieval Christian practice, borrowed at least in part from Judaism, that had been maintained among Chris-

31. *Id.* at 267.
32. *See* McClendon, *supra* note 17.
33. See Exodus 21:14; Numbers 35:25; Deuteronomy 19:11.

tians from the time of Constantine.[34] In both biblical and medieval Christian manifestations, asylum kept the offender from the vengeance of the law as it offered methods of mediation by which, as Rodes puts it, "the unjust marauder was deterred from his wicked purpose by the awe of the Divine Presence, and the seeker of just vengeance was brought to exalt mercy over justice and to make peace with his adversary."[35] The alternative in Reformation England became not reconciliation but a chance for the offender to "abjure the realm."[36]

Another example—and both of these are more symbols of hope than models—is the practice, in Jewish law, for loans to the poor. Lending to the poor, the Rabbis taught, is a *mitzvah*. If the loan involved pledged property the borrower needs, the lender cannot keep the pledge.[37] Lenders are required to make "arrangements" for poor borrowers who are not to be left without the benefit of their furniture, tools, farm animals, and of such food as they have on hand. A loan to a poor person for the repayment of a prior loan was prohibited—so that the prior lender would have an opportunity to forgive the prior loan.[38]

## SEEKING THE PEACE OF THE CITY

The third problem, given a theology of community constituted by forgiveness, and consequent on a distinction between the community of the faithful and the surrounding society (in some situations, between the community of the faithful and the state), asks what attitude the community of believers is to take toward the welfare of the surrounding society—toward the common good, if you like. As the prophet Jeremiah put it, the faithful are to "seek the welfare of any city to which [God has] carried you off."[39]

34. Jewish law came to distinguish between intentional homicide and accidental homicide—a distinction with warrant in the Torah. Rabbi Hertz claims that this distinction meant that the Jewish practice did not lead to the maintenance of "nurseries of criminals," as in ancient Greece and Rome, nor to refuges for "criminals of every description," as in the medieval church. *The Pentateuch and Haftorahs* 721 n.15 (J. H. Hertz ed., 1987).

35. Robert E. Rodes, Jr., *Ecclesiastical Administration in Medieval England: The Anglo-Saxons to the Reformation* 52–54 (1977).

36. Robert E. Rodes, Jr., *Lay Authority and Reformation in the English Church* 276 (1982). A feminine instance, within Islam, is described in Fatima Mernissi, *Women, Saints, and Sanctuaries,* 3 Signs 101 (1977).

37. Cf. Exodus 22:24.

38. Menachem Elon, *The Principles of Jewish Law* 262, 628–30 (1974); *see also* Exodus 22:24.

39. Jeremiah 29:7.

Part of this answer is that the community of believers is prophetic, enjoying and practicing "a holiness that requires prophetic protest and action directed at any situation where people's lives are being diminished or destroyed."[40] "The most important and most subversive thing the church can do now," Walter Brueggemann says, in one of his pessimistic moods about late-twentieth-century America, is to "refuse to give up on the world and its promised transformation." It is a mistake for those who believe in a community constituted by forgiveness to "act as though the world gets to vote on its long-term future."[41]

Brueggemann suggests here, as he does in much of his scholarship, that the meaning of what Christians call the Old Testament is that there is a reality that is alternative to the "real world" that is first described and then ruled by legal order. The Hebrew prophets, he says,

> have an alternative perception of social reality that they insist is true and for which they want to create working space and allow for social possibility to emerge. . . . The prophetic is not understood primarily as denunciation or rejection, unless it is clear that there is a positive alternative available that, in fact, is true, gives life, and really functions. . . .
>
> The truth is that because of the enormous fear in our social context, our government and its allies have constructed for us a fanciful world of fear, threat, security, and well-being that has little contact with the data at hand.

And, to us lawyers: "Because we are managers and benefactors of the system, we find it easy and natural to accept this imagined world as real. . . . The system . . . creates disproportion . . . [and] creates a set of lenses so that we look and genuinely do not see."[42] Brueggemann proposes a political agenda, an agenda that would ponder the parable of the prodigal son and conclude that Jesus there proposes a notion that is civilly controversial, particularly as it also proposes to forgive those who are not repentant. "Our cooperation in God's purposes," Robert E. Rodes, Jr., says, "is powerfully impeded by unjust economic and social structures"—particularly when God's purposes are the great commandment of Judaism and Jesus to love one's neighbor.[43] (Rodes teaches that liberation from oppression includes liberation of the oppressors—liberation of poor and rich alike from their unjust institutions—because the poor cannot love institutions that oppress them, and because the rich, "if the rich understood their

40. Jones, *supra* note 18, at 4.

41. Brueggemann, *supra* note 28, at 43, 51.

42. *Id.* at 223–25.

43. Robert E. Rodes, Jr., *Law and Liberation* 2 (1986).

true interests," would hate the institutions that make them rich. His perception depends on understanding that the prosperity of the prosperous is complementary to the suffering of the poor.[44])

But there is a problem within the problem here, raised by reading Scripture, particularly the scriptural teachings Jews and Christians preserve on the matter of forgiveness of unrepentant enemies. It is this: where are those who forgive to determine what to be prophetic about? The Anabaptist tradition (and, for the most part, the Baptist tradition) points to the community of believers, what the Anabaptists called the believers' church, both for the description of the reality of which Brueggemann speaks and for provisional answers on how and when to seek the welfare of the city. "We can afford to begin with the gospel notions themselves and then work out from there," John Howard Yoder said, "rather than beginning with the 'real world' out there (someone else's definition of 'the nature of things') and then trying to place the call of God within it. . . . The fulcrum for change and the forum of discernment is the moral independence of the believing community as a body."[45]

Yoder and his tradition would excuse themselves from some political action. They do not buy into Reinhold Niebuhr's moral theology of necessary evil.[46] It is not quite clear in Brueggemann's more mainline Protestant scholarship that the believing community itself is such a forum. Nor is it clear in the scholarship of Robert E. Rodes, Jr., which is often similar to Brueggemann's in its prophetic clarity. Rodes speaks from the Catholic tradition, and counsels courage, but he does not forswear violence.[47]

When they are clear on what they are doing, those in the believers' church pick and choose: they may, as the Anabaptists do, decline "the sword" of lethal government power—which probably means they will not seek most political offices in modern America, and, for those who are lawyers, will practice law selectively. Yoder says they can "serve the world but are not called to rule it."[48] Yoder emphasizes that this nonviolent stance does not counsel turning aside from those who serve (patriotically) the lethal power of the government. He makes

44. See id. at 4, 52.

45. John Howard Yoder, *Body Politics: Five Practices of the Christian Community Before the Watching World* 76 (1992).

46. This is the theme of what is probably Yoder's most influential book, John Howard Yoder, *The Politics of Jesus* (2d ed. 1994).

47. See Thomas L. Shaffer, *The Christian Jurisprudence of Robert E. Rodes. Jr.*, 73 Notre Dame L. Rev. 737 (1998).

48. Yoder, *supra* note 45, at 74; *see also* Shaffer, *supra* note 47.

the obvious distinction between the person who serves and the office in which she serves; he finds it compatible with prophetic witness to approach and deal with the person in public office in that person's terms and from that person's frame of reference: "It may very well be, if this [person] is engaged in an activity . . . which a more sensitive or more informed Christian conscience would not permit, that in the process of responding to the gospel he might come to the conclusion that his office is incompatible with his faith," Yoder said. "But it is improper to begin with this conclusion. It is impossible to impose this logic on him before beginning the conversation. . . . What we ask of him does not cease to be gospel by virtue of the fact that we relate it to his present available options."[49]

Wendell Berry's stories and essays about the farming communities of northern Kentucky suggest a focus. Berry, whose politics is not obviously theological, finds no hope for large American political order unless its imposition on the citizen is mediated through the sort of local, familial communities he writes about. "The concerns of public and private, republic and citizen . . . are not adequate for the shaping of human life," he says. "Community alone, as principle and as fact, can raise the standards . . . without which the other two interests will destroy one another."[50] Community—local civil community, in that earthy sense—holds promise, I think, for the peaceful participation of the community within it that is constituted by forgiveness (the believers' church). More promise than larger governments which wage war and fashion the bureaucracies that oppress and exploit. There will be happy coincidences of purpose between these two kinds of communities, even if, as I think, the coherence necessary for political action remains the agenda of the community of the faithful within the local civil society.

The discernment and coherence of biblical politics, in communities constituted by forgiveness, is for the believing community itself. Its "constant inventive vision for the good of the larger society," its "witness reminding those in power of the continuing injustices of their regime," need only be consistent with the "general moral values to which [the wider society] has no spiritual or logical commitment." Yoder wrote, "The testimony that the risen Christ is Lord also over the world is to us the reason for speaking to the state, and the biblical witness concerning the reason for the state's continued existence enables us also to guide this testimony with definite standards." He summarized

49. John Howard Yoder, *The Christian Witness to the State* 25 (1964).
50. Wendell Berry, *Sex, Economy, Freedom, and Community* 119 (1993).

these standards as (1) faithfulness to "the church's clear conviction," (2) consistent behavior in the church's management of its own affairs, and (3) that "the church should speak only when it has something to say."[51]

The Christian, Yoder said, "*accepts* the powers that be and speaks to them in a corrective way." And this, at the margins, without either practicing or counseling violence: "The choice between violence, which is always the easiest way, and justice, which is more difficult, more dangerous, and superficially less efficacious, is always a question of faith."[52]

51. Yoder, *supra* note 45, at 19–21.
52. *Id.* at 41–42 (emphasis added).

# "Incendiaries of Commonwealths": Baptists and Law

*Timothy L. Hall*

My aim in this essay is to chart the intersection between law and the particular communities of faith whose members have known themselves as Baptists. I do so with trepidation, though, because Baptists have traditionally been more than a little hesitant to be spoken for. A rather diverse assortment of souls have taken shelter under this theological standard: John Bunyan and Harvey Cox; Martin Luther King, Jr., and Jerry Falwell; William Jefferson Clinton and Jesse Helms. Even the names Baptists have chosen for themselves testify more to fractiousness than to unity, and to as sharp a readiness to distinguish themselves from one another as to distinguish themselves from other stripes of Christians.[1] The Revolutionary generation witnessed Gen-

1. *See,* for example, the Covenant of Cherokee Creek Baptist Church (1783) of Washington County, North Carolina (now Jonesboro, Tennessee), which launches its statement of faith with a difference-regarding declaration: "As the professors of Christianity are so divided in their principles and practice that they cannot hold communion together and passing by the several classes of pedobaptists. There are several classes of Antepedobaptists, with which we cannot agree. Namely, the Seven Day Baptists, the non-Sabbath Baptists, and those that

eral Baptists, Regular Baptists, Free Will Baptists, Separate Baptists, Dutch River Baptists, Permanent Baptists, and Two-Seed-in-the-Spirit Baptists.[2] Today's list contains different entries, but is not any more brief. In fact, a faithful polyphony has been one of the defining marks of Baptists.

## BAPTIST THEOLOGY

More than any other theological feature, a radically individualized concept of salvation has directed the course of Baptist thought. Baptists fixed their attention on the narrow gate to which Jesus commended his disciples in the Sermon on the Mount and imagined it as a kind of turnstile through which each soul had to pass individually, separated at the moment of entry from both those who had passed before and those who would follow. Guided by this imagery, early Baptists repudiated the practice of infant baptism. They rejected the willingness of the mainstream Reformation to perpetuate an Abrahamic covenant in which infant baptism replaced circumcision and placed the children of believers in a special relationship with God.[3] Baptists insisted that entrance into the community of Christ required faith on the part of the entering believer. They also insisted that baptism should be a sign of this personal faith. Infants, lacking capacity for saving faith, were inappropriate subjects for this symbolic representation. Early Baptists thus repudiated their own infant baptisms and elected to be baptized again, earning the epithet showered promiscuously on the wide variety of believers who opposed infant baptism: Anabaptists ("rebaptizers").

For most Protestants, infant baptism confirmed a covenant community that embraced children and adults in spiritual fraternity. Baptists also believed in a spiritual community, though the community they envisioned was one in which the ties of human kinship and fraternity played no salvific role. The intimate transaction between God and believer was not mediated by a preexisting community of faith. Before the community of faith was the solitary soul. Cyprian insisted that "he cannot have God as a father who does not have the Church as a mother," but Baptists found mostly incomprehensible this maternal conception of the church.[4] They emphasized instead the unmediated encounter be-

---

dip three times in baptism, with all of which we cannot agree." *Baptist Confessions, Covenants, and Catechisms* 213 (Timothy George and Denise George eds., 1996).

2. Gordon S. Wood, *The Radicalism of the American Revolution* 333 (1992).

3. For a general survey of the Baptists' arguments against infant baptism, *see* 1 William G. McLoughlin, *New England Dissent* 26–48 (1971).

4. Cyprian, *De ecclesiae unitate,* chapter 6 (Bevenot ed. 1971).

tween God and the individual, an encounter that required, in the words of the London Confession of 1644, an early statement of English Baptist principles, no "qualifications, preparations, terrors of the law, or preceding ministry of the law, but only and alone the naked soul, as a sinner and ungodly to receive Christ."[5]

Opponents of these Baptist views saw something more than theological nicety at stake. To more mainstream heirs of the Reformation, the repudiation of infant baptism evidenced not simply a spiritual apostasy but a social apostasy as well. The idea of covenant that sustained the practice of infant baptism for many Protestants sustained as well a more expansive social vision in which men and women entered into a covenant to be ruled by God and his laws. To attack, as Baptists did, the idea of covenant that made the practice of infant baptism meaningful was to attack its social manifestations as well, and such Protestants as the Massachusetts Bay Puritans saw only alarm and confusion in this funda- mental challenge to their experiment in holy commonwealth. They attempted to express the destructive capacity of opposition to infant baptism through im- ages of fire and combustion and branded Anabaptists "incendiaries of com- mon-wealths."[6] By this label they asserted that the erroneous theological views of colonial Baptists would inevitably spill over into the political world, the world of faith into the world of politics and law. The Puritan judgment that Baptist scruples about infant baptism would topple the social order was, of course, polemical exaggeration. Predicting the ruinous consequences of dissent is a favorite pastime of the orthodox. But the notion that Baptist principles might yield a unique perspective on political life and on law is not at all far- fetched.

## SOUL LIBERTY

New England Puritans translated their alarm at Baptist tendencies into law and harried Baptist heterodoxy with the lash of legal sanction.[7] Baptists also con- fronted the law's hostile face in the royal colonies where Anglican preeminence was sustained by legal sanction. Accordingly, the formative Baptist experience with law had to do with lawbreaking rather than lawmaking. Those whom so- ciety marginalizes seldom have leisure to craft theories of law: they are too busy

5. The London Confession (1644), in *Baptist Confessions, Covenants, and Catechisms, supra* note 1, at 43.

6. *The Laws and Liberties of Massachusetts* 1 (1648).

7. *See id.* at 2.

dodging the whip. Even after the earliest colonial Baptists made an uneasy peace with Puritan and Anglican establishments, a second wave of Baptists who emerged after the Great Awakening, sometimes called New Light Baptists, suffered a renewal of harsh treatment.[8] In all, Baptists suffered under one or another religious establishment in the New World for nearly 150 years. Even once they obtained freedom from the whip, Baptists tended to be of poor enough circumstances not to be much consulted on issues of law. The experience left its mark. When confronted thereafter about the appropriate relation between religion and law, Baptists tended to emphasize convictions associated with their long exile from political fraternity. A steadfast devotion to religious liberty, which the Baptists tended to refer to as "soul liberty," has occupied the central place in their understanding of law.[9] Indeed, it has occupied a central place, even, in their understanding of faith.[10]

The privatization of faith implicit in the Baptist concept of "soul liberty" inevitably challenged the millennia-old assumption that faith required the support and protection of the civil magistrate. Baptists thus became opponents of religious establishments and fierce advocates of religious liberty not merely out of a self-serving desire to escape the burdens of Congregational and Anglican establishments. The very heart of their theology dampened any desire by them to step into the role of persecutor and favored religious establishment once their increasing numbers in the eighteenth and nineteenth centuries gave them a measure of political power. In fact, theological principle—and not simply political expediency—led Baptists in the main to repudiate the notion of state-supported churches and, until relatively recent times, made them generally comfortable with metaphors that described the appropriate relation between government and religion in terms of a "wall of separation."[11] The one-time

8. For the distinction between "old" Baptists, whose roots run back to mid-seventeenth-century colonial America and New Light Baptists, who separated from established churches during the Great Awakening and ultimately migrated to Baptist principles, *see* Martin E. Marty, *Pilgrims in Their Own Land: Five Hundred Years of Religion in America* 150–54 (1990).

9. For the long Baptist struggle on behalf of religious freedom, *see especially* William G. McLoughlin, *Soul Liberty: The Baptists' Struggle in New England, 1630–1833* (1991).

10. *See,* for example, the professed devotion to religious liberty as one of five defining characteristics of Baptists in Towards a Baptist Identity: A Statement Ratified by the Baptist Heritage Commission in Zagreb, Yugoslavia, July, 1989, reprinted in Walter B. Shurden, *The Baptist Identity: Four Fragile Freedoms* 66 (1993).

11. *See* Baptist Distinctives and Diversity and Disagreements and Differences of Emphases Among Baptists, *reprinted in* Shurden, *supra* note 10, at 72 (suggesting as one point of agreement among Baptists their commitment to "a basic separation between church and state").

Baptist Roger Williams made this metaphor a centerpiece of his own understanding of law's relation to faith, and Thomas Jefferson summoned it again
most famously in his letter to the Danbury Baptists.[12]

## FAITH AND LAW

Baptists' opposition to infant baptism earned them denunciation among the
New England Puritans as "Anabaptists," the Puritan denigration for everything
radical in the spiritual world. In fact, however, early American Baptists were
distant both geographically and—at least in some ways—theologically from
the Continental Anabaptists. Although Baptists followed the Anabaptist wing
of the Radical Reformation in repudiating infant baptism, they did not similarly distance themselves from the concept of the "sword." One does not find
within doctrinal statements of colonial Baptists, for example, anything quite
like the Anabaptist insistence that the use of force—even the legal use of
force—was inconsistent with Christian faith and a matter in which believers
could have no part.[13] Baptists steadfastly repudiated the use of force in matters
of religious conscience but did not posit any fundamental tension between the
life of faith and other exercises of lawful force.

By (often disadvantaged) social circumstances and theological inclination,
though, Baptists seldom imagined themselves as creators of law. They confronted the law most directly when it barred their way or attempted to direct
their paths down routes foreign to Christ. They challenged the law on these occasions, not with visions of establishing the kingdom of righteousness through

---

12. Williams used the metaphor as a dirge upon the death of the church occasioned by its
alliance with government under the reign of the Roman emperor Constantine. "The faithful labors of many witnesses of Jesus Christ, extant to the world, abundantly proving, that
the Church of the Jews under the Old Testament in the type, and the Church of the Christians under the New Testament in the antitype, were both separate from the world; and that
when they have opened a gap in the hedge or wall of separation between the garden of the
Church and the wilderness of the world, God has ever broke down the wall itself, removed
the candlestick, and made his garden a wilderness, as at this day." Mr. Cottons Letter Lately
Printed, Examined and Answered, in 1 *The Complete Writings of Roger Williams* 108 (1963).
For Jefferson's letter, see Letter from Thomas Jefferson to Messrs. Nehemiah Dodge and
Others, a Committee of the Danbury Baptist Association in the State of Connecticut (Jan.
1, 1802), in *Thomas Jefferson: Writings* 510 (Library of America ed. 1984).

13. *See,* for example, the statements to this effect in the Schleitheim Confession. *Creeds of
the Churches: A Reader in Christian Doctrine from the Bible to the Present* 287–89 (John H.
Leith ed. rev. ed. 1973).

this challenge, or of pulling down idolatrous strongholds, but of simply gaining freedom to follow Christ. Pietists find themselves at odds with totalitarians of all stripes, because totalitarians will not grant them liberty to follow Christ. Even when the law was not attempting to stifle their pilgrimage after Christ, Baptists tended to view the law as a relatively remote force ordained by God. Early Baptist confessions of faith rarely address the issue of law other than to paraphrase New Testament texts commending subjection to lawful authorities and prayers for those authorities. The 1644 London Confession's treatment of the civil magistrate is an example of this kind of paraphrasing. The "civil magistracy," it declared, "is an ordinance of God set up by God for the punishment of evil doers, and for the praise of them that do well; and that in all lawful things commanded by them, subjection ought to be given by us in the Lord; and that we are to make supplication and prayer for kings, and all that are in authority; that under them we may live a peaceable and quiet life in all godliness and honesty."[14] The confession's chief aspiration was simply that God might "provide such mercy for us, as to incline the magistrates' hearts so far to tender our consciences, as that we might be protected by them from wrong, injury, oppression and molestation, which long we formerly have grounded under."[15] Here, Baptist piety imagines itself mostly the object of law rather than the author of it. It seeks liberty to pursue a life in keeping with the principles of Christ rather than political or legal power to assure the dominion of these principles.

By their emphasis on spiritual individualism, Baptists unleashed theological principles capable of devouring the foundations of Christendom. The nature of these principles might have pushed Baptists solidly into the ranks of H. Richard Niebuhr's "Christ Against Culture" category, though Baptist piety has seldom exhibited the stern isolationism of certain monastic orders or of some Mennonite groups.[16] Many Baptists have, in fact, held theological views consistent with Niebuhr's cartography. Emphasizing the need for believers to

14. The London Confession, supra note 5, at 47. See also the New Hampshire Confession of 1833, which says of civil government only that it is ordained by God "for the interests and good order of human society" and that it ought to be "prayed for, conscientiously honored, and obeyed" except when such obedience conflicted with the demands of Christ. New Hampshire Confession of 1833, in *Baptist Confessions, Covenants, and Catechisms, supra* note 1, at 135 (1996).

15. *Id.* at 48.

16. H. Richard Niebuhr, *Christ and Culture* (1951). See also Michael W. McConnell, *Christ, Culture, and Courts: A Niebuhrian Examination of First Amendment Jurisprudence*, 42 DePaul L. Rev. 191 (1992).

separate from the unbelieving world, they found little value in political engagement, including engagement in lawmaking. They placed first priority in communicating the gospel to an unbelieving world and viewed attempts to use law to create a more desirable world as a dangerous distraction from this priority. They located the kingdom of Christ primarily within the hearts of individual believers and, by doing so, deprived every earthly kingdom—including the kingdoms of Christendom—of sacred pretensions.[17] The external world was for them a place of pilgrimage rather than a permanent or semipermanent residence fit for godly renovation. One could not, they believed, construct the kingdom of Christ out of worldly rubble. One could only traverse the rubble carefully, in search of a heavenly city. The most that believers could expect from the world's wilderness was a peaceful coexistence, a kind of spiritual detente between citizens of the world and citizens of the heavenly kingdom.

Now the idea of coexistence between citizens of the world and citizens of Christ's kingdom was hardly a product of Baptist originality. Augustine had expressed a similar view centuries before:

> This heavenly city, then, while it sojourns on earth, calls citizens out of all nations, and gathers together a society of pilgrims of all languages, not scrupling about diversities in the manners, laws, and institutions whereby earthly peace is secured and maintained, but recognizing that, however various these are, they all tend to one and the same end of earthly peace. It therefore is so far from rescinding and abolishing these diversities, that it even preserves and adapts them, so long only as no hindrance to the worship of the one Supreme and true God is thus introduced. Even the heavenly city, therefore, while in its state of pilgrimage, avails itself of the peace of earth, and, so far as it can without injuring faith and godliness, desires and maintains a common agreement among men regarding the acquisition of the necessaries of life, and makes this earthly peace bear upon the peace of heaven.[18]

Augustine may have referred to his magisterial city as a sojourner, but the images with which he dressed it suggested settledness, bulk, and even veiled power. Baptist piety, on the other hand, envisions a church too dispersed in its pilgrimage to qualify as a city, even a heavenly one, and too weak in the balance of worldly power to play the dominant role in present affairs implicit in Augustine's vision. Pietistic Baptists are not likely to see much point in attempts to

17. The Kingdom of God, declares the most prominent Southern Baptist creedal statement of the twentieth century, "is the realm of salvation into which men enter by trustful, childlike commitment to Jesus Christ." The Baptist Faith and Message (1963), in *Baptist Confessions, Covenants, and Catechisms, supra* note 1, at 143.

18. Augustine, *City of God,* book XIX, sec. 17, 696 (Marcus Dods trans., 1993).

use the law to serve the noble ends envisioned for Augustine's city. They, unlike Augustine, are estranged from the world, and strangers seldom make good mayors.

## "CHRISTIAN" VALUES

The Baptist pietism I described in the previous section seems to me the natural outworking of general Baptist principles. In fact, many Baptists have embraced a pietism that disinclined them to pay much attention to law, so long as the law was not harassing them. But there have always been Baptists who departed from this mold to one degree or another. Walter Rauschenbusch, the advocate of the "social gospel," and Martin Luther King, Jr., are but two Baptist counterexamples. In fact, a good many Baptists have remained on speaking terms with Christendom, even when their theological principles might have made them implacably hostile to it. Many Baptists—perhaps even most—hesitated to imagine a society consistent with their spiritual individualism. They had demolished the foundations of Christendom by their sustained opposition to religious establishments but were satisfied to continue tramping about on its now rickety superstructure. Kindred in many ways with the more radical Roger Williams, they nevertheless were unwilling to follow his lead in sounding the dirge for Christendom.[19] The Massachusetts Puritan John Winthrop has found more than a few disciples among Baptists: eager champions of a holy commonwealth, more enamored of Old Testament law than of New Testament gospel.

For example, even before the 1980s found many Baptists joining ranks with conservative political actions groups like the Moral Majority, the chief creedal statement of the Southern Baptists had envisioned a fair amount of commerce between the City of God and the cities of the world. In a paragraph devoted to "The Christian and the Social Order," the *Baptist Faith and Message* announced that "every Christian is under obligation to seek to make the will of Christ Supreme in his own life and in human society." To be sure, the statement emphasized, "means and methods used for the improvement of society and the establishment of righteousness among men can be truly and permanently helpful only when they are rooted in the regeneration of the individual by the saving grace of God in Christ Jesus." But the *Baptist Faith and Message* rushed significantly beyond this reiteration of pietist principle when it encouraged Chris-

19. I explore Roger Williams's thought in *Separating Church and State: Roger Williams and Religious Liberty* (1998). *See also* Edmund Morgan, *Roger Williams: The Church and the State* (1967) and Perry Miller, *Roger Williams: His Contribution to the American Tradition* (1953).

tians to make the standards of the Kingdom visible in the workaday world: "Every Christian should seek to bring industry, government, and society as a whole under the sway of the principles of righteousness, truth, and brotherly love. In order to promote these ends Christians should be ready to work with all men of good will in any good cause, always being careful to act in the spirit of love without compromising their loyalty to Christ and His truth."[20] These final two sentences seem to admit the possibility that "industry, government, and society as a whole" might be made subject to the principles of "righteousness, truth, and brotherly love" through cooperative ventures with the citizens of the world. It is, I think, but a short step to conclude, as modern-day Puritans do, that if the citizens of the world will not cooperate, then Christians must use power in all its manifold forms—political action and economic boycotts being favorite contemporary varieties of power—to *make* the world's citizens subject to these principles. Traditional Baptist piety, on the other hand, would be profoundly skeptical of the ability of power, or even cooperative ventures, to produce real righteousness or truth or brotherly love. These are fruits of the regenerated life, not of caucus or clout.

I suggested earlier that Baptist principles seem to lend themselves to a "Christ Against Culture" stance. Why, then, have so many Baptists—and now perhaps, more than ever before—adopted different visions of the relation between Christ and culture? There are three key reasons. In the first place, Baptist sectarianism has tended to evolve into denominationalism over time. Early Baptists were ardently sectarian, identifying themselves as aliens in a strange land and withdrawing from other congregations of believers to form what they believed were more authentic communities of faith. As Niebuhr has suggested, though, sects tend to evolve into denominations over time.[21] They become less otherworldly and less ready to distance themselves from other believers. For Baptists, this transformation has dulled the edge of pilgrim sensibilities and made many Baptists quite comfortable with the present world and less absorbed with the world to come. They have put down deeper social roots than many of their colonial forebears and are increasingly eager to make the world in which they presently find themselves more hospitable to their moral and theological sensibilities. To do so, they have turned more deliberately toward law and social activism as a tool to transform the society about them into one that more closely mirrors their values.

20. *Baptist Faith and Message, supra* note 17, at 145–46.
21. *See* H. Richard Niebuhr, *The Social Sources of Denominationalism* 17–21 (1929).

In the second place, many Baptists—along with other late-twentieth-century evangelicals—have been inspired to champion "Christian" values in the face of increasing moral pluralism. Baptists have traditionally agreed that the task of law was not to convert men and women but to restrain their sinful tendencies in some semblance of order. The law was not an evangelist, only a constable. But according to what values is the law infused with content? Here, many Baptists assumed that the law with which the magistrate subdued bad men as ordained in Romans 13 should reflect moral principles consistent with Christian teaching.[22] Unlike Roger Williams, who steadfastly insisted that the business of law and of governing did not require a Christian underpinning, these Baptists were comfortable to find civil shelter within the moral residuum of Christian commonwealth that survived legal disestablishment.[23] They did not have to speak of the need for law to reflect "Christian" values. America, they were confident, was still a Christian nation even if they themselves had been midwives of religious disestablishment.

By the second half of the twentieth century, however, many conservative Christians wondered whether America's "Christian" character had ceased to be a reality and was now only an aspiration. For these believers, the law could no longer be assumed to reflect Christian principles but had to be made to reflect these principles by the concerted effort of Christians within the public sphere. Baptists, increasingly, are numbered among these believers. Although Baptists have made sporadic forays into the public arena to influence the content of law, these episodes appear to have increased over the past two decades or so. Now many Baptists may be found among the numbers of believers who resolutely insist that the laws and public life of the United States should reflect Christian values. By this I do not mean that such Baptists would use the force of laws to establish Christianity as anything like an official religion. Rather, they are increasingly happy to use the law to impose moral and social norms consistent with their understanding of Christian teachings.

Even Roger Williams's deconstruction of the Puritan establishment assumed that the superstructure of law could be erected upon the framework of shared moral principles, a natural law accessible to individuals without regard to their

22. *See* 2 McLoughlin, *supra* note 9, at 752.

23. For Williams's insistence that governing did not require a foundation in Christian beliefs, *see, e.g.,* Roger Williams, The Bloody Tenent of Persecution, in 3 *Writings of Roger Williams* 246 (1963) ("A Subject, a Magistrate, may be a good Subject, a good Magistrate, in respect of civill or morall goodness, which thousands want, and where it is, it is commendable and beautiful, though Godliness which is infinitely more beautiful be wanting").

membership in the community of Christ.[24] But moral pluralism has challenged this confidence that democratic systems can find common cause around
a set of fundamental moral principles. Baptists and other conservative Christians could at one time assume that any such set of agreed-upon principles
would be consistent with Christian norms of moral conduct. But bitter debates
concerning such subjects as abortion and gay rights have shattered this confidence. As a result, many Baptists—faced with seemingly intractable moral differences about these issues—no longer see any purpose in finding a neutral
moral language in which to speak but are happy to reassert their allegiance to
"Christian" values.

Finally, Baptists have attempted to colonize public life with "Christian" values at least partially as a defense against aggressive variants of secularism, which
consign faith to the category of pre-Enlightenment superstition and would be
happy to purge it from the American scene. Endless skirmishes in the ongoing
culture wars have no doubt imbued some Baptists with the conviction that secularists are not satisfied with detente but insist, instead, on domination. If
there must be a winner in this struggle between belief and unbelief, they reason,
then let us see that it is belief. If we must choose between a secular America,
hostile to faith and the values it generates, and a "Christian America," why
then, they determine, let it be "Christian America."

This renewed allegiance to a "Christian America" in which Christian values
predominate is inconsistent with more deeply rooted Baptist principles and, in
fact, harmful to the cause of Christ. The Romans 13 authority of the civil magistrate to punish bad conduct does not require a foundation of Christian values. Otherwise, Roger Williams argued, God, who ordained this authority,
would have left in a poor state all those nations in which the principles of
Christ have not flourished. The Apostle Paul insisted that God's law was not the
peculiar possession of the righteous but that it had been universally minted on
the human heart. "When Gentiles, who do not possess the law, do instinctively
what the law requires, these, though not having the law, are a law to themselves.
They show that what the law requires is written on their hearts, to which their
own conscience also bears witness; and their conflicting thoughts will accuse or
perhaps excuse them on the day when, according to my gospel, God, through
Jesus Christ, will judge the secret thoughts of all."[25] We would do better to locate the standards used by the Romans 13 magistrate in some notion of natural

24. *See* Roger Williams, The Bloody Tenent Yet More Bloody, in 4 *Writings of Williams*
365 (1963).

25. Romans 2:14–16. All biblical quotations are from the New Revised Standard Version.

law, ascertainable in circumstances where saving faith is absent. This divine inscription on the human conscience, and not any peculiarly "Christian" values, is the basis for secular law. Calling "Christian" the principles inscribed by God has at least three harmful consequences.

First, it jeopardizes the ability of Christians to make common cause with non-Christians to establish right principles of law. It is difficult to rouse support for "Christian" values among those who do not acknowledge Jesus as Christ. Even if the values themselves are a matter of common agreement, citizens who do not follow Christ must inevitably bridle at attaching to common principles the name of a Messiah whom they do not serve. Christians themselves would be no more likely to find common cause with Moslems, for example, around agreed-upon moral principles that were championed as Islamic values.

Second, clearly implicit in the current enthusiasm for a renewed commitment to "Christian" values is the assumption that if nonbelievers will not join in support of these values, then Christians will nevertheless exercise political power to enforce these values over the protests of nonbelievers. Although the creation of law inevitably summons the use of force to prevail over the views of dissenters, it is simply inconsistent with the character of Christ to summon his name as blessing on such uses of force. The gospel of peace becomes associated with the sword. Here the Anabaptist reluctance to link the cause of Christ with the sword is justified. I differ, perhaps, as Baptists traditionally have, in thinking that a follower of Christ might be involved in using the sword as a magistrate, say, without linking the cause of Christ explicitly to this use. The world has its kingdoms, and Christians may participate in their governance, but they follow a Lord who claimed that His kingdom was not of this world. To summon the name of Christ to exercises of law and political power in the world's kingdoms is to invest him with kingdoms He has—for the present at least—renounced.

Third, most references to "Christian values" as a basis for political activism seem to me to suggest a stunted vision of Christian principles, and one that hardly flatters Christ. When "Christian values" becomes nothing more than a synonym for "traditional middle-American conservative values," then the cause of Christ will have suffered. In fact, if we use the phrase "Christian values" at all, shouldn't we understand these to be the peculiar rules which Christ established for His kingdom in such New Testament discourses as the Sermon on the Mount?[26] The values of Christ's kingdom—nonretribution and sacrifi-

---

26. *See* Stanley Hauerwas and William H. Willimon, *Resident Aliens: Life in the Christian Colony* 172–80 (1989).

cial love, for example—are not precepts of the law, nor should they be. It dilutes the awesome severity of these values to imagine that they might be produced by mere legislative fiat. In truth, of course, no one seems in much of a hurry to translate Christ's commands into law. We will search the legal databases in vain for A Bill for Requiring Everyone to Forgive a Brother for Four Hundred Ninety Offenses or A Bill for Requiring Everyone to Carry the Roman Pack Twice as Far as the Law Has Heretofore Required.

It is possible, though, to tame the demands of Christ to make them palatable for legal enforcement efforts. The surge of enthusiasm for "Christian" values, in particular, entices followers of Christ to label as Christian values that are scarcely more than law-abidingness. There is nothing uniquely Christian, for example, in refraining from harming others—especially the innocent—or in being faithful to one's commitments, including one's marriage commitments. These, among both those who believe in Christ and those who do not, amount to minimum duties of civic life. They are, consequently, moral duties appropriate for enforcement by legal sanction. Jesus, though, admonished his disciples that the one who satisfies only such minimum standards is scarcely worthy of commendation. "So you also, when you have done all that you were ordered to do, say, 'We are worthless slaves; we have done only what we ought to have done.'"[27] The call of Christ is to something more than good citizenship, something more than stolid Republican conservativism. But the constant trumpeting of calls for "Christian values" seems to suggest otherwise.

What contribution can Baptist pietism make to law, then? Very little, I suspect. This theological perspective denies to law the mantle of either inherent divinity or diabolicalness. It denies the law divinity by seeing law as radically separate from the gospel. It denies the law diabolicalness by seeing law as an imperfect institution, to be sure, but one charged by God with a limited but necessary task. From this perspective, faith does not subvert law, except when law attempts to wrap its doings in the mantle of faith. Then faith may prick the pretentiousness of law by repudiating any kinship with law. Nor does faith oppose law, unless law claims a dominion and a purpose that is idolatrous.

The law does not need to be tethered to Christ, and the cause of Christ neither needs to be nor profits from being tethered to the law. To every Pilate who would trap Christ in the political turmoil of the moment, He answers, "My

27. Luke 17:10.

kingdom is not of this world."[28] The world must have its kingdoms, and these kingdoms must have their laws, but Christ refuses to be anointed as ruler of any of them, until "the kingdom of the world has become the kingdom of our Lord and of his Messiah."[29] Baptists have generally located this coronation in an apocalyptic future. In the meantime, as aliens and pilgrims, we should be wary of those who would fix the location of Christ in any particular worldly place or institution, whether in "Christian" America or in the law.[30]

28. John 18:36.
29. Revelations 11:15.
30. *See* Matthew 24:26.

# On Liberty and Life in Babylon:

# A Pilgrim's Pragmatic Proposal

*Richard F. Duncan*

> By the waters of Babylon, there we sat down and wept, when we
> remembered Zion.
> On the willows there we hung up our lyres.
> For there our captors required of us songs, and our tormentors,
> mirth, saying "Sing us one of the songs of Zion!"
> How shall we sing the Lord's song in a foreign land?
> —*Psalms 137:1–4 (rsv)*

My purpose here is not to present a grand theory of the role of Christians in society. Nor is my goal to convince you that Christians should embrace libertarianism as a political theory or Biblical principle for all times and all places. I am neither a theologian nor a political scientist. I write as a sinner who has accepted Christ as Savior and as Lord, as a husband of a Christian wife, as a father of five children, and as an academic lawyer who teaches and writes about constitutional law. Although this essay is addressed to fellow "pilgrims" wandering in contemporary America, I hope other readers—particularly readers with a strictly secular worldview—will find this conversation interesting.[1]

---

1. Portions of this essay are adapted from Richard F. Duncan, *Public Schools and the Inevitability of Religious Inequality,* 1996 BYU L. Rev. 569.

The reference to Babylon in the title of this essay is meant to convey my understanding of what it is like to live as a pilgrim in a postmodern secular state. Just as the Jewish people wandered in exile in ancient Babylon, Christians wander today in an America that has rejected our God—indeed, in an America that often seems to be waging war against our God.[2] I no longer take it for granted that America is a decent place in which children can grow and flourish. Like many others, I now realize that the motto "God and country" no longer rings true. Rather, I have reluctantly begun to accept that all too often today "the question is 'God *or* country.'"[3] That is an easy choice for me—I choose God. I struggle here not for grand theories but for pragmatic solutions to the many problems faced today by Christian parents as we struggle to raise godly children in an increasingly depraved and depraving culture.

Our society is deeply divided over the meaning of good and evil. We tell clashing stories about things that matter a great deal, things such as abortion, marriage and family, education, the role of religion in the public square, and the ethics of human sexuality. The sociologist James Davison Hunter has observed that this culture war is a struggle between starkly polarized moral communities and that it represents "a strain upon the course of democratic practice."[4] If the functions of government were, as Richard Epstein has suggested, "limited to preserving order, protecting property rights and enforcing contracts, as was the Founding Fathers' intention," people on both sides of the culture war could live in peace in the ample demilitarized zone of private life.[5] Of course, each side would be free to try to persuade the other about the meaning of the good life, but neither could employ the coercive power of government to impose its values on the private lives and enterprises of the other. However, we live in an era of Big Government, an age in which the state—with its carrots and sticks—exercises great control over our lives and families.

My "pragmatic proposal" for pilgrims in Babylon suggests that we recognize that Babylonian law will typically reflect the morality and values of Babylon,

2. In 597 BCE, King Nebuchadnezzar of Babylon captured the city of Jerusalem and "carried into exile all Jerusalem," leaving behind "only the poorest people of the land." 2 Kings 24:14 (NIV). *See generally* Paul Johnson, *A History of the Jews* 78–79 (1987); *The Works of Josephus* 272–76 (William Whiston trans., 1987). Psalm 137, the source of the epigraph, is a poignant poem about the grief of the Jewish exiles during the Babylonian captivity.

3. Symposium, *The End of Democracy? The Judicial Usurpation of Politics,* First Things, Nov. 1996, at 20 (emphasis in original).

4. James Davison Hunter, *Culture Wars: The Struggle to Define America* 316 (1991).

5. Richard A. Epstein, *The Welfare State's Threat to Religion,* Wall St. J., July 27, 1994, at A15.

not those of Jerusalem. Thus we need to reduce significantly the size of the state, particularly that part of the state that limits our ability to raise God-fearing children and to pursue happiness in a manner that is pleasing to God. My proposal does not ask Christians to accept libertarianism as the orthodox Biblical theory of government; I am merely suggesting that Christians living in contemporary America might do well to support policies that limit the power of government to control our lives and businesses. In other words, in spite of our different theological traditions, we ought to be able to agree that a small Babylonian government is better than a large Babylonian government.

## SETTING FREE THE CAPTIVE AUDIENCE

> The fear of the Lord is the beginning of knowledge, but fools despise wisdom and discipline.
> —*Proverbs 1:7 (NIV)*

The selective funding of education in secular government schools guarantees religious inequality in our polity. It imposes on religious parents what even supporters of "common schools" call a "brutal bargain."[6] We must choose between declining the single largest benefit most families receive from local government and countenancing assimilation of our children into a dominant secular culture by means of a governmental institution that exists for the very purpose of inculcating "common" secular values. More than a century ago, John Stuart Mill warned about the danger of allowing government to direct the education of children. In his classic defense of individual freedom, *On Liberty,* Mill explained how government schools are inherently destructive of religious liberty and freedom of thought: "A general State education is a mere contrivance for moulding people to be exactly like one another: and as the mould in which it casts them is that which pleases the predominant power in the government, whether this be a monarch, a priesthood, an aristocracy, or the majority of the existing generation, in proportion as it is efficient and successful, it establishes a despotism over the mind, leading by natural tendency to one over the body."[7] Instead of schools run by government, Mill supported what he called "diversity of education" and parental choice.

6. Peter Beinart, *Degree of Separation,* New Republic, Nov. 3, 1997, at 6 (quoting Norman Podhoretz).

7. John Stuart Mill, *On Liberty* 106 (1859) (Stefan Collini ed., Cambridge University Press 1989).

As Richard Baer puts it, "the basic structure of American education is *inherently* discriminatory and *unavoidably* involves serious forms of censorship. . . . Parents are forced to submit their children to a government-controlled school system that promotes a particular set of favored values."[8] Moreover, the legal rules governing public schools are weighted heavily against families with serious religious perspectives, because we are not permitted to use the political process to seek inclusion of our values and perspectives in the common curriculum. This is so because under prevailing Supreme Court interpretations of the Establishment Clause, public schools may not sponsor religious values or perspectives. Indeed, the Court has gone so far as to strike down a law requiring public schools to provide "balanced treatment" for creation-science and evolution. The Court held that the law, which merely required the teaching of "scientific evidences" for both creation and evolution, was enacted for the primary purpose of "endors[ing] a particular religious doctrine" and therefore was inconsistent with the Court's understanding of the Establishment Clause.[9]

Kathleen Sullivan argues that a playing field slanted against religious citizens is a good thing and that the Constitution "entails the establishment of a civil order—the culture of liberal democracy—for resolving public moral disputes." Thus "the war of all sects against all" is ended by a truce which privileges secular factions and relegates religious citizens to the margins of organized society. The public classroom may be used to advance secular ideologies and visions of the good and, concludes Sullivan, "protection for religious subcultures lies in exit rights. . . . The solution for those whose religion clashes with a Dick and Jane who appear nothing like Adam and Eve is to leave the public school."[10]

There is abundant evidence that religion has been cleansed from the public school curriculum.[11] The leading study of textbook bias—conducted by Paul

8. Richard A. Baer, Jr., *Public Education as "Brutal Censorship,"* This World, Summer 1988, at 110 (emphasis in original).

9. *Edwards v. Aguillard,* 482 U.S. 578, 580–81, 594 (1987).

10. Kathleen M. Sullivan, *Religion and Liberal Democracy,* 59 U. Chi. L. Rev. 195, 198, 214 (1992).

11. For a list of sources, *see* Richard F. Duncan, *Public Schools and the Inevitability of Religious Inequality,* 1996 BYU L. Rev. 569, 578 n. 45. There is at least some evidence that "the study of religion has expanded in the last 10 years" in some textbooks and curricula. Gilbert T. Sewall, Religion and the Textbooks in *Curriculum, Religion, and Public Education* 79 (James T. Sears and James C. Carper eds., 1998). But even Sewall acknowledges that "a double standard now operates in society and culture, whereby media and courts, sympathetic to the claims of ethnicity, disability, or sexual orientation, for example, vigorously exclude tra-

Vitz, a professor of psychology at New York University, for the United States Department of Education—concluded that public school textbooks are seriously biased and that "the nature of the bias is clear: Religion, traditional family values, and conservative political and economic positions have been reliably excluded from children's textbooks." For example, Vitz's study of social studies textbooks for grades one through four—books designed to introduce children to U.S. society—found that not one of the books contains even "one word referring to any religious activity in contemporary American life." One particular social studies book contains thirty pages on the Pilgrims without even one word or image "that referred to religion as even a part of the Pilgrims' life." Remarkably, one sixth-grade reader went so far as to censor a story authored by the Nobel laureate Isaac Bashevis Singer, eliminating all references to God. As Vitz observes, this censorship "not only represent[s] a clear case of removing God from our textbooks, but [it] also transforms the story." The author's narrative of "small town Jewish life in Eastern Europe is . . . falsified," and all of the students who are assigned this textbook are poorer as a result.[12]

Vitz also discovered that the textbooks present a biased view of family life in America. For example, social studies textbooks for grades one through four contain "countless references" to mothers and other women in professions and occupations in the workplace, but there is "not one citation indicating that the occupation of a mother or housewife represents an important job, one with integrity, one that provides real satisfactions."[13]

Sullivan believes the establishment of a strictly secular civil order in public education will produce a lasting peace, a kind of Pax Secularis between otherwise hostile religious sects. But there is no peace. The public schools have become one of the primary battlegrounds in the culture war.[14] The reason the Pax Secularis has failed in public education should be apparent. It is the reason described so eloquently more than fifty years ago by Justice Jackson in *West Virginia State Board of Education v. Barnette:*

> As governmental pressure toward unity becomes greater, so strife becomes more bitter as to whose unity it shall be. Probably no deeper division of our people could proceed from any provocation than from finding it necessary to choose what doctrine

ditional religious thought from respectable discourse on public life and the education of the young." *Id.* at 83.

12. Paul C. Vitz, *Censorship: Evidence of Bias In Our Children's Textbooks* 1–4 (1986).

13. *Id.* at 38.

14. *See generally* Stephen Bates, *Battleground: One Mother's Crusade, the Religious Right, and the Struggle for Control of Our Classrooms* (1993).

and whose program public educational officials shall compel youth to unite in embracing. Ultimate futility of such attempts to compel coherence is the lesson of every such effort from the Roman drive to stamp out Christianity as a disturber of its pagan unity, the Inquisition as a means to religious and dynastic unity, the Siberian exiles as a means to Russian unity, down to the fast failing efforts of our present totalitarian enemies. Those who begin coercive elimination of dissent soon find themselves exterminating dissenters. Compulsory unification of opinion achieves only the unanimity of the graveyard.[15]

Because public schools are "intentionally designed to influence the values, habits, and behavior of the rising generation," and "since people do not agree on which values, habits, and behaviors should be encouraged," public school curricula will always be controversial; and because the education of their children is one of the things that matters most to nearly everyone, the battle for control of the curriculum will often be very bitter and divisive.[16]

Christians are called to be fools for Christ, but we are not foolish. We understand that the "peace" we are offered in the public schools is Esau's bargain; and we will not barter the hearts and minds of our children for a bowl of red pottage.[17] A secular education is neutral toward religion only in the sense that it marginalizes all religious perspectives about what is true, what is good, and what is beautiful. As Michael McConnell has put it so eloquently, "A secular school does not necessarily produce atheists, but it produces young adults who inevitably think of religion as extraneous to the real world of intellectual inquiry, if they think of religion at all."[18]

In our struggle to protect and nurture the hearts and minds of our children here in Babylon, Christians must adopt a libertarian strategy. We must stop fighting symbolic wars over prayer in the public schools and concentrate our efforts on transforming the way our society structures educational benefits. The proper role of government in a pluralistic society is not to provide a one-size-fits-all secular education to a captive audience of impressionable children from many diverse religious and cultural backgrounds; rather, government should facilitate parents' educational choices for their children by funding a quality education for each and every child.

15. 319 U.S. 624, 641 (1943).

16. Diane Ravitch, *The Great School Wars: New York City, 1805–1973: A History of the Public Schools as Battlefield of Social Change* 403–4 (1974).

17. See Genesis 25:29–34 (King James).

18. Michael W. McConnell, *"God Is Dead and We Have Killed Him!": Freedom of Religion in the Post-modern Age,* 1993 BYU L. Rev. 163, 181.

Parents who wish to protect their children from being made part of a captive audience for the government's educative speech currently have a right under the Due Process Clause to exit from public schools. This is so because compulsory public schooling laws were declared unconstitutional in *Pierce v. Society of Sisters*. In *Pierce* the Supreme Court strongly condemned attempts by government "to standardize . . . children by forcing them to accept instruction from public teachers only" and used equally powerful prose in recognizing both the right and the duty of parents to "direct the upbringing and education" of their children.[19]

However, the Court persists in allowing the state to do indirectly that which it is forbidden to do directly; by withholding tax-supported funds from children who attend nongovernment schools, the state "exerts powerful—and highly questionable—financial pressure on dissenting parents to conform their educational choices to the majority's values by enrolling their children in public schools."[20] In other words, selective funding effectively coerces parents to allow government to do what *Pierce* forbids it to do—"standardize" children by forcing them to attend public schools.

As Stephen Gilles has argued, "Selective funding of public schools [also] raises profound free speech problems," because it is intended to, and in fact does, discriminate against parental educative speech on the basis of viewpoint. He reasons that "a person's freedom of speech includes the right to select and employ other persons to speak on his or her behalf." Political candidates, for example, often employ staff and public-relations firms to convey their message to voters, and persons wishing to influence public policy often hire experts, lawyers, and other representatives to present their views to public officials. Similarly, observes Gilles, parents may express educational messages to their children either directly, or indirectly through the schools of their choice. He argues that the government engages in viewpoint discrimination of parental educative speech when it subsidizes the educative speech of parents who share the values and beliefs taught in public schools while denying funding for the educative speech of dissenting parents. "The result is powerful, though indirect, governmental pressure on dissenting parents to conform their educative speech to the majority's preferred values."[21]

It is not my purpose here to present a rigorous analysis of the constitutional-

19. 268 U.S. 510, 534–35 (1925); *see also Meyer v. Nebraska*, 262 U.S. 390 (1923).
20. Stephen G. Gilles, *On Educating Children: A Parentalist Manifesto*, 63 U. Chi. L. Rev. 937, 942 (1996).
21. *Id.* at 1018–25.

ity *vel non* of public schools. Rather, I hope merely to convince readers that the government school monopoly in education threatens basic notions of human liberty and justice. As Gilles points out, even the familiar notion of Rawlsian justice suggests that it is unreasonable for the majority to insist on an educational system in which "the children of dissenting parents are to be taught the state's established wisdom concerning the human good" day in and day out for thirteen years of formal schooling. Picture the class of committed and loving parents, behind Rawls's veil of ignorance, deciding between competing schemes for the education of children. Because these committed parents do not know whether their values and beliefs will be in the majority or the minority, which educational scheme will they most likely prefer? Gilles submits that there would be a "consensus in favor of exclusive parental authority," because most of us care more about the educational interests of our own children than we do about controlling the education of other children. Thus we are likely to "care more about having the undisturbed authority to educate our children in accord with our conception of the good than we do about expanding that authority to encompass the formal schooling of children whose parents adhere to different conceptions of the good."[22]

In a free and just society, government has no business commandeering an audience of impressionable children for inculcation in the ideas, beliefs, perspectives, and attitudes of those who hold the reins of political power. The government is free to speak and celebrate whatever it chooses. But it suppresses the fundamental freedoms of thought and belief formation when it requires our children to show up and pay attention to its messages.

Moreover, the censorship of religion in public schools required by the Court's modern Establishment Clause decrees stacks the deck against religious families by ensuring that our beliefs and perspectives cannot be taught in government schools. Selective funding of education guarantees religious inequality in two respects. Some religious families—the lucky ones who can afford to educate their children in private schools—suffer only an economic penalty by losing a large public benefit when they choose to exit from public schools. A larger class of religious families suffer a far worse fate—the "compulsory socialization" of their children in strictly secular government schools. As Stephen Arons puts it: "The present method of financing American education discriminates against the poor and the working class and even a large part of the middle class by conditioning the exercise of First Amendment rights of school

22. *Id.* at 969–70.

choice upon an ability to pay while simultaneously eroding the ability to pay through the regressive collection of taxes used exclusively for government schools."[23]

My pragmatic proposal to fellow pilgrims in post-Christian America is to demand that our government let our children go—without penalty. We pay taxes to finance education, and our children are entitled to their fair share of these benefits whether they attend public, private, or parochial schools. This proposal seeks nothing more than basic justice and equal regard for all citizens in a nation as culturally and religiously diverse as ours. Pluralism is not honored by a system of education that tries to fit all children into a one-size-fits-all secular mold. We should remove our children from government schools and withhold our support from any system of education that does not respect the right of every child to an appropriate elementary and secondary education.

Christians believe that God is real and that the "fear of the Lord is the beginning of knowledge."[24] Therefore a secular education does not even begin to transmit true knowledge to students. Phillip Johnson has said it best: "If God really does exist, then to lead a rational life a person has to take account of God and his purposes. A person or a society that ignores the Creator is ignoring the most important part of reality, and to ignore reality is to be irrational."[25] Johnson is right, and therefore America's Godless public schools are irrational. It is time that we pilgrims begin to act accordingly.

### THE LIBERTY TO MAKE LASTING MARRIAGE VOWS

> "Haven't you read," he replied, "that at the beginning the Creator 'made them male and female,' and said, 'For this reason a man will leave his father and mother and be united to his wife, and the two will become one flesh'? So they are no longer two, but one. Therefore what God has joined together, let man not separate."
> Matthew 19:4–6 (NIV)

Remember when the law viewed marriage as a lifetime relationship and served to hold us accountable to live up to the promises we made to our spouses and children? In the past half-century, we have witnessed a radical redefinition

23. Stephen Arons, *Compelling Belief: The Culture of American Schooling* 211 (1983).

24. Proverbs 1:7 (NKJV).

25. Phillip E. Johnson, *Reason in the Balance: The Case Against Naturalism in Science, Law, and Education* 7 (1995).

of marriage "from a relationship that could be legally terminated before the death of one of the spouses only for grave reasons, if at all, to one which is . . . terminable upon the request of one party."[26] Indeed, the "apparent normative goal of modern divorce law" is not to help spouses keep their promises to one another and to their children but rather to ensure a "quick and easy" termination of marriages that are no longer satisfactory to at least one spouse.[27] In other words, the law has moved away from facilitating the continuation of marriages and instead treats marriage as "a contract terminable at will by either party."[28]

Professor Elizabeth Scott argues that this radical transformation of divorce law may reflect the preferences of unhappy couples desiring to end a marriage but probably does not embrace most people's concept of marriage and family.[29] In particular, traditional Christians typically don't view marriage as a relationship designed to last only so long as romantic love remains. We take lifetime vows seriously, and we expect the law to respect us enough to take our commitments seriously.

The quick and easy divorce laws of post-Christian America have codified a culture of divorce.[30] The norm of moral or religious duty that animated traditional marriage has been discarded and a new paradigm of self-realization and personal satisfaction has taken its place. The effects of this paradigm shift have been dramatic. Marriage in postmodern America has become something of an oxymoron—a "non-binding commitment" that "may begin with optimistic hopes that it will endure, but that survives only as long as each spouse's needs are met."[31]

I was born almost a half-century ago in an America that seems many eons and many galaxies removed from the America I live in today. In the world in which I was raised, children expected to grow up in an intact family. As I think back upon the friends and friendly acquaintances of my youth, I honestly cannot remember even one whose parents were divorced. In the modern throwaway culture of quick and easy divorce, however, children grow up with an ex-

26. Mary Ann Glendon, *Abortion and Divorce in Western Law: American Failures, European Challenges* 64–65 (1987).

27. Elizabeth S. Scott, *Rational Decisionmaking About Marriage and Divorce,* 76 Va. L. Rev. 9 (1990).

28. *Id.* at 17.

29. *Id.* at 22.

30. *See* Barbara Dafoe Whitehead, *The Divorce Culture* (1996).

31. *See* Scott, *supra* note 27, at 10.

pectation of separation. Our children live in a world in which "family love comes and goes. Daddies disappear. Mommies find new boyfriends. Mommies' boyfriends leave. Grandparents go away. Even pets must be left behind."[32] In a society like ours in which divorce is commonplace, "family breakup becomes a defining event of . . . childhood itself."[33] Moreover, the prevailing norm in family law takes as given that one dissatisfied spouse has a unilateral right to divorce without regard to the interests of the other spouse or of any possible detriment to his or her children.[34] There is no good reason why this sad story of what marriage has come to mean in Babylon should be imposed on those who wish to make a long-term investment in a marriage-for-life. The law must be changed to allow couples who wish to enter into marriages that are not easily broken an option to do so.

I am not arguing here for a repeal of "no-fault" divorce laws. I believe these laws have done a great deal of harm to families and especially to children, but, writing as a pragmatist, I recognize that so long as so many hearts are so hard, no-fault divorce is politically untouchable.

I suggest, rather, that marriage laws be amended to allow couples an *option* to enter into something like the "covenant marriages" that have been recognized in Louisiana. In other words, the law should allow couples to choose between a "no-fault" marriage-at-will model and a "covenant" marriage-for-life model. If a husband and wife are willing to be held accountable to a lifelong marital vow, the law should respect their commitment by holding them accountable to their freely chosen covenant. Under Louisiana law, for example, if a couple elects to enter into a covenant marriage, "divorce requires proof of fault in the nature of adultery, conviction of a felony and a sentence of imprisonment at hard labor or death, abandonment (for one year), physical or sexual abuse of a spouse or child of the parties, habitual intemperance or cruel treatment and a period of time living separate and apart thereafter."[35]

My proposal does not demand that the law impose my view of marriage on anyone else. It is a purely libertarian proposal that merely asks that the law respect the commitments of competent adults who wish to make lifelong mar-

32. Whitehead, *supra* note 30, at 11.

33. *Id.*

34. *See* Scott, *supra* note 27, at 27.

35. Katherine Shaw Spaht, *Louisiana's Covenant Marriage: Social Analysis And Legal Implications,* 59 La. L. Rev. 63, 107–8. (1998). In addition, "either spouse may obtain a divorce upon proof of living separate and apart for two years." *Id.* at 108.

riage vows. Those who freely enter into covenant marriages are asking the state to leave their marriage alone unless certain serious grounds for divorce exist.

Divorce is state action of a particularly intrusive nature. Under no-fault divorce laws, one party can unilaterally declare a marriage broken and petition the state to issue coercive decrees intimately and profoundly affecting the other party and the couple's children. Perhaps no-fault divorce is what some people want, but there are others who wish to unite in marriages that cannot be broken so easily. Why shouldn't the law honor the choices of couples who wish to make lifelong commitments to each other and their children?

It is not my intention here to endorse any particular covenant-marriage law. I am simply suggesting that marriage laws be amended to allow a man and a woman to choose to make a binding marital commitment to each other and to their children. This legal option should require premarital counseling to ensure informed consent, establish that marriage is a lifetime commitment that can be broken only for certain specified reasons involving grave circumstances, and provide that each party must formally and solemnly declare his or her commitment to a lasting marriage. The Louisiana covenant-marriage law specifies a declaration that eloquently captures the essence of what I am proposing:

> We do solemnly declare that marriage is a covenant between a man and a woman who agree to live together as husband and wife for so long as they both may live. We have chosen each other carefully and disclosed to one another everything which could adversely affect the decision to enter into this marriage. We have received premarital counseling on the nature, purposes, and responsibilities of marriage. We have read the Covenant Marriage Act, and we understand that a Covenant Marriage is for life. If we experience marital difficulties, we commit ourselves to take all reasonable efforts to preserve our marriage, including marital counseling.
>
> With full knowledge of what this commitment means, we do hereby declare that our marriage will be bound by Louisiana law on Covenant Marriages and we promise to love, honor, and care for one another as husband and wife for the rest of our lives.[36]

The covenant-marriage option permits us to choose to be legally accountable to our loved ones for the promises we make respecting the permanence of marriage. It permits a man and a woman to make a mutual commitment—for better or for worse, for richer or for poorer, in sickness and in health—to remain together in a lifetime marriage that is bigger and more important than the

36. La. Rev. Stat. Ann. § 9:273A(1) (West 2000).

personal satisfaction and self-realization of either spouse. This option allows a couple to build a life together on a secure foundation. It emphasizes responsibility, cooperation, and a commitment to success as the accepted norms for behavior in marriage.[37] It does not ask the state to help us keep our promises to our spouses; it merely allows a man and a woman to agree that the state may not terminate their marriage upon the unilateral petition of one spouse unless serious grounds for divorce are established.

The best gift we can give our children is the promise that their parents are together for life. A covenant-marriage option does not require anyone to make such a promise; it merely respects our decision to choose to marry for life. Pilgrims in a post-Christian society should seriously consider this countercultural (and libertarian) proposal.

### RELIGIOUS FREEDOM IN THE WELFARE/ REGULATORY STATE

> Samuel told all the words of the Lord to the people who were asking him for a king. He said, "This is what the king who will reign over you will do: He will take your sons and make them serve with his chariots and horses, and they will run in front of his chariots. Some he will assign to be commanders of thousands and commanders of fifties, and others to plow his ground and reap his harvest, and still others to make weapons of war and equipment for his chariots. He will take your daughters to be perfumers and cooks and bakers. He will take the best of your fields and vineyards and olive groves and give them to his attendants. He will take a tenth of your grain and of your vintage and give it to his officials and attendants. Your menservants and maidservants and the best of your cattle and donkeys he will take for his own use. He will take a tenth of your flocks, and you yourselves will become his slaves. When that day comes, you will cry out for relief from the king you have chosen, and the Lord will not answer you in that day."
> 1 Samuel 8:10–18 (NIV)

The "ever-expanding reach of government" in postmodern America poses a grave threat to Christians and other religious subgroups.[38] When the size of government is limited—as in the night watchman state, in which the role of government is confined for the most part to protecting citizens against the un-

37. See Scott, supra note 27, at 50.
38. Richard A. Epstein, *The Welfare State's Threat to Religion*, Wall St. J., July 27, 1994, at A15.

lawful use of force and fraud—religious citizens will only rarely come in conflict with the law. However, when the arm of government reaches into every corner of life with its carrots and its sticks—as in the modern welfare/regulatory state—there will often be conflicts between religious lifeways and the law.

Moreover, when you combine a large, activist state with a view of nonestablishment that requires religion to retreat as government advances, the state of religious freedom sinks even lower. A government that ignores property rights and other secular liberties is not likely to tread lightly on religious freedom. As Richard Epstein observes, "Many of the greatest threats to religious liberty stem from insufficient protection of individual liberty in economic affairs."[39]

Consider the case of Evelyn Smith, a devout Christian who was widowed when Paul Smith, her husband of thirty-two years, died in 1987. Mrs. Smith's primary source of income is rent generated by four apartments left to her as a legacy by her husband. Mrs. Smith's pilgrimage in that part of Babylon known as California took a turn for the worse when she refused to rent to an unmarried couple, who wished to cohabit in one of her apartments, because she "believes that sex outside of marriage is sinful, and that it is a sin for her to rent . . . to people who will engage in nonmarital sex on her property." The unmarried couple filed a complaint against Smith with the California Fair Employment and Housing Commission, and after protracted litigation the California Supreme Court held that the state fair-housing laws protected unmarried cohabitants from discrimination and that Mrs. Smith was not entitled to a religious freedom exemption.[40]

A full and complete analysis of the court's decision in *Smith* is beyond the scope of this essay. I wish to focus on only one significant thread of the case: the court's refusal to recognize that Smith's religion was "substantially burdened" by the coercive impact of a law requiring her to do what her religious conscience condemned as a sin. The court held that Smith's religious freedom was not substantially burdened because she had the option of "selling her units and redeploying the capital in other investments." In other words, when people of faith choose to engage in commercial activities in California they waive their right to religious freedom. If the state's restrictive commercial laws conflict with the exercise of religion, believers are free to go out of business or move to

39. *Id.*

40. *See Smith v. Fair Employment & Hous. Comm.*, 51 Cal. Rptr. 2d 700, 703–22 (1996), *cert. denied*, 521 U.S. 1129 (1997). Mrs. Smith's story was reported at some length in *People* magazine. *See* Montgomery Brower, *Living in Sin? Not in Her Apartments, Vows Christian Landlady Evelyn Smith,* People, Dec. 11, 1989, at 113.

a more tolerant state. The "legal and dignity interests" of unmarried cohabitants were too important to yield, even a little, to the demands of God on Mrs. Smith's business ethics.[41] The world has indeed turned upside down, and good has become evil and evil good.

When we hear of a case in which a church is prohibited from expanding its building because it has been declared a historic landmark, or one in which a Christian landlord such as Mrs. Smith is treated as an outlaw because she could not in good conscience lease an apartment to an unmarried cohabiting couple, we shake our heads and express dismay that religious freedom is taken so lightly in our society.[42] Although this insight about religious freedom is valid, it only scratches the surface of what is wrong with the state of our liberties. The root of the problem is not that religious liberty is slighted but that property rights and economic liberties are disrespected. The modern welfare/regulatory state routinely tramples on our inalienable right to the pursuit of happiness by regulating and taxing almost every aspect of our lives and businesses.

The path to religious freedom in our society lies in an explosion of privatization, in a radical shrinking of the role of government in the lives of its citizens. As government retreats, religion will be free to advance. As government programs are cut and resources are returned to private citizens, we will be free to educate our children as we believe is best, to support causes we believe are right and good, to live our lives in accordance with our understanding of the good life and based upon our own theories of justice.

Peter Berger, a well-known and respected sociologist, has observed that if India is the most religious nation in the world and Sweden the most irreligious, then America is best understood as "a nation of Indians ruled by Swedes."[43] I think it is time we Indians take back control of our lives, our families, and our property from the Swedes who govern us. Although the night watchman state is unobtainable (and undesirable) in our complex modern society, if we Christians are to be free to live our lives and raise our families in a manner that is pleasing to God, we must make room for ourselves and our lifeways by reducing the power and ubiquitousness of the secular state.

41. *Smith,* 51 Cal. Rptr. 2d at 716.
42. *See, e.g., City of Boerne v. Flores,* 521 U.S. 507 (1997).
43. *See* Phillip Johnson, *The Swedish Syndrome,* First Things, Dec. 1993, at 48.

**Section 4** Dualists: Christ and Law in Tension

Luther shared the Anabaptist belief that the use of law is in tension with the pure message of Christ's gospel, but he believed that in a fallen world its use is necessary. He argued that Christians should participate in the state but cannot expect it to reflect Christ's teaching. David M. Smolin's essay gives us some historical background to Luther and the Anabaptists and analyzes how they adopted such different responses to the fallen nature of the state. He also contrasts Lutheran and Anabaptist views of the state with those of Calvinists and Catholics. According to Marie A. Failinger and Patrick R. Keifert, Lutherans understand Christians to be living a twofold life in the world: as human beings, they are bound by the natural law and are responsible for ensuring that the positive law reflects those demands to serve the neighbor; as saved by Christ, they are freed from the law to live responsively to the gift of grace. Failinger and Keifert discuss the Lutheran vision of law, always reflecting both the distortions of sin and God's co-creative activity, and thus both "wrathful and loving, punishing and nurturing, restraining and freeing."

# A House Divided? Anabaptist and Lutheran Perspectives on the Sword

*David M. Smolin*

What is the relationship between Jerusalem (religious faith) and Rome (the state)?[1] This question takes a distinctive form for the Christian Church, which seeks to follow the teachings and example of Jesus. Jesus instructed the disciples to "resist not an evil person" and warned that "all those who take up the sword will perish by the sword."[2] His followers had hoped that He would restore Israel politically and militarily, but Rome crucified Him. The New Testament portrays the apostles asking the resurrected Jesus when the kingdom would be restored to Israel, but they receive only an indirect answer from their Lord, who then ascends into heaven.[3] We don't come as innocents to these questions, for as children of Christendom we have blood on our hands. Christendom began around 311 CE, when Con-

---

1. An earlier version of this essay appeared in 47 J. Legal Ed. 28 (1997) and is used with permission. This essay is a significantly expanded version of a speech originally presented in January 1995 at the Law Professors' Christian Fellowship Conference entitled Following Christ in the Legal Academy.

2. Matthew 5:39; 26:52.

3. *See* Acts 1:6–9.

stantine claims to have seen the vision of the Cross athwart the midday sun and the words "by this sign conquer."[4] Christendom embodied the hope that an entire civilization, including the sword, including government, including force and war, can be Christian, even though Christians worship a Lord who declined a political kingdom and went to die on the cross. Many theological traditions have wrestled with this dilemma; I will emphasize here the Lutheran and Anabaptist perspectives and then compare them to Roman Catholic and Calvinistic approaches.

## ANABAPTISTS AND THE SWORD

Anabaptists broke with the rest of the reformation in several related ways. First, they rejected infant baptism and insisted on voluntary, adult, believer's baptism; this is why they were labeled Anabaptist, which means "baptized again." Second, Anabaptists became nonresistant: they denied that a Christian may take up the sword. Adult baptism and nonresistance were a part of their broader program of constituting a pure church of those who would follow the example and words of Jesus.

The classic nonresistant Anabaptist statement is found in the Schleitheim Confession of 1527, written by Michael Sattler, who (along with most of the signatories) was martyred. The confession states:

> The sword is ordained of God outside the perfection of Christ. It punishes and puts to death the wicked, and guards and protects the good. In the Law the sword was ordained for the punishment of the wicked and for their death, and the same [sword] is [now] ordained to be used by the worldly magistrates.
>
> In the perfection of Christ, however, only the ban is used for a warning and for the excommunication of the one who has sinned, without putting the flesh to death—simply the warning and the command to sin no more.[5]

Within this statement is an implicit two-kingdom theology, and an accompanying tension, which early nonresistant Anabaptism shares with Luther. The statement implies a kingdom of Christ whose citizens are obligated to follow the counsels of Jesus in the Sermon on the Mount. Citizens of this kingdom should turn the other cheek, should not return evil for evil but instead should

---

4. *See, e.g.,* Henry Chadwick, *The Early Church* 126 (1967); Michael Grant, *Constantine the Great* 138–41 (1993).

5. The Schleitheim Confession, in *Creeds of the Churches* 281, 287 (John H. Leith ed., 3d ed. 1982).

overcome evil with good. Citizens of Christ's kingdom are limited to those who follow the way of Jesus, which Jesus marked by teaching and example. Jesus' followers should be willing to go nonresistantly to their deaths, as Jesus did.

On the other hand, Sattler does not advocate pacifism. The sword is "ordained of God" and is necessary in this fallen world. Sattler therefore accepted the common Christian view that the basic functioning of human society requires the restraint of evil through the sword. However, although Sattler was not an anarchist or pacifist, he insisted that the use of the sword marked a lower kingdom beneath the perfection of Christ. The sword is necessary in this world but has no place in Christ's kingdom.

The Anabaptist rejection of infant baptism and insistence on believer's baptism embodied their rejection of Christendom and thus constituted a repudiation of more than a millennium of church history. After Constantine's conversion, the church and Christians had gradually become politically empowered. It became advantageous in a worldly, political sense to be Christian, and the church was filled with "converts" of doubtful piety. The subsequent collapse of the Roman Empire created a great void, which the church sought to fill through the creation of the Holy Roman Empire. There was competition for political power between church and empire, and between East and West. Some viewed the church as virtually a department of the state, with the emperor as the head of Christendom; in the West the papacy attempted, at one time, to assert control over both spiritual and political realms. The Western divisions of jurisdiction between church officials and emperors, or between the spiritual sword and the military-political sword, did not splinter the overall unity of Christendom, which was conceived as the rule of God over an entire civilization.

Under Christendom, membership in society required baptism; once a people were "converted," infant baptism guaranteed membership to succeeding generations. Religious outsiders, such as the Jews, were denied membership in society. Thus the Jews were at various times forced to wear distinctive clothing, murdered, forcibly converted, barred from various economic pursuits, expelled, and segregated into ghettos. Heretics were considered worse than thieves because they stole souls; thus the church would use its spiritual authority to announce people heretics, and then turn them over to the civil ruler, who would provide some suitably gruesome (and lethal) punishment.

By rejecting infant baptism, the Anabaptists not only rejected Christendom but also charged even Reformational Christendom with being "the world," the very antithesis of Christ's kingdom. In the biblical sense, "the world" comprises all within human society, and within the human individual, that seeks to operate autonomously from God, and thus is in rebellion against God. "Do not love the world, or anything that is in the world, or the love of the Father is not in you," warns John.[6] Believers' baptism, nonresistance, and the rejection of the oaths by which Christians were bound politically to Christendom thus constituted doctrines and practices by which the Anabaptists sought to establish a faithful church separated from Christendom.

The Protestant reformers and the Roman Catholic Counterreformation sought to reform, control, and reunify Christendom; only the Anabaptists repudiated the vision of a united Christian civilization. The various Protestant reformers were able to implement their religious programs spiritually and politically within specific cities or territories—Calvin in Geneva, Zwingli in Zurich, and Luther in northern Germany. These Protestant reformers, along with the Roman Catholic Church, all retained infant baptism and granted political authorities a broad role in establishing "true" Christianity and rooting out "false religion." They, or their followers, spread their various teachings to other lands. It was this religious competition among the reformers, and between the Roman Catholic Church and the reformers, that helped foment the wars of religion. Civil wars of religion in England, Scotland, and France, and the wars between Lutheran, Reformed, and Roman Catholic jurisdictions, all were born of the competing Christian visions of Christendom.

The Anabaptist rejection of Christendom apparently arose largely from their political and military failures. In the ferment of the Reformation, some Anabaptists supported the peasants' demands for rights, but the peasant revolt was crushed in 1525. Other Anabaptists initially hoped that Zwingli would implement their views in Zurich, but Zwingli disappointed them. Faced with an inability to pursue their religious program in the traditional territorial, military, and political manner of Christendom, Anabaptists developed an alternative vision—a vision for which they were martyred in large numbers.[7]

The account of the trial and punishment of Michael Sattler is a significant example of Anabaptist martyrology. His tongue was cut out, his body torn with red hot tongs, and finally he was burned. His crime was his nonresistant Christian faith.[8] The church has long believed that the "blood of the martyrs is the seed of the church," that the heroic martyrdom of the early Christians con-

6. See 1 John 2:15; see also 1 John 2:16.

7. See generally Denny Weaver, Becoming Anabaptist (1987); James M. Stayer, Anabaptists and the Sword (1976 ed.).

8. See Thieleman J. van Braght, Martyrs Mirror 416–20 (Joseph F. Sohm trans., 1987).

tributed spiritually to the cultural, religious, and political triumph of the church over its oppressor, the pagan Roman Empire. One does not have to agree with every tenet of Anabaptism to wonder at the spiritual significance of Christendom martyring a significant group of nonresistant Christians. In God's judgment and providence, did the large-scale martyring of the nonresistant Anabaptists lead to the demise of Christendom? Is this spent blood the reason that the great churches and cathedrals of Europe have become, in Nietzsche's words, the "graves of God," or in less religious terms, the monuments of a spent civilization?

This speculation is based on the special biblical significance of the shedding of innocent blood and of martyrdom. From the blood of Abel to that of God's prophets, and finally to that of Jesus Christ, the shedding of innocent blood is portrayed as invoking a particularly strong response of judgment from God. So it is a worthy Christian theological project to enquire about the providential and eschatological significance of the Jewish Holocaust.[9] The mass-murder of God's original chosen people and the subsequent reestablishment of the state of Israel are momentous events. Is it significant that both the martyrdom of the nonresistant Anabaptists and the Jewish Holocaust occurred in the midst of European Christendom? Could the political reempowerment of the Jews in their original homeland signify the end of Christendom, an end that had its spiritual roots in that earlier martyrdom of the Anabaptists? Has the innocent blood shed by Christendom, and by the heirs of Christendom, sealed up, for all time, its time of glory, and led, in God's providence and judgment, to its permanent demise? Or will God's judgment of European Christendom, for its role in these two crimes, allow for its future continuation?

## LUTHERAN TWO-KINGDOMS THEOLOGY

It is fascinating to see how close Martin Luther's theology is to Anabaptist theology, and yet what sharply different practical conclusions Luther draws. Luther agreed with the Anabaptists that Christians were obligated to follow Jesus' words and example, and hence to be nonresistant. Christians, according to Luther, need "no temporal law or sword" and would not even go to court to defend their interests. Furthermore, Luther taught that "the world and the masses are and always will be un-Christian, even if they are all baptized and Christian

9. *See, e.g.,* David P. Gushee, *The Righteous Gentiles of the Holocaust, A Christian Interpretation* (1994).

in name." Thus Luther (as of 1523) agreed with the nonresistant Anabaptist charge that Christendom and its people were largely coterminous with the "world." "There are few true believers, and still fewer who live a Christian life, who do not resist evil and indeed themselves do no evil," conceded Luther.[10]

Luther nonetheless insisted that a true nonresistant Christian, who for his own sake would not even seek legal redress, let alone direct vengeance, should be willing to wield the sword as a means of service to others. It is necessary for the world and one's neighbor that there be those "who arrest, prosecute, execute, and destroy the wicked, and who protect, acquit, defend, and save the good." Wielding the sword is a service of love to one's neighbor and a work ordained by God, according to Luther. Thus, according to Luther, one could simultaneously be a nonresistant Christian and a hangman: "You suffer evil and injustice, and yet at the same time you punish evil and injustice; you do not resist evil, and yet at the same time, you do resist it. In the one case, you consider yourself and what is yours; in the other, you consider your neighbor and what is his. In what concerns you and yours, you govern yourself by the gospel and suffer injustice toward yourself as a true Christian; in what concerns the person or property of others, you govern yourself according to love and tolerate no injustice toward your neighbor. The gospel does not forbid this; in fact, in other places it actually commands it."[11]

Luther goes so far as to argue that "it would even be fine and fitting if all princes were good, true Christians. For the sword and authority, as a particular service of God, belong more appropriately to Christians than to any other men on earth." Thus, for Luther, God's ordination of the governing authorities, as announced by Paul in Romans 13:1, necessarily implies the appropriateness of Christian participation, because it renders such participation a service to God. "Now it would be quite un-Christian to say that there is any service of God in which a Christian should not or must not take part, when service of God is actually more characteristic of Christians than of anyone else," declares Luther. Thus political service becomes, like marriage or farming, one of the many honorable "callings which God has instituted."[12]

Luther, however, does not lose his head in praise of princes. His pessimistic assessment of Christendom extends as well to rulers:

10. *See* Martin Luther, On Governmental Authority (1523), in *The Protestant Reformation* 46, 54, 48, 47 (Hans J. Hillerbrand ed., 1968).

11. *Id.* at 54, 51, 52.

12. *Id.* 53, 53, 53.

You must know that since the beginning of the world a wise prince is a mighty rare bird, and an upright prince even rarer. They are generally the biggest fools or the worst scoundrels on earth; therefore, one must constantly expect the worst from them and look for little good, especially in divine matters which concern the salvation of souls. They are God's executioners and hangmen; His divine wrath uses them to punish the wicked and to maintain outward peace. Our God is a great lord and ruler; this is why He must also have such noble, highborn, and rich hangmen and constables. He desires that everyone shall copiously accord them riches, honor, and fear in abundance. It pleases His divine will that we call His hangmen gracious lords, fall at their feet, and be subject to them in all humility, so long as they do not ply their trade too far and try to become shepherds instead of hangmen. If a prince should happen to be wise, upright, or a Christian, that is one of the great miracles, the most precious token of divine grace upon that land. Ordinarily the course of events is in accordance with the passage from Isaiah 3[:4], "I will make boys their princes, and gaping fools shall rule over them"; and in Hosea 13[:11], "I will give you a king in my anger, and take him away in my wrath." The world is too wicked, and does not deserve to have many wise and upright princes. Frogs must have their storks.[13]

Luther further argued that heretics should not be restrained by the sword or force because it was a spiritual matter entrusted to the church. The temporal power could not crush heresy, warned Luther, "even if it were to drench the world in blood."[14] This admonition, along with Luther's broader teaching that princes should not serve as "shepherds," or spiritual authorities, was not followed in practice. Luther's Reformation depended on the spiritual and military leadership of princes; in the splintered Christendom created by the Reformation, the rule frequently was that "the religion of the prince is the religion of the people." Thus the practices of Luther and his followers led to mini-Christendoms consisting of nation-states with state churches; the sword and government played an overwhelming role in religious matters, both within and between these nation-states.

Luther's two-kingdoms theology, coupled with the Lutheran concepts of "orders of creation" and "callings," ultimately led some manifestations of Lutheranism in a statist, socially conservative direction. Christ's kingdom became primarily the realm of justification by faith, an inner matter of piety and of the individual's relationship with God. The church was the place where this faith was planted and nourished by the preaching of the gospel, right teaching of doctrine, and the administration of the sacraments. The political realm, like

13. *Id.* at 61.
14. *Id.*

that of marriage, the family, and various kinds of work and trades, were orders of creation; they implied relationships of reciprocal obligations, including the obligation of subjects to obey their rulers. The separation of these orders of creation from gospel principles left them, in principle, untransformable; Christians could infuse their callings and roles with devotion, service, and love but could not alter these apparently fixed arrangements. A Christian subject devotedly obeyed and served his ruler and his country; a Christian tradesman worked diligently in service of his neighbor, family, and nation. The charge that this Lutheran conservatism led to the capitulation of most of Germany's church to the Nazis can be debated; it is clear at a minimum, however, that some German theologians came to see service to the German people *(volk)* as the highest expression in this world of Christian service. Thus it seems as though Lutheranism in practice often lost touch with both the Anabaptist dream of a transformed, separated church and with the Calvinist dream of a Biblically patterned and transformed polity. Aside from an inner piety, service to God came to be understood, at least by some Lutherans, virtually exclusively in terms of serving and affirming the (untransformable) orders of creation.

In a more positive vein, however, Lutheran two-kingdoms theology claims to offer a realistic assessment of the condition of the world, and of politics, in this time between the two comings of Jesus, as well as erecting a possible bulwark against a politicization of the faith. Against all utopian, transformative visions, two-kingdoms theology informs us that this world has been, is now, and ever will be filled with evil, suffering, and death; no fundamental change will come until Jesus returns. Justice and love will not reign on this earth, in a political sense, until the return of Jesus.[15]

On one level, it is difficult to take seriously Luther's image of a hangman or king executing people all day, and then, a day's bloody work done, heading home to an evening of turning the other cheek. Those who hold the power of the sword generally must defend themselves and their own authority and interests with the sword. A ruler may claim that his self-defense is done for the sake of the people he rules (or "serves"), but then what is left of his claim not to defend his own interests? After all, any one of us could find someone (spouse, parent, child, friend) for whose benefit we must defend ourselves. What, then, would be left of the principle of nonresistance?

---

15. *See generally* Carl E. Braaten, *Justification* 171–82 (1990) (discussing the doctrine of the two kingdoms); Carl E. Braaten, *God in Public Life: Rehabilitating the "Orders of Creation,"* in First Things, 32–38 (Dec. 1990).

On another level, however, Luther's paradox underscores and seeks to resolve the dilemma of the nonresistance position, which appears unloving in its refusal to protect others. Any parent or spouse can appreciate that a refusal to protect one's loved ones from harm would seem a terrible dereliction of the duty of love; the famous New Testament passage on love (or "charity") declares, after all, that love "always protects."[16] The use of force by government is, at its best, simply this impulse toward protective love, writ on a larger scale. Victims of violent crime or survivors of war crimes or invasions can appreciate the necessity of force in protecting the innocent. Is a refusal to use force to stop the Hitlers of this world really the moral high ground?

In addition, nonresistant communities face the charge of being moral freeloaders, because they benefit from the protections provided by police, jails, and the military, and yet refuse to share the difficulties and burdens of providing these protections. This difficulty can be overcome, to a limited degree, by alternative service. Nonetheless, it can appear hypocritical to declare oneself too pure to participate in the use of force, when one is significantly benefiting from the willingness of others to so participate.

The nonresistant Anabaptists were not unaware of these difficulties. Thus the Schleitheim Confession acknowledged the question of "whether a Christian may or should employ the sword against the wicked for the defence and protection of the good, or for the sake of love."[17] The answer of the Schleitheim Confession was that Christians, as Christ's members or body, must follow His ways and teachings; because Jesus refused the sword and political power and taught his disciples likewise, then all Christians must do likewise.[18] Any attempt to justify Christians exercising the sword as magistrates must, the Anabaptists thought, produce an internally divided and contradictory man and church ("body"). Thus the response to Luther's paradox of a nonresistant hangman would be to invoke Jesus' saying that "every kingdom divided against itself will be destroyed."[19]

Anabaptists can further argue that in any event there will always be people willing to bear the sword; in an evil world driven in large part by the desire for power, those willing to employ force will not be lacking. Furthermore, God's nonresistant church will always be a minority, and so questions of what would happen if "everyone" were nonresistant are irrelevant. It is not God's will that

16. 1 Corinthians 13:7.
17. *Creeds of the Churches, supra* note 4, at 288.
18. *Id.* at 288–89.
19. *See id.* at 289.

the church should rule the world; the mission of the church, instead, is to stand apart as an alternative society that embodies the teachings and presence of the lamb of God. God intends there to be a sharp contrast between world and church; Christians bearing the sword blur this contrast and make it more difficult for the church to fulfill its mission.

Lutheranism in the end is more paradoxical than Anabaptism, because Luther (at least initially) accepted many Anabaptist premises, and yet in practice and effect Lutheranism's propensity toward state churches and social conservatism became a bulwark of Christendom. Lutheranism theoretically frees the Christian from trying to impose the gospel by force, only to command or encourage the Christian to lend an often bloody hand to the glory of the fatherland. Some Lutherans who reject these Lutheran propensities toward state churches and nationalism have largely substituted a pietistic apoliticalism. However, other Lutherans—such as those who at great cost resisted Hitler— remind us that there are theological resources within the Lutheran tradition to actively oppose the idolatrous pretensions of tyrants and totalitarian states. Viewed positively, Lutheranism's account of callings, office, and orders of creation encourages a life of responsible service to others while providing a potent antidote to political, ideological, or personal hubris. Thus the complex paradoxes of Lutheranism offer more promising alternatives than either authoritarian statism or apolitical quietism, despite the tendency of some of Luther's followers in those directions.

## ROMAN CATHOLIC AND CALVINIST
### PERSPECTIVES

Roman Catholic and Calvinist theology share a one-kingdom, multiple-jurisdiction approach. Both have traditionally embraced the view that Christians should seek to embody the reign of God through the rule of Christendom.

Calvin seems to experience none of the tensions of Luther and the Anabaptists in regard to Christians as rulers employing force. Calvin's overarching awe of the sovereignty of God leads him to view the use of the sword by Christians as an expression of God's rule. For Calvin, God is glorified in judgment as well as in mercy. Thus there is no higher or more glorious calling than that of civil ruler. Any apparent tension between the use of the sword and the commands and example of Jesus is easily resolved by reference to the concept of office. God Himself has placed the sword in the hand of the ruler, and there is nothing contrary to the gospel in employing it. The individual Christian does not seek vengeance, but the ruler has the glorious office of carrying out God's vengeance.[20]

Calvin is an untroubled child of Christendom in declaring that the civil ruler has the obligation to establish right religion and uproot false religion.[21] He further perceives the right of political revolution in terms of office; individuals are forbidden to revolt, but lesser magistrates can, and sometimes should, defend the people from "licentious kings."[22] Calvin's further desire that every area of life be remade to the glory of God makes Calvinism a revolutionary force. Some attempted revolutions, like that in France, were crushed; other revolutions, like those of Knox and the English Puritans, had their seasons of relative political and military success. The United States can be seen as an outworking of the Calvinist impulse toward creating entire societies dedicated, in every function and sphere, to the glory of God.

Calvinism eventually repudiated Calvin's view that political rulers should have authority to punish false religion or irreligion. This change, however profound, is in Calvinistic terms merely an adjustment of jurisdiction and does not alter the broader hope of bringing all of society under the reign of God. Thus American and Dutch Calvinism has embodied the hope that every sphere and function within society, including government, church, family, university, and labor, can be brought under the reign of God, and has linked that concept to religious freedom and the institutional separation of church and state.[23] Thus the United States' institutional separation of church and state was historically a new expression of, rather than a repudiation of, the Christendom vision. Adjusting the relations between church and state, and the respective jurisdiction of each, did not remove for Calvinists the ultimate accountability of both church and state to the sovereign God.

The Western church is characterized by the development of a multijurisdictional view of church-state relations. Thus within Roman Catholicism there eventually emerged an elaborated distinction between church and state, and between the spiritual "sword" of the church and the military-political sword of

20. *See, e.g.,* 2 John Calvin, *Institutes of the Christian Religion* 1485–1521 (J. McNeill ed., 1960).

21. *See id.* at 1488, 1495 (civil government has the "duty of rightly establishing religion"; civil government "prevents idolatry, sacrilege against God's name, blasphemies against his truth, and other public offenses against religion from arising and spreading among the people").

22. *See id.* at 1510–21.

23. *See, e.g.,* Abraham Kuyper, *Lectures on Calvinism* (1931).

temporal rulers. The Roman Catholic division of authority between pope and emperor, church and empire, represents the forerunner of the Calvinistic view of jurisdiction and office. The Thomistic division between nature and grace, in which the greater, particularistic gifts of grace and revelation build upon the lesser, universal goods of nature and reason, similarly undergirds Luther's two-kingdoms theology, and its view of the political realm as a lesser kingdom.

Roman Catholicism, as the Western church's historical form of Christendom, therefore contains the presuppositions from which the various Reformational versions of Christendom developed. It was not until the Second Vatican Council, however, that Roman Catholicism officially embraced religious freedom for non-Catholics.[24] Vatican II, moreover, does not repudiate the possibility of an established church but merely requires that the state grant religious liberty and toleration to all religions.[25] John Paul II frequently addresses his teachings to all people of goodwill and urges upon rulers the adoption of laws consonant with "natural law." There are few religious leaders more involved in politics and the temporal realm, in the broad sense, than John Paul II. His concern for a broadly just social order touches virtually every aspect of the political order, including social, moral, and economic issues. It seems likely that John Paul II hopes for a resurgence of a purified Christendom in the new millennium: a Christendom with religious liberty and toleration, but still a form of Christendom.

Thus both Roman Catholicism and Calvinism still retain the Christendom vision: the hope that the world can and will be brought progressively under the reign of God, in large part through the involvement of Christians in all spheres of life, including politics. The apostasy, secularization, violence, immorality, and crimes against humanity of the twentieth century have chastened these hopes but have not as yet induced these churches to adopt an Anabaptist view of the church as a powerless alternative society in a necessarily wicked world.

It is an ancient but practical bit of wisdom that God will not thank us for doing what he has not asked us to do. Christians since Constantine have evidenced great zeal, and sometimes great folly and cruelty, in seeking to conquer the world in the name of Christ's cross. In spite of its many cruelties and abuses of power, Christendom represents the idealistic hope that power can serve the

---

24. *See* Declaration on Religious Freedom (Dignitatis Humanae), *reprinted in The Documents of Vatican II* 672 (Walter M. Abbott ed., 1966).

25. *See id.* at 685.

ends of God and justice, and that right and might can be joined in this world. The broader question, however, is whether God has asked the church (and Christians) to rule the world. What is the mission of the church during this time between the two comings of Jesus? Is it to embody Jesus by creating an alternative society that eschews political power? Or is it to represent the reign of God through grasping and using political and military power?

A rejection of the Christendom dream would not necessarily represent a complete abandonment of Christian involvement in the political arena. The Old Testament gives us examples of faithful Jews who served God in political office in the great pagan empires. Joseph in Egypt, Daniel in Babylon, and Esther and Mordecai in Persia used their offices to protect God's people and to provide for the common good of the peoples of the pagan empires they served. The Mennonite scholar John Howard Yoder has argued for Christian participation in the political process based on the church's place as a minority challenging the world to do greater justice.[26] It is possible to participate as a Christian in the political sphere, even if one eschews the hope of the world becoming Christianized. Political involvement changes its character, however, if it is based on the hope of ruling the world in the name of God.

For the Christian, questions of law and government are intertwined, even if unconsciously, with theological questions. Do we consider law and government a lower "kingdom" with a minimalist purpose of providing some degree of social order? Do we view secular law and government as accountable to natural law or God's law? Can a sphere as important as law and government be viewed as autonomous, without relationship to the Creator and Ruler of the Universe? Is a search for racial or economic justice properly based in biblical norms, and if so, should those norms be made explicit? To what degree is a contract-based marketplace to be viewed as separate from ethical constraint? How is the sphere of the family and personal life to be related to the jurisdiction of government? The content and structure of every subject area of law present multiple theological challenges that cannot be answered without application of an implicit theology of government and the state.

Because even theologically literate Christians are often unclear about the meaning and purpose of their political activities, it is hardly surprising that non-Christians, and particularly the secularized American elites who dominate the academy, wonder about the goals of Christian political activism. Are Christians attempting to resurrect Christendom? If Christendom were ever

26. *See, e.g.,* John Howard Yoder, *The Priestly Kingdom* (1984).

reestablished, would some sort of inquisition or crusade follow? For many Jews, Muslims, and secularized Americans, the Moral Majority and the Christian Coalition resurrect painful memories of persecution, intolerance, and wars of religion.

Though understandable, such fears are exaggerated. The version of "Christendom" that the religious right seeks to resurrect embraces religious freedom, civil liberties, and the institutional separation of church and state, and thus implicitly rejects the medieval Christendom paradigm upon which many of these fears are based.

It is wrong, moreover, to assume that theologically conservative Christians are always politically conservative. A significant percentage of evangelicals and traditionalist Roman Catholics are politically liberal on economic issues and thus have a natural affinity with the Democratic Party. It was the born-again Democrat Jimmy Carter who helped bring evangelical Christianity back into public prominence. The American press has discovered, when the pope visits America, that on economic, as opposed to social issues, John Paul II sounds like a liberal. Furthermore, although American Christianity has historically been dominated by a single-kingdom Christendom paradigm, the prominence of Baptists and others from the free-church tradition within the conservative evangelical movement tends to pacify the more aggressive aspects of the Christendom model. Finally, there is a radical-left minority within the broader traditionalist Christian movement, both within evangelicalism and Roman Catholicism, that is intensely antiwar and identifies spiritually and politically with the poor and marginalized. Thus secular academics should not presume that Christian involvement in politics invariably is oriented toward the political right.

On the other hand, many traditionalist Christians do believe that our Western secularized culture has unleashed a "culture of death" embodied, among other things, in elective abortion, euthanasia, and a violent and sexually charged mass media, and that a rejection of traditional virtue and morality, including sexual morality, is an important contributor to this culture.[27] Moreover, some perceive, behind the veil of official "secular" elite culture, hostile ideologies that function in the place of traditional religions in the lives of their adherents. Others go further and perceive, behind and alongside such ideologies, a modern resurgence of that ancient enemy of monotheism, paganism.[28]

27. See Pope John Paul II, Evangelium Vitae, in Origins 689 (April 6, 1995).
28. See, e.g., Thomas Molnar, Paganism and Its Renewal, 31 The InterCollegiate Rev. 28 (Fall 1995).

Indeed, there is a kind of "religious warfare" in this world. How could Christians think otherwise, when Scripture commands us to be engaged in spiritual warfare?[29] Both the nonresistant Anabaptist and the Calvinist warrior accept the inevitability of spiritual warfare; they merely disagree about whether politics and force may be used as a secondary means supplementing the primary scriptural means of prayer, Scripture, and virtuous living.

So it is understandable that some who embrace the dominant leftist ideologies of the legal academy evidence an instinctive aversion to all forms of orthodox Christianity. Many academics understand that the sexual and reproductive "freedoms" that their ideologies promote are viewed by orthodox Christians as social poisons, and that the cultural and sexual revolution that they seek to complete is broadly viewed by traditionalist Christians as a path to societal suicide. This revolutionary agenda seeks to mainstream as social goods "alternative families," elective abortion, and active euthanasia, and to marginalize permanent marriage, parenthood, and the traditional family as outmoded pathologies; it interprets our contemporary social ills as the birth pains of a new age struggling against reactionary religious and cultural forces. Faithful Christians cannot fail to find themselves labeled the "enemy" by those who have identified traditional religion and family life as the primary obstacles to their political and cultural aspirations.

It may be reassuring to some to understand that politics and law, for Christians, are not the ultimate or most important means or ends of spiritual warfare. Because Christianity is not merely an ideology, it can survive both political power and political powerlessness, and the respective and collective sins and temptations endemic to each situation. Both Marxism and democratic capitalism are meaningless without governments that practice and enforce them; Christianity can and will thrive, regardless of whether a single government of this earth embraces or even tolerates it. Marxism and democratic capitalism tend to become discredited when particular governments and individuals abuse power in their name; Christianity somehow remains credible, even when it is misused for base political and military objectives. This capacity of the church and Christianity to survive under a variety of relationships to political power is evidenced in their history; it means that neither power nor powerlessness ultimately will prevent the church from accomplishing her mission in this world. This independence from political circumstances allows Christians the luxury—what merely political creature could afford it?—of loving, even in

29. *See* Ephesians 6:10–20.

word and deed, our enemies. It points beyond the church, and her abuses and sins, to a voice and a power that calls to all, and to whom we all someday will give an account. For the message of Christianity is not ultimately about political power, but about the power of God, and not merely of that, but equally so of His mercy and forgiveness to those who are powerless to save themselves.

# Making Our Home in the Works of God: Lutherans on the Civil Use of the Law

*Marie A. Failinger and Patrick R. Keifert*

> If anyone attempted to rule the world by the gospel and to abol-
> ish all temporal law and sword on the plea that all are baptized
> and Christian and that, according to the gospel, there shall be
> among them no law or sword—or need for either—pray tell me,
> friend, what would he be doing? He would be loosing the ropes
> and chains of the savage wild beasts and letting them bite and
> mangle everyone, while insisting that they were harmless, tame,
> and gentle creatures.
> —*Martin Luther, "On Temporal Authority"*

> The fact is that in the sight of God those who are most devoted
> to the works of the law are farthest from fulfilling the law, be-
> cause they lack the Spirit that is the true fulfiller of the law, and
> while they may attempt it by their own powers, they achieve
> nothing.
> —*Luther, "The Bondage of the Will"*

In the past two centuries, the Lutheran witness has focused so critically and incessantly on grace, for which the law's condemnation
merely prepares us, that Luther's "first" or "civil" use of the law is often

overshadowed.[1] Indeed, Luther's insight that salvation cannot be a human work—that recognition of one's need for salvation is itself a gift of God—is so radical and extreme as to lead a careless reader to believe that in the moment of faith, the law vaporizes like a Romulan warrior into the ions of space.[2] Or Christians might imagine salvation as jurisdictional: for a Christian to pass over into grace is to leave behind a godless country for a new land overflowing with love and all good virtues. The Lutheran insight into law's civil or political use in God's creative governance offers a very different vision, one that startles modernity. Modern culture offers two stark choices: the optimistic view of law as dynamic means toward a good society and human perfection (a view shared by liberals, utopians, and Marxists, among others); or law as an evil embodiment of oppressive power that should be, but is not, governed by equality and relationality (as some in the critical legal studies movement, for example, would argue). The Lutheran vision is perhaps more fitting to a matured pluralistic culture, whose hope in a new land of (material-political) milk and honey has been shaken by limitation, the end of the frontier and uncomplicated civilization, and dashed prospects of a universal formula for peace. For the Lutheran insight into law is at once darkly realistic that evil is inevitable even within law and blithely optimistic that law can do good in this world; it imagines law as wrathful and loving, punishing and nurturing, restraining and freeing. It is fully egalitarian in its condemnation; fully inclusive in its demand for justice and care.

1. The underplaying of the first, "civil" use of the law is a profound effect of the Enlightenment. Luther's premodern doctrine that the grace of law is an expression of creation and human reason has collided with (especially American) modernism, which substitutes secular for "sectarian" theological categories: in modernism, creation becomes nature, reason becomes science, and law claims to be less human—"not of men but reason [alone]."

2. Alister E. McGrath argues that Luther's distinctive breakthrough was to reject the claim of the "via moderna" that humans played a limited but crucial part in their own salvation by recognizing their need for salvation and appealing to God to bestow God's covenantal offer of salvation on them. Luther denied that human beings played any part at all in their own salvation. Alister E. McGrath, *Luther's Theology of the Cross* 88–90, 128–36 (Cambridge, 1990). See Martin Luther, The Bondage of the Will, *in Martin Luther's Basic Theological Writings* 181 (Timothy Lull ed., Fortress 1989). This anthology is cited throughout because of its availability. Because this essay is a contemporary interpretation rather than a history of Lutheran doctrine, our sources are primarily Luther or late-twentieth-century Luther scholarship. As shorthand, we will refer to "Lutheran" claims as though they were uniform, even though Lutheran thought is very diverse, and others within various Lutheran communities and in other Protestant traditions read Luther differently.

For Luther, to receive the gift of grace is not to pass, as it were, from the country of law to the new and very different country of loving freedom. Nor do mainstream Lutherans view the world as dualist, an untransformable world of law in which Christians must serve within fixed, static systems of authority and a completely separate faith-kingdom where they are obligated to live out Christian principles, a common Protestant interpretation of the two-kingdoms doctrine.[3] To be a Christian in the world is more like being the salt in a bland meal, the yeast in a loaf of bread. The salt and yeast are distinctive and yet not separate; for the world to be fully what it is, that Christian spice, that leavening is required. Christians have no need of the law, Luther writes, and in the very same moment, they are unrepentant lawbreakers, needing law to order and nurture human relationship.[4] They participate simultaneously within the grace of the law and the grace of the promise of life in Jesus Christ. Or as Luther also claimed, there are so few true Christians who live purely out of grace among so many sinners (even those who profess to be Christian) that the law is vitally necessary to restrain evil and demand good. Even these few true Christians who have no need of the law must obey the law for the sake of others who do need it, just as sinners are justified by grace through faith, not just for their own sake but for the sinner's "neighbors"—that is, for all creatures.[5]

## PRINCIPLES FOR UNDERSTANDING THE POLITICAL USE OF LAW

Because Lutheran understandings about law are complex and deliberately open-ended, they offer guidance about the making, interpretation, and administration of law mostly by preclusion: they can rule out some claims altogether and act as a corrective to any jurisprudence demanding to be embraced as ultimate, flawless, or final justice. Yet although Lutheran doctrine does not definitively point to a particular school of legal thought as most theologically correct, it yields some important principles for understanding the political use of law.

3. *See, e.g., supra* this volume, David Smolin, A House Divided? Anabaptist and Lutheran Perspectives on the Sword.
4. Martin Luther, On the Freedom of the Christian, *in Martin Luther's Basic Theological Writings, supra* note 2, at 601, 606, 610, 613–14 (hereinafter The Freedom of the Christian).
5. *See* Martin Luther, On Temporal Authority, *in Martin Luther's Basic Theological Writings, supra* note 2, at 663, 665, 668–69 (hereinafter On Temporal Authority).

### Formation and Justification of Law

In its civil use, law is the demand of God for preservation and re-creation of the world, expressed through such orders of creation as the family and the state. In the Lutheran view, aligned in a distinctive way with the natural-law tradition, law is largely the product of human reason, which is itself a gift of God to all human beings.[6] Lutherans reject both the concept that human law is divinely spoken word for word, a narrative continuous with the Giving of the Law at Sinai; and a Deist view that because God's creative activity is over, law is fully the work of created beings capable of managing their own affairs. Mainstream Lutheran theology rejects the notion that the world's evil makes it untransformable or obliges Christians to separate themselves to follow the way of Jesus as some Christian traditions believe.[7] For Lutherans, through the continuing creative activity of human beings, every moment of which God makes possible and makes new, law comes forth, and Christians participate on virtually the same footing as others in that activity. Lutherans affirm the natural-law view that human beings are endowed with the inherent ability to determine right from wrong by reasoning from their own experience and surroundings, and thereby to make law that will both nurture human life and punish and deter wrong.[8] Yet they would argue that human will and demonic forces often obscure the right.[9]

### Central Focus of Law

In the Lutheran view, law, like any other human enterprise, must be theocentric, but it is neither salvific nor theocratic. That is, in its civil use, law does not

6. B. A. Gerrish, *Grace and Reason: A Study of the Theology of Luther* 22, 25–26 (Oxford 1962) (quoting Luther's Sermon on the Seventh Sunday after Trinity, on Romans 6:19–23). Luther likened reason to a tool that, properly used, makes things clear, but in itself "do[es] not guarantee sound results." *Id.* at 22. Although Luther repudiated a nominalist doctrine of justification, he remained a nominalist on creation and law, believing that God was daily creating the world and changing its orders in relation to His purpose, by stark contrast to realist natural lawyers like Thomas Aquinas.

7. *See* H. Richard Niebuhr, *The Kingdom of God in America* 41–42, 70–73 (Wesleyan University Press, 1988).

8. Gerrish, *supra* note 6, at 22, 74 n.5; Heinrich Bornkamm, *Luther in Mid-Career, 1521–1530* 115 (E. Theodore Bachmann trans., Fortress 1983).

9. In fact, Luther argued that original sin was so deep a corruption of nature that reason cannot understand it. Martin Luther, The Smalcald Articles, in *Martin Luther's Basic Theological Writings, supra* note 2, at 516 (hereinafter *The Smalcald Articles*); George Forell, *Faith Active in Love: An Investigation of the Principles Underlying Luther's Social Ethics* 143 (Augsburg, 1954).

establish a relationship between human beings and God that can result in their perfection or salvation; there is no set of laws that, if kept, would result in humans' repair of the breach they have caused with God. Nor can humans form a set of laws that fully captures God's will for humankind, or look to God's Word for an immediate "yes" or "no" to resolve a particular justice conflict. Because God can make good things from God's creation, even creation corrupted by evil or unbelief, Lutherans have always claimed that justice can come from those who do not accept God as the center of their understanding. Still, God's will for the good of creation is an ever-present reality even in lawmaking and application; law that pretends otherwise is a distortion of the truth.

**Purpose of Law**

The law's purpose is to serve the neighbor in a way that reflects our situatedness in particular contexts. The debate about what serves the neighbor, though, is clearly open-ended, meant for the application of human reason. Lutherans accept that the law can and must be both wrathful and nurturing. As David Smolin observes in his essay in this volume, the Lutheran tradition is not "pacifist": law must be used to restrain, deter, and punish, by physical force if necessary, those who evilly destroy the neighbor. Yet law also has a constructive role in nurturing that same neighbor, by empowering and limiting human institutions so that they serve human need. In particular, law helps to preserve the world by recognizing, defining, and critiquing historical social relations critically at the core of human community, identified by Luther in the sixteenth century as the church, the household (oeconomia), and the state. The Lutheran tradition, however, has always recognized that, as God's co-creative work, new orders will come into existence as human need demands, and even the traditional orders must be adapted to human need as it changes over time.

**Legal Interpretation and Jurisdiction**

Following a central Lutheran insight, legal interpretation must account for the complex reality that human reason is both good and flawed, and that human imperfection and evil will always distort reason as law is formed, interpreted, and applied. This fundamental reality suggests a division of legal power that insists that civil authority must seek to correct other agencies of human community while it is continually self-critical, watching for signs that its own delusions masquerade as public good.

## THE WORK OF OUR HANDS: FORMATION
## OF LAW

In American academic circles, the justification of law by process has been a re-curring theme. Any number of legal theorists have suggested that majoritarian process is an essential condition of making law morally valid because it is wrong for people to be governed by those laws to which they cannot consent. Yet "pure" majoritarians are difficult to find, though many qualified majoritar-ians would prefer pure democracy if it could be practiced under ideal condi-tions.

Recognizing law as a gift that is yet accursed, Lutherans stand almost outside of these efforts to describe an ideal majoritarianism because they recognize both the important insights and the equally significant flaws in this discussion. First, Lutherans must applaud the instinct of majoritarianism, which is to rec-ognize the conscience of the individual person, one critical location of God's creative activity along with communities and institutions. Lutherans accept that human beings have been endowed with tremendous powers to reason about their own situation in the world, to find a way to nurture, preserve, and extend all of creation. Humans' ability to imagine themselves metaphorically in those worlds that they cannot physically observe (from an atom's composi-tion to the reaches of space) and to make the world into usable processes and objects seems almost limitless in many areas; and this vast power, harnessed to tackle the problems of human social relations, must inspire and deserve awe. Thus each person's conscientious ethical and practical reasoning, as trained upon a problem of justice in our society, deserves the respect of any political or-der. For Lutheran theorists, the majority's views, which represent a multiplicity of such judgments, and the conscientious claim of the dissenting individual are both entitled to the respect due the activity of a creature of God, a view that recognizes the inherent goodness of creation's diversity.

Yet the magnificent power of human reason is put to the test by the awesome strength of human evil and demonic power in the world, powers that lie both within and without the heart and soul of every human person. There is no pure reason; it is always corrupted by the human will. Or as Luther would put it, "Satan has blinded reason to the natural law and has covered this law with a veil."[10] In more psychological terms, self-interest, self-justification, and self-

10. Paul Althaus, *The Ethics of Martin Luther* 27 (Robert C. Schultz trans., Fortress 1972) (paraphrasing *D. Martin Luthers Werke: Briefwechsel* (Weimar, 1930–48)).

delusion are at every moment present in the formation and application of the law. Citizens must thus simultaneously rejoice in those aspects of democratic governance that encourage the development of community through human reason and still reject the claim that any democratic decisionmaking process makes law morally right per se, or that process criteria dispositively decide the law's moral validity. With Tocqueville and others, Lutherans recognize that majorities no less than individuals can make law blind to the needs of the other, and that they can use the power of reason to make evil law seem morally right or even morally responsive to a set of "facts" about human need that exist only in the mind of the majority. Thus democratic majorities can as easily as dictatorships imagine that children do not starve in their society, or argue that they should starve for many perfectly plausible reasons, not the least of which is that the majority has decided they should.

From a Lutheran perspective, however, modern proposals to recognize the "tyranny of the majority," which may relocate political power to oppressed groups or even reconfer it on individuals and private institutions, are not necessarily better solutions. No one can avoid the sins of the will: it is as likely (perhaps more likely) that one individual claiming in conscience to be exempt from positive law is driven by the sins of self-interest and self-delusion as it is that the majority's decision is so flawed; it is as likely that an oppressed minority will use power corruptly as will a self-satisfied majority.

Luther himself generally expressed a preference, among two evils, for some amount of organized tyranny in the person of the ruler (or majority) over the chaotic tyranny of individual choice. Although we cannot know how much of that preference is context driven, coming out of the political chaos of the later Reformation period, Luther often demanded that Christians accept the created order of government until its activities were no longer tolerable, though he did not hold a consistent position on rebellion throughout his life. His conclusions driven by practical realities he observed, Luther once suggested that Christians should not revolt against a clearly evil ruler unless the ruler was so insane that he could not listen to reason, for while there was the chance to change the ruler's mind toward good, a short-term tyranny was preferable to destruction of society through political chaos.[11] On another occasion, Luther chided rebel leaders about the widespread human suffering caused by the rebellions of his time, suggesting that revolt more often brings evil in the form of human pain

11. George Forell, Luther's Theology and Domestic Politics, in *Martin Luther: Theologian of the Church* 113–14 (Word and World, 1994).

and death than does living under the yoke of a tyrant.[12] Luther regarded with suspicion rebels' claims that revolt was necessary to secure human liberty, because he believed that freedom as humans understood it was largely illusory. Perhaps because he saw that the sins of rebellions are too often visited upon the innocent rather than the guilty, Luther strongly urged his followers not to destroy the foundations of authority; and yet he almost gleefully lobbed grenades against its walls and roof.

Following Luther, most Lutherans have expressed fairly conservative views on the right to overturn authority through rebellion, while many have fiercely challenged particular laws and decisions of the authority. Thus even though Christians should stand against the authority of a particular government (itself part of God's design) only when that authority has jeopardized the preaching of the Gospel *(in statu confessionis),* they are in every time and place obliged to demand justice for the neighbor, no matter how pure or democratic the "process" of lawmaking has been. Although Lutheran doctrines of the two kingdoms and the orders have been distorted in some times and places to justify quietism (as in some American Lutheran settings) or even cooperation with evil regimes (as in Nazi Germany), the central tradition is equally adamant that citizenship is a mandatory human vocation, whether citizens exercise the authority as the democratic equivalent of "princes" or live under nondemocratic authority. Far from authorizing passivity in the face of authority, Lutheran doctrine demands active participation in law; every adult must view his or her citizenship as a calling, just as he or she would view a role as a parent, or a worker, or a church member. As to government service, Luther taught, "you should esteem the sword of governmental authority as highly as the estate of marriage, or husbandry, or any other calling that God has instituted. Just as one can serve God in the estate of marriage, or in farming or a trade, for the benefit of others— and must so serve if his neighbor needs it—so one can serve God in government, and should serve if the need of his neighbor demands it."[13]

Thus Christian participation in the formation and reformation of law must be respectful of authority; supportive of those who try valiantly to carry out the law; and equally, incessantly and frankly critical of any moment when the law is designed, interpreted, or enforced unjustly. A Christian, then, can be respectful of the office of policing necessary for community protection, cog-

12. Luther noted that God would punish the tyrannical ruler, and if God chose not to do so, it might be because of sins that we are not prepared to admit. *Id.* at 114–15.

13. On Temporal Authority, *supra* note 5, at 674.

nizant of the difficult task each officer faces, while protesting every instance in which the police selectively enforce the law, brutalize vulnerable citizens—even those who are not innocent—or overlook evil that should be addressed.

## THEOCENTRICITY AND THE PURSUIT OF POLITICS WITHOUT IDOLS

Lutheran theology originated in a historical context in which God's creative activity and sovereignty were unquestioned, at least in political arguments. Contemporary Lutherans face serious conceptual challenges in a pluralistic culture that has no such consensus, rejecting *any* theology as a possible basis for political justification. American Lutherans have recognized—indeed would have to recognize—our particular form of government with its modern gloss on church and state as a form of blessing, and must applaud its role in eradicating civil violence wrongfully justified by religious belief. Yet it would be impossible for Lutherans to accede to the "common sense" that God is no longer continuously involved in the creation and re-creation of human society (though finding a metaphor to describe that involvement, both direct and through human action and institutions, is difficult). For God's creating and sustaining activity is not restricted to some human realms, not lost in the past or waiting in the future. It is embedded in each judge's decision, each legislator's vote, and each administrator's enforcement of the law.

Other Christian and non-Christian alternatives proposing to resolve this dilemma obscure or deny one critical aspect of God's creative activity. The separatist move, requiring Christians to withdraw as much as possible from the affairs of the world so that God's work can be more fully expressed in a "purer" community of belief and action, leaves behind a part of the created world to which Christians are called to minister. The secularist move, to confine religious worldviews and expressions to a private or at least nonpolitical sphere, similarly denies the sovereignty of God over all creation. The theocratic move, demanding that law recognize and swear allegiance to a theocentric understanding of social life through coercion, not only risks the God-given conscience of the religiously other. It also pretends to an idolatry backed by force: for humans to be God by demanding allegiance of mind and heart to a particular interpretation of God's will, as they are likely to do according to Lutheran doctrine, is almost worse than to allow the forces of the Devil to have free rein over part of the given world.

So the Lutheran conundrum. For a Lutheran to stand mute about God's creative activity in "secular" discussions about law and government is not ethically (theologically?) possible any more than it should be possible for a Lutheran to bracket his understanding about God's action in the world when he thinks through problems of justice and care with other Christians. Yet to demand that law precisely reflect their particular theological beliefs is equally problematical for Lutherans because of the ethical demand to care for the neighbor, a demand that includes respect for his difference and his different conscience. At the very least, however, Lutherans can stand in prophetic critique of the pretensions of anthropocentric lawmaking, even if they cannot find a simple substitute; the Lutheran claim that law is made for the ordering of human society is critically different from the claim that human beings are the center of the universe. As merely the most obvious illustration, Lutherans must be deeply and vocally disturbed by environmental law that considers uses of the earth solely according to human desires, needs, and material aspirations, while equally rejecting fanciful projects that "preserve" nature with a pristine aestheticism that diminishes those human beings whose suffering (famine, disease, impoverishment) can be alleviated through careful management of resources.

Lutheran recognition of the pretension that human knowledge or values constructed from the past, a present consensus or an anticipated ideal future, are the primary, infallible material from which law is created opens a space for political dialogue with others of differing beliefs. Lutherans believe that Christians can make distinctive theological arguments for the justice of particular legal measures or structures while joining theologically differing citizens to reach consensus or even compromise on practical outcomes. They do so recognizing that Christian confession is no predicate or indispensable condition to judicial or legislative virtue: those who are "secular" or other-religious, and even evil rulers, can be instruments of justice in the world. Thus Christians can fight over the message without rejecting the messenger; they can recognize the competence and virtue of an other-believing judge or legislator or executive—and even the rightfulness of that lawmaker's decisions—while disagreeing with her justifications for law.

Third, Lutherans can deny the power of "isms" that create legal structures around them, particularly those that pretend to perfectionism. Even if they accept the insights on the human condition that have given rise to some of these "isms," Lutherans must unalterably oppose any juridical strategy that promises the salvation or ultimate perfection of individual human beings or human community. Thus although Lutherans can, for instance, accept the Marxist recognition that modern society has alienated human beings from their own work, they cannot accept the ultimate conclusion that humans can, by themselves, achieve reunification of the spiritual and material by a political programme, whether it is the dictatorship of the proletariat or unfettered capitalism.

## THE NEIGHBOR'S GOOD IN THE WORK OF THE LAW

Simply put, the central focus of the civil law is to serve the neighbor. Lutherans view the responsibility to love one's neighbor as *the* critical insight of the natural law, not as a "Christian duty." It is a seeming paradox of Lutheran theology that Christians do make a loving response to the neighbor because they are saved by grace, while at the same time they with others are bound by the natural law to respond in love. Thus for Lutherans the "law of love" is neither distinctly Christian nor a form of obligation imposed on one by virtue of one's salvation. As an insight of natural law, loving service is a demand upon all persons who can exercise reason and a call to which all humans are accountable, irrespective of their religious beliefs or salvation, irrespective of whether they are virtuous or thoroughly evil, rulers or ruled.

Thus civil law is not only permitted but required to reflect God's demand that the neighbor be served. That this prescription is exceedingly general does not suggest its complexity. First, Lutheranism accepts the paradox that law is situated as well as universal: to do justice, law must always reflect the circumstances of those who demand justice and the historical, cultural, and political setting in which justice is dispensed. Second, Lutheranism imagines "doing justice" as a complex relation driven by virtues, not rules. Third, the notions of both "service" and "neighbor" are broadly defined to embrace a strong ethic of responsibility to the whole world.

Although Lutherans understand justice to be contextual, the situatedness of law does not imply the partiality of justice, nor justify the use of power to escape justice or to exclude any groups from its protection. Luther described a radical egalitarianism in the application of the law, although its application to Christians is complicated. Thus Luther could say, "All who are not Christians belong to the kingdom of the world and are under the law," while demanding that even those few who are Christians in faith and deed obey the law. They must obey, not only as a loving example to the ungodly but also because "no one is by nature Christian or righteous; but altogether sinful and wicked, [so] God through the law puts them all under restraint so they dare not wilfully implement their wickedness in actual deeds."[14] Moreover, the "neighbor" to whom both government and individuals owe the duty of care is not defined by relationship or history; he or she is identified only by need, for "a man does not live for himself alone in this moral body to work for it alone, but he lives also for all men on earth; rather, he lives only for others and not for himself."[15] Thus Luther could counterintuitively call for exercise of the sword on behalf of others even while one should not be prepared to defend oneself.

In addition, Luther rejected relativism on justice: he accepted that the natural law is the foundation for our reasoning about justice. Yet Lutherans have not imagined natural law as a set of fixed, universal principles, objectively separate from the world to which they apply and static from age to age. Rather, they have understood natural law as a dynamic, ever-changing source of knowledge about God's demand of, and concern for, human well-being, a source for correction of human short sightedness and self-interest, but reliant on human reason to apply natural law to particular controversies in particular periods.

Second, justice is the fruit of legislative and judicial virtue, not arid application of abstract principles to the facts; it is the result of the natural call to love the neighbor, expressed as "I should do as I would be done by." As Luther claimed, "For when you judge according to love you will easily decide and adjust matters without any lawbooks. But when you ignore love and the natural law you will never hit upon the solution that pleases God, though you have devoured all the lawbooks and jurists. Instead, the more you depend on them, the further they will lead you astray."[16]

Third, though the concept of service to the neighbor may seem "soft," in fact, Lutherans have explicitly articulated how the law preserves, including Luther's well-known, seemingly pessimistic emphasis on its restraint of the wicked. Luther's writings particularly stress the use of law in incapacitating and generally deterring wrongdoers: "The unrighteous do nothing that the law demands; therefore, they need the law to instruct, constrain and compel them to do good. . . . [If the law did not restrain them], men would devour one an-

---

14. *Id.* at 664.

15. The Freedom of a Christian, supra note 4, at 616.

16. *Id.* Luther's description of the lawmaker's tasks reflects his ambivalence at times on whether Christians are particularly suited to govern: he demands "true confidence [in God] and earnest prayer," love and Christian service toward those ruled, "untrammeled reason and unfettered judgment" toward subordinates; and "restrained severity and firmness" toward evildoers. On Temporal Authority, *supra* note 5, at 700, 702.

other, seeing that the whole world is evil. . . . No one could support wife and child, feed himself and serve God. The world would be reduced to chaos. . . . [God] has subjected [those who are not true believers] to the word so that, even though they would like to, they are unable to practice their wickedness, and if they do practice it they cannot do so without fear or with success and impunity."[17] Luther's primary focus here is the protection of citizens who fall prey to the wrongdoer's harm, though retribution plays a minor chord in Luther's work: while exhorting Christians to let themselves be "despoiled and slandered" if necessary, he demands that they seek "vengeance, justice, protection and help" on behalf of others.

Positive law also serves to correct human behavior and to teach those who have not been transformed by grace what is expected of them under the natural law. Luther was fairly realistic about the fact that citizens have different intellectual, moral, and spiritual capabilities for discerning what natural law requires, and viewed positive law as one way of teaching those who could not think deeply about questions of natural justice, or whose other duties did not permit sustained reflection on these issues.

One function of the civil law that has been most overlooked in some American Lutheran communities is its role in nurturing individuals and the community. Luther believed that government had an affirmative responsibility to care for public needs, anticipating that governments might provide not only police protection and criminal justice but also fire protection, medical care, and public education.[18] In some cases, such as education, Luther saw these responsibilities as a public function because the family was unable or unwilling to do its duty: parents were not always competent to educate, and many lacked time to spare from meeting the basic material needs of the family.[19] In other areas, such as medical care, he considered it efficient for cities and states to care for those who needed it, noting that governmental hospitals and nursing homes

17. *Id.* at 665, 664.

18. Martin Luther, Whether One May Flee from a Deadly Plague, and Martin Luther, To the Councilmen of All Cities in Germany That They Establish and Maintain Christian Schools, *in Martin Luther's Basic Theological Writings, supra* note 2, at 711–12, 738, 743 (hereinafter referred to as Plague and To the Councilmen, respectively).

19. Luther noted that even if some parents "lack the goodness and decency to educate their children," they should not be neglected merely because their parents were ne'er-do-wells. In fact, Luther pointed out that such uneducated children, the product of cruel homes, would "poison and pollute other children until at last the whole city is ruined." To the Councilmen, *supra* note 18, 711–12.

would be "a fine, commendable, and Christian arrangement to which everyone should offer generous help and contributions, particularly the government."[20]

It is important to reemphasize, however, that Lutherans have traditionally distinguished the civil use of the law from spiritual uses of the law. Most important, these distinctions have emphasized that obedience to the law cannot repair the breach between human beings and God and, in terms of one's salvation, is virtually beside the point, because even the perfect keeping of the law, were it possible, is not a sufficient work in God's sight.

Within a discussion of the civil use of the law, moreover, this clear distinction between God's spiritual realm and God's earthly realm would make Lutherans skeptical of political movements, legal structures, or programs that purport to provide a complete answer to the ills of society, or even to the needs of a particular individual. To suggest, for instance, that a criminal-corrections program or a set of welfare regulations will "reform" an individual in both heart and mind is to deny the spiritual aspects of human existence and to brashly pretend to a competence that is God's alone. Luther did respect the power of law to encourage positive patterns of behavior, if not internal reformation, both by teaching what is expected and by threatening sanctions if those expectations were not met. Moreover, he believed that children could be taught what moral activity was expected of them and, to a limited extent, schooled in moral virtues. Yet Luther was skeptical about the role of education in changing the heart and will of sinful human beings, who knowing what they should do refuse to accept or do it. And because Luther saw that sinful human beings would create flawed social systems, the agencies of social and economic life could be also expected to reflect self-aggrandizement, dishonesty, and distortion of the common good, even as they could nurture, sustain, and protect human community.

The Lutheran focus on human responsibility as defined by an individual's office, a concept that rejects the former primacy of priestly and religious callings, drives this constructive understanding of the law. Luther uses the term *office* or *station (Stand)* to define the life-place into which all people are put to make their contribution to the need of the neighbor.[21] The focus of moral

20. Plague, *supra* note 18, at 743.

21. There is some inconsistency in the way Lutheran writers use these terms. The noted Lutheran ethicist Paul Althaus suggests that Luther used the terms *station, orders, duties, institutions, offices, functions,* or *hierarchies* somewhat interchangeably, especially after 1522. Paul Althaus, *The Ethics of Martin Luther* 36, 39 (trans. Robert C. Schultz, Fortress, 1972). Others might distinguish between the great orders or governances, such as family, and the

judgment in shaping law must be on the unique and multiple offices one occupies as a worker, parent, spouse, or citizen. These offices must be exercised diligently by the person who occupies them so that certain critical human orders that make it possible for human beings to flourish may be maintained. Thus the office of parent is vital to the flourishing of the age-old order of the household *(oeconomia)* or family; the office of pastor to the order of the church; the office of judge to the functioning of the state. Individuals occupy these orders not primarily by personal choice but rather by being found where they are, though Lutherans would not understand by this that people are "fated" into orders and have no control over their destiny.

The concept of office both constrains and permits freedom, as understood by moderns. The constraints of an office are those responsibilities that the person who holds this office is bound to meet diligently and do well, even if his immediate choice would be to escape them. On the other hand, the orders are shaped by the ongoing co-creative activity of God, so that definition and contours of these orders may change from age to age, because the key principle defining the orders is whether they meet human need as reflected in God's will for God's creation. As a simple example, the fact that the state was aristocratic in medieval times does not settle the question of what form of state best meets human needs in modern times. Similarly, the fact that women and men held certain responsibilities in the family in Luther's time does not forever lock them into "natural" and unchanging roles.

Modern law defines with some complexity those orders and institutions believed to be essential for the flourishing of human community. For instance, corporate forms are largely dictated by the states; marriage is a statutory contract embracing defined responsibilities of spouses toward each other and their children; and vast bodies of rules define even the constraints on government. Because for Lutherans the orders are constantly being created and revised, the state bears a heavy responsibility in trying to think through how these orders should be continuously restructured to preserve human community. Extremely individualistic or static conceptions of orders would be incompatible with both the form and the fluidity characteristic of these orders. On one hand, traditional Lutherans would not accept a state in which all responsibilities were designed by individual contract, so that moral and legal accountability would ap-

---

specific role or office, such as father, that the person occupies within those orders; or between office or station *(Stand),* those places where we are to obey God, and a person's vocation *(Beruf),* to which he knows God has called him.

ply only to those duties that one "chooses," because they do believe that individuals are called into offices by God and the neighbor's need. Moreover, they would be skeptical about whether an individual, given the power to "choose" the terms of his engagement with others, would order his responsibilities fully to serve his neighbor. For instance, it is likely, Lutherans would suggest, that most individuals, if permitted to "choose" their marital responsibilities, would look to their own self-interest before considering the interests of even a beloved spouse.

On the other hand, law must structure these critical human institutions in a sufficiently flexible way that people can meet the varied offices they occupy or vocations to which they are called. Thus marriage law that utilized a monolithic and static concept of gender or parentage to define women's and men's obligations so rigidly that it did not account for conflicting callings of particular individuals would be wrong. For instance, legal regulation of family roles or economics that would make it difficult for a spouse to practice her vocation as a healer, or for a father to support children from his first marriage, would be problematical.

## OFFICE, JURISDICTION, AND INTERPRETATION:
## THE CONSEQUENCES OF RESTRAINT

The concept of office or vocation within these orders of creation also sets boundaries on the extent to which the state should be involved in forming and regulating human institutions, and how it should be structured to do so. The central anthropological paradox, that human beings are a good creation of God and at the same time deeply sinful, self-trusting, and self-regarding creatures, must necessarily be at the heart of good-faith attempts to define the diverse responsibilities of those who occupy various offices within the order of the state. Those who define offices and those who hold them must be other-critical, willing to hold accountable other office holders who exceed their trust and their competence, while self-critically ensuring that they themselves do not venture beyond either their duties or their gifts because of arrogance, greed, or delusions that they alone have properly understood the good.

Thus the Lutheran view of legal authority would not only be concerned about limiting power, as we usually contemplate when we discuss separation of powers or protection of the press as a check on the excesses of other branches of government. It would also demand the development of an affirmative understanding of the competencies and weaknesses of different branches and offices in government, and would expect them to create structures that account for their weaknesses and exercise their competencies. Indeed, Luther even allowed that some offices are simply intrinsically evil: though the office of "soldier" is "a ministry of love and a vocation," the office of "torturer" is still morally wrong.[22]

To take the most debated example in American constitutional jurisprudence—the limits of judicial review—Lutheran conceptions of the orders and the realities of human sin would counsel simultaneously for robust judicial review and careful, reflective judicial restraint. In matters in which reason suggests that the state has exceeded its bounds under natural law, by ignoring the needs of its citizens, by protecting power of those officeholders who are abusing them, or by excluding the vulnerable from the human community, a judge would be duty-bound to use the power of his office to counter the state's action, even if positive law supported it. Similarly, in the Lutheran view, majorities and institutions can be just as corrupt as individuals, so a legal regime that put its entire faith in majoritarian decisions or individual rights, neglecting the sin inherent in both individuals and institutions, would be soon corrupted. Conversely, even a morally insightful Lutheran judge would be careful about substituting his personal judgment for the legislature, whether democratic or not, if the legislature were acting within the appropriate boundaries of its office to restrain and protect, and the process of deliberation reflected lawmakers' careful exercise of their unique competence and consideration of what the need of the neighbor requires.

A Lutheran judge might similarly, for example, express the need for judicial restraint in overturning laws whose effectiveness requires broad democratic input, while rejecting the power of the majority to define without challenge what rights of citizenship and respect are due those groups excluded by our society. Such a judge would have a developed theory of the limits and gifts of executive (as opposed to legislative) decisions, of the federal government as opposed to a state or local government, of government regulation at all compared to social constraints leveled by public institutions other than the state.

Rather than viewing the problem of jurisdiction solely as a problem of balancing power or restoring the hegemony of one branch of government over another, a Lutheran would ask about where the officeholder or the branch of government is situated; and what resources it has at its disposal. A debate about the

22. Gustav Wingren, *Creation and Law* 3–4 (Ross MacKenzie trans., Oliver and Boyd 1958).

respective powers or "rights" of the state and federal governments under the Constitution might be transformed into a debate about what decisions each branch of government is uniquely situated to make and to enforce due to its ability to understand context, its historical contributions to a well-ordered and just society, its resources (including human ones), and its historical tendencies toward oppression of various kinds.

Internal to each branch of government, the problem of creating and interpreting the law would be similarly viewed in the context of conflicting demands that would rule out absolute positions of interpretation. A strict positivism or textualism that rejected the role of human reason and compassion in determining the need of the neighbor in a particular case would be equally as unappealing to Lutherans as a jurisprudence of unreflective personal prejudices or instincts not geared to the search for earthly well-being from within the tradition of natural principles of justice. A Lutheran interpretive scheme would be marked by flexibility, for God can make things new in the world, and yet respect for the text and tradition as the embodied wisdom of others who have fought different evils and made the same—or other—mistakes.

For Lutherans, the ambiguous terrain of the postmodern world is familiar territory. To turn one's face toward God is to escape neither the darkness of the present world nor its possibility. It is not, indeed, to turn one's face at all, but to find the abruptly and momentarily unmasked hiddenness of God in the most daily of difficult tasks, the making of law for the good of the neighbor. In this territory of law, hope acknowledges its own powerlessness, wrath is love, and those who stand placed in God's world burst into a future they have made and unmade with their own hands, crafted and yet crippled. Lutherans stand against every attempt to define the civil law as salvation or soulless, as paramount or irrelevant, for they see the preserving hand of God moving imperceptibly in the human debate about the law for the neighbor's welfare. For Lutherans, law is bound authority, creative restraint, suspicious passion for life. It is not an "either" to the "or" of the gospel, but makes its own home in the works of God.

# Part III Christian Perspectives on Substantive Areas of the Law

In this part, we present six examples of Christian approaches to substantive areas of the law. Each author draws on one or more of the Christian traditions that have been discussed earlier. Clearly, among and within Christian communities there are differing views on many of the issues raised in these essays. The coverage here is not comprehensive, but we hope these essays will illustrate our claim that Christian perspectives can contribute usefully to the analysis of practical legal questions.

# God's Joust, God's Justice: An Illustration from the History of Marriage Law

*John Witte, Jr.*

> History is God's theatre, . . . God's jousting place.
> —*Martin Luther*
>
> All things are ruled and governed by the one God as He pleases,
> but if God's motives are hid, are they therefore unjust?
> —*St. Augustine,* City of God

In the spring of 1995 I visited the great Saxon capital of Dresden. I stood on the banks of the Elbe River at the site of the Frauenkirche—the monumental domed church, consecrated in 1734, graced by one of Johann Sebastian Bach's greatest organ concerts in 1736 and celebrated in German music, art, and literature ever since.

It was a sobering moment. For the great church lay in ruins. A guide explained that the church did not survive the firebombing of Dresden near the end of World War II. On February 13 and 14, 1945, 773 Allied bombers emptied their payloads on Dresden. No bombs hit the church directly. But the fires were enough. First the art, the woodwork, the pulpit, the organ, and the altars were consumed. As the fires penetrated more deeply, scores of people hidden in the church's catacombs were burned to death. Eventually, the intense heat of the fires weakened the church so much that it simply collapsed under its own weight. Large chunks of the dome, charred and cracked, still lay where they had fallen some fifty years before. A large piece of the steeple still protruded from the ground at a grim angle. Only one wall of the nave still stood, its top jagged and pocked where the roof had torn away.

It was also an exhilarating moment. For stretching out from the wall of the nave in all directions were dozens of rows of scaffolds, where workers were storing the ten thousand odd pieces of stone that had been collected from the rubble of the fallen church. The Frauenkirche, the guide informed me, would be reconstructed, using as many of the original stones as possible. A giant blueprint assigned each of the recovered stones to its original place in the structure. New stones were being collected from the same quarry that had been mined for the original construction. A massive outpouring of charity had made this reconstruction possible.

I have often given thanks for that brief moment on the banks of the Elbe River. For this small frame captured several themes that are at the center of my life—as a Christian believer and as a legal historian.

The story of the Dresden church is a metaphor of life. Construction, destruction, and reconstruction. Work, judgment, and purgation. Birth, death, and resurrection. Creation, fall, and redemption. These are the stages of life. These are the passages of faith. The old must pass away so that the new may come forth. We must die so that we can be reborn. Our bodies must be buried so that they can be resurrected. Our works must be burned so that they can be purified. Our bonds must be broken so that we can be reconciled. This is the nature of biblical religion.[1] It gives life its power. It gives pain its purpose. It gives time its pattern.

These basic biblical themes—that time has a pattern, that history has a purpose, that life has an end of reconciliation—inform my understanding of history. The Bible teaches that time is linear, not cyclical. Biblical history moves forward from a sin-trampled garden to a golden city, from a fallen world to a perfect end-time. Our lives move, circuitously but inevitably, toward a reconciliation with God, neighbor, and self—if not in this life, then in the life to come; if not with the true God, then with a false god; if not in the company of heaven, then in the crowds of hell.

1. Matthew 24–25; John 11:25–26; Romans 6:5–11, 8:18–38; 1 Corinthians 3:10–15; 1 Corinthians 15:12–57; 2 Corinthians 5:1–5, 16–19.

## CONFESSION AND PROFESSION

Human history cannot be fully understood without reference to this divine mystery. God is beyond time yet has chosen to reveal a part of Himself within it. Through the creation and incarnation, God pours out a measure of His being and grace. Through the law and Gospel, God sets forth a measure of His word and will. Through miracles and messengers, God puts forth a measure of divine power and judgment. All of history, in Martin Luther's words, is "a demonstration, recollection, and sign of divine action and judgment, how God upholds, rules, obstructs, rewards, punishes, and honors the world, especially the human world."[2] We are within time, yet we are able in part to transcend it. Through our conscience and imagination, we gradually discover something of the meaning of God's plan for each creature. Through our creativity and experimentation, we slowly uncover something of the majesty of God's plan for the creation. Through our liturgies and epiphanies, we slowly uncover something of the mystery of God's incarnation for the church. Through our texts and traditions, we gradually accumulate something of the wisdom of God's revelation for all people.[3]

To be sure, God's plan and our history are not identical. God's plan consists of much more than what God chooses to reveal to us or what we are able to discern of it. Much of what we see appears to be the work of a concealed God, even at times a seemingly capricious God. In Luther's colorful image, history is "God's mummery and mystery," "God's joust and tourney." History is "God's theatre," in which the play cannot be fully understood until it ends and until we exit.[4] To equate one act or actor, one speech or text, with the divine play itself is to cast a partial and premature judgment. To insist on one interpretation of the play before it ends is to presume the power of eternal discernment. To judge the play on the basis of a few episodes is to insult the genius of the divine playwright.

Human history, in turn, consists of much more than our conscientious struggle to follow God's word and will in our lives, to reflect God's image and immanence in our world. Much of what we see in our personal lives is the "war between our members," the struggle between the carnal and the spiritual, the sinner and the saint.[5] Much of what we see in our collective lives comprises the

2. 50 *D. Martini Luthers Werke: Kritische Gesamtausgage* (repr. ed. 1964–68) 383–84.

3. For further discussion, *see* E. Harris Harbison, *Christianity and History* (1964).

4. *See* 15 *Luthers, supra* note 2, at 32 ff., 50, 383 ff.

5. Romans 8:1–17; James 4:1.

sinful and savage excesses of corrupt creatures, the diverse and perverse choices of free human agents. But there is simply too much order in our world, too much constancy in our habits, too much justice in our norms for us to think that the course of human events is not somehow channeled by God's providential plan.

God is thus both revealed and concealed in history. "All events," as John Calvin put it, "are governed by God's secret plan."[6] If God were completely revealed in history, there would be no reason for faith. History would simply be a mechanical execution of a predetermined plan. There would be no eternal mystery for which faith could yearn. But if God were completely concealed in history, there would also be no reason for faith. History would simply be a random and rudderless exercise of chaos. There would be no eternal justice in which faith could trust. "Somewhere between those two the Christian has to find his [or her] own balance between concealment and revelation."[7]

This is the balance I try to find in my work as a Christian legal historian. For me history is more than a series of tricks that we play on the dead, or that the dead play on us. History is more than simply an accidental chronology of first one thing happening, and then another. For me history is also a source of revelation, a collection of wisdom. The archive is a treasure trove. Old books are windows on truth. The challenge of the Christian historian is to search within the wisdom of the ages for some indication of the eternal wisdom of God. It is to try to seek God's revelation and judgment over time without presuming the power of divine judgment. It is to try to discern God's justice within God's joust.

## LAW AND RELIGION IN THE HISTORY
## OF MARRIAGE

These basic convictions about history inform my work on the interaction of law and religion in Western history, and they have been informed by the same. I start with the assumption that God is both hidden and revealed in human laws and that human laws in turn both reflect and deflect divine values. I believe that the patterns of human laws over time will reflect something of the meaning of religious truth and that the patterns of religious truth over time in

6. *See* John Calvin, *Institutes of the Christian Religion* (1559), bk. 1, chap. 16.2 (F. L. Battles, trans., J. R. McNeill ed., 1954).

7. Harbison, *supra* note 3, at 102.

turn will reflect something of the measure of divine laws. Law will reveal a religious dimension. Religion will reveal a legal dimension.

Western history bears out these assumptions. In the Western tradition, systems of law and systems of religion have coexisted from the beginning. The contents of these legal and religious systems, of course, have differed dramatically over time and across cultures. At points they have converged or contradicted each other. Every religious tradition in the West has known both theonomism and antinomianism—the excessive legalization and the excessive spiritualization of religion. Every legal tradition has known both theocracy and totalitarianism—the excessive sacralization and the excessive secularization of law. But the dominant reality in the West is that law and religion stand not in monistic unity or in dualistic antinomy but in dialectical harmony. Each political community struggles to balance law and religion by counterpoising justice and mercy, rule and equity, discipline and love. Each religious tradition strives to come to terms with law by striking a balance between the rational and the mystical, the prophetic and the priestly, the structural and the spiritual. Each legal tradition struggles to link its formal structures and processes with the beliefs and ideals of its people.[8]

This dialectical interaction has allowed the spheres and sciences of law and religion to combine and to cross-fertilize each other in a variety of ways. For example, law and religion interact conceptually. They embrace overlapping concepts of sin and crime, covenant and contract, righteousness and justice. Law and religion interact formally. Both have interlocking patterns of liturgy and ritual, common habits of tradition and precedent, shared sources of authority and power. Law and religion interact methodologically. They maintain analogous hermeneutical methods of interpreting texts, casuistic and rhetorical methods of argument and instruction, systematic methods of organizing their doctrines. Law and religion relate professionally. Both have officials charged with the formulation, implementation, and demonstration of the norms and habits of their respective fields. Law and religion interact institutionally, through the multiple relations between political and ecclesiastical officials and institutions.[9]

The "binocular of law and religion" allows us to gain a closer and better view of many familiar ideas and institutions that have been studied principally

8. *See* Harold J. Berman, *The Interaction of Law and Religion* 133–42 (1974); *see also* Harold J. Berman, *Faith and Order: The Reconciliation of Law and Religion* x–xii (1993).

9. *See* sources and fuller discussion in John Witte, Jr., *Law, Religion, and Human Rights,* 28 Colum. Hum. Rts. L. Rev. 1, 3–8 (1996).

through the monocular of law or the monocular of religion.[10] As an illustration, permit me to focus on the interaction of marriage law and theological norms in the history of the West. We are the heirs of two traditions of marriage and family life—one rooted in Catholic and Protestant Christian theology, a second rooted in Enlightenment secular theology. Each of these traditions has contributed a variety of familiar ideas and institutions to our marriage law—some overlapping, some conflicting. It is in the overlapping and creatively juxtaposed legal contributions of the Christian and Enlightenment traditions that we see both enduring religious values for marriage and enterprising legal pathways of reform.

## The Western Tradition

The Western tradition has, from its beginnings, offered four perspectives on marriage and the family. A spiritual perspective regards marriage as a religious or sacramental association, subject to the creed, code, cult, and canons of the religious community. A social perspective treats the family as a social estate, subject to special state laws of contract, property, and inheritance and to the expectations and exactions of the local community. A contractual perspective describes the family as a voluntary association, subject to the wills and preferences of the couple, their children, their dependents, their household. Hovering in the background, and often adduced in support of these three perspectives, is a naturalist perspective that treats the family as a created or natural institution, subject to natural laws. In Voltaire's quip: "Among Christians, the family is either a little church, a little state, or a little club" blessed by God and nature.

These four perspectives are in one sense complementary, for each emphasizes one aspect of this institution—its religious sanction, its social legitimation, its voluntary formation, or its natural origin. These four perspectives have also come to stand in considerable tension, however, for they are linked to competing claims of ultimate authority over the form and function of marriage—claims by the church, by the state, by family members, and by God and nature. Some of the deepest fault lines in the historical formation and the current transformations of Western marriage ultimately break out from this central tension of perspective. Which perspective of marriage dominates a culture, or at least prevails in an instance of dispute—the spiritual, the social, the contractual, or the natural? Which authority wields preeminent, or at least

10. The quoted phrase is from Jaroslav Pelikan, Foreword, *The Weightier Matters of the Law: Essays on Law and Religion* xii (John Witte, Jr. and Frank S. Alexander, eds., 1988).

peremptory, power over marriage questions—the church, the state, the couple, or God and nature operating through one of these parties?

Catholics, Protestants, and Enlightenment exponents alike have constructed elaborate models to address these cardinal questions. Each group recognizes multiple perspectives on marriage but gives priority to one. Catholics emphasize the spiritual (or sacramental) perspective of marriage. Protestants emphasize the social (or public) perspective. Enlightenment exponents emphasize the contractual (or private) perspective. In broad outline, the Catholic model dominated Western marriage law until the sixteenth century. From the mid-sixteenth to the mid-nineteenth century, Catholic and Protestant models, in distinct and hybrid forms, dominated Western family law. In the past century, the Enlightenment model has emerged, in many instances eclipsing the theology and law of the Catholic and Protestant traditions of marriage and the family.[11] A brief snapshot of each of these traditions follows.

### The Catholic Inheritance

The Roman Catholic Church first systematized its theology and law of marriage in the course of the Papal Revolution of the twelfth and thirteenth centuries.[12] In that era the church came to treat marriage and the family systematically in a threefold manner—at once as a natural, contractual, and sacramental unit. First, the church taught, marriage is a natural association, created by God to enable man and woman to "be fruitful and multiply" and to raise children in the service and love of God. Since the fall into sin, marriage has also become a remedy for lust, a channel through which to direct one's natural passion to the service of the community and the church. Second, marriage is a contractual unit, formed by the mutual consent of the parties. This contract prescribes for couples a lifelong relation of love, service, and devotion to each other and proscribes unwarranted breach or relaxation of their connubial and parental duties. Third, marriage, when properly contracted between Christians, rises to the dignity of a sacrament. The temporal union of body, soul, and mind within the marital estate symbolizes the eternal union between Christ and His church. Participation in this sacrament confers sanctifying grace upon the couple and the community. Couples can perform this sacrament privately, provided they are capable of marriage and comply with rules for marriage formation.

11. *See* sources and discussion from John Witte, Jr., *From Sacrament to Contract: Marriage, Religion, and Law in the Western Tradition* 1–15 (1997).

12. For further development of the argument in this subsection, *see id.* 16–41, 221–26.

This sacramental theology placed marriage squarely within the social hierarchy of the church. The church claimed jurisdiction over marriage formation,
maintenance, and dissolution. It exercised this jurisdiction through both the pen-
itential rules of the internal forum and the canon law rules of the external forum.

The church did not regard marriage and the family as its most exalted estate,
however. Though a sacrament and a sound way of Christian living, marriage
was not considered to be so spiritually edifying. Marriage was more a remedy
for sin than a recipe for righteousness. Marriage was considered subordinate to
celibacy, propagation less virtuous than contemplation, marital love less whole-
some than spiritual love. Clerics, monastics, and other servants of the church
were to forgo marriage as a condition for ecclesiastical service. Those who could
not were not worthy of the church's holy orders and offices.

The medieval Catholic Church built upon this conceptual foundation a
comprehensive canon law of sexuality, marriage, and family life that was enforced by church courts throughout Christendom. Until the sixteenth century,
the church's canon law of marriage was the law of the West. A civil law or common law of marriage, when and where it existed, was usually supplemental and
subordinate to this canon law.

Consistent with the naturalist perspective on marriage, the canon law punished contraception, abortion, infanticide, and child abuse as violations of the
marital functions of propagation and child rearing. It proscribed unnatural relations, such as incest and polygamy, and unnatural acts, such as bestiality and
buggery. Consistent with the contractual perspective, the canon law ensured
voluntary unions by dissolving marriages formed through mistake, duress,
fraud, or coercion. It granted husband and wife equal rights to enforce conju-
gal debts that had been voluntarily assumed, and it emphasized the importance
of mutual love among the couple and their children. Consistent with the sacramental perspective, the Church protected the sanctity and sanctifying purpose
of marriage by declaring valid marital bonds to be indissoluble, and by dissolving invalid unions between Christians and non-Christians or between parties
related by various legal, spiritual, blood, or familial ties. It supported celibacy
by dissolving unconsummated vows to marriage if one party made a vow to
chastity and by punishing clerics or monastics who contracted marriage.

The medieval canon law of marriage was a watershed in the history of Western law. On the one hand, it distilled the most enduring teachings of the Bible
and the Church Fathers and the most salient rules of earlier Hebrew, Greek,
and Roman laws. On the other hand, it set out many of the basic concepts and

rules of marriage and family life that have persisted to this day, in Catholic, Protestant, and secular polities alike.

## The Protestant Inheritance

The Protestant reformers of the sixteenth and seventeenth centuries supplanted the Catholic sacramental model of marriage with a social model.[13] Like Catholics, Protestants retained the naturalist perspective of the family as an association created for procreation and mutual protection. They largely retained the contractual perspective of marriage as a voluntary association formed by the mutual consent of the couple. Unlike Catholics, however, Protestants rejected the subordination of marriage to celibacy and the celebration of marriage as a sacrament. According to common Protestant lore, each person was too tempted by sinful passion to forgo God's remedy of marriage. The celibate life had no superior virtue and was no prerequisite for ecclesiastical service. It led too easily to concubinage and homosexuality and impeded too often the access and activities of the clerical office. Moreover, marriage was not a sacrament. It was instead an independent social institution ordained by God, and equal in dignity and social responsibility with the church, state, and other social units. Participation in marriage required no prerequisite faith or purity and conferred no sanctifying grace, as did true sacraments.

Calvinist Protestants emphasized that marriage was not a sacramental institution of the church but a covenantal association of the entire community. A variety of parties played a part in a marriage. The marital couple themselves swore their betrothals and espousals before each other and God—rendering all marriages triparty agreements with God as party, witness, and judge. The couple's parents, as God's bishops for children, gave their consent to the union. Two witnesses, as God's priests to their peers, served as witnesses to the marriage. The minister, holding the spiritual power of the Word, blessed the couple and admonished them in their spiritual duties. The magistrate, holding the temporal power of the sword, registered the parties and their properties and ensured the legality of their union. The involvement of parents, peers, ministers, and magistrates in the formation of a marriage was not an idle or dispensable ceremony. These four parties represented different dimensions of God's involvement in the marriage covenant, and were thus essential to the legitimacy of the marriage itself. To omit any of these parties was, in effect, to omit God from the marriage covenant. Protestant covenant theology thus helped to inte-

---

13. For further development of the argument in this subsection, *see id.* 42–193, 226–68.

grate what became universal requirements of a valid marriage in the West—mutual consent of the couple, parental consent, two witnesses, civil registration, and church consecration.[14]

As a social or civil estate, Calvinists and other early Protestants argued, marriage and the family were no longer subject to the church and its canon law but to the state and its civil law. To be sure, church officials should continue to communicate biblical moral principles respecting sexuality and parenthood. Church consistories could serve as state agents to register marriages and to discipline infidelity and abuse. All church members, as priests, should counsel those who seek marriage and divorce, and cultivate the moral and material welfare of children. But principal legal authority over marriage and the family, Protestants taught, lay with the state, not the church.

In spite of the bitter invectives against the Catholic canon law by early Protestant theologians—symbolized poignantly in Luther's burning of the canon law and confessional books in 1520—Protestant rulers and jurists incorporated much of the traditional canon law of marriage within the new civil law. Traditional canon law prohibitions against unnatural sexual relations and acts and against infringements of marital and procreative functions remained in effect. Canon law procedures treating wife and child abuse, paternal delinquency, child custody, and the like continued. Canon law impediments that protected free consent, that implemented biblical prohibitions against marriage of relatives, and that governed the relations of husband and wife and parent and child within the household were largely retained. These and many other time-tested canon law rules and procedures were as consistent with Protestant theology as with Catholic theology and were transplanted directly into the new state law of marriage.

The new Protestant theology of marriage, however, also yielded critical changes in this new civil law of marriage. Because the reformers rejected the subordination of marriage to celibacy, they rejected laws that forbade clerical and monastic marriage and that permitted vows of chastity to annul vows of marriage. Because they rejected the sacramental concept of marriage as an eternal enduring bond, the reformers introduced divorce in the modern sense, on grounds of adultery, desertion, cruelty, or frigidity, with a subsequent right to remarry at least for the innocent party. Because persons by their lustful nature were in need of God's soothing remedy of marriage, the reformers re-

14. *Id.* 94–113, 243–49, and elaboration in John Witte, Jr., *Between Sacrament and Contract: Marriage as Covenant in John Calvin's Geneva,* 33 Calvin Theological J. 9–75 (1998).

jected numerous canon law impediments to marriage not countenanced by Scripture.

After the sixteenth century, these two Christian models of marriage lay at the heart of Western marriage law. The medieval Catholic model, confirmed and elaborated by the Council of Trent in 1563, flourished in southern Europe, Iberia, and France, and their colonies in Quebec, Latin America, Mexico, Florida, Louisiana, and other outposts in the southwestern United States. A Lutheran social model of marriage dominated portions of Germany, Austria, Switzerland, and Scandinavia, together with their colonies. A parallel Calvinist social model flourished in Geneva and in portions of Huguenot France, the Pietist Netherlands, Presbyterian Scotland, and Puritan England and New England. Something of a hybrid among these Christian models prevailed in Anglican England and its many colonies along the Atlantic seaboard.

### The Common-Law Inheritance

The basic ideas and institutions of marriage born of these earlier Christian models lay at the foundation of the Anglo-American common-law tradition. Until well into the nineteenth century, leading common-law authorities in England and America spoke regularly of marriage as a "state of existence ordained by the Creator," "a consummation of the Divine command to multiply and replenish the earth," "the highest state of existence," "the only stable substructure of social, civil, and religious institutions."[15] Standard legal texts described marriage as "a public institution of universal concern" and as "a sacrament . . . of primary concern, transcendent in its importance both to individuals and to society."[16] The United States Supreme Court spoke regularly of marriage as "more than a mere contract," "a sacred obligation," "a holy estate," "the foundation of the family and society, without which there would be neither civilization nor progress."[17]

At the same time, nineteenth-century Anglo-American common law treated marriage much the same way that Catholic and Protestant communities had done since the sixteenth century. With ample variations across jurisdictions, the common law generally defined marriage as a permanent monogamous

15. W. C. Rogers, *A Treatise on the Law of Domestic Relations* 2 (1899); 1 Joel Bishop, *New Commentaries on Marriage, Divorce, and Separation* 3–7 (1891).

16. 1 Chester G. Vernier, *American Family Laws: A Comparative Study of the Family Law of the Forty-Eight American States* 45 (1931–38).

17. *Maynard v. Hill*, 125 U.S. 190, 210–11 (1888); *Reynolds v. United States*, 98 U.S. 145, 165 (1878); *Murphy v. Ramsey*, 11 U.S. 15, 45 (1885).

union between a fit man and a fit woman of the age of consent, designed for mutual love and support and for mutual procreation and protection. It required that betrothals be formal and that marriages be contracted with parental consent and witnesses. It required marriage licenses and registration and solemnization before civil and/or religious authorities. It prohibited marriages between couples related by various blood or family ties identified in the Mosaic Law. It discouraged, and in some states involuntarily annulled, marriage where one party was impotent or had a contagious disease that precluded procreation or endangered the other spouse. Couples who sought to divorce had to publicize their intentions, to petition a court, to show adequate cause or fault, to make permanent provision for the dependent spouse and children. Criminal laws outlawed fornication, adultery, sodomy, polygamy, incest, contraception, abortion, and other perceived sexual offenses. Tort laws held third parties liable for seduction, enticement, loss of consortium, or alienation of the affections of one's spouse. Churches, synagogues, and other mediating structures were given roles to play in the formation, maintenance, and dissolution of marriage, and in the physical, moral, and intellectual nurture of children.

### The Enlightenment Inheritance

Exponents of the eighteenth- and nineteenth-century Enlightenment introduced a new theology of marriage that gave priority to the contractual perspective.[18] The essence of marriage, they argued, was neither its sacramental symbolism nor its covenantal associations nor its social service to the community and commonwealth. The essence of marriage was the voluntary bargain struck between the two married parties. The terms of their marital bargain were not preset by God or nature, church or state, tradition or community. These terms were set by the parties themselves, in accordance with general rules of contract formation and general norms of civil society. Such rules and norms demanded respect for the life, liberty, and property interests of other parties, and compliance with general standards of health, safety, and welfare in the community. But the form and function, and the length and limits, of the marriage relationship were to be left to the bargain of the parties themselves.

Enlightenment exponents predicated this understanding of marriage on a new theology of deism, individualism, and rationalism. First, they taught, God was no longer to be viewed as an active agent in the daily affairs of human be-

---

18. For further development of the argument in this subsection, *see* Witte, *supra* note 11, at 194–215, 268–73.

ings, including their daily marital lives. God had created the human and natural world with its own laws and processes and thereafter left the world to run on its own—occasionally perhaps intervening with acts of miracle or *force majeure*. The doctrine of deism undercut the traditional notion that God was somehow a necessary party to every marital contract, or that His church was a necessary agent in every scheme of marital governance. Second, the individual was no longer to be viewed primarily as a sinner seeking eternal salvation or a saint exercising a godly vocation within the church, state, and household. According to basic Enlightenment theology, each individual was created equal in virtue and dignity, vested with inherent rights of life, liberty, and property, and capable of pursuing independent means and measures of happiness without involvement from any other person or institution. The doctrine of individualism rendered anachronistic the traditional notion that marriage was somehow a spiritual estate or a social calling that demanded the involvement of priests, parents, and peers in its formation and maintenance. Third, reason was no longer to be viewed as the handmaiden of revelation; rational disputation was no longer to be subordinated to homiletic declaration. The rational process, conducted privately by each individual and collectively in the open marketplace of ideas, was considered a sufficient source of private morality and public law. The traditional notion that a law of marriage had to be grounded in Scripture and conscience, in nature and custom, or in the lawmaking functions of church, state, and various mediating structures gave way to a positivist theory of law as the command of the popular sovereign alone.

This contractarian model of marriage, already adumbrated by John Locke in his *Two Treatises of Government* (1689), was elaborated in endless varieties and combinations from the early eighteenth century onward.[19] The Enlightenment was no single, unified movement but a series of diverse ideological movements, in various academic disciplines and social circles throughout Europe and North America. For all the variations on its basic themes, however, the Enlightenment contractarian construction of marriage was quite consistent in its formulation of marriage as contract and quite insistent on the reformation of traditional marriage laws along contractarian lines.

Exponents of the Enlightenment advocated the abolition of much that was considered sound and sacred in the Western legal tradition of marriage. They urged the abolition of the requirements of parental consent, church consecra-

19. John Locke, *Two Treatises of Government* I.9, I.47, I.98, II.2, II.77–83, and *see* discussion in Witte, *supra* note 11, at 179–93, 267–68.

tion, and formal witnesses for marriage. They questioned the traditional teaching of heterosexual monogamy and of male headship within the household, calling for the absolute equality of husband and wife to receive, hold, and alienate property, to enter into contracts and commerce, to participate on equal terms in the workplace. They castigated the state for leaving annulment practice to the church and urged that the laws of annulment and divorce be both merged and expanded under exclusive state jurisdiction.

Much of this contractarian gospel for the reformation of Western marriage law was too radical to transform the law of the nineteenth century. But it did anticipate much of the agenda for the transformation of marriage law in the twentieth century, particularly in the United States.

In the early part of the twentieth century, state legislatures passed sweeping new laws to govern marriage formalities, divorce, alimony, marital property, and child support. Marriages became easier to contract and easier to dissolve. Wives received greater protections in their persons and in their properties from their husbands, and greater independence in their relationships outside the family. The state began to replace the church as the principal external authority governing marriage and family life. The Catholic sacramental concept of the family governed principally by the church and the Protestant concepts of the family governed by the church and broader Christian community began to give way to a new privatist concept of the family, whereby the wills of the marital parties became primary. Neither the church nor the local community nor the *paterfamilias* could override the reasonable expressions of will of the marital parties themselves.

In the past three decades, the Enlightenment call for the privatization of marriage has come to greater institutional expression. Antenuptial, marital, and separation contracts that allow parties to define their own rights and duties within the marital estate and thereafter have gained increasing acceptance. Implied marital contracts are imputed to longstanding lovers. Surrogacy contracts are executed for the rental of wombs. Medical contracts are executed for the abortion of fetuses. Requirements of parental consent and witnesses to most of these contracts have largely disappeared. No-fault divorce statutes have reduced the divorce proceeding to an expensive formality. Lump-sum property exchanges now often substitute for alimony. Traditional criminal prohibitions against most sexual offenses have become dead letters in most states. Traditional tort suits for alienation of affections and loss of consortium have become largely otiose.

While consensual intimate relationships between adults have become increasingly impervious to state scrutiny, nonconsensual conduct has become increasingly subject to state sanction. Many state courts have opened their dockets to civil and criminal cases of physical abuse, rape, embezzlement, and fraud by one spouse or lover against the other. The ancient "marital exemption" in the law of rape, which often protected abusive husbands from criminal prosecution, is falling into desuetude. Fading too is the ancient spousal exemption in evidence law that discouraged spouses from testifying against each other. The arm of the state no longer knocks at the bedroom door with the same ease that it did in the past. But today if a distressed party opens the bedroom door for it, the state will reach deeply into the intimacies of bed and board and punish severely those who have abused their autonomy.

To be sure, these exponential legal changes are, in part, simple reflections of the exponential changes that have occurred in the culture and condition of American families in the past three decades—the stunning advances in reproductive and medical technology, the exposure to vastly different perceptions of sexuality and kinship born of globalization, the explosion of international and domestic norms of human rights, the implosion of the Ozzie and Harriet family in the wake of new economic and professional demands on wives, husbands, and children. But we have also been witnessing the precocious rise of an Enlightenment contractarian model of marriage that has eclipsed Protestant and Catholic models of marriage and the legal ideas and institutions which those models introduced.

## ADMINISTERING OUR LEGAL LEGACY
## ON MARRIAGE

As responsible administrators of this Christian and Enlightenment legal legacy, we can neither wax nostalgic about a prior golden age of marriage and the family nor wax myopic about modern ideals of liberty, privacy, and autonomy. We cannot be blind to the patriarchy, paternalism, and plain prudishness of the past. Nor can we be blind to the massive social, psychological, and spiritual costs of the modern sexual revolution. Traditionalists must heed the maxim of Jaroslav Pelikan that "tradition is the living faith of the dead; traditionalism is the dead faith of the living."[20] Wooden antiquarianism, a dogmatic indifference to the changing needs of marriages and families, is not apt. Modernists must heed the instruction of Harold Berman that "we must walk into the fu-

20. Jaroslav Pelikan, *The Vindication of Tradition* 65 (1984).

ture with an eye on the past."[21] Chronological snobbery, a calculated disregard for the wisdom of the past, also is inapt.

The achievements of the Enlightenment in reforming the traditional theology and law of marriage cannot be lost on us. It took the contractual radicalism of the Enlightenment to force the Western tradition to examine and reform itself—to grant greater respect to the rights of women, children, and religious minorities, to break the monopoly and monotony of outmoded moral and religious forms and forums respecting sexuality, marriage, and the family. While some Christian denominations may have retrieved or conceived their own resources to achieve these reforms, it was the Enlightenment critique that forced these traditions to reform themselves and the state to reform its laws. This was no small achievement.

Just as the Enlightenment tradition still has much to teach us today, so do the earlier Christian traditions of the West. Both Catholic and Protestant traditions have seen that a marriage is at once a natural, religious, social, and contractual unit; that in order to survive and flourish, this institution must be governed both externally by legal authorities and internally by moral authorities. From different perspectives, these traditions have seen that marriage is an inherently communal enterprise, in which marital couples, magistrates, and ministers must all inevitably cooperate. After all, marital contracts are of little value without courts to enforce them. Marital properties are of little use without laws to protect them. Marital laws are of little consequence without canons to inspire them. Marital customs are of little cogency without natural narratives to ground them.

The modern lesson in this is that we must resist the temptation to reduce marriage to a single perspective, or to a single forum. A single perspective on marriage—whether sacramental, social, or contractual—does not capture the full nuance of this institution. A single forum—whether the church, state, or the household itself—is not fully competent to govern all marital questions. Marriage demands multiple forums and multiple laws to be governed adequately. American religious communities must think more seriously about restoring and reforming their own bodies of religious law on marriage, divorce, and sexuality, instead of simply acquiescing in state laws. American states must think more seriously about granting greater deference to the marital laws and customs of legitimate religious and cultural groups that cannot accept a mar-

21. Harold J. Berman, *Law and Revolution: The Formation of the Western Legal Tradition* v, vii (1983).

riage law of the common denominator. Other sophisticated legal cultures—
Denmark, England, India, and South Africa—grant semiautonomy to Catholic, Hindu, Jewish, Muslim, and Traditional groups to conduct their subjects'
domestic affairs in accordance with their own laws and customs, with the state
setting only minimum conditions and limits.[22] It might well be time for the
United States likewise to translate its growing cultural pluralism into a more
concrete legal pluralism.

The Western tradition has learned, through centuries of hard experience, to
balance the norms of marital formation and dissolution. There was something
cruel, for example, in a medieval Catholic canon law that countenanced easy
contracting of marriage but provided for no escape from a marriage once properly contracted. The Council of Trent responded to this inequity in 1563 by establishing several safeguards to the legitimate contracting of marriage—
parental consent, peer witness, church consecration, civil registration—so that
an inapt or immature couple would be less likely to marry. There was something equally cruel in the rigid insistence of some early Protestants on reconciliation of all married couples at all costs—save those few who could successfully
sue for divorce. Later Protestants responded to this inequity by reinstituting the
traditional remedy of separation from bed and board for miserable couples incapable of either reconciliation or divorce.

The modern lesson in this is that rules governing marriage formation and
dissolution must be balanced in their stringency—and separation must be
maintained as a release valve. Stern rules of marital dissolution require stern
rules of marital formation. Loose formation rules demand loose dissolution
rules, as we see today. To fix the modern problem of broken marriages requires
reforms of rules at both ends of the marital process. Today, more than twenty
states have bills under discussion seeking to tighten the rules of divorce, without corresponding attention to the rules of marital formation and separation.
Such efforts, standing alone, are misguided. The cause of escalating divorce
rates is not only no-fault divorce, as is so often said, but also no-faith marriage.

A promising course is suggested by the 1997 Louisiana covenant-marriage
statute, which seeks to reform both ends of the marital process. At the time of
their marital formation, couples may choose either a contract marriage with at-

---

22. *See, e.g.,* Dicey and Morris on the Conflict of Laws 697 ff. (12th ed., 1993); Alan Reed,
*Transnational Non-Judicial Divorces: A Comparative Analysis of Recognition Under English
and U.S. Jurisprudence,* 18 Loy. L.A. Int'l & Comp. L.J. 311 (1996).

tendant rights to no-fault divorce, or a covenant marriage, with more stringent formation and dissolution rules. In forming a covenant marriage, the parties must receive detailed counseling from a licensed therapist or religious official, must read the entire covenant marriage statute, and then must swear an oath, pledging "full knowledge of the nature, purposes, and responsibilities of marriage" and promising "to love, honor, and care for one another as husband and wife for the rest of our lives." Divorce is allowed such covenanted couples only on proof of adultery, capital felony, malicious desertion or separation for more than a year, or physical or sexual abuse of the spouse or one of the children. Formal separation is allowed on any of these grounds, as well as on proof of habitual intemperance, cruel treatment, or outrages of the other spouse.[23]

This is a cleverly drawn statute that seeks to respect both the virtues of contractual calculus and the values of the disestablishment clause of the First Amendment. It goes a long way toward incorporating the historical lesson that rules of marriage formation and dissolution must be balanced. The statute has been attacked, predictably, as an encroachment on sexual freedom and the rights of women and children, as a "Trojan horse" to smuggle biblical principles into American law, and as a throwback to the days of staged and spurious charges of marital infidelity which no-fault statutes sought to overcome. But given the neutral language of the statute and its explicit protections of both voluntary entrance and involuntary exit from the covenant union, such objections are largely inapt. The statute should help to inject both a greater level of realism into the heady romance of prospective couples and a greater level of rigor into the state's law of marriage formation and dissolution.

The stronger objection to the Louisiana statute is not that it jeopardizes liberty but that it trivializes covenant.[24] The statute effectively reduces "covenant" to a super–marriage contract between the husband and wife alone. Historically, however, marriage covenants involved parents, peers, ministers, and magistrates as well, who served at least as checks on each other and the prospective couple, if not as representatives of God in the covenant formation. The Louisiana law replaces all four of these parties with a licensed marital counselor. Moreover, the Louisiana law leaves it to the state to decide the terms of the mar-

23. Act 1380 (1997), amending and reenacting Louisiana Civil Code, Articles 102 and 102 (amended) and R.S. 9:235 and 245(A)(1) and enacting R.S. 9:224(C) and 225(A)(3), Part VII of chap. 1 of Code Title IV of Code Book I of Title 9 of the La. Rev. Statutes (1950).

24. For a pristine modern exposition on marriage covenant, *see* Max L. Stackhouse, *Covenants and Commitments: Faith, Family, and Economic Life* (1996).

ital covenant, the credentials of the marriage counselor, and the contents of the marriage oath. Historically, however, churches and synagogues defined these matters for themselves, without much state interference.

The Western tradition has learned to distinguish between annulment and divorce. Historically, annulment was granted when a putative marriage was void from the start, by reason of some impediment that lay undiscovered or undisclosed at the time of the wedding. Divorce was granted when a marriage once properly contracted was dissolved by reason of the fault of one or both of the parties after their wedding. The spiritual and psychological calculus and costs were different in these decisions. In annulment cases, a party may discover features of the marriage or spouse that need not, and sometimes cannot, be forgiven—that they were manipulated or coerced into marriage; that the parties are improperly related by blood or family ties; that the spouse will not or cannot perform expected connubial duties; that the spouse misrepresented a fundamental part of his or her faith, character, or history. Annulment in such instances is prudent, sometimes mandatory, even if painful. In divorce cases, by contrast, the moral inclination (and, for some, the moral imperative) is to forgive a spouse's infidelity, desertion, cruelty, or crime. Divorce, in such instances, might be licit, even prudent, but it often feels like, and is treated as, a personal failure even for the innocent spouse. The historical remedy was often calculated patience; early death by one spouse was the most common cure for broken marriages. In the modern age of fitness and longevity, this remedy is usually less apt.

The modern lesson in this is that not all marital dissolutions are equal. Today, most states have simply collapsed annulment and divorce into a single action, with little procedural or substantive distinction between them. This is one (forgotten) source of our exponentially increased divorce rates; historically, annulment rates were counted separately. This is one reason that religious bodies have become largely excluded from the divorce process; historically, annulment decisions were often made by religious bodies and then enforced by state courts. And this is one reason that no-fault divorce has become so attractive; parties often have neither the statutory mechanism nor the procedural incentive to plead a legitimate impediment. Parties seeking dissolution are thus herded together in one legal process of divorce—subject to the same generic rules respecting children and property, and prone to the same generic stigmatizing by self and others.

Finally, the Western tradition has also recognized that marriage and the family have multiple goods and goals. This institution might well be rooted in the natural order and in the will of the parties. Participation in it might well not be vital, or even conducive, to a person's salvation. But the Western tradition has seen that the marriage and family are indispensable to the integrity of the individual and the preservation of the social order.

In Catholic and Anglican parlance, marriage has three inherent goods, which Augustine identified as *fides, proles, et sacramentum.*[25] Marriage is an institution of *fides*—faith, trust, and love between husband and wife, and parent and child, that goes beyond the faith demanded of any other temporal relationship. Marriage is a source of *proles*—children who carry on the family name and tradition, perpetuate the human species, and fill God's church with the next generation of saints. Marriage is a form of *sacramentum*—a symbolic expression of Christ's love for His church, even a channel of God's grace to sanctify the couple, their children, and the broader community.

In Lutheran and Calvinist parlance, marriage has both civil and spiritual uses in this life. On the one hand, the family has general "civil uses" for all persons, regardless of their faith. Marriage deters vice by furnishing preferred options to prostitution, promiscuity, pornography, and other forms of sexual pathos. Marriage cultivates virtue by offering love, care, and nurture to its members, and holding out a model of charity, education, and sacrifice to the broader community. Ideally, marriage enhances the life of a man and a woman by providing them with a community of caring and sharing, of stability and support, of nurture and welfare. Ideally, marriage also enhances the life of the child, by providing it with a chrysalis of nurture and love, with a highly individualized form of socialization and education. It might take a village to raise a child properly, but it takes a marriage to make one.

On the other hand, the family has specific "spiritual uses" for believers—ways of sustaining and strengthening them in their faith. The love of wife and husband can be among the strongest symbols we can experience of Yahweh's love for His elect, of Christ's love for His church. The sacrifices we make for spouses and children can be among the best reflections we can offer of the perfect sacrifice of Golgotha. The procreation of children can be among the most important Words we have to utter.[26]

---

25. Augustine, On Original Sin, chap. 39 [xxxiv], in 5 *A Select Library of Nicene and Post-Nicene Fathers of the Christian Church,* Second Series 251 (Philip Schaff and Henry Wace, eds., repr. ed., 1952).

26. *Cf.* John E. Coons, The Religious Rights of Children, *in Religious Human Rights In Global Perspective: Religious Perspectives* 172 (John Witte, Jr. and Johan van der Vyver, eds., 1996) ("In a faint echo of the divine, children are the most important Word most of us will utter").

# Human Nature and Criminal Responsibility: The Biblical View Restored

*Phillip E. Johnson*

At the beginning of *The Selfish Gene,* Richard Dawkins poses the question "What is man?" and in answer quotes with approval George Gaylord Simpson's comment that "all attempts to answer that question before 1859 are worthless and that we will be better off if we ignore them completely."[1] Eighteen fifty-nine was the year of publication of Darwin's *Origin of Species,* and what Dawkins and Simpson meant was that Darwin did not just say that humans descended from monkeys. What Darwinian theory came to mean is that human beings, like other animals, are a part of nature and hence can in principle be completely comprehended in terms of material causes that are accessible to scientific investigation. In the words of the evolutionary geneticist Richard Lewontin, "We exist as material beings in a material world, all of whose phenomena are the consequences of material relations among material entities."[2] To put the same point in the neg-

1. Richard Dawkins, *The Selfish Gene* (Oxford University Press, 1989 ed.) (hereinafter *TSG*).
2. Richard Lewontin, *Billions and Billions of Demons,* New York Review of Books, Jan. 9, 1997.

ative, scientific materialists see no need to invoke a mysterious "soul" or spiritual dimension to understand human nature. Scientists comprehend living organisms in terms of their chemistry, particularly their genes, and the environmental influences (also material) to which they are subject. Scientific explanations of human nature and behavior thus are framed in terms of some combination of heredity and environment, because the ruling assumption is that these factors exhaust the possibilities.

In short, human behavior, like all other natural phenomena, is caused. From a scientific materialist point of view, it is virtually meaningless to say that a person "chose" to commit a particular action. What is important is to understand what combination of genetic or environmental circumstances caused him to commit this action rather than a different one. In the more logically rigorous versions of this model, the human subject itself—the "I" in "I choose"—is taken to be merely a placeholder for causative factors that we do not yet understand. It follows that the rational approach for a discipline of criminology is to discover the "root causes" of crime, whether genetic, psychological, or sociological—and having discovered them, to ameliorate them. Blame and retributive punishment are seen as relics of prescientific superstition, premised on a view of human nature that science has discarded.

This scientific materialist view is often qualified in important ways, indeed in ways that may seem to contradict its central point. I will get to the qualifications in due course, but for now I want to inquire into the influence of the basic premise of scientific causation upon criminal law. How did the scientific revolution that occurred after 1859 change our notions of criminal responsibility, and was the change a success or a flop?

The inquiry is important because the criminal law handed down to us by pre-Darwinian legal authorities has traditionally been based on quite different assumptions. Perhaps the clearest example is the classic *M'Naghten* definition of the insanity defense, which takes its name from an English decision in 1843, just sixteen years before the publication of *Origin of Species*. According to the *M'Naghten* rule, an accused is excused from criminal punishment (but usually remitted to civil commitment) only if "at the time of committing the act, the party accused was laboring under such a defect of reason, from disease of the mind, as not to know the nature and quality of the act he was doing, or if he did know it, that he did not know he was doing what was wrong."[3]

3. The specific wording of the *M'Naghten* rule is quoted from *United States v. Freeman*, 357 F. 2d 606 (2d Cir. 1966), one of the leading opinions that broke from *M'Naghten* to adopt the supposedly more liberal American Law Institute test.

The concept of human responsibility assumed by that legalistic formula finds its metaphysical support in biblical theism, not scientific materialism. First, there is no reference to free will, or to the opposing concept of compulsion, because the law conclusively presumed that human adults have freedom to choose between good and evil. What the test puts in issue is not the defendant's freedom but his knowledge of the wrongfulness of his act. Second, the knowledge in question is not of legal wrongfulness but of moral wrongfulness. As the old maxim says, ignorance of the law is no excuse. What responsible persons are deemed to know is not that the law forbids murder, theft, perjury, and adultery (as it once did) but that such deeds are wrongful and would be so even if the law permitted them. If God is the ultimate source of morality, then the concept of a moral order independent of positive law makes sense. Matter by itself has no morality; nor does Darwinian evolution. When there is no transcendent authority, morality can be constructed only by human choice, which is why variations on the theme of a social contract have come to have such importance in contemporary moral theory.

When a person does know right from wrong, the *M'Naghten* standard holds him responsible for his choice. There is no concept of an irresistible compulsion to commit evil deeds because the defense is based solely on cognitive factors. Persons who do not know the nature and moral quality of their acts are analogous to small children, who may say "Bang! Bang!" and point a loaded pistol at a playmate without grasping the consequences of what they are doing. This is a very narrow exception to the general rules of responsibility, and successful insanity defenses are consequently rare. Successful defendants under *M'Naghten* are also generally so incapable of living in normal circumstances that there is no question of granting them freedom. Liberal reformers have often thought that a broader defense would more adequately take account of the irrationality of much criminal behavior, but they never had a clear idea what to do with nearly normal people who commit crimes and are not convicted. The problem became particularly acute when public policy turned to deinstitutionalizing the mentally ill. If insanity acquittees were treated like other mentally ill people, they would be speedily released to the streets. If they were confined in an institution because they had committed a crime, then in what sense could they be said to have been acquitted?

Be that as it may, Darwinism at its flood tide certainly did influence our ideas of criminal responsibility, but only temporarily. The main point of entry was through the insanity defense, as reformulated by the Model Penal Code of the American Law Institute (hereafter ALI), which represents the elite of the legal profession. At its high-water mark around 1980, the ALI test was the law in every federal circuit court and in about half of the states. The ALI version of the insanity defense proposed that "a person is not responsible for criminal conduct if at the time of such conduct as a result of mental disease or defect he lacks substantial capacity either to appreciate the wrongfulness of his conduct or to conform his conduct to the requirements of law."[4] Superficially, this formulation may seem no more than a modest expansion of the *M'Naghten* rule. It retains the concept of knowledge of wrongfulness, only broadening the defense to excuse one who "knows" that his conduct is wrongful but lacks substantial capacity to "appreciate" this very point. The radical difference is in the introduction of a new excuse for a defendant who lacks "substantial capacity . . . to conform his conduct to the requirements of law." This new element reflected a philosophical position called "soft determinism," which is best described as an uneasy halfway house between the scientific model (behavior is caused) and the common-law model (behavior is chosen). For soft determinists the question is one of degree, rather than either/or, and criminal acts represent a continuum between freely chosen at one pole and totally compelled at the other. The jury, guided by expert testimony, was expected to locate the particular defendant's act on the continuum and somehow to decide whether that location fell inside or outside the imaginary boundary of "substantial capacity to conform."

Other tests of mental incapacity that flourished during the same period (around 1960) reflected the same soft determinist philosophy and the same logical quagmire over where to draw the boundary between free will and compulsion. The District of Columbia's *Durham* formula, judicially enacted in 1954 and replaced by the ALI formula in 1972, said that an accused should be found not guilty by reason of insanity if his act was the "product of a mental disease or defect."[5] The California Supreme Court grafted a mental-illness defense onto its definition of "malice aforethought" so that a killer who could not control his conduct would be convicted of manslaughter rather than murder.[6] All these

4. Model Penal Code § 4.01 (1974).
5. *United States v. Brawner,* 471 F.2d 969 (D.C. Cir. 1972) (overruling *Durham v. United States,* 214 F.2d 862 (D.C. Cir. 1954)).
6. *See People v. Gorshen,* 51 Cal.2d 716 (1959). The California defense of "diminished mental capacity" was eventually abolished by a combination of legislation and a ballot initiative in the early 1980s. There was a bipartisan reaction against the diminished-capacity defense after a notorious case in which a disappointed politician named Dan White assassinated two popular public officials in San Francisco and was convicted only of manslaughter. Because one element in the psychiatric defense involved an assertion that White behaved impulsively

tests came to grief once they were tested in practice, for reasons I will explain presently, and so they are best understood as reflecting a cultural and ideological moment rather than a permanent trend in the law.

In my opinion the vogue for these soft determinist defenses, which aimed to split the difference between scientific and traditional understandings of human action, is best explained by two circumstances. First, the defenses flourished (in the sense of being approved by scholars and appellate judges) during a period in which the death penalty was being vigorously attacked, and eventual abolition of capital punishment seemed probable. Allowing expert witnesses the greatest leeway to present mitigating circumstances as scientific knowledge seemed an effective way of reducing the number of death penalty verdicts during the period while the abolition movement was gathering support. Progress (if that is the correct term) in this direction was halted in 1976 by the Supreme Court's decision in *Gregg v. Georgia.*[7] The Supreme Court decision probably reflected the fact that the death penalty opponents by then had lost their case decisively in the court of public opinion.

Second, the mid-twentieth century was a period of scientific hubris sparked by such genuine triumphs of technology as radar, nuclear bombs, antibiotics, insecticides, the polio vaccine, and space travel. It seemed that science, accompanied by the scientific materialist ideology, provided the most promising way to deal with previously intractable social problems such as crime. Soft determinism could be justified as an illogical but practical compromise between the traditional and scientific models for the time being, with the expectation that the scientific model would eventually triumph. Progress (again, if that is the correct term) in this direction was set back in 1968 by the Supreme Court's decision in *Powell v. Texas,* in which the very liberal Justice Thurgood Marshall's opinion held that a chronic alcoholic may be punished for public intoxication notwithstanding an apparent scientific consensus that "alcoholism is a disease."[8]

The ALI insanity defense outlived its historical moment, mainly because juries ignored it. All it took was for the defense to have tangible consequences in a highly publicized case, and immediately a bipartisan consensus appeared in support of a return to the *M'Naghten* rule.

---

after gorging himself on high-sugar foods, the lenient verdict was popularly attributed to "the Twinkie defense."

7. 428 U.S. 153 (1976).

8. 392 U.S. 514 (1968).

The seminal event was the attempted assassination of President Ronald Reagan by John Hinckley, who hoped to attract the attention of a movie star he was stalking by this daring act of self-sacrifice. By traditional standards Hinckley was dead-bang guilty of attempted murder and related crimes. But he came to trial in a federal court in the District of Columbia, in a legal culture that by this time had absorbed not only the letter of the ALI defense but also its spirit. Hinckley, whose parents were both wealthy and devoted to him, had the benefit not only of the ALI standard, and of the testimony of expert witnesses with sterling scientific qualifications, but also of the general principle of evidence that the burden of proof rests on the prosecution, not the defense. Thus the federal rule required the prosecutor to prove beyond a reasonable doubt that a demented man, who had attempted to assassinate a president for utterly bizarre reasons, was not insane. Ordinarily one can rely upon a jury to ignore unrealistic legal standards, but the Hinckley jury surprised everyone by taking the judge's instructions seriously and returning a verdict of not guilty.

Hinckley himself gained little or nothing by the verdict. The courts remitted him to civil custody in a secure mental hospital, and there he remains to this day, though most civil committees are released after a few months of treatment. But the prospect of his release convinced the public that it was the legal standard that was insane, and that a standard as loose as that of the ALI insanity defense could permit rich people to buy a verdict. The resulting counterrevolution led Congress to take the issue away from the judges by enacting a modernized version of the *M'Naghten* rule, omitting the defense for a defendant who "lacks substantial capacity to conform his conduct to the requirements of law" and placing the burden of proof squarely on the defense. The federal Insanity Defense Reform Act of 1984 now provides as follows:

> (a) Affirmative defense. It is an affirmative defense to a prosecution under any federal statute that, at the time of the commission of the acts constituting the defense, the defendant, as a result of a severe mental disease or defect, was unable to appreciate the nature and quality or the wrongfulness of his acts. Mental disease or defect does not otherwise constitute a defense.
>
> (b) Burden of Proof. The defendant has the burden of proving the defense of insanity by clear and convincing evidence.[9]

Superficially, one might have interpreted the public reaction to the Hinckley verdict as a victory of popular opinion over the experts. The trouble with this interpretation is that the American Psychiatric Association (APA), the official

9. 18 U.S.C. § 17 (2000).

voice of the psychiatric profession, enthusiastically agreed with the popular decision. The APA's 1982 *Statement on the Insanity Defense* was clear in its conclusion but confused in its reasoning.[10] It started by assuming that the basis of criminal punishment is moral culpability and that there must therefore logically be a defense for defendants who do not possess free will and therefore cannot be said to have "chosen to do wrong."[11] Despite this soft-determinist rationale for the insanity defense, the APA recommended that the law drop the concept of lack of free will and go back to the *M'Naghten* formula. Why? The APA statement explained that psychiatric testimony about whether a defendant understood the wrongfulness of his act "is more reliable and has a stronger scientific basis" than does psychiatric testimony about whether a defendant could control his behavior. The APA acknowledged that "psychiatry is a deterministic discipline that views all human behavior as, to a good extent, 'caused.'"[12] On the other hand, the APA admitted that psychiatrists disagree about how these deterministic presuppositions should affect the moral and philosophical question of whether a person is responsible for his conduct. Expert testimony about volitional capacity (free will) is therefore likely to be confusing to the jury, and psychiatrists like other people are therefore content to restrict psychiatric testimony to the old standard of "knowledge of wrongfulness."

I do not take this mishmash seriously. If scientific psychiatry views all behavior as caused, then psychiatrists never should have undertaken to draw a line between behavior that is caused and behavior that is chosen in the first place. Yet eminent psychiatrists were involved in drafting the ALI standard, and the legal experts thought that the psychiatrists were pleased with it. Why did psychiatrists not object from the beginning that the crucial dividing line between caused behavior and chosen behavior does not exist? Why does the APA continue to say that there should be a defense for those defendants who lack free will if nobody has free will? And what scientific content does the concept of "wrongfulness" have? One reason the federal courts rapidly adopted the ALI test was that the psychiatrists had told them that the old *M'Naghten* formula was so unsatisfactory that expert witnesses even found it necessary to commit "professional perjury" to couch their testimony in terms of right and wrong when they really wanted to testify that the defendant lacked free will.

A better explanation for the APA's changed attitude was that the psychiatric profession had changed drastically between the 1950s and the 1980s. The ex-

10. American Psychiatric Association, *Statement on the Insanity Defense* (1982).
11. *Id.* at 8.
12. *Id.* at 9.

perts who had supported the broadened insanity and diminished-mental-capacity defenses were mainly Freudian in orientation and had ambitions for political and social reform that far outstripped the modest therapeutic value of their "talking cure." The result was that they promised a great deal more than they could deliver, in terms both of a scientific understanding of why people commit crimes and of a practical knowledge of what to do about it. The subjectiveness of Freudian explanations led to the notorious courtroom "battle of the experts" and consequent public ridicule of the psychiatric profession as witch doctors or "headshrinkers." By 1982 psychiatric medicine had turned away from psychoanalysis in favor of innovative drug therapies that were genuinely effective in mitigating psychotic behavior. Greater knowledge led to greater modesty, and most psychiatrists now found the pretentious claims of the Freudians absurd. In short, psychiatry wanted to escape from an embarrassing situation, and going back to a much narrower test offered a way out.

By the end of the twentieth century, the idea of replacing retributive justice with a scientific search for the "root causes" of criminal behavior was virtually dead. There has been some confusion about this in the public mind because of a few high-profile cases in which a fashionable "abuse excuse" has seemed to be successful. The leading example was the first trial in the notorious Menendez brothers case in Los Angeles County, California. The brothers, who had coldbloodedly murdered their wealthy parents, claimed that they acted in self-defense because the parents were planning to kill them to cover up a history of sexual abuse. The defense managed to muddy the waters enough with this preposterous story that the jurors could not agree on a verdict. That was embarrassing for the criminal justice system, but it did not do the defendants any good. On retrial the judge ran a tighter ship, and the jury had no difficulty convicting both brothers of first-degree murder, with resulting sentences of life imprisonment without possibility of parole. The anomalous outcome of the first Menendez trial, like the highly publicized acquittal of O. J. Simpson shortly afterward in the same court system, probably owed more to postmodernist relativism and its "victim perspective" than to anything even distantly related to science.

The failure of the scientific materialists to change the criminal law permanently stems from the inherent shortcomings of the attempt to understand human nature and the human predicament in exclusively scientific categories. Even the most dedicated scientific materialists tend to be ambivalent about applying their theories to the mind, and especially to the problem of moral choice. At the beginning of *The Selfish Gene*, for example, Richard Dawkins asserts that "we, like other animals, are machines created by our genes" solely for the purpose of reproducing their own genetic kind. Although there are special circumstances under which genes might encourage a limited form of altruism (mainly for the benefit of close relatives), ruthless selfishness must be the norm because our genes have survived by emulating "successful Chicago gangsters." Dawkins's bleak conclusion is that "much as we might wish to believe otherwise, universal love and the welfare of the species as a whole are concepts that simply do not make evolutionary sense."[13]

On the very next page (and without a shred of scientific justification), Dawkins tosses this vision of a gangster world overboard, calling on his readers to rebel against their genetic creators in the name of the very concepts that simply do not make evolutionary sense. "Be warned that if you wish, as I do, to build a society in which individuals cooperate generously and unselfishly towards a common good, you can expect little help from biological nature. Let us try to *teach* generosity and altruism, because we are born selfish. Let us understand what our own selfish genes are up to, because we may then at least have a chance to upset their designs, something that no other species has ever aspired to."[14] But where did those ideals come from, and how can they be anything but nonsense in a world ruled by gangster genes? Dawkins the moral prophet winds up endorsing something very much like the biblical view of human nature that generated the *M'Naghten* rule. Man may be born in sin, but he has the capacity to know good from evil and to choose the good. Indeed, Dawkins in his moralizing vein seems to agree with Pope John Paul II, who is the farthest thing from a scientific materialist. The pope's 1996 statement granted approval to a vaguely defined principle of evolution, with the very significant qualification that "theories of evolution which, in accordance with the philosophies inspiring them, consider the spirit as emerging from the forces of living matter or as a mere epiphenomenon of this matter, are incompatible with the truth about man. Nor are they able to ground the dignity of the person."[15] That is why concepts that simply do not make evolutionary sense may be the most important concepts of all.

13. *TSG, supra* note 1, at 2.

14. *Id.*

15. The complete text of the pope's 1996 letter on evolution to the Papal Academy of Sciences is reprinted in *First Things*, Mar. 1997, at 28–29.

# Christianity and

# Environmental Law

*John Copeland Nagle*

In the beginning, Genesis tells us, God created the heavens, the earth, and all of the creatures on the earth. Sometime thereafter, but still nearly four thousand years ago, God gave the law to Moses. The combination of the two—environmental law—is largely the product of our own generation.

Of course, the story is not nearly that simple. Genesis, the rest of the Old Testament, and various passages in the New Testament are replete with stories and instructions regarding this earth and our obligation to care for it. The law that developed from God's initial commandments included a host of provisions governing the use of land, animals, and the other aspects of God's creation. That law, in turn, informed traditional common-law concepts that established rights and duties of people with respect to creation. Slowly, statutory enactments supplemented those common-law doctrines as particular environmental problems were thought to need legislative attention. What we know as environmental law in the United States today is largely the result of an explosion of congressional activity beginning in the late

1960s and the subsequent executive, judicial, and legislative revisiting of the issues arising from that extensive body of federal statutes.

The Christian voice was missing from much of the debate that produced today's environmental law. Indeed, one famous essay blamed Christianity for modern environmental problems because it saw nature in exclusively utilitarian terms.[1] The ethical and philosophical foundations of environmental law were often left unstated, or to the extent they were debated, the ethical arguments proceeded from assumptions inspired by Eastern religions, Native American spirituality, New Age thought, and a host of pantheistic and nontheistic philosophies.

That has changed. The past few years have brought a bounty of scholarly writings and political advocacy designed to bring Christian thought to bear on environmental problems. Countless books have been written about how Christians should think about environmental issues.[2] Shortly before becoming vice president, Al Gore published a book expressing the relation between his religious beliefs and his commitment to environmental protection.[3] Likewise, Senator Joseph Lieberman has proclaimed, "If you believe in God, I think it's hard not to be an environmentalist, because you see the environment as the work of God."[4] As secretary of the interior, the federal official responsible for the enforcement of numerous environmental laws and the management of our national parks and other ecologically valuable lands, Bruce Babbitt described

1. Lynn White, Jr., *The Historical Roots of Our Ecological Crisis,* 155 Science 1203 (Mar. 10, 1967).

2. Some of the most helpful books are Calvin B. DeWitt et al., *Caring for Creation: Responsible Stewardship of God's Handiwork* (1998); Michael S. Northcott, *The Environment and Christian Ethics* (1996); Fred Van Dyke et al., *Redeeming Creation: The Biblical Basis for Environmental Stewardship* (1996); Robert Booth Fowler, *The Greening of Protestant Thought* (1995); Richard A. Young, *Healing the Earth: A Theocentric Perspective on Environmental Problems* (1994); Peter DeVos et al., *Earthkeeping in the Nineties* (1991); James A. Nash, *Loving Nature: Ecological Integrity and Christian Responsibility* (1991); Francis A. Schaeffer, *Pollution and the Death of Man: The Christian View of Ecology* (1970).

3. Al Gore, *Earth in the Balance* (1992). In his chapter entitled "Environmentalism of the Spirit," Gore explains that "in my own religious experience and training—I am a Baptist—the duty to care for the earth is rooted in the fundamental relationship between God, creation, and humankind." *Id.* at 244. Later he surveys a variety of world religions because "this panreligious perspective may prove especially important where our global civilization's responsibility for the earth is concerned." *Id.* at 258–59.

4. Richard Pérez-Peña, *Lieberman Cites Religion as Foundation of Environmentalism,* New York Times, Oct. 19, 2000 (quoting Senator Lieberman).

the environment as a religious issue.[5] Among religious leaders, Pope John Paul II has spoken of the need to care for God's creation, as has the evangelist Billy Graham.[6] The National Religious Partnership for the Environment combines the efforts of the Evangelical Environmental Network, the National Council of Churches of Christ, the United States Catholic Conference, and the Coalition for the Environment and Jewish Life to speak out about current environmental questions.[7] Those groups and others have lobbied Congress to maintain protections afforded to endangered species, to resist the expansion of private property rights, and to aggressively combat global warming.

All of this occurs at a time when a sweeping body of environmental law is already in place but when advocates from all sides are expressing discontent with the status quo. In part this is because many of the easy environmental problems have been solved: rivers do not catch on fire, hazardous wastes are no longer simply buried in back lots, and cities are not hidden beneath a cloud of factory emissions. Instead, the Endangered Species Act (ESA) that Congress passed to protect the bald eagle is now employed to save the Delhi Springs Flower-Loving Fly, and the Clean Air Act that cut emissions from factories now threatens to make cars more expensive and force people to ride in car pools. The discontent with the status quo also results from the fear that further environmental progress will come at the cost of jobs, increased taxes, and other undesirable side-effects—or that environmental progress will be sacrificed for more jobs, lower taxes, and less government regulation. But the efforts to change environmental laws have met an impasse in Congress, where years of hearings and debate have yet to achieve the reauthorization of the ESA, the Clean Water Act, or the federal Superfund scheme for cleaning up hazardous wastes.

Perhaps the best explanation for the dissatisfaction with the status quo and the inability to change it lies in the lack of a consensus about why we protect the environment and what legal obligations should be imposed to accomplish those ends. How one chooses between an endangered butterfly and a mosquito eradication program, and how one decides who should pay to clean up a con-

5. *See, e.g.,* Bruce Babbitt, *Between the Flood and the Rainbow: Our Covenant to Protect the Whole of Creation,* 2 Animal L. 1 (1996).

6. *See* Pope John Paul II, The Ecological Crisis: A Common Responsibility, *in* Roger S. Gotlieb, *This Sacred Earth: Religion, Nature, and Environment* 235 (1996); Billy Graham, *Does God Care About Animals?* Chattanooga Free Press, Feb. 27, 1997.

7. For additional information about the National Religious Partnership for the Environment, see its web site at http://www.nrpe.org.

taminated but abandoned inner-city factory depend upon one's views of the environment and of law. It is probably no coincidence, then, that the debate over the relevance of Christianity to the environment has occurred at a time of confusion in environmental law. But what is the distinctively Christian message about environmental law? How would environmental law be different if it were purposely founded on Christian principles? This essay seeks to address such questions.

## THE CHRISTIAN VIEW OF CREATION

Christian teaching on creation, like other Christian teachings, is rooted in the Scriptures. The Bible offers more than a description of the relationship of God to humanity. Numerous passages recount the relationship between God and the rest of the world, beginning with God's creative acts and ending with His ultimate plans for all of creation. The following paragraphs summarize several themes that emerge from the Bible's account of creation.

### God Created the World

The opening sentence of the Bible states that "in the beginning God created the heavens and the earth."[8] The balance of the first chapter of Genesis records how God created plants, fish, animals, birds—and finally, men and women. That chapter also describes how God brought order to the world by separating light from darkness, land from water, and the earth from the heavens. The way in which God did all of this is notable in two respects. First, God created the world out of nothing. As the apostle John later wrote, "Through him all things were made; without him nothing was made that has been made."[9] Second, God created by His word. The creation story repeatedly describes how God spoke and "it was so."[10]

### God Pronounced the Creation to Be Good

When God created each part of creation, He "saw that it was good."[11] These statements suggest three interconnected explanations for the goodness of cre-

---

8. Genesis 1:1. All scriptural quotations are to the New International Version (NIV), unless otherwise indicated.

9. John 1:3.

10. *E.g.*, Genesis 1:7, 9, 11, 15, 24. *See also* Psalms 33:6 ("By the word of the Lord the heavens were made").

11. *E.g.*, Genesis 1:10, 12, 18, 21, 25.

ation: creation is good because God created it, creation is good because God proclaimed that is was so, and creation is intrinsically good as shown by God's response to it. Creation reflects God and it honors God. Today creation suffers the consequences of the entry of sin into the world, but that simply shows that the current state of creation does not reflect the original goodness that God saw.

### God Is the Owner of All Creation

David wrote that "the earth is the Lord's, and everything in it."[12] The idea of God as the owner of creation pervades the creation account, the Old Testament saga of the people of Israel, and the parables that Jesus told in the New Testament. God charges humanity with certain responsibilities for creation, but God's authority and control over His creation supersedes both the creation itself and humanity's role in it.

### God Gave Humanity Dominion over Creation

The most controversial verses in the Bible for environmentalists appear at the end of the first chapter of Genesis, where God gives men and women "dominion" over all other creatures and commands humanity to "fill the earth and subdue it."[13] Historically, these commands have been cited to justify actions that treat the provision of resources needed—or wanted—by humanity as the only purpose of creation. Much of the recent Christian environmental scholarship questions that understanding. Indeed, the word *dominion* is used elsewhere in the Bible to describe a peaceful, servant rule.[14] Moreover, God exercises dominion Himself, and the examples of God's rule—and His rule of creation in particular—belie any suggestion that dominion equals exploitation.[15] Thus one writer has identified three models of dominion—servanthood, kingship,

12. Psalms 24:1. *Accord Deuteronomy* 10:14 ("To the Lord your God belong the heavens, even the highest heavens, the earth and everything in it").

13. Genesis 1:26, 28 (New King James Version (NKJV)).

14. *E.g.,* Leviticus 25:43 ("Do not rule over [your slaves] ruthlessly, but fear your God"); Ezekiel 34:4 ("You have not strengthened the weak or healed the sick or bound up the injured. You have not brought back the strays or searched for the lost. You have ruled them harshly and brutally"); 1 Kings 4:24 ("For he ruled over all the kingdoms west of the River, from Tiphsah to Gaza, and had peace on all sides").

15. *See, e.g.,* 1 Peter 4:11 (letter of Paul referring to "Jesus Christ, to whom belong the glory and the dominion forever and ever"); Matthew 20:26–28 (teaching of Jesus that "whoever wants to be great among you must be your servant, and whoever wants to be first must be your slave—just as the Son of Man did not come to be served, but to serve, and to give His life a ransom for many"); Psalms 147:8–9 (praising God because "He covers the sky with

and stewardship—that support a Christian obligation to actively care for creation.[16]

## God Charged Men and Women with the Responsibility of Caring for Creation

God placed Adam in the Garden of Eden so that Adam could "tend and keep it."[17] What it means to "keep" creation is illustrated by the priestly request that "the Lord bless you and keep you" and by God's placement of an angel at the east of Eden to "guard" the garden after the fall.[18] The obligation to care for creation is further demonstrated by the understanding of the command to exercise "dominion" described above. The story of Noah obeying God by saving all species from the flood, God's subsequent covenant with the entire creation, and God's encouragement of all creatures to multiply and fill the earth provides yet another example of our duty to care for creation.[19] Conversely, the Bible teaches that God will judge those who injure the earth.[20]

## God Alone Is Worthy of Worship

The first commandments that God gave to Moses on Mount Sinai were that "you shall have no other gods before me" and that "you shall not make for yourself an idol in the form of anything in heaven above or on the earth beneath or in the waters below. You shall not bow down to them or worship them."[21] The Scriptures then recount numerous instances where people violated those commands by worshiping a variety of other beings: golden calves, Baal, silver and gold gods, angels, the starry host, and unknown gods.[22] In short, people "ex-

---

clouds; he supplies the earth with rain and makes the grass grow on the hills"); Matthew 6:26, 29 (teaching of Jesus in the Sermon on the Mount reminding that God feeds the birds and clothes the grass).

16. *See* Young, *supra* note 2, at 170–77.

17. Genesis 2:15 (NKJV).

18. Numbers 6:24; Genesis 3:24 (using the word *guard* to translate the same Hebrew word translated as "keep" in Genesis 2:15).

19. Genesis 6:1–9:17. I discuss the implications of the story of Noah in more detail in John Copeland Nagle, *Playing Noah,* 82 Minn. L. Rev. 1171, 1216–59 (1998).

20. *See, e.g.,* Revelations 11:16–18 (indicating that "the time has come . . . for destroying those who destroy the earth").

21. Exodus 20:3–4.

22. *See, e.g.,* Exodus 32:1–5 (a golden calf); 1 Kings 16:31 (Baal); Isaiah 46:6 (silver and gold gods); Jeremiah 13:10 (other gods); Zephaniah 1:5 (the starry host); Acts 17:23 (an unknown god); Colossians 2:18 (angels).

changed the glory of the immortal God for images made to look like mortal man and birds and animals and reptiles."[23] The consequences that befell the people who worshiped the creation instead of the creator demonstrates the seriousness with which God takes these commands.

### Creation Has Suffered the Effects of the Entry of Sin into the World

The fall of humanity that occurred when Adam and Eve sinned affected the rest of creation, too. The immediate result was God's curse of the ground so that it produced thorns and thistles and so that much more work was required to obtain food from the land.[24] The fall also alienated people from other creatures, with later passages describing how God used animals to exercise His judgment against humanity.[25] Animals, plants, and the rest of creation suffer themselves because of human actions and because of God's judgment against human sin.[26]

### God Will Redeem His Creation

The entire creation is included in many of the covenants that God announces throughout the Bible. For example, God established a covenant with Noah, his descendants, *and* every living creature on earth that never again would a flood destroy all life on earth.[27] In his letter to the Romans, Paul writes: "The creation waits in eager expectation for the sons of God to be revealed. For the creation was subjected to frustration, not by its own choice, but by the will of the one who subjected it, in hope that the creation itself will be liberated from its bondage to decay and brought into the glorious freedom of the children of God. We know that the whole creation has been groaning as in the pains of childbirth right up to the present time."[28] Other passages describe how this earth will be destroyed in the day of judgment, only to be replaced by a new earth.[29]

This is far from an exhaustive list of themes relating to creation that run through the Bible. It gives a sense, though, of the premises from which Christians approach environmental issues. To be sure, the details of God's relation to

23. Romans 1:23 (NIV).
24. Genesis 3:17–19.
25. *See, e.g.,* Leviticus 26:22; Numbers 21:6; Ezekiel 5:17.
26. *See, e.g.,* Hosea 4:1–3; Jeremiah 7:20; Isaiah 24:5–6.
27. *See* Genesis 9:8–11; *see also* Hosea 2:18; Colossians 1:15–20.
28. Romans 8:19–22.
29. *E.g.* 2 Peter 3:7, 10; Revelations 21:1.

creation—past, present, and future—have prompted debates between Christian traditions, and they continue to do so. Nonetheless, the biblical account of creation contains abundant instruction for those who seek to fulfill God's purposes for His creation today.

## APPLYING CHRISTIAN THOUGHT TO ENVIRONMENTAL LAW

This perspective yields a number of questions. What is the relation between humanity and other creatures? When do human needs justify actions that are harmful to the rest of creation? When must people make sacrifices for the good of the rest of creation? When must people sacrifice so that other people can better enjoy the goodness of creation? What significance do the utilitarian arguments for environmental protection have for Christians?

These questions, important as they are, address just half of the problem. A Christian approach to environmental law must be based not only on a Christian view of creation but on a Christian view of law. The essays that appear throughout this book explain that the Christian tradition encompasses several theories of law. These theories generate another group of questions when they are applied to the specific role of the legal system in protecting creation. When is it appropriate to write Christian environmental principles into statutory law? Can Christian teachings about creation be expressed through secular terms so that they are acceptable to those who are not Christians? When should those of other (or no) religious faiths be commanded to respect creation in the way suggested by Christian teaching? Who should bear the burden of environmental protection efforts?

I cannot hope to answer all of these questions here. What I shall attempt instead is to explain how one Christian—namely, me—tries to take the Christian teaching on creation and a Christian understanding of law and apply them to several current problems in environmental law. In particular, I will discuss the relation between people and other creatures, the relation between Christian teaching and legal obligations to protect the environment, and the legal consequences of the Christian obligation to care for those most in need.

### The Relation Between People and Other Creatures

Christian teaching places humanity above other creatures, but far below God. Thus I am persuaded by those who characterize the Christian view of creation as theocentric—God centered—rather than biocentric (all creatures are created equal) or anthropocentric (humans are at the apex of the world). This view has numerous implications for environmental protection efforts, and for environmental law in particular.

Biblical teaching anticipates that people will rely upon animals and plants for food, clothing, and other needs. That teaching also indicates, however, that God cares for the rest of creation and expects us to care for it. Indeed, God's care extends to the whole of creation, as best illustrated by his command to Noah to bring two of each kind of creature on the ark so that every species would be saved.[30] It appears, then, that we should not choose merely to preserve the creatures that we like—or need—and ignore those that have no appeal to us.

Yet we confront many situations in which creation threatens us. That should not come as a surprise; the Old Testament records numerous instances in which the people of Israel struggled to survive amid an apparently hostile creation. The modern situations may be even more troubling. Mosquitos are a threat to human health, so we try to eradicate them.[31] We are even more zealous in our efforts to destroy the smallpox virus, or more recently, the AIDS virus. We do so because we see such creatures as threats to our health or very survival, with no apparent compensating benefits. When Christians take such actions they distinguish themselves from those who proclaim that every form of life has an equal right to exist, even at the expense of the health and survival of humanity or other creatures.

The issue is not limited to circumstances where the survival of another species is at stake. In suburban Denver, for example, mountain lions have attacked children as subdivisions have sprung up in previously unsettled land and as the traditional checks on the mountain lion population—other predators and human hunting—have disappeared. The fatal attacks have sparked a debate about who belongs there—the people or the mountain lions—with many claiming that the value of human life dictates that the mountain lions be moved, and many others insisting that the people, not the mountain lions, are out of place.[32] The conflict is being replayed in suburbs around the country as

30. I discuss the Biblical rationale for protecting endangered species in Nagle, *supra* note 18, at 1217–30.

31. *Cf.* 16 U.S.C. § 1532(6) (authorizing the secretary of the interior not to list an endangered insect species that "constitute[s] a pest whose protection under the [ESA] would present an overwhelming and overriding risk to man").

32. *See* James Brooke, *Cougars Clash with Colorado Suburbanites,* N.Y. Times, Sept. 3, 1997.

the numbers of bear, deer, and other animals grow even as their historic habitat is increasingly occupied by new human habitations. The debate is still more intense when wild animals are returned to their historic habitat, as in the efforts to reintroduce the grizzly bear to Idaho and wolves to New Mexico and Arizona. In those cases the assertion that people are out of place sounds harsh to Christian ears, but it has echoes in traditional legal doctrines, and it requires us to ask which places we are leaving for the other members of God's creation.[33]

### The Relation Between Christian Teaching and Legal Obligations

Which Christian teachings should be written into public law? Because that question admits of no clear answer generally, there can be no confident conclusions about the relation between Christian environmental teaching and federal environmental statutes. Yet that question lies at the heart of any effort to craft an approach to environmental law that is faithful to Christian teaching.

Consider the Christian duty to preserve endangered species. The Bible supports the claim that God wants us to work to prevent any of the species that He created from going extinct. The very diversity of creation itself—and God's labeling it as "good"—attests to the divine pleasure with an abundance of different animal and plant creatures. God's command to Noah to build an ark to accommodate two members of all of the world's species shows an even more direct indication of God's concern about preserving all kinds of life. Indeed, the story of Noah offers a better reason for protecting *all* species than the stated purposes of the Endangered Species Act itself, which overlook seemingly unimportant species by mentioning only the utilitarian reasons for preserving endangered species.[34]

The next step for those seeking to honor the biblical concern about endangered species is to confront the different reasons why species become endangered in the first place. Some species have become extinct or on the brink of extinction because of natural causes. Other species suffer from poaching, pol-

---

33. *Cf. Indiana Harbor Belt R.R. Co. v. American Cyanamid Co.,* 916 F.2d 1174, 1181 (7th Cir. 1990) (Posner, J.) (suggesting that as between the use of land for rail transportation of a hazardous chemical and as a residential community, the inappropriate use may be the residential one); *Spur Industries, Inc. v. Del E. Webb Dev. Co.,* 494 P.2d 700 (Ariz. 1972) (employing the "coming to the nuisance doctrine" to require the residents of a new subdivision to pay for the moving costs of a neighboring cattle feedlot whose presence predated the subdivision by many years).

34. *See* 16 U.S.C. § 1531(a)(3).

lution, and other harmful human activities. But the greatest threat to the continued existence of most endangered species is habitat destruction. The land that has served as the home for countless species is being transformed into residential developments, shopping malls, commercial offices, amusement parks, and a myriad of other human structures. Some species thrive amid human populations, but many others do not, and that latter group has fewer and fewer places to call home.

Protecting endangered species, then, requires the protection of habitat. Most land in the United States is privately owned, so anyone can do the math and reach the obvious conclusion: endangered species can be preserved only if private landowners will preserve them. Christian teaching provides one incentive for private landowners to manage their land in a way that is friendly to any endangered species that are—or could be—living there, but that incentive counts for little for those who have no desire to obey Christian teaching in the first place. Of course, Christians are hardly the only ones to demonstrate a concern about endangered species. Whatever the motivation, the efforts made by ranchers and developers to accommodate their land to the needs of endangered species are among the most heroic in the environmental movement today, though many of them might disclaim the label of environmentalist. Moreover, such secular groups as the Nature Conservancy have accomplished much by using charitable donations to purchase the habitat of endangered species in this country and elsewhere. But all of those voluntary efforts to preserve endangered species have proven inadequate. In other words, not enough people feel a religious or ethical obligation to manage their land in a way that preserves endangered species.

Thus the Endangered Species Act prohibits landowners from interfering with the habitat of any endangered species that lives on their land. In particular, the ESA makes it illegal to "take" an endangered species, the term *take* is defined to include any "harm" to an endangered species, the U.S. Fish and Wildlife Service interprets *harm* to include the destruction of the habitat of a particular endangered species, and the Supreme Court has upheld that interpretation.[35] The result is that the habitat of endangered species is protected against many actions that could interfere with that species.

But that prohibition has been controversial because it creates a perverse in-

35. *See Babbitt v. Sweet Home Chapter of Communities for a Greater Or.,* 515 U.S. 687 (1995) (upholding the Fish and Wildlife Service's interpretation of the "harm" to an endangered species prohibited by 16 U.S.C. § 1331(19)).

centive. If you discover oil on your property, the market value of your property increases dramatically. But if you discover an endangered species on your property, the value of your land plummets because the ESA may prohibit you from developing it. Indeed, an endangered species can be compared to hazardous waste in the effect that both legal designations have on property value. Thus it should not be surprising that some property owners have surreptitiously tried to destroy endangered species that they discovered on their property, or that landowners have destroyed a species before it could be formally listed as endangered under the ESA.

Or consider the problem that occurs when an endangered grizzly bear attacks a rancher's sheep. The ESA prohibition on killing the attacking animal to protect livestock means that the law requires the landowner to sacrifice his real estate *and* his livestock. The law requires that sacrifice in order to promote the greater public interest in the preservation of an endangered species. Moreover, the rancher assumes all of the costs of securing the public interest because the ESA's prohibition on killing the grizzly bear does not constitute a government taking of the rancher's property without compensation, at least according to the Ninth Circuit.[36] (When the Supreme Court refused to review the Ninth Circuit's decision, Justice White wondered whether there is any difference between that application of the ESA and a hypothetical law that prohibited storekeepers from harassing thieves who wanted to clear their shelves bare.[37]) Concerns about the fairness of that result have prompted some environmental groups to compensate landowners in such circumstances. Defenders of Wildlife, a leading environmental group, has established a Wolf Compensation Trust that has been used to pay more than $115,644.77 to 116 ranchers whose livestock was killed by wolves in Arizona, Idaho, Montana, New Mexico, Wyoming, and Alberta.[38]

A Christian environmental ethic should encourage individuals to contribute to such efforts. One of the reasons that it should do so is a recognition of the predicament of a landowner who confronts a wolf attacking his livestock and who is mindful of the biblical teachings about God's creation. Such a landowner should refrain from taking any actions that would harm an endangered

36. *Christy v. Hodel,* 857 F.2d 1324, 1334–35 (9th Cir. 1988), *cert. denied,* 490 U.S. 1114 (1989).

37. *Christy v. Hodel,* 490 U.S. 1115, 1115–16 (1989) (White, J., dissenting from denial of certiorari).

38. Defenders of Wildlife, *Wolf Compensation Trust* (visited June 6, 2000) <http://www.defenders.org/wolfcomp.html>.

species, whether or not the law speaks to the question.[39] But the landowner does so at potentially significant cost with few countervailing benefits. To be sure, some species provide utilitarian benefits that should be considered in any such cost/benefit analysis. But many species lack any substantial utilitarian benefits, and even for those species that are valuable, that value accrues to society at large while a small number of landowners are often asked to pay the cost of preservation. This placement of disproportionate costs on a small number of landowners while the whole society shares the benefits is hard to justify, particularly for landowners who do not share Christian beliefs or any other religious or ethical imperative to preserve endangered species.

Such concerns help explain the frequent demands that landowners should be compensated by the government when a regulation prevents the landowner from using his or her property. No court, however, has found that the Fifth Amendment's Just Compensation Clause requires payment to a landowner subjected to ESA regulation.[40] Undeterred, private property advocates have promoted legislation that would require compensation whenever the ESA causes the value of a landowner's property to decrease by a specified amount. One Christian response to such arguments is that all land belongs to God, and therefore takings legislation is inappropriate to the extent that it pays landowners for doing something—including protecting habitat—that we should do anyway. That is the position articulated in a thoughtful monograph prepared by the Christian Environmental Council (CEC). The emphasis on the biblical teachings with respect to land strongly affirms the relative positions of God as owner and people as stewards. More specifically, the CEC monograph notes that our ownership of land occurs in the context of our obligation to act as stewards of the land, and that the value of land cannot be measured in purely material terms.[41] I would expect a Christian landowner to heed these principles. But that does not necessarily prove that landowners—Christian or not—need not

39. I do not intend to trivialize the importance of protecting one's livestock. Indeed, the Bible contains several stories that emphasize the value of livestock and the need to protect livestock from attacking animals. *See, e.g.,* 1 Samuel 17:34–35; Luke 15:4–7. Nonetheless, I conclude for the reasons discussed above that the need to preserve a species from extinction outweighs the protection of one's livestock.

40. *See, e.g., Good v. United States,* 189 F.3d 1355 (Fed. Cir. 1999), *cert. denied,* 120 S. Ct. 1554 (2000).

41. Ann Alexander et al., *"This Land Is Your Land, This Land Is God's Land": Takings Legislation Versus the Judeo-Christian Land Ethic* 11–12 (1996). I served as a member of the CEC's Advocacy Committee and participated in the preparation of the monograph, though my views are somewhat different from those expressed there.

be compensated when their activities are circumscribed by federal regulation, however worthy. The Constitution's Takings Clause itself becomes meaningless if legal property rights are qualified by the biblical teaching that God is the true owner of the land. Rather, the scope of the takings doctrine is limited by the obligation to use land in a way that does not interfere with one's neighbors—a principle that follows nicely from both the teachings of Jesus and traditional nuisance law.[42] Thus stated, the question for endangered species legislation is whether it serves that end by protecting our animal and plant neighbors from human activities that would destroy them.

It is unlikely that the Congress that wrote the ESA viewed the creatures it protects as neighbors to whom we owe a duty. The stated purposes of the ESA refer to the utilitarian benefits that people receive from the protection of endangered species rather than the benefits that the species receive themselves.[43] Even the interpretations of the ESA that depend upon the law's moral underpinnings frame that morality in utilitarian terms.[44] But Jim Ball posits that other creatures do qualify as our neighbors for purposes of the Great Commandment. Moreover, Ball argues that the protection of the habitat of an endangered species is entitled to legal sanction because it involves "a minimum standard of public justice whose intention is to prevent serious harm."[45] That is the language of nuisance law, thus placing actions necessary to protect the habitat of endangered species outside the property rights protected by current Takings Clause jurisprudence. But Ball argues only that the law should protect endangered species habitat; he does not necessarily oppose government compensation to those whose land must now be managed consistent with such habitat. Indeed, the very claims that Ball relies upon in support of an obligation to protect habitat—God's special concern for the powerless—might also support the compensation of certain landowners. And the premise from which Ball begins— that other creatures qualify as our neighbors for purposes of Jesus' commands— is a plausible but hardly inevitable understanding of the biblical text.

42. *Compare* Matthew 22:39 (teaching of Jesus to love your neighbor as yourself) *with* Restatement (Second) of Torts § 821D (explaining that one engages in a nuisance if he or she interferes with someone else's use and enjoyment of their land).

43. 16 U.S.C. § 1531(a)(3).

44. *See National Ass'n of Home Builders v. Babbitt,* 130 F.3d 1041, 1046–49 (D.C. Cir. 1997) (opinion of Wald, J.) (justifying the ESA as necessary to prohibit the use of interstate commerce for immoral purposes), *cert. denied,* 118 S. Ct. 2340 (1998).

45. Jim Ball, A Christian Defense of Species Protection and Habitat Preservation (1997) (unpublished manuscript on file with the author).

The solution that I find most attractive balances the Christian teaching about wildlife and landownership with the need for even-handed justice in the application of environmental law. Professor William Treanor advocates narrowly focused takings legislation that seeks to compensate those most harshly affected by government regulation. He proposes to compensate landowners when "unanticipated regulations destroy a significant portion of the total assets of a property owner."[46] The three qualifications ensure that someone who was aware of applicable government regulation or who is a repeat player who loses on one investment but gains on others need not be compensated. Compensation is provided, though, to the small landowners who could lose their life's savings, the individuals most deserving of compensation and those whose predicament has informed much of the current debate.

Notice that Treanor does not ground his proposal in specifically Christian commands, nor does this general resolution of the controversy depend upon exclusively Christian principles. It also rests on ideas of the importance of endangered species and the meaning of landownership that some Christians will endorse while others will not. And those ideas are contested among those outside the Christian community, too. The reason I like this approach is that it seeks to simultaneously accommodate the biblical concern about protecting wildlife and preserving species, the practical need to protect habitat, and the general principles of equity and justice that prevent the government from placing a disproportionate burden on any individuals. This may not be the only solution that satisfies all of these desires, but it illustrates how biblical teaching can be applied to one of the more controversial environmental issues of our day.

### The Obligation to Care for Those Most in Need

Christian teaching emphasizes the duty to care for the elderly, the sick, and all of those whose ability to care for themselves is impaired.[47] This idea has numerous applications in the environmental-law context. The recent controversy over the Environmental Protection Agency's Clean Air Act (CAA) particulate standards focuses on this issue. The regulations imposed by the CAA are designed to protect human health. But whose health? It would be possible to draft

46. William Michael Treanor, *The Armstrong Principle, the Narratives of Takings, and Compensation Statutes,* 38 Wm. & Mary. L. Rev. 1151, 1155 (1997).

47. *See, e.g.,* Psalms 72:12–14. For a collection of similar passages, *see* Cry Justice 27–76 (Ronald J. Sider ed., 1980).

regulations that allow the amount of pollution that an average person can tolerate, or that most people could tolerate. The CAA, however, requires that the standard be set according to the lesser tolerance of the most vulnerable groups: children, the elderly, and those suffering from various asthmatic ailments.[48]

Likewise, the presence of a disproportionate number of hazardous waste facilities, landfills, and other environmentally threatening sites in poor communities is of special concern to Christians. The concern is compounded when those communities prove to be the home of racial minorities as well. Such environmental racism—with the concomitant desire for environmental justice—has become one of the leading environmental issues of our time.[49]

The law has not developed as quickly as has the academic literature on the subject. Lawsuits designed to protect poor and minority communities from environmental harms have failed for a variety of reasons.[50] In 1994 President Clinton issued an executive order directing federal agencies to address any disproportionately high adverse environmental impacts of their programs.[51] That order cannot give rise to any rights in court, but it has been invoked in several EPA administrative proceedings. Most recently, EPA Administrator Browner advised Louisiana to reconsider a proposed manufacturing facility because it would be built in an area that is already branded "cancer alley" because of the presence of many refineries and chemical factories.[52] The company decided to build its facility elsewhere, thus saving the community from further pollution but denying it much desired employment as well.

Christians should applaud the attention that is being paid to the effects of

48. *See* William H. Rodgers, Jr., *Environmental Law* 158 (2d ed. 1994).

49. *See generally The Law of Environmental Justice: Theories and Procedures to Address Disproportionate Risks* (Michael B. Gerrard ed., 1999).

50. *See, e.g., Rozar v. Mullis,* 85 F.3d 556 (11th Cir. 1996) (rejecting equal protection and Title VI challenges to the siting of a landfill); *R.I.S.E., Inc. v. Kay,* 768 F. Supp. 1141 (E.D. Va. 1991) (rejecting an equal-protection challenge to the siting of a landfill), *aff'd,* 977 F.2d 573 (4th Cir. 1992). The only lawsuits that have succeeded in the lower courts have identified an implied private cause of action to enforce the prohibition on federal funding of grant applicants that discriminate on the basis of race. *See generally* Bradford C. Mank, *Is There a Private Cause of Action Under EPA's Title VI Regulations? The Need to Empower Environmental Justice Plaintiffs,* 24 Colum. J. Envtl. L. 1, 37–53 (1999) (discussing the cases making this argument).

51. Exec. Order 12898, *reprinted in* 59 Fed. Reg. 7,629 (1994).

52. *See, e.g., EPA Orders Louisiana to Re-Evaluate Controversial Clean Air Permit,* Inside EPA, Sept. 12, 1997, at 16. Note, too, that the area is the subject of John Grisham, *The Pelican Brief* (1992).

pollution on poor and minority communities. Indeed, the Bible commands us to work on behalf of those who lack the resources or ability to protect themselves.[53] Whether the law should take the further step of providing poor communities with special protections against environmentally harmful activities presents a harder question. The Bible does not contain many examples of legal commands that are inapplicable to the poor and oppressed; in fact, some passages explicitly reject such treatment.[54] But the consistent biblical message demands that laws designed to apply equally to all be enforced in such a way that does not favor the wealthy and the powerful. That environmentally harmful landfills and industries are found much more frequently in low-income and minority communities demonstrates that the biblical command to protect the poor and the vulnerable has not been satisfied. Perhaps, then, remedial action to protect those communities from the introduction of further harms would be appropriate.

The modest obligation to "address" these issues that is contained in the environmental justice executive order may offer the wisest approach at this time. It offers a way to try to level the playing field when the concerns of local residents who already confront a disproportionate share of environmental harms are in danger of being overwhelmed by economic development. But it also recognizes that sometimes the local residents are ambivalent themselves. To forbid certain kinds of economic development in poor and minority areas would be to dictate to the residents of those communities that they must not place a higher value on creating more jobs. A legal regime that acknowledges each of these perspectives without prejudging any of them fits well with Christian teachings because it requires the question to be addressed while empowering the affected communities to decide how to answer it.

Christianity has much to say about the environmental challenges that we face in this country and throughout the world today. That message is only now beginning to be heard within the increasingly polarized debate over such issues as the price we should pay for clean air, who should bear the cost of cleaning up hazardous wastes, and how to protect endangered species. The sight of thoughtful Christians reading the same Bible and coming to different conclusions about environmental law could be frustrating, but it should not be sur-

---

53. *See, e.g.,* Proverbs 31:9 (instructing to "defend the rights of the poor and needy").
54. *E.g.,* Exodus 23:3 (commanding "do not show favoritism to a poor man in his lawsuit").

prising in light of disagreements among Christians about all sorts of legal and political issues, nor should it be a cause for concern. It might even be desirable. For above all else, Christianity is about reconciliation. It is foremost about the reconciliation of men and women to God, but it is also about the reconciliation between God and all of the members of His creation. The promise of such reconciliation, and the promise of a day when God will re-create this broken world, provides a message of hope that the current debates over environmental law would do well to hear.

# Can Legal Ethics Be Christian?

*Joseph G. Allegretti*

In 1975 the theologian James Gustafson asked the provocative question, "Can ethics be Christian?"[1] Gustafson did not deny that Christians have been talking and writing about ethics since the time of St. Paul. He did not deny that Christianity has always included a wide range of ethical prescriptions and prohibitions. But, he asked, what is distinctive about Christian ethics? In what way is Christian ethics really Christian, not merely philosophical ethics dressed up in religious garb?

I want to ask an analogous question: can legal ethics (or professional responsibility—I will use the terms interchangeably) be Christian? What can Christianity contribute to our thinking about legal ethics? How will a Christian legal ethics differ from a secular legal ethics?

I will divide my reflections into three parts. First, I will begin by considering whether there is any role at all for religion in legal ethics. Does legal ethics need religion? If so, why? Second, assuming that religion does have a role to play in legal ethics, I will ask the more specific question: is it possible to talk about a Christian legal ethics? If so,

---

1. James M. Gustafson, *Can Ethics Be Christian?* (1975).

what would this mean? Third, I will close with a few conclusions about the relation between Christianity and legal ethics.

## WHY LEGAL ETHICS NEEDS RELIGION

In general, the discipline of legal ethics has developed without strong ties to religion or religious thinking. There are exceptions, particularly the work of law professor Thomas Shaffer, to which I will return. By and large, however, books and articles about legal ethics rarely discuss religion or explore its relevance for legal ethics. Most legal ethics textbooks contain little if any mention of religion or religious ethics. The study of legal ethics is the study of court cases, bar association opinions, a few philosophers such as Kant and Mill, and (especially) the codes of professional responsibility that govern the profession.

What have been the results of approaching legal ethics in this manner? I would argue that there are a number of drawbacks to studying legal ethics divorced from religion. Consider the following.[2]

### Ignoring Religion Overlooks an Important
### Source of Wisdom

Religions such as Christianity deal with questions about the meaning and purpose of human life. They have something to say about the role of law as a restraint on violence and coercion, the duties owed to the secular state, and the relation between justice and love.

As the bioethicist Daniel Callahan has observed, no one can deny that religions "have provided a way of looking at the world and understanding one's life that has a fecundity and a uniqueness not matched by philosophy, law, or political theory."[3] All this is ignored, however, when we exclude religion from the study of legal ethics.

### Ignoring Religion Encourages Legal Ethics to
### Become Legalistic

In his study of the history of bioethics, Callahan notes that the neglect of religion "leaves us too heavily dependent upon the law as the working source of

2. My discussion of the shortcomings of a secularistic legal ethics owes much to an article by Daniel Callahan, a leading bioethicist, in which he points out the defects of an exclusively secular approach to bioethics. Daniel Callahan, *Religion and the Secularization of Bioethics,* 20 Hastings Center Rep. Special Supplement 2 (July–August 1990).

3. *Id.* at 2.

morality. The language of the courts and legislatures becomes our only shared means of discourse."[4]

A similar problem afflicts legal ethics. Legal ethics is usually taught as a subject of substantive law akin to torts and corporations. Students are trained in the interpretation of the various codes of professional responsibility and in the court decisions applying those codes.[5] The focus of the typical legal ethics course is on teaching students the "law of lawyering" that regulates the profession.[6]

This code-based and legalistic approach has its advantages.[7] Rules *are* important and should be taught. At their best, rules give lawyers practical guidance that can help them choose wisely when they confront difficult ethical questions. Furthermore, rules announce the agreed-upon minimums below which a lawyer cannot fall without incurring sanction, and they thereby provide a basis for lawyer accountability.

Rules, however, are only a part of the moral life. The problem with approaching legal ethics as a course in rules is that it tempts us to embrace the illusion that rules constitute the whole of the moral universe. Too often morality and legality are conflated, and anything legal is assumed to be moral. The result is a legal ethics of the bottom line.[8]

In fact, rules ignore many of the most interesting and important issues in legal ethics. Rules cannot tell a lawyer whether a tactic or a strategy that can be employed should be employed. Rules cannot empower a lawyer to be caring or courageous. They provide no guidance at all for the lawyer who is grappling with fundamental questions that the rules ignore—questions like the ends of

4. *Id.* at 4.

5. There are two codes of professional responsibility in widespread use today: the American Bar Association Model Code of Professional Responsibility (1969) and the American Bar Association Model Rules of Professional Conduct (1983). Most states have adopted the Model Rules. For a useful survey of the history of lawyer regulation in America, *see* David Luban and Michael Millemann, *Good Judgment: Ethics Teaching in Dark Times,* 9 Geo. J. Legal Ethics 31 (1995).

6. It is no surprise that the leading treatise on legal ethics is entitled *The Law of Lawyering.* Geoffrey C. Hazard and W. William Hodes, *The Law of Lawyering: A Handbook on the Model Rules of Professional Conduct* (2d ed. 1990, with annual supplements).

7. For an overview of the importance of rules in legal ethics, as well as their limitations, *see* Roger C. Cramton and Susan P. Koniak, *Rule, Story, and Commitment in the Teaching of Legal Ethics,* 38 Wm. & Mary L. Rev. 145 (1996).

8. *See* James Elkins, *Moral Discourse and Legalism in Legal Education,* 32 J. Legal Educ. 11 (1982). The subsequent quotation from Elkins is at 19–20.

lawyering or the morality of violating the rules themselves. As James Elkins reminds us, "Concentration on the minimum requirements imposed on all lawyers obscures the choice of a standard for the individual lawyer, a choice that affects personal integrity, self-image, and human aspiration (the spirit as well as the letter of the law)."

## Ignoring Religion Devalues Questions of Character

When we exclude religion from discussions about legal ethics, we are encouraged to keep our values to ourselves or to hide them beneath a veneer of rationality and supposed impartiality.

Our religious beliefs and values, however, are an integral part of our self-identity. They help to make us who we are.[9] When we exclude religion from legal ethics, we find it exceedingly difficult to address questions of character and virtue. There is a risk that we will end up ignoring the most important things about ourselves—who we are and wish to be, what particular communities and traditions have formed us, how we see our lives played out against the backdrop of eternity. None of this seems relevant to a legalistic legal ethics.

But how can I decide what to do in a particular situation without some prior sense of who I am and who I want to be? As the theologian Stanley Hauerwas observes, "The kinds of quandaries we confront depend on the kind of people we are and the way we have learned to construe the world through our language, habits, and feelings. . . . The question of what I ought to *do* is actually about what I am or ought to be."[10]

As Hauerwas reminds us, our religious convictions are themselves a kind of ethics.[11] For example, when I turn to a particular issue or problem in legal ethics, such as the duties owed by a lawyer to clients or adversaries, I do so with an understanding of myself as a disciple of Christ called to live out the gospel message of love, justice, and reconciliation.[12] That is the starting point for

9. Here I am defining religion broadly, in a way similar to the approach of the theologian Paul Tillich. Tillich conceived of religion as that which concerns us ultimately. He often used the word *faith* to refer to this quality of ultimate concern. *See* Paul Tillich, 1 *Systematic Theology* 11–12 (1951); Paul Tillich, *The New Being* 152–60 (1955); Paul Tillich, *Dynamics of Faith* (n.d.).

10. Stanley Hauerwas, *The Peaceable Kingdom: A Primer in Christian Ethics* 117 (1983).

11. Hauerwas, *supra* note 10, at 16 ("Our convictions embody our morality; our beliefs are our actions").

12. *See, e.g.,* Joseph Allegretti, *Rights, Roles, Relationships: The Wisdom of Solomon and the Ethics of Lawyers,* 25 Creighton L. Rev. 1119 (1992).

my reflections. My character provides the context within which I make my choices.

Furthermore, there are times when the rules authorize lawyers to decide for themselves how to act—the rules, for example, often permit but do not require certain behavior. How can I decide what to do in such a case without first reflecting upon my understanding of myself as a lawyer and a human being? To ignore religion is to risk excluding fundamental questions of character and virtue.

### Ignoring Religion Helps Perpetuate the Status Quo

When we focus too narrowly on ethics as a matter of rules and principles, we tend to perpetuate the status quo. In bioethics, for example, the emphasis on law and rights has led to a "reluctance to question the conventional ends and goals of medicine, thereby running the constant risk of simply legitimating . . . the way things are."[13]

The same is true of legal ethics. When we focus exclusively on codes and cases, we often develop moral tunnel vision; we take the existing structures and values of the legal system and profession for granted and debate how a lawyer should act within the constraints of those structures and values. We spend most of our time tinkering around the edges of the system.[14]

Religion can provide a corrective. Although it may at times sanctify the status quo, at its best religion provides a challenge to the status quo. It forces us to look more deeply at the existing norms of the profession. Christianity, for example, affirms that God is the God of the whole world, even the legal system, and that God stands in judgment over all human institutions, including the legal profession. Religion can bring a countercultural edge to our reflections that might otherwise be lost.

For all these reasons, legal ethics suffers when it adheres too rigidly to a secularistic, legalistic mindset. We need to find a place in legal ethics for religion and religious thinking alongside law and philosophy.

13. Callahan, *supra* note 2, at 4.

14. *See* Charles Kammer, Vocation and the Professions, *in The Annual of the Society of Christian Ethics* 153, 167–68 (Thomas W. Ogletree ed., 1981) ("Codes have limited effect because they are set within the current horizons of law and medicine. These horizons are assumed to be normative and the codes address only issues concerning how a person, practicing within one of the already established professions, should conduct him or herself. What is missing is any attempt to address the adequacy of the structures and values of the existing professions").

I am not alone in this view. For two decades, Thomas Shaffer of Notre Dame Law School has bucked the dominant orthodoxy by bringing an explicitly religious dimension to the study of legal ethics. The titles of two of his many books leave no doubt about his approach: *On Being a Christian and a Lawyer* and *Faith and the Professions.*[15]

For much of his career, Professor Shaffer has been a solitary voice crying in the wilderness. Recently, however, there have been signs of a growing interest in the relation between religion and legal ethics.[16] We may be poised at the brink of a new era in legal ethics in which religion is allowed to play an integral role— not uniquely privileged, to be sure, but not uniquely disadvantaged either.

Even if we agree that religion has a role to play in legal ethics, we are left with the challenge of determining what that role should be. What can religion contribute to legal ethics? Or, to return to Gustafson's question, can there be a legal ethics that is distinctively Christian? What might this mean?

## WHAT CHRISTIANITY CAN CONTRIBUTE TO LEGAL ETHICS

When Gustafson asked "Can ethics be Christian?" his answer was yes, because "religion *qualifies* morality." It does so because "certain action-guiding values and principles can be inferred from religious beliefs as normative for those who share some common Christian experience and reality."[17] I would add that even those who are not Christian may benefit from exploring the ways in which Christian values and principles shed light on ethics in general and legal ethics in particular.

Gustafson identified three ways in which religious beliefs can qualify ethics.[18]

15. Among Shaffer's many writings examining the relation between religious faith, ethics, and lawyering, *See American Lawyers and Their Communities* (with Mary M. Shaffer, 1991); *Faith and the Professions* (1987) [hereinafter *Faith and Professions*]; *American Legal Ethics* (1985); *On Being a Christian and a Lawyer* (1981) [hereinafter *On Being a Christian*]. For a number of commentaries on Shaffer's work, along with comments by Shaffer, *see* 10 J.L. & Religion 277–366 (1993–94).

16. *See, e.g.,* Symposium, *The Relevance of Religion to a Lawyer's Work: An Interfaith Conference,* 66 Fordham L. Rev. 1075 (1998); Symposium, *Faith and the Law,* 27 Texas Tech L. Rev. 911 (1996); *Can a Good Christian Be a Good Lawyer? Homilies, Witnesses, and Reflections* (Thomas A. Baker and Timothy W. Floyd, eds., 1998); Joseph G. Allegretti, *The Lawyer's Calling: Christian Faith and Legal Practice* (1996) [hereinafter *The Lawyer's Calling*].

17. Gustafson, *supra* note 1, at 173.

18. *Id.* at 173–79.

First, religion affects the reasons for being moral. Second, religion affects the character of human agents. Third, religion affects what Gustafson calls the "points of reference" that a person looks to for guidance when confronting a moral problem. Let us consider the significance of each of these elements for the development of a distinctively Christian approach to legal ethics.

### Christianity Affects the Reasons for Acting Ethically

Christians believe that our experience of God requires us to be moral. Our experience of God as Creator, Redeemer, and Sustainer; the feelings of love, gratitude, dependence, repentance, and obligation that this experience of God evokes; our fear of judgment and our hope of salvation—all these give us reasons for acting in a certain way.[19] Ethics is the real-world embodiment of our religious beliefs.

How is this relevant to legal ethics? As a starting point, it reminds us of something so obvious that it deserves repeating. Many lawyers are religious, whether they are conventional churchgoers or not. A goodly percentage of these are Christians. Christian lawyers want not only to obey their profession's codes of conduct but to live in harmony with their own deepest values. They want to live lives of purpose and meaning.

Codes and laws cannot give these lawyers the sustenance they desire. As Allen Verhey and Stephen Lammers note, "Members of religious communities—or many of them, at any rate—want to make [the] choices they face with religious integrity, not just impartial rationality."[20] They want to do what is right, not only what is legal. They want to be faithful to their God.

This may sound abstract, but Gustafson suggests a more concrete way of making the point. Christians believe that they are called to imitate God, especially as God has been revealed in the life, death, and resurrection of Jesus. As God has acted, so should we act: "God seeks justice for the weak and the fatherless; God seeks to maintain the rights of the afflicted and the destitute; God seeks to rescue the weak and the needy; God seeks their deliverance from the hand of the wicked. Go and do likewise. God has met men's [and women's] deepest needs in love; men [and women] thus are to meet the deepest needs of their neighbors in love."[21]

19. *See id.* at 82–116.
20. *Theological Voices in Medical Ethics* 5 (Allen Verhey and Stephen E. Lammers eds., 1993).
21. Gustafson, *supra* note 1, at 116.

The story of Jesus reveals that God's love for human beings knows no bounds. God loves each of us equally and unconditionally. We in turn are called to love one another as God has loved us. Indeed, "the biblical message . . . is that in treating persons we are in an important sense treating God."[22] The story of the Last Judgment in Matthew's Gospel makes the point graphically: "Truly, I tell you, just as you did it to one of the least of these who are my family, you did it to me."[23]

This has important implications for legal ethics. Consider, for a moment, how this way of thinking might influence our relationships with clients. I encounter and serve my God as I encounter and serve my clients. Lawyers and clients are called to form a moral community—a kind of covenant—in which each respects and honors the other as made in the image and likeness of God. My task as a lawyer is not only to give competent legal advice, though that is always required, but to serve as the moral companion of my client, encouraging my client to be the kind of person she can be at her best rather than helping her do what she can get away with at her worst.[24]

In the same way, Christians are committed to justice for the weak and the disenfranchised, not because of the pronouncements of their profession but because of their religious convictions. God is a God of justice and liberation. Jesus himself came to fulfill the words of Isaiah—to preach good news to the poor, release to the captives, sight to the blind, and liberty for the oppressed.[25] Can we who are his disciples do otherwise?

### Christianity Shapes Character

The exclusion of religion from legal ethics tempts us to ignore questions of character and virtue. A typical law school textbook in legal ethics consists primarily of a series of legal cases or hypothetical problems. Class discussion typically focuses on what a lawyer should do in various situations: Can a lawyer do this? Should she do that? What do the codes and courts require or permit her to do?

This emphasis on rules and cases is not all bad. Christian ethics is not anti-

22. Hessel Bouma III et al., *Christian Faith, Health, and Medical Practice* 58 (1989).

23. Matthew 25:40. All Biblical citations and quotations are from the New Revised Standard Version.

24. I discuss this model of the lawyer-client relationship in more detail in Joseph Allegretti, *Lawyers, Clients, and Covenant: A Religious Perspective on Legal Practice and Ethics*, 66 Fordham L. Rev. 1101 (1998).

25. Luke 4:18–19.

nomian, and a Christian approach to legal ethics should not ignore the importance of rules in providing guidance and accountability for lawyers. Indeed, Christian lawyers may feel an obligation to participate in the drafting and enforcement of legal ethics rules to ensure that the rules promote (or, at the very least, do not undermine) the gospel values of respect for persons, equal rights for the poor and the rich, and justice as a matter of substance as well as procedure. Certainly, Christian lawyers should not hesitate to voice their criticism of legal-ethics rules that serve the narrow self-interest of the legal profession rather than the common good of society.

A Christian perspective on legal ethics, however, necessarily transcends a narrow concern for rules and regulations. Issues of character cannot be ignored. The Christian experience of God has consequences for the kind of persons we become. Our religious values shape our character; certain virtues, certain dispositions, ensue.

A person nurtured by the Christian story will see the world in a distinctive way. As Bruce Birch and Larry Rasmussen explain: "What all good stories do is draw us into their world. And what powerful stories, like the Jesus story, do is mold people's identities and their sense of the world and reality. Powerful stories create a basic orientation for those who are drawn into them. They foster and hone sensitivities. They help form commitments and convictions. They yield insight, and inspire. They create and shape virtue, value, vision, and obligation. And not least, they solicit our involvement—we want to hear more! All this creates a certain framework for decision making."[26]

What is distinctive about the character of Christians is *not* that we are formed and shaped by stories and traditions but that we are formed and shaped by the particular stories and traditions of Israel, Jesus, and the Christian church. As Gustafson says, "The sort of persons Christians ought to become is informed and influenced (that is, qualified) by the Christian story."[27]

### A Turn Toward Narrative

What are the implications for legal ethics? Perhaps most importantly, the Christian focus on character and story invites us to shift the emphasis away from rules and problems to broader questions of personhood and virtue.

26. Bruce C. Birch and Larry L. Rasmussen, *Bible & Ethics in the Christian Life* 106–7 (revised and expanded ed., 1989).

27. Gustafson, *supra* note 1, at 176.

The use of narrative in teaching legal ethics is often associated with the work of Thomas Shaffer.[28] For Shaffer, stories provide the best avenue for addressing questions of the moral life. Stories come before principles and rules. As Shaffer explains: "Our stories are the sources of our moral notions and our moral notions are prior, in time and logic, to our classifications, our categories, and our principles. . . . To put that another way, a moral notion becomes something we see and can talk about because of a story. A moral notion is displayed and understood in a narrative context better than it is displayed and understood in a context of issues, quandaries, decisions, acts and principles."[29]

Stories enflesh and make real the cold hard facts of a moral problem or dilemma. They help us to understand—in a way that codes and case law cannot—why a person does what she does, at what cost, and for what reasons. A legal ethics grounded in narrative will encourage students to probe the meaning of their lives, to examine the forces that have shaped them into the persons they are, and to confront the question of who they want to be as lawyers and as human beings.

Underlying all this, of course, is the story of Jesus. If we ask what kind of person a Christian should be, we naturally point to Jesus. Be like Jesus, and be like those who have followed Jesus through the centuries. Hauerwas puts it simply: "Christian ethics is not first of all an ethics of principles, laws, or values, but an ethic that demands that we attend to the life of a particular individual—Jesus of Nazareth."[30]

This does not mean that Christians must slavishly imitate the particulars of Jesus' life, but that we should seek to embody in our lives the same openness to God and loving self-sacrifice that marked his life. The humility, the compassion, the commitment to justice and to the outcast, the radical devotion to the God of Israel, the courage to challenge those in authority and deflate the pretensions of all worldly powers, the willingness to trust in a God who brings life from death and resurrection from a cross—these are hallmarks of the character of persons molded by the story and traditions of the Jesus we call the Christ.

If we take the story of Jesus seriously, we must admit that our character and values may put us into conflict with the norms and values of the wider community, including the legal profession. As Christians we may find ourselves em-

28. *See* note 15, *supra.* Shaffer's use of narrative is examined in Leslie E. Gerber, *Can Lawyers Be Saved? The Theological Legal Ethics of Thomas Shaffer,* 10 J.L. & Religion 347, 353–54 (1993–94).

29. Shaffer, *Faith and Professions, supra* note 15, at 14.

30. Hauerwas, *supra* note 10, at 75–76.

bodying values that are in tension with or contrary to the prevailing professional notions of what constitutes a "good lawyer."

For example, many would argue that a "good lawyer" is one who serves her client alone, regardless of the consequences for other people. The Christian lawyer, however, will try to balance her duties as a zealous advocate with her obligations to other people and to society at large. Consider a divorce case. A "good lawyer" is expected to fight vigorously for her client's right to custody of the children. But what if the client is a bad or an abusive parent? The Christian lawyer cannot ignore the wishes and interests of the children whose well-being is at stake. Or consider a corporation that is engaged in an activity that is legal but harmful to society. The "good lawyer" is free to devote herself unreservedly to her client's interests, but the Christian lawyer must also consider the injury being done to the common good.

More generally, the legal profession and legal system may foster an amorality and disregard for the consequences of our actions that are inconsistent with the Christian vocation to follow God in all things.[31] For a person shaped by the stories of Jesus, this is no small matter. I would agree with Shaffer that a Christian approach to legal ethics must not shy away from confronting the one question that most of us would prefer to ignore: *Can a Christian be a lawyer?*[32] By holding that question open, by facing it anew each and every day, we acknowledge that the gospel stands in judgment over all human institutions, and that the Christian lawyer is called to be a Christian first and a lawyer second.

How might these characteristics of a character-based, narrative-based ethics be given reality in a legal ethics course? Let me provide one example of how stories can be used to focus attention on character rather than rules.

I often have my students read and compare the lives of two lawyers: Ivan Ilyich, from Leo Tolstoy's *The Death of Ivan Ilyich,* and Thomas More, as we meet him in Robert Bolt's play *A Man for All Seasons.*[33] As we attend to these stories, we learn something of what it means to be a lawyer and a person of faith.

Ilyich is an agreeable man and an agreeable lawyer, but he is a person and a

31. The classic treatment of the alleged amorality of lawyers is Richard Wasserstrom, *Lawyers as Professionals: Some Moral Issues,* 5 Hum. Rts. 1 (1975).

32. Shaffer, *On Being a Christian, supra* note 15, at 32.

33. Leo Tolstoy, *The Cossacks, Happy Ever After, The Death of Ivan Ilyich* (Rosemary Edmonds trans., 1960); Robert Bolt, *A Man for All Seasons* (Vintage Int'l ed., 1990). An analysis and comparison of these stories appears in Allegretti, *The Lawyer's Calling, supra* note 16, at 110–24.

lawyer with little sense of himself as a moral agent. He stands for nothing, cares for nothing, and wants only to be successful and respected by his peers and social superiors. *There's no there there.* And so . . . Ivan ends up wasting his life. Only on his deathbed does he realize that he has failed to live the life he should have.

In contrast, More is a man with an "adamantine sense of his own self."[34] He desires success, as did Ilyich, but he does not covet success at any cost. He is willing to compromise and to serve his king, but at the same time he knows that "there is a little . . . little area . . . where I must rule myself." More puts first things first. He realizes that his loyalty to his king, his profession, his job, his family—all these are important, but not as important as his loyalty to God. God comes first, and More is willing to go to his death rather than betray the one true God whom he loves and serves.

These stories invite us to consider where we place our own loyalties. There are many gods who demand our worship. Some are disguised as country, money, or altruism. Sometimes it is our client, profession, or system of justice that we turn into gods. More's life, and Ivan Ilyich's in contrast, ask us to ponder our own lives, character, and choices. What do I put first? What do I worship? Whom do I serve?

By focusing upon character and virtue, rather than solely upon rules and principles, I hope to encourage my students (and myself) to engage the study of legal ethics at a deeper, more personal, and ultimately more satisfying level. A Christian approach to legal ethics does not avoid the most basic of questions: who am I and who am I called to be?

### Christianity Provides Distinctive Points of Reference to Guide Moral Choices

As Gustafson observes, Christianity provides us with certain points of reference that can help us make moral choices. Certain key symbols and theological concepts are used to interpret the moral significance of events and to help believers discern what God is enabling and requiring them to do.[35] Once again, the role of Jesus is paramount, for he is the best indicator of who God is and who God calls us to be.

In short, certain principles and values can be inferred from the Christian story, and especially from the story of Jesus. These should guide the Christian

---

34. Bolt, *supra* note 33, at xii. The subsequent quotation from Bolt appears at 59.
35. Gustafson, *supra* note 1, at 176–78.

who is facing a moral decision. Gustafson explains: "For those for whom there is a compelling clarity to the experience of God through the scriptures and Jesus, it is worthwhile to infer rationally the principles and values that would direct a 'way of life' that is grounded in Jesus and the scriptures. Those for whom Jesus has this authority ought to be guided by certain moral principles and values in their actions."[36]

These principles and values do not eliminate the need for moral reflection, but they do provide a starting point, as well as a kind of trajectory, for our moral deliberations. There are broad themes in Scripture, for example, that do not give unequivocal answers to the ethical issues facing lawyers but that do suggest the attitudes and perspectives that should guide the Christian lawyer.

Sometimes, of course, Christians disagree on what these central themes and principles are (or they agree on the themes but disagree on how to apply them). Nevertheless, there would be broad agreement on many of these core values and principles. The centrality of love, for example. Respect for creation. Service to those who are less fortunate. A commitment to peace, justice, and liberation. The need for repentance. The willingness to forgive as we are forgiven.

How do these basic Christian themes and values influence my own approach to legal ethics? As one example, consider the Sermon on the Mount, where Jesus enjoins his followers not to resist evildoers, even if they are dragged into court: "You have heard that it was said, 'An eye for an eye and a tooth for a tooth.' But I say to you, Do not resist an evildoer. But if anyone strikes you on the right cheek, turn the other also; and if anyone wants to sue you and take your coat, give your cloak as well; and if anyone forces you to go one mile, go also the second mile. . . . You have heard that it was said, 'You shall love your neighbor and hate your enemy.' But I say to you, Love your enemies, and pray for those who persecute you."[37]

I do not pretend that lawyers or anyone else can live this out perfectly in their personal or professional lives. I think of the Sermon on the Mount in the way that Reinhold Niebuhr did—as an impossible possibility.[38] No finite and sinful human being will ever love as selflessly or as sacrificially as Jesus teaches. Lawyers cannot help but fall short of the ideal in their treatment of clients and adversaries.

But that does not mean that we can ignore the Sermon on the Mount, how-

36. *Id.* at 162.

37. Matthew 5:38–44.

38. *See* Reinhold Niebuhr, *An Interpretation of Christian Ethics* (1935) (especially chapters 2–4).

ever much we would like to forget it and get on with our everyday lives. Although Jesus' ethic of total love is impossible for us to fulfill, it remains relevant to our daily life, for it always judges us and challenges us. We can always approximate the Sermon more fully in our lives, even if we can never live up to it completely.

As a Christian, I am called to live out the Sermon on the Mount. As a Christian lawyer, I am called to do so, too. There is no exception for lawyers, advocates, or trials. The Sermon on the Mount provides an orientation for my thinking, a moral bias in favor of reconciliation, peacemaking, and love of enemies.

This has certain necessary implications for the way I envision the role of the lawyer in litigation.[39] I believe that as a Christian I should be slow to sue and slow to encourage others to sue. I believe that an important part of my professional duty is to help my clients "count the costs" of litigation—not only the economic costs, but the psychological, emotional, and moral costs as well. I believe that I should actively explore with my client such alternatives to litigation as mediation and arbitration. Furthermore, even in the midst of a trial, I should do whatever I can to extinguish the flames of bitterness and hatred, not fan them. Even though litigation is often justified, it remains a form of state-sanctioned coercion, and I should try to restrain its force, not give it full rein to devastate the lives of litigants, lawyers, and third parties.

The Sermon on the Mount is not the end of my ethical reflection, but the beginning. It provides a presumption—to use legal terminology, which seems appropriate—in favor of reconciliation and against litigation and "hardball" tactics.

Consider a second example.[40] There is currently a vigorous debate within the legal profession about the extent to which lawyers and the profession have a moral duty to provide uncompensated legal assistance to the poor. Usually, the *pro bono* debate is treated as another proposed regulation of lawyers, and the discussion focuses on technical, legalistic questions: Is mandatory *pro bono* akin to slavery, as critics hyperbolically claim, or is it a natural correlate of belonging to a learned profession that is afforded substantial autonomy and status in society? If *pro bono* is made mandatory, how will the duty be enforced? How many hours will a lawyer be required to donate each year? The questions proliferate as

39. These themes are developed in more detail in Allegretti, *The Lawyer's Calling, supra* note 16, at 81–109.

40. *See* Allegretti, *The Lawyer's Calling, supra* note 16, at 60–63.

lawyers turn their fertile, disputatious minds to the problem. Often the underlying question of the lawyer's duty to serve is lost amid the endless debates about the what and the how of any proposed plan.

But what if we approach the issue from a different perspective? What if we begin with the story of Jesus, who came to bring good news to the poor, release to the captives, and freedom to the oppressed?[41] What if we ponder the words of Jesus at the Last Judgment, where he says that each of us will be judged by how we have treated the hungry, the thirsty, the naked, the stranger, and the prisoner? What if we consider as well the teachings of the Hebrew prophets— Amos, Isaiah, Jeremiah, and the rest—who insist that God demands not pious rituals but lives dedicated to justice for the poor and the outcast? Doesn't Isaiah exhort us to "cease to do evil, learn to do good; seek justice, rescue the oppressed, defend the orphan, plead for the widow?" Doesn't Jeremiah proclaim that to know God is to do justice to the poor and the needy?

To approach the question of *pro bono* in this way is to see it in a new light. For the lawyer who seeks to live out her Christian faith, *pro bono* can never be a matter of philanthropy alone. It is not something extra that we do in addition to our other more important and more lucrative work. It is what God expects, what God demands. To repeat Jeremiah's challenge: If we want to know God, we must do justice to the poor and the needy.

This does not resolve all questions about the duty of *pro bono*. Lawyers will still disagree about whether the duty should be made mandatory through rules of professional conduct, or left to each individual lawyer to decide. Lawyers will still disagree about the extent of the duty, how it should be structured, and so on.

But our Christian faith provides a trajectory for our thinking about the issue. Each of us, in our own way, regardless of what the profession requires us to do, should use our legal talents—our God-given gifts—to serve the poor and bring justice to the oppressed. This entails some sort of legal work for the needy.

When we examine the possible relation between Christianity and legal ethics, we must guard against two fundamental and opposing errors. First, we must avoid the simplistic assumption that we can interpret the Christian faith tradition in a way that will give us clear and unambiguous answers to the myriad ethical problems that arise in the practice of law. Second, we must not rush to

41. Luke 4:18–19. The subsequent scriptural references in this paragraph are to Matthew 25:31–46 (Last Judgment); Isaiah 1:16–17; Jeremiah 22:15–16.

the other extreme and conclude that Christianity has nothing to contribute to busy lawyers wrestling with ethical questions in their work.

What we have seen, instead, is that Christianity does exert an important influence upon legal ethics. Christianity gives us reasons to be moral, it shapes our character in distinctive ways, and it engenders certain basic values and principles that can guide our moral choices.

For all these reasons, we must agree with Gustafson. Can legal ethics be Christian? Yes, it can—and it should be, for those who see themselves as disciples of Christ, who want to be not only lawyers who happen to be Christian but Christian lawyers.

There is one final point that needs to be considered. In the minds of some, doing legal ethics from a religious perspective smacks of indoctrination. Won't the legal ethics teacher who seeks to bring a faith perspective to her work end up "preaching" rather than "teaching"? Won't she, subtly or not so subtly, try to impose her values upon her students, many of whom are not Christian or are not interested in bringing a Christian perspective to the subject?

I must admit that I am far less worried about the risk of indoctrination than I was when I began teaching. For one thing, I find my law students unwilling to accept anything I say on blind faith. More important, most of my students come to legal ethics already imbued with the pragmatic, positivistic, and relativistic mindset of the law school, what Roger Cramton has called "the ordinary religion of the law school."[42] My job is not to indoctrinate my students but to remind them that the accepted view of law and lawyering as value neutral and unconcerned with morality is itself a pervasive and powerful form of indoctrination.

All teaching comes packaged in a worldview. My task is to be clear about where I am coming from, explain the reasons why I feel as I do, and respect those who think differently. Often I make the pragmatic judgment to translate my faith values into secular language, depending upon the occasion and the audience. This is not a "selling out" of my values but an expression of respect for my students and a recognition that God speaks to each of us through the prism of our own history, experiences, traditions, and values.

In the end, the most important thing that I can do for my students is not to teach them the law of lawyering, or to teach them anything at all, but to model

42. Roger C. Cramton, *The Ordinary Religion of the Law School Classroom*, 29 J. Legal Educ. 247 (1978).

for them the kind of person and lawyer that I am called to be as a disciple of Jesus.[43] What does God require of me, or you, or any Christian? Simply this: to do justice, love mercy, and walk humbly with our God.[44] As long as we keep this in mind, and keep before us the example and inspiration of Jesus, our legal ethics will be Christian.[45]

43. James Gordon makes this point well: "A faithful faculty member shows her students in a concrete way that the integration of intellect and faith is possible, and she proves it with evidence no less convincing than the power of her own life." James D. Gordon III, *The Importance of Religiously Affiliated Law Schools,* 37 Cath. Law. 183, 186 (1996).

44. Micah 6:8.

45. The author gratefully acknowledges the assistance of Creighton law student Tricia O'Hare, class of 1998. The author wishes to thank Bob Cochran for his advice and suggestions.

# A Historical Perspective on Anglo-American Contract Law

*C. M. A. Mc Cauliff*

The law of contracts might hardly appear to be a prime candidate for an expression of Christian beliefs and attitudes. For Christians, however, faith is relevant to all aspects of life, including economic relations. The Christian tradition demands that contract law, like all law in society, be viewed from the focal point of justice. Justice in this tradition is a complex tapestry of principles woven from many historical periods—classical antiquity, medieval Christendom, the Reformation, the Enlightenment, and our own period. At a minimum, however, it demands that the parties to a contract, as well as the society in which their contract takes place, receive what is due.[1]

Many who place themselves within the Christian tradition use a natural-law approach and find in the concept of justice a connection between law and an objective morality.[2] The long history of contracts,

1. The author wishes to thank Harold J. Berman, Mitu Gulati, Joseph M. Perillo, George W. Conk, Marianne Calabrese, and Peter D. Post for their gracious suggestions and comments.
2. According to natural-law theory, which had a basis in Christian theology and Aristotelian philosophy, "human law derived ultimately from, and was to be

which deals with keeping promises and performing obligations, provides examples of Christian judges whose opinions can be analyzed in accordance with principles of Christian morality within the natural-law tradition. This commentary will concentrate mainly on two British jurists, Lord Mansfield, who lived in an age of waning faith during the eighteenth century, and Lord Denning, who lived in our own age of religious pluralism and multiculturalism. The opinions of these two judges frame the nineteenth century. During that time, the long Christian tradition based on natural law grew less influential as positivism in law and materialism in society came to dominate legal thinking. Nevertheless, these two judges applied timeless Christian values to particular legal problems and provided powerful solutions to the important legal questions of their day. Lord Denning, who used explicitly Christian language in his writings, considered justice primarily an application of the commandment to love one's neighbor. He said that "precepts of religion" had become a habit of mind for English judges over the centuries and therefore "the guide to the administration of justice." It was significant to him that "the common law of England has been moulded for centuries by judges who have been brought up in the Christian faith."[3] In their particular Christian appropriation of the natural-law tradition, these judges sought to give each one what is due under the circumstances, in accordance with the natural-law concept of commutative justice.

As a positive notion, law refers to rules promulgated by duly constituted governmental bodies, without intrinsic moral or normative content. Under a positivist view contracts might reflect whatever values the parties seek to pursue. Thus in a commercial setting the parties might seek profit without regard to other values. In contrast, justice reflects a moral measure of the law in question by putting profit into the context of a contractual relation that reflects good faith and fair exchange. Justice demands a sense of fairness both for the parties in question and for society as a whole. Although fairness does not mean exactly the same thing to every lawyer exercising practical reasoning and analysis, the natural-law tradition was comfortable with a range of circumstances roughly providing what is due in each case. This sense of commutative justice maintains

---

tested ultimately by, reason and conscience." *See also* Lon L. Fuller, *The Morality of Law* (1964).

3. Alfred Thompson Denning, *The Changing Law* 109 (1953). When he died on March 6, 1999, Lord Denning was the oldest peer in England, having retired as Master of the Rolls in 1982.

balance between contracting parties in such commercial relationships as sales, loans, and leases through the voluntary exchange of goods of equal value.[4]

Several contract doctrines reflect the passion for justice that Christianity demands. The theories of contract liability, including reliance, benefit conferred, and bargain, as well as several doctrines designed to moderate the sometimes harsh rigor of contract formation, such as duress and mistake, commend themselves to Christians.[5] Even damage rules may serve this function of not permitting one party to take unfair advantage of another, when, for example, the price of a commodity changes after the contract is made. Concern for the poor in the Judaeo-Christian tradition is reflected in scrutiny of contracts of adhesion and in prohibition of usurious interest rates in consumer contracts.[6] The requirement of bargaining in good faith and principles of restitution round off an equitable approach to contracts. I shall tie these aspects of contract jurisprudence to Christian beliefs and to the timeless concerns of justice and natural law we inherited in a Christianized form through Thomas Aquinas from Aristotle and those who came before him.[7]

## THE DEVELOPMENT OF MODERN
## CONTRACT LAW

Modern contract law gradually began to be formed from Christian principles in the late eleventh and the early twelfth centuries throughout Europe, though

4. Aristotle, *Nicomachean Ethics* V.ii 1130b *in Introduction to Aristotle* (Richard McKeon ed., 1947). The damage rules comport with considerations of justice. For example, both Aristotle, *Nicomachean Ethics,* IV.vii 1127a–1127b, and Thomas Aquinas, *Summa Theologiae* II-II, q. 88, a. 3 found it wrong simply to break a promise. *See also* Anthony J. Lisska, *Aquinas's Theory of Natural Law* 5 (1996), *Nicomachean Ethics, supra,* V, 1130b–1133b.

5. Harold J. Berman, The Religious Sources of General Contract Law *in Faith and Order: The Reconciliation of Law and Religion* 186, 194 (1993), describes the moral theory of contract law in a decalogue of canonists' principles from the enforcement of agreements without formalities if the purpose was reasonable and equitable to the nonenforcement of unconscionable contracts, citing Johannes Barmann, *Pacta sunt servanda: Consideration sur l'histoire du contrat consensual,* 13 Revue internationale de droit compare 18–25 (1961).

6. Friedrich Kessler, *Contracts of Adhesion: Some Thoughts about Freedom of Contract,* 43 Colum. L. Rev. 629 (1943); John T. Noonan, Jr., *The Scholastic Analysis of Usury* (1957) and Raymond De Roover, *The Concept of the Just Price: Theory and Economic Policy,* 18 J. Econ. Hist. 418 (1958) deal with medieval just-price theory.

7. *See* Stephen A. Siegel, *The Aristotelian Basis of English Law: 1450–1800,* 56 N.Y.U.L. Rev. 18 (1981); James R. Gordley, *Review of Grant Gilmore, The Death of Contract,* 89 Harv. L. Rev. 452 (1975).

of course contracts and contract law existed long before that both in Christian and other traditions. In England, Bracton represents the trained, administrative judge with systematic knowledge whose insights from Roman law were simply second nature. Bracton's generation of lawyers and judges had a familiarity with Roman law, took a natural-law approach, and saw "problems as a whole and made solutions work."[8] By the fifteenth century, royal courts accepted contract cases through writs, ecclesiastical courts applied Roman principles through canon law, county and local courts applied customary law, and the chancery (usually headed by clerics) used broad Christian principles to fashion equitable results. All these courts operated side by side in medieval England.[9] This remained so until the law-reform era during the puritan revolution of the seventeenth century, which abolished all but the common-law courts and the chancery. Matters formerly heard in ecclesiastical courts came under the jurisdiction of the common law.[10] Between the medieval period, which indirectly reflected the natural-law analysis of life common to Western societies at that time, and the nineteenth-century positivism of John Austin, came the period of Christian Reformation, when many natural-law doctrines were reworked. This reworking brought about a transformation in the approach toward contracts throughout Europe.[11]

Those who reformed the Christian religion also reformed law, and contract law changed from its medieval, moral basis in just performance to a new foundation in bargain, which the reformers treated from the moral perspective of the decision to make a bargain. In a deft portrayal of the changes in commercial attitude in seventeenth-century Puritan England, Harold Berman shows that the law shifted its focus from the moral wrong of the defaulting promisor to "the binding character" of the agreement and the rightful expectations of the promisee. To the Puritans, freedom of contract meant choosing whether to contract, but once the contract was made, the parties became absolutely bound

8. S. F. C. Milsom, *Historical Foundations of the Common Law* 41–42 (1981).

9. Berman, *supra* note 5, at 196–97. The chancery's jurisdiction was designed to serve the poor and incompetent, enforce fiduciary obligations (trusts), and grant personal remedies of specific performance and injunctions. For more extensive treatment of these areas, *see* John H. Baker, *An Introduction to English Legal History* 44–154, 360–426 (3d ed. 1990).

10. Contracts had generally been actionable at common law, but ecclesiastical courts had jurisdiction over litigation for breach of faith. Richard H. Helmholz, *Assumpsit and Fidei Laesio*, 91 Law Q. Rev. 406 (1975).

11. James Gordley, *The Philosophical Origins of Modern Contract Doctrine* 68–133 (1991).

so that the entire focus was on the bargain itself.[12] Puritan religion arose from a conception of God as the God of rules and order and from the willingness of the people to enter into a covenant with that God for a certain result, thus demonstrating that their faith had saved them.[13] This conception of God was harsher and more exacting than the forgiving, loving God of the medieval world. Nevertheless, the Puritans shared the biblical recognition that God is faithful and keeps His bargains. Emphasizing the literal theological meaning of a covenant between God and the people, Professor Berman shows that in Puritan theory, breaking a contract leads to war and chaos, as the English Civil War during the 1640s was interpreted in their theory.

When Christianity was widely accepted, contract law reflected Christian values both implicitly and explicitly, and judges applied these values in cases adjusting the rights of contracting parties. Between the seventeenth and twentieth centuries, contract liabilities were reshaped in accordance with the changes in philosophy to meet religious, social, and economic circumstances. During this time, "the authority of Aristotle was challenged and ultimately destroyed by the founders of modern critical philosophy. One of the casualties was his theory of distributive and commutative justice. . . . When modern philosophers rejected Aristotle's conception of human nature, they pulled out the prop that supported his ideas about just distribution of wealth and equality in exchange."[14] Thus the Aristotelian virtue of keeping faith was disregarded. Under the tutelage of Jeremy Bentham, the merchants realized that they could use Parliament to make laws suited to their need for allocating and controlling their risk and liability from contracts.[15] When the Puritan religious foundation for the covenant was no longer socially compelling, the idea of the individual's free will remained to expand and fill the conceptual void without the Christian content.

Thus the secular concept of freedom of contract, based on individual autonomy, isolated these economic relations from moral understanding and social relations. The secularized idea of contract became nothing more than market efficiency, stripped of other connotations. Although the efficiency of markets

12. Berman, *supra* note 5, at 201–5, citing John Witte, Jr., *Blest Be the Ties that Bind: Covenant and Community in Puritan Thought,* 36 Emory L. J. 579, 595 (1987).

13. Christopher Hill, *The Century of Revolution, 1603–1714,* 80–86 (1961).

14. James Gordley, *Enforcing Promises,* 82 Cal. L. Rev. 547, 556 (1995). *See also* James Gordley, Natural Law Origins of the Common Law of Contract, *Towards a General Law of Contract* 367, 420, 463.

15. Patrick S. Atiyah, *Rise and Fall of Freedom of Contract* 342 (1979).

was good commercially as an engine of wealth creation and of good-faith business relations, it received such exaggerated status during the nineteenth century that it prevented other models from receiving adequate recognition.

In spite of this increasing separation of contract from moral considerations over the centuries, the traditional natural-law notions and concerns of justice continued to resonate in moral conscience and in parties' basic sense of what is right. Chief Justice of the King's Bench Lord Mansfield, who received a Christian education at the Westminster School in London, gave his decisions at a time when commutative justice was being forgotten in the clear simplicity of the morals of the marketplace.[16] Mansfield nevertheless retained the old virtues of justice and moral conscience, which he expressed in the new context of merchants' needs and the new philosophy emphasizing the will of the parties to a contract. Although in many instances Lord Mansfield brought the customs of merchants within the purview of the common law, he adhered to the requirements of justice informing merchants' transactions. Translating the timeless value of justice into the contemporary commercial situation, his commercial decisions exercised profound influence on Anglo-American law. From the beginning, Mansfield appealed to "Justice and Truth."[17] In *Moses v. Macferlan,* Mansfield balanced justice for the parties and justice for the society in which the parties made their contract. *Moses* was an action to recover money on a theory of unjust enrichment arising from "the ties of natural justice" and equity. Mansfield's holding provided for restitution on this fact pattern. According to Mansfield, law had to take account of morality, and laws that deterred people from taking unjust advantage of others were "very beneficial, and therefore much encouraged."[18] Moral obligation was the hallmark of Mansfield's jurisprudence.[19]

Mansfield's moral-obligation cases centered on three qualities: "an affirma-

16. 1 James Oldham, *The Mansfield Manuscripts and the Growth of English Law in the Eighteenth Century* 8–9 (1992).

17. *Windham v. Chetwynd,* (1757) 1 W.Bl. 95, 97 Eng. Rep. 377, 387 (K.B.).

18. *Moses v. Macferlan* (1760) 2 Burr. 1005, 1010, 97 Eng. Rep. 676, 680 (K.B.). Peter Birks, *English and Roman Learning in Moses v. Macferlan,* 37 Curr. Legal Probs. 1 (1984).

19. In *Hawkes v. Saunders,* (1782) 1 Cowp. 289, 290, 98 Eng. Rep. 1091 (K.B.), Lord Mansfield stated that when a party "is under a legal or equitable obligation to pay, the law implies a promise, though none was ever actually made. A Fortiori, a legal or equitable duty is a sufficient consideration for an actual promise." Mansfield equated moral obligation and consideration for purposes of validating a contract, stating that "under a moral obligation, which no court of law or equity can enforce," a promise will be deemed to have consideration from "the honesty and rectitude" of the situation.

tion of a prior moral duty, a promise supported by consideration grounded in
conscience, and a promise that was enforceable in chancery when specific relief
was available."[20] According to Sir David Parry, in the eighteenth century,
"moral obligation was regarded as the primary factor making promises enforceable"; the general climate still favored freedom of contract with the Puritan religious connotation that if the parties freely entered into a contract, it was enforceable and not lightly to be rejected or to have damages substituted for
actual performance.[21] The example Mansfield provided gave guidance to his
immediate contemporaries before a reaction against Mansfield's views set in
and—after the long period of this reaction passed—to later generations as
well.[22]

As jurists in the eighteenth and nineteenth centuries moved away from
Mansfield's focus on moral obligation, the bargained-for-exchange theory grew
stronger. In that theory, past consideration is deemed inadequate to trigger
contract liability, and Mansfield's moral obligation is irrelevant to the strong
bargainer. If one party acts prior to the exchange of considerations, then no
contract liability exists. Because no consideration may be given until after the
exchange of promises, it is easier to determine contract liability. The bargained-
for-exchange theory allows the parties to contract for anything to which the
parties willingly give their mutual assent.

"Enlightenment faith," according to Professor Berman, "found expression,
in nineteenth-century contract law, in the overriding principles of freedom of
will and party autonomy." Nineteenth-century jurists "cut the general law of
contract loose from its moorings in a religious—more specifically, a Christian—belief system."[23] In the nineteenth century, the philosophy underlying
contract liability was positivism, a set of principles that did not seek to conform
the law to morality as commutative justice. The professed aim of positivism
was to ascertain the law as a matter of fact without worry about whether the law

20. Kevin M. Teeven, *Mansfield's Reform of Consideration in Light of the Origins of the Doc-trine,* 21 Mem. St. U.L. Rev. 669, 693 (1991). For more on Lord Mansfield's concept of fair-ness, *see* James Oldham, *Reinterpretations of 18th Century English Contract Theory,* 76 Geo. L.J. 1949–91 (1988), and C. M. A. Mc Cauliff, *A Theme of Fairness Revisited: Lord Mansfield's Legacy for a Holistic Theory of Contract Today* in 17 Denning L.J. 67–91 (2000).

21. David H. Parry, *The Sanctity of Contracts in English Law* 51 (1959).

22. *See, e.g., Rann v. Hughes,* (1778) 7 T.R. 350, 101 Eng. Rep. 1014 (H.L.) (overruling Lord Mansfield's view of consideration in *Pillans v. Van Mierop* (1765), 3 Burr. 1663).

23. Berman, *supra* note 5, at 190. *See also* Owen Chadwick, *The Secularization of the Euro-pean Mind in the Nineteenth Century* (1975).

is just.[24] Under positivism the view of contract as merely a bargained-for exchange of promises triumphed. Government reflected the merchants' concerns by narrowing liability to help protect merchants and limiting contractual liability to the bargain theory. In the bargained-for-exchange theory, the negotiated exchange of promises creates expectations among parties. With the exchange of promises, the parties know exactly what they are supposed to receive under the contract. Only when that expectation is not met is liability triggered. This narrow version of contract liability facilitated business during the uncertain conditions of early industrialization. The development of the bargain theory of contracts reflected the political theory of an individualist period in which fairness arguably played a less important role. The bargain notion was designed to set an artificially narrow range of contract liability.

Much of the wider Christian context in society was gone by the time Lord Denning, a strong Christian, achieved prominence after World War II; he looked back to Lord Mansfield for inspiration as a judge.[25] Lord Denning powerfully asserted that Christian morality informs the doctrines of English common law.[26] I was present at a lay sermon he preached about Christian morality as the foundation of English law. This struck me deeply because although I had not yet gone to law school, I knew that the constitutional separation of church and state would probably mean a judge in the United States would not have said that.[27] When soon thereafter I went to law school in the United States, I never forgot that in order to be just, the laws must reflect morality. I thought often about that sermon as I studied contracts and business associations and in my own teaching have often related the reasoning and results in cases to a moral understanding of the law.

24. *See* H. L. A. Hart, *Positivism and the Separation of Law and Morals,* 71 Harv. L. Rev. 593 (1958); Frank S. Alexander, *Beyond Positivism: A Theological Perspective,* 20 Ga. L. Rev. 1089 (1986); David Lyons, *The Connection Between Law and Morality,* 36 J. Legal Educ. 485 (1986).

25. Alfred T. Denning, *The Way of an Iconoclast,* 5 J. Soc'y Pub. Teachers of Law (n.s.) 77, 80–81 (1960).

26. Lord Denning (Baron Denning of Whitchurch), *The Family Story* 205–7 (1981). *See also* Andrew Phang, *The Natural Law Foundations of Lord Denning's Thought and Work,* 1999 Denning L.J. 159, 162 n.12, who quotes Lord Denning on another occasion: "Without religion there can be no morality and without morality there can be no law."

27. At the beginning of England's legal year (the opening of the Michelmas Term, here secularized as the first Monday in October, when the Supreme Court begins its term), Lord Denning regularly preached a lay sermon at the Temple Church for the Lawyers' Christian Fellowship, of which he was president from 1950 until 1987 and then patron until his recent death. (I was privileged to attend several of these services.)

Although Christianity is only one approach in a pluralistic society, the work of great Christian lawyers and judges may still stamp a field, as Lord Denning's books and opinions amply demonstrate. Lord Denning, who remains for me an inspiration, explained, "Religion concerns the spirit in man whereby he is able to recognise what is truth and what is justice: whereas law is only the application, however imperfectly, of truth and justice in our everyday affairs." Lord Denning contrasts the approach of the objective, formalist judge with Denning's own approach to doing justice: "He is indifferent to the merits. Going by the strictness of the law. Heedless of hardship to one side or the other. No raising or lowering of his voice. No ornament or colour in his words. Precise and accurate. . . . Coming ultimately—and with professed reluctance—to a decision contrary to the justice of the case. Wiping crocodile tears from his eyes." Lord Denning rejected that approach because justice in the particular case is sacrificed by leaving out "real life." Denning begins with the circumstances of the actual parties in the case. He uses the parties' names to remember who they are as human beings rather than merely their litigation posture as plaintiff and defendant. "In telling the story, I set out the merits—I rely on them—I do not scorn them because the merits go to show where justice lies." To that end, Lord Denning did not say, "'I regret having to come to this conclusion but I have no option.'" Rather, he found, "There is always a way round. There is always an option—in my philosophy—by which justice can be done."[28]

### BENEFIT CONFERRED AND RELIANCE

Lord Denning believed that "our conception of justice is only the Christian teaching of love" and quoted the late Archbishop William Temple to the effect that "the primary form of love in social organisation is Justice."[29] Some of Lord Denning's contract opinions reflect the notion that Christian morality may still inform decisionmaking. Two cases involving contract liability illustrate these principles. In the first case, Stuart Eves told his partner Janet Eves that he was going to put the house where they lived in both their names. He never in fact did so, using the excuse that Janet was under twenty-one years of age. In accordance with Stuart's promise, Janet worked hard to help rehabilitate the old

28. Quoted by Phang, *supra* note 26, at 162 from a typescript by Lord Denning preserved at the Hampshire Record Office. *See also* Alfred T. Denning, *The Due Process of Law* 67–73 (1980).

29. The Influence of Religion on Law 17, published by the Lawyers' Christian Fellowship as a pamphlet in 1989.

house, but she received no compensation for her work.[30] Stuart then evicted her and sold the house. In the second case, Eric Tanner said in Josephine Tanner's presence that he would put a house in both their names. Although Josephine had a rent-controlled flat, she thereupon gave it up to move in with Eric, the father of her twins. Soon after, Eric wished to evict the three of them, leaving Josephine no place to go with her children.[31]

Lord Denning's decisions in these cases imposed contract liability. His opinions are examples of natural-law analysis. Natural law, whether from the Greek philosophers, Christian interpreters, or modern secular theorists, is "the embodiment in legal rules and concepts of moral principles derived from reason and conscience."[32] A natural-law perspective emphasizes the connection between law and morality. As Aristotle and Aquinas philosophically envisioned in their times, laws were to be based on reason and fairness. Today, natural law has commended itself to secular as well as Christian theorists.[33] Although there are widely different conceptions of natural law, the common thread among them is that law is value laden and that the purpose of the law is to establish justice. Morality—that is, justice—is the goal of law. Lord Denning's approach to decisionmaking (on the merits, that is, the equities, of the case) meets the natural-law requirement of reaching a just decision. Natural-law theorists assert that the authority of law depends on its capacity to secure justice and that although the legal obligation to obey the law may be absolute, the moral obligation to obey the law depends on the justice of the laws themselves.

In *Eves,* had the court not found a contract, Janet would have conferred a

---

30. *Eves v. Eves* [1975] 1 W.L.R. 1338. This principle of recognizing the labor given to the other party goes back to *Dilwyn v. Llewelyn* (1862) 4 D.F. & G. 517 (son's expenditure on father's land supplied a valuable consideration); *see* D. E. Allan, *An Equity to Perfect a Gift,* 79 Law Q.Rev. 238 (1963). The same notions of equity prominent in the thought of Aristotle and Aquinas and the decisions of Lord Denning survive in the United States; *see Watts v. Watts,* 405 N.W.2d 303 (Wis. 1987) (Shirley S. Abrahamson, J.); *cf. Pyeatte v. Pyeatte,* 661 P.2d 196 (Ariz. Ct. App. 1982). *Justice, Lord Denning and the Constitution* 1–3 (Peter Robson and Paul Watchman eds., 1981) criticizes Lord Denning's approach.

31. *Tanner v. Tanner* [1975] 1 W.L.R. 1346.

32. Berman, *supra* note 5, at 290.

33. *See* Ronald Dworkin, *Law's Empire* (1986) (*see* John T. Noonan, *Hercules and the Snail Darter,* New York Times Book Review 12 (May 25, 1986)), John Rawls, *A Theory of Justice* (1971). Some Christians have restated the principles of natural law for contemporary society, most prominently the Australian John Finnis. John Finnis, *Natural Law and Natural Rights* 86–89 (1980). The decisions of Lord Mansfield and Lord Denning are easily explainable with reference to the criteria Finnis sets forth.

benefit on Stuart without any compensation. In *Tanner,* Josephine relied on the statement that Eric would put the house in both their names and thereby suf- fered the loss of her rent-controlled flat. A positivist might say with perfect doc- trinal propriety that neither Janet nor Josephine had a contract. The bargained- for-exchange theory would not yield recovery for either Janet or Josephine because neither case involved an explicit agreement in advance that a particular commodity was being offered, that acceptance was to be rendered in a particu- lar way, and that a particular consideration was to be exchanged. But natural law understands that Janet's work in fixing the house deserves compensation and that Josephine relied on Eric's conduct in giving up her flat.

In both cases, the existence of at least one of the three traditional contract el- ements, bargain, benefit, or detriment, is in question, but through natural law we may avoid the requirement of that element through the theories of benefit conferred and reliance. In neither case was there a bargained-for exchange as classical nineteenth-century law envisaged in a contract. In Janet's case, there was no traditional consideration. In order to achieve equity, the law inferred that Stuart's moral obligation to Janet for the benefit she conferred on him by fixing up the house served as consideration to support the contract. In Josephine's case, there was no offer and acceptance of a bargained-for exchange, but Josephine did suffer a detriment in relying on Eric's promise when she gave up her rent- controlled flat. Again, to do justice, the court found that Josephine's action in reliance on Eric's promise resulted in a binding contract.

In Janet's case, the theory of liability that compensated her for her work in fixing up the house is benefit conferred. It builds on the Aristotelian notion of equality of exchange at the foundation of the moral understanding of restitu- tion and economics alike.[34] This theory allowed her to recover a share of the proceeds from the sale of the house. Janet's case is consistent with the rule of Mansfield's case on moral obligation *(Hawkes v. Saunders),* which allowed moral obligation as sufficient consideration to support a subsequent promise to pay if the promisor has received a material and substantial benefit.[35] Janet con- ferred a benefit on Stuart, which gave rise to a moral obligation on his part to compensate her.

In Josephine's case, the issue is whether she might stop Eric from evicting her because of her reliance on Eric's expressed intent to put the house in both their

34. *See* Gordley, *Enforcing Promises, supra* note 14, at 597.
35. The principle of quasi-contract recognized the benefit-conferred theory in the United States. A. W. Brian Simpson, *A History of the Common Law of Contract: The Rise of the Action of Assumpsit,* 489–505 (1987).

names. She can use detrimental reliance. If a promisor reasonably expects his promise to induce action or forbearance, and it does, then the promise is binding. Josephine won.[36] The justice of not requiring bargained-for consideration in family situations, charitable contributions, other gratuitous grants, and bailments should have been self-evident. This sense of wholeness, however, had receded from judicial consciousness for a time due to the strength of the bargain principle, which overflowed its commercial boundaries and swamped other relations. Beyond the marketplace, bargaining often plays no role in relations that may nevertheless give rise to contractual obligations.

In both these cases, Lord Denning reached results that did justice between the parties. In both cases, the defendants would otherwise have escaped without any responsibility for their actions—Stuart would have pocketed all the money gained from Janet's work in fixing up the house, and Eric would have been able to leave Josephine worse off for having trusted his promises. The principles behind Lord Denning's language are that Stuart should not gain through Janet's loss and that Eric's promises to Josephine should not cause her a loss of housing. Because one party has disregarded the other, the law steps in and attempts to do justice between the parties as far as possible. Ultimately, for a Christian these attitudes are based on the principles of commutative justice and Jesus' command to love one's neighbor as oneself. Lord Denning in doing justice between the parties reflects a Christian interpretation of natural law and the equity of the law. The fair person outside the natural-law tradition—and indeed, outside the Christian tradition entirely—frequently reaches the same result as the Christian, and in the cases of Janet and Josephine would almost certainly do so but would not go beyond fairness to faith in explaining the morality of the decisions. Natural law itself recognizes the human desire to do justice through reason. For lawyers and judges, part of living a Christian life is to draw the connections and express the principles of Christian morality inherent in cases and situations we meet in practice. By doing this Lord Denning stamped the law of contracts with a Christian character for all to see.

## MISTAKE AND DURESS

The concepts of mistake and duress are also manifestations of fairness that might be informed by Christian faith to prevent liability falling on a party who

36. In the United States, Josephine would likely be successful in a contract action against Eric based on reliance under the rule codified in the Restatement of Contracts § 90 as promissory estoppel.

has entered into a contract under a mistaken impression or without free will. As the bargain theory grew stronger, mistake and duress became more important in providing the means to avoid the imposition of liability in extenuating circumstances. Sometimes the doctrine of mistake can rescue parties from a contract that should never have been made.

An example of a mistake in bargaining is *Wood v. Boynton,* in which a woman brought a gemstone to a jewelry store to sell.[37] She did not know what kind of stone she had, and because quartz is as common as diamond is rare, she accepted payment of $1.00 for a white topaz (which looks like a diamond without the brilliance). In fact, the stone was a rough diamond, worth between $700 and $1,000. The court held that the purchasing jeweler had no duty to disclose the results of his preliminary examination under the jeweler's loupe. Commentators see this situation as an assumption of risk not proper for the application of the doctrine of mistake.[38] But to me the difference in the parties' knowledge about gems warrants a wholly different answer. I have difficulty accepting a "conscious ignorance" or caveat emptor argument when a member of the public or a consumer deals with a merchant or professional.

In this case, the striking disparity between the price of one dollar and the low-end value of $700 calls for the equitable extension of the Roman law principle of extreme injury, *laesio enormis,* to attack inadequacy of price and an unequal bargain. This doctrine gave rise to the remedy of rescission for a vendor who sold for less than half-price.[39] Moral ideals of a fair exchange recommended this doctrine to medieval theorists. The failure to apply the doctrine of mistake in this case remains inexplicable to me on Roman law, equitable and Christian principles alike. The jeweler did no work to acquire the stone. The woman simply walked into the store probably needing money, perhaps even for necessities. Under a moral approach to contracts, it is unjust for the jeweler to have kept the ring at the woman's expense—a clear case of unjust enrichment. The jeweler simply took advantage of the woman and the court allowed him to keep this windfall, to the shame of the law. At the very least, the court should have permitted the woman to split the low-end value of the diamond with the

37. *Wood v. Boynton,* 25 N.W. 42 (Wis. 1885).

38. John D. Calamari and Joseph M. Perillo, *The Law of Contracts* § 9–26 (4th ed. 1999).

39. Aquinas affirmed this doctrine. Thomas Aquinas, *Summa Theologiae, supra* note 4, at II-II, q. 77, a. 1, ad 1 reflects the Roman law notion of *laesio enormis.* John P. Dawson, *Economic Duress and the Fair Exchange in French and German Law,* 11 Tul. L. Rev. 345, 364–65 (1937) explains that the doctrine under the influence of Christian morality went far beyond its Roman origins into the "recesses of medieval thought."

jeweler. Applying Christian principles through natural law, it is difficult to see how it is a just result to uphold the sale of the gemstone at one dollar.[40]

With the increasing dominance of the bargain theory of contract during the nineteenth century, the need grew for a principled basis at common law on which to avoid some contracts. The doctrine of duress has grown as a response. In *Lloyds Bank Ltd. v. Bundy,* Lord Denning surveyed a series of cases in which relief was given against unfair contracts and then concluded that English law "gives relief to one who, without independent advice, enters into a contract upon terms which are very unfair or transfers property for a consideration which is grossly inadequate, when his bargaining power is grievously impaired by reason of his own needs or desires, or by his own ignorance or infirmity, coupled with undue influence or pressures brought to bear on him by or for the benefit of the other."[41] Thus Lord Denning stated a general common-law principle of protecting the weaker party when there is inequality of bargaining power. Although one of the leading commentators suggested that "without express legislative authority" the cases could not reach such a result, Lord Denning was not willing to concede the powerlessness of the courts in the absence of legislation.[42]

### THE CENTRALITY OF COMMUNITY IN NATURAL LAW

In literature, the exaggerated ideas of the unique power of the nineteenth-century bargain are reflected in the image of the raw individual from *The Last of the Mohicans* and later in *The Fountainhead:* taming nature, achieving wealth, and triumphing over adversity. The hero is pitted in a contest of individual combat against the invisible hand of nature or the market.[43] Community

40. Nevertheless, in England mistake and duress have limited scope despite the efforts of Lord Denning. *See Magee v. Pennine Ins. Co. Ltd.* [1969] 2 Q.B. 507 and *Howard Marine and Dredging Co. Ltd. v. A. Ogden (Excavations) Ltd.* [1978] Q.B. 574.

41. *Lloyds Bank Ltd. v. Bundy* [1975] Q.B. 326, 339.

42. Guenther H. Treitel, *The Law of Contract* 384 (9th ed. 1995), citing several opinions by other judges unwilling to face uncertainty in the law and recognizing the power of the legislature to deal with unfairness in consumer contracts. Lord Denning stated his broad principle of relief against inequality of bargaining power before some of the consumer legislation (such as the Unfair Contract Terms Act (c. 50) 1977 and Unfair Terms in Consumer Contracts Regulations (S.I. 1994 No. 3159)) had been enacted.

43. James Fenimore Cooper's character Hawkeye was a frontiersman in *The Leatherstocking Tales* (1823–41). Ayn Rand's novels *The Fountainhead* (1943) and *Atlas Shrugged* (1957) are

nowhere plays a role in the achievement of these lone rangers who single-handedly reap the reward of their contracts. For the Christian tradition, in contrast, community is central.

Jesus was never a "lone ranger." He always had with Him the presence of His heavenly Father. He also lived in a family. We prayerfully remember them, saints all: his parents Mary and Joseph, grandparents Ann and Joachim, aunt Elizabeth, uncle Zacharias, and cousin John, and his friends, Martha, Mary, and Lazarus, and Mary Magdalene, to say nothing of the twelve apostles. We read of his lineage from David. Jesus was rooted in his community and would never have bothered to do the work of salvation if it were not for us, his spiritual community. Surely, then, contracts are better served if the view of contracts as the lone, isolated commercial deals between two bargaining strangers gives way to a less dysfunctional paradigm of contractual relationships.

The historical assessment presented in this essay argues that owing to natural-law principles, contract law was concerned with the community's good rather than only the merchants' interests. Contract theories of benefit conferred and reliance allocated the risks among the parties once they had interacted with each other and did not leave liability solely within the control of the sharply bargaining party. These theories served to extend the ties that bind the contracting parties. They are more equitable and fairer than the sole theory of bargaining, reflecting the natural-law principles that parties desiring to contract accept the obligations that enable the parties to deal with each other and carry out their purpose. From the rich natural-law tradition, a Christian approach to contracts will always concern itself with the community's good.[44]

All three theories (reliance, bargain, and benefit conferred) seek to protect the reasonable expectations of the parties. But the theories of reliance and benefit conferred encompass notions of fairness, equity, and justice that place lim-

---

best described as hymns to individualistic capitalism. For a study in judicial individualism, *see* Anita Ramasastry, *The Parameters, Progressions, and Paradoxes of Baron Bramwell*, 38 Am. J.L. Hist. 322 (1994). The Bible, starting with the Book of Genesis, shows the multiplicity of creation and the context of individuals living together in society. Similarly, Aquinas wrote that people have "a natural inclination to know the truth about God and to live in society." Aquinas, *supra* note 4, q. 94, a. 2.

44. A merchant who sells goods at a fair price is likely to have repeat customers with long-term commercial relationships. That model provides a better structure for employment contracts, which demand good faith in order to succeed. *See* Mark B. Greenlee, *Maps of Legality: An Essay on the Hidden Role of Religious Beliefs in the Law of Contracts*, 4 Regent U.L. Rev. 39 (1994). Leases, service contracts, and partnerships also work better in the context of community.

its on what one sharp bargaining party can exact. These natural-law philosophies and contract theories helped to formulate the contract-liability theories
society uses today. With the renewed emphasis on fairness and morality in Anglo-American jurisprudence, all three contract liability theories are now being
used, and thus some checks exist on how far bargaining can insulate the sharp
bargainer from contract liability. Commutative justice—giving each contracting party what is due—retains a place of primacy for Christians. Fortunately, at
present this primacy is also reflected in contract and commercial law through
the Restatement of Contracts (Second) and the Uniform Commercial Code.
Should this position change, as it did during the nineteenth century, the needs
of justice will again inspire committed Christians, such as Lord Mansfield and
Lord Denning, to seek reformation of contract law. For as long as human history continues, reform and renewal will be as necessary in human laws as they
are in the individual human heart.[45]

---

45. C. M. A. Mc Cauliff, *Law as a Principle of Reform: Reflections from Sixteenth-Century
England,* 40 Rutgers L. Rev. 429 (1988).

# Tort Law and Intermediate Communities: Calvinist and Catholic Insights

*Robert F. Cochran, Jr.*

Tort law is commonly thought to be individualist in character.[1] Some tort law theorists celebrate its individualistic character.[2] Others lament it.[3] But tort law theorists have failed to give attention to a countervailing strain in tort law. Many tort rules are not individualist in character; many were designed to protect and many others to make demands on intermediate communities—the families, religious congregations, and other associations that stand between the individual and the state.

These tort law rules can best be understood based on what I will call

1. *See, e.g.,* Robert A. Baruch Bush, *Between Two Worlds: The Shift from Individual to Group Responsibility in the Law of Causation of Injury,* 33 UCLA L. Rev. 1473, 1473 (1986); Richard L. Abel, *A Critique of Torts,* 37 UCLA L. Rev. 785, 831 (1990); Richard A. Epstein, *A Theory of Strict Liability,* 2 J. Legal Stud. 151, 203–4 (1973); David Owen, *The Moral Foundations of Products Liability Law: Toward First Principles,* 68 Notre Dame L. Rev. 427, 498–99 (1993).

2. *See* Owen, *supra* note 1, at 498–99, and Epstein, *supra* note 1, at 203–4.

3. *See* Robert M. Ackerman, *Tort Law and Communitarianism: Where Rights Meet Responsibilities,* 30 Wake Forest L. Rev. 649, 651 (1995) and sources cited therein.

"intermediate communitarian" theory, a theory drawn from Calvinist and Catholic social thought, but which is likely to find support in other religious and nonreligious traditions. Intermediate communitarian theory recognizes that intermediate communities are crucial to the health of both the individual and the broader society. As to tort law, intermediate communitarian theory can play both a descriptive role, helping us to identify and understand the intermediate communitarian strain that has generally gone unnoticed in the torts literature, and a normative role, suggesting ways that tort law might both protect and make demands on intermediate communities in the future.

## INTERMEDIATE COMMUNITARIAN THEORY

### Calvinists and Sphere Sovereignty

Abraham Kuyper (1837–1920) was a philosopher, a theologian, founder of the Free University of Amsterdam, and prime minister of Holland. In his social philosophy, Kuyper responded to Rousseau's Enlightenment individualism and Hegel's collectivism with the notion of "sphere sovereignty." Kuyper shared the traditional Calvinist belief in the sovereignty of God. In his speech at the founding of the Free University, he said, "There is not a square inch in the whole domain of our human existence over which Christ, who is Sovereign over *all,* does not cry: 'Mine!'"[4] But he also believed that God "delegates his authority to human beings." God delegates authority to the state, but He also delegates authority to other entities, each of which is sovereign within its sphere. Kuyper recognized the church, the state, families, universities, guilds, and other associations as having spheres within which they are sovereign. He recognized two special responsibilities for the state: "[The State] must provide for sound mutual interaction among the various spheres, insofar as they are externally manifest, and keep them within just limits. Furthermore, since personal life can be suppressed by the group in which one lives, the state must protect the individual from the tyranny of his own circle." Nevertheless, Kuyper warned, "Do not forget that every State power tends to look upon all liberty with a suspicious eye." The state should not become an octopus, stifling the whole of life.

Sphere sovereignty has its roots in Calvin's thought. Calvin saw the church

4. Abraham Kuyper, *Sphere Sovereignty* (1880) (trans. George Kamp) *in Abraham Kuyper: a Centennial Reader* 488 (1998). Quotations that follow in the text are from 466, 468, and 472.

and the state as separate entities, each with its own God-given authority. Neither is subordinate to the other. The Calvinist ideal is a free church in a free state. Just as under the government of the Protestant churches, all believers and congregations are of equal standing, so are all citizens and groups within a nation.[5]

Kuyper found the basis for sphere sovereignty "in the order of creation, in the structure of human life," but also in Scripture. He cited the examples of Jews and Christians resisting the governing authorities, as well as the "Lord's maxim concerning what is God's and what is Caesar's."[6]

### Catholics and Subsidiarity

The Catholic notion of subsidiarity received its first expression in Pope Leo XIII's encyclical *Of New Things (Rerum Novarum)* in 1891.[7] He presented subsidiarity as an alternative to the individualism of unrestrained capitalism and the collectivism of Marxism. Leo had strong language for each. Capitalists should pay their workers wages sufficient to provide for their families; socialists should respect the right of private property. Leo emphasized the importance of institutions between the individual and the state remaining independent, using language similar to that of Kuyper. According to Leo, state administration of property would "bring State action into a sphere not within its competence." In addition, "A family, no less than a State, is . . . a true society, governed by a power within its sphere."

Nevertheless, there appears to be greater room for interaction between the family and the state under subsidiarity than under sphere sovereignty. "If a family finds itself in exceeding distress, utterly deprived of the counsel of friends, and without any prospect of extricating itself, it is right that extreme necessity be met by public aid, since each family is a part of the commonwealth. In like manner, if within the precincts of the household there occur grave disturbance of mutual rights, public authority should intervene. . . . But the rulers of the State must go no further: here nature bids them stop."

In *Of New Things,* Leo also discussed the importance of other intermediate institutions. The church, private benevolent foundations, labor unions, and religious orders all serve the needs of human beings and all face the danger of in-

5. Abraham Kuyper, *Calvinism* 96, 106, 63 (1943).

6. Kuyper, *supra* note 4, at 480.

7. Pope Leo XIII, *Of New Things* (1891), *reprinted in The Papal Encyclicals in Their Historical Context* 166 (Anne Fremantle ed., 1956) (hereinafter *Papal Encyclicals*). Quotations that follow in the text are from pages 168, 171, 172, and 187–89.

terference from the state. Leo's special concern in *Of New Things* was the relationship between business and labor. Here, again, he preferred a limited role for the state. Wages and working conditions should be improved through organizations of employers and workmen and strong labor unions, "in order to supersede undue interference on the part of the State."

Subsidiarity has received further development in papal encyclicals since *Of New Things,* most recently in Pope John Paul's *Centesimus Annus, The Economics of Human Freedom,* an encyclical commemorating *Of New Things*' one hundredth anniversary. John Paul wrote, "*The principle of subsidiarity* must be respected: a community of a higher order should not interfere in the internal life of a community of a lower order, depriving the latter of its functions, but rather should support it in case of need and help to coordinate its activity with the activities of the rest of society, always with a view to the common good. Needs are best understood and satisfied by people who are closest to them, and who act as neighbors to those in need."[8] Under the Catholic notion of subsidiarity, "Communities must enable and encourage individuals to exercise their self-responsibility and larger communities must do the same for smaller ones."[9]

Like sphere sovereignty, subsidiarity is grounded in both human nature and in Scripture. John Paul said, "In the Christian vision, the social nature of man is not completely fulfilled in the state but is realized in various intermediary groups, beginning with the family and including economic, social, political, and cultural groups that stem from human nature itself and have their own autonomy, always with a view to the common good."[10]

Leo quoted Ecclesiastes 4:9–10 to illustrate the very practical value of community. *"It is better that two should be together than one; for they have the advantage of their society. If one fall he shall be supported by the other. Woe to him that is alone, for when he falleth he hath none to lift him up."*[11]

Although there are differences between the Calvinist doctrine of sphere sov-

8. Pope John Paul II, *Centesimus Annus, The Economics of Human Freedom* (1991), *reprinted in* Richard John Neuhaus, *Doing Well and Doing Good* 285, 301 (1992); for a similar description of subsidiarity, *see* Pope Pius XI, *Quadragesimo Anno* (1931), *reprinted in Papal Encyclicals, supra* note 7, at 228, 230.

9. Jean Bethke Elshtain, Catholic Social Thought, the City, and Liberal America, in *Catholicism, Liberalism, and Communitarianism* 97, 105 (Kenneth L. Grasso et al. eds., 1995), *citing* Joseph A. Komonchak, *Subsidiarity in the Church: The State of the Question,* 48 The Jurist 298, 301–2 (1988).

10. *See* Pope John Paul II, *supra* note 8, at 289–90.

11. Pope Leo XIII, *supra* note 7, at 189 (emphasis in the original).

ereignty and the Catholic doctrine of subsidiarity, their similarities are greater than their differences. There is probably greater interaction among the Catholic subsidiary communities than among the Calvinist sovereign spheres. Nevertheless, both doctrines recognize the importance of intermediate communities, for the sake of individuals as well as of society, and both recognize the dangers that either individualism or totalitarianism creates for intermediate communities.

## The Value of Intermediate Communities

Intermediate communities are important for several reasons. First, they have inherent value. As Peter Berger and Richard John Neuhaus have noted, the megastructures of modern life (big government, big business, big unions) are "typically alienating, that is, they are not helpful in providing meaning and identity for individual existence," but in the modern world's alternative, private life, "the individual is left very much to his own devices, and thus is uncertain and anxious."[12] In a sense, in modern America we are all homeless.[13] Intermediate communities provide opportunities for fellowship, friendship, and meaning.

Second, intermediate communities are the source of the psychological and moral formation of individuals. In the words of Michael Sandel, community is "constitutive" of the self. For most people, intermediate communities are a source of personal identity. As Alasdair MacIntyre has said, "[I] inherit from the past of my family, my city, my tribe, my nation, a variety of debts, inheritances, rightful expectations and obligations. These constitute the given of my life, my moral starting point."[14] The experience of living in community teaches people how to relate to and treat others. This is especially true of the family. As Mary Ann Glendon has said, "[In the family,] citizens acquire the capacity to care about the common good"; "people learn to view others with respect and concern, rather than to regard them as objects, means, or obstacles"; and "a boy or girl develops the healthy independence of mind and self-confidence that enables men and women to participate effectively in government and to exercise responsible leadership."[15] From love of the smaller community,

12. *See* Peter L. Berger & Richard John Neuhaus, *To Empower People* 2 (1977).

13. *Cf.* Elshtain, *supra* note 9, at 106.

14. *See* Alasdair MacIntyre, *After Virtue* 220 (2d ed. 1984).

15. *See* Mary Ann Glendon, *Rights Talk: The Impoverishment of Political Discourse* 129 (1991).

love of the larger society can, we hope, grow. Tocqueville called communities "little schools for citizenship."[16]

Third, intermediate communities provide "social services," both to their own members and to other people. The family is the greatest "social-service provider." Some suggest that the United States is now going through crises in education, child care, and health care. But the problems that we have are minuscule compared with what they would be if families did not voluntarily meet a substantial portion of all of these needs. The costs of reproducing these services through government or market transactions would be overwhelming.

Most religious communities teach that members should care for one another, but they also teach that their members have a social responsibility beyond the religious congregation. "The most anomic individuals in our society, the denizens of skid row for example, are cared for almost exclusively by voluntary associations, usually religious in character."[17] Studies show that people from religious congregations are the most active in both charitable giving and public-service volunteering.[18]

Not only do intermediate communities provide many social services to many people, they probably do a better job of providing services than does the state. Care by communities is likely to be more individualized, more tailored to the specific problems faced by those in need, than the care given by the state. As Pope John Paul II has said, "Needs are best understood and satisfied by people who are closest to them, and who act as neighbors to those in need."[19]

Finally, intermediate communities can provide a source of moral insight to the state and the surrounding culture. Religious communities draw from a source of values beyond the state. This can give them strength to speak a moral voice to the broader community. In the United States, the American independence, antislavery, child labor–reform, labor-rights, prohibition, antiwar, civil-rights, and pro-life movements all have had religious leaders among their leaders. In England the fight against the slave trade, in Eastern Europe the fight against Communism, and in South Africa the fight against apartheid all were

16. *See* Mary Ann Glendon, *Communitarian Wager,* Responsive Community, Summer 1992, at 56 (quoting Alexis de Tocqueville).

17. Berger and Neuhaus, *supra* note 12, at 32.

18. *See, e.g.,* Robert Franklin, *Charitable Giving Up 7.3% in U.S.,* Minneapolis-St. Paul Star-Trib., May 29, 1997; *Religiously Affiliated Americans Remain Most Generous,* Dallas Morning News, Oct. 12, 1996 (citing a 1996 Gallup Independent Sector survey); Cindy Kranz, *So You Want to Volunteer,* Cin. Enquirer, May 15, 1997.

19. *See* Pope John Paul II, *supra* note 8, at 301.

led by religious communities.[20] The religious leaders in all of these movements operated in the tradition of the Hebrew prophets, who challenged the state and the culture on behalf of the poor and oppressed.

## TORT LAW'S INDIVIDUALIST CHARACTER

Tort theorists have tended to view life through individualist lenses. Robert A. Baruch Bush summarizes the "individual responsibility" principle underlying American tort law: "The individual is responsible for all he does, but for only what he does."[21] Robert Ackerman says, "Modern tort law represents a perverse triumph of radical individualism."[22] Tort law's individualist character is epitomized for many by the tort rule that says one need not go to the aid of someone who is in danger: if you see a child drowning or a blind person stepping in front of a car, you have the right to remain silent and enjoy the show. Mary Ann Glendon says, "Buried deep in our rights dialect is an unexpressed premise that we roam at large in a land of strangers, where we presumptively have no obligations toward others except to avoid the active infliction of harm."[23]

## TORTS LAW'S TREATMENT OF
## INTERMEDIATE COMMUNITIES

I agree that tort law is primarily individualist in character. Nevertheless, little noted by tort-law theorists in any systematic way have been a host of torts rules that are not individualist. These rules were designed to protect or impose responsibilities on the same intermediate communities that the doctrines of sphere sovereignty and subsidiarity identified as so important to human flour-

20. *See, e.g.,* James W. Skillen, Toward a Contemporary Christian Democratic Politics in the U.S., *in Christianity and Democracy in Global Context* 85, 89 (John Witte, Jr. ed., 1993); Aldon D. Morris, *The Origins of the Civil Rights Movement, Black Communities Organizing for Change* 4–8 (1984); Stephen V. Monsma, *Pursuing Justice in a Sinful World* 5 (1984); Mary L. Gautier, *Church Attendance and Religious Belief in Postcommunist Societies,* 36 J. for Sci. Study Religion 289, 289–90 (1997) (Poland and Eastern Europe); Joseph Punjer, Contribution of the Reformed Churches to the Fall of Communism in Hungary and Romania *in Research on Democracy and Society: Democratization in Eastern and Western Thought* 111–32 (F. D. Wells, et al., eds., 1993).

21. Bush, *supra* note 1, at 1474.

22. *See* Ackerman, *supra* note 3, at 651.

23. Glendon, *supra* note 15, at 77.

ishing—the families, friendships, religious congregations, neighborhoods, charities, labor unions, and towns that lie between the individual and the state. I will consider first several rules designed to protect intermediate communities, then several rules that were designed to make demands on them. My point is not that all of these rules are good rules. In some cases, these rules may have even been counterproductive, causing damage to the intermediate communities that they were designed to protect.

I focus primarily on rules of law that affect families and religious congregations, two of the communities that have been of primary concern within both the Calvinist doctrine of sphere sovereignty and the Catholic doctrine of subsidiarity. The family and the religious congregation have received substantial attention from tort law. This is not surprising, since they are the most common, the closest, the most intense, and the most active intermediate communities. They are the intermediate communities that have provided the most care and service to people. They are communities with power, power that can be used for good or ill.

### Protecting Intermediate Communities

A significant number of traditional tort rules were designed to protect the family. Spousal immunity, parental immunity, and the parental discipline privilege protected defendants from suit by their spouses and children. These rules were designed to reinforce authority within the home and to insulate "families from the vagaries and rancorous effects of tort litigation."[24] In recent years, most jurisdictions have overturned spousal and parental immunities, though they have retained the parental privilege for reasonable parental discipline.

Under the alienation-of-affections cause of action, a spouse could seek recovery against a third party who had maliciously or intentionally interfered with the marital relationship. However, many states have abrogated this cause of action. Among the justifications that courts have given for abrogation are "changed social concepts of family solidarity . . . [and] increased freedom of association between each spouse and the outside world."[25]

Associational immunity protected unincorporated associations in many jurisdictions from liability to members and from liability for the torts of one member against another, and charitable immunity protected charities from lia-

24. *Renko v. McLean*, 697 A.2d 468, 478 (Md. 1997) (retaining the doctrine of spousal immunity).

25. *Lentz v. Baker*, 792 S.W.2d 71, 75 (Tenn. 1989).

bility for injuries to their beneficiaries.[26] Most jurisdictions have abandoned associational and charitable immunity in recent decades.[27]

In defamation and privacy causes of action, courts recognized a qualified immunity that enabled communities to protect themselves. A defendant who communicated to someone to protect a common interest was subject to liability only if the defendant communicated the information beyond the protected community, acted primarily from ill will, or negligently communicated a false statement.[28] This qualified immunity rule has been undercut in recent years. In 1989 the Oklahoma Supreme Court held a church and its leaders subject to liability for advising its members to withdraw fellowship from a member who continued to engage in an adulterous affair.[29] In an earlier day, it is likely that the church's advice would have been protected as a communication in the common interest of the community.

### Imposing Responsibilities on Intermediate Communities

A second group of tort rules impose special responsibilities on intermediate communities. There are even communitarian aspects of the rule that for many epitomize the individualistic character of tort law, the no-duty-to-rescue rule. The law does not impose a duty to aid strangers, but it does impose a duty to aid those with whom the plaintiff has a special relationship. Special relationships giving rise to an affirmative duty of care include the common carrier–passenger, innkeeper-guest, landlord-tenant, employer-employee, jailer-prisoner, hospital-patient, school-pupil, business owner–customer relationships.[30] Here the law attempts to expand the range of relationships within which citizens care

26. On associational immunity, *see MacDonald v. Maxwell*, 655 N.E.2d 1249, 1250 n.1 (Ind. 1995); *Calvary Baptist Church v. Joseph*, 522 N.E.2d 371, 374 (Ind. 1988); *Cox v. Thee Evergreen Church*, 836 S.W.2d 167, 169–70 (Tex. 1992); *Zehner v. Wilkinson Mem'l United Methodist Church*, 581 A.2d 1388, 1389 (Pa. 1990); *Marshall v. Int'l Longshoremen's & Warehousemen's Union*, 371 P.2d 987, 990 (Cal. 1962).

27. *See* Daniel A. Barfield, Note, *Better to Give Than to Receive: Should Nonprofit Corporations and Charities Pay Punitive Damages?* 29 Val. U. L. Rev. 1193, 1194–95, 1197 n.15 (1995) and cases cited therein.

28. *See Prosser and Keeton on the Law of Torts* § 115, at 828–30, 832–35 and § 117, 868 (W. Page Keeton et al. eds., 5th ed. 1984). *See also* Restatement (Second) of Torts §§ 652F & G.

29. *Guinn v. Collinsville Church of Christ*, 775 P.2d 766, 766, 783 (Okla. 1989).

30. *See Prosser, supra* note 28, at § 56, 383; *see also Funkhouser v. Wilson*, 950 P.2d 501, 508–9 (Wash. Ct. App. 1998).

for others. The law acts to create communities among people who might not generally see themselves as being in a community. As we have seen, tort law traditionally prohibited suits among people within the closest community—the family. It left it to the affection and goodwill of people within families to generate care for those who suffered injuries.

Tort law also imposes a duty to protect third parties from people with whom one has a special relationship.[31] Relationships giving rise to such a duty include parent-child, employer-employee, and psychotherapist-patient. For example, parents who know of the dangerous behavior of their children and fail to take reasonable steps to control them are subject to liability for the torts of the children. The legislatures in many jurisdictions have also adopted statutes that impose strict liability on parents for their children's torts.

In addition to parental responsibility for their children's torts to third parties, many jurisdictions hold parents subject to liability for torts that they commit against their children. Within some jurisdictions, the abrogation of parental immunity merely opened parents to the same responsibilities to their children that other citizens have. New York, for example, has limited the abrogation of parental immunity to those cases in which liability would have been imposed on the parent had he been an unrelated person.[32] Under this rule, a parent is subject to liability to a child for negligent driving (since reasonably safe driving is a duty that courts impose on every citizen), but not for negligent supervision (since supervision of children is not a duty that courts impose on every citizen). Other states, however, have imposed liability on parents for failure to reasonably comply with the special responsibilities of parenthood. The California Supreme Court adopted such a rule, stating: "The standard to be applied is the traditional one of reasonableness, but viewed in light of the parental role. Thus, we think the proper test of a parent's conduct is this: what would an ordinarily reasonable and prudent *parent* have done in similar circumstances?"[33] This amounts to liability for parental malpractice.

Tort law may create similar risks for religious congregations. The abolition of associational and charitable immunity exposed religious congregations to liability on the same basis as other businesses. The religious congregation is subject to liability when a parishioner or visitor slips in the parking lot. Plaintiffs in

31. *See Prosser, supra* note 28, at § 56, 383–85 and cases cited therein.
32. *Holodook v. Spencer,* 324 N.E.2d 338, 346 (N.Y. 1974).
33. *Gibson v. Gibson,* 479 P.2d 648, 653 (Cal. 1971).

a few cases have attempted to push the liability of religious congregations much further.[34] They have alleged "clergy malpractice." In some of these cases, the plaintiff has claimed that the clergy failed to provide reasonable pastoral counseling. A few lower courts have allowed clergy malpractice claims, but so far they have been reversed on appeal.

Courts generally have held clergy liable for having sexual relations with counselees and children, but they generally have held that religious congregations are not subject to vicarious liability in such cases because the clergy have been acting outside of the scope of their employment.[35] In some cases, however, courts have found churches liable for the sexual activities of their clergy based on negligent supervision. Courts have held churches subject to liability where they know of a clergy member's proclivity toward sexual exploitation and fail to take reasonable steps to control him.[36] Under such a rule, the fact finder may need to evaluate the reasonableness of the religious congregation's disciplinary steps toward clergy. Other courts have rejected such claims as an improper interference within religious matters.[37]

## INTERMEDIATE COMMUNITARIAN TORT LAW THEORY: SOME PRELIMINARY CONSIDERATIONS

This overview of torts, families, and religious congregations illustrates that tort law is far from purely individualist in character. Many rules have given special consideration to intermediate communities, either providing special protection to communities and their leaders or imposing special responsibilities on them. The overview reveals two trends in the law:

1. The rejection of rules that provided special protections for intermediate communities; and
2. The imposition of responsibility on intermediate communities for failing to fulfill responsibilities according to the standards of the broader society (for

34. *See, e.g., Nally v. Grace Community Church,* 763 P.2d 948, 949–50 (Cal. 1988) and *F.G. v. MacDonell,* 696 A.2d 697, 700 (N.J. 1997).

35. *See, e.g., Swanson v. Roman Catholic Bishop of Portland,* 692 A.2d 441, 445 (Me. 1997); *Destefano v. Grabrian,* 763 P.2d 275, 284, 287 (Colo. 1988).

36. *See, e.g., Erickson v. Christenson,* 781 P.2d 383, 386–87 (Or. 1989); *Smith v. O'Connell,* 986 F.Supp. 73, 81 (D.R.I. 1997).

37. *See L.L.N. v. Clauder,* 563 N.W.2d 434, 441 (Wis. 1997); *Pritzlaff v. Archdiocese of Milwaukee,* 533 N.W.2d 780, 790 (1995); *Schmidt v. Bishop,* 779 F. Supp. 321, 332 (S.D.N.Y. 1991).

example, the failure to act as "reasonable" parents or "reasonable" religious congregations).

These trends in tort law are squeezing intermediate communities from both ends of the ideological spectrum. From the individualist end, individuals—for example, children and members of religious congregations—are winning cases against intermediate communities with the argument that communities have no basis for making claims on them. From the collectivist end, the broader society is imposing standards on intermediate communities as to their internal operations. Intermediate communities are losing to an alliance of individuals and the state. In recent years, tort law has moved power to the individual and the state at the expense of intermediate communities.

My point is not that intermediate communities should always win in conflicts with individuals or the state. As the doctrines of both sphere sovereignty and subsidiarity recognize, the state has a role to play in regulating the interaction between intermediate communities and protecting individuals within intermediate communities. Tort law might be a means whereby the larger community can encourage smaller communities to exercise their self-responsibility and advance the common good. Nevertheless, as sphere sovereignty and subsidiarity also warn, the state poses dangers to intermediate communities. Tort law can destroy the very communities that it seeks to call to greater care.

The state should give communities some protection from tort liability based on Hippocrates' first law of moral duty: Do no harm. Tort liability can harm communities in several ways. Obviously, tort liability can impose financial responsibilities on communities, in the form of damages or of insurance payments. These can be very destructive, especially for smaller and poorer communities. But in addition, the fear of tort liability may lead communities to alter their practices. Tort liability may cause some communities to become passive or dependent and lose their vibrancy as the state takes over the responsibility to set their standards. If communities are not allowed to resolve their internal affairs, there is little reason for their existence. Like individuals, as communities exercise responsibility, they are likely to grow in the ability to exercise responsibility.

Not only should courts hesitate to impose tort liability on communities because tort liability damages them, internal community practices are likely to accomplish many of the goals of tort law without state intervention. There is generally no need for the state to create incentives for members of communities to care for one another. Within most communities, there is an internal affection between members. Members of families, religious congregations, and other close communities generally care for and nurture one another naturally in ways that the law could not command (and our culture could not live without). Tort law generally can rely on this internal affection to govern relationships between community members. When there is injury within a community, people within the community may be better able to fashion a remedy than those from the outside. For example, if a member of a family or religious congregation is injured, the family and religious congregation may provide meals, comfort, and other forms of care that may better meet the injured party's needs than money damages.

There are reasons for protecting communities from tort liability, but there are also areas where state regulation of communities through tort law may be appropriate. The ultimate goal of the state, as well as communities, should be to protect individuals. Under the theories of both sphere sovereignty and subsidiarity, the state may intervene in intermediate communities in order to protect individuals. Communities have power; they should use that power to benefit people, not to harm people. In some situations, where communities have caused harm to people, the state should provide a remedy to the injured party.

In their study of intermediate communities, Peter Berger and Richard John Neuhaus make the following recommendation: *"Public policy should protect and foster mediating structures,* and *Wherever possible, public policy should utilize mediating structures for the realization of social purposes."*[38] It may be that tort law can pursue both of the ends suggested by Berger and Neuhaus—both protecting intermediate communities and utilizing them for social purposes. To some extent, this is a matter of balancing two interests that are in conflict. Using intermediate communities for social purposes may undercut their authority and damage them. Nevertheless, there may be ways that courts and legislatures can hold such communities responsible, without undercutting their power and discretion. In the following sections, I shall consider some ways that tort law might treat intermediate communities within the familiar bases of tort liability: intent and recklessness, negligence, and strict liability.

### Holding Communities Responsible for Intentional and Reckless Injury to the Person

Tort law should give communities substantial discretion, but in cases in which there is a high risk of serious injury and communities or their leaders act with

---

38. Berger and Neuhaus, *supra* note 12, at 6 (emphasis in the original).

intent or recklessness as to that risk, courts should hold those communities and those leaders responsible. In such cases, tort liability may serve as a needed supplement to the incentives of criminal law. Cases raising this issue include those in which a member of the clergy engages in sexual relations with a child or counselee, a parent maliciously injures a child, or a parent or religious community denies a child urgently needed medical care.

Clergy who engage in sexual exploitation of children or adult counselees should be subject to liability for the damage that they cause. In these cases, liability helps to protect individuals and reinforces the norms of both the religious community and the broader community. In such cases, courts have rightly stated that clergy may be held individually liable on battery, intentional infliction of emotional distress, and breach of fiduciary relations theories.[39] The more complex question is whether the sins of the clergy should be visited on the religious congregation. I shall discuss in subsequent sections the possibility of imposing liability on religious congregations under negligence or strict liability theories when their clergy engage in sexual exploitation.

Some early decisions granted parental immunity, even in cases where parents caused malicious or reckless injury.[40] Courts today are agreed, however, that parents should be subject to liability.[41] Admittedly, a tort suit by a child against a parent may cause conflict within the home, but the incentives of tort liability may be needed to deter child abuse. Protection of children, the culpability of the parents, and fairness to the children justify this limited interference with family autonomy.

The third case is much more difficult than the other two. Where parents or religious leaders deny a child medical care for religious reasons, they not only are acting based on religious convictions but generally are doing what they believe to be in the child's best interests. Nevertheless, in these cases, the interests of children are sufficiently important and there is a sufficiently broad and a suf-

39. *See, e.g., Byrd v. Faber,* 565 N.E.2d 584, 587 (Ohio 1991) (battery); *Destefano v. Grabrian,* 763 P.2d 275, 286 (Colo. 1988) *(en banc)* (intentional infliction of emotional distress); *Bear Valley Church of Christ v. DeBose,* 928 P.2d 1315, 1321 (Colo. 1996) *(en banc)* (breach of fiduciary relations).

40. The first explicit recognition of parental immunity occurred in 1891 in *Hewlett v. George,* in which the Mississippi Supreme Court denied a daughter's claim for false imprisonment against her mother, who had committed her to an insane asylum. The Court based its decision on concern for "the peace of society, and of the families composing society." 9 So. 885, 887 (Miss. 1891).

41. *See, e.g., Attwood v. Attwood,* 633 S.W.2d 366, 370 (Ark. 1982); *Barnes v. Barnes,* 603 N.E.2d 1337, 1342 (Ind. 1992).

ficiently strong consensus concerning proper medical care that the state should intervene and impose tort liability.[42] The danger to the child may be sufficiently great that the failure of the parents to act may properly be deemed reckless. The risk of tort liability may provide a needed incentive for the parent either to provide medical care or to notify state officials of the child's condition so that they can provide medical care.[43]

### Liability for "Unreasonable" Community Care

When we move to cases against communities and their leaders based on allegations of mere negligence, the argument for respecting community autonomy becomes stronger. The argument for community autonomy is especially strong in cases in which the community is alleged to have failed to exercise reasonable care in performing community functions, such as raising children or pastoral counseling. As noted previously, some courts have adopted negligent-parenting and "clergy malpractice" theories. There is a great danger that through such rules, the state can control parental and religious practices.

As to the matter of child discipline, parents are in a particularly difficult position under current tort doctrine. They can be subject to liability for either too much discipline or too little discipline. In claims brought by a child alleging excessive parental discipline, a "parent is privileged to apply such reasonable force or to impose such reasonable confinement upon his child as he reasonably believes to be necessary for its proper control, training or education."[44] In claims

42. For example, in *Lundman v. McKown*, 530 N.W.2d 807 (Minn. Ct. App. 1995), a diabetic child died after three days of Christian Science care. "Although juvenile-onset diabetes is usually responsive to insulin, even up to within two hours of death, the Christian Science individuals who cared for Ian during his last days failed to seek medical care for him—pursuant to a central tenet of the Christian Science religion." *Id.* at 813–14. The Minnesota Court of Appeals allowed the natural father to recover from the mother, the stepfather, and a Christian Science nurse practitioner. The court held that the state's compelling interest in the child's life overcomes the free exercise–of–religion protection. *See id.* at 818; *see also Prince v. Massachusetts*, 321 U.S. 158, 170 (1944).

43. Michael McConnell has suggested to me that the best compromise is a statute that would require parents who wish to rely on spiritual healing to notify state protective officials of the child's symptoms. The state can then take temporary custody for purposes of authorizing medical care. Such notification does not violate Christian Scientist beliefs. The parents can continue to provide Christian Scientist healing, in addition to the medical care that the state provides. Such a statute would leave the possibility of a torts suit if the parents failed to notify the authorities of a child's illness.

44. Restatement (Second) of Torts § 147(1) (1965).

brought by a third party against parents for an injury caused by their child, parents are subject to liability if they knew of the child's dangerous tendencies and failed to take reasonable remedial measures.[45] In both types of cases, the parent is held to a reasonableness standard, but the existence of both types of claims gives parents little or no discretion. If they err in either direction, they are subject to liability. The dilemma of parents is worse than mere lack of discretion; they may be in trouble no matter what they do. Given the differences in views about child discipline in our culture, a spanking might lead some juries to impose liability on parents for battery to their child, and the failure to spank the child in the same circumstances might subject parents to liability to a third party for failure to exercise reasonable control over the child.

Some jurisdictions subject a parent to liability to a child not only for unreasonable discipline but for unreasonable supervision as well. As noted previously, California holds parents to a reasonable-parent standard. In a pluralistic culture, where there is so much disagreement about the way to raise children, society should not dictate such matters. As Justice Rogosheske of the Minnesota court has said, allowing a negligent parenting cause of action, "creates [a] potential for judgments discriminating against parents whose conduct does not conform to prevailing community standards."[46] Only in the most extreme cases, such as those involving maliciousness or reckless endangerment, should courts intervene to judge parental decisions.

Clergy malpractice claims create a similar danger of imposing society's values on and discriminating against minority communities. In *Nally v. Grace Community Church,* parents sued a church, alleging that it was responsible for their adult son's suicide. The parents' expert witnesses, members of the clergy from other denominations, sought to establish "the standard of care to be followed by pastoral counselors" when confronted with a suicide risk.[47] But imposing liability on such a basis would dictate uniformity for religious congregations. The state has no business creating a common religious standard, in the absence of a compelling justification.

As suggested above, courts properly impose intentional tort liability on clergy who engage in sexual exploitation of children or counselees. Such claims do not require the state to create a common religious standard; clergy actions

45. Restatement (Second) of Torts § 316.

46. *Anderson v. Stream,* 295 N.W.2d 595, 603 (Minn. 1980) (Rogosheske, J., dissenting).

47. The California Court of Appeals held that such evidence should be admitted into evidence, 240 Cal. Rptr. 215, 221 (1987), but it was reversed on appeal by the state supreme court, 763 P.2d 948, 953 (Cal. 1988).

can be judged against the reasonable expectations of counselees. But cases against religious congregations alleging negligent supervision of such clergy can create problems that are similar to the problems of the clergy malpractice claim. Negligent supervision claims may require the state to evaluate the reasonableness of the religious congregation's practices.[48] As the Wisconsin Supreme Court has said, rejecting a negligent supervision claim, "Such claims would require a court to develop a 'reasonable cleric' standard of care, which would involve the interpretation of church canons and internal church policies."[49] In such cases, religious congregations have communitarian incentives to see that their clergy do not exploit children and counselees; they provide such services in order to care for members' needs. But religious congregations also have incentives to protect their clergy. As the noted Catholic natural-law theologian Germain Grisez has acknowledged, "I believe that the real problems presented and revealed by the conduct of priests [who take sexual advantage of young counselees] have hardly been acknowledged by bishops [and] that thus far they have developed no adequate policy or procedure for dealing with those problems."[50] It may be that religious congregations need the additional incentive of tort law to encourage greater oversight. In the following section I shall suggest a method of encouraging oversight without imposing a uniform religious standard on congregations.

## Simultaneously Broadening the Accountability of and Preserving the Discretion of Communities Through Limited Strict Liability

As noted previously, there are significant reasons for both giving discretion to communities and holding them responsible. It may be that the tensions between these two goals can be reconciled in some cases by imposing limited strict liability on intermediate communities. Under such a rule, intermediate communities would be accountable for results but would have autonomy as to means.

Communities often claim that they know their members better than out-

---

48. In general, attempts to impose *respondeat superior* liability on churches have failed. *See, e.g., Moses v. Diocese of Colo.,* 863 P.2d 310, 330 n.28 ("When a priest engages in oral sex with a mentally ill parishioner, the priest is not acting within the scope of employment").

49. *See L.L.N. v. Clauder,* 563 N.W.2d 434, 441 (Wis. 1997).

50. Germain Grisez, *The Way of the Lord Jesus,* vol. 3, *Difficult Moral Questions* 751 (Franciscan 1997).

siders and that they are best able to train and discipline their members. A rule of strict liability would encourage communities to prevent injury but allow them to determine, in light of their wisdom and insights into their members, how best to do so. Although a system of strict liability creates the greatest possibility of liability, it is not as intrusive a standard as negligence. A strict-liability rule does not apply an external standard, as does a negligence rule. It leaves communities to determine what action is least likely to cause loss. It internalizes the decision-making process. A strict-liability rule would tell communities that they can chart their own course but that they bear the responsibility for the results. The law would encourage care without interfering with the inner workings of communities. It may be that a limited strict-liability rule is the best approach to parental responsibility for their children's torts and to religious congregations' responsibility for sexual exploitation by their clergy. Through a limited strict-liability rule, courts may be able to hold communities responsible without micromanaging them and undercutting their authority.

Many states have statutes that impose limited strict liability on parents for the torts of their children. Statutory limits vary greatly.[51] My preference is for a rule that imposes strict liability on parents for any type of tort committed by a child, with a fairly high limit. Parents should have a strong incentive to control their children, but this responsibility should not ruin a family.

Similarly, courts or legislatures might impose limited strict liability on religious congregations when their clergy engage in sexual exploitation. In my opinion, such liability should be imposed only when the religious congregation or clerical supervisors are on notice of the clergy member's propensity toward sexual exploitation. Only then does the congregation know of the need for special action. Strict liability would avoid having the state evaluate the reasonableness of the religious congregation's response. Nevertheless, strict liability would create an incentive for the church to take effective steps to protect children and counselees.

In cases of clergy sexual exploitation there should be a significant limit on a religious congregation's damages. There is a great risk that juries will punish minority religious groups.[52] As Judge Noonan reminds us, "Respect for the reli-

---

51. *See* L. Wayne Scott, *Liability of Parents for Conduct of Their Child Under Section 33.01 of the Texas Family Code: Defining the Requisite Standards of "Culpability,"* 20 St. Mary's L.J. 69, 72–73 and appendix A (1988).

52. *See, e.g.,* the jury verdicts in the following cases: *Wollersheim v. Church of Scientology,* 260 Cal. Rptr. 331, 353 (Ct. App. 1989) (punitive damages of $25 million for shunning the plaintiff, encouraging church members to break existing contracts, and threatening plain-

gious beliefs of others is particularly difficult when one does not share [their] beliefs."[53] Legislatures might impose damage limits in such cases, and courts should freely exercise the option of *remittitur* in cases in which there is the danger of religious prejudice.

Concerns with corrective justice, individual rights, practical court administration, and economic efficiency have all influenced the development of tort law. Protection of intermediate communities has also been, and should continue to be, an important factor in this development. As both the Calvinist doctrine of sphere sovereignty and the Catholic doctrine of subsidiarity have taught, the health of both individuals and the broader society depends on our having strong intermediate communities. I do not suggest that intermediate communities should always win in conflicts with individuals or the state, but a balance of power will benefit individuals, intermediate communities, and the state.

---

tiff); *George v. International Soc'y for Krishna Consciousness,* 262 Cal. Rptr. 217, 221 (Ct. App. 1989) ($32 million in compensatory and punitive damages for "brainwashing" plaintiff); and *Lundman v. McKown,* 530 N.W.2d 807, 815 (Ct. App. Minn. 1995) ($5.2 million in compensatory damages against mother, stepfather, and Christian Science practitioner and $9 million in punitive damages against the church for death of diabetic child, discussed *supra* at text accompanying note 42). Most of these verdicts were reduced by judicial grant of remittitur.

53. *EEOC v. Townley Eng'g & Mfg. Co.,* 859 F.2d 610, 624 (9th Cir. 1988) (Noonan, J., dissenting).

# Contributors

*Joseph G. Allegretti,* Douglas T. Hickey Professor of Business, Siena College, Loudonville, N.Y. Professor Allegretti previously was the A.A. and Ethel Yossem Professor of Legal Ethics at Creighton University School of Law. Professor Allegretti has published widely in law reviews and in theology and spirituality journals. He is the author of *Loving Your Job, Finding Your Passion: Work and the Spiritual Life* (2000) and *The Lawyer's Calling: Christian Faith and Legal Practice* (1996).

*Albert W. Alschuler,* Wilson-Dickinson Professor at the University of Chicago School of Law. Alschuler recently published *Law Without Values: The Life Work and Legacy of Justice Holmes* (2000). Among his more than seventy law review articles is "Rediscovering Blackstone," 145 *University of Pennsylvania Law Review* 1 (1996), winner of the American Society of Legal Historians' Sutherland Prize for the year's best article on English legal history.

*Stephen M. Bainbridge,* Professor of Law at the University of California, Los Angeles. Professor Bainbridge teaches and writes mainly on corporate law topics. His recent publications include *Securities*

*Law: Insider Trading* (1999); "Corporate Decisionmaking and the Moral Rights of Employees: Participatory Management and Natural Law," 43 *Villanova Law Review* 741 (1998); and "Community and Statism: A Conservative Contractarian Critique of Progressive Corporate Law Scholarship," 82 *Cornell Law Review* 856 (1997).

*Harold J. Berman,* Robert W. Woodruff Professor at Emory University School of Law. Professor Berman's books include *The Nature and Functions of Law* (1996, 5th ed. with William R. Greiner and Samir N. Saliba), *Law and Revolution: The Formation of the Western Legal Tradition* (1983, winner of the 1985 ABA Scribes Book Award), and *Faith and Order: The Reconciliation of Law and Religion* (1993).

*Gerard V. Bradley,* Professor of Law at Notre Dame University. Professor Bradley's books include *Church-State Relations Today* (1987), *Set No Limits* (ed. with Robert L. Barry) (1992), and *Catholicism, Liberalism, and Communitarianism* (1995, ed. with Kenneth L. Grasso and Robert P. Hunt). He is coeditor (with John Finnis) of *The American Journal of Jurisprudence* and serves as president of the Fellowship of Catholic Scholars.

*Angela C. Carmella,* Professor of Law at Seton Hall Law School. Professor Carmella's publications include "A Theological Critique of Free Exercise Jurisprudence," 60 *The George Washington Law Review* 782–808 (1992), and "Mary Ann Glendon on Religious Liberty: The Social Nature of the Person and the Public Nature of Religion," 73 *Notre Dame Law Review* 1191–1216 (1998). She has been a member of the Religious Liberty Committee of the National Council of Churches since 1988 and was elected to the Catholic Commission on Intellectual and Cultural Affairs in 1997.

*Stephen L. Carter,* William Nelson Cromwell Professor at Yale University School of Law. Professor Carter is the author of more than one hundred articles. His books include *God's Name in Vain: The Wrongs and Rights of Religion in Politics* (2000), *Civility: Manners, Morals, and the Etiquette of Democracy* (1998), *The Dissent of the Governed: A Mediation on Law, Religion, and Loyalty* (1998), *Integrity* (1996), *The Culture of Disbelief: How American Law and Politics Trivialize Religious Devotion* (1993), and *Reflections of an Affirmative Action Baby* (1991).

*W. Burlette Carter,* Professor of Law at George Washington University. Professor Carter's publications include *Christopher Columbus Langdell and the Rise of the American Law School* (2001), "Reconstructing Langdell," 1 *Georgia Law Review* 32 (1998), and "Can This *Culture* Be Saved? Another Affirmative

Action Baby Reflects on Religious Freedom," 95 *Columbia Law Review* 473 (1995).

*David S. Caudill,* Professor of Law at Washington and Lee University. Professor Caudill's publications include *Lacan and the Subject of Law: Toward a Psychoanalytic Critical Legal Theory* (1997), *Radical Philosophy of Law: Contemporary Challenges to Mainstream Legal Theory and Practice* (1994, ed. with Steven J. Gold), *Law, Belief, and Criticism* (1989), and numerous law review and journal articles.

*Robert F. Cochran, Jr.,* Louis D. Brandeis Professor of Law at Pepperdine University School of Law. Professor Cochran is author of *Lawyers, Clients, and Moral Responsibility* (1994, with Thomas L. Shaffer), *Cases and Materials on the Rules of the Legal Profession* (1996, with Teresa Stanton Collett), and *The Counselor at Law* (1999, with John M. A. DiPippa and Martha M. Peters). He is the author of more than twenty law review articles, including "Introduction to Christian Perspectives on Law and Legal Scholarship," 47 *Journal of Legal Education* 1 (1997).

*Teresa Stanton Collett,* Professor of Law at South Texas College of Law, Texas A&M University. Professor Collett is the coauthor of *Cases and Materials on the Rules of the Legal Profession* (1996, with Robert F. Cochran, Jr.). Her articles include "Seek No Evil, Speak No Evil, Do No Evil: Client Selection and Cooperation with Evil," 66 *Fordham Law Review* 1339 (1998).

*Davison M. Douglas,* Professor and Director of the Institute of Bill of Rights Law at William and Mary School of Law. Professor Douglas's books include *School Busing: Constitutional and Political Developments,* vols. 1 and 2 (ed., 1994), *Reading, Writing, and Race: The Desegregation of the Charlotte Schools* (1995), and *Redefining Equality* (1998, ed. with Neal Devins). His articles include "The Limits of Law in Accomplishing Racial Change: School Segregation in the Pre-*Brown* North," 44 *UCLA Law Review* 677 (1997).

*Richard F. Duncan,* Sherman S. Welpton, Jr., Professor of Law at University of Nebraska College of Law. Professor Duncan serves on the Grant Review Committee of the Alliance Defense Fund. His books include *The Law and Practice of Secured Transactions* (1987, with William H. Lyons), and he has written numerous law review articles and essays on religious liberty, the right of privacy, equal protection, and other constitutional law issues.

*Marie A. Failinger,* Professor of Law at Hamline University. Professor Failinger has been the coeditor of the *Journal of Law and Religion* since 1988. She has written numerous law review articles and book reviews and has served on

Evangelical Lutheran Church in America task forces on church and state issues.

*George E. Garvey,* Professor of Law at the Catholic University of America. Professor Garvey is the author of *Economic Law and Economic Growth: Antitrust, Regulation, and the American Growth System* (1990, with Gerald J. Garvey) and *Affirming the Sanctity of Human Life: Exploring How the Jewish Community Can Work to Reduce Abortion* (1999, with Chris Gersten).

*Leslie Griffin,* Associate Professor, Santa Clara University School of Law. Professor Griffin is the author of "Good Catholics Should Be Rawlsian Liberals," 5 *Southern California Interdisciplinary Law Journal* 297 (1997); "'We Do Not Preach, We Teach': Religion Professors and the First Amendment," 10 *Quarterly Law Reports* 1 (2000); "The Relevance of Religion to a Lawyer's Work: Legal Ethics," 66 *Fordham Law Review* 1253 (1998); and other essays.

*Timothy L. Hall,* Professor of Law, University of Mississippi Law School. Professor Hall's books include *Separating Church and State: Roger Williams and Religious Liberty* (1998), and *Biographical Dictionary of Supreme Court Justices* (2001). His law review articles include "Educational Diversity: On Viewpoints and Proxies," 59 *Ohio State Law Journal* 551, (1998) and "Sacred Solemnity: Civic Prayer, Civil Communion, and the Establishment Clause," 79 *Iowa Law Journal* 35 (1993).

*Marci A. Hamilton,* Thomas H. Lee Chair in Public Law, Benjamin N. Cardozo School of Law, Yeshiva University. Professor Hamilton is a visiting professor of law at New York University School of Law, 2000–2001. Her publications include "Free? Exercise," *William and Mary Law Review* (2000); "Religion and the Law in the Clinton Era: An Anti-Madisonian Legacy," 63 *Law and Contemporary Problems* 359 (2000); "Vouchers, the Establishment Clause, and Power," 31 *Connecticut Law Review* 807 (1999); "Reply," 31 Connecticut Law Review 1001 (1999); and "The Constitutional Rhetoric of Religion," 20 *University of Arkansas at Little Rock Law Journal* 619 (1998).

*Phillip E. Johnson,* Jefferson E. Peyser Professor at the University of California, Berkeley. Professor Johnson's books include *Criminal Procedure* (2d ed., West, 1994), *Criminal Law* (5th ed., 1995), *Darwin on Trial* (1993), *Reason in the Balance* (1995), and *The Wedge of Truth* (2000).

*José Roberto Juárez, Jr.,* Professor at St. Mary's University School of Law. Professor Juárez is the author of "The Supreme Court as the Cheshire Cat: Escaping the Section 1983 Wonderland," 25 *St. Mary's Law Review* 1 (1993); and "The American Tradition of Language Rights: The Forgotten Right to Government in a 'Known Tongue,'" 13 *Law and Inequality Journal* 443 (1995).

*Patrick R. Keifert,* Professor of Systematic Theology, Luther Seminary, St. Paul, Minnesota; adjunct professor, Hamline University School of Law. Professor Keifert serves as a contributing editor of the *Journal of Law and Religion.* His books include *Welcoming the Stranger: A Public Theology of Worship and Evangelism* (1992) and *The Congregation After Christendom* (forthcoming), as well as the chapter "Law and Gospel" in *A New Handbook of Christian Theology* (eds. Donald W. Musser and Joseph L. Price, 1992).

*Catherine M. A. Mc Cauliff,* Professor of Law at Seton Hall University School of Law. Professor Mc Cauliff's articles include "Mother Teresa's Legacy to Lawyers," 28 *Seton Hall Law Review* 765 (1998, with Paula A. Franzese); and "Law as a Principle of Reform," 40 *Rutgers Law Review* 429 (1988). She is the author of the revised edition of *Corbin on Contracts,* vol. 3A, §§ 622–771 (1999).

*Michael W. McConnell,* Presidential Professor of Law at the University of Utah. Among Professor McConnell's many law review articles are "Religious Freedom at the Crossroads," 59 *University of Chicago Law Review* 115 (1992); "The Selective Funding Problem: Abortions and Religious Schools," 104 *Harvard Law Review* 989 (1991); "The Origins and Historical Understanding of Free Exercise of Religion," 103 *Harvard Law Review* 1409 (1990); "An Economic Approach to Issues of Religious Freedom," 56 *University of Chicago Law Review* 1 (1989, with Richard Posner); and "The Role of Democratic Politics in Transforming Moral Conviction into Law," 98 *Yale Law Journal* 1503 (1989).

*Elizabeth Mensch,* Professor of Law at Buffalo University. Professor Mensch is the coauthor (with Alan Freeman) of *Property Law,* 2 vols. (1992 [U.K.], 1993 [U.S.]), and *The Politics of Virtue: Is Abortion Debatable?* (1993). Her articles include "The History of Mainstream Legal Thought," in *The Politics of Law* (1982, David Kairys, ed.; rev. 1990, 1998), and "The Colonial Origins of Liberal Property Rights," in *Critical Legal Studies* (1992, James Boyle, ed.).

*John Copeland Nagle,* Associate Professor of Law at Notre Dame Law School. Professor Nagle's articles include "Playing Noah," 82 *Minnesota Law Review* 1171 (1998); and "A Twentieth Amendment Parable," 72 *New York Law Review* 470 (1997).

*H. Jefferson Powell,* Professor of Law and Divinity at Duke University. Professor Powell's books include *Languages of Power* (1991), *The Moral Tradition of American Constitutionalism: A Theological Interpretation* (1993), and *The Constitution and the Attorneys General* (1998). His articles include "The Original Understanding of Original Intent," 98 *Harvard Law Review* 885 (1985); and

"The Gospel According to Roberto: A Theological Polemic," 1988 *Duke Law Journal* 1013 and 5 *Modern Theology* 97 (1989).

*Thomas L. Shaffer,* Robert E. and Marion D. Short Professor of Law Emeritus, University of Notre Dame. Shaffer's books include *The Planning and Drafting of Wills and Trusts* (1972; 2d ed., 1979; 3d ed., 1991, with Carol Ann Mooney; 4th ed., 2001, with Carol Ann Mooney and Amy Jo Boettcher); *On Being a Christian and a Lawyer: Law for the Innocent* (1981); *American Legal Ethics* (1985); *Faith and the Professions* (1987); *American Lawyers and Their Communities* (1991, with Mary M. Shaffer); and *Lawyers, Clients, and Moral Responsibility* (1994, with Robert F. Cochran, Jr.). In addition, he is the author of more than 250 law review articles.

*David M. Smolin,* Professor of Law at Samford University. Professor Smolin's articles include "Church, State, and International Human Rights: A Theological Appraisal," 73 *Notre Dame Law Review* 1515 (1998); "The Jurisprudence of Privacy in a Splintered Supreme Court," 75 *Marquette Law Review* 975 (1992); and "Regulating Religious and Cultural Conflict in a Postmodern America: A Response to Professor Perry," 76 *Iowa Law Review* 1067 (1992).

*John Witte, Jr.,* Director, Law and Religion Program and Jonas Robitscher Professor at Emory University. Professor Witte's books include *Law and Protestantism: The Legal Teachings of the Lutheran Reformation* (forthcoming, 2002), *Religion and the American Constitutional Experiment* (2000), *Proselytism and Orthodoxy in Russia: The New War for Souls* (1999, with Michael Bourdeaux), *Sharing the Book: Religious Perspectives on the Rights and Wrongs of Proselytism* (1999, with R. C. Martin), and *From Sacrament to Contract: Marriage, Religion, and Law in the Western Tradition* (1997). He is also the author of more than ninety articles and book chapters.

# Index

Lincoln, C. Eric, 142
*L.L.N. v. Clauder,* 563 N.W.2d 434, 441
  (Wis. 1997), 496, 502
*Lloyds Bank Ltd. v. Bundy,* 1975 Q.B. 326,
  483
Locke, John, 11, 66–68, 248, 418
*Lundman v. McKown,* 530 N.W.2d 807
  (Minn. App. 1995), 499–500, 503–4
Luther, Martin, 247, 415
—on the Christian's role re. the state, 374–
  79, 394–403
—on the civil use of the law, 386–403
—on God's sovereignty, 386, 406, 408
—on offices and orders of creation, 376–
  77, 399–403
—on revolution and submission to the
  state, 66, 392–93
—and two kingdom theology, 9–10, 376–
  77, 388, 393

MacCormick, Neil, 285
Macedo, Stephen, 50
MacIntyre, Alasdair, 279–81, 490
MacKinnon, Catharine A., 97
Madison, James, 8, 10, 14
—role in framing the Constitution, 294,
  297–306
Maimonides, Moses, 49
Mansfield, Lord William Murray, 471, 475–
  76
Maritain, Jacques, 189
Marriage, 183–86, 362–66, 411–25
Marsh, Charles, 25–26, 43–44
Martínez, José Antonio, 172
Mason, George, 298, 300
McClendon, James William, 328n, 334
McConnell, Michael W., 359, 500n
Mediating institutions, 87–90, 486–504.
  *See also* Calvinism: sphere sovereignty;
  Catholic Church, The: subsidiarity
Mill, John Stuart, 187, 356
Ming, William R., 137
*Mississippi University for Women v. Hogan,*
  458 U.S. 718 (1982), 203

*M'Naghten's Case,* 8 Eng. Rep. 718 (H.L.
  1843), 427–34
Model Penal Code, 428–29
Moore, Michael, 101, 103–5
Morality and law, 285–86
More, Thomas, 463–64
Morris, Gouverneur, 299–300, 303–4
*Moses v. Macferlan,* 2 Burr. 1005, 1010, 97
  Eng. Rep. 676, 680 (K.B. 1760), 475
*Murphy v. Ramsey,* 11 U.S. 15 (1885), 416
Murray, John Courtney, 258n, 262, 271n

*Nally v. Grace Community Church,* 763 P.2d
  948 (Cal. 1988), 496, 501
National Conference of Catholic Bishops,
  272
National Council of Churches, 248–49
Natural law, 60, 243–44, 269–70, 277–78,
  309
—Baptist view of, 349–51
—the Bible, relationship to, 272–76, 277–
  78
—as corrective to the moral relativism of
  modern law, 100, 105–6
—critics of, 278–82
—judges and, 287–90
—and justice, 272–76, 470–75, 479–81
—Lutheran view of, 389, 396–98
—new classical theory of, 282–86
—and positive law, 270, 284–86, 287–89
Neuhaus, Richard John, 490–91, 498
Niebuhr, H. Richard, xiii, 198–99, 241–52,
  256, 345, 348
Niebuhr, Reinhold, 151–62, 337, 465
Novak, Michael, 211, 222

Okin, Susan Moller, 204–5
*Olmstead v. United States,* 277 U.S. 438
  (1928), 85, 187
Olthuis, James, 125–26
Originalism, 287–88

Parry, David H., 476
Parsons, Susan Frank, 197